Marge and Julia

UNIVERSITY PRESS OF FLORIDA

Florida A&M University, Tallahassee
Florida Atlantic University, Boca Raton
Florida Gulf Coast University, Ft. Myers
Florida International University, Miami
Florida State University, Tallahassee
New College of Florida, Sarasota
University of Central Florida, Orlando
University of Florida, Gainesville
University of North Florida, Jacksonville
University of South Florida, Tampa
University of West Florida, Pensacola

MARGE & JULIA

THE CORRESPONDENCE BETWEEN
Marjorie Kinnan Rawlings and Julia Scribner Bigham

EDITED BY

Rodger L. Tarr, Brent E. Kinser, and Florence M. Turcotte

UNIVERSITY PRESS OF FLORIDA

Gainesville | Tallahassee | Tampa | Boca Raton

Pensacola | Orlando | Miami | Jacksonville | Ft. Myers | Sarasota

Frontispiece: Marjorie Kinnan Rawlings (*top*) and Julia Scribner (*bottom*) circa their first meeting in 1939. Courtesy of the Department of Special and Area Studies Collections, George A. Smathers Libraries, University of Florida.

27 26 25 24 23 22   6 5 4 3 2 1

Library of Congress Cataloging-in-Publication Data
Names: Tarr, Rodger L., editor. | Kinser, Brent E., editor. | Turcotte,
Florence M., editor.
Title: Marge and Julia : the correspondence between Marjorie Kinnan
Rawlings and Julia Scribner Bigham / edited by Rodger L. Tarr,
Brent E. Kinser, Florence M. Turcotte.
Description: 1. | Gainesville : University Press of Florida, 2022. |
Includes bibliographical references and index.
Identifiers: LCCN 2021047944 (print) | LCCN 2021047945 (ebook) | ISBN
9780813069289 (hardback) | ISBN 9780813070063 (pdf)
Subjects: LCSH: Rawlings, Marjorie Kinnan, 1896-1953—Correspondence. |
Bigham, Julia Scribner—Correspondence. | Authors, American—20th
century—Correspondence. | Florida—Intellectual life—20th century.
Classification: LCC PS3535.A845 Z48 2022 (print) | LCC PS3535.A845
(ebook) | DDC 816/.52—dc23/eng/20211013
LC record available at https://lccn.loc.gov/2021047944
LC ebook record available at https://lccn.loc.gov/2021047945

The University Press of Florida is the scholarly publishing agency for the State
University System of Florida, comprising Florida A&M University, Florida Atlantic University,
Florida Gulf Coast University, Florida International University, Florida State University, New
College of Florida, University of Central Florida, University of Florida, University of North Florida,
University of South Florida, and University of West Florida.

University Press of Florida
2046 NE Waldo Road
Suite 2100
Gainesville, FL 32609
http://upress.ufl.edu

For Anita, Chesney, and Helen,
who have enriched our lives in countless ways

Contents

Figures

Special Thanks

The editors wish to acknowledge the critical support
of the Marjorie Kinnan Rawlings Society,
whose grant in memory of their founder, Phil May Jr.,
significantly enhanced the outcome of this volume.

Acknowledgments

THE EDITORS WISH to thank also the following individuals for their kind and invaluable assistance in the editing of this volume: Maggie Ashley, Western Carolina University, for her work on the transcriptions; Elizabeth Dunn, research services librarian, David. M. Rubenstein Rare Books and Manuscript Library, Duke University, for help in identifying the Duke family associated with Nancy Camp; Richard and Carol Gaugh, for their support of Rodger Tarr in the use of various research tools; Sheila Bacon Greenleaf, for providing information about the Culver Family of St. Augustine, Florida; Dave Kinner, Dean of the College of Arts and Sciences, Western Carolina University, and the University of Florida Foundation for their generous subventions of the index; Ashley Q. Lear, professor of humanities, Embry-Riddle University, for her response to queries concerning Ellen Glasgow; David Nolan, independent scholar and expert in Florida culture and history, for sharing his extensive knowledge of Norton Baskin and St. Augustine; Anne Pierce, Rawlings Farm, Cross Creek, for her answers to questions regarding the contents of Rawlings's home; David Southern, managing editor, Carlyle Letters Project, Duke University Press, for his assistance in identifying the Duke family associated with Nancy Camp; Adrienne Rusinko and Anna Lee Pauls, Mudd Manuscript Library, Department of Special Collections and Manuscripts, Princeton University, for assistance with navigating the Scribner Archive at Firestone Library, Princeton University; Carol Anita Tarr, professor emeritus, Illinois State University, for reading, editing, and emending the Introduction, in addition to providing the idea for the edition's title; Charles Tingley, senior research librarian, St. Augustine Historical Society, for help in identifying several lost names and places; and Celine Hickey for creating digital scans of the letters. The editors would also like to thank the members of the Marjorie Kinnan Rawlings Society and the Friends of the Marjorie Kinnan Rawlings Farm for their long-standing friendship and shared devotion to the legacy of Marjorie Rawlings, her writings, and her home.

Editorial Note

THIS VOLUME COMPRISES the entire correspondence of Marjorie Kinnan Rawlings and Julia Scribner Bigham known to the editors, which is housed in Special Collections, Smathers Library, University of Florida. Other relevant primary documents are held in the Scribner Archive at Princeton University, in the Rawlings Collection at the University of Florida, and in the Tarr Rawlings Collection at the University of South Carolina. A small number of documents are in private hands. Some letters, very few, are missing, likely destroyed, lost, or misplaced by either Rawlings and/or Bigham in situ, or later by Bigham, who was named Rawlings's literary executor and who formally assumed that role upon Rawlings's death in 1953. Norton Sanford Baskin, Rawlings's widower, was aware of her role as executor and delivered the manuscripts to Bigham after Rawlings's death. As a result of this clarity of possession, it seems safe to say that the bulk of the correspondence is printed here: 201 letters, notes, and wires. The archive is remarkable in the breadth of its size, quality, and time span, representing all fourteen years of their friendship. And, as a history, the archive reveals a great deal about the current literature, publishing practices, and evolving socio-political-cultural milieu, especially World War II, from the first communication in 1939 to the last in 1953.

Every effort has been made to preserve the integrity of the letters. With a few exceptions, all of Rawlings's letters were typed; without exception all of Bigham's letters were handwritten. Each writer's habits of composition are protected. Rawlings had peculiar habits, such as indicating a long-dash with three typed hyphens (---). When in a hurry she used on occasion a hyphen (-), or a medium-dash (—). The editors have attempted to present these three styles by use of the hyphen, en dash, and em dash. Bigham writes in a range of moderately clear to excessively scratchy, and because she uses various papers—such as tablet paper, plain paper, watermarked paper, and onion-skin paper—the condition of her holographs varies in terms of their readable condition. Further, her punctuation seems to vary depending upon the type of pen and paper, or whether she was writing in a moving train, which she often did. Usually, her handwriting is very small and frequently difficult to parse. Her hand features the particular habit of using a short dash (similar to a hyphen on a typewriter) either to break up or to punctuate long sentences. She often uses her version of a dash instead of a period. The editors represent her unique dash by using an en dash. At times, she also writes very long and complicated sentences without any punctuation whatsoever. Only on rare occasion have her sentences been emended for clarity with editorial punctuation. When altered, the punctuation is placed in brackets. Words that are impossible to decipher on either scans or the holographs are marked with [????] and [illegible]. Non-substantive typographical and spelling errors—such as "teh" for "the" or "Proffessor" for "Professor"—are silently corrected. However, when an error or misspelling is deemed potentially substantive, [*sic*] is used to preserve the fabric of the letter and as an indication of the writing process.

Rawlings's miscues were often the result, as she freely admits, of alcohol or anger or both, which sometimes resulted in faulty typing, such as "weeek" for "week," or failing to use a capital at the beginning of the sentence. When Bigham thought she had misspelled a word, she often would put "?" above the word or simply write, "I cannot spell." The spelling of "hemorrhage" was a source of particular annoyance. She also disapproved of Rawlings's off-again, on-again use of a capital I instead of a 1 in her dates (I943 instead of 1943). Rawlings, a former newspaper copyeditor, is less demonstrative. She often just excises the offending word and continues on with the preferred substitute; in other instances she returns to excise words and insert alternatives above the line. All emendations made by the editors are placed in square brackets ([ ]). Underlining in the letters is indicated as it appears in the holographs, by single underline, double underline, or triple underline. To preserve the habit of the times, wires (telegrams) are printed in capital letters. Authorial excisions are indicated with angle brackets (< >) and above line insertions with (^ ^). All excisions are provided when they can be read and when they are not just one or a few letters of a word, or ??? to indicate illegibility. Translations of foreign language expressions are provided in the notes.

The letters are presented consecutively by date of composition. A *Header* is provided to indicate: The author of each letter, the date of the letter, whether the letter is typed or handwritten and signed (TLS, ALS), and the length of the letter (e.g. 4 pp.). The *Header* also provides a description of the postmark (PM), the address (AD), the return address (RA) if there is one, the type and contents of the letterhead on stationery (LH), and other relevant postal markings such as Air Mail or Special Delivery. Often the place of composition does not match the postmark address—for example, the letter was composed at Crescent Beach but mailed in Citra, FL, or the letter was composed in Far Hills, NJ, but mailed in New York City. On occasion, the letters were delivered to an incorrect address and then redirected. This post office action is also provided, especially because it is important to the dating of undated letters and/or to the whereabouts of the addressee. Every effort has been made to date undated letters, either from context and/or from previous and subsequent letters. Editor-dated letters are presented in brackets—for example, [11? September 1941] means that the editors have estimated with as much certainty as possible that the letter was written on the eleventh day of September 1941. There are several variations of this system, such as [11 September? 1941], which means the letter may have been written on the 11th day of a month in 1941, but there is less certainty of the month. The dating is further complicated by the fact that with rare exception stamps have been removed, perhaps for collecting. On occasion, the removal of the stamp compromises the postmark. Most letters are dated on the first page, but not always completely. For example, letters might indicate "11 September," but not give the year. For letters that simply use the day of the week, such as "Tuesday," the perpetual calendar was used to provide, if possible, the actual date. In the archive, there are three undated fragments, which are placed properly with explanation in the notes.

The following abbreviations are used in the *Header*:

ALS: Autograph Letter Signed   TLS: Typed Letter Signed
ANS: Autograph Note Signed   TNS: Typed Note Signed
PM: Postmark   AD: Address
RA: Return Address   LH: Letterhead

Explanatory Notes are provided to assist the reader in understanding the content and context of the letters. The correspondence mentions four groups of families: The Rawlingses, the Baskins, the Scribners, and the Bighams. When possible and appropriate, the names and the birth and death dates of each family member mentioned are provided. In the case of the Charles Scribner lineage, various numbers have been adopted by the Scribner family over the years. For the sake of clarity, the following is a chronological enumeration: Charles Scribner I (1821–1871), Charles Scribner II (1854–1930), Charles Scribner III (1890–1952), Charles Scribner IV, aka Jr. (1921–1995), Charles Scribner V, aka III (1951–). Charles Scribner III is the father of Julia Scribner (1918–1961). Julia married Thomas James Bigham Jr., on 24 May

1945. The bulk of Julia's letters, both in number and in length, published here was written while she was a Scribner. Individuals and allusions mentioned in the letters that the editors were unable to locate are labeled in the notes as "Not Identified." To shorten and to facilitate references, the following abbreviations are used

JSB: Julia Scribner Bigham
MKR: Marjorie Kinnan Rawlings
NSB: Norton Sanford Baskin

In their capacity as "explanatory," the notes are intended to explain in as much detail as possible the myriad allusions and the complicated, often elusive biographical, bibliographical, geographical, and historical references contained in the letters. The correspondence is also intimately personal, a quality reflected in the plethora of innuendos, inside jokes, and comic interludes, not to mention topics such as private reports on medical conditions, substantive descriptions of World War II and the harrowing efforts to get Norton Baskin back from the India-Burma theater, and heartfelt pronouncements treating the innumerable trials and tribulations of profession and of marriage and of feelings. The temptation to explain their explanations is great, and would be for any editor. But, unless essential for clarity and context, interpretations of intent and affective content are left to the reader of Rawlings and Bigham's conversations.

A Word on the Provenance

RODGER L. TARR

ACCORDING TO THE DIRECTIONS of Rawlings's will, all of her unpublished manuscripts were to be delivered to her literary executor, Julia Scribner Bigham. It was Rawlings's express wish that each and all of her manuscripts not already at the University of Florida were to be delivered to Bigham, who had agreed also to take on the onerous task of protecting and, if she saw fit, of publishing any previously unpublished writings she deemed worthy. Rawlings's only directive to Bigham was not to publish "trash." Dutifully, Rawlings's widower, Norton Sanford Baskin, delivered the material to Bigham. The manuscript archive entrusted to Bigham is a much larger archive than one might expect. It includes: the manuscript of *South Moon Under* (1933); unpublished short stories; start-ups of short stories, poems, and letters; and the full-manuscript of *Blood of My Blood,* a 183-page inquiry into family, both Kinnans and Traphagens, but especially into Rawlings's mother Ida May Traphagen Kinnan (see Ann Blythe Meriwether, ed., *Blood of My Blood.* University Press of Florida, 2002). After Julia Scribner Bigham's death in 1961, the archive, which was supposed to be sent to the University of Florida Library, came into the possession of her husband, Thomas James Bigham Jr., who later needed to liquidate assets for financial reasons. The archive was found by Anne "Anda" Scribner Bigham Hutchins in "two boxes" in the attic of the Bigham home in Massachusetts (see Eliot Kleinberg, "Blood War," *Chicago Tribune,* 9 September 1990).

The archive was offered for sale to the University of Florida, the representatives of which apparently did not want to pay for it. The date of the offer is not clear, but certainly it would be 1987 or before. Meanwhile, Norton Baskin had forgotten all about the archive. Understandable, since he was already in his upper eighties. In 1988, Thomas Bigham, feeling sufficiently rebuffed by the University of Florida, contacted through Charles Scribner III [aka

V] a New York bookseller, Glenn Horowitz, who agreed to sell the collection. Nothing untoward whatsoever, such sales are made on a regular basis. Horowitz first priced the archive at $75,000, and later dropped the price to $40,000, then to $25,000. The Seajay Society paid Horowitz $12,500, a veritable bargain. We are very fortunate that the Bighams found the archive and did not choose to destroy it or just pack it away for posterity. Preservation is the key here. We are all grateful for the decision to sell it, for contained in the archive are the letters Marjorie Kinnan Rawlings wrote to Julia Scribner Bigham, published here for the first time. The letters that Bigham wrote to Rawlings were already in the Rawlings Collection at the University of Florida, and are also published here for the first time.

In the interests of transparency, I entered into the story in 1987–1988. I was a Rawlings collector and had amassed a substantial collection of her books, manuscripts, and letters (see Rodger L. Tarr, *Marjorie Kinnan Rawlings: A Descriptive Bibliography.* University of Pittsburgh Press, 1996). As with any collector, my antennas were always up. A reputable California bookseller, whom I had dealt with on a regular basis, Thomas Goldwasser, contacted me that the archive was for sale for $40,000, a sum beyond my means. I contacted my friend, the celebrated book collector, Matthew Bruccoli, who responded, "Buy it! I will go in half with you!" Matthew's word was his bond. I immediately contacted Goldwasser, who within a week wrote with the bad news: the archive had been sold. Disappointment reigned supreme. All book collectors know the feeling of such disappointment when one loses a treasure. Afterward I learned that the archive had been bought by the Seajay Society, a nonprofit literary society headed up by James B. Meriwether, another celebrated book collector, at the University of South Carolina. Bruccoli was a distinguished professor at the same institution and was a friend of Meriwether. Yet, inexplicably, Bruccoli and Meriwether apparently never had occasion to discuss the purchase, perhaps because Meriwether was keeping its purchase close to his vest. All book collectors understand this paranoia as well. Never mind! The archive was lost to me. I then mentioned it in passing to a newfound friend, Phil May Jr., whose father was Rawlings's attorney, and who possessed the best Rawlings collection in the world, bar none. May was nonplused. He knew nothing of the archive. He immediately contacted Baskin, his very good friend, who became immediately incensed by the whole affair. Why? Baskin felt that the archive belonged to him as "Personal Representative" of the Rawlings estate and that it should have been returned to him by the Bighams once Julia Bigham died.

However, the issue of ownership continued in dispute, complicated by the Bigham assertion that certain parts of the archive, never identified, were "given outright" to Julia Scribner Bigham by Marjorie Kinnan Rawlings and, thus, were not part of the archive. The most significant gift, remembered by the Bighams as the "novel about Rawlings's mother," was *Blood of My Blood*. The Bighams profess that early in the friendship Rawlings came to realize that Julia Bigham's psychological problems were caused by her mother, Vera Scribner, with whom she did not get along, a fact certainly confirmed by the letters in this volume, and one recognized clearly by Rawlings, who also had a conflicted relationship with her own mother. To ease Julia's pain, it is the memory of the Bighams that Rawlings "gave" Julia *Blood of My Blood* with the stipulation she "never give it away or let it to be published" (telephone conversation of Hildreth Bigham McCarthy and Rodger Tarr, 10 September 2020). In a letter to Baskin on 6 July 1988, Charles Scribner III [aka V] addresses this very issue: "If I had ever suspected that there might possibly arise any questions concerning the provenance or ownership of my aunt's various personal papers which I encouraged my cousins to arrange to have transferred to a safer place than a farmhouse attic, I certainly would have called or written to you to set your mind at rest. For I believed at the time . . . and am reassured—that the only papers preserved among my aunt's personal belongings were letters and manuscript fragments that Marjorie Rawlings mailed and gave to her over the many years of their close friendship. I am certain that any 'literary estate' papers were properly handled by my aunt before her death." Scribner concludes, "I was able to locate in our firm's archives at Princeton two documents that make it clear that Aunt Dule [Julia] was scrupulous about seeing to it that estate papers . . . were sent to the Rawlings collection in Florida. She—like my father [Charles Scribner IV]—was not a person who would ever confuse business or other people's matters with her own personal property" (photocopy, unpublished letter, Tarr collection). In effect, Scribner is making the argument that the whole of the archive was given to Julia by Rawlings, including the complete manuscript of *South Moon Under,* and thus was the property of the Bighams by inheritance. In a long letter of response to Scribner on 15 July 1988, Baskin vigorously disputes the assurances of Scribner III [aka V]: "I note that you suggest that over the years Marjorie sent Julia certain letters, or even manuscripts, that were given to her personally and were not part of the estate. This is hard for me to believe, and I am sure it is not true." Baskin then challenges Scribner to locate a letter confirming such gifts: "This I am sure you will not be able to produce" (photocopy, unpublished letter, Tarr collection). Difficult words exchanged between two friends. In spite of several attempts to smooth the waters, neither Scribner nor Baskin would alter his position. The line in the sand had been drawn. Legal proceedings by Baskin were inevitable, despite his protestations to the contrary.

In 1990 all hell broke loose! Baskin filed a lawsuit on 17 May against the Seajay Society, which had bought the archive, in the U.S. District Court South Carolina in Columbia, South Carolina, demanding the return of the archive, but not mentioning the issue of the alleged gifts. Meriwether refused categorically to return anything. The fight was on. Baskin was at an immediate disadvantage, since the laws of possession somehow differ between South Carolina and Florida, Baskin's residence. Letters of deposition flew back and forth like an avian migration. The lawsuit was finally heard, and the judge took it all under advisement. The case presented interesting issues, not the least of which is who exactly owns the rights to literary manuscripts that have been sold? It is a bit like asking if you purchased a Warhol painting from an art dealer, does Warhol still own the paint and/or the painting? A tricky, if not sticky wicket. The judge pondered the case, under South Carolina law, for more than a year. Most interested parties had fallen asleep. Tort law to civilians can be excessively boring. But not to Norton Baskin, who believed that there was the principle of lawful possession here. In the end, after thousands of dollars in legal fees were spent, he lost. The judge ruled against Baskin and in favor of the Seajay Society, deciding that Baskin had forfeited his rights to the archive because he had made no claim for it for such a long time—from 1961, when Julia Bigham died, to 1990, when he filed the lawsuit.

James Meriwether, at the First Annual Rawlings Conference at the University of Florida in 1988, assured me that the archive would be protected, an assurance that was made months later on 12 August 1988 in a letter to Baskin by Charles Scribner III [aka V]: "Copies of my aunt's papers (including Rawlings' manuscripts) will be presented to the Collection at Florida in the not-too-distant future. At the moment, they are in the hands of a distinguished scholar [James Meriwether] who is studying them with his students" (photocopy, unpublished letter, Tarr collection). Jim was a man of his word. The manuscripts have been preserved, but thus far only the holographs of the letters from Rawlings to Scribner have been delivered to Florida. Meriwether died in 2007, but not before he assisted his wife, Anne Blythe Meriwether, in the editing and publication of *Blood of My Blood*.

From here, my personal interest in the archive shifted completely from collecting to scholarly pursuit. Again, in the interests of transparency, I contacted Robert O. Meriwether, an attorney and James Meriwether's son. I asked if I could see the archive. He put me off, indicating there were family issues to settle. I contacted him again sometime later, and once again he put me off, always politely. As I remember, we spoke on the telephone as well. No dice. I gave up. Greener pastures lay before me. Norton Baskin, who shared so much lore about Rawlings with me, died in 1997. My treasured friend Phil May followed in 2019. Each believed to the end that justice had not been served. My friends were now gone, and as far as I could ascertain so was the archive—that is, gone to me. Then, as a bolt out of the blue, came the news from Florence Turcotte, university librarian in charge of the Rawlings Papers: the University of Florida had acquired from the Seajay Society a part of the Rawlings archive, thanks to Nicholas G. Meriwether, a son of James B. Meriwether, and currently the head of the Grateful Dead Archive at the University of California, Santa Cruz. Manna from Heaven. I could now rest in peace, knowing for certain that at least some of the manuscripts are now preserved forever. Scholarship is greatly indebted to Robert and to Nicholas. Little could I imagine that a year later I would be contracted by the University Press of Florida to edit the Rawlings-Bigham letters with Brent E. Kinser and Florence Turcotte. More manna from Heaven. Perhaps Shakespeare is correct, "All's Well That Ends Well."

. . .

One word more . . .

Just as I was about to put the "Provenance" issue to bed, satisfied that I had thoroughly covered each sequence in the controversial story, I looked once more in one of my more dusty Scribner files. Fortuna struck again. From the nether regions of the file out jumped a letter from Julia Scribner Bigham to Norton Baskin on the very subject of the transfer of the manuscript archive to her by Baskin that sheds new light on the subject of ownership. The revealing letter is in response to her trip to confer with Baskin on how best to deal with the archive now that she was officially the literary executor. That meeting, according to Baskin, took place approximately "three weeks" after Rawlings's death on 14 December 1953, so probably early in 1954. As Baskin recalls to Charles Scribner III [aka V] on 15 July 1988, "Within three weeks, I called her [Julia Bigham], and she came to the cottage at Crescent Beach. . . . All of Marjorie's papers had been moved from Cross Creek to Crescent Beach. She sorted things into three groups—things that she wanted to take with her, things she wanted sent immediately to the University of Florida, and things she wanted destroyed" (photocopy, unpublished letter, Tarr Collection). In her undated letter in response to the 1954 meeting, Bigham effusively "thanks" (underlined three times) Baskin "from the bottom of all our hearts for what you did for us," and then apologizes for the tardiness of her letter because of a "spate of ill health on our return."

Bigham then provides and/or confirms facts that heretofore have not been in full evidence. Most notably she asserts, "Norton, I am crazy about that childrens [*sic*] story of Marjorie's that you gave me, and I feel very strongly that it should be published. I think it is a lovely charming thing. Marjorie's poetry working in its best form with no false notes. I feel it could only add to her position and is too fine and original to be let languish. Don't you agree?" The story is *The Secret River*, edited by Bigham and published by Scribners in 1955. What Bigham's words imply is that she had not previously seen the manuscript of the story, even though Scribners must have had a copy, the one that Maxwell Perkins had been considering for publication when he died in 1947. Her letter also seems to indicate that Bigham knew little of the manuscript before this moment in time. It also does not undermine the oft told story that Baskin had found the manuscript by accident on a closet shelf in his home. What is also known is the manuscript of *The Secret River*, at least one version of it, became a part of the larger archive put up for sale by the Bigham family in 1988. As Bigham reports to Baskin in 1954, I have "spoken to Buzz [Charles Scribner IV] and Wallace [Meyer]" about it, "but haven't shown it to anyone yet as page 9 is missing & I guess it is probably among the manuscripts you are sending." Here we learn for the first time that Baskin has not yet sent the rest of the archive to Bigham. For certain we now know that Rawlings did not "give" the manuscripts as a "gift" to Bigham, for otherwise she would already have had them and they would need not be sent. Thus, the assertion by Charles Scribner III in his letter to Baskin on 6 July 1988 that the archive in question was "among my aunt's personal belongings" is mistaken, since Scribner III claims to Baskin that the archive consists of "letters and manuscript fragments that Marjorie Rawlings mailed and gave to her over the many years of their close friendship. I am certain that any 'literary estate' papers were properly handled by my aunt before her death" (photocopy, unpublished letter, Tarr Collection).

Thus, since the manuscript archive was still in the hands of Baskin in 1954, Bigham had no proprietary claim to it whatsoever. The archive was merely on temporary loan to her as literary executor, and as Rawlings's will directs, it was to be sent to the University of Florida once Bigham had completed her tasks as literary executor. Not "copies" of the manuscripts, the original holographs. Rawlings's will makes no provision for "copies" to be made for the Scribner Archive at Princeton University Library. Why? Because the manuscript archive was not the property of Julia Scribner Bigham or Princeton University. Likewise, the will makes no provision that Baskin could claim ownership, as Rawlings's widower or "Personal Representative" as asserted in the lawsuit" (*Baskin v. Seajay Society* 1990). Under the clear provisions of the will (Section Thirteen), the manuscript archive was from the outset the property of the University of Florida:

> Thirteenth: I direct that immediate custody of my complete library, wherever situated, all manuscripts, all notes, all correspondence and all literary property of any kind, be delivered to my friend, Julia Scribner Bigham, whom I hereby designate as my literary executor, with the power and duty of destroying any notes, manuscripts, or correspondence which, in her sole discretion, she determines should be destroyed. Such remaining property shall continue in her custody so long as she considers it desirable in the performance of her duties as my literary executor and then shall be delivered by her to the Library of The University of Florida at Gainesville, Florida, to whom I shall give and bequeath all of such property subject to the prior right in my said literary executor of access to and use of all of such property. My said literary executor shall have the sole right to determine what publication shall be made of or from such property and material. All net returns, proceeds, profits, and royalties therefrom, after reimbursement of expenses incurred by my said literary executor and payment made of reasonable compensation to her, shall constitute income to be held by my trustee hereafter named for disposition as hereafter provided.

> (Reproduced in Robert D. Middendorf and Rodger L. Tarr, "The Will of Marjorie Kinnan Rawlings." *Journal of Florida Literature* 15 [2007]: 125–40)

As the will makes abundantly clear, Bigham was only the caretaker of the manuscript archive, although she was given sole authority to publish or to destroy material at her discretion while it was in her possession. Most important, however, nowhere does the will state, imply, and/or hint that Bigham could at any time claim ownership of the property. One might now ask, why didn't Julia Scribner Bigham forward the archive to the University of Florida as she was instructed? The answer is a tragic one. For the last five years of her life, Bigham suffered from the painful onslaught and the inevitable conclusion of metastatic breast cancer (telephone interview, Hildreth Bigham McCarthy, with Rodger Tarr, September 2020). Bigham was, in effect, incapacitated during the final years of her life. Rawlings would be the last to be critical of Bigham for not fulfilling her final duty as literary executor to see that the archive "be delivered by her" to the University of Florida. Bigham is not culpable. If anything, the fault lies with the will, which does not provide for disposition in the event of Bigham's untimely death. Indeed, our eternal gratitude goes to Bigham, who packed away and thus preserved the manuscripts from harm. Perhaps out of her love for Rawlings she even envisioned a project with the manuscripts, a project that the final years of her fatal illness prevented. Thus, the manuscript archive lay silent from 1961, the year of Bigham's death, arranged carefully in two boxes until 1987, when Anne Bigham Hutchins, Bigham's third daughter, found it in the attic while looking for material of value to help her father address his financial hardship. The elderly Thomas James Bigham Jr. and his four children knew nothing of the provision in Rawlings's will that the archive was, in fact, the property of the University of Florida. Had they known this, it is absolutely certain they would have forwarded the archive to the University of Florida. These are honorable people. All they knew is that they uncovered two boxes of Rawlings's manuscripts, which they thought belonged to their mother, and which they thought the sale of which might help alleviate their father's financial distress. One might argue that Charles Scribner III, who would have had no direct access to the will, should have questioned that such a valuable archive might not have been given to Julia Scribner Bigham "free and clear." Yet from the outset he is adamant in his belief that the archive belonged to "Aunt Dule" [Julia]. As he writes to Baskin on 12 August 1988, "Incidentally, I am also happy to report that a full set of copies of my *aunt's* papers (including Rawlings' manuscripts) will be presented to the Collection at Florida in the not-too-distant future (see also photocopy, unpublished Scribner III letter on 19 July 1988 to Jean Preston, Curator of Manuscripts, Princeton University, Tarr Collection). Again, Scribner assured Baskin, "At the moment they [the manuscripts] are in the hands of a distinguished scholar [James Meriwether] who is studying them with his students" (photocopy, unpublished letter, Tarr Collection). Since the archive had already been sold and delivered to the Seajay Society, Scribner III must be referring to an assurance from James Meriwether. For certain Charles Scribner III is no thief in the night. He too is honorable, a man with a stellar reputation (I myself have benefitted from his myriad kindnesses). But the unquiet truth is he should have made certain that the archive did, indeed, belong to the Bighams by inheritance before he arranged for its sale. For once it was sold to the Seajay Society, all he could arrange conclusively, using his considerable influence, was for "copies," not the originals, to be deposited at the University of Florida. Baskin protested vigorously, this time through his close friend Phil May Jr., who writes to Scribner III on 20 August 1988: "Also, Norton feels that the *original* manuscripts/typescripts, not copies should go to the estate collection at the Univ of Florida" (photocopy, unpublished letter, Tarr Collection). Scribner III, somewhat irritated by all the fuss, responded to May on 23 August 1988,

"Please don't worry about my aunt's 'Rawlings' papers. I am assured that they—the *originals*—have been 'earmarked' for the Collection in Florida, after the scholars and students studying them have concluded their work" (photocopy, unpublished letter, Tarr Collection). To date, some thirty-two years later, only the Rawlings to Bigham letters, published in this volume, have been deposited, although there is the hope that through the good graces of Nicholas Meriwether the rest will soon be forthcoming.

In the end of ends, the conundrum is that everyone, except Norton Baskin, just assumed that the archive was a "gift" by Rawlings to Bigham and thus rightfully belonged to the Bigham descendants, including apparently the bookseller Horowitz, who, through Scribner III, handled the sale, the exact date of which is not known. However, it was likely in December or January 1987–1988 (unpublished letter, Thomas Goldwasser to Rodger Tarr, 6 January 1988). Should James Meriwether be held accountable because he bought the archive on behalf of the Seajay Society? Of course not. I too would have purchased it, had I been given the opportunity. As a manuscript and rare book collector, it was a splendid opportunity for Meriwether to acquire a valuable collection. Perhaps he could have been more accommodating with Norton Baskin, Rawlings's widower, who was ancient in age at the time and who was adamant in his demands that the archive belonged to him, even though Rawlings's will says differently. To paraphrase John Milton, confusion quickly confounded. And had the lawyers on both sides done their homework, the Baskin lawsuit would have been thrown out of court. Rawlings's will would have prevailed. Julia Scribner Bigham never "owned" the manuscript archive, thus her family had no right to sell it. As Rawlings's literary executor, Bigham was the valued caretaker. As Rawlings's will directs unequivocally, she intended from the outset that the University of Florida library be the owner. However, because of the decision of a South Carolina judge conferring ownership to the Seajay Society, the best the library can hope for now is to be the "final" owner, and, thus, short of a successful appeal to the South Carolina courts, ownership depends upon the largess of the Meriwether family. From my perspective, hope continues to spring eternal. The Grateful Dead eloquently anticipate such a transition:

> A box of rain will ease the pain
> And love will see you through.

Introduction

How I wish you were my daughter!

You are exactly what I should choose if I could have a daughter,

and I would be the right sort of mother for one like you.

Marjorie to Julia

My parents . . . are so generous with everything they can give.

What you gave me is what they cannot give.

Julia to Marjorie

THE DISCORDANT HARMONY and nuanced drama that pervade the relationship of Marjorie Kinnan Rawlings and Julia Scribner Bigham reach crescendo in these two declarations of filial devotion, born out of a love finally impossible to define. And even to attempt definition of their special bond is to rob both of what they prized most, their privacy. Yet the intellectual depth and the historical importance of what they express in these letters demands examination, especially because the exchanges are such compelling manifestations of female discourse as it exists in, responds to, and transcends the overwhelming presence of patriarchy and its omnipresent voice. Here, there is no need to employ a Bechdel-Wallace test to determine whether two named women are present and having a conversation that does not involve men. Whether they are discussing literature, music, current events, men, women, friends, celebrities, gifts, family, health, drinking, parents, or sex, their correspondence continually interrogates their identities and roles in the patriarchal world in which they lived and wrote their lives. They are two women talking, in the most intimate and comfortable ways, outside the presence of men.

When they first met on 3 December 1939 at the Scribner estate "Dew

Hollow," Marjorie, a seasoned forty-three-year-old, had reached a pinnacle most writers can only fantasize. She had been awarded the Pulitzer Prize for *The Yearling* (1938), the rite-of-passage bildungsroman of a Cracker boy who must shoot his pet deer to ensure his family's survival. Julia, then a precocious twenty-one-year-old, was already confronting the demons of maturation, haunted by a pedigree emblazoned upon her by a male publishing dynasty of epical proportion, the House of Charles Scribner's Sons. What makes their association all the more remarkable is that Marjorie was from the middle class, Julia from the upper crust. Normally such twain seldom join, at least in the profoundly intimate manner represented in this correspondence. But it did, largely because *The Yearling*, composed under the tutelage of the celebrated editor Maxwell E. Perkins, was not only a Pulitzer-Prize novel, it was an unexpected bestseller for Scribners, and as such a much-needed financial infusion for the press. There is no evidence that Julia, still a more sophisticated teenager than settled adult, knew anything substantive about *The Yearling*, other than it was making "daddy" (aka Charles Scribner III) a lot of money. It is not surprising, therefore, that the Scribners would make a celebratory stop in Jacksonville some two months after their first meeting to visit their newly crowned novelist before continuing on to the lavishness of West Palm Beach. What is surprising, shocking really, is that they agreed to make the ninety-mile trip through the formidable scrub over to Cross Creek, the isolated home of Marjorie, a hamlet then so remote that only the most knowledgeable Florida Crackers knew exactly where it was. One can only imagine what the socially crested Vera Gordon Bloodgood Scribner, spouse of Charles III and mother of Julia, thought when she was confronted by a front gate overwhelmed by wild flowers that gave entry to a mostly sand yard that in turn enveloped a Cracker house built crudely on pilings. The Scribner home in Far Hills, New Jersey, was grand and stately; the Rawlings home on the partly unpaved road to Cross Creek was beset by age, sagged precipitously, seemingly held up by an open lean-to garage that partly hid the "Kohler," a sometimes-reliable generator and only source of electricity.

Even more astonishing, the Scribners agreed to stay the night of Sunday, 25 February 1940. Marjorie's reports suggest that Vera, the not-always-present but almost-always-critical mother, was requisitely polite, even though upon arrival she came down immediately with a "vicious" headache. The reaction of Charles III is not known, no doubt because his nobility of character was not challenged by the vastness of the scrub or the quaintness of Marjorie's struggling orange grove. Julia, whom Rawlings described as a "most unusual person," fell immediately in love with what she saw. She begged off the return to Jacksonville and the onward journey toward the luxury of West Palm Beach. Instead she stayed two weeks with Marjorie, returning to New York on 11 March. It was paradise found for Julia. Not only did she not have to dress up for formal dinners, she actually had to dress down to accommodate the vagaries of a wilderness heretofore unimagined by her. An alumna of the fashionable Foxcroft School in Middleburg, Virginia, she now had to be instructed on how to avoid poisonous snakes, to dodge massive alligators, and to eat what she and Marjorie shot or caught, cooked in a Dutch oven over an open fire while camping in the scrub. Julia was used to the pastoral life of New England. She was no innocent. She understood the rugged New England grandeur made famous in the poems of Robert Frost. But this was different. Cross Creek represented frontier life, where a single mistake in judgment could prove costly, even fatal. Julia loved the adventure. And Marjorie loved her for loving it. In a fortnight, their lifetime bond was set. Marjorie became Julia's confidante, in effect her mother by proxy. Equally important, Julia became the daughter that circumstance had denied the too-often child-lonely Marjorie.

The sheer wonder and the full breadth of their letters are astonishing. No subject is off limits; no pursuit beyond dignity. The letters are a diary of their passions, of their fears, and more often than expected of their hurt. They chronicle a history of two disparate but kindred souls determined to survive and to flourish in spite of the barriers placed before them, not the least of which the male culture that, wittingly or unwittingly and always systemically, controlled their space. Whatever the obstacles, they stood their ground, argued their case, and suffered fools reluctantly. Julia had been raised in the closed—to her stifling—atmosphere of "Scribner's Sons," where posh and preferment were the raisons d'être. Marjorie, on the other hand, was confronted daily by the ubiquitous Crackers, who viewed her as an outsider, a Yankee—an appellation she resented—and who evaluated her largely through the telescopic lens of the so-called Late Unpleasantness, known in the North as the Civil War. Even more unfathomable to Marjorie were the Blacks, whose ancestors had survived not only the agonies of chattel slavery but the shackles of ineffective Reconstruction as well. Jim Crow laws were alive and flourishing, enforced rigorously by the Klan. Resentments ran deep. The aristocratic Julia knew little of the Black or of the White culture of the South, since she was kept from it all by her Scribner exclusivity. Marjorie's Cross Creek opened up a whole new world to Julia. Both Marjorie and Julia seemed to share a mutual concern for social justice, at least in theory. However, Marjorie's social fuse was too often short, owing to adverse experiences; Julia's fuse seemed shorter, owing to her elitist expectations. In response to all of the often absurd circumstances they were placed in because they were women, their keynotes are persistence and irreverence. The Foxcroft-refined Julia peppers her language with variations of "shit," her favorite expletive. In a particularly revealing description to Norton, Marjorie claims that she is often astonished by Julia's language: "[S]he curse[s] worse than I do. She has so many of my characteristics . . . that it does seem as though she were my daughter, or at least closer kin than anyone in her own family. As a matter of fact, she is more vulgar than I, and uses words I should not dream of using. I picked her a choice navel orange the other day, and as she peeled it, she said gloomily, 'A bird did something on it.' I said Nonsense, and please to show me any such thing. . . . She simply shouted across the grove, 'I guess I know bird shit when I see it!'" (*Love Letters* 289). The truth is Marjorie revels in Julia's defiance of social decorum, much the same defiance she herself had exhibited before her sorority at the University of Wisconsin when she dared call for racial justice in 1918.

As time passed, Marjorie made a serious effort to confront the contradiction between her racial attitudes and her behavior. She was aware of and worked hard to conquer her own prejudice, but as these letters demonstrate she was not doing a very good job of it. Sadly, Marjorie tossed about racial epithets with abandon, especially when she was drinking, and especially toward her maids and grove workers. Julia was more circumspect, perhaps more liberal, but she could do and did little or nothing to silence her mentor. Early on Julia sensed that the Black culture of Cross Creek was an ever-present and much-needed emolument for Marjorie. After all, it was the Blacks who chopped her grove, cooked her food, cleaned her home, and in return suffered her racist outbursts. It was in the end a utilitarian compromise. Marjorie needed the Blacks, and the Blacks came to need Marjorie. Truth be told, the White denizens of Cross Creek, the so-called Crackers, wanted nothing to do with the menial chores consigned to the so-called niggers. The Crackers, who like the Blacks possessed an uncommon sense of nobility that defied their circumstances, hunted and fished and distilled corn squeezin's with and for Marjorie, with their first step always one ahead of the law. In the most meaningful way, the Crackers also were indispensable to Marjorie because they provided her not only with the food of life but also with the food that nurtured her literary soul, and ambition. These letters dramatically convey that mutual interdependence, between Yankee and Cracker and Yankee and Black, as Marjorie informs and instructs Julia on the subtleties of human endeavor—more precisely, human endeavor as Marjorie perceived it, mainly through the contradictory interactions with her employees. Idella Parker, who Marjorie famously later called her "perfect maid," provides the emblem of this paradox. Idella begins her tenure at Cross Creek with Marjorie describing her to Julia as "the new nigger" (25 November 1940). By the next year, after Idella complains that she is afraid she will be replaced by the daughter of Martha Mickens, Adrenna, Marjorie tells Julia, "did I hurry to assure her that there was no thought of such a thing, that I could not ask [for] a better maid than she, Idella" (9 March 1941). Marjorie's altered sensibility is unfortunately short-lived as she continues in the next sentence: "Adrenna is a born trouble-maker, and she and Martha will be up to plots to drive off my good Idella. I can outwit men, but am a feeble thing against niggers. They have the same low cunning that Pat [her dog] has, and it makes you feel very foolish" (9 March 1941). For her part, Julia seems mainly to have ignored such racist disquisitions on the help, as in her next letter. The travails of Cross Creek go unmentioned, but she thanks Marjorie for the gift of salt-water taffy, commends her on the progress of her new "novel" (*Cross Creek*), and regales her with the wonders of Classical music ([31 March]). Three months later, the tide of Marjorie's racial rhetoric changes again: "My maid Idella, who has been with me since October, is still the answer to prayer. . . . She doesn't drink, she isn't interested in men, she borrows my books, and likes the same movies I like!" (23 June 1941).

In spite of her perpetual backsliding, Marjorie tried hard to treat the Blacks with kindness and understanding. She gave them food, paid them by comparison high wages, got them out of jail, and listened to their stories and litany of sorrows, all at the risk of alienating the Crackers and other white bosses trying to hire workers. In several instances, the Blacks she oversaw became her friends. And she vigorously defended them against the verbal onslaught of the Crackers and on occasion her friends in Ocala and in Jacksonville. Her treatment of Parker and Martha "Old Martha" Mickens, to whom she was indebted equally for helping her, are but examples of her conflicted prejudice. The two of them, most prominent among many others, helped Marjorie not only to maintain a relatively comfortable lifestyle but to survive in rural Florida in the 1940s. For a middle-aged, divorced woman such survival was an accomplishment. For the Blacks in her employ it was nearly a miracle.

The intimate nature of these letters reflects the personality of the relationship. Julia was not only a listener; she was an advocate. Nowhere is her advocacy more apparent than in her blunt, daughterly approach to one of Marjorie's enduring foibles, her abuse of alcohol. Marjorie had been a social drinker since her student days at the University of Wisconsin. As a young married, not entirely prepared for the vicissitudes of wedlock, Marjorie's taste for alcohol did little for her domestic situation as her immature husband Charles "Chuck" Rawlings struggled to make ends meet, eventually turning to a nomadic life as a traveling salesman in an attempt to save what was already a decaying marriage. Marjorie did not help matters. She was volatile, given to fits of temper and to irrational judgment, especially if alcohol were involved. In a futile quest to save themselves from themselves, the struggling couple, at Marjorie's insistence and with Marjorie's inheritance, bought in 1928 a seventy-four-acre orange grove in north-central Florida with the idea of reversing their fortunes. The cup of naiveté flooded over. Both were determined to be successful writers, Marjorie more so than Charles. To make matters worse, they knew absolutely nothing about running an orange grove. From the outset they became dependent upon the locals, both the Blacks and the Crackers, for the native knowledge necessary to survive much less to eke out a living. Marjorie adapted; Charles did not. In March 1930, Marjorie placed her first story, "Cracker Chidlings," with the prestigious *Scribner's Magazine*. The more ambitious novella "Jacob's Ladder" followed in December. In March 1933, her first novel, *South Moon Under,* inspired by the lore conveyed to her by both Black and White, was published by Charles Scribner's Sons. In the space of three years, Marjorie had risen toward the zenith of literary accomplishment, a height impossible to imagine for a young woman who just a decade before was writing newspaper copy for the *Louisville Courier-Journal* and occasional poetry for the *Rochester Times-Union.* Yet Marjorie's newfound success came at a price, for it served only to exacerbate the tensions between her and Charles. Alcohol fueled domestic conflict and abuse. She continued to seek expiation through her work, not the least of which was her explosive, thinly veiled, Freudian-laced exposé of her marriage in "Gal Young Un," the winner of the O. Henry Memorial Prize for the best short story of 1932. None of this placated Charles Rawlings. His response was to throw hollandaise dressing in her face in contempt. No amount of trial and error could repair the fracture. They were divorced in November 1933.

Nevertheless, the die had been cast. By the time Julia came into her life, alcohol had become a nemesis for Marjorie, in spite of which she continued to place short stories and to oversee the orange grove. Her second novel, the moderately successful but unremarkable *Golden Apples,* was published by Scribners in 1935. Destiny seemed finally on her side. She had what she needed most, the full attention of Maxwell Perkins. Oddly enough, he suggested she next consider a "boy's book." Marjorie was reluctant at first to accept what she perceived as an intellectually unrewarding topic. She did not want to become known as a children's writer. But Perkins's sway was enormous. She succumbed. A transfiguration took place. In 1938, from her heart and from her soul emerged not a children's book but "a book about a boy," *The Yearling,* winning her the Pulitzer Prize in 1939 and with it international stardom. Wealth and fame were laid before her. Once the protégé of the esteemed editor Perkins, she was now his personal friend. He was now "Max" instead of "Mr. Perkins." She dined with the Scribners and their literati; she met with Thomas Wolfe in New York, carrying Perkins's message to shorten his manuscripts; she met with Scott Fitzgerald in Asheville, again at the behest of Perkins, to see if he was writing or drinking (they got drunk); she became good friends with Margaret Mitchell, later attending as an honored guest the premiere of the movie based upon *Gone with the Wind* in Atlanta; and MGM bought the rights to *The Yearling* and in consequence Hollywood became her oyster. She was now a celebrity, a writer awash in the wildness and the wilderness of recognition. She was sought after as a speaker, receiving adulation from thousands. She suffered from losing the solitude she needed to work. Yet she also was lonely. She had a lover, but, as she surmised, no one to love her. In some of her more poignant letters, she warns Julia about this fated loneliness for which, she believed, all women are destined. She was consumed by a private loneliness celebrity served only to complicate. Little could Marjorie have imagined that Julia Scribner was about to come into her life. Meanwhile, at Foxcroft School, Julia was a debutante with a destiny she also could scarcely foresee. She loved her father beyond measure, but she had difficulty abiding the wiles of her socialite mother, a circumstance that parallels Marjorie's experiences with her father and mother. In both cases, the problem was the mother. And, as incredible as it might seem for a Scribner girl, Julia seemed to cling desperately to a new vision of feminine, to the notion that a woman's life "should exceed [her] grasp," or indeed what exactly is "Heaven for"?

The year is 1939. Suddenly, provocatively, and completely beyond expectation, a bright star swam into Marjorie's ken—her name, Julia Bloodgood Scribner. A youthful twenty-one, Julia was already fighting the loneliness that wealth could not abate. She needed a sympathetic mother to share the depths of her despair. She found that surrogate mother in Marjorie Kinnan Rawlings, who often felt a lack in not having the companionship and the love of a child. Borrowing the inimitable metaphor of John Donne, their two souls, like two candles, melted into one. Julia was the anodyne Marjorie needed; Marjorie was the comforting mother Julia did not have. As time passed, Julia visited regularly, on more than one occasion staying for a month or longer. Julia came to depend on Marjorie as much as Marjorie depended upon her. Julia had arrived just in time. They philosophized on topics ranging from Julia's need (in Marjorie's view) to have a love affair, to

Marjorie's need (in Julia's view) to read more philosophy, to Julia's need (in Marjorie's view) to find a proper vocation, to Marjorie's need (in Julia's view) not to drink and drive.

Late in 1938 or early in 1939, Marjorie met Norton Sanford Baskin, a shy, demure man, with whom Marjorie fell in love almost instantly. A hotelier from Union Springs, Alabama, Norton was both in awe of and afraid of Marjorie, who in turn wanted more than "weekend love." In one of her more remarkable letters, Marjorie proposes marriage, but not before she expresses frustration with Norton's seeming ennui on the subject of matrimony, which, confesses Marjorie, "makes me flare out at you in my ill or drunk unguarded moments" (*Love Letters* 39). The importance of Norton in Marjorie's mercurial life cannot be overstated, and she recognized both the fact and foundation for it, as she wrote to him while he was away during the war: "That is your particular triumph, so much higher than being United States Senator or Ernest Hemingway----*being* such a *luminous* person that everyone who comes within range warms his hands at your lovely flame. God knows I have warmed myself at your fire. . . . Oh darling, come back to me" (*Love Letters* 380). But, as deep as her feelings for Norton clearly were, from the outset of their relationship in 1940, Julia provided what Norton could not, the love of a child for her mother.

Then, just as their immediate filial love was solidifying into permanence, the "Day of Infamy" interrupted. On 7 December 1941, the Japanese Imperial Navy attacked Pearl Harbor. On the days following what President Roosevelt called a "dastardly attack," the whole of the United States was in a panic. Roosevelt asked and Congress answered by declaring war on Japan, 8 December, and on Germany, 11 December. Air raid sirens went off daily in New York, for without fail someone out there in the wide firmament was certain that a German bomber was seen flying toward the city. Irrationality, an understandable irrationality, gripped the nation. Both Marjorie and Julia faced the chaos that no one could have imagined with typical strength. Julia was in New York; Marjorie at Crescent Beach with her husband Norton, whom she had married less than two months before. Instead of retreating to the safety of the Scribner estate in New Jersey, Julia became immediately proactive. She volunteered as a "spotter" and took rigorous lessons on how to identify enemy aircraft. She spent lonely, cold days atop various hills, waiting for the German bombers to appear. She also volunteered to take lessons on how to recognize German agents and German espionage. She later became a "dancer" at the USO Clubs, created to give the troops a break before being shipped off to war. It was not easy. In one letter she complains in obvious exhaustion, "I'm thoroughly sick of being a one woman USO camp" ([late May

1943]). The letters from Julia to Marjorie are amazingly detailed, a veritable history of the times. The letters are, in effect, war diaries, riveting accounts of how women took over as the men prepared for what was too often the inevitable, death. Julia even canceled planned trips to Florida, pointing out with pride that she simply could not abandon her various volunteer assignments in New York. Marjorie was more removed, although there was a constant fear that the Germans would come ashore along the Florida beaches. Still, like Julia, she persisted, fully committed to the war effort. At the urging of the celebrity-editor Clifton Fadiman, she agreed, somewhat reluctantly, to write pro-America statements for Fadiman's various literary engines. After she wrote the now-lost article, "The Southern Soldier and the Negro," deemed "too controversial" by the Writer's War Board to publish because it defended Black soldiers against prejudice, Marjorie became disillusioned with the shrill propaganda of these nationalist organs. She had reason. In 1943, Norton volunteered without her knowledge and began dodging death as a volunteer ambulance driver for the American Field Service in the India-Burma theater. She wrote Norton almost daily imploring him to be careful, and then she repeated her terror to Julia. Her letters to Julia are filled with World War II anecdote, most of it from Norton, after it had survived censorship. Marjorie had been supporting the troops since the advent of the war. She received hundreds of letters from the troops, praising her books that they read in the Armed Services Editions and asking for her prayers as they prepared to go into battle. Her responses to them, meant to allay their fears, stand as testimony to her commitment. Her letters were the letters of a mother to her sons. Marjorie agonized over their content. Because of these letters and because of Norton's to Marjorie, her letters to Julia on the war are more personal than Julia's more descriptive accounts. Asked by the grieving parents, Marjorie paid this impassioned, universal tribute to one soldier, Caleb Milne, a stretcher bearer, who was killed by a German mortar shell in North Africa on 11 May 1943, while giving aid to a wounded French Legionnaire: "What does it take to teach us? How and when shall we learn? Shall we continue to kill off our Rupert Brooke's, our Joyce Kilmer's, our Caleb Milne's, and be as stupid as before?" (*Uncollected Writings* 309). Taken together, the correspondence of Julia and Marjorie presents a compelling history of World War II, firsthand accounts of what Marjorie came to consider the "appalling madness" of war.

Yet, even in the face of this monstrous human conflict, Julia had time to instruct Marjorie on literature and music. At times her letters are overwhelming, sentence after sentence, paragraph after paragraph punctuated with critical commentary and reading suggestions. Through Scribners, Julia had ready (and free) access to the latest fiction and nonfiction to appear on the market. And, of course, she also had the advantage of reading in proof what Scribners was about to publish. Numbers and access were on Julia's side. She often asks if Marjorie knew this novel or that novel, and if not she would send it to her immediately, but not so much as a gift but as an expectation to receive evaluation in return. Marjorie responds with equal gusto, as on 19 May 1944: "[M]any thanks for the books, which I have just finished and shall return shortly. I enjoyed particularly the Sender 'Counter-Attack in Spain,' and it seemed to me to be 'For Whom the Bell Tolls' without love in a sleeping-bag." Julia was a serious aficionado of matters literary. She was by any standard amazingly well-read. And for Marjorie literature was her life's blood. But the exhausting exchanges would finally come to an end. By Julia's own testimony, before marriage she spent many of her afternoons in the New York Public Library. She was particularly interested in philosophy and would complain to Marjorie, expecting immediate response, about writers and critics she did not like or just thought absolutely silly in their credo, especially the famed critic Edmund Wilson whom she found "a drip." Foxcroft had taught her well. She was discerning, except perhaps for her unqualified devotion to Charles Péguy, the Catholic socialist, whom she plagued Marjorie about incessantly. Julia was not only persistent; she was doggedly persistent. Names flew from her pen like ether from eternity. Marjorie held her own, much to the amazement of this youthful dynamo: "I can't put down a vision of you thirsting for more and bigger and longer books. It's quite shocking the way you consume them. I cannot read them slowly enough (if they are good). . . . When I read little bits at a time and gnaw over each chapter as I go I do better – but it is a great handicap to my ambition to be widely read" ([21 March 1944]). Ignoring Julia's protestations of deficiency, Marjorie's letters display a pride, a motherly pride, in her surrogate daughter's accomplishment, not the least of which was her knowledge of music, but especially Classical and Romantic symphony and opera. Julia's knowledge of literature pales in comparison to her knowledge of music and opera. She discusses symphonies and arias and oratorios with expert knowledge. Nothing escapes her prodding eye. Her favorite composer was Bach and without doubt her favorite Bach was the Mass in B-flat Minor. In one letter, she advises Marjorie—who was planning to attend a performance of the Mass at Rollins College—on what to anticipate, movement by movement, as an experienced teacher might, somewhat irreverently, advise an advanced pupil: "The Crucifixus is heavy with pain & that is unless they play it straight with much academic reverence for Bach, in which case don't blame him for *their* emotional short comings. At the end it broadens out from the rather limping theme of 'crucifixus' and falls very slowly 'passus' with an awful finality to 'sepultus est' which fades and fades into nothing. Then! be somewhat prepared because the 'Et resurrexit' should leap up! And if your spine doesn't curl then you can damn the Rollins choir to hell" ([24 February 1941]). Julia attended symphonies and operas with the verve of a teenager, but also with the analytical eye of a seasoned critic. Her letters are filled with deft evaluation. She became, in the face of Marjorie's already fine-tuned understanding of high culture, Marjorie's symphonic and operatic teacher, advising her on what and what not to attend. In effect, when it came to music, to philosophy, and to certain areas in literature, the roles of teacher and of student were reversed. The mentee became the mentor. And in that shift the true wonder of this correspondence comes to fruition, for in the end, their conversations on music and literature and the authority that they exude on the subjects represent an astonishing community of two, unrestricted by the patriarchal forces that would question both their ability and their right to discuss such matters on such a level of intimacy. If these letters can be defined by anything, they are a woman speaking to a woman completely free from the fetters of male intrusion.

It would be misleading, however, to imply that all was so serious in their relationship. Quite to the contrary, joie de vivre was a mantra they fully embraced. Few experiences seemed too outrageous for them. Adventure was their oyster-opening sword. They hunted and fished and cooked in the Florida scrub, almost always with a male guide. One of the more intriguing episodes took place when the two of them went hunting in a remote area and Julia fell into the moccasin-infested water neck-deep and upon emerging had to strip, wearing only the male guide's coat as her clothes dried over an open fire while Marjorie cooked wild game in her Dutch oven. Much hilarity resulted from that experience. On another occasion, the two of them set out with a male guide from the U.S. Forestry Department on a monthlong trek through the forests of the South in order that Marjorie could gather material for an article she was commissioned to write, later published as "Trees for Tomorrow." But more was at stake than the trees. Perhaps Julia's teasing, some whispered flirtation—fully supported by the scheming Marjorie—attracted the guide, who apparently fell head over heels for Julia. With an abundance of caution Julia abandoned the trip after three weeks, leaving the married Marjorie to deal with the aftermath. Being her usually forthright self, Marjorie writes of her experience with their guide: "The shape I was in that night, it's God's mercy, I am fat and forty and just didn't appeal to him. But something told me to keep him away from you. Write me all the dirt" (11 November 1942). Being her usually prudent self, Julie waits some six months to respond ([late May 1943]), acknowledging that she received a silver leaf brooch as a gift, which came with an "un-father-of-3-children like note[.] I was quite upset, and toyed (for the first time in my life) with the melodramatic idea of sending it back," which she did not. Julia was now safe in the confines of New York. All perfectly innocent, except Julia and Marjorie did not think so. After a month in the woods, Marjorie was relieved to get back to the safer life of Black intrigue and Cracker conflict at Cross Creek. Marjorie and Julia also traveled frequently together in the North, especially in the Berkshires of Western Massachusetts, and the outcome was by their testimony always the same—they laughed uproariously, ate sumptuously, and talked constantly. Even unexpected snowstorms did little to impede their zest for adventure. Marjorie and Julia were forever up to some tomfoolery, often instigated by Marjorie who dragged potential suitor after potential suitor before Julia, each and all rejected after some designation of unworthiness. There was at least one instance, however, when their behavior backfired; they both became infatuated with the same man, which proves to be one of the enduring stories found in the letters.

The man in question even gave himself a name, Perry Patterson (aka Caleb Perry Patterson). In what may be one of the great literary hoaxes of the twentieth century, this genuine trickster, armed with the self-proclaimed Patterson nom de plume, first wrote to Marjorie in the summer of 1942, complimenting her on her work and then asking if she would help him, a self-declared budding writer. He offered his tragic story of wounds in battle at Dunkirk, how he read from *The Yearling* to children in an "air raid shelter" in London, and how he suffered the perils of convalescence in a military hospital in Canada. Marjorie's "heart melted." Miraculously, the wounded Patterson had somehow made his way to New York City to do "camouflage work." Patterson's story, writes Marjorie, is the "most heart-breaking I have ever heard" (21 August 1942). Perhaps in light of the hundreds of letters from servicepeople she was receiving, without examining motive, Marjorie fell hook, line, and sinker for the blather of "Mr. Patterson." They exchanged more letters. After all, how could Marjorie ignore the cri de coeur of a Dunkirk survivor? Without permission and quite innocently, of course, she offered to introduce him to Julia, the daughter of one of the most powerful publishers on planet Earth. The adroitly fawning Patterson immediately contacted Julia, who was so swayed by his words that she not only invited him to visit her in New York, she invited him to meet her father at Dew Hollow, a mansion reserved for literary royalty. This self-proclaimed wounded veteran, who further alleged that he was on a temporary furlough from the Canadian military hospital, arrived at Julia's doorstep in very short order. The vaunted Charles Scribner III was so taken aback by the righteous soliloquies of Patterson that he offered him a preliminary contract to publish a children's novel pre-titled *Zubu*. The sycophant Patterson eventually left, after apparently making his romantic interest in Julia known, but not before he "borrowed" her typewriter, which not surprisingly he never bothered to return. It took months before Marjorie and Julia realized, reluctantly, that they had been deceived by Patterson, who continued to write them, now allegedly from England, where he had retreated to be inspired. How Charles III dealt with the deception is not clear, although his silence speaks for itself. Marjorie and Julia never let the subject die. In their fertile imaginations, Patterson became an obsession. And, in spite of their stated outrage, it is clear that they both hoped to the bitter end that Patterson would magically appear, novel in hand, to explain his behavior. He never did, of course. This colossal hoax is told here for the first time, providing one more instance of the compelling lives of these two remarkably complex women.

Whatever negative impact the Patterson saga had upon them, or their confidence about romantic entanglements, it did not blunt their interest in sex, both as a theoretical topic or as a physical reality. The supposedly more sophisticated Marjorie took the lead here, assuring the purportedly innocent Julia that her life would be altered for the good if she would just consider having an affair, not for love, just for sex. "L'affaire Patterson" morphed into l'affaire Julia, whose self-confessed virginal life irritated Marjorie. With all the opportunities Julia enjoyed, Marjorie was incredulous that Julia was a virgin. With no psychoanalytic training whatsoever, and warned not to mix psychiatry and friendship by her physician Dana Atchley, Marjorie plunged right in, "The hell with Dr. Atchley---I am going to say what I think. I think that after a happy and sheltered childhood, you found maturity unpleasant, for several reasons: sexual frustration and sexual guilt (but you should feel none, as masturbation is the medically accepted substitute for the desirable sex relation)" (19 May 1944). There seems little question that Julia was intrigued by the thought. In one letter, she confesses rather openly that she is frustrated with her sexuality, especially after her friend Catherine Gilpin announces her marriage: "The sad part is that I am the last rose left blooming alone, all my friends being now in someone's buttonhole. So there is no one to plan a gay spinsterhood with, (Cath and I had often considered that contingency), and there is an end to girlhood friendship, to put a pleasant thing in sickening words. . . . And friendship becomes adult – firmer founded, but not so exciting and full of adventurous possibilities – and *don't* for *Godsake* bring the vulgar side of your mind to bear on that innocent phrase" ([late May 1943]). Marjorie, the quasi-committed Freudian—witness again "Gal Young Un"—sees Julia's response as an expression of her psychological immaturity. In an effort to shake Julia to the core, Marjorie in yet another letter introduces the generally verboten subject of masturbation, which Marjorie claims is perfectly normal. She goes so far as to posit the notion that by avoiding masturbatory sex Julia is becoming abnormal. Once again, Marjorie assumes the guise of the psychiatrist, bluntly arguing that Julia needs to begin to masturbate or else be condemned to a life of "sexual guilt," a psychosomatic condition that is the logical outcome of "sexual frustration." Julia, the master tactician, counters by assuring Marjorie that she does not feel like her mental life is in jeopardy just because she has never masturbated. She asks Marjorie to trust her and assures her that her psychological being is in decent order, at least insofar as sex is concerned. Marjorie would have none of it. She was convinced that Julia was the living emblem of the frustrated female, which leads Marjorie to the conclusion that "her illness is neurotic . . . and if she doesn't get straightened out soon, is going to make an awfully eccentric old maid" (*Love Letters* 261). Unwittingly, of course, Marjorie is taking the position of the male chauvinist who assumes all an unhappy woman needs is good sex. Julia is refusing to be put into that position. The subject of sex and the implications of sexuality are not a passing fancy in the letters. That the two of them would even be having such discussions indicates the mutual trust shared. Marjorie, within reason, is profoundly serious, but what she does not seem to recognize is that Julia, within reason, is equally serious. Buried somewhere in such mother-daughter-like exchanges is the wider issue of male sovereignty, and on this subject both are pro-female, if not decidedly feminist. In the end, they are always two women talking to each other with the jointly held goal of creating the lives they "wished to live" on their own terms, to borrow the keynote from Ann McCutchan's recent biography of Rawlings.[1]

This desire for self-determination only exacerbated the plague of patriarchy from which both Marjorie and Julia suffered the whole of their adult lives. Male power, male dominance, male privilege, call it what you will, was an ever-present reality with which they had to cope, sometimes artfully, sometimes generously, and sometimes angrily. In the letters they are forever analyzing male ego, tossing the names of male friends and male writers around both in earnest and in jest, and on occasion in contempt. They discuss through sarcasm and irony Julia's many suitors, serious as some were, as if she were Snow White and they one of the Seven (or more) Dwarfs. It seemed as if the men in Julia's life all suffered hamartia, a fatal flaw that excluded each of them from a permanent place in her life. For Marjorie, it

---

1   Ann McCutchan, *The Life She Wished to Live* (New York: Norton, 2021), xviii.

was different. She had the love of Norton, the hotelier and the raconteur, another "born storyteller" as Margaret Mitchell once referred to Marjorie. Yet, as Marjorie confides to Julia, he was not everything she wished, a striking confessional. She further confesses to Julia that she has loved only "one man" in her life, and he was married with children, hence off limits: "Married to a man whose work a woman considers useful enough so that she can give herself to his life, is probably the best female life, but after that, doing a type of work for which she is fitted, and which she loves, is next best. I have never had the former---the one man I was in love with, whose work seemed valuable to me, was married, and conditions were such that I was the first to admit that he could not become un-married, to marry me---. And without work of my own, I don't know what I should have done" (9 August 1944). Marjorie then warns Julia that she must give up her current "parasitic life" as a Scribner. Either find a man whose work she finds "useful" or find work that she "loves." Julia responds in a sympathetic tone: "I think you are right about the work angle, and unquestionably much of my *personal* depression is due to my unuseful existence and unused potentialities. I also agree that the logical place for me would be in CSS [Scribners]. The only trouble is that I haven't the faintest desire to work there" (29? August 1944).

Then, all of a sudden, the subject of marriage, raised by Marjorie, took on new meaning. Julia first fell in love with an Episcopal priest, much her senior, who was married with children and grandchildren, hence also off limits. Then, within a year, she met and married, on 24 May 1945, another Episcopal priest, this one attached to the General Theological Seminary in New York City. Marjorie was in shock, partly because Julia had kept it from her until her engagement announcement was to appear in the *New York Times*. Never mind. Earlier, in October 1941, Marjorie had kept her pending marriage to Norton from Julia. Point, counterpoint. Nevertheless, Marjorie's hurt is palpable in both her letters to Norton and to Julia. Thomas James Bigham Jr. was his name. He came with pedigree. His father, Thomas James Bigham Sr., was the Reverend Canon of the Episcopal Church in Pittsburgh, Pennsylvania. In her letters Julia does everything she can to justify her choice to Marjorie. "Tom," as Julia calls him, was not Marjorie's choice. Simple as that. To be sure, Marjorie was polite, even encouraging, but Julia had already anticipated her disappointment in her first, carefully crafted announcement and introduction that she was engaged to marry Bigham: "I think you will like him, Marge, though maybe not at once. He is terribly reserved and wears a slightly formidable moustache. The first time I met him I thought he was awful then the second time I must have said to myself there is a man I could marry. And you know, I had not been able to say that to myself for about

8 years" (16 February 1945). More astonishing, Marjorie did not attend the wedding ceremony, begging off, but only after Julia suggests that it would be better if she came "some other time than the actual wedding." That wound could never fully heal. Vera Scribner, the biological mother, was determined to host a socialite wedding that, most notably, did not include the surrogate mother, Marjorie. Julia complains bitterly to Marjorie about the nastiness of Vera, who, among other things, did not like Tom:

> Muddy [Vera] took the news even worse than I had expected, and is not becoming as resigned as I thought she would. So she is taking out all her disappointment and resentment over this unsocial marriage I am making, but having a wedding to end all weddings. To make up for the fact that I am not marrying a Vanderbilt or a future Master of Foxhounds, I am being subjected to a Vanderbilt wedding.
>
> Marjorie, you know how I hate such affairs. They are the very apotheosis of everything I loathe in the life I have led, and now this even in my life which means so much and so deeply has to be made into a sort of garish nightmare. I can assure you that on no point have I been asked what I would like. . . . What with this and the continued sniping at Tom, and endless references to this or that person who is "so in love'" meaning of course that I'm not, I get pretty worn down. Muddy has seen Tom just once since we've been engaged, at which point with icy smile and an edgy voice she said "Well, I never thought I'd have you for a son-in-law[.]" That sort of slowed up conversation and shortly afterward she left!
> (26 March 1945)

Marjorie tried to keep up her own conversation with Julia, and the letters from Julia kept coming, albeit at a far slower pace after the wedding. The understanding Marjorie wrote more often and more than once forbade Julia to write in return. The once unfettered, at times ebullient Julia seemed blindsided by the rigors of marriage. She could no longer spend afternoons in the New York Public Library. And she could only attend her beloved opera after negotiation. She detested cleaning and cooking. She demanded to have a servant and got one, but at a cost. She was obliged to worry even more about finances, a concern that begins to dominate her letters. The once Miss Julia Scribner was now addressed as Mrs. Thomas J. Bigham. When Julia became pregnant, Marjorie asked if she could be the godmother, even announcing to Maxwell Perkins that she *was* to be the godmother. The best laid plans were not to be. Episcopal High Church orthodoxy, issued forth by rational male edict, forbade that a woman who was not baptized function as a godmother. Makes sense if you believe in edicts, which leads Julia to opine about the "blindfolded quality of all laws." Not the words Marjorie expected. Raised by a God-fearing Methodist, Marjorie had not been baptized. Julia openly suggests, through "Tom," that baptism is easy enough to accomplish. Not for the prideful Marjorie. She refused to do what male principle demanded. Once again Marjorie was confronted by what she saw as obstinate maleness, and once again she did not blink. But what she lost over principle she could never gain back through love. She rejected the will of her "daughter" and in consequence lost the comfort of a "goddaughter," although Marjorie claimed the right anyway: "I can only say that I shall still think of myself as godmother, spiritual and in every way, to your child. If the House of Scribner should fall, and I should still have an orange grove; if the formal god-mothers should enter whore-houses, presumably disqualifying themselves; if anything in this uncertain world should ever give your child any need of me in any possible fashion, I should nurture it to the best of my ability with sustenance, with spiritual comfort and a passing on of the deep love I feel for you" (2 March 1947). Julia had actually invited the declaration, for when it came to naming the child, the authority and the wishes of the biological mother were replaced by the surrogate, as she tells Marjorie: "I don't like the name Vera anyway, and that amount of pressure arouses every ounce of my resistance so that I just *can't – won't*. I am seriously considering Hildreth which was Muddy's father's name and which I have always liked very much. How does it strike you?" (26 February 1947). Marjorie responds with an obvious sense of happiness: "I am surprised that Vera should insist that a girl be named for her. It is Tom's and your child, so stand firm. I think 'Hildreth' would be an enchanting name" (4 March 1947). Hildreth Julia Bigham, a baby girl, was born on 1 April 1947, and subsequently was christened without Marjorie, and yet with her. And the Baskins did get to see Julia and Hildreth on occasion, and as the fates granted, the child seemed especially to love the attention of Norton, which he gave happily and without reservation. As for Marjorie, as always she rose again to the occasion, supporting Julia with fulsome letters of encouragement and of love as Julia continued her long journey through postpartum anxiety that finally turned to clinical depression.

In spite of her never ending trials and tribulations, Julia's devotion to Marjorie never wavered. But it was now tempered by a new reality. Marriage, motherhood, and theological obligation had taken her once-heralded freedom. She tried to resurrect her interest in becoming a professional photographer, but the pressures of life were too much. The migraines increased, seemingly in proportion to her domestic anxieties. Julia's fragility worsened. Marjorie, whose own health issues were increasing dramatically, did everything a surrogate mother could. She insisted that Julia visit her as often as possible, probably with the silent hope that Tom would not be tagging along. Tom, as Marjorie confided to Norton, is too "High Church," too interested in administering rather than ministering Christian virtue. Nonetheless, when she could, Julia came for brief visits to Cross Creek and to the oceanfront cottage at Crescent Beach. But for the most part, domestic itineraries would permit only weekend visits, usually to Van Hornesville, New York, where Marjorie had bought an old farmhouse in 1947. They did see each other when Marjorie came to the city on Scribner press business or to be evaluated at Harkness Pavilion Hospital. Marjorie seldom stayed with the Bighams. Various excuses were always given to alleviate the pain of betrayal Julia must have felt, as the circumstances of her life seemed to compel her to put aside her surrogate mother. To avoid bothering the overwrought Julia, Marjorie claimed she preferred a hotel, or even the Scribner estate at Far Hills. On 29 August 1951, Julia's second daughter was born, Mary Kirkpatrick Bigham. Her birth was welcomed by Marjorie, but any meaningful interaction between Mary and Marjorie has not come to light. Once again, Julia suffered nausea throughout the pregnancy and this time serious hemorrhaging after the birth. After Mary's arrival, the number of letters from Julia goes into steep decline, but the substance of the ones she writes are vintage Julia, always appealing to the wisdom of Marjorie's motherly attitudes toward her. Visits also declined. Because of the circumstances of each, there seemed little time for them to rekindle their once nomadic ways. Also, by 1951, Marjorie's health was slipping rapidly. Being unable to complete the revisions of the manuscript of *The Sojourner* led her to fits of creative doubt. Without Perkins, who had died suddenly in 1947, to her an "unspeakable grief," Marjorie became a writer beyond restraint, although the editors at Scribners, including Charles Scribner III himself, worked diligently to buttress her fragile ego.

The year 1952 could hardly have been worse. On 11 February, Julia wired Marjorie that Charles Scribner III, second only to Maxwell Perkins in Marjorie's eyes, had died after only a brief illness. Julia had lost "daddy," Marjorie had lost "Charlie," and nothing ever again could be the same. Only weeks later, the distraught Marjorie suffered a coronary spasm at Cross Creek and was rushed to Riverside Hospital in Jacksonville, where she spent three weeks in recovery, at which point she was warned that she must give up cigarettes completely, drink only in moderation, and watch her diet carefully. The good news was she completed the revisions of the manuscript of *The Sojourner* in April and packed it off to Scribners. Light was supposed to appear at the end of the tunnel. It did not. Aunt Ida Tarrant, Marjorie's beloved ward, died in June. Then, in July her forever obstreperous and financially insolvent brother showed up at Crescent Beach with his infant son Jeffrey, whom he had taken from his estranged wife. Arthur Houston Kinnan quickly became Marjorie's agony. Julia's recurrent health problems added yet another cross to bear. Within months Marjorie was back to her destructive habits. Yet, for a brief period, Marjorie's own life seemed in recovery. In October, she and Norton left for an extended trip to Great Britain and Ireland, partly planned by Julia. On 4 January 1953, the albatross was lifted from her soul. *The Sojourner,* nearly ten years in the making, was published by Scribners. Rested and with a renewed sense of purpose Marjorie headed to Virginia in February to begin research for a projected biography of Ellen Glasgow, largely from materials provided to her by Glasgow intimates. Her letters to Julia from Richmond are aglow with her discovery of hitherto unknown and private information about Glasgow. For the almost two months she was there, Marjorie seemed less dependent upon alcohol, cigarettes, and food. Unhappily, however, Julia began to slide further into depression. She spent the summer of 1953 under the care of a psychiatrist in neighboring Pennsylvania. Marjorie despaired that Julia was doomed to a life of mental anguish. Shakespeare's assurance that "All's Well That Ends Well" proved a myth. Marjorie's myriad issues returned in force. After a brief return visit to Richmond in late October–early November to shore up Glasgow sources, she returned to Florida exhausted. On 14 December, she was rushed to Flagler Hospital in St. Augustine from Crescent Beach. This time the fates were unforgiving. Her rich and ruinous life came suddenly to an end. Marjorie Kinnan Rawlings died of a ruptured aneurysm that night. Julia had lost her "mother." Just what her immediate response was is lost in the vaults of history. She flew to Florida to minister to Norton's agonies. Her last recorded words to Marjorie were as they always had been: "Love, Julia." The two candles that long ago had melted into one, became one again.

The tenacious Julia was not to be silenced, however. As Marjorie's literary executor, she advocated before Scribners' editors the unpublished children's story, *The Secret River,* begun under the guidance of Maxwell Perkins. She was determined to see it into print. Where Perkins had seen the mixing of racial issues and childhood fantasy as a problem, Julia did not see this as an impediment. How else might a Black child safely act in a world of racial divide? Fantasy seemed the perfect vehicle to express the collision between wonder and reality. Julia also had strength on her side. Charles Scribner IV (aka Jr.), her brother, was now the president of Scribners. On 23 May 1955, an especially large print run of 18,000 copies was published. *The Secret River* was named runner-up for the prestigious John Newbery Medal, given to the most distinguished children's book of the year. Yet Julia was not done. In 1956, she followed with yet another accolade to her surrogate mother, *The Marjorie Rawlings Reader,* which she edited and to which she added an introduction. Among the selections, Julia included the full-text of the novel *South Moon Under,* with this insight on Marjorie's depiction of the Crackers: "There is much hardship and sorrow and tragedy in this book, but here, possibly more than any other of her books, Marjorie Rawlings has conveyed the quality of these people who drew her sympathy—their gallantry, their grace of spirit and [their] bitter struggles for survival." Julia adroitly observes that the Crackers were the "well-spring of Marjorie Rawlings' inspiration and the lodestar of her writing talent. . . . Through her they have gained a place in the literature of their country, and through them that literature has been enriched by the achievement of an outstanding writer" (*Rawlings Reader* xviii–xix).

Julia bore two more children, a third daughter, Anne "Anda" Scribner Bigham ([Hutchins], b. 1955), and a son, Thomas J. "Jake" Bigham Jr. (1957–2007). Then, on 26 October 1961, the *New York Times* printed the startling announcement: Julia Bloodgood Scribner Bigham had died, a victim of breast cancer at the age of forty-three. Just eight short years after Marjorie's death, the faithful light of the remaining candle was snuffed out.

Death, however, need not be final. To our good fortune, the written incarnation of Marge and Julia talking to each other is enshrined forever in these magnificent letters.

I would rather be talking to you than writing to you – not just because of the way I feel about writing, but because of the way I feel about you.

Julia to Marjorie

Memories of Mother

HILDRETH JULIA BIGHAM MCCARTHY, MD

I THOUGHT I DID NOT HAVE many memories of my mother except as a constant presence in my life; but in remembering moments with her, I now realize how very vivid her memories are for me. I will share some of these memories to perhaps give some context to her letters. Clearly, I knew her after these letters were written.[1] The person I knew was the married woman and mother she became.

My mother, Julia Scribner Bigham, was not a shrinking violet, not an invalid (as described by her brother [Charles Scribner IV, aka Buzz] in his book, *In the Company of Writers*), nor in any way incompetent. She was the person who taught me to cook, to drive, to ride, and most of all to think for myself. She did not coddle her children (though Mary and I thought she coddled the two younger ones, Anda and Jake, too much—Anda for her blond curls and Jake for his gender.) Mary and I always competed strongly for her attention and felt we deserved more spoiling by Mother. Our father [Rev. Thomas James Bigham Jr.] was always addressed quite formally as Father and Mother was Mother. She had called her parents by nicknames, Muddy and Daddy. Our father did not approve and was worried that overfamiliarity would turn into Pops or Poppa, which he certainly would not have been comfortable with. I don't believe Mother was so anxious about being a

---

1   Hildreth Julia Bigham, "Hildy," eldest daughter of Julia Scribner Bigham, kindly and generously agreed to write this reminiscence of her mother. The editors are beyond grateful, not only for Hildy's singular memories, here set down for the first time, but also for her many contributions to the substance of the explanatory notes. Hildy would want us to acknowledge that her sister, Mary Kirkpatrick Bigham Binks, contributed in draft, and that her youngest sister, Anne "Anda" Bigham Hutchins, is to be credited with finding the Rawlings letters published in this volume in the attic of their family home. Hildy's only brother, Thomas James "Jake" Bigham Jr., the youngest of the four, died in an accident in 2007.

Mummy or Muddy, because she did not rise to the bait like Father did when we teasingly called him "Dad."

Mother probably did not want, however, to continue the names she had with her parents. She had enough difficulties with Granny not to have to also assume her mother's name by her own children. As far as language and accents go, she actually consciously worked to lose her "to the manor born" accent and vocabulary when she was at Foxcroft. She could hear it in her family and her classmates and did not want "the man on the street" to know her background from her speech and assume she was "high and mighty." I remember no accent from Mother, but her brother and her mother and my great aunt all sounded like they came from a 1930's high-society movie, which in a way they did. Mother sounded like a newscaster. I think she listened to the radio to emulate the voices. She also had wonderful swear phrases like "Holy cats and dogs," "Jiminy Crickets," and "Gadzooks." She liked to call police "cops." All of which, her mother, Granny, highly disapproved of hearing, even Father complained at times of her slang. Mother was very uncomfortable with the bounty and living large that she had been brought up with and did not want to be associated with it.

I do not believe it was in opposition to her mother's glamour that she eschewed fashion, cosmetics, and jewelry; but rather her deep conflict over the haves and have-nots. She never complained of Granny's wonderful clothes or high style of living, except when it appeared extravagant, like never taking public transportation in New York City, only a taxi. When she married, she wanted a plain gold band ($18) and would not wear a diamond. Her mother, famously, always wore her own mother's engagement ring (7 carats) together with an equally large cabochon sapphire on her right hand and large square-cut sapphire with diamond surround engagement ring on her left with her platinum wedding band. I, without such thoughts or concerns, wondered why Mother allowed herself to be so out of fashion and plain. She had inherited diamond rings, why not wear one? To me as a child, Granny was very glamourous and to be idolized and emulated. Why wasn't Mother more like Granny?? Having lived through the Great Depression, Mother told me that she was deeply disturbed by the life she led while many others suffered for even basic comforts around her. She would tell me about rationing she experienced during the war and the continued poverty she had seen in the south. She abhorred the racism she witnessed. She was an original member of the NAACP. Her words actually made an impression on her selfish, self-centered child.

Mother didn't graduate from Foxcroft. Summer before her senior year, she had a terrible riding accident in New Marlborough that broke her femur. She and Granny were out for a ride in The Preserve, her grandfather's land, when her horse broke through a culvert and fell. She spent almost six months in traction and during that time had to have one operation to rebreak the leg as it was not in good alignment. As she was about seventeen and her brother fifteen, perhaps that is why he thought of her as an invalid. She was in bed for almost a year. There was no pinning of bones at that time and immobility in traction was the only way to allow such a big bone to heal. She recovered and rode again, but not with the same fearless confidence that her mother exemplified. She still loved horses and was still a beautiful, though more careful, rider. I was lucky enough to have her as my primary teacher of horse management and riding. She also did teach my father to ride and even took him foxhunting on old Jack, who was famous for only having one eye. Father was a diligent student, but galloping around was not really his cup of tea. When I was about six, Mother and Father bought an old farmstead, Ford Hill, in Sheffield, Massachusetts, to summer in. As Father was a professor at General Theological Seminary, he had three months off in the summer. The whole family relocated to the country: Mother, Father, children, cook, nursemaid, and cat. Granny sent up the horses and pony from Far Hills, New Jersey.

Ford Hill suffered from disrepair and neglect when we got it. There were many large old elm trees that had died from Dutch Elm disease. My poor father was required by Mother to learn how to fell large trees and then they would cut them up and make bonfires. Father was never very outdoorsy as compared with Mother, but he was a very good sport about all the dangerous and strenuous work required. They also put in a good-sized vegetable garden. Digging out of the sod was a big job, but they were both very pleased with the results. Mother loved fresh corn and they planted some rows of sweet corn. It would just sprout and then disappear. One early morning she caught the crows eating the new row of seeds. She and Father put up a scarecrow with Father's old work clothes, and reseeded. Next day the crows were eating the seed from under the scarecrow. She asked a local farmer and he suggested hanging a dead crow, as crows were smart and would respect that "scarecrow." More seed in the ground and the crows came back. She got her .22 Hornet rifle (one of her several competition and varmint guns) and shot a crow from her bedroom closet. We had corn that summer, but weeding in the garden was distasteful as the dead crow smelled really bad.

Mother was a very good shot and liked to compete, but pretty much gave it up after getting married. The only other time I saw her shoot was at a woodchuck on a hill where we wanted to graze horses. You could see the hillside from the dining room table and the woodchuck usually would be out when we had dinner. Mother set up the rifle by the little outside porch and, of course, the woodchuck didn't show up for several days. Then one day at lunch he was out under the apple tree on the hill. She crept out to the porch and got him with one shot. It was quite a distance and she had no scope. The guests at lunch that day were quite impressed. Father didn't shoot, but didn't seem to mind having an Annie Oakley at his side.

Fly fishing had also been one of her sports, but I never saw her fish or knew of her taking a trip to do so. I think Granny may have told Mother that she would have to give up her shooting, fishing, and photography trips to make a successful marriage. Granny would have been full of advice and it was hard to brook her. Granny, herself, boasted that she had never let her husband, Charlie, sleep a night away from her. She would even go with him on business trips. (My father confided to me that it was a bit of a burden for grandfather to have his wife along on patently "men-only" business trips.) Mother would have very likely taken Granny's advice to heart, however, as she did respect her authority and wisdom in family matters.

Mother developed many skills that her schools and upbringing had over-looked. She complained of not even knowing how to wash out her stockings when she arrived at boarding school, so she may have overcompensated, learning many other untaught skills. She took basic cooking instruction from her mother's cook (and from Marjorie, no doubt). She never felt herself to be a good cook, but she was able to impart to me her basic skills of cooking an egg or hamburger to order, making a white or marinara sauce and frying chicken livers so they were as good as pâté. Her hunting skills made lobsters a favorite for guests and she would always broil them, not boil, by pithing them with her hunting knife in the kitchen, to the dismay of our young, Irish aspiring cook. Somewhere along the line, Mother also learned carpentry. Her carpentry tools were organized and carefully selected. She would repair tables and chairs, but was also able to design and build. She made me a large built-in bookcase in an alcove when I was twelve that was even wired for my fish tank. She designed and built the cabinets for her hi-fi and records, planning the wiring and installing the switches. Tools for the garden, clear-ing the land, and the stable were all selected by Mother. She never did get the hang of sewing on a button, though. Granny could paint, so Mother said she couldn't. Granny could dye and set her own hair; Mother could barely brush her own. Granny liked to be the center of attention in a room; Mother preferred to sit quietly and have a conversation.

Mother and Granny had a very close, although also strained relationship. They were, unfortunately, very different people. Granny could not understand Mother's sensibilities about society and did not share many of her interests. Mother studied fine art and enjoyed going to museums. She also loved classical music and was more than just an opera buff. She built her own hi-fi and had a large collection of music, classical and opera. She would follow the operas with her libretto both at home and at the auditorium. She was not a casual listener. When she took me to *The Magic Flute*, I already knew the music from the record we would often play, but insisted I read the libretto in translation. (I was about seven.) I just wanted to see the costumes and hum along with the music. Granny would compete with Mother in many fields, but admitted that she had no taste for music.

It was unfortunate for my mother, that finishing high school and being encouraged to pursue her interests further in college were strongly discouraged. Granny saw college for women as only a place for women who would have to work to support themselves and not quite "the thing." It would have been unthinkable for her brother, Charles Scribner, not to go on to Princeton in his father's footsteps; but not necessary, and vaguely middle-class, for a girl. Granny had not graduated from her high school but had gone to Russia for an extended visit with her Belgian cousins in St. Petersburg. There was no reason to worry that Mother missed her senior year and, therefore, never graduated or to try to make it up (anyway that might all collide with her debut year.)

Mother, however, did put her foot down about "coming out." She would not do it. She asked her father's sister to instead do a "Grand Tour" of Europe. Her Aunt Louise also enjoyed museums and culture and they had a fine trip together. I believe that trip to Europe was the only one she took until the month before her death when she and Father went to find a place for the family to live in Oxford for his sabbatical the following year. They also visited Paris and she had portrait photographs taken by her old dear friend and mentor, Charles Leirens. There were almost no photographs of Mother from after her marriage. She did not like snapshots and would rarely pose for formal pictures. She was the photographer, not the model. The fact that she had the photographs taken must have been very upsetting for both my mother and father—the realization that she was very sick and not getting better. She had spent much of the summer in her bed with metastatic breast cancer and liver failure. In Paris she had her hair done and then spent all day in bed except for the photography sessions. Father only mentioned that time to me once.

I'm not sure when Mother started suffering from the debilitating migraine headaches that the whole family was so accustomed to. As a child I remember her in the darkened bedroom and with the radio at barely audible classical music and an ice bag on her forehead. Probably almost once a week, rarely for more than a day; these headaches would take hold. She underwent psychoanalysis to try to rid herself of their intrusion into her life. When they were gone, there was no residual of the pain from the day before. Granny even competed with Mother over the headaches, describing to me how she had gone "blind" for a day with a headache. Granny did not ever take to bed with a headache in all the years I knew her. One of Father's theories about the headaches that they often occurred on a Thursday, which was the cook's night off. I remember Father cooking omelets for us children with mother resting in the bedroom. He thought that she always felt inadequate to prepare and present a meal. A surprise to me as I thought her a wonderful cook. Another trigger for the headaches was her developing her pictures in the bathroom darkroom she had set up. He said to me that he could rely on a headache coming on if she started developing and working with her pictures. Whether the chemicals or the lost hopes and ambitions of becoming a significant photographer set off the migraines, the pain would come. Father told me that he insisted that Mother stop developing her own pictures. I believe he had very mixed feelings about that request as he knew that her dream of being a photographer was important to her; but he felt that the pain was more than he could bear, much less for herself.

Growing up with Mother's regular and repeating headaches, I got very used to her in the darkened room for a day or an evening and then right as rain the next day. Her battles with two C-sections, morning sickness with the last two pregnancies, oophorectomy, radical mastectomy, hysterectomy were always ones that she won, it seemed to me, as she would be up and going full speed in a short time. She may have been fragile, but she was tough and brave and not complaining. The last year of her life when the cancer was in her liver, she would still go uptown shopping to Bloomingdale's to get some clothes for us children. She asked the cook (the wonderful, young Irish woman who was frightened by the lobsters) before going out if a particular dress suited her as her skin had turned greenish overnight. (Recounted to me more than once by that cook, Maureen Maloney.) She would go get Cobalt radiation treatments (harsh and burning compared to today's treatments) and then pick me up at school to go to dancing lessons, saying she just felt a little tired.

Mother died at forty-one with four children and an all too short marriage to the man she adored, admired, respected, and loved. Father never really recovered from her death. He lived without her for another twenty-nine years, missing her daily. I was only fourteen and the youngest, my brother, four. I was the child lucky enough to have had the most years with her. Memories are so flavored by our own self, so this is just a portrait from my perspective. Fourteen is a difficult time for the relationship of many daughters with their mothers. It certainly was for me, from wearing lipstick to the length of my skirt. So many minor conflicts occurred to blur the love and esteem I had for her at that time. She taught me to think for myself. "Use your head, Hildy" was a favorite phrase, which meant she would not tell me "how to do it." Self-esteem and confidence were instilled and nurtured. I never had a migraine.

The Letters

The Rise of Intimacy

1939–1942

Do take good care of your entrails, and don't stray one celery stalk from your diet.

[JSB to MKR, 18 March 1940]

Aside from the great bond of the same diet, the same antagonisms
and the almost identical profanity, I think you are a grand person.

[MKR to JSB, (22? March 1940)]

MKR to JSB, 14 December 1939. TLS, 1 p. AD: Miss Julia Scribner |
Dew Hollow | Far Hills | New Jersey. PM: OCALA | DEC 14 | 10 PM |
1939 | FLA. LH: Marjorie Kinnan Rawlings | Hawthorn, Florida.

December 14, 1939

Dear Julia:

You were a dear to send me the books. I have been up to my ears since I
reached home, but I couldn't resist dipping into "The Wind in the Willows",[1]
and it is enchanting. I had to take a quick look at the Hans Christian Andersen, too, and it seems there are two stories in the edition that are new to
me.[2] I look forward to grand evenings by my fire with the new fare. When
you come across something good, and new to you, do ^you^ have the frantic
feeling of wondering what else you're missing?

I'm feeling very luxurious about books. Mr. Breck[3] did send me "The Revolt of the Masses".[4] I've just been able to read a few pages of that, and it is
terrific---not in the slang sense---but actually. It is such solid food that I
think I shall be able to digest only a few pages at a time.

It is grand to be home in my grove. The orange and grapefruit and tangerine trees look as though they were hung with Chinese lanterns. I hate
selling my crop, and just will not sell the trees right around the farmhouse.
I'm getting a box off to your family in a few days. It will not be packed in a
fancy way, but it will be right from my own trees, and shipped the day it's
picked.

I enjoyed being with all of you so much.[5] And all my thanks for the good
books.

---

1   Kenneth Grahame (1859–1932), *The Wind in the Willows* (London: Metheun, 1908), children's
novel set in Edwardian England and featuring the anthropomorphic characters Mole, Rat, Toad,
and Badger.

2   Hans Christian Andersen (1805–1875), Danish author, best remembered for his fairy tales.

3   Mr. Breck: Perhaps Joseph Breck, a book dealer in Boston, Massachusetts.

4   José Ortega y Gasset (1883–1955), Spanish philosopher, author of *La rebelión de las masas* (1930),
published in English as *The Revolt of the Masses* (New York: Norton, 1932).

5   MKR writes to Aunt Ida Tarrant, Charles Rawlings's great aunt by marriage (Silverthorne 83) on
Tuesday, 5 December 1939, that she spent Sunday, 3 December (date inferred), with the Scribners
at their estate Dew Hollow, Far Hills, New Jersey (see unpublished MS, Special Collections, UF).
MKR had met with Charles Scribner III (1890–1952) a number of times at his New York office
when she came to visit Maxwell E. Perkins (1884–1947), her renowned editor. However, this visit
to Dew Hollow was apparently the first time she had met Vera Scribner (1891–1985), the wife of
Charles Scribner III, and the children Julia Scribner (1918–1961) and Charles Scribner IV (aka Jr.,

My best to you—

Marjorie <u>K. R.</u>

. . .

MKR to JSB, 4 February 1940. TLS, 1 p. LH: Marjorie Kinnan Rawlings | hawthorn, florida. Envelope is missing.

Feb. 4, 1940

Dear Julia:

I sounded out your father on the idea of your driving down with them when they go to Palm Beach[1] and spending a week with me. I was delighted when he wrote that he was sure you would like to come. So I'm writing you direct---and hope nothing will happen to prevent your coming.

We have so many tastes in common that I think you would like my quiet life---and there are some awfully nice day-trips we could make---Bok tower, Silver Springs,[2] and any other places that may appeal to you.

I specified a week, as I really would like to have you that long, and feel sure you would find enough to interest you for that time. I think we'd enjoy a day or two over at my cottage right on the ocean. It might even be warm enough for a swim, although our cold winter in the South has made me think I'm not far enough in the tropics. In case you wonder about clothes, don't know what you'll need after you leave me, but here you'll only want the simplest sports clothes, with one informal dinner dress for possible festivities.

1921–1995). MKR was staying at the St. Moritz in New York. On Saturday, 2 December, she had delivered her lecture, "Regional Literature of the South," before the National Council of Teachers of English, which was subsequently published in the *English Journal* 29.2 (February 1940): 89–97, and in *College English* 1.5 (February 1940): 81–89 (see Tarr, *Bibliography*, C613). On Tuesday, 5 December, MKR gave a lecture at Columbia University, followed by a "small party" given in her honor by Adelin Sumner Briggs Linton (1899–1977), a friend from her University of Wisconsin days (*Selected Letters* 180, and *Love Letters* 45). However, it was that Sunday at the Scribner estate on 3 December that proved monumental. MKR and the much younger JSB bonded instantly. MKR immediately invited JSB to Cross Creek. JSB arrived on 25 February and stayed for two weeks, leaving on 11 March (*Selected Letters* 183). The importance of the visit cannot be overemphasized, as MKR writes to Norman Stanley Berg (1908–1978) on 18 March: "Had a lovely two-weeks' visit from young Julia Scribner. One of the grandest youngsters I've ever known" (*Selected Letters* 185).

1 Charles Scribner III and Vera Scribner visited MKR at Cross Creek on 25 February 1940 on their way to Palm Beach (see Silverthorne 179 and *Love Letters* 47). With the Scribners was their daughter Julia, who, rather than return to New York with her parents, chose to stay for two weeks, departing on 11 March.

2 Bok Tower, north of Lake Wales, Florida, garden and bird sanctuary opened in 1929, and Silver Springs, Florida, a group of artesian springs on the Silver River, an attraction since the 1870s.

I can almost certainly drive you to Palm Beach or wherever you go from here. There's a wonderful jungle garden[1] I'd like to show you on the way.

Marjorie K. R.

. . .

JSB to MKR, 11 and 13 March 1940. ALS, 5 pp. PM: NEW YORK. N.Y. | MAR 14 | 7 AM | 1940 | STA. K. AD: Mrs. Marjorie K. Rawlings | Cross Creek | Hawthorne | Florida. [In JSB's hand, bottom left corner]: AIR MAIL.

<u>Monday</u> [11 March 1940][2]

Dear Mrs. Rawlings:

It seems that cruel Fate[3] decided that it was not enough that I be torn from your arms,[4] but I must be thrown into the arms of – <u>Mr. Snead</u>.[5] As I collapsed on my seat, I saw him leaning happily across the aisle at me, and in response to my feeble recognition, he sat down beside me and, timetable en main embarked on an analysis of the probable lateness of our train at every stop from Hawthorne to NYC. I couldn't take it, so at about Wilmington Del. I picked up my book and asked him if I couldn't give him something to read. This I am sure was your influence, and I must hand it to you it worked. He went back across the aisle. But still no peace. I wanted to stare moodily out the window and brood about what a happy time I had, and how much I would miss you, and what I would say in this letter, but I had to read, because every time I looked up from the book Mr. S. started a conversation. I finished <u>The Constant Nymph</u>,[6] and I thought it was good, but not as good as the authorities quoted in the blurb said it was.

---

1 If coming from Cross Creek, perhaps Cypress Gardens, opened in 1936, near Winter Haven, Florida, not far from Bok Tower (see 45, n. 2). Or, if coming from Crescent Beach, perhaps the reference is to McKee Jungle Gardens, opened in 1929, as a tropical hammock near the Indian River Lagoon, Vero Beach, FL.

2 JSB began this letter on Monday, 11 March 1940, and completed it on Wednesday 13 March.

3 A common trope, made famous by the theologian and author Albert B. Simpson (1843–1919), "When I cannot understand my Father's leading, And it seems to be but hard and cruel fate, Still I hear that gentle whisper ever pleading, God is working, God is faithful—Only wait."

4 An allusion to *Macbeth* 5.3.15–16. Macbeth asserts that he cannot be killed by a man born of woman, and Macduff responds that he "was born from his mother's womb / Untimely ripped." He then slays Macbeth.

5 Mr. Snead is not identified.

6 Margaret Kennedy, *The Constant Nymph* (London: Heineman, 1924; Garden City: Doubleday, 1925), a best-selling novel about a fourteen-year-old girl who falls in love with a gifted composer

We had dinner together, of course. Discussed golf, fishing and the trouble Mrs. Snead had in obtaining in Ocala a copy of <u>The Yearling</u> to bring to the picnic for you to sign. Horrid! And Fate was guilty of what I considered a crude stroke—the only vegetable the Seaboard[1] offered was broccoli with hollandaise.[2]

I lay for hours next morning in the dark green gloom of my berth to avoid breakfast with S. which I succeeded in doing, but I felt quite dark green and gloomy for the rest of the day. I managed to out stay him for lunch too, but that was easier because I was very interested in <u>The Loon's Feather</u>.[3] And so Trenton.[4]

There is a great deal I would like to say here, but I ^only^ seem to be able to curse and "blunder around" in my head and not a single coherent sentence leaks down from my brain to my hand. I am so very grateful and gratitude seems a particularly difficult thing to express.

Oh Hell with my inarticulateness – I[5]

It is now Wednesday – I looked back on <??> Tuesday morning at the page which was originally here, and my objective critical eye was blinded with horror. It read like a poem I had written in bed during a fit of insomnia. Cruel morning light![6] Why my most profound and noble feelings have looked so bloody on paper I don't know. I would like to tell you in poised but glowing prose how very happy I was with you, (and I don't mean just "having a good time["]), how much I miss you and how lonely I am when I think

---

who in turn marries the girl's beautiful cousin. The front slip cover of the first American edition featured three blurbs. "The year has certainly not yet produced a novel up to *The Constant Nymph* in all around excellence" (*New York Evening Post*); ". . . its gorgeously reckless humor, its lovely tenderness, its full ribald understanding of the cruel urgency of life . . . yes, a thrilling and intolerable book" (Christopher Morley); "One of the best new novels, old or new, that has ever absorbed the reader's attention" (Augustine Birrell, *The New Statesman*).

1   The Seaboard Coast Line Railroad ran from Tampa to Jacksonville and then on to New York City.

2   A reference to Charles Rawlings, who in anger at what he thought was an ill-prepared meal threw hollandaise sauce in MKR's face. The threatening episode is mirrored in "The Pelican's Shadow" (*Short Stories* 195).

3   Molly Beaver [Iola Fuller Goodspeed], *The Loon Feather* (New York: Harcourt, Brace, 1939), a historical novel set in the Mackinac region of Michigan, the manuscript of which MKR read for the Michigan Hopwood Award, calling it a "rare beauty" (*Max and Marjorie* 401–02).

4   Trenton, New Jersey, approximately 43 miles from the Scribner family home in Far Hills, New Jersey. From New York City, the distance is approximately 46 miles.

5   JSB ends her letter abruptly and then begins again two days later, on Wednesday, 13 March.

6   Perhaps an allusion to Gertrude Dix (1867–1950), who used the phrase in her short story "Veronica's Mill" (*Pall Mall Magazine* 21 [1900]: 306–319): "[L]ife with all its mockery of gaiety and brightness, which passes in a night-time, and leaves nothing for the cruel morning light but trampled turf and a few broken toys on the ground" (312).

of something I would like to talk to you about or see something I think you would enjoy, and, most of all, how proud I am of your friendship. The best I can do is <leave> to give you this blue print. I think you will understand it.

I have just come from Scribners. The first person I saw there was Mr. Perkins.[1] We had a completely unsatisfactory dialogue on my Fla. visit. Per usual, I couldn't understand him and he couldn't understand me, and so we walked awkwardly away from one another, <out of hand>. The office is full of some wild story about you, M. Mitchell, and the GWTW premiere.[2] Something about a cocktail party given by a newspaper woman and you sat down in a chair just as M.M. was about to sit in same chair and she fell on the floor necessitating a trip to the hospital and much adhesive binding before she was fit to attend premiere. I told them it might be true, but if so I ^!^ would probably[3] have heard it two or three times from various people during my visit. Everyone asked fondly after you, your orange grove and your work. I felt tempted to say that you were working on 2 novels—four-act play, an autobiography and an epic poem, but truth won.[4] I had another alarming chat with Mr. P. We went down in the elevator together and he turned on me sharply and said: "You should be here working on this floor." I looked uncomprehending and he said "We (editorial "we" I suppose) have always felt you should be in here." I stuttered something about I hadn't done very well with the charge account sheets, quite conscience-stricken and he said, "you should be doing publicity work." Just what that is, or how I would go about it I don't know, but he has shocked me into thought.

Good God, white camellias have just arrived! Which reminds me that I have to get dressed and go through with this awful evening. I wish I could be more blasée about these situations, but I have terrible indigestion already. Well, axe in hand to the slaughter.

Give my love to Bob, Cecil & Norton[5] and take lots, as much as you want, for yourself.

---

1 Maxwell Evert Perkins (1884–1947), first served as a mentor to MKR and later became a close personal friend. See *Max and Marjorie*, Introduction 1–24.

2 MKR and her intimate friend Norton Sanford Baskin (NSB; 1901–1997) were the personal guests of Margaret Mitchell for the film premiere of *Gone With the Wind*, a gala event held in Atlanta on 15 December. At a luncheon on 14 December, hosted by Macmillan (her publisher), Mitchell allegedly hurt her back when she missed her chair and landed on the floor (Pyron 377). In a letter dated [23? March 1940] MKR denies categorically that any of this happened, pointing out that Mitchell had a bad back for many years before.

3 JSB circles "probably" and draws an arrow to the "!" she inserts above the line indicating that she knows better than to split the modal verb.

4 Actually, MKR had begun work seriously on the manuscript of *Cross Creek* (1942).

5 Robert Camp Jr., Cecil H. Clarke, and NSB. MKR referred to them as the "three musketeers who

Julia

p.s. I did lose my best roll of film, the seals at Marineland,[1] etc. I have an awful feeling I left it chez Driftwood, but if you see a little aluminum cylinder that's it.

I hope you don't feel slighted that I write you on this paper, but my notepaper is cute and blue with JBS at the top and I feel uncomfortable on it.

. . .

JSB to MKR, 18 March 1940. ALS, 4 pp. AD: Mrs. Marjorie K. Rawlings | Cross Creek | Hawthorne | Florida. PM: NEW YORK. N.Y. | MAR 19 | 5:30 PM | 1940 | STA. K.

Monday [18 March 1940]

Dear Mrs. Rawlings:

There are some books on their way to you and I want to prepare you for them. There is not a copy of The Y. to be signed. I was afraid that it would be rather a shock. If you can't bear it, drop me a postcard and I will have one sent (illustrated edition, of course).[2]

I forgot to ask you whether you had read 7 Gothic Tales,[3] but I didn't see a copy around your bookcase, so I took a chance and sent it. I think it is one of the most fascinating books I have ever read, even more fascinating than The Innocent Voyage.[4] I read it last fall when I was in New Marlboro shooting and it used to put me in a terrific state of mind. My mind would get so far off its beaten track and so lost that it took me a couple of hours chasing partridge across the N.E. hills before it come home and integrate with the body of Scribner, the mighty huntress.[5]

---

are like brothers to me" (*Max and Marjorie* 359). Clarke was the manager of the Marion Refrigeration Co. in Ocala.

1 Marineland, a noted Florida tourist attraction south of St. Augustine. Baskin in March 1946 became the manager of the two restaurants and the bar. Driftwood was a rental cottage on the property. MKR found the cylinder in her car (see her letter dated [22? March 1940]).

2 JSB is referring to the "Pulitzer Prize Edition" of *The Yearling* (New York: Scribners, 1939), "With pictures by N. C. Wyeth" (Tarr, Bibliography, A3.3.b).

3 Isak Dinesen [Karen Blixen] (1885–1962), Danish novelist, *Seven Gothic Tales* (New York: Harrison Smith and Robert Haas, 1934).

4 Richard Hughes (1900–1976), English novelist, *Innocent Voyage* [*A High Wind in Jamaica*] (New York: Harper, 1929).

5 An allusion to Diana, the Roman goddess of the hunt.

In case you get temporarily discouraged with Florida, where "there is no Spring," you can visit awhile in Vermont where they have an excellent Spring.

N.E Year[1] is a far cry from <u>Gothic Tales</u>, and the writing pretty stark unadorned beside Mrs. Dinesen's vintage wine prose, but there is something to be said for Vermont spring water, I think, and sentences can afford to be plain when one can feel so much of living behind them.

I am sending you also one of my favorite "neglected first novels."[2] I think it's a <u>hell</u> of a good book.

Last, and I'm afraid least, the little wildflower book <u>with</u> <u>pictures</u>.[3]

Another box which you should have soon contains a jar of nice <u>black</u> buckwheat honey. I saw it at the Flower Show, among Burpee's seeds,[4] aluminum lawnmowers, flower perfumes, soilless plant growers, oriental rugs, etc., etc. It took great courage to buy it, because the counter was festooned with cages of live bees. But I reminded myself it was one of our <u>very</u> few mutual likes and I braved the insects. It ought to go well with Drenna's hot biscuits.[5]

The point of this letter is to tell you positively must not write so much as a postcard to say that these sundry articles have arrived. I remember with horror your stacks of mail, and I like to think of your sigh of relief for one letter that does not have to be written. With this understood you will not mind if I send you an occasional book? I cannot bear the thought that I would be gone and forgotten but for the buttons on your playsuit, which I tore swan-like from my breast.[6]

My window here looks out on the vast comfortable form of the Metropolitan Museum. On its numerous ledges, the N.Y.C. pigeons are making love. It must be Spring. – It is also very distracting. I like being next to the Museum, though. There are so many things inside that I love. I seem to feel them all the way across Fifth Avenue.[7]

---

1 Muriel G. Follett (1904–1992), American writer, *New England Year: A Journal of Vermont Farm Life* (Brattleboro, VT: Stephen Daye Press, 1940).

2 Not identified.

3 Not identified.

4 Burpee Seed Co., founded in 1876, known for its vegetable and flower seeds and for its catalogue.

5 Adrenna Mickens (1899–1960), daughter of "Old Martha" Mickens, who worked as a maid and a cook for MKR.

6 The story of the informal playsuit is lost, but JSB may be alluding to the widely known poem by Sarojini Naidu (1879–1949) "The Gift of India" (1915), in which dead soldiers from India in World War I are identified as "Priceless treasures torn from my breast" (l. 4), and also perhaps to Charles Swann, whose repeated attempts to forget his wife Odette are recorded in *Swann's Way*, volume 1 of Marcel Proust's *In Search of Lost Time* (1913–1927). Odette is named after the queen of the swans in Tchaikovsky's ballet *Swan Lake*. See JSB's letter dated [13 July 1942].

7 Charles Scribner's Sons address is 153–157 Fifth Avenue. The Metropolitan Museum of Art is

I still find hating alone awfully dull after having such a congenial fellow hater. I can't seem to work up the same healthy passion as I did before. Except musical hates – on that subject I am my old violent self. There is only [one] person who is as violent as myself on that subject, my dear friend and ex piano teacher.[1] I drove to New Rochelle yesterday and we spent the afternoon in fierce conversation and intense debate with occasional interruptions when her children (ages 3 and 1 1/2) would fall down or start eating cigarette butts out of the ashtray. Marge would deal with these crises without stopping a discussion of how one should conduct the Hallelujah chorus from <u>The Messiah</u>[2] with vocal and histrionic illustrations, but I couldn't take the children so calmly and so spent half the time rescuing them from what I considered imminent dangers. I was so exhausted when I got home that today I have succumbed to my brother's grippe.[3] I trust there are no germs enclosed with this letter.

Which reminds me that this thing is pages too long already. I must let you get on with your other fan letters.

Do take good care of your entrails, and don't stray one celery stalk from your diet.[4]

Love,

Julia

. . .

MKR to JSB, [22? March 1940]. TLS, 2 pp.; ALS, 2 pp. PM: Illegible. AD: Miss Julia Scribner | Dew Hollow | Far Hills | New Jersey. [In MKR's hand at top of envelope and obscured by stamp]: Airmail Sp[ecial | Deli[very].

At the beach

Friday [22? March 1940]

Dear Julia:

---

located at 1000 Fifth Avenue.

1   Not identified.

2   Georg Friedrich Handel (1685–1759), German-British composer, *The Messiah* (1742), an oratorio composed in English.

3   Charles Scribner IV, aka Jr. (1921–1995).

4   MKR suffered from recurrent bouts with diverticulosis, which became particularly severe in 1940. On one occasion NSB was summoned home from Alabama to rush her to a hospital in Jacksonville.

You need never fear a duty-letter from me. That is a low form of hypocrisy that I should not inflict and never have on anyone I care for. Of course there may be times when you wonder casually whether I am dead or alive---but you may know then that I am entertaining "persons" who could have written about the tobacco night-riders[1] if they had only cared to bother, shagging Jody's and what-not from the gate[2]---and thinking about you. It is much better to be thought of fondly than to be written to with curses.

I wish you could be here at the beach today. The air is warm but very alive, and the sea is an incredible moonstone blue. Faithful Lant has just finished measuring for Adrenna's apartment,[3] figuring out to the last splash the relation of toilet to lavatory, and is now painting the grimy kitchen. "By God, Morge," he said, "some bastard must have spit tobacco juice on them cabinet doors." The stain proved to be coffee. He is to do the rest of the work while I am away on my so-called lecture trip. Then Adrenna can entertain in style.

You were certainly at the Creek during the lean period. The light plant is now impeccable, the garden is full of African daisies, calendulas, delphinium, forget-me-nots, bachelor-buttons, baby's breath and schizanthus---Dora and Lady both came across with calves,[4] so that you could have kept your nose in a bucket of milk all the time—milk so rich the cream is almost saffron. Sorry! Dora's calf was a bull, and Adrenna asked me suspiciously what I meant to do with it. I said it had better be put out of the way at once. She said, "Oh, Mrs. Rawlings---Dora's own!" Much as I despise Dora, I couldn't stand that, so the calf is to be made a steer and allowed to grow

---

1 Vigilantes, mainly in Kentucky and Tennessee, who protested, often violently, the monopolistic practices of The American Tobacco Company, owned by James. B. Duke (1856–1925) of Durham, North Carolina.

2 MKR seems to be referring to an inside joke held with JSB, possibly involving someone who claimed that she or he "could have written" from the start, or "gate," the kind of story MKR wrote in *The Yearling*, thus demeaning her accomplishment. In *The Yearling*, Jody's pet deer Flag, like a "night rider," tramples the Baxters' tobacco crop (382–83) before eating the corn that seals his doom (392–93, 401–02). MKR's phrase "shagging Jody's and what-not" possibly refers to a term that entered the military lexicon around 1939, a "Jody," the generic name of a boy at home having sex with the girlfriend or wife of a soldier serving overseas.

3 Lant is the protagonist in *South Moon Under* (New York: Scribners, 1933), who survives by making moonshine. It is argued that he is modeled upon MKR's good friend and handyman Leonard Brinkley Fiddia (1901–1958), who taught her much about Cracker lore, including one of her favorite expressions, "Christian-hearted sons of bitches" (*Love Letters* 37). MKR is referring to the small garage in the front driveway below the Crescent Beach cottage. When Idella Parker came to work for her, the apartment, actually a room attached to the garage, was already completed. Later MKR converted the whole into larger living quarters for Idella (*Idella* 46–47).

4 Dora and Lady, MKR's two cows, whose two calves, Chrissy and Cissy, respectively, were the offspring of Ferdinand the Bull and the source of considerable bawdy humor (*Cross Creek* 263–66).

beef size, when presumably Dora won't give a damn. Adrenna said, even if Dora don't suckle it, she can look at it in the pen and know it's her'n." It's awful to have your help more sensitive than you are. I go around feeling like a brute half the time. We also have flocks of new biddies and one of the Mallards is about to hatch. Pat had a handsome lady-friend brought to him to do his duty, and Cecil said,[1] "Now if Pat has puppies, that leaves only you and Adrenna unaccounted for." Adrenna had a polite fit of mirth when I passed this on and said, "Well, I wouldn't care." I have never felt quite so infertile. Producing stories simply does not give you that lush feeling, although of course a writer can look at her words in their bound pen and know they're her'n.

This last week before I barge off for Shreveport is crammed with visitors. Malvina Hoffman and a friend are coming Sunday to spend a day or two, Bob Camp's sister from Durham and her husband (one of the Duke heirs, but a dear regardless)[2] and three small children and two nurse-maids arrived a few days ago and there is much partying going on, and my Macmillan friend Norman Berg arrives Monday or Tuesday to play with Norton and me a couple of days,[3] and somewhere in between there must be time found to see a film a weird man wants to show me on the life of the otter.

By the way, Bob's brother-in-law is having great fun with Kodachrome pictures.[4] They have shown to be shown by projection, like movies, but the colors are infinitely lovelier than the home movie films. He has some gorgeous stuff, and for the first time I am tempted to see what I could do in our country with a color camera. Your film showed up, bent behind the car seat. I think the film itself is all right and will send it on.

The MGM people are here, beginning the animal sequences and back-

---

1   Pat, MKR's pointer, who was run over and killed on Christmas Eve 1941. Cecil Clarke.

2   Malvina Hoffman (1887–1966), novelist. Robert Camp Jr., who later did the illustration for the dust jacket of *Cross Creek* and for the illustrations in *Cross Creek Cookery* (1942). Nancy (Davenport) Camp Harrity (1911–1987) married, on 1 June 1936, Edwin (Edward) Buchanan Lyon Jr. (1911–1992), the great-grandson of Washington Duke (1820–1905), founder of the tobacco company W. Duke & Sons, which would eventually become the American Tobacco Company under the leadership of his son, James Buchanan Duke (1856–1925). According to the 1940 census, the Lyons had two children, Edward (5) and Nancy (2), and a stepson Rorry Harrity (6), Nancy's son by a previous marriage to Joseph Richard Harrity (1908–1973). The census also lists two female servants in their household: Georgia Underwood (housemaid) and Della Crowe (children's nurse). The Lyons were divorced in 1947.

3   Norman S. Berg, sales manager for Macmillan in Atlanta and often credited for helping to secure the contract for *Gone With the Wind*.

4   35mm slides, popularized by Kodak, were displayed through a projector.

grounds in the Scrub.[1] Jody is not yet selected, though a delightful looking Tampa boy is favored. The film is to be in technicolor, which should help.

I have really missed you terribly. I can't tell you how much I enjoyed you. Aside from the great bond of the same diet, the same antagonisms and the almost identical profanity, I think you are a grand person.

With, love,

Marjorie[2]

Books and honey arrived safely, and am delighted with both. The honey is too good to be true.

Forgot to say that the story about Margaret Mitchell and the chair and the accident and me is the most amazing canard I've run into in a long time.[3] Margaret had an operation shortly after the première for abdominal adhesions.[4] She had been putting it off until after the première. I just saw Margaret once, at a luncheon.[5] We posed together for the news photographer. At the woman's Press Club cocktail party I didn't even see her. There was no incident of any sort—no chair—nothing! She did not fall down at any time! Somehow, the "adhesive tape" in your story must be the adhesions!

Marjorie

Am sending you a birthday something via your father's secretary.[6]

. . .

MKR to Scribner Secretary, n.d. [22? March 1940]. ALS, 1 p. PM: Special Delivery stamp torn and PM smudged. AD: Secretary to [Charles Scribner] | 597 Fifth Ave [Inserted in pencil: Mar 1940] | New York City. RAD: [circled in MKR's hand] Air Mail | Special Delivery. Envelope stamped: SPECIAL DELIVERY | VIA AIR MAIL.

---

1   In a letter to Perkins, 17 April 1939, MKR writes, "The MGM movie people were in Florida doing a Tarzan picture, and while here their camera man was commissioned to take shots of The Yearling country" (*Max and Marjorie* 397). MGM began filming *The Yearling*, starring Spencer Tracy, in 1941. The filming was scrubbed as a result of expensive delays and actor disenchantment. In 1946, it was produced, starring Gregory Peck, Jane Wyman, and Claude Jarman Jr., and used many of the animal and outdoor scenes filmed in 1941.

2   MKR then includes a handwritten postscript on Cross Creek stationery.

3   See JSB's letter on 11 March 1940.

4   Abdominal adhesions are fibrous scar tissue that form on organs in the abdomen.

5   The luncheon given by Mitchell's publishers Macmillan and Co.

6   Mr. Watson. First name not identified.

Envelope stamped: Fee Claimed by Office | of First Address. LH:
Marjorie Kinnan Rawlings | Hawthorn, Florida

[22? March 1940][1]

May I trouble you to have the Victrola[2] record shop from which Julia Scribner buys her records, send her $10. worth of new operatic or symphonic records that they think she would like, with privilege of exchange if she wants something else?

This is for her birthday the 26th.

Thanks so much
Marjorie K. Rawlings[3]

. . .

JSB to MKR. [31 March 1940], ALS: 4pp. PM: NEW YORK, N.Y. | APR 1 | 12 [P?]M | 1940 | STATION [Illegible]. AD: Mrs. Marjorie Kinnan Rawlings | Cross Creek | Hawthorn | Florida | AIR MAIL.

Sunday [31 March 1940]

I notice that this letter goes on for pages without a new {par}, so just wink your proofreading eyes as you read it.[4]

Dear Mrs. R:

Ever since I have been 22 I have felt like the individual in the picture. That is the only reason that l didn't write days ago. I wanted to tell you at once that yours was the most unexpected and the nicest birthday present[5] I've ever had, but, as you can see, the flesh was in bad shape. – Christmas even without Santa Claus has still most of the excitement and atmosphere that it used to have–but birthdays lose their glamour pretty thoroughly. The presents under the bed and parties with magicians and Mickey Mouse movies and

---

1   Written in what appears to be MKR's hand on the envelope: Mar 1940. Since MKR mentions in her letter on Friday, 22 March, that she is sending JSB a birthday present via a Scribner secretary, it seems reasonable to date this letter as Friday, 22 March, as well. JSB's birthday was 26 March.

2   RCA Victrola was a leader in record making and recording, especially of Classical music.

3   This is an early example of MKR's signature, where she does not write out her middle name.

4   JSB inserts this postscript at the top on p. 1 as a reading heuristic for MKR.

5   JSB was born on 26 March 1918, making this her twenty-second birthday.

Jack Horner pies, snappers,[1] pink, blue and white cake and ice cream in the shape of animals are gone forever. Now my few immediate relations scratch off a check, and that, together with a few bitter thoughts on the wasted year just past and the wasted year about to come, is about all there is to a birthday. I suppose the day starts getting festive again when one reaches 75—that is if and when one reaches 75.

Well, this particular birthday started off worse than usual. I woke up with a headache--no one remembered to wish me "Happy Birthday", and the checks were a hollow joy because they have to be sunk into new tires for the car. In the afternoon I was sitting in the hotel[2] alone & distinctly mopey, when a large package of records arrived "from Marjorie K. Rawlings." And so that lousy Tuesday the 26th was changed into one of the best birthdays I've ever had. I couldn't figure how the records got there and happened to be just what I wanted and how you had remembered that insignificant date. Daddy[3] explained some of it when he got home. It seems that Mr. Watson (Daddy's sec.),[4] stricken with horror by the strange assignment, appealed to my cousin George,[5] who shares an office with him. George is also a record collector, and we had been discussing by the grace of God, our respective collections. I told him that I had all the Beethoven symphonies except the 4th,[6] and I also had raved about the Franck <u>Variations</u>[7] that I heard at Bob Camp's. I got them both. As far as I am concerned the 4th is from now on Beethoven's Cross Creek Symphony.

---

1 Mickey Mouse, iconic cartoon character created by Walt Disney Co. in 1928. Jack Horner pies are named after the Mother Goose nursery rhyme "Little Jack Horner" (c. eighteenth century, see below). Modern-day pies are gifts, not always food, that children wrap on Christmas Eve and leave for Santa Claus, among others. Snappers are very popular at birthday parties and pop when stepped upon.

    Little Jack Horner
    Sat in the corner,
    Eating a Christmas pie;
    He put in his thumb,
    And pulled out a plum,
    And said, "What a good boy am I!"

2 Not identified.

3 Charles Scribner III.

4 The first name of Mr. Watson is not identified.

5 George M. Schiefflin Jr. (1905–1988), JSB's paternal cousin.

6 Ludwig von Beethoven (1770–1827), German composer, whose Symphony No. 4 was composed in 1806 and first performed publicly in Vienna in April 1808.

7 César Auguste Franck (1822–1890), French composer, whose work influenced French Romanticism. *Symphonic Variations* was composed in 1885.

I'll never know how you remembered the date. Perhaps it was our Astrology magazine.[1] I shall have to buy a year's subscription out of gratitude.

From your letter I gather that Cross Creek is in such an orgy of "flowering" and "fruiting" that I'm ^sure^ by now Adrenna is great with Albert's child[2] and you are about to write another story. I wish you both an easy "birthing" though I hope <it isn't going to> that you will be delivered long before Adrenna. 9 months is reasonable for a baby but a short story is a less complex organism – better make it a novel.

The weather here, as you have no doubt been told daily in the Fla. papers, has been setting new records for God awfulness. Day before yesterday, what with my physical and mental decline and a freezing November rain I decided that a.) I was much too exhausted ever to recover from said decline, and b.) the earth was too exhausted to push up another Spring. Today has proved both conclusions erred toward pessimism. I have recovered physically to the extent of taking a vigorous (due to the horse) ride and washing my car, and mentally, well I can't think of any mental exercise beyond reading the Sunday papers at breakfast. As for the Spring, it really arrived today. We had a thunderstorm, and then the sun came out and made a beautiful rainbow. Tonight the frogs are giving a few tentative croaks. I get up every few minutes and go to the window to listen for peepers,[3] but they are not awake yet. In about another week our Garden Pond Symphony will be quite deafening. We have a couple of bass viol frogs that rock the house.

I don't know whether this will arrive before you leave on your lecture tour, if it does I wish you luck and caution you not to succumb to the temptation of roughage even on pain of starvation. If you don't get this till you and the Oldsmobile have staggered back, I hope that it was a great success and that you are not too "tired in the arms" from signing autographs.

With ever so many thanks and much love,

Julia.

P.S. It kills me that you have defeated me in the amount of stamps on letters, but I'm afraid that if I put a Special Delivery it will cost you 50¢ to have it

---

1   Perhaps the *World Astrology Magazine*.

2   Albert: Not identified. In 1939, Adrenna's husband was B. J. Sampson, although as MKR records with exasperation, there were a "succession of Negro men who occupied one half of the tenant house" with Adrenna, most notable among them Enmon, Jeff Davis, and Sherman, each of whom MKR liked and each of whom was finally rejected by Adrenna (*Cross Creek* 190–91).

3   Peepers, tree frogs, whose chorus is said to signal the advent of spring.

brought out, so I generously give in and will content myself with a spot of sealing wax on the flap.

Double P.S. Thank God you found the film, because the other roll is something awful! The only half-decent prints are a portrait study of Jib,[1] which I shall send you, and a handsome picture of bathing beauties taken underwater in the Photo Sub of Silver Springs[2] which I think I shall send Norton as a souvenir of our trip to Silver.

. . .

MKR to JSB, 6–7 May 1940. TLS, 4 pp. PM: Hawthorn | May 8 | 1940. AD: Miss Julia Scribner | <Dew Hollow> | <Far Hills> | <New Jersey> | New Marlboro | Berkshire County | Mass.

Went to Jacksonville last week for the Philadelphia Symphony Orchestra. Ormandy did Tchaikovsky's Fifth Symphony[3] so that my hair literally stood on end, and knives went all through me. Thought I had lost the capacity to respond to music but realized I just hadn't been hearing good music.[4]

Monday [6 May 1940]

Dear Julia:

I should be writing to mothers of Jodys and to students who demand "the story of your life"[5] (as if I'll tell that to anyone but the angel Gabriel,[6] and then only under compulsion) so I'm writing you instead---and don't you like letters that are pleasures and not duties!

I have an awful tragedy to report, knowing that I will get ribald hoots

---

1   Jib, MKR's tabby cat.

2   JSB is referring to the glass-windowed boats, Silver Springs called them "Subs," from which tourists were able to observe and to photograph what was going on underwater.

3   Eugene Ormandy [Jenö Blau] (1899–1985), conductor of the Philadelphia Symphony Orchestra. Pyotr Ilyich Tchaikovsky (1840–1893), Russian composer of the Romantic Period, composed Symphony No. 5 in E Minor in 1888.

4   This postscript is typed in at the top of p. 1.

5   MKR is referring to the fan mail she receives regarding *The Yearling* (New York: Scribners, 1938) and its iconic character, Jody. Grateful for the attention, MKR tried to respond to every letter, which soon became an overwhelming task. Scribner records detail that by 1940 *The Yearling* had sold in excess of 240,000 copies (see Tarr, *Bibliography*, A3.1.a, p. 39). In 1939, MKR was awarded the Pulitzer Prize for the novel and her fame was thereby secured.

6   Gabriel, an archangel of God in Hebraic tradition, who appears three times in the Bible, notably as a messenger to the prophet Daniel.

from you instead of sympathy. Mary Jane Tigert[1] is this week marrying the tall snooty track star whom, out of all Gainesville, I chose to insult---. Needless to say, I have not been invited to the wedding. It is probably difficult enough for him to take the leap without my disapproving countenance in one of the pews.

I wished for you on my trip to Louisiana, and would actually have asked you to join me for the two-weeks' round except that the lectures were hard enough on me without making anyone else share them.[2] But I struck that part of the country at the height of the spring and it was unbelievably beautiful. Across the Gulf of Mexico section the ti-ti was in full bloom,[3] and the dogwood, and through Alabama the azaleas, and wisteria so old and huge that a vine often covered the whole of an immense pine tree. I had a grand day in New Orleans, the most heavenly food in Galatoire's,[4] where the waiter helped me figure what herbs we could leave out of various dishes so that I could eat them. I bought some lovely old Sheffield[5] there for use at the cottage. Swung by Natchez, and it is a dream of the ante-bellum south. Drove 15 hours in a driving rain to have a week-end with my friends in Louisville.[6] Nashville---Tallahassee---then, thank God, home. Will give a talk gratis at my own university in October,[7] then am through with such foolishness.

I'm so glad you got the records[8] you wanted without the trouble of exchanging them. I remembered the date of your birthday, and had an idea that the 22d was one of those that isn't any fun. 30 is bad---and 40---I expect

---

1   Mary Jane Tigert (1917–1998) married William Blaine Thompson Jr. She was the daughter of John J. Tigert (1882–1965), the president of the University of Florida 1928–1947, and Edith Jackson Tigert (1887–1987), both friends of MKR.

2   MKR went on a multiday lecture tour through the Deep South, the itinerary of which she describes to Maxwell Perkins in a letter on 1 April 1940: "I leave in the morning for 12 days, speaking in Shreveport, La. . . . Nashville, Tenn. . . . Chattanooga, Tallahassee---home April 13" (*Max and Marjorie* 449).

3   Ti-ti is the Cracker term MKR used to refer to *cyrilla racemiflora*, aka "leatherwood" or "Swamp Cyrilla," which has showy white clusters of flowers in the spring.

4   Galatoire's, the famous restaurant on Bourbon Street in the French Quarter of New Orleans, whose signature dishes are Creole inspired.

5   MKR writes in a letter to NSB on 2? April 1940, "I prowled on in through the old silver shops [of New Orleans], and bought some English Sheffield serving dishes much too nice for the way I live, at the Creek or the Cottage" (*Love Letters* 48).

6   Lois Clark Hardy (1893–1983), MKR's sorority sister at the University of Wisconsin, and James Edward Hardy (1895–1951), her husband.

7   University of Wisconsin.

8   MKR had asked a Scribner secretary to have RCA Victrola records sent to JSB for her birthday. See MKR's letter dated [22? March 1940].

to mind 45---then after that I hope I won't care. But you mustn't talk about a wasted year. Nothing is wasted, for anyone intelligent and sensitive enough to learn and respond and enjoy. And what we are is so much more important than what we do.

I think Max[1] is right about the desirability of your doing something in Scribner's editorial department. I can see you as understudy to Max, and loving it.

The movie of The Yearling is postponed for lack of a boy, deer and a weatherbeaten hound.[2] I went the other day to the abandoned clearing that I used for locale, and found that the movie-ites had re-created a setting exactly as I imagined it. The place was charming. Next time you're here we'll go over.

Have been at the beach cottage a good deal off and on. Am just back from a week-end there. Had thought I was safe from the world that is too much with us,[3] when Mr. and Mrs. Owen D. Young called on me. They have a place three miles south of Marineland. Invited me to a tea, which I ducked, but will call on them, for they are really very sweet. Was sound asleep when I heard a rap at the door,[4] slipped on a house coat and shuffled to the door. A strange man asked if Mrs. Rawlings lived there---Yes---could he see her. I said "I'm afraid not". Well, "I am Owen D. Young, and Mrs. Rawlings' friends, Dr. and Mrs. Tigert, said she lived here and Mrs. Young and I just wanted to call."[5]

---

1   Maxwell Perkins, MKR's editor at Scribners, suggested on several occasions that JSB join Scribners on a more formal basis, once speculating that her interests in photography would make her ideally suited for the publicity department. Her marriage to the Rev. Thomas James Bigham Jr. (1911–1990) in May 1945 effectively ended any prospects of a position of authority at Scribners.

2   In 1938, MGM purchased the rights to The Yearling for $30,000. By 1940, production had begun on the film, which was to star Spencer Tracy (1900–1967) as Pa Baxter and Anne Revere (1903–1990) as Ma Baxter. In May 1940, filming was delayed in part because a national search was underway to find an actor to play Jody Baxter. Later that month, Eugene Edenfield "Gene" Eckman (1927–2009) and his mother Mamie (1895–1978), who lived at 1536 Mozley Drive, Atlanta, Georgia, were invited to Hollywood so he could audition for the role. On 6 July, The Atlanta Journal-Constitution reported that Eckman and five other southern boys were in Hollywood as finalists. Eckman was given the role, and on 26 August it was reported that he was in Hollywood playing with the animals that were to appear with him in the movie. The following year, The Yearling was abandoned after the shooting of only a few scenes because of the hot, rainy weather, and actor discontent, which in turn led to significant cost overruns. MGM lost nearly $500,000. Eckman, according to Elizabeth Heffelfinger ("'Seems like bein' hard is the only way I can stand it': The Softening of Ma Baxter in Clarence Brown's Adaptation of The Yearling," Journal of Florida Literature 17 [2009]): 59–82), "was crushed and left the business" (63).

3   MKR is alluding to "The World Is Too Much with Us" (1807), a sonnet by the English Romantic poet William Wordsworth (1770–1850).

4   MKR is alluding to "The Raven" (1845) by Edgar Allan Poe (1809–1849), American poet, fiction writer, and critic, known especially for the macabre: "While I nodded, nearly napping, suddenly there came a tapping, / As of some one gently rapping, rapping at my chamber door" (ll. 3–4).

5   MKR is describing here her first meeting with Owen D. Young (1874–1962) and Louise Powis

Well, Hell, "Come on in." But if there's much of that sort of thing, I'll have to look for a further outpost. Had Thornton Wilder[1] down to lunch when I was there lately, the most adorable person. Do you know him? He put on an interpretation of Finnegan's Wake,[2] I thought at first facetiously, but bless Katy he meant it. It [seems] that the book is written in five languages, and there are three-way puns in English, French and Latin, and if you don't get it it's just your tough luck. After Wilder explained a lot of it, Norton said to him, "Wouldn't it have been simpler if three or four of you had gotten together with Joyce and just talked it over?"

Ferdinand the bull[3] is Coming Into His Own, and I had to buy a nose-ring for him yesterday. I do hate to do that to him, but everyone tells me I will regret it bitterly if I don't. I stroked his nose last week, and the other day tried it again and he pawed the earth. That's gratitude for you.

The romance between Albert and Adrenna is not going so well. Albert tried to get ten dollars out of me and when I asked what he wanted it for, just jerked his thumb toward Adrenna. She knew nothing of the intended touc[h][4] and the suspicion has come to all of us that Albert was just trying to marry her for her money---. The rest of the family is very much down on him, So I'm hoping that if I hold firm financially, Albert will just drift off. His charm was not substantial, and I found he was very uppity on closer acquaintance. When a bunch of us went to the cottage this week-end, I took Martha as company for Adrenna, and all seemed happy. Martha was crazy about the place and said she would spell Adrenna off this summer when I go

---

Young (1897–1965) who owned "Washington Oaks," once a plantation, now a state park, three miles south of Marineland. Owen D. Young was a businessman, lawyer, diplomat, and founder of RCA. The Youngs and MKR soon became very close friends. It was the Youngs who convinced MKR to buy her summer home in Van Hornesville, New York, where they also owned an estate and various farms.

1   Thornton Wilder (1897–1975), American novelist and playwright.

2   James Joyce (1882–1941), Irish novelist, *Finnegan's Wake* (London: Faber & Faber, 1939). In a letter to NSB on 7 September 1943, MKR claims to be disappointed by the novel, "It seems actually spiteful of him to have done 'Finnegan's Wake,' as though he held food just out of reach of hungry people. Perhaps, he thought, if you were avid enough, like Thornton Wilder, you would make great leaps and get hold of the meat" (*Love Letters* 123).

3   Some of the more humorous passages in *Cross Creek* involve Ferdinand the bull, who had suddenly come of "breeding age." MKR had raised him from a calf, but now "Ferdinand was a very large bull of ferocious tendencies. . . . I was appalled by his size. . . . Now he was a mammoth thing. . . . I recall a poll on the most dangerous animals in the country, and the Jersey bull was at the head of the list." As Little Will Mickens adroitly points out to the endangered MKR, "'He don't like womens no more . . . Jes' cow-womens.'" (264–66).

4   Hole in MS. Speculation is that the word is "touch," as Albert was trying to "hit up" MKR for some money.

over. She said, "Sugar, if I didn't have me a husband, I'd follow you anywhere in the world."

Tuesday [7 May 1940]

Just went in to Island Grove to vote. One of the local ladies was standing within arrestable distance from the polls damning our present governor, an old ass who is running for the U.S. Senate[1]. She shrilled, "I wouldn't vote for him for dog-catcher at Cross Creek." I slunk in and out---.

Pat[2] is the father of six puppies and more are expected in a week from another good friend of his. I get my choice and neither Pat nor I has any use for them.

And so to work--love--- Marjorie (over)

I never thought to ask you whether you preferred to call me "Mrs. Rawlings" or if you wouldn't rather use the Marjorie. Wish you would do as you like about it. Don't like to insist on the first name after a shock I had at a cocktail party Bob[3] gave for some visiting friends! He spoke of "Alice" this and "Alice" that as "Alice" turned out to be about 80 years old, putting down the martinis with a palsied hand---[4]

. . .

MKR to JSB 22 July 1940. TLS, 2 pp. PM: Hawthorn | Jul | 24 | 1940 | FLA. AD: Miss Julia Scribner | Dew Hollow | Far Hills | New Jersey

July 22 [1940]

Dear Julia:

I was just "fixing", as we say, to write you a good long letter when yours came---and as the Nicholas Brady rye[5] had not, I thought I had better wait

---

1 Fred P. Cone (1871–1948) was governor of Florida (1937–1941), and rather than seek a second term he ran for U.S. Senate. He was defeated in the Democratic primary by Charles O. Andrews (1897–1946), who was elected and died in office.

2 Pat, MKR's pointer dog.

3 Robert Camp Jr.

4 This second postscript is in MKR's hand.

5 Rye whiskey from the estate of Nicholas Frederic Brady (1878–1930), New York businessman and philanthropist who managed and expanded a massive fortune left to him by his father Anthony N. Brady (1841–1913), industrialist. In 1906, Brady married Genevieve Garvan (1880–1938). Both devout Catholics (they were created Papal Duke and Duchess in 1926), she decided to donate their estate on Long Island, "Inisfada," to the Catholic Society of Jesus, known as the Jesuits. On 6 March 1937, she married William Babington Macaulay (1893–1964), Irish minister to the Vatican. The art and furnishings of Inisfada were systematically auctioned off in May 1937; see *New York Times*, 25

until its safe arrival. When it did come, and the notice, and Norton picked it up at Hawthorn and brought it over to the cottage, I was deeply involved in patriotic duties---a speech in Jacksonville,[1] with much hullabaloo, the proceeds go to the Red Cross---and on the heels of that, an article boosting the American way of life---more of that in a minute---and the pleasant things, as usual, had to wait. I should have sent you a picture postcard saying the rye had arrived and a letter would follow, but every day I thought I would find time to write you, as I wanted.

I could spank you for being so extravagant about the rye. You must not do such things for me. But I must admit I was tickled to death to have it. Norton and I opened one bottle and had a reverent sample. The stuff is more like a fine brandy than any whiskey I have ever tasted. It is smooth as satin---and most deceptively mild. We sipped it with awe and were grateful that our drunkenness is still eclectic enough so that we can appreciate a drink as choice as that. After the one drink we put it aside and decided to save the rest for very special occasions---and for showing off. I have two or three snooty friends---Bob Camp's nasty mother for one---to whom it will be an evil joy to say, in offering the rye, "Just a little thing a friend sent me from the Nicholas Brady cellar." One special occasion I want to save some for is your next visit to see me. You can certainly take one sip!

What are your summer plans? Unless you have something very exciting planned, I am sure you would enjoy two weeks with me at the ocean cottage. It is always cool and breezy there---as a matter of fact, most of Florida in the summer is much cooler than New York. When the whole Atlantic blows in on you, straight across from Spain---or is it north Africa?---you are bound to be cool. I know you will think of the work I am supposed to be doing, but I really do think I could do considerable work while you were there. The day's schedule would be something like this: Arise from 7 to 8, take a walk with Pat on the beach, have a swim, come in for breakfast. Read the paper. Then one of us could take the terrace (which I have had screened) and the other the living room, and I could work while you read. Lunch. Talk. Work and reading or what have you. I never work after about five in the afternoon in any case. A swim again, dinner, and whatever we wanted to do in the evening. How does it sound?[2]

I am stuck at the Creek for ten days, thanks to a very nervy friend of mine

---

Feb. 1937: 25, and 16 May 1937: 85. The contents of the wine cellar were sold by the wine and spirit dealer M. Lehmann, Inc., New York, beginning in May 1940, including a cache of Stewart Pure Rye Whiskey, "90 proof 4/5 qt. Made 1913," priced at $65 per case (*New York Times*, 24 May 1940: 12).

1 MKR's Red Cross speech is not identified.
2 JSB came at the end of August and stayed for three weeks (Silverthorne 186).

(Macmillan's southern trade manager) who got married and asked for my cottage for his honeymoon.[1] Why should I provide another woman with a honeymoon I don't quite see, but I hated to refuse, since even much-married people (he had just gotten rid of wife no. 1)[2] don't do it so very often. But it is very stuffy inland, and I entertain the kindly hope that before their time is up they will be cutting each other's throats.

I understand exactly the type of distress you are going through. It is simply that you have a terrific mental and emotional energy that is not being used. As to the emotional energy, nothing can be done about that until your path crosses the path of <man> a man you can care for who cares for you. As to the mental energy, I think you should get into some work---going on with your voice, or going into editing at Scribner's---that will give your very fine mind an opportunity to use itself. And you would find that the mental absorption takes care of a lot of the emotional damning. But you are the last person in the world who should be either idle or doing something futile.

I loved your letter. Letters should be either completely perfunctory, or like yours.

Let me know your plans and whether you'd like to come down.

Marjorie

. . .

MKR to JSB, 7 August 1940. TLS, 2 pp. PM: SAINT AUGUSTINE | AUG 7 | 8:30 PM | 1940 | FLA. AD: Miss Julia Scribner | care of J. Macy Willets | New Marlboro | Massachusetts.[3]

August 7 [1940]

Dear Julia:

Your letter just came with the good news that a summer visit fits in with your plans, and that you are not upset by an invitation from a working hostess.[4] I think you are the only person I would dare much [make] such a proposition to, and certainly the only one I could conceive of as a guest around

---

1 Norman Berg and Julie Berg. JSB was there at Crescent Beach, and as MKR reports to Baskin in a letter dated [21? August 1940], "Julia . . . is simply violent on the subject of Julie. . . . She is even furious at her beloved Pat [the dog] because he lay at Julie's feet. She said that girl is obviously not in love with Norman" (*Love Letters* 53).

2 Josephine Greer Berg (d. 2006).

3 Josiah Macy Willets (1889–1940), husband of Gladys August Bloodgood Willets (1889–1978), the sister of Vera Gordon Bloodgood Scribner (1891–1985), the mother of JSB.

4 This sentence suggests that JSB's letter accepting MKR's invitation is missing.

whom I could really work. I want terribly to get the book[1] done by the end of September, for I go to my university at Madison, Wisconsin October 8 to give a lecture for the benefit of the Scholarship Fund,[2] and what work I haven't finished by then, stands a jolly good chance of not being touched until next summer. Florida winters are more than I can manage as far as work is concerned.

Really, the Nicholas Brady rye[3] should have been the birthday present. How on earth did you remember <u>my</u> birthday?[4] Yours was easy, being so soon after I saw you. Ordinarily I can't remember from one week to the next under what sign my friends were born. But as in the case of the choice rye, I cannot be hypocrite enough to say I'm sorry the creamer and sugar bowl are coming. You see, the cottage has turned out so much fun that I brought most of the old Sheffield[5] I bought over here---and I still have no sugar and creamer to use at the Creek with my tremendously old family pewter coffee-pot. So no one gets your set for a wedding present unless you want it back when you take the plunge.[6]

I'm glad you passed up the matrimony if there was the least question in your mind. Marriage is a little like death---if you're of a loyal and earnest nature, it lasts so long---. And once an unfrivolous woman is in it, she tends to make the best of it, as I did, and suffers in silence.[7] Marriage should happen only when there is absolutely no question in your mind. I know that it is possible to become attached to someone with whom you were not originally terribly in love, but it is much better and safer to start out with a good margin of feeling!

---

1   *Cross Creek* (New York: Scribners, 1942). See Tarr, *Bibliography*, A5.1.

2   On 19 September 1940, MKR wrote to Maxwell Perkins, "My trip to Madison, Wisconsin will be a brief one just for the one lecture for the Benefit of the Alumni Scholarship Fund. I am going at my own expense. It seems little enough to do for one's own college" (*Max and Marjorie* 469). Apparently MKR's experience exceeded her grandest expectation. The lecture on fact and fiction went well. She was then fêted by both the students and the faculty (Silverthorne 188–89). She also met the novelist Sinclair Lewis (1885–1951) and the architect Frank Lloyd Wright (1867–1959). MKR describes her adventure to Beatrice H. "Bee" McNeill, a close friend at the University of Wisconsin, in a letter on 24 June 1941, as an "absolutely perfect experience. The old school did everything but turn out the band" (*Selected Letters* 202).

3   Nicholas Brady Rye Whiskey.

4   MKR was born on 8 August 1896.

5   English Sheffield dishes MKR bought in New Orleans during her lecture tour in April 1940. See letter to NSB on 3? April 1940 (*Love Letters* 48).

6   That is, when she gets married. This reference to marriage further suggests that there is a JSB letter missing.

7   MKR is referring to her unhappy marriage to Charles "Chuck" Rawlings whom she met at the University of Wisconsin, whom she married in New York in May 1919, and from whom she was divorced on 10 November 1933.

Just as I was settling down to hard work at the cottage, I had to give it up to a friend for his honeymoon.[1] He was a "rejected suitor" and when he went off on a fresh trail and found him a wife, he decided I was his best friend and calmly asked for my cottage. When I came back to it, there was a very grateful note from him, saying that the cottage had been his Shangri-la. Hell, it was mine, too---.[2]

I have to leave again in the morning for another Christian duty. Aunt Ida[3] has been having me with her on her birthday ever since she's been in Florida, and it is one of her big moments. She planned originally this time "a sort of reception", then when Norton quietly eased her out of that idea, she compromised for an outing with a dozen or so of my friends at Rainbow Springs.[4] I'd give anything not to have to leave, but truth to tell, I can't take my work seriously enough to put it ahead of the human element.

Any time you are through with what you are doing up yonder will be fine for me. I'll meet you in Jacksonville whenever you say. You might enjoy coming down by boat on the Clyde-Mallory line.[5] If you do, be sure you get an ocean-side stateroom, preferably well forward, to get the usual south-east breezes of this time of year.

Adrenna is still delinquent and at last reports will be home in September, so I am putting up with old Martha's devotion and ignorance until then, rather than break in a new girl.[6] Fortunately Martha likes it here at the beach. She drives me nuts, but I should be fussy about who is behind the broom and over the dishpan.

Bob Camp is upset about the proposed draft[7]---he is 29---as he is work-

---

1 Norman and Julie Berg, the latter Berg's second wife.

2 MKR wrote NSB about the Bergs' stay using much the same qualified and at times resentful language: They left the cottage in "good shape," but the "tub and toilet dirty. . . . I knew the bastard would put me further on the spot by being terribly grateful. 'The cottage was his Shangri-la, etc. etc. Etc.' Hell it was mine, too" (*Love Letters* 51).

3 Aunt Ida Tarrant, great aunt of Charles Rawlings, MKR's first husband. Aunt Ida, known for her malapropisms, was beloved by MKR. She lived in Ocala, then in St. Augustine, Florida, and spent considerable time with MKR at Cross Creek.

4 Rainbow Springs, a natural spring north of Dunnellon, Florida.

5 Clyde-Mallory Steamship Co.

6 Adrenna's absences had become the stuff of legend. MKR liked her, needed her, but despised her repeated disappearances. On 24 May 1940, MKR's exasperation reared its racist head when she writes to Perkins, reporting that this time "Adreina [*sic*] had eloped with a worthless nigger, half her age, to St. Petersburg. . . . Old Martha, her mother, is a great spiritual satisfaction to me, but can't even make a decent cup of coffee. Martha is more crushed than I by Adrina's delinquency, for it is a reflection on her training" (*Max and Marjorie* 458).

7 On 16 September 1940, Congress enacted the Selective Training and Service Act requiring all males between twenty-one and forty-five to register for the draft. By the end of World War II, more than ten million men had registered.

ing for his one-man show in New York in October, but I doubt if he is husky enough to exempt the army until they have used up the truck-drivers.

Until later, with love,

Marjorie

Please do use the Marjorie.[1]

.   .   .

MKR to JSB, 23 August 1940. TLS, 2 pp. AD: Miss Julia Scribner | care of Charles Scribner | 597 Fifth Avenue | New York City. PM: SAINT AUGUSTINE | AUG 24 | Saint Augustine | 8^{30} PM | 1940 | FLA. LH: Marjorie Kinnan Rawlings | Hawthorn, Florida.

Friday [23 August 1940]

Crescent Beach RFD
St. Augustine, Fla.

Dear Julia:

Expect you had better have my beach address---it is as above. For a telegram, that would be 'phoned to the filling station[2] near me, and then delivered to me. That address would be by 'phone, Crescent Beach 2, Via St. Augustine.

Weather warm, but always pleasant on top of the dune, and the ocean water grand.

Don't know what kind of help we'll have while you're here, but there will be someone who can at least clean up, and the restaurant, The Dolphin, a few miles below at Marineland, has already proved a boon to me, so at worst we can have dinners there. You could hardly fare more lightly at breakfast than you did under Adrenna's ministrations! The black hussy, as her own mother fondly calls her, has not yet returned, and last week old Martha, who had me about crazy anyway, got enough of the beach and was strangely and suddenly ill when I took her to the grove for a day. Have the promise of a maid from St. Augustine,[3] whom I am to see today, and since you don't mind foregoing

---

1   The postscript is in MKR's hand.
2   Junko's, where MKR was able to buy convenience items and gasoline.
3   Most likely Dorothy May, about whom MKR wrote in a letter to NSB dated [1? August 1940], "Dorothy has already spoiled me for coping with Martha's droopiness and incompetency. Certainly wish I could take the little nigger home with me for the winter, but have no illusions about its working. Dreamt last night that Adrenna was back at the grove" (*Love Letters* 53).

style in any case, know you won't mind. Just wanted to warn you in case I have one of the freaks who seem to come my way.

Well, the pewter cream and sugar are utterly <u>charming</u>. Don't think I ever saw any I liked better. Don't believe I could even bear to give them back to you for a wedding present! They look absolutely pre-Revolutionary, much older than the coffee pot I shall use them with, but a perfect complement.

I went home to spend my birthday with Aunt Ida,[1] and they were in that day's mail, so it seemed very festive. You were grand to track down anything so perfect. But I want that to be the end of your recklessly extravagant things for me.

Let me have a line or a wire about your plans---it makes no difference to me, but want to catch Bob and Cecil and Norton together for a week-end when you are here, and the three are sometimes illusive.

Found a piece of paper on my door one day when I had been away, "To the Queen of the Beach", and signed "The Count of Ocala", and in between a sketch of a horse's rear labeled "Multum in parvo",[2] so knew Bob had stopped by---.

My love,
Marjorie

. . .

MKR to JSB, [23? September 1940]. ALS, 3 pp. Envelope is missing.

Monday [23? September 1940][3]

At the Creek

Julia my dear:

I was delighted to read in Tom Wolfe's new book[4] a statement about writers that seems to explain so much. He said that he was really lazy, that all creative people were lazy, but that lazy people get a terrific amount done in

---

1 Aunt Ida Tarrant. MKR's birthday 8 August.

2 *Multum in parvo*: Latin for "much in a little." Camp was soon to become a well-known artist and illustrator, thanks in some measure to the support of MKR.

3 Written in a second hand at the top of p. 1: [1940]. Since JSB left on 17 September, the only two possible Mondays are 23 or 30 September, before MKR left for her lecture at the University of Wisconsin. Because of the immediacy of JSB's departure on 17 September and the subsequent tone of the letter, 23 September has been chosen.

4 Thomas Clayton Wolfe (1900–1938), American novelist and short fiction writer, *You Can't Go Home Again* (New York: Harper & Brothers, 1940). Published posthumously. Wolfe died on 15 September 1938.

the end, more than energetic people, because they know they are lazy and a frightful sense of guilt and self-knowledge torments them, so that they end up with bursts of energy, self-driven and at last accomplishing. I could perfectly well have written you long ago, so won't pull any fancy line about all I've had to do. Yet, actually, this is the first peaceful moment I've had.

I took Aunt Ida[1] back to the cottage with me to spend last week, and she loved it. It was my Girl Scout act for the summer, but her pleasure was more than compensation. Work would have been a fatuous effort, for she was so happy to have someone to talk to that even when I pretended to be deep in creation (actually getting caught up on those letters "Thank you so much for your generous comment on The Yearling. I am sorry, but I cannot criticize manuscripts---["]) she would make some excuse to trot in to exchange ideas.

Unfortunately, she was constipated, and went around lamenting "Here I am with someone to talk to and all these good things to eat, and I have to take Carotid-and-Bile tablets."

I <u>loved</u> Winnie-the-Pooh.[2] It <u>hurts</u> me that you could doubt me. I shall say no more. I am saving "Out of Africa"[3] for a lean day. Thanks a lot for the catalogue, but perhaps fortunately, the picture is not the Gauguin I coveted.[4] The one I saw was much larger, and the proportions were reversed. Mine was at least 3 or 4 feet wide and about 3 feet deep, and it was almost entirely landscape. Just the suggestion of the old house at the left, and if there were figures, they were hazier, and at the right, and were not an important part of the scene. But keep your eyes open in the galleries and catalogues---you may run across it some day. It is all lovely greens and yellows, the most exotic and dreamy yet restful thing you can imagine.

An express package is waiting for me in St. Augustine, which I'll pick up tomorrow when I go over, and I imagine it is the Grant Wood flower prints.[5] From the weight, it must be a much larger book than I thought. I am so anxious to see them.

Now <u>please</u> don't send me another thing. I picture your Buick without tires and panting without gasoline, and you having to borrow Buzzy's pajamas[6] because you have spent all your money and can't afford any of your own.

---

1   Ida Tarrant, who lived in Ocala at this time.
2   A. A. Milne (1882–1956), English poet, novelist, and playwright, *Winnie-the-Pooh* (London: Methuen, 1926).
3   Isak Dinesen, *Out of Africa* (London: Putnam, 1937).
4   Paul Gauguin (1848–1903), French Impressionist. The work MKR refers to has not been identified.
5   Grant Wood, American artist.
6   Charles Scribner IV (aka Jr.), JSB's brother, nicknamed "Buzz."

I'm sending you a small painting of the Fort Marion arch that you liked, done by a St. Augustine man.[1] You may not like it at all, so have no scruples about throwing it out if you don't. I think I'd feel safer picking hats for anyone, than pictures. Actually, I didn't even pick this. I just happened to have it.

I was much surprised at Bob's transparent 'phoning of you on the excuse of news about the folks. From his report, you rather stalled the young man off a bit, though he didn't take it that way. It seems you were very vague as to where you'd be in October. Don't think you need be afraid of his trying to be more than a friend. He seems a pretty confirmed celibate.

Well, I am all of a twitter getting ready to go to Madison[2] for a week of teas, dinners etc., the sort of thing I usually duck, but at the hands of old friends think it will be fun. There is just an outside chance that Norton will be able to go to the fair after Oct. 13, and if he should find he can get away, I'd go right from Chicago and meet him in New York. Wonder if the best exhibits will be taken down early? Would hate to strain a point and find Flushing Meadows in ruins.[3]

You did <u>miracles</u> with Max.[4] He must have written me that very day. Exactly the marvelous criticism I hoped for. He thinks that basically my material is good, but suggested another line of attack that will take care of my problems. When I get back from Madison I shall pitch in with joy and abandon and there will be no more stalling.

Came home from the cottage to find confusion worse confounded[5] at

---

1 Fort Marion painter: Not identified.

2 MKR's lecture "Fact and Fiction" was delivered on Tuesday, 8 October, in the Union theater. She "was enthusiastically received by an audience of more than 1000 listeners." A check for $750.00, representing the profit from the event, was presented to the University of Wisconsin, then the largest donation of its kind ever given (*Wisconsin Alumnus* 42.1 [November 1940]: 8).

3 MKR is referring to the New York World's Fair, which opened on 30 October 1939 and closed on 27 October 1940. The Fair was held in Flushing Meadows, New York, and its theme was The World of Tomorrow. Among other things, TV was formally introduced, and the opening was broadcast on W2XBS (now WNBC).

4 Maxwell Perkins's influence on the writing of *Cross Creek* was pervasive. See especially his letter to MKR on 20 September 1940 (*Max and Marjorie* 470–73). MKR met with Perkins in New York circa 26 October, but she continued to have problems with the control of fact and fiction (*Max and Marjorie* 474–75). Perkins knew how to handle MKR's misgivings as a writer and counseled her on 28 November, "I can easily imagine that the difficulties of shaping the material are great, but it is part of the inevitable process. Of course you need not be strictly bound by fact. In such a book you can move things around rightly so long as you give the poetic truth. But you know all about that anyhow" (*Max and Marjorie* 476). This was all Rawlings needed to hear. She moved on painfully but inexorably to conclusion.

5 An allusion to John Milton (1604–1674), *Paradise Lost* (1667): "With ruin upon ruin, rout on rout, / Confusion worst confounded" (2.995–96), describing the fall of Satan.

the Creek. Jealousy between Cracker Snow and Nigger Will,[1] which flared up into Snow's cussing out poor innocent Will shamefully. Will cleared out, leaving me wondering why I torment myself trying to cope with the help problem here, when there are steam-heated apartments with simple window-boxes and janitors. Then this morning Will came back to give formal notice, which gave me a chance to talk nobly <and> ^about^ one for all and all for one,[2] ending with Will and me almost in fraternal tears and everything rosy. Will said, "I'll go get a dollar from Mama to pay the man what brought me, and then I'm gettin' down to work." So apartments hold no more appeal, and I shall begin my garden.

I missed you unconscionably after you left. You don't seem like a new friend at all, but someone who has been dear to me as long as I can remember. I am only afraid that when you get over the stomach ulcers, I will not be what Christopher Robin would call A Good Influence. I still feel guilty about the two Scotches in which I encouraged you.[3]

My love,

Marjorie

. . .

MKR to JSB, 5 October 1940. TLS, 2 pp. PM: HAWTHORN | OCT | 19 [year illegible] | [FLA]. AD: Miss Julia Scribner | Dew Hollow | Far Hills | New Jersey. LH: Marjorie Kinnan Rawlings | Hawthorn, Florida

October 5 [1940]

My very dear Julia:

I am terribly distressed about the doctors' exploratory yearnings.[4] But if

---

1 Feldon Snow Slater (1909–1997), MKR's grove man, and "Little Will" Mickens, who worked in the grove (See *Cross Creek*, Chapter 8, and Stephens 28–29).

2 A nostrum that appears through literature and government. It is the unofficial motto of Switzerland and was popularized by Alexandre Dumas (1802–1870), French author of *The Three Musketeers* (1844).

3 JSB was with MKR in late August until 17 September 1940, for approximately three weeks (postcard to Ida Tarrant, 17 September, unpublished document, Special Collections, University of Florida). In a letter to Tarrant the next day, MKR relates what wonderful company JSB proved to be (unpublished letter, 18 September 1940, Special Collections, University of Florida). MKR writes to Maxwell Perkins on 19 September 1940, "I enjoyed Julia Scribner's visit immensely. She is most unusual and very mature" (*Max and Marjorie* 469). Christopher Robin is A. A. Milne's son, to whom he addressed *Winnie-the-Pooh*.

4 JSB has obviously been for a checkup by physicians, most likely for what is causing her migraine

several good ones are in complete agreement, suppose it is right. Just be sure in your own mind that there is something mechanically wrong, over and above the nervous tension to which you are liable. When your nerves tie up in a solid ball, you can feel anything in the world. Yet there were times when you were with me, when I knew you were perfectly happy and had nothing on your mind (but spiders), when you showed that something wasn't behaving properly.

I think the Denver trip sounds grand. It is hard to resist an appeal like that, and I think you'll really enjoy giving in to it.

Well, the exquisite Grant Wood[1] is now hanging where I imagine you visualized it---over the console in the cottage hall. The frame matches the blond mahogany wood exactly, and the print shows up beautifully there from all angles. I love it. I had imagined a small folder of several small individual flower prints---I didn't realize you were speaking of one large composite. This is much more satisfactory, for it can be looked at and enjoyed all the time. The frog is completely ingratiating.

I did hate to leave the beach, but the fall planting is going forward here at the farm, and that is great fun. I leave tomorrow for my week in Madison.[2] The New York trip doesn't look very promising. Will let you know of course if anything materializes.[3]

Did a very careless thing---two or three days after you left a wire came, and I opened it without noticing that it was for you. Saw that it was too late for you to do anything about it and set it aside to include when I wrote you---and forgot all about it until now. My apology to you and your fri[end]![4]

Much love,

Marjorie

---

headaches. MKR's references to this event and in the next paragraph to JSB's contemplation of going to Denver suggest that JSB's letter is missing.

1   Grant Wood (1891–1942), foremost American Regionalist painter, best known for the iconic *American Gothic* (1930). MKR is referring to the Wood lithograph *Wildflowers* (1939), hand colored by Wood's sister Nan, sent to her by JSB, which is at present hanging in the home at Cross Creek. Nan Wood posed as the woman in *American Gothic*. The frog is at the bottom left of the lithograph and is integrated among the flowers.

2   Where MKR delivered her lecture at the University of Wisconsin in October 1940. MKR apparently went by train (*Max and Marjorie* 469) on 6 October. The lecture was on 8 October. She was back at Cross Creek on 26 October 1940, when she wrote Perkins about the MS of *Cross Creek* (*Max and Marjorie*, 474–75).

3   MKR did go to New York at the end of October to see Maxwell Perkins about persistent plotting and character issues in the manuscript of *Cross Creek* (see *Max and Marjorie* 474).

4   An ink blot and tear in the MS obscure what seems to be "friend."

. . .

MKR to JSB, 26 October 1940. TLS, 8 pp. PM: CITRA | OCT | 26 |
FLA. AD: Miss Julia Scribner | Dew Hollow | Far Hills | New Jersey.
LH: Marjorie Kinnan Rawlings | Hawthorn, Florida.

October 26 [1940]

Dearest Julia:

Well, Cross Creek has settled down into the somnolence of Saturday afternoon. The help has all been paid off---"given their time", they call it---
and gone to town to buy grits and white bacon and make a payment on the
battery-set radio. Pat is asleep on the veranda, a West Indian ground dove is
having a quiet dip in the bird bath, and the cows and chickens are comfortably between meals and so are silent. Even the ducks, who scream for supper
an hour before anything else is hungry, are drowsing under a jasmine bush
by the front steps. The only sound in many minutes has been a bee's droning
and Brice's[1] rooster down the road. It is good to be here, and to be writing to
a dear friend.

I am hoping that after the utter quiet we shall have a rain, for I came
home to a bad drought, and even the glossy green orange trees are dusty. I
rashly told the help that they couldn't be trusted to make a rain while I was
away, but to give me a few days and I'd get us one. It would be nice to come
across---. Then I should not only have prestige, but the broccoli and lettuce
plants could be set out, and my bare yard be planted to rye grass and sprigs[2]
of the new blue St. Augustine. My old-type St. Augustine finally disappeared
under the appetite of a bug to which it is susceptible, and while I was gone
I had the whole yard flat-hoed to make a new start. There are almost no
flowers on the place at the moment---Vincas, which aren't much help in the
house---French marigolds from Martha's yard---Turk's-cap blooming, but
no good for cutting, as they simply melt---so when ordering flowers in Ocala
yesterday for ill friends, I treated myself to some stunning chrysanthemums
which the florist called "Dotys". They are absolutely compact balls, about
the size of an orange, and I have them in lavenderish pink and lemon-yellow
tipped with bronze. I always feel a combination of guilt and triumph when I

---

1 William Riley "Old Boss" Brice (1861–1945), MKR's closest neighbor, a "frail little man" who
"wandered down from Georgia as a boy, nearly sixty years ago . . . to die" (*Cross Creek* 13).
2 Sprigging, the planting of small clumps of St. Augustine grass approximately six inches apart
with the hope, often fatal, that they would grow together. The "old type" St. Augustine was likely
Floratam and the "new Bitterblue," which was denser and less susceptible to insect damage.

buy flowers for myself, for many times at very broke moments I have passed up, if not one loaf of bread, at least a filet mignon, and bought hyacinths or calendulas for the soul.

Norton and I reached home Wednesday noon, not very tired, and so glad that we had taken the New York trip.[1] We enjoyed every minute---except Sunday [20 October] morning, when too consistent night-clubbing finally took its toll. I had to call a hotel maid to pack for me, not daring to run the risk of leaning over to open a drawer or pick up a shoe, and Norton's voice on the 'phone about eleven was definitely wan and pale. We managed to meet at the bar about two, and after three Alexanders each---an appalling drink usually, but the most divine pick-up---I had the strength to telephone Far Hills,[2] to say good-bye. I was sorry to miss you, but I had little to offer---. I had meant to call two good friends before leaving, but couldn't even make that. But our heads while heavy, were unbowed, and we left town under our own power---or that of Norton's new Dodge. What finished us was Saturday night [19 October]. We ran into a good friend, a most convivial poet, Daniel Whitehead Hickey,[3] and went out with him and his lady to the Penthouse Club.[4] Norton came as close there to getting into trouble as he ever will again. He simply couldn't get tight enough to brawl or / ^be^ bad-tempered, but a Willkie-ite[5] almost made a fight of it all by himself. He asked Norton about the South's voting, and Norton innocently said that of course his home state of Alabama was solidly for Roosevelt. "Why?" asked his new friend, and Norton didn't notice the glint in his eye. "Because," says Norton amiably, "he takes care of us and we love to be taken care of. And when he's elected again, he's going to give every WPA worker at least two free nights a week at the Plaza." His friend shouted, "Those ignorant Alabama Crackers are going to put that bastard back in the White House". Norton said to the shouter's---as it turned out, lady-friend---"I think your father's going to have a stroke. Look how purple he

---

1 Wednesday was 23 October. MKR and NSB had gone to New York ostensibly to talk with Maxwell Perkins about the progress of the manuscript of *Cross Creek*. "It was good to see you, if only so briefly," she wrote to Perkins on 26 October 1940. "We manage to come to our understandings very nicely by letter, but there is always somehow a reassurance in the personal contact" (*Max and Marjorie* 474).

2 Far Hills, New Jersey, the home of the Scribners.

3 Daniel Whitehead Hicky (1900–1976), Georgia poet, who enjoyed considerable popularity and who was considered by many to be the poet laureate of Georgia.

4 The Penthouse Club, 30 Central Park South, overlooked Central Park.

5 A reference to Wendell L. Willkie (1892–1944), 1940 Republican candidate for president, who tried unsuccessfully to defeat Franklin D. Roosevelt (1882–1945). MKR and NSB were friends of Willkie and entertained him at Cross Creek, at Crescent Beach, and at the Castle Warden.

is. You'd better take him home." And the man was on the verge of a stroke, and he was purple, and the woman did take him home! Norton thought it was all very friendly and nice, and I can't even now convince him that he very nearly had A Man's Death Laid at His Door.[1]

We did have such a good time seeing you---and you were so grand to us--- and we liked Dave[2] so much.

Don't miss Gertrude Stein's article in the November <u>Atlantic</u>. It is marvelous, in itself, and as a sequel to <u>Paris France</u>.[3]

Please keep me in touch with your plans. When your doctors are prowling about over and in you, have they checked nerve pressure and that sort of thing from your horse-injured backbone for that nausea and headaches and so on? I get the most amazing relief from stomach-touchiness and pain, from massage, my own backbones and what-not liking to act funny. Of course, the X-rays are infallible in showing the stomach thing, but I have wondered about the other.

I think I shall get by with my carousing without an "attack".[4] It is grand to be so definitely on the up-grade. A trip that long would have laid me flat, even a year ago. Pat[5] would send his love if he were awake and could speak, and Norton would if he were here, so I'll include theirs with mine. Pat was coldly furious on my return, and the next day found the car door open and jumped in and would not be budged. He <u>knew</u> I had been at the beach without him, and the car just was not going to leave again without him. I had to take him to Gainesville and everywhere for two days to reassure him.

I brought home my new colored girl[6] Thursday, and things seem very hopeful. I had a frightful shock this morning, however. Looking for string to tie up a book, in the pantry, my eye fell on Emily Post's "Etiquette".[7] I had visions of Bob and Cecil being facetious, and cried out, "Where on earth

---

1 Perhaps a reference to Luke 16:20, where the starving Lazarus was "laid at the gate" of a rich man who rejected his entreaties for food.

2 Dave, a beau of JSB, unidentified.

3 Gertrude Stein (1874–1946), "The Winner Loses: A Picture of Occupied France." *Atlantic Monthly* 166 (November 1940): 571–83. In the article, Stein addresses what it is like to live in German occupied France. Stein's memoir, *Paris France* (New York: Scribners, 1940; London: Batsford, 1940), is a stream-of-consciousness retrospective on the French people and culture before the German occupation.

4 MKR is referring to her ongoing bouts with diverticulosis.

5 MKR's pointer dog.

6 Idella Parker. See *Idella: Marjorie Rawlings' Perfect Maid* (Gainesville: University Press of Florida, 1992), and *Idella Parker: From Reddick to Cross Creek* (Gainesville: University Press of Florida, 1999).

7 Emily Post, American writer on manners, best known for *Etiquette* (New York: Funk and Wagnalls, 1922).

did that come from?" Idella said, "That's my copy." I must have showed my distress, Emily being as useful at Cross Creek as a zebra, for Idella said rather apologetically, "I didn't have anything else to read." I made a mental note that I'd try to change her reading habits, so when she had finished her work today I offered her something. We went to the bookstore together and I began looking around for Kathleen Norris[1] or something like that, saying, "I don't know whether I have the kind of book you like or not." Says Idella, "There's one book I want very much to read, The Yearling"------

Now I don't know whether I'll be upset if she doesn't like it---or if she does---

Lots and lots of love,

Marjorie

. . .

MKR to JSB, 25 November 1940. TLS, 2 pp. PM: HAWTHORN | NOV | 26 | 1940 | FLA. AD: Miss Julia Scribner | Far Hills | New Jersey.

November 25, 1940

Dearest Julia:

I have thought about you a lot and worried about you. Do let me have a line as to how things are going.

I am in a perfectly vicious mood, and wish you were here to go barging off some place with me until I quiet down. I'm having the usual trouble with the goddam book,[2] and my lovely young grove across the road is frozen brown. A perfectly unheard-of early freeze ambled in about ten days ago. We had had a two months' drought and the trees were in bad shape from that, and when the temperature suddenly dropped to 2 two nights in succession, they just couldn't take it in their condition, in spite of firing.[3]

---

1   Kathleen Norris (1880–1966), American writer, best known for her novel *Certain People of Importance* (Garden City, NJ: Doubleday, Page, 1922), whom MKR compared favorably (*Love Letters* 156) to Jane Austen (1775–1817).

2   The book is the manuscript of *Cross Creek*. MKR, who was having trouble with the chronology of the narrative, repeats these sentiments in a letter to Maxwell Perkins the next day, 25 November, "I am having a perfectly evil time with the book. . . . Have torn up half a dozen beginnings" (*Max and Marjorie* 475).

3   Firing refers to methods used to ward off a hard freeze in a citrus grove. There are varying methods, such as building small fires throughout the grove or using smudge pots to produce dense smoke. However, once the temperature reaches 28°F and stays there for a number of hours, most firing techniques do not work. MKR spared little in expressing her anguish to Perkins about the freeze: "I am in a furious mood. A perfectly unprecedented freeze came in a week or so ago, and in

The only bright spot is my new darky maid,[1] who is too good to be true. Think the Lord is holding her like a carrot in front of my nose, to lure me into a sense of comfort and security, and plans to snatch her away just as I settle down in peace. My trust in Providence is about as firm as the trust of the family canary in the family [c]at.[2] Though expecting to be singled out for peace and comfort, is rather unwarranted egotism, after all, isn't it. By the way, the well-dressed and demure café au lait Dorothy,[3] made off with all the sheets and towels that belonged to the maid's room at the cottage.

Have had one good week-end there. Norton and Cecil and I went to a good football game in Jacksonville[4] and then spent Saturday night and Sunday at the beach, and it was swell. We even went in swimming and after the first shock the water was great. Went down to the Dolphin bar[5] and had my first Zombie. They shouldn't call it that, for Zombies are the living dead, and the drink is the resurrection of the prone.[6] Idella, the new nigger, has a sister at the colored normal school in St. Augustine,[7] and I had her down to keep Idella company. She thanked me for a pleasant week-end and said fervently, "Anything to get away from the campus." Idella has been reading my books and is enthusiastic. Don't know whether to salve my pride by believing she's just diplomatic, or whether to accept the fact that I have found the group-audience I write for.

Yesterday, Sunday, Martha came over to see me. She said, "Little Will[8] done jus' exactly like you tol' him." I said, "Fine, what did he do?" She said,

---

spite of firing my young grove across the road, it is a brown, hopelessly looking mess, and I loathe to look out at the damage. Not for any money reasons, but because something beautiful and satisfying is now hideous and depressing" (*Max and Marjorie* 475).

1 Idella Parker.

2 A fold in the MS obscures part of the text, but it seems likely that MKR has typed "cat."

3 Dorothy May, MKR's former maid at Crescent Beach.

4 The University of Florida defeated the University of Georgia 18-13 on 9 November.

5 At Marineland, then managed by NSB.

6 Zombie, a cocktail that requires at least four different kinds of rum: ½ oz. white rum, 1½ oz. golden rum, 1 oz. dark rum, and ½ oz. 151-proof rum, the last folded in with a teaspoon after the first three are combined and poured over ice.

7 Florida's oldest black college/university, founded in 1879 as the Florida Baptist Institute, located in Live Oak. The school relocated to Jacksonville in 1882 because of racial tensions and was renamed the Florida Baptist Academy. It then was moved to St. Augustine and renamed as the Florida Normal and Industrial Institute, with emphasis on teacher training. It remained there from 1918 to 1968. It was then moved to Miami and renamed as Florida Memorial University. Idella Thompson Parker's sister, Eliza Thompson Bickers (1923–) attended the school while it was in St. Augustine, as did her brother, Edward Milton Thompson, who was later killed in World War II in 1944. Zora Neale Hurston (1891–1960), the celebrated African American novelist, taught there and invited MKR to give a lecture on 5 July 1942 (Lillios, *Crossing the Creek* 15).

8 William "Little Will" Mickens, son of Martha Mickens, did grove work for MKR, when, as MKR observes in *Cross Creek*, he was not "drunk" (23).

"You tol' him any time he take a notion to get drunk, not to go makin' no trouble on the highway. You tol' him in that case to get hisself a bottle and get drunk at home. Well, he did it."

Norman and Julie[1] breezed in, expecting to have a happy three days vacation with me, and by the grace of God I was in bed, with a dash of flu or an intestinal attack or something, so all I had to do was stay put and tell them to go ahead and use the cottage. I felt like a dog afterward, for Norman trusts me! Did put Norman to good use, though, sent him to Gainesville to pick out a gun for a belated birthday present for Norton, who fell in love last year with dove shooting. Got a 28-gauge Remington pump. Have been out once with Pat on quail and he did beautifully. After all his spoiling and his whimsies, it is wonderful to see him settle down to work. But you can be darn well sure he wouldn't do it if he didn't want to! But that's why I enjoy him as a hunting dog---it isn't a matter of harsh discipline, but something he is crazy about, and willing to cooperate on. His son Patou, that Cecil is training for Bob, is the spitting image of him, almost as big as he is, and going to make a fine dog. Cecil had Patou out the other day and to my surprise Pat was an enthusiastic host. He had despised him as a puppy.

Well, my dear, I still miss you. Let me have a bit of news.

Much love,

Marjorie

. . .

MKR to JSB, 1 January 1941. TLS, 3 pp. PM: HAWTHORN | JAN | 2 | 1941 | FLA. AD: Miss Julia Scribner | Far Hills | New Jersey.

Jan. 1, 1941[2]

Dearest Julia:

Indeed, yes, this forbidden liquor reached Florida safely, and the express agent apologized for not delivering it in person. The Mount Vernon rye is an extra-special, because I don't buy rye that good, but the Herring cherry brandy is a super-colossal special because I couldn't buy it here if I would.[3]

---

1   Norman and Julie Berg.

2   MKR used a capital "I" for 1 in her dates. This so irritated JSB that MKR eventually agreed to use the proper 1.

3   George Washington Rye Whiskey, produced at the Mount Vernon distillery. For MKR's spelling of "Heering," see her letter on 4 August 1941.

I shall save it for next summer for Singapore slings[1] for the chosen few. It is far too good for the common people. But once again, and quite futilely, you shouldn't do so much for me. I think of your gifts first as your thoughtfulness, and then in terms of tires for your car.

Now as to the wood ducks---and the illegal liquor shipment enters into this, too. Are you trying to get me put in the jail house? I HAVE NO MIGRATORY FOWL PERMIT.[2] I have been keeping that fact from the all-seeing Uncle Sam, because when I want to eat a duck I raised myself, I don't want to have to report its demise to the Roosevelts.[3] And you have to go and put me on their list marked "Inquiries". I have two alternatives---eating the flock spotly [sic], or letting the federal troops march in to arrest me---and in the latter case you have a sacred obligation to keep me in rye and cherry brandy, during my time of incarceration. For I WILL NOT take out a permit. The ducks are not only as free as I am, but a hell of a lot freer, for I have to make a living and they don't. They could leave for a federal game preserve any time they wanted to, but no, they hang around and root up my Italian rye grass and shriek to be put in their pen at night. Wild Mallards fly over and call them and they answer, "We're sitting pretty. Come on down and go on relief with us." The pen is NOT confinement, it is safety from their enemies, as they know, and I WILL NOT TAKE OUT A PERMIT. So as to your idea of wood ducks, I can only quote a woman who had entertained me and to whom I sent a copy of "When the Whip".[4] She wrote, "I know we will enjoy the stories, but even if we don't, we appreciate the thought."!!!!!!!!!

So if you insist on adding wood ducks to Cross Creek, bring them down some time in a suitcase and YOU run the risk.

The liquor is much more to the point.

We have had a gay and hectic Christmas season, with visitors here from hither and yon. Bob Camp's sister Nancy and husband[5] were here for the holidays and I did my bit with quail shooting and a duck hunt and what-not.

---

1 Singapore Sling, a gin-based drink.

2 The Migratory Bird Hunting and Conservation Stamp Act (1934) required hunters to purchase a Federal Migratory Waterfowl Hunting Stamp, known as a "Duck Stamp," in addition to a state hunting license.

3 Franklin D. Roosevelt (1882–1945), the 32nd president of the United States, and Eleanor Roosevelt (1884–1962), the first lady. Although not a Democrat, MKR especially admired Eleanor and was her guest at the White House on 1–2 April 1941.

4 When the Whippoorwill— (New York: Scribners, 1940). See Tarr, Bibliography, A4.1.

5 Nancy Camp, sister of Robert Camp Jr., and Edward B. Lyon, her husband. See MKR's letter dated [22? March 1940], 53, n. 2.

Mrs. Grinnell,[1] my sportswoman-fishing friend, is still at the Marion Hotel,[2] and I have had to do things for her. And so on.

At a New Year's Eve party last night, Bob lamented to me that after having phoned you long distance and ordered special stationary on which to write you, you wrote him on practically toilet paper. I told him you always wrote me on toilet paper and I was pleased to death, because I myself wrote to people I despised on fancy paper and wrote to those I esteemed on very practical paper. He is evidently hard hit and I am tempted to tell him that he muffed any chance with you he may ever have had, by not showing up at the proper time when you were here. If he is definitely out as far as your heart is concerned, I really think the best thing you could do would be to write him in great confidence that you are formally engaged and wanted him to be "the first to know". Otherwise he will be on your trail from now on. The "engagement" would go no further, distance being what it is.

I had an amazing letter from Martha Gellhorn H. from Cuba, opening, "I wonder if you could do something for Mrs. Roosevelt." My thought was that Eleanor wanted the address of Wally Simpson's dentist, or wanted somebody reliable to shoot Franklin. (Have you heard that Roosevelt is dickering with Billy Rose to buy the Aquacade? Yes, indeed, it's the only way he can see to keep Eleanor Holm.) It turns out that Martha G. wants me to find a spring vacation place for Mrs. R and secretary.[3]

I'm so glad you're having such a good time. Wish I could join you for about a third of it. The schedule sounds more strenuous than my musical ear could take. That feeling of guilt you have is very familiar to me. I suffer from it all the time. I never feel that I have earned my leisure, or a vacation, or anything. I am free from it only a few minutes at a time, after having cleaned

---

1 Mrs. Oliver Cromwell "Bill" Grinnell, MKR's fishing companion in Bimini. Grinnell, a noted angler who wrote the introduction to *American Big Game Fishing* (New York: Derrydale Press, 1935), shared her knowledge with Ernest Hemingway (1899–1961), some of which figures in *The Old Man and the Sea* (New York: Scribners, 1952).

2 Marion Hotel, Ocala, once managed by NSB.

3 Martha E. Gellhorn (1908–1998), American journalist, married Ernest Hemingway in 1940, and was divorced from him in 1945. Wallis Warfield Simpson (1896–1986), twice-divorced, whom Edward VIII, Duke of Windsor, abdicated the throne in 1937 to marry. Billy Rose [William S. Rosenberg] (1899–1966), American impresario, conducted *Aquacade*, a music, swimming, and dancing show at the New York World's Fair in 1939, starring Johnny Weissmuller (1904–1984) and Eleanor Holm (1913–2004). Holm, who won an Olympic gold medal in swimming in 1932, starred with Weissmuller in the film *Tarzan's Revenge* (1938), and was married to Rose from 1939 to 1954. Weissmuller won five Olympic gold medals in swimming in 1924 and 1928. It is likely that MKR is having fun with the name Holm, using it as a pun for "home." Presumably, Gellhorn was scouting getaway spots for Mrs. Roosevelt and her intimate friend Lorena Hickok (1893–1968), an American journalist.

out the dresser drawers or gotten caught up on the mail. I think I'd feel free right after each book, except that then Carl Brandt[1] keeps writing me, "And now the book[2] is off, how about some stories?" I don't know where the guilt comes from, except that anyone with lots of mental energy knows secretly how much more he could get done than he does, if he is troubled really to "put out". But there is also a certain satisfaction in going right ahead and having a good time, guilt or no guilt---like playing hooky.

I'd been having some peculiar symptoms and went to the hospital in Jacksonville for two days for a flock of tests.[3] Found all kinds of silly little things wrong---metabolism terribly low, absolutely no hydrochloric acid in the stummick, a dash of anemia and what-not. Correctives all very simple, but I have a whole carton of pills and pellets to keep track of. Feel better already and in a little while ought to be able to lick my weight in wild-cats---or federal duck investigators. If the latter come, you don't mind my saying the Mallards are YOUR ducks, do you? I think they're just what you need at Dew Hollow.

All nonsense aside, the wood ducks were a sweet (if impractical) thought--- and the liquor is both sweet and practical.

Lots of love,

Marjorie

· · ·

MKR to JSB 3 February 1941. PM: Ha[wthorn] | [PM obscured] | FLA. Postal Stamp over PM: BUY U. S. SAVINGS | BONDS | ASK YOUR POSTMASTER. Second PM for Rerouting: NEW YORK, N.Y. | FEB 6 | 8³⁰ P.M. | 1941. AD: Miss Julia Scribner | <Far Hills> | <New Jersey> | c/o Paul Moore, Esq | South Ocean Boulevard | Palm Beach | Florida.[4] AIR MAIL [in MKR's hand]. Air Mail stamp.

---

1   Carl Brandt, MKR's literary agent in New York, pressing her for short stories to sell.
2   *When the Whippoorwill—*, itself a collection of stories, was published in April 1940.
3   Riverside Hospital.
4   Rerouting is in a second hand. Paul Moore Sr. (1886–1959), widely successful American businessman, employed the American architect Addison Mizner (1872–1933), who specialized in Mediterranean and Spanish Revival, to design his 14,550 sq. ft. home on 1820 S. Ocean Blvd., Palm Beach, Florida. Moore's wife, Fanny Mann Hanna Moore (1885–1980), was a proponent of Planned Parenthood and the American Birth Control League and the first female director of the Episcopal Church Foundation. Their home became the center of social life at South Beach. Charles Scribner III and Vera Scribner, his wife, visited there on a number of occasions, often with JSB.

Feb. 3, 1941

Dearest Julia:

The fine rye is down the hatch, but the Herring's cherry brandy still waits for summer and Singapore slings.[1] I looked longingly at it today, in a black mood, but cracked open a bottle of Martell brandy[2] instead. I have an added tenderness for anything Danish since the last mail, in which I was told that my intrepid Danish publisher is buying and bringing out "Golden Apples".[3] I feel at moments that I should turn back all foreign royalties, then I remember how much of my hard-earned pelf our Franklin[4] is taking from me in order to give guns to Britain, and I decide that I am already doing my bit for that illusion called democracy and that utter fake called civilization.

I was at the cottage a week-end or so ago, and Norton and I had drinks at Marineland, and I sent you some of the salt water taffy on which we gorged last summer. I got some for myself and it didn't taste half as good as it did when we ate it together, sure that we were sure tearing up our respective systems. Speaking of systems, mine seems to be rocking on a bit better since the tests and consequent pellets, and a minor operation ^on some "anal crypts"^ that were perhaps a focus of infection. It is hell to be full of energy and to be held back by being under par most of the time, as you know. I was in the hospital just a few days for the operation and drove home alone under my own steam, but with a very tender tail.[5]

I have really been working very hard on the book and am making progress, even though yesterday's work often has to be thrown to the fire today. I've done a little quail shooting, and yesterday had the best hunt I've ever had. Two men and I[6] went on horseback and we found seven covies [sic], and it was fine shooting. I had sworn to my God I would never get on a horse again, but they assured me Old Jim was entirely reliable. So he took the bit in his teeth and headed back for the stables, and it took all three of us to stop him, and then he reared back again and again because he was frustrated, and finished up by stepping in a hole and falling down---all of which they said he had never done before. But it was a fine day, and we went in lovely wild country through marshes and hammocks and around lakes. Pat performed magnificently, and

---

1   Heering's; see MKR's letter on 4 August 1941.

2   Martell brandy, most likely Martell's VOP (Very Old Pale) Cognac.

3   *Golden Apples* (New York: Scribners, 1935). *Gyldne Frugter*. Trans. Kirsten Restup (Copenhagen: Jespersen, 1940). See Tarr, *Bibliography*, A2.1 and E6.

4   President Roosevelt in a radio broadcast on 29 December 1940 promised, under the Lend-Lease Program, to give Great Britain military supplies to aid in its war with Nazi Germany.

5   MKR had surgery at Riverside Hospital in Jacksonville, Florida. See her letter on 1 January 1941.

6   Two men: Not identified.

my hard-boiled friends said he was the best dog they had ever hunted behind. This was not flattery, for they said we were going in country where no dog could last more than three hours---and we hunted without a stop for nearly seven---and as you know, sportsmen tell the truth about dogs.

I forgot to tell you about Daniel Whitehead Hickey's book of verse.[1] I ordered several copies, and asked to have him sign them for the designated friends. He had no ulterior motive, and left New York a day or two after we did. I wanted to help swell his sales---surely a Scribner understands that:--- and I really like his poetry. You must not be so cynical. Some people are worse than you think, but most of them are better. Also, Margaret Mitchell, who is an astute psychologist, flatly denies the charge against him of pansyness.[2] She and her husband[3] spent several days with me last month and we had an awfully good time. I took them into the Yearling country and they were fascinated. I think she is doing another book---may God have mercy on her soul, and on the reviews---.

This is just to say hello---I must dress to go to dinner in Gainesville.

Lots of love,

Marjorie

. . .

MKR to JSB, 5 February 1941. Telegram.

WESTERN UNION
CH109 38 DL XC=ISLAND GROVE FLO 5 130P
MISS JULIA SCRIBNER= 1941 FEB 5 PM 2 17
CARE PAUL MOORE SOUTH OCEAN BLVD=[4]
YOU RASCAL WHY DIDN'T YOU LET ME KNOW YOU WERE HERE
WAS THINKING THE OTHER DAY HOW MUCH I'D LIKE TO SEE
YOU. WILL MEET YOU SUNDAY[5] AND WONT LET YOU GO UNDER
A WEEK. LOTS OF LOVE=
MARJORIE.

---

1   Daniel Whitehead Hicky, *Wild Heron* (New York: Harper, 1940).

2   Pansyness—that is, effeminate or homosexual.

3   John Marsh (1895–1952), the second husband of Margaret "Peggy" Mitchell (1900–1949). Mitchell never wrote another book. She was hit and killed by a taxi on Peachtree Street in Atlanta on 11 August 1949.

4   See MKR's letter on 1 January 1941, which was forwarded from New York to Palm Beach.

5   Sunday, 9 February 1941.

MKR to JSB, 7 February 1941. Telegram.

WESTERN UNION
CH113 49 DL=GAINESVILLE FLO 7 653P 1941 FEB 7 PM 7 44
MISS JULIA SCRIBNER=
CARE PAUL MOORE SOUTH OCEAN BLVD=[1]

JUST CANT HEAR OF YOUR NOT SPENDING A LITTLE TIME WITH
ME. WE CAN SPEND A FEW DAYS AT THE BEACH AND THE SUN IS
AS GOOD AS AT PALMBEACH. IT IS FOOLISH TO GO NORTH NOT
FEELING BETTER.[2] DO WANT A DECENT VISIT WITH YOU PLEASE
ARRANGE IT.
LOVE=
MARJORIE.

. . .

JSB to MKR, [24 February 1941]. ALS, 14 pp. Envelope is missing.

Monday. [24 February 1941][3]

Dearest Marjorie –

Did you think I was dead, as the old line runs, – or did you just think I was damn self-preoccupied louse. Happily, this time at least, the death theory is closer to the truth.

I put in a hectic time when I got back to N.Y. Four concerts and two operas in what was left of the week. Added to the musical activity was the terrific strain of writing three letters – to the Moores and Bob.[4] I felt no such compulsory politeness toward you – might as well confess it – and so I put off writing you until last week, or so I thought at the time, never dreaming of the hordes of bacteria which were to invade my poor systems. I came out here last Sunday, and had to spend the entire day and night hearing about Buzz's[5] love affair which is doing very badly. I wore myself out trying to con-

---

1 See MKR's telegram of 5 February 1941.
2 There seems to be a communication from JSB missing, in which she says she is not feeling well.
3 Written in a second hand at the top of p. 1: [Early 1950's?]. Contextual evidence confirms that this date is incorrect.
4 Paul and Fanny Moore, and Bob Camp Jr.
5 Buzz, Charles Scribner IV (aka Jr.), son of Charles Scribner III and Vera Scribner, was JSB's

sole and encourage him. He seems to have the most awful effect on women – they always treat him in the most bitch-like manner. He gets humbler and more attentive than ever and I have to try to stiffen his morale and persuade him somehow into an indifferent and hardboiled attitude. I got him to go out with some other girls, which I am sure will put this love of his back into his pocket, but I am not sure I <u>like</u> the idea of her being in his pocket. I'm quite disillusioned with her myself. Well – anyway – Monday I awoke with tonsillitis but I went into NY anyway because that night was Lydia's Carnegie Hall concert,[1] and I had been looking forward to it for so long and was so full ^of^ hopes that it would be a big success that nothing short of pneumonia would have kept me away. Sad to relate – it was a dreary flop. Not that anything drastic happened – in fact Lydia sang magnificently and musically everything was quite correct, but the fire, the something which is called by a dozen names – art, interpretation, oomph, or in my language "guts", that was not there. Lydia has always been a bit short on this angle, but we (I and Mr. Alves[2] et al) felt that her opera season had developed her temperament and her ability to project it, and preparing for this concert she showed some of the real stuff. It was just one of those things. Everything <just> went flat the night of the concert and she couldn't get a damn thing into the songs except her beautiful voice. I was tremendously disappointed, and I felt awfully sorry for her because she has worked like a dog and all of her family and friends had come on from Michigan and points both east and west, and we who had had previews were expecting a crashing success. To have to face all those people <u>and</u> yourself must have been grim. I know that I put in a horrible day Tuesday knowing that I must call her and wondering what the hell to say.[3] The press notices were so cold she could at best use them on her head instead of an icebag. Needless to say my tonsillitis was not at all improved by the evening's outing, and so I retired to bed for a week – just got up yesterday [Sunday, 23 February].

I tried to write you twice during the week. Got a table-tray and pad and

brother. Lover: Not identified.

1 Lydia Summers, a contralto, was praised for her interpretations of Bach B Minor Mass: "One of the greatest delights . . . is the difficult technical demands of Bach's complicated score . . . [Summers] rose to the challenge of this marvelous music" (*Orlando Morning Sentinel*). "That rare thing among women, a true Bach singer" (*Montreal Gazette*). "Magnificent . . . tone production was magnificent throughout" (*Montreal Daily Herald*). "Full of volume, flexibility with a remarkable timbre" (*Chattanooga Times*). Source: 1941 newspaper blurbs.

2 Carl Waldemar Alves (b. 1888?), a voice teacher, specializing in operatic training.

3 It is not clear why JSB "had to call" Summers, unless she was writing a review. No indication that JSB was employed to do so has surfaced. However, this letter to MKR, written in a reviewer style, could have been the seedbed for such a review.

pencil, but each time I wrote about half a page and then collapsed. I just felt too limp, particularly mentally. I remembered that you used to do your best work with a fever, but it certainly doesn't help me any – in fact I couldn't spell anything beyond C-A-T. Maybe I had a bit too much.

I'm all recovered now, except that today my right tonsil is sore again. I imagine that they will just get better and worse, worse and better for a couple of months – unless, of course, I progress to something more serious, like a touch of pneumonia.

It was wonderful to see you, Marjorie, and it did my heart so much good, just that one day at Cross Creek, that I wished there was something wrong with it so that it could have been made sound. Well, I shall hoard the "extra soundness" for some rainy day when I have been cruelly treated by an egomaniac composer or some such perfidious creature. I hated to leave more every hour I was there, and when I got on the train I felt so miserable about going away that I wanted to jump off the end of the train and walk back down the track, however as I am not by nature impulsive nothing came of it.

I thought all the way up on the train about you going to the B Minor Mass, and have often thought of it since and <u>today</u> I borrowed a complete record-ing of it and have just finished going through the entire thing score in hand. This is a lot of listening – it takes Rollins a whole day[1] but I have just gulped it down on top of dinner, and if I wasn't at work on this letter I would begin right at the beginning again now. I shall die of disappointment if you don't go.[2] How I wish I could go with you, I would so infect you with my passion-ate enthusiasm and love that you <u>couldn't</u> be bored or think it scholarly and tiresome. If you only go to half, by all means go in the evening even if it is twice as inconvenient. The first half is, of course, magnificent, but aside from the opening Kyrie and the Qui Tollis,[3] which is I think the most beautiful single number in the work, it is not so dramatic or so emotionally moving as the second half.

The second half starts ^with^ the Nicene creed.[4] First a chorus in two

---

1 It took the day and the evening for the Rollins College choir to sing the whole of Bach's B Minor Mass. The Winter Park Bach Festival in conjunction with Rollins College presented Bach's B Minor Mass on 27–28 February, as part of Rollins College Founders' Week. In the *Rollins Sandspur* 46.17 (19 February 1941): 5, the college newspaper in its subheader of its leader announces that "Bach's B Minor Mass To Be Given In Entirety."

2 MKR did not go. Instead, she had to entertain old friends, one of them ill, at Crescent Beach. In her letter on 9 March 1941, MKR laments, "After I read your letter, I wish that I had just ditched them and gone to Bach."

3 Liturgical prayer (Kyrie) that the Lamb of God (Agnus Dei) takes away (*qui tollis*) the sins of the world.

4 Nicene Creed, in Latin as in Bach's Mass *Symbolum Nicaenum*, profession of the Christian faith

parts, first very broad and solemn and then allegro, which takes you as far as "all things visible and invisible." Then a peach of a duet for Sop. And Alto. Just sit back and close your eyes and listen to how marvelously the two voices weave in and out, sing together and sing against each other. I must add here as my most valuable tip on how to hear the B Minor Mass that the more you close your eyes or keep them buried in a score the better, because the chorus is <u>always</u> composed of the weirdest looking people making the most <u>awful</u> faces and generally being as distracting as possible. I think I went to two B Minors without hearing a note, but I got to know most of the Oratorio Society so well that I recognize them on the street all the time. The same goes for soloists who usually look <u>very</u> – agonized or cute or smug or scared to death – and always, again, distracting. Once you notice some very odd alto or tenor you will find yourself taking a terrible interest in them and you just <u>have</u> to keep looking them up to see how they are coping with some difficult sounding part – and good-bye Bach's music. I never look out of my score, except if I lose my place (which is also distracting) in which case I look solemnly at my lap and catch up on the next number. Well, now Lydia and the Sop have finished the duet, together I hope. Of course you <didn't> ^won't^ have your eyes closed you will be looking at Lydia trying to decide what she is like. I do hope you won't find any interesting types in that damned chorus, though, because now comes the climax of the mass. God, if they will only do these three choruses with understanding. I don't think anything more wonderful has ever been written. There are just three bars of introduction to the "Incarnatus", but see if you cannot feel in them the wonder and mystery. The altos start first and then the 2nd sops and then the 1st sops a fourth higher. If you can work your way through my construction to the meaning of this sentence, you're hot.[1] T<here>his is a wonderful effect I think, <from> because it starts with a falling phrase which comes in higher and higher. Notice at the very end – "homo factus est" the way the "est" comes down with what seems to me a [*sic*] atmosphere of quiet <but, or,> and, complete consummation – "the word made flesh". The Crucifixus is heavy with pain & that is unless they play it straight with much academic reverence for Bach, in which case don't blame him for <u>their</u> emotional short comings. At the end it broadens out from the rather limping theme of "crucifixus" and falls very slowly "passus"

---

adopted in the city of Nicaea (present-day Turkey) at the First Ecumenical Council of Bishops. The Creed, as in Bach's Mass, is divided into three sections, which are devoted to the Father, the Son, and the Holy Spirit.

1 This sentence is a note in the margin with no clear point of insertion.

with an awful finality to "sepultus est" which fades and fades into nothing. Then! be somewhat prepared because the "Et resurrexit" should leap up! And if your spine doesn't curl then you can damn the Rollins choir[1] to hell. It is a sad fact that many choruses consider that they are doing nobly if they don't lose their places in the Resurrexit and to hell with what the words mean or the music is trying to get across. However, from what you say, this chorus probably works a good deal over the Mass and is enough at home to really be able to sing the thought as well as the notes. After these three great choruses which go through "And he shall come again, with glory, to judge both the quick and the dead; whose kingdom shall have no end," there is a bass aria. I am sure it would seem like a swell aria anywhere else, but to me it always seems anticlimactic here. It carries the creed through "one Catholic and Apostolic church." Then a big chorus "Confiteor unum baptisma" which weaves around in a complex way until you will probably be reminded (if you are in a biblical mood) of "all we like sheep have gone astray, <and> ^we^ have turned everyone to his own way." But about then all five parts miraculously come together and the music slows way down and there is a wonderful broad impressive statement of "expecto resurrectionem mortuorum". Then it goes twice as fast as before through "the Life of the world to come. Amen." And that finished the Credo, the Sanctus is next. I think I talked to you about it when I was at Cross Creek. Suffice it to say that it is the swellest sounding chorus in the work. Notice that while the upper voices have long holds or runs the basses boom the musical design strong and steady underneath. I like the first part – Holy, Holy, Holy, Lord God of Hosts – better than the "Heaven and earth etc." There is a lovely tenor aria next "Blessed is he who cometh in the name of the Lord". But it always seems too high for the tenors I have heard and the only emotion they can manage at that range is one of tearful agony which I think is quite inappropriate to the text. Maybe this guy will do better. Then there is a very exciting chorus, "Osanna". The voices are divided into eight parts and they have a hell of a fine time yelling at each other – it sounds fine too. It is a real spine tingler, and I think very illustrative of the wonderful muscular virile tunes that Bach could write. It's so full of spirit I wonder how it can sit so dryly on the score beside me, – I don't think the most academic treatment could make it <u>sound</u> dry. Then Lydia sings the most beautiful <u>aria</u> in the Mass, the "Agnus Dei" This is a "slow" Bach aria at its very best with a lovely long melody and full of the sweetness and tender-

---

1   The Rollins College choir in 1941 was made up of sixty members (*Rollins Sandspur* 46.17 [19 February 1941], p. 3).

ness he had without even a hint of slush. The "Qui tollis" chorus has much the same feeling. And then the last chorus, "Dona nobis pacem." After all the wonderful choruses of the first half, and the Credo, the "Life of Christ" three, the Sanctus, the Hosanna in this half, Bach still had one more just as magnificent as any of them. The sustained inspiration of the Mass grows more incomprehensible for me each time I hear it. And when I think of his St Matthew and St John Passions and his hundreds and hundreds of concertos, suites, etc, etc, most of them perfection it seems as far beyond my understanding as the number of stars in the sky. – Well, back to the Mass the Dona nobis starts a very fervent humble prayer that rises very gradually to a cry. I don't think it is possible to sing this chorus now without an awful load of pain in that cry, and I don't think Rollins choir, even if they preserve till then a frigid academicism, can sing it with less than their whole hearts – and if they sing it with their hearts, which is the way all of it must be sung, then you will understand what I have been trying to tell you – then you will be standing upon a peak, and seeing a reach of gold. This climb up is not so difficult. It takes no great mental strain, but just that you should listen with your heart as well as your ears, but the climb down, if you have reached the summit, is painful as I am realizing now having just turned off the phonograph and closed the score and remembered that I must brush my teeth and go to bed. If you really get "into" the thing, (and you shouldn't feel disappointed if you don't in your first hearing), you will probably experience my trouble which is a terrific desire to hit the first person who speaks to you.

I do hope all this will not have a reverse effect and turn your heart against Bach. I shall be quivering with anxiety until I hear about it – But don't you lie to me, Marjorie! I had much rather be told that you still think Bach is a mathematical bore then have you soothing me with a sickly enthusiasm. I am from way off here slightly suspicious of your female with the musical education who is going with you. Don't you let her get all dull and technical about it. I mistrust people with musical educations. Too often they know all about music technically and still don't have any more feeling for it than a flea. I don't know half as much as they do, but I love twice as much, and as with all the arts love is the gold that buys the way in and knowledge is only silver. I wish I could send you the price of admission, because though I'm a bit light on silver I have gold to spare, but I'm afraid that is no more practicable than the digestive juice project. At least I can send love – a good deal of it.

Julia

I will write again soon about all the other things <u>besides</u> the BMM.

By the way, if you feel so inclined and I know that you are very enthusiastic and courageous about such, to me, terrifying things, go back and see Lydia.[1] I know she would be most pleased and overcome. She has looked on me with new interest and respect since she heard I was a friend of yours. Your musical friend may be the "green room" type, who insists on congratulating soloists. If Lydia isn't good as hell I shall eat my <u>10 gal.</u> hat, because I have heard her sing it and she can really do it right. However, singers are never to be trusted.

FOREWORD

It is now Tuesday [25 February] morning and I am looking aghast at Monday night's work. My first ^thought^ was to throw it quickly <u>far</u> away, but it kills me to throw away twelve pages of effort and there is no time to write another twelve or even to purge this one. I cannot understand why words like "mystery: and "wonder" look all right when someone else writes them and perfectly godawful when I do. I suppose it has something to do with where you put them. In the paper this AM there is a review of the new Behrman play[2] that says – "his agility of thought and his magic of phrase evaporate when he assumes an earnest manner," which sure is me all over except that I never get so far as agility or magic but just a reasonable English that I can read without blushing. It is a great cross because I am really very earnest in thought and feeling but I have to stick to light blasphemy to keep from embarrassing myself and any poor listener.

With no little effort of courage I send this along anyway, because I think if you will bravely pick your way over the soft spots and go around such swamps as the part about Bach's inspiration, (the miracle of inspiration is a constant wonder to me, and I ponder on it all the time. Usually it leaves me quite speechless, but this time unfortunately only almost speechless. I can detect a heavy influence of Alves there).[3] I think you will really find it somewhat helpful. I know when I started listening to music Mr. Alves's little "watch for this" and "watch for that" were a great help. I guess I heard this Mass four or five times before I even noticed that three bar opening of the Incarnatus. It was just a wisp of music to orient the chorus – and then suddenly

---

1   Lydia Summer was the soloist in New York not at Rollins College. The meaning here is not clear, unless JSB is speaking in metaphor.

2   Samuel N. Behrman (1893–1973), American playwright, biographer, and screen writer, *The Talley Method* (1941). Rev. *New York Times* (25 February 1941): 25.

3   Carl Alves, see JSB's letter dated [24 February 1941].

last summer at the Berkshire Festival, I really heard it and I almost fainted at how wonderful it was and how in the hell had I missed it.

And then the place in the Confiteor where it broadens out for the "expecto resurrectionem mortuorum" – that's something to be waiting for. It's like going on a road that's new to you. It's good to have someone tell you to watch when you get to this village for a wonderful house or tree. Not that you couldn't see the tree for yourself, but you might happen to be looking the other way. And too, I think that looking for and recognizing special places makes the road much shorter. – I hope it will.

. . .

MKR to JSB, 9 March 1941. TLS, 3 pp. PM: OCALA | MAR 9 | 9 PM | 1941 | FLA. AD: Miss Julia Scribner | Far Hills | New Jersey.

March 9 [1941]

Dearest Julia:

Such a sad story to tell you! I came back from the cottage, where I had taken two friends, presumably just for over-night---and our stay lengthened into four days---to find your letter, with its fascinating interpretation of the Bach mass.[1] Meantime, because of the friends, I had missed the mass, to which I had planned to go. The friends were a couple who used to live in Florida, and I was very fond of them. The man had been very ill and was here recuperating. On their way north again, I suggested that they go to the cottage and they could take their train from St. Augustine. They were totally unable to get reservations, and it was four days before they could get away. They had no car, and we thought from hour to hour they would get the reservations, and I couldn't just abandon them on a sand dune while I dashed off to Rollins.[2] Also, I couldn't take them there with me, as it was necessary for them to get away as soon as they could. After I read your letter, I wished that I had just ditched them and gone to Bach. What we'll have to do, is to hear the mass together sometime, even if it's only on the Victrola. You made me feel that I just haven't heard anything until I've heard this.

Ocala had a little musical evening last night. Fray and Braggiotti[3] were

---

1   See JSB's long letter on Bach, dated [24 February 1941].
2   Rollins College, Winter Park, Florida, where the Bach Mass, sung by the Rollins College choir, was presented on 23–24 February in conjunction with the Bach Festival of Winter Park.
3   Jacques Fray (1903–1963) and Mario Braggiotti (1905–1996), formed a piano duo and were a

here and Bob and Rebecca[1] had a party for them afterward. To me there is something tragic about traveling musicians, unless they are so great that they can dictate the atmosphere, or reject it. Fray was a glum looking person who played the interludes, and Braggiotto was an enormous wild-looking person who fair tore hell out of his piano. They came on to the bare bleak stage of the local auditorium, with white sheeting for backdrops, an American flag pinned perilously amidships, and looked out over the half-filled hall, whose acoustics are something to wake up screaming about. I murmured to Norton that they reminded me of the Lives of the Hunted.[2] They had a grand program, Bach and Debussy and Rachmaninoff,[3] but soon realized they had the audience, for the most part, in over its head, so cancelled two good Debussy numbers and played The Blue Danube[4] instead. For their encores, something happened that would make a swell New Yorker cartoon. The wild looking Braggiotti stood up and pointing to the dour Fray said, "I want to play a classical composition, but Fray wants to swing."

The Camp party[5] was very gay and again the awful happened. A friend of Rebecca's is one Alice Huebner,[6] a pianist who has accompanied and coached several Met singers. She is married to one Borodine, grandson of the Russian composer. She is just as good if not better than Fray and Bragiotti. Rebecca insisted on Alice'[s] playing, on the very good Camp piano which due to the frivolity of Ocala life was in desperate need of tuning. The lower octaves either did not register at all, or came out with the sound of a Jew's-harp. Alice discovered the unhappy condition of the piano, and being a good sport, went ahead and played, scarcely touching the lower register, to hide its inadequacy. Whereupon one of the local beauties, married to a rich man, in a loud voice said "Bragiotti says you play all right, but you don't use your left hand." Norton seldom gets upset, but he made obscene gestures of choking to death the Ocala fair.

---

sensation in the United States for nearly nineteen years, but had to disband when the war broke out in 1941.

1   Robert Camp Sr. and Rebecca Camp (1885–1977), his wife.

2   Ernest Seton-Thompson (1860–1946), *Lives of the Hunted: Containing a True Account of the Doings of Five Quadrupeds & Three Birds, and Elucidations of the Same, Over 200 Drawings* (New York: Scribners, 1901). Seton-Thompson was one of the founders of the Boy Scouts of America in 1910.

3   Claude Debussy (1862–1928), French composer. Sergei Rachmanioff (1873–1943), Russian composer.

4   Johann Strauss II (1825–1899), Austrian composer of "The Blue Danube" in 1867.

5   Rebecca and Robert Sr.

6   Alice Huebner Borodine (1902–1980) was married to Karol Robert Borodine (1909–1987). Alexander P. Borodin (1833–1887), Russian composer.

Well, we are in a fair way to start another Mess at the Creek. Old Martha went down to St. Petersburg to visit the ill Adrenna, and wrote my new grand Idella (not me) that she would be home soon---bringing Adrenna with her. Idella naturally assumed that the recalcitrant Adrenna was to replace her, and did I hurry to assure her that there was no thought of such a thing, that I could not ask [for] a better maid than she, Idella. But Adrenna is a born trouble-maker, and she and Martha will be up to plots to drive off my good Idella. I can outwit men, but am a feeble thing against niggers. They have the same low cunning that Pat[1] has, and it makes you feel very foolish.

You don't follow the New Yorker, do you? I had a story in the Feb. 22 issue that you might enjoy.[2]

And was your Marineland salt water taffy at Far Hills when you got there? If not, let me know, as I can't let them gyp me out of two bucks. They make me furious in any case. They took a picture of me when they entertained Stephen Vincent Benet[3] there a few weeks ago, and sent me a copy to autograph for their publicity department. "Please autograph this picture," they wrote, "and give us a one-line description of Marineland." If it weren't that Norton and I should hate to be barred from their bar, I'd give them a one-line description they'd never forget---. I'm not accustomed to having my literary services bought for a 60 cent lousy lunch.

I gave a reading at Rollins last week on the Animated Magazine,[4] and never expect to be in weirder company---Archduke Otto of Austria, with the Empress Zita wandering around like a lost soul with a big white cross over a black bosom; Maurice Maeterlinck, speaking in an exquisite and by-the-audience-totally-ununderstood-French, and his actress wife called "Countess", the Governor of Florida, and Faith Baldwin---.[5]

---

1   MKR's pointer dog.

2   "Jessamine Springs." *New Yorker* 17 (22 February 1941): 19–20. See Tarr, *Bibliography*, C615.

3   Stephen Vincent Benét (1898–1943), American poet, novelist, and short fiction writer, perhaps best known for his epic poem *John Brown's Body* (1928).

4   The so-called *Animated Magazine* of Rollins College was not a publication, but rather an event, often as a part of Founders' Day week, at which time speakers were invited to read from their works or discuss their lives at the invitation of the college president Hamilton Holt (1872–1951). MKR and Holt became friends, and she was invited to several events. MKR's presentation was on Sunday, 23 February. See *Rollins Sandspur* (21 February 1941): 4; see also Anna Lillios and Brent Kinser, "The Rawlings/Holt Correspondence," *The Journal of Florida Literature* 17 (2009): 9–56.

5   Arch Duke Otto of Austria: Otto von Habsburg (1912–2011), the last Crown Prince of the Austro-Hungarian Empire, 1916–19. Empress Zita (1892–1989), the last Empress of Austria and mother of Otto. Maurice Maeterlinck (1862–1949), Belgian poet and playwright, whose wife, Renée Dahon (1893–1969), was a popular French actor. Spessard L. Hollard (1892–1971), governor of Florida from 1941 to 1945. Faith Baldwin 1893–1978), American writer of romance fiction.

I have had to begin the book once again and am suffering terribly.[1] Otherwise, life is very pleasant.

Lots of love,

Marjorie

. . .

JSB to MKR, [31 March 1941]. ALS, 3 pp. PM: FAR H[ILLS] | [illegible] | AP[RIL] | 1941 | N. J. AD: Marjorie Kinnan Rawlings | Cross Creek | Hawthorn | Florida. RA: J. Scribner | Far Hills, N.J. VIA AIR MAIL envelope.

Monday [31 March 1941][2]

Dearest Marjorie:

If someday I develop into a spoiled creature who expects everyone to remember her birthday[3] and to do something about it, I think you will be a little bit to blame. Thank God I am not yet quite that bad and I was very much surprised and pleased and made very happy by you remembering my quite unimportant anniversary. I certainly didn't expect you would – I don't understand how you did as I only kept it in my family's minds by frequent mentionings. The book is really swell.[4] It was snatched away from me immediately by my aunt and my mother[5] who seemed to feel that they could appreciate it much more than I could. I have finally gotten it back and am enjoying it very much – botanist that I am, I still felt I had better know a little about horticulture and I am really learning. The pictures are very inspiring too, as you know I have a vague ambition to <tell> take a series of wild flowers in Kodachrome.[6]

I finally caught up with your story[7] in the New Yorker and I thought it was damn good. The writing is very sharp and neat and "visual" and it cer-

---

1   *Cross Creek*. Yet four days later MKR writes to Perkins on 13 March 1941, "I feel much encouraged, and think my job is just not to let a careless narrative style run away with me" (*Max and Marjorie* 484).

2   Written in a second hand on the envelope: Apl. ? / 1941

3   JSB's birthday was on 16 March.

4   Book on wild flowers: Not identified.

5   Aunt: Louise Scribner Schieffelin (1883–1963); mother: Vera Gordon Scribner (1891–1985).

6   Kodachrome, a type of color film used in photography, introduced by Eastman Kodak in 1935.

7   "Jessamine Springs," *The New Yorker*, February 22, 1941: 19–20. Reprinted in *The Marjorie Rawlings Reader*, 355–60. See also Tarr, *Short Stories* 320–25, and Tarr, *Bibliography*, AA2, AA4, C615.

tainly sticks in the mind. It's sort of depressing I must say. That round soft little Reverend – I forget his name keeps popping into my head and then, perhaps unreasonably, I associate myself with him and I'm not sure why, maybe the situation – you think you're doing fine and then, wham! – that gets home – or maybe it's the human relationship mess which is usually a mess on account of people talking different languages even if they're not as literally different as Chubby's case. Anyway, it makes me think about these things which maybe a big surprise to you as maybe you were just writing about a traveling preacher and not these philosophical whatnots. Probably I have just had tonsillitis once too often and my outlook is dark and gloomy. (Really Marjorie, "God Is My Buddy"! Tsk.)[1]

I did get the saltwater taffy[2] and with the cooperation of the family and my dog who <u>loves</u> it I have eaten my way through both boxes, all but a few hybrid numbers with stripes that usually turn out to be clove which we all hate. When I get very hungry, though, I even eat clove so in time they will be assimilated too.

By the way – two things I keep forgetting in every letter – if you will send me the measurements of the desk I will do something about that piece of leather – and for God's sake send the waffle recipe[3] as our cook gets worse with every try.

Probably it is just as well you didn't go to the B Minor Mass, as you would likely have been 50% sickened by my description and 50% expecting the skies to crash open and a lot of shiny angels fly down dropping golden orbs of perfect song, and so you would have been about 100% disappointed. I just heard my yearly performance at Carnegie last week, and it was not at all up to scratch.[4] I'm glad you weren't there – a lot of the things I feebly wrote about weren't either, the "imponderables" as Daddy[5] would say. This year it looks as if I would get 4 B Minors as I have one next month

---

1 "God Is My Buddy" is the name of the sermon that Reverend Thomas J. Pressiker delivers to the Kiwanians in "Jessamine Springs."
2 MKR sent saltwater taffy from Marineland to JSB. See MKR's letter on 9 March 1941.
3 For the "desk," see MKR's letter on 21 April 1941. For the "waffle recipe," see MKR's letter on 16 July 1942.
4 The Oratorio Society of New York, with Albert Stoessel (1894–1943) conducting and the Hall of Fame Singers of New York University augmenting, gave its annual performance of Bach's Mass in B-Minor for the 15th consecutive year at Carnegie Hall on 25 March 1941. In his overall positive review, the American music critic Howard Taubman (1907–1966) admits, "The chief danger of this annual rite of Spring is that it may become routine. There were moments last night when one felt a heaviness and a lack of variety in the interpretation" (*New York Times*, 26 March 1941: 26).
5 Charles Scribner III.

in Newark, at the Bach Festival in Bethlehem in May and at the Berkshire Festival in August.

Daddy tells me that you wrote Max that your novel is really coming right at last.[1] I was very happy to hear that and I hope it behaves from now on. Perhaps now you will be finished by summer and able to take the New England motor trip we were thinking of. I can't remember who you were going to visit up there – someone poetic, wasn't it?

I have had tonsilitis again since I wrote you and am now in bed with a cold which seems to be insinuating its way into my sinuses – at least they are full of pain at the moment. Naturally, I guess my thoughts are all rotten somber and I am feeling very discouraged with my character, my past, my present, my future and everything else. Even the blessed spring-like sound of robins in the unspring-like twilight outside my window doesn't cheer me one bit – merely adds a romantic touch to my melancholy. Still – it is nice to hear them and the weather may really improve soon.

If I only felt a little better I would go into the next room and console my spirits ^with^ the kindred melancholy of Brahms, Mahler and Sibelius. Then I could perhaps cheer myself up with some Beethoven or Mozart.[2] They are so good for the spirits these two – so free of soul and strong. Free is what they are – particularly Beethoven and so they are often sad or tormented etc., but never despairing because despair is loss of freedom. Well, no discourses tonight.

I will write soon again and give you some news of my plans, etc. Right now the most pleasant things are tinged with gloom and I find myself unable to rise above the pain in my face.

Hope you are in good shape – No longer anemic or lacking in digestive juices.

Much love,

Julia

---

1   After a lot of negative letters expressing her frustration with the manuscript of *Cross* Creek, MKR's attitude brightened, writing to Maxell Perkins on 14 March 1941, "I just finished reading over the 'Cross Creek' manuscript. . . . I do not believe I was as far off as I thought. . . . [I]n fact the writing itself is not too bad" (*Max and Marjorie* 484).

2   JSB contrasts the Romantic works of Johannes Brahms (1833–1897), German composer, pianist, and conductor; Gustav Mahler (1860–1911), Austro-Bohemian composer; and Jean Sibelius (1865–1957), Finnish composer and violinist with the Classical works of Ludwig von Beethoven (1770–1827), German composer and pianist; and Wolfgang Amadeus Mozart (1756–1791), Austrian composer, pianist, and violinist.

MKR to JSB, 21 April 1941. TLS, 4 pp. PM: HAWTHORN | A[PRIL] | 2[1] | 194[1] | FLA. AD: Miss Julia Scribner | Dew Hollow | Far Hills | New Jersey.

April 21, 1941

Dearest Julia:

I have great sympathy for your attempt to maintain the aesthetic point of view in this period when one is considered beyond the pale who does not plunge into the building of little bomb shelters in the back yard and the collecting of old shoes for the English. I have been through exactly the same thing, aggravated by being besieged to serve on committees for all the outraged of the world, and to write propaganda for democracy. The last assault came from the Florida Defense Council,[1] which has only after long correspondence taken No for an answer. This was definitely embarrassing, for the accusation is likely to be made that I am willing to draw sustenance from Florida but am unwilling to help the citizenry figure out what to do in the event of an aerial attack. I suppose my mission would have been to sell Floridians on the idea that they are in danger and must make ready, for ye know not when the son of a bitch cometh.[2]

Yet it seems to me that much more is at stake than any nation, and that the ultimate salvation of a sorry world depends on as many as possible keeping a detached point of view, and seeing things from the historical and cosmic angle, rather than from the immediate one. No one can do this better than the aesthete, and it is not out of the way to remember that the glory that was Greece was a matter of culture more than a matter of military prowess. It seems to me that we are in the complete mess of the moment solely because we have not put into practice our almost universal

---

1 The [Florida] State Defense Council was authorized in 1941 by then Governor Frederick P. Cone (1871–1948) and concerned every aspect of defense from civilian morale to airplane spotting. Incoming Governor Spessard Holland (1892–1971) chaired the council, which was disbanded at the end of the war in 1945. MKR was beleaguered with charitable and political mailings asking for her time and her money, as she complains to Maxwell Perkins in a letter written in January 1941: "I continue to get a flood of literature asking for money and cooperation for everything connected with the world's mess---China's Children, Exiled Writers, Committee for Aiding the Allies, Committee for Keeping Us Out of the War, Hoover's Committee to Feed Europe, somebody else's committee to block such feeding. I send checks to a few and just tear up the rest of the stuff" (*Max and Marjorie* 480).

2 That is, Hitler. Compare the injunction by Jesus in the Bible: "I must work the works of him that sent me, while it is day: the night cometh, when no man can work" (John 9:4).

ideals and the best of our ideas. It is certainly not going to right anything in the long run, to build up hate, to fight, to win, and then, as we did after the last war, to settle down complacently in the same ruts of stupidity and greed and injustice. I hold no brief for the German aggressions, but I also hold no brief for past American and French and English aggressions. Germany is only doing what we did in the past, and we are interested, especially Britain, only in maintaining the status quo, whether that is right or wrong. The same principles hold in the fight between capital and labor.[1] I suppose that it would be very undesirable to have any one race, such as the Germans, dominate the world under their ideas of superiority of that one race. I object violently to the hypocrisy of the moment, by which the entirely natural and understandable inferiority complex of the Germans is damned as something unheard of in all of time; by which they are labeled utterly black and the English and Americans utterly white. Entrenched position, whether that be of an individual or of a nation, when it is too powerful and has too great a share of things, is always going to be challenged by the have-nots.[2]

Some of us, and the more the better, must remain aloof from temporary hates, if only that, when the fighting is over---if ever---there is a nucleus left that has never lost sight of the fact that the only permanently good and valuable things lie in our mutual and raceless[3] heritage of literature and music and art, on the aesthetic side, and in our ideals of a better-balanced social order, on the practical side. I for one am not going to be drawn into the maelstrom if I can help it. I went through a great struggle and period of suffering, feeling that I should function as a citizen and not as an aesthete or artist, but I came to the conclusion that it was much more to the point to go ahead minding my business and doing my work. If the great invasion ever comes, of course I'll man a machine gun at Cross Creek, but meantime, until the world is ready to talk sense, I prefer to have nothing to say and to

1 MKR is likely referring to the discord in Congress (and in the Supreme Court) over the policies of the "New Deal," initiated by President Franklin Roosevelt to protect workers from the Capitalist Conservatives. By 1939, the "New Deal" had waned in the face of war in Europe, although its effects remained controversial.

2 MKR's conservatism is not new. She supported Wendell Willkie (1892–1944), who represented "Big Business" in his unsuccessful run for the presidency against Roosevelt in 1940. Of course, in her comments here, MKR could not have anticipated the Japanese attack on Pearl Harbor eight months later on 7 December.

3 MKR is attempting to make a distinction between "race" and "racism"—that is, raceless means that literature, art, and music are not defined by race, but instead exist beyond the politics of the moment and instead reside in the world of universality. Her position is not unlike that of Matthew Arnold (1822–1888), who in *Culture and Anarchy* (London: Smith, Elder, 1869) makes the distinction between Hebraism (MKR's "race") and Hellenism (MKR's "raceless").

let anybody squabble that wants to. I do not consider it selfish to keep one's sanity and sense of values.

I do hope the rearrangement of your insides will make you feel better.[1] I can't agree with your "Granny" about the affidavit, for a husband who wouldn't take your simple word about your virginity, would be one you wouldn't care to go through life with.[2]

"My Trip to Washington"[3] is too long a story to write, but remind me to tell it when I see you next. I have been interrupted so much that a few days away seemed a trifle. The three aunts[4] have come and gone, thank God, and I see no further punishment on the horizon. Two of the younger aunts have devoted a whole year, in which they had planned a trip to South America--- and in one's sixties it's a good idea to do the things one wants to---to trying to breathe the breath of life into the oldest aunt, Luella, who is 78 and never having been interested in much of anything, naturally at that age finds little zest anywhere. The woman is just a Zombie, shuffling about with a vacant air and speaking only to utter something meaningless out of the distant past. It would be a great kindness to her just to let her fade away. Life is valuable only when one considers it so.

The book continues to be agony.[5] I have discarded untold chapters. Sooner or later I shall get at the reason I wander off-key, and then it will not go so slowly and painfully.

I'm glad you liked the Rev. Pressiker story.[6] I have no idea where I found him, but he was a symbol to me of the people who will never "belong". Edith Pope[7] said he broke her heart, not only for himself, but for "the loneliness of the whole damn human race."

---

1   JSB's operation was a tonsillectomy. See MKR's letter on 23 June 1941.

2   If MKR is referring to a specific person in JSB's life, that person has not been identified. See 100, n. 1. As to the issue of virginity, the topic has not come up in the letters extant, but of course that does not mean that a letter might be missing. Granny: Louise Flagg Scribner (1862–1948), wife of Charles Scribner II (1854–1930).

3   MKR was the guest of Eleanor Roosevelt at the White House from 1 to 3 April, writing NSB in considerable detail on 1 April about the experience of sleeping in Lincoln's bed: "I simply don't feel good enough to sleep in it---there is dust on the marble-topped center table---so I feel almost at home----And the help has an easy a welcome as Martha [Mickens]----On 2 April she continues: "I have been quite an orphan at the White House. . . . I called Miss Thompson, Mrs. R's very jolly secretary, and asked to see her. I told her I'd never been as lonesome in my life as at the White House!" (Love Letters 57–58). Secretary: Malvina "Tommy" Thompson (1893–1953).

4   Three aunts: Edith Wilmer Kinnan (1873–1980), Grace Isabell Kinnan (1868–1977), and Luella Hermine Kinnan Black (1861–1945).

5   The manuscript of Cross Creek.

6   "Jessamine Springs." See JSB's letter dated [31 March 1941].

7   Edith Pope (1869–1974), novelist from St. Augustine, a close friend of MKR.

Yes, I'm very glad that Dave[1] is removing himself from your life. I should have been lovely about it if you'd married him, but I think he would make a very difficult husband.

My health is so much better these days that I can't believe it is I. Evidently the low metabolism and so on were much to blame for everything I felt. Unfortunately the thyroid extract hasn't taken off a single pound, possibly because subconsciously I've thought I could eat more and get away with it.

I can't account for Bob's epistolary indifference. He bragged about getting a long letter from you, so I know the contact still seems pleasing to him. He is working very hard and I don't see much of him. He doesn't come to lots of the picnics and parties that we more frivolous people indulge in. He has just finished doing over my old Tole tray,[2] and it is a treasure. I insisted on magnolias, to his annoyance, as he wanted to do a stylized landscape, then he got interested in the magnolias and the job is altogether too good for anything as practical as a tray. I shall swing from the chandelier onto anyone who puts a highball glass on it.

I should really love to have you track down some leather for my old desk. It should be thin, you know. The center piece is 7½ by 13 and ¾ inches, and the two side pieces are each 10 by 15 ½ inches. Don't break your neck doing me this favor, as I'll have the desk done over in the fall.

Norton was sorry to hear you had had a minor operation[3] and wanted to know whether you were at home, to send you flowers. I said you almost certainly would be in town, where, I didn't know, and getting flowers delivered to Far Hills was probably as difficult as to Cross Creek. I'm so glad the major operation is called off.

Well, back to work. Am going to Jacksonville tomorrow for the Phila. Symphony,[4] with great joy.

Lots of love,

Marjorie

Tell your publishing Papa[5] that there is just no end to the uses of a book. Last night I started through the first bathroom on my way to my room to bed. Fortunately, the light was on, for stretched across my path through the bathroom was a small moccasin. We stood eyeing each other while I tried to figure out a practical means of disposing of him. I didn't dare leave

---

1   Dave, not identified, but apparently the individual referenced at 99, n. 2.
2   An enameled decorative tray, from the French *tôle peinte*, meaning painted sheet metal.
3   JSB's tonsillectomy. See MKR's letter on 23 June 1941.
4   Philadelphia Symphony, then directed by Eugene Ormandy (1899–1995).
5   Charles Scribner III.

him to go for my gun, for he would have darted away, to reappear later in some more inconvenient place and period. And the gun was not quite the thing after all, for it seemed silly to shoot a good bathroom full of holes. I knew no one at the tenant house would hear me ^call,^ for it was after their bedtime.

Conveniently at hand behind <the> ^me^ on the chest in the small bedroom were two volumes. One was the Sears Roebuck catalogue. I reached for this and heaved it at the moccasin. It hit him a glancing blow, enough to bother him, and he went into twists and convulsive coils that indicated he was hurt enough for me to approach him closer. The other volume was a well-wrapped copy of The Yearling that someone had sent me for autographing. I took The Yearling and beat the moccasin to death---.

I told black Will about it this morning and he was terribly tickled. We agreed that it was mighty handy to write books---.

. . .

MKR to JSB, 23 June 1941. TLS, 8 pp. PM: OCALA | JUN 24 | 10 PM | 1941 | FLA. AD: Miss Julia Scribner | Far Hills | N.J. RA: Marjorie K. Rawlings [in MKR's hand] | Hawthorn. Fla. LH: Marjorie Kinnan Rawlings | Hawthorn, Florida

June 23 [1941]

Dearest Julia:

I am obliged to remark that your doctors seem to be playing both ends against the middle---

No one knows much better than I the frustration of trying to track down the remote source or sources of a vague illness, and I can only hope it won't take you as long as it did me. I hope by now you are getting over the tonsillectomy but as I remember mine, it is at least three weeks before you can forget how abused you've been.

I am at the Creek for a few days, to get a new planting of St. Augustine grass started on my lawn. We had had a long terrific drought and when I went to the beach two weeks ago, things here at the grove looked as if they would never grow again. Everything was parched and brown. Now our rainy season has set in, and I returned to a tropic jungle. It rains heavily every afternoon, the earth steams, and vegetation grows inches in a night. It is the ideal time for starting new grass, and I have twenty-five bushels of sprigs coming as a start.

I have been enjoying Crawlings-by-the-Sea[1] immensely, and getting steady work done. A lot of it is lousy but at least I am getting it out of my system. It is going so steadily that I believe the first draft will be finished by the end of August, barring accidents, and since I mean to do a lot of re-writing, I think I shall bring the manuscript to Max[2] and then take a breather before I go back at it, and if it works out that way I'll hope we can get together for a mountain jaunt or something. I may be too optimistic about time, but I am so in the swing that no matter how bad a hang-over I may have, or even if I am ill, I turn out my minimum wordage every day.

Remember that South Moon Under was published on the day in 1933 that all the banks closed,[3] I am fully expecting this book to come from the press the day the first German bomb is dropped on New York.

Bob is working hard too and getting lots of good new stuff done.[4] Even Aunt Ida[5] likes some of his new things. "Rob is improving," she said. She has a genius for getting names funny. It is always Lindenburgh.[6] After one of his radio talks she said, "I didn't like Lindenburgh on the 'phone. He sounded so smudge."

I had a horrible experience last Tuesday night. When I was in Washington Senator Pepper[7] asked if I wouldn't give a reading at Camp Blanding[8] some time. I said of course and hoped he'd forget it. But there came a letter from one of the generals, and then a 'phone call (ashamed to say I have a 'phone at the beach now) asking me to come that night.[9] I felt no qualms about it

---

1   JSB called MKR's Crescent Beach cottage "Crawlings-by-the-Sea" because she was afraid of the large number of spiders in residence there (David Nolan, *The Houses of St. Augustine* [Sarasota: *Pineapple Press*, 1995], p. 84).

2   On 6 May MKR writes to Maxwell Perkins, "I am going ahead steadily on 'Cross Creek.' It does not please me, for the most part, but I couldn't stand the frustration so have gone on and let it have its head." On 23 June, she reports, "'Cross Creek' goes steadily, though much of it is bad, but the thing to do is to get it down on paper. Barring accidents, I should have the first draft by the end of August, and then I think I'd like to bring the manuscript to you and discuss it with you" (*Max and Marjorie* 485, 488).

3   On 6 March 1933, President Roosevelt declared a four-day bank holiday in order to give Congress the time to address the monetary crisis. *South Moon Under* was published on 2 March (Tarr, *Bibliography*, 7, n. 3).

4   Robert Camp Jr. would create the illustration for the dust jacket of *Cross Creek*.

5   Aunt Ida Tarrant, the great aunt of Charles Rawlings.

6   Charles A. Lindbergh (1902–1974), American aviator, who made the first solo flight across the Atlantic in 1927.

7   Claude D. Pepper (1900–1989), represented Florida as a U.S. senator from 1936 to 1951 and as U.S. representative from 1963 to 1989.

8   Camp Blanding, near Starke, was created for the Florida National Guard in 1930.

9   Tuesday, 17 June.

at all, planning to read "Benny and the Bird Dogs",[1] which the University of Florida boys like, and thinking the humor was elemental enough to appeal to any drafted farmhand or mechanic.

I had been ill in bed all day with a minor attack, and it was a sticky-hot evening. I drove from the beach to the camp and dinner with the general was very pleasant, with the band serenading us through the meal, mint juleps and all quite OK. There are nearly 50,000 men there and each brigade has its own recreation hall, holding about 400, bare wooden barns. I was to read at 7:30 to the Florida Brigade, and then at 8:30 to the Alabama Brigade. The reading had not been publicized, I was just Tuesday night "Dramatics". Wednesday is Chapel, Thursday Mass Singing, Friday Boxing. Perhaps the boys expected Gallagher and Shean, or a nautch dancer.[2] Anyway, they got me, and after a couple of sentences they began walking out on me. Every few paragraphs two or three would get up and go. I didn't mind at the beginning, for the early leavers knew what they didn't want. But it slayed me to have some of them go when I was almost at the end and thought I had them, In all, a fourth or a third of the Florida boys walked out.

I wanted to ask the general if we couldn't skip Alabama, but the men who had stayed had seemed to like it and applauded generously and I didn't want to be a poor sport. But when the second bunch began leaving, as I stood literally dripping sweat, it seemed to me I could not go through it again. I closed the book and I said, "I don't believe you Alabama boys like this story." The general jumped up and called out, "What about it, Alabama? Do you want her to go on with the story?" A generous number applauded, and I said, "All right. I love to read and I'll read to any one man as long as he wants to listen." Only about a tenth of Alabama walked out, but I have never had a more ego-destroying experience. My one comfort was to think to myself as a new batch would clear out, "Go on out, you bastards. You probably like Gene Autry."[3]

It was rather hard to go back to my typewriter the next day. My feeling was, "Somebody's been kidding me about my work being liked."

---

1   "Benny and the Bird Dogs." *Scribner's Magazine* 94.4 (4 October 1933): 193–200. Tarr, *Bibliography*, C597. Rpt. *Short Stories* 198–215. One of MKR's "Quincey Dover" stories, about a Cracker who sells his dogs to unsuspecting Yankees, who learn too late that the dogs are trained to return home at the earliest moment.

2   A vaudeville comedy act founded in 1910 featuring Ed Gallagher (1873–1929) and Al Shean (1868–1949). "Nautch girls" were Indian court dancers who by the early twentieth century had become negatively associated with prostitution.

3   Gene Autry (1907–1998), known as "The Singing Cowboy," whose immensely popular radio and TV shows began in the 1930s. His most famous song at the time was "Back in the Saddle Again" (1939).

Of course a lot of the draftees are of the lowest class---one man who set out to hold extra classes at the camp found he had to drop the subject and teach a lot of the men to <u>read</u> <u>and</u> <u>write</u>---but I thought a funny story spoke the universal language.

I see the Popes[1] once or twice a week. We are going floundering at night next Sunday. You go at the end of ebb tide and the beginning of the incoming tide, whenever that is dark, use a flash light and a spear along the edge of the surf, and get the flounders as they lie half-submerged in the sand where they've come in to feed. They are delicious eating and I imagine you know that filet of sole on most menus is flounder.

My maid Idella,[2] who has been with me since October, is still the answer to prayer. Nothing is ever too much for her, and loves having company and protests that it's not necessary when I give her extra money after a hard week. Saturday I had ten men for dinner, and after my suggestion that we get in a helper for her, she said she'd rather handle it alone than bother with a stranger. She handled it so smoothly you'd have thought there were two butlers working with her. After Adrenna's groans and Martha's futility and Dorothy's thieving it is too good to be true.[3] She doesn't drink, she isn't interested in men, she borrows my books, and likes the same movies I like!

I get very homesick for you, and how I should like to have you come to the beach for a few weeks, but there is no use in fooling myself about working when anyone is around, and if I don't get this book done, either Max or your father will disown me, or I'll blow up of frustration, so I mean to stay with it and hope to see you in about 2mos.

Lots of love,

Marjorie

---

1   Verle Pope (1903–1973), prominent Florida legislator from St. Augustine, and Edith Everett Pope (1905–1961), the novelist, both close friends of MKR and NSB.

2   Idella Ruth Thompson Parker (1914–2015), whom MKR referred to in *Cross Creek* as the "perfect maid. . . . I feel perfectly sure that the Lord sent me Idella" (191, 203). Parker, who played an indelible role in MKR's life, worked for her from 1940–1950, with various interruptions. She was instrumental in developing the recipes for *Cross Creek Cookery* (New York: Scribners, 1942). But, most important, Parker was with MKR during both her trials and her tribulations. Simply put, the impact Parker had upon MKR's life during the eventful 1940s cannot be overestimated. See, Parker with Mary Keating, *Idella: Marjorie Rawlings' "Perfect Maid"* (Gainesville, University Press of Florida, 1992). Later, Parker played a prominent role in the Marjorie Kinnan Rawlings Society and served as a Lifetime Honorary Trustee. Her second book, with Bud and Liz Crussell, *From Reddick to Cross Creek* (Gainesville: University Press of Florida, 1999), expands upon her relationship with MKR.

3   Adrenna Mickens, daughter of Martha Mickens who was the acknowledged matriarch of Cross Creek. Dorothy May worked for MKR at Crescent Beach.

. . .

MKR to JSB, 4 August 1941. TLS, 2 pp. PM 1: SAINT AUGUSTINE
| AUG 4 | 7 PM | 1941. PM 2: NEW YORK N.Y.| AUG 7 | 7:30 PM
| 1941. AD: Miss Julia Scribner | \<Dew Hollow\> | \<Far Hills\> |
\<New Jersey\>. [Written to the left of the excised address] c/o Mrs J
M Willets | New Marlboro | Berkshire Co. | Mass.[1] LH: MARJORIE
KINNAN RAWLINGS | HAWTHORN, FLORIDA.

Aug. 4, 1941

Dearest Julia:

Your munificent and magnificent birthday gift of Herring's cherry brandy
caught me at the Creek during the few days I was there.[2] You are psychic! By
the way, I am not going to celebrate birthdays any more. I am not shy about
it, deliberately giving my birth date a few years ago to various agencies, including Who's Who,[3] against the day when I should mind telling. I decided
to have it out before I minded, so that in later years I could not go back on
it. So this must be your last birthday gift. I told Norton I was through with
birthdays, and he said he had ordered me a portable bar for the cottage, and
that we would just call it a memento for the Ides of August.[4]

You may be interested to know that I am finishing the first draft of my
present book under the power of one of your year-old gifts. You remember
that you sent me two bottles of choice rye from the Nicholas Brady cellars,
bought at God knows what cost. I guzzled one and saved the other.[5] I came
back to the cottage last night, to go into the home stretch on the book, was
out of whiskey, and cracked open the other bottle. I decided that nobody
would appreciate it more than I, and it might help the God damn book. As a
result, I have done as much today as in any other three days. Hurray for rye
and Julia! (And me.)

The cherry brandy will tide me over, via Singapore gin slings, after the
Brady rye is gone.

---

1   PM 1 indicates where the letter was originally sent from St. Augustine on 4 August. PM 2 indicates that the letter was redirected from New York on 7 August. Written in a second hand to the
right of the address are some mathematical figures.
2   Heering's Cherry Liqueur, produced since 1818 by the Danish distiller Peter Heering. Here and
elsewhere MKR spells "Heering" as "Herring," as in the oft-pickled fish, perhaps in jest.
3   Originally *Marquis Who's Who*, a biographical listing of prominent people, founded in 1898.
4   In the Roman calendar Ides (calendar) of August is on 13 August. MKR's birthday is 8 August.
5   See MKR's letter on 7 August 1940, 66, n. 3.

I am working like a self-conscious dog at a field trial. Much of the book is lousy, but after Max tells me so, I shall go at it again.

I must pass on to you an excerpt from a letter from Edith Pope, written while I was on my recent brief sojourn at the Creek. As I stopped at Junko's[1] to fill up with gas to go to the Creek, they asked me if I had seen my friend. My friend turned out to be Norman Berg and Julie and his brat by his first marriage. / ^He had taken a cottage a couple of miles south of me.^[2] / I quote from Edith's epistle:

"You didn't flee to the Creek to avoid Norman Berg, I trust? The idea has its points but is impractical. He's going to be here for a month, complete with Julie. We ran into him last night at Junko's. He had his little boy with him, a dirty, seraphic looking child with a lower lip like a Louis Phillipe[3] rose, who looked at you out of angel eyes and spoke in whining monosyllables. The one time the kid managed a sentence, 'Les go, Poppa,' he was so charmed by it that he tried it up and down the scale, ending in a tired scream. It was hard to believe that Julie is not his true mother."

Wish me luck, both as to the damn Bergs and the damn book.
Lots of love and thanks.

Marjorie

. . .

MKR to JSB, 18 September 1941. Telegram.

WESTERN UNION TELEGRAM
NF12 64 NT=STAUGUSTINE FLO SEP 18
MISS JULIA SCRIBNER=
FARHILLS NJ=
HAD EXPECTED TO FOLLOW TIMOROUSLY ON HEELS OF
MANUSCRIPT[4] BUT AM MOVING AUNT IDA[5] TO STAUGUSTINE
OCTOBER FIRST AND MUST STAY TO SEE HER THROUGH. STOP.
PLAN TO COME TO NEW YORK THEN FOR VACATION. STOP.
COULD YOU TAKE ABOUT A WEEKS' DRIVE WITH ME THEN

---

1 Junko's, the gas station and the small grocery near MKR's Crescent Beach cottage,

2 Insertion typed above the previous sentence. Norman Stanley Berg (1908–1978) and Julie Berg, his second wife. Josephine Greer Berg (1918–2006), Berg's first wife, was the mother of his son, Norman S. Berg Jr.

3 Louis Philippe (1773–1850), King of France from 1830 to 1848.

4 *Cross Creek.*

5 Aunt Ida Tarrant.

THROUGH NEW ENGLAND IN WHICH CASE SHALL I BRING
MY CAR OR CAN I BORROW YOURS.[1] RETURNING HAWTHORN
TODAY. LOVE=
MARJORIE
717A SEP. 19.

. . .

MKR to JSB, 21 September 1941. TLS, 2 pp. Envelope is missing. LH:
Marjorie Kinnan Rawlings | Hawthorn, Florida.

Monday [21 September 1942]

Dearest Julia:

Am back at the Creek and will be here until October first, when I hope to head north for a bit of change.[2]

Had been in too much turmoil with the book to write you about the grand leather for my desk---I thought you were just to hunt it out for me, not to make me a present of it. I'll just have to get even with you some other way. It is correct as to size, color perfect, and I am taking the desk for doing over to my man in Gainesville this week.

Norton mailed you a copy of a local newspaper telling about his buying of an old show-place in St. Augustine, which he will convert into a small first-class hotel. It has all the atmosphere in the world, lovely grounds etc. Unless everything goes to pot, he can't help but make a success of it. He plans to open early in December.[3] Ocala is in public mourning over his leaving.[4] His board of directors presents him with sterling silver, etc., but I think it is marvelous he is to have his own place.

Since I am at the beach half of the year anyway, and will go over oftener through the winter now that Norton is to be in St. Augustine, I decided Aunt

---

1   The proposed trip was delayed. On 1 October, MKR she was admitted to Harkness Pavilion, where she had tests under the supervision of her chief physician, Dana W. Atchley, MD (1892–1982), a prominent doctor and expert in electrolyte balance whose patients included JSB and many celebrities. On 12 October, she checked into the Hotel New Weston, where on 13 October she writes to NSB, "Julia and I leave at two this afternoon" for the Berkshires. "We'll take everything very leisurely---both by inclination and doctor's advice" (*Love Letters* 64). MKR was back at Cross Creek by at least 23 October, when she sent a wire from Island Grove to NSB discussing the details of their upcoming wedding on 27 October in St. Augustine (*Love Letters* 65–66).

2   MKR actually left earlier, since she was checked into Harkness Pavilion on 1 October. See above, MKR's telegram on 18 September 1941, 107, n. 1.

3   NSB hoped to open the Castle Warden on 7 December 1941. Verle Pope warned him via MKR that he should not pay more than $22,000 for the hotel (*Love Letters* 60).

4   NSB managed the Marion Hotel in Ocala before purchasing the Castle Warden.

Ida[1] would enjoy being in St. Augustine, and she is to live in a lovely boarding place, the nicest in town, and I will pay the difference between what she can afford and their rather high rates. Think she will be happier not trying to keep house, and being among other people.

When I wired you suggesting a trip through New England, had in mind driving through some of the mountainous country, if it will not be too late then for the autumn foliage. If the idea appeals to you, can perhaps take the boat up and bring my car, or as I suggested, borrow yours. I'd enjoy driving back, but to drive both ways takes so long.

Max is to write me today about my manuscript,[2] so I'll soon know whether it is at all possible or not. I hope you will decide to become a prostitute long before you decide to become a writer. It is hellish work, even when you can get it---the writing.

Tuesday [22 September 1941]

A wire from my blessedly thoughtful Max says he thinks the book will turn out "very fine and unusual", with revision not difficult, but requiring some more study on his part. What a relief.

Have wondered why I have had no answer to my wire to you. I sent it last Thursday, and your letter spoke of an engagement this week with Bob, so feel sure you are at home. Let me have a note at Hawthorn.

Much love,

Marjorie

. . .

MKR to JSB, 23 September 1941. TLS, 1 p. PM: CIT[RA] | SEP[T] | 23 | 1941 | FLA. AD: Miss Julia Scribner | Far Hills | New Jersey. LH: Marjorie Kinnan Rawlings | Hawthorn, Florida

Wednesday [Tuesday, 23 September 1941]

---

1 Aunt Ida Tarrant.

2 Maxwell Perkins wrote to MKR on 15 September, "The manuscript has come, and I'll take it home with me." On 16 September, he wired MKR, "MUST HAVE WEEKEND TO GIVE FULL AND QUIET READING TO MANUSCRIPT BUT AM GREATLY ENJOYING IT. On 22 September, he wired again, "Think Cross Creek will make very fine and unusual book." On 29 September, MKR learned what she wanted to hear from Perkins: "'Cross Creek' may be queer, but it is lovely, and it is human. . . . I think it is a very rare book, and that while you will, of course, improve it in a revision, you have nothing to feel anxiety about" (*Max and Marjorie* 495, 498–99).

Dearest Julia:

Your letter came today,[1] and so glad the idea of a jaunt with me appeals to you. Do hope the neurologist continues to help your headaches, whether it's with nicotinic acid or crystal gazing. I had decided I needed a good psychiatrist, but Norton and Edith Pope talked me out of it. Edith said I might never write again if I were normalized,---and that would be a break for me! Norton was afraid I would be completely changed, and I should think that would be a break for him or any of my friends! They convinced me my moods of depressions are not manic-depression, but physical exhaustion and made me promise to have a checkup at Medical Center or somewhere like that.[2]

Yes, it was I who ordered the Bartram's Travels for you. One of the MGM executives, Frank Whitbeck, is literate, collects rare firsts etc., and has recommended me and the Argus bookshop to each other. I had an order in with them for an old edition of Bartram, and when the re-print came out they sent me one. I thought you would enjoy it so ordered a copy for you.[3]
Will let you know my plans when they are set.

Think we'll have fun.

Love

Marjorie

. . .

MKR to JSB, [23 October 1941]. TLS, 3 pp. PM: CITRA | OCT 23 | 1941 | FLA. AD: Miss Julia Scribner | Far Hills | New Jersey. Stationery and envelope: Hotel New Weston | Madison Avenue at 50th Street | New York, N.Y. RA: Typed by MKR under the hotel logo:

---

1   This JSB letter appears to be missing.

2   Worried about her outbursts of temper toward NSB, MKR checked into the Harkness Pavilion in New York on or about 1 October, and she writes to NSB about the experience: "The first doctor to come in is an eminent psychiatrist," who was also the "coordinating diagnostician" and who told MKR, "'Emotional disturbances may be causing most of the trouble.'" After a battery of tests, Dr. Atchley provided encouraging news that led MKR to conclude, "My rages . . . have nothing to do with you" (*Love Letters* 61–63).

3   MKR professed to have once owned a first edition of William Bartram (1739–1823), *Travels* (1791), and that she discovered the "termites had completely destroyed it." Later she writes to NSB that Scribner's [Rare Book Shop] "found me another first edition" (*Love Letters* 438, 529). Frank Whitbeck (1882–1963) was the longtime head of publicity at MGM, particularly known for the creation of trailers for films. Argus Book Shop, Chicago, Illinois.

Rawlings | Hawthorn, Florida. [Written and circled in MKR's hand]:
Air Mail. Envelope: Stamped twice: VIA AIR MAIL. Air mail stamp.

Hawthorn, Florida

Thursday [23 October 1941]

Dearest Julia:

Have no stationery of my own at the Creek, but find this in my luggage and know you are one who won't be confused by it![1]

My God, the glory in which I not only arrived home, but in which I left New York! Robert Van Gelder[2] of the NY Times came for an interview the morning I left,[3] and I sailed down to the lobby, dripping orchids, daring him to ignore them and describe me as a wholesome country-woman. I carried them in the box on the train, and dampened the paper under them, and they are still fresh and impressive. Have folks coming for dinner tonight, and plan to floor them with my elegance. If it were not for what I hope they did to Van Gelder, I would scold you thoroughly, but under the circumstances am grateful. It was a darling and improvident thing for you to do.

Had something of a struggle to reach the Creek. This part of Florida got part of a hurricane[4] and there had been fourteen inches of rain in three days. There was a washout fifteen miles north of Gainesville and the train had to be detoured hundreds of miles, the passengers for Gainesville being taken off at a way station and autos sent to ferry them in to the town. Idella,[5] waiting with my car (and Pat) at the station, was told the train would not come to Gainesville and the passengers were coming by car "through the country." So, very intelligently, she dashed back to the Creek to see if there was a wire from me directing her elsewhere. When she was not at the station, knew I could count on her not doing anything stupid, so waited patiently, and in due time she arrived back. Pat[6] was so glad to see me that he could not conceal it, and when he recovered his habitual sense of injustice, he had committed himself and it was too late to act sore.

We go to the cottage Saturday, more or less permanently, for the weather

---

1 The letter is typed on Hotel New Weston stationery.
2 Robert Van Gelder (1904–1952), American critic and essayist, especially known for his columns in the *New York Times* on celebrities and famous people.
3 MKR left New York by train on 21 October. See unpublished letter to NSB on 21 October (Special Collections, University of Florida Library).
4 On 20 October, a hurricane came ashore near Cedar Key on the west coast of Florida, causing heavy rain and flood damage.
5 Idella Parker.
6 Pat, MKR's pointer dog.

is still warm. So use the address Crescent Beach RFD, St. Augustine. The duck-eating problem was solved for me, as most of the new hatch has turned out to be drakes. There was a preponderance of drakes last year, so the new ones can be eaten with a clear conscience, as otherwise they would literally kill the ducks with love.

I did have such a good time on our trip.[1] Your bright ideas on the side trails were the best of all.

The desk is here,[2] and looks very <u>distinguished</u>.

Well, have a lot of <correspo> ^work of all sorts^ to do.[3] Just wanted to say hello---can't begin to thank you for the blaze of glory.[4]

Lots of love, and my very best to all the family.

Marjorie

. . .

JSB to MKR, [29 October 1941]; ALS: 2pp. PM: NEW YORK. N.Y. | OCT 29 | 4 - PM | 1941. AD: Mrs. Norton Baskin | Crescent Beach R.F. D. | St. Augustine | Florida

Wednesday [29 October 1941][5]

Dearest Mrs. Baskin!

You old close-mouthed so and so – you might have warned me that you were going to take the plunge at once so that I could have marshalled telegrams and wedding presents etc. I was, or am, caught absolutely with my pants down.[6] Someone told me they had read it in the paper. I didn't even see it myself – you know I only read the drama and music news.

---

1   MKR is referring to the weeklong trip that she and JSB took through New Hampshire and Vermont after MKR's checkup at Harkness Pavilion from 1–14 October, as she writes to NSB in a letter dated [13? October 1941]: "Julia and I leave at two this afternoon" for the Berkshires. "Won't go into details on doctor's findings, but briefly the medical picture is exactly the same—physical condition neither better nor worse. . . . People with diverticulosis as extensive as mine . . . are perfectly comfortable as long as they stay on their diet" (*Love Letters* 64).
2   JSB helped MKR get her desk repaired. See JSB's letter dated [31 March 1941].
3   Not the least of which, MKR was preparing for her marriage to NSB four days later in St. Augustine on 27 October, an event JSB did not find out about until after. See JSB's letter dated [29 October 1941].
4   That is, the orchids JSB sent to MKR, described above in paragraph two.
5   Written on Gladstone Hotel stationery. Written in a second hand at the top: 10-29-41.
6   MKR married NSB on 27 October. It is curious that MKR did not inform JSB about the marriage, for she writes to Perkins on 27 October [1941], "As you will know by this time, Norton Baskin and I are being married this morning. I am terribly happy about it" (*Max and Marjorie* 502).

Well anyway I think it's swell and I hope that every year you'll wonder more and more why you didn't do it before. (Hmm – poetry!).

There is no use my sweating a pint or so and chewing several hotel pens to pieces trying to express how hard I am wishing for your happiness – because I am sure you know.

My best love to you both,

Julia

. . .

MKR to JSB, [1? November 1941]. TLS, 4 pp. Envelope is missing.
LH: Marjorie Kinnan Rawlings | Hawthorn, Florida

Crescent Beach RFD

St. Augustine [1? November 1941][1]

Dearest Julia:

I thought I picked out the one sure way of getting word / ^to you^ of Norton's and my marrying before it was in any paper. I didn't know whether you would be at Far Hills or in town---and one telegram seemed to cover everything---so I wired your father[2] immediately after the ceremony Monday the 27th, saying, "Please tell Julia, Max and Whitney."[3] And a friend sees it in the paper and tells you Wednesday! Tell your father he will never be the first to know, again! Didn't mean to surprise you that way--- but of course we were trying to do it so simply that there wouldn't be upheavals and wedding presents and what-not. We decided on Saturday to do it on Monday, and by Monday afternoon we were both so nervous that we couldn't see how anybody got through it who planned way ahead, a church ceremony and so on. We just asked the Popes[4] separately to do us a favor about 4 in the afternoon and dragged them down to the court house to act as witnesses. I didn't really want Aunt Ida,[5] because I didn't want

---

1   JSB sent her letter dated [29 October 1941], saying that she knew nothing about the marriage until it was over. Allowing two days for the letter to reach MKR at Crescent Beach, the tentative date for this letter is 1 November, and it could be later, of course.

2   Charles Scribner III. The fact that MKR now addresses him as "Charlie" is evidence of her growing personal relationship with the Scribner family.

3   Maxwell Perkins and Whitney Darrow, the latter sales manager and later vice president at Scribners.

4   Verle and Edith Pope.

5   Aunt Ida Tarrant.

anybody being weepy and making an effort at maintaining any formalities, but Norton, sweet thing that he is, said it meant so much more to her to be on hand than for us not to have her, that I must do it. Edith Pope said afterward she thought it literally would have killed Aunt Ida not to have been there. Of course she did weep, called Norton "a thief in the night"---which struck me as riotously funny when I've been hot on his trail for eight years---raising Cain with Verle for smoking while the judge was filling out the certificate, and fair swooned because Edith, all unprepared, arrived in red slacks.[1]

I insisted that I had already had my trip, which would do for a honeymoon trip, but Norton was tired of St. Augustine, so we drove down Friday to Palm Beach and had a good time watching them get ready to open those fascinating shops, the Everglades Club[2] and so on, and tracking down attractive bars.

Norton and I are terribly pleased with ourselves for landing each other. We think we're a wonderful couple. He said he felt like a man who'd sold somebody a gold brick, but doesn't have to leave town, because the customer is perfectly satisfied, and it turns out that all her life she's wanted a gold brick. The St. Augustine matrons had already begun plotting against him, and I feel I snatched him just in time from a den of entirely female lions.[3]

I had a nice wire from your father,[4] and a darling note from Max,[5] but no word from Whitney. I suppose Charlie didn't tell him either, and if he saw it in the paper, he would probably sulk.

We are all agog over plans to turn the fourth floor of the Castle into a penthouse apartment. We need a good architect to plan, as we'll have to make an adroit use of space, there not being very much. But if done right, it should have a great deal of Bohemian charm. I love roof-tops anyway. The

---

1   See the wedding photograph (*Max and Marjorie* 66), which was taken in front of the St. Johns County Court House.

2   The Everglades Club in Palm Beach was originally intended as a hospital for World War I veterans when it was financed by the billionaire Paris Singer in 1918. But when the war ended, it was changed to an exclusive and discriminating social club and remains so. How MKR and NSB gained entrance is not clear, since the club was open only to members and their guests.

3   An oblique reference to the story of Daniel in the lion's den, who was not eaten "because I was found blameless before Him" (*Daniel* 6:22).

4   Not located.

5   See *Max and Marjorie* (503), where the note and a facsimile are reproduced. Clearly affected by the news, Perkins writes, "Anything that makes you happy makes me happy. I hope someday I'll see Norton Baskin for I'm sure I should like anyone who loves you, & should have much in common with him too. All good fortune to you both."

place seems oddly to call for modern furnishings, although the Castle itself is being done in an old fashioned way. Norman had some charming Marie Laurencin[1] pastel or wash drawings framed for the bedrooms.

Now Julia, NO wedding present! One reason we did it the way we did! Presents are not given for either courthouse or shotgun weddings. Charlie says you're 100% better. So glad![2]

Much love,

Marjorie

. . .

JSB to MKR, [9–10? December 1941].[3] ALS, 5 pp. Envelope is missing.

Tues. & Wed. [9–10? December 1941][4]

---

1 Marie Laurencin (1883–1956), French artist and printmaker, especially known for her impressionistic drawings of vulnerable women.

2 The text after "Charlie says" is written in MKR's hand.

3 Written in a second hand at the top of p. 1: Perkins sent galley proof "up to galley 23" to MKR on 5 December 1941 (*Max and Marjorie* 505). MKR acknowledges on 12 December that "Proofs through galley 59 are here" (506) and she returns them on 17 December (508). On 22 December, she writes, "I will try very hard to get the rest of the proofs back to you by Friday" (508), and on 27 December she confesses, "Just had to do some Christmas preparing and couldn't finish the proofs any earlier" (509). On 2 January 1942, Perkins writes, "'Cross Creek' is now all in pages" (511). On 5 January, Perkins assures her, "We are in page proofs, and a good many of them go to you today" (513). On 12 January, MKR writes, "I am sending today page proofs through page 212, and will have the rest in your hands by Friday" (513). On 14 January, Perkins assures, "Another good thing is that we shall be able to publish in the middle of March" (515).

4 This tentative date is based upon the urgency and the fear expressed in the opening paragraphs of the letter. The historical chronology is paramount: On, Sunday, 7 December, the Japanese attacked Pearl Harbor while the Brooklyn Dodgers were playing the New York Giants at the Polo Grounds before 55,051 fans. During this football game announcements were made that various military personnel should report immediately to their headquarters. The game continued. The fans were not informed of the attack, apparently out of fear that any announcement might cause widespread panic. By Monday, 8 December, the general populace was fully aware of the attack and a combination of fear and resentment spread throughout the city, punctuated by two major air raid warnings that day as rumors spread that bombers were seen flying toward the city from the Atlantic Ocean. That same day, President Roosevelt delivered the "day of infamy" speech before Congress, declaring war on Japan, which did little to quell a growing sense of panic. On Tuesday, 9 December, crowds gathered outside the Nippon Club and the Japanese Embassy. Resentment had turned to anger. On Tuesday, like Monday, two more major air raid alerts were sounded, each based on heightened rumor that the Japanese were preparing to invade. Blackouts were declared through the country. See also 115, n. 2. It was during this period of national emergency that JSB wrote this letter to MKR—namely on Tuesday (9 December) and Wednesday (10 December). JSB's letter is, in effect, a firsthand report of some of the most chaotic moments in U.S. history, and as such is of

P.S. I have decided the first sentence shows definite
Alves influence – uncomforting thought![1]

Dearest Marjorie:

Well, just a few minutes ago the All Clear sounded on our second, and I hope final, air raid alarm for the day. No one, I think, was altogether sure whether it was a hoax or on the level. Everyone I saw felt obliged to be humorous about it, but so damned much has happened in the last 48 hours that some of the confidence and the "it can't happen here" has been shaken out of us.[2]

I was having lunch with a couple of friends in a restaurant and we all ordered an extra large lunch in case there was something in the rumors which at that time were flying hot and heavy. We wanted to have all our favorite food anyway to console ourselves. I had to dash up to Granny's house after lunch to meet Sandy.[3] Sirens were screaming all over the city and the radio in the taxi was on full force & bulletins pouring in and an announcer hysterically telling everyone to keep calm. People were instructed to get into houses and keep away from doors and windows. And then, they blew a siren over the radio that practically blew _me_ into the front seat with the driver it was so loud. All the time the driver was yelling over the radio his theories on the situation. According to him, the English fleet were in the Atlantic so how could any planes get over them. I couldn't see that that was such an airtight situation but argument was impossible if one cared anything for one's vocal chords. All up and down 66th street maids came to windows and looked as if they were going to jump out and one came out on the street. She looked to me as if she was going to head for the nearest manhole and dive in.

Sandy had to go right home as his mother had been phoning frantically

---

immensurable significance. That she downplays her fear is indicative of her tough outward personality, a cover for her actual fear for her own well-being and that of the Scribner family, many of whom lived and worked in the city. The address of Scribners was Fifth Ave. at 48th St.

1   The postscript, in JSB's hand, also inserted at the top of the page. Carl Alves, JSB's music teacher; see JSB's letter dated [24 February 1941].

2   The *New York Times* reported on 10 December 1941 that the previous Army Air Force Headquarters notified local authorities that "hostile aircraft were approaching New York from the Atlantic" (1). The ensuing alarms caused invasion panic in the city and elsewhere on the east coast. The Japanese attack on Pearl Harbor, 7 December 1941, had greatly increased anxiety about air raids in New York City, and this concern continued into the new year. More than 2,000 air raid wardens were assigned to protect the annual New Year's Eve celebration in Times Square (*New York Times*, 28 December 1941: 1). On 8 January, the *New York Times* reported an increase of air raid wardens in New York to 220,028 (8).

3   Granny, Louise Flagg Scribner, wife of Charles Scribner II (1854–1930), who lived at 12 East 38th St., New York, New York. Sandy Dillon, a beau of JSB.

ordering him to return at once to the safety of Far Hills.[1] I laughingly refused an offer to be evacuated. Even now it seems days ago and a huge practical joke (which it was) but we conjectured at the time whether if things got worse the roads might not be in a couple of days almost completely impassable traffic being what it is on a holiday here.

It certainly made an exciting two hours—humorous but a little nerve-wracking too. I must confess that as Granny and I were left by the evacuating Sandy and I went upstairs to read my record catalogues I didn't feel quite so placid as I looked, and when the house began to vibrate from the roar of planes (trucks in the block) my pulse doubled up a bit and I don't think I would have been very surprised by a couple of explosions. One doesn't have an imagination for nothing. Well, so much for our N.Y. A.R.[2] Alarm, which probably seems quite vulgar and noisy to a contemplative countryman like yourself. We city folks must have our excitement.

There is one thing that is worrying me more than the bombs at the moment, and that is when am I going to get my hands on some more galleys of your book. I hope there are lots more, and I am beginning to wish that I hadn't wolfed down the first forty at such a terrific speed. I can easily understand how Mr. Brandt[3] was kept up all night. I got ahold of it one night when I had to arise the next AM at six to go duck hunting. It ruined my sleep quota. I loved the stories I knew and I loved the one I hadn't heard. Mr. Swilley[4] made me laugh so loud I found my poor dog looking at me with obvious alarm. I'm not sure whether I enjoyed most reading about the places I had seen or the ones that were new to me. I do know that I simply must see the River Styx.[5]

Granny has an expression she uses when she wants to be particularly complimentary about someone. She says they "have juice". I think your book has plenty of juice and I hope you don't mind the New England expression stuck on your Florida book. I can't hazard any more lines on the subject because it is one of my unfortunate peculiarities to be articulate about things I <u>don't</u>

---

1   Far Hills, a borough in Somerset County, New Jersey.

2   A.R., air raid alarm.

3   Carl Brandt, MKR's agent, head of the firm of Brandt & Brandt, New York.

4   Swilley, see *Cross Creek* (128–37), whom MKR describes as a "cross between an Indian and one of those travelling quacks known as medicine men" (128). Upon the recommendation of [Feldon] Snow Slater (1909–1997), MKR hired him to do some hoeing in the grove.

5   River Styx *Cross Creek* (49–51), about which MKR observes, "'It is not given to many to cross the Styx and live to tell it'" (*Cross Creek* 51). In Greek mythology, the river that forms the boundary between Hades and the corporeal world. The River Styx in Florida is on CR 346 between Cross Creek and Micanopy (Stephens 20).

like, and enthusiasm is my ruination –verbally speaking. I'd better relapse into speechless admiration.

I am living in town with Granny now and am studying Columbia[1] catalogues to see about courses I should take to improve myself. I will write soon and submit the project to you.

Much love,

Love to Norton too, Julia

P.S. That bowl I sent you reminded so much of the color scheme at the beach that I couldn't resist it. Probably it is wrong enough to be impossible. If so it might come in handy as a Xmas present and you can always explain to me that you threw it at Norton or vice versa.[2]

· · ·

MKR to JSB, 13 December 1941. TLS, 2 pp. PM: SAINT AUGUSTINE | DEC 13 | 11^{30} AM | 1941 | FLA. AD: Miss Julia Scribner | Far Hills | New Jersey.

Crescent Beach RFD

St. Augustine, Fla. [13 December 1941]

Dearest Julia:

I hate to admit how glad I am that you ignored my Stop signal and went right ahead and got us a wedding present. God, it's beautiful! But surely you must have chosen it with the cottage in mind. That divine turquoise blue and the fade-out into the lavender-purple are too perfect in the living room here. What is to become of our new penthouse life? The crushed-grape shade tones in with the colors we plan to use in the Castle apartment, but the decorator says the turquoise is the wrong blue. But since we'll be at the cottage most of the time in the summer, and since I will escape here practically every day, it suits me perfectly.

I am very happy that your car is new, otherwise I should have thought of

---

1   Columbia University.

2   The bowl was a gift in celebration of the Baskins' wedding, not a Christmas gift, which accounts for JSB's comment, in jest, that if MKR did not like it she could regift it as a Christmas present. See MKR's letter on 13 December 1941, where she acknowledges the bowl as a marriage gift, and on 2 January 1942, where she asserts that the bowl should have counted as a Christmas gift. JSB is alluding to the episode when Charles Rawlings in a fit of rage threw hollandaise sauce at MKR because the preparation did not suit his taste.

the divine bowl as an alternative to new tires for your Buick, and possibly, incidentally, your life. Now it means only that you will have to forego a bunch of concerts. But that is your life blood, too. Well, all life is compromise, isn't it? Anyway, the bowl is magnificent and you can be sure any sacrifice is not in vain.

After five weeks of marriage, Norton and I have reached our first domestic crisis. I knew it would happen, and was prepared for it, and Thank God met it like a lady and a sport. As it happens, Norton has about thirty male satellites / ^(I shouldn't dare count the female satellites)^ who are simply mad about him, follow him wherever he goes, and expect a welcome. He is so damn nice to everybody, whereas you and I are nice to a very few. Yesterday two of his followers found him very deep in work at the Castle, so descended on me at the cottage. They were incredibly drunk, waved me in from the beach where I was walking with Pat[1]---waving, to be exact, a bag of grapes and a bottle of Scotch---and in a nice way took over the cottage. I had met the pair just once before. I imagine that, sober, they would be quite charming gentlemen. Drunk, they promptly collapsed, and Norton came home to find them sound asleep in the guest room. We left them sleeping and went off to Marineland for dinner. Norton was so crushed that I had to cheer him up by telling him that they weren't as much of an affliction as the aunts,[2] who don't give you a break by passing out.

Glad to report that I've been feeling grand ever since I came home. I do hope your B plus did the trick and you are really free of the headaches. Afraid we'll all need our health in the next five or ten years---.[3]

I've found all sorts of stunning things that can be done with the blue and wine bowl. There is a tropical plant here like a papaya, the rice plant, that has sprays of marvelous creamy bloom much like the wild plum, but denser and much more exotic. One spray in the bowl fair takes your breath. The dwarf Calla lilies are grand in it, too, and when I have no flowers at all, it is completely decorative per se. I don't need to tell you not only how thrilled we are with it, but how much I appreciate the agonies you must have gone through in finding something so perfect. Can't even try to thank you.

Work on the Castle has run into its first bad snag. Everything seemed to be going smoothly for the wind-up, when the traps arrived for the toilets,

---

1   Pat, MKR's beloved pointer dog, who just over a week later on Christmas Eve was run over and killed at Cross Creek. MKR was distraught. See her letter on 2 January 1942.

2   Likely Wilmer Kinnan and Grace Kinnan.

3   MKR is referring to the war. The Japanese bombed Pearl Harbor on 7 December, and President Roosevelt declared war on Japan the next day before Congress in his famous "day of infamy" speech.

and proved to be a job the government rejected, and they just aren't useable at all, and where and how to get them is suddenly a Problem. Unless Norton sets up a line of outhouses under the magnolias and live oaks, the whole hotel may be held up for several weeks more. Anyway, the pre-Christmas opening he had hoped for is impossible. Such an ignominious delay.

However, when you come down, we still have our choice of Creek or cottage.

I am deep in proofs.[1] Poor Pat hasn't been hunting yet and is wild. He knows it's time and can't understand why I sit with papers.

Lots of love, old dear.

Marjorie

.   .   .

MKR to JSB, 2 January 1942. TLS, 2 pp. (postscript on the verso of p. 2 in MKR's hand). PM: SAINT AUGUSTINE | JAN 3 | 11 AM | 1942 | FLA. AD: [in holograph] Miss Julia Scribner | 9 East 66th St. | New York City.

Jan. 2, 1942

Dearest Julia:

I'm in bed, at the end of one of my attacks---the first I've had since I went to New York, which isn't bad---and should be writing polite notes, but I'm damned if I'm going to write to anyone today to whom I have to be polite. I shall write for pleasure until I'm tired, then quit altogether.

Thank God you did intend the gorgeous bowl for the cottage.[2] It simply makes the living room.

I do not know what I am going to do about your extravagance. The bowl should have been Christmas, wedding, birthday and Armistice Day presents for years to come. Then comes the buckwheat honey, and I think what a grand Christmas present, except that you shouldn't have bothered. THEN comes the choicest 1921 champagne. Who do you think you are---Barbara Hutton?[3] And of course you know all my weak spots, and your gifts hit them

---

1   *Cross Creek.*

2   This comment indicates that a JSB letter is missing.

3   Barbara Woolworth Hutton (1912–1979) was once dubbed the "richest woman in the world." She was married and divorced seven times. She died nearly bankrupt, her fortune exhausted by lavish living and poor financial decisions. She was married to the actor Cary Grant (1904–1986) from 1942 to 1945.

square. Anyway, the champagne will be saved until your visit, and you and Norton and I shall crouch together, perhaps during a blackout,[1] and drink it together.

He thinks he can open Castle Warden in about a week. Our apartment won't be ready for a couple of weeks after that and I'll probably steal a little time at the Creek after he opens and before our nest is ready. I had a good offer to rent the farmhouse for the four months of the winter season, and found myself totally unable to do it. I got in an utter panic at the thought of not being able to go to it. Norton found the Culvers[2] prowling through the Castle the other day and had a good visit with them. He liked them immensely, and said they fair died laughing when he told them that your father had written me please not to give him any more messages for you, that he had mislaid you again, and you could probably be found only at the Metropolitan.[3] I'll drop around and see them some day. They live just around the corner from Norton's place.

Well, I have the saddest possible news. We went to the Creek for Christmas, and Christmas Eve Pat was run over and killed right in front of the house. Fortunately, it was almost instantaneous. But to say that Christmas was ruined is putting it mildly, and when we came back to the cottage, Idella and I could not bear to look at the beach. I don't need to tell you how I feel about it. He had been my one close companion during my worst and loneliest years. The sweethearts had come and gone, and the maids, and the grove hands, but there was always Pat.

Norton and I, thank God, can always get a laugh, and we have had a good one even out of this. Edith and Verle Pope went to Rebecca Camp's Christmas night party with us, and Edith was very much upset / ^about Pat^ on my account. She told Bob and Cecil[4] and Norton how glad she was that it hadn't happened before my marriage. She turned to Norton and said, "You can more or less take his place."

Norton said, "I suppose so. I just hope nothing happens to Dora."[5]

I'm so glad you got "juice" from my book.[6] I'd rather have that kind of re-

---

1 MKR refers to the repeated blackouts (lights turned out and/or curtains closed) that were ordered during World War II. Jacksonville and the immediate area were considered prime targets for the Germans. MKR acted as a "plane spotter" during this time of civil panic.

2 Henry Brundage Culver (1869–1946), attorney and master model ship builder, and Irma Asch Culver (1875–1952). The Culvers were a part of the St. Augustine literary scene, which included MKR's friend, the celebrated poet Stephen Vincent Benét (1898–1943).

3 Metropolitan Museum of Art and / or the Metropolitan Opera.

4 Possibly Robert Camp Sr., but more likely Bob Camp Jr. and Cecil Clarke.

5 MKR's cow, but also MKR's nickname for herself.

6 *Cross Creek.*

action than any other. Hope you've had the rest of the proofs and continued to like it. I thought Bob's jacket[1] was swell.

You said you didn't have the Audubon bird book,[2] so I sent that to Far Hills. I'm anxious for you to see the originals to which I blew myself.

When can you come down? There's no reason for waiting until our apartment at the Castle is done, as we probably wouldn't spend much time there anyway. Any time that suits you is grand for me, and we both look forward so much to your coming. Give me a few days' notice in case I had some special duty on hand, but otherwise just name your date and come ahead. I think Idella[3] and I will just have to have another dog, and I am considering getting one of the fawn colored Cocker puppies. A small dog will fit in better, moving about a lot and living part of the time in a hotel apartment, and Cockers are smart and lovable but not sissy. Do you know of any breed better for my purposes? Loads of love, and hope to see you soon.

Marjorie

I told Norton I mentioned him, in passing, several times in "Cross Creek." He asked if I used any adjectives about him. I said I hadn't, and he put me in stitches quoting from The Rover boys,[4] who, under all circumstances, were "fun-loving" Dick, "serious Tom" and "romantic" Harry. He said he didn't ask for a character delineation, but out of 150,000 words, it did seem to him I could spare <a "debonair"> an adjective.

. . .

**JSB to MKR, [16 January 1942]; ALS: 5pp. PM: NEW YORK, N.Y. |
JAN 18 | 4³⁰ PM | 1942. VIA AIR MAIL envelope. Stamped: VIA AIR
MAIL.**

Friday [16 January 1942]

Dearest Marjorie:

Thank you for asking me down. I'm afraid I just can't make it this winter. The Civilian Defense in NY[5] might collapse if I left. It was becoming increas-

---

1   Robert Camp Jr., his illustration for the dust jacket of Cross Creek.

2   John James Audubon (1785–1851), American artist and naturalist, best known for his paintings of birds, most famous of which is the multivolume folio Birds of America (London, 1827–38).

3   Idella Parker.

4   The Rover Boys, a series of books for young adults by Arthur M. Winfield [Edward Stratemeyer (1862–1940)]. The original boys were Tom, Dick, and Sam.

5   The Office of Civilian Defense (OCD) was created by Franklin Roosevelt on 20 May 1941, with

ingly embarrassing to explain why I, who felt so strongly and audibly that everyone should do his duty toward the community, was doing nothing. After all, I have no children, no job, not even a husband – no excuse in other words. And so now I am involved in a welter of courses to prepare me for "Motor Corps" and my dear new car (it's really beautiful) and I are on call 24 hrs a day 7 days a week – a situation which I <u>hope</u> no one takes advantage of. Oh what an unhappy combination I am! An ardent believer in community spirit and organization and yet an equally ardent anarchist. Well, this may make a citizen of me, dull prospect, in spite of the aura of political sanctity with which I have always decorated that responsibility. Two of my courses I really look forward to – mechanics and map reading. Not without some apprehension though, for I have always felt that I would shine in those lines, and now I have horrid fears that perhaps I may be completely outclassed by some city slickers and chic debutantes. That would really be a blow to my pride. My way with a screwdriver and pliers is to me, I imagine, what cooking is to you – so feel for me.

I'm afraid Columbia is out now too.[1] None of the courses I want to take will fit into my heavily occupied week.

I love the Audubon. I get as much fun from both the wild flowers in the plates as I do from the birds. That's heresy, no doubt, but I am so botanically minded. What plates do you have?[2]

I was relieved to hear that the champagne arrived safely. I was quite worried. It would be such a sacrilege if it were dumped out at the Fla. border or guzzled by some petty official. I won't hear of your saving it till I come and ^help to^ drink up my own present. I intended it just for you and Norton and my feelings will be hurt if you don't have it all to yourselves. For once don't be generous to your friends.

Also, I can't understand this Barbara Hutton business. What a silly idea – why I <u>never</u> thought I was Barbara Hutton, I'm Doris Duke![3]

---

the expressed purpose of preparing the populace for war, which included on-site training for every possible contingency.

1   Columbia University, New York.

2   MKR owned several Audubon prints and gave one to JSB. In her letters to NSB she refers to the "pale green Audubon"(*Love* Letters 138); "Audubon is green tones" (186); "all but one of the Audubons came through with damage only to the frames, and the other one is by no means ruined" in Castle Warden fire (399); "I put up the Audubon, and noticed, as I should have before, that it is not a genuine one, only a chromolithograph done in 1860" (448); "Julia thought the Audubon was lovely" (532).

3   Doris Duke (1912–1993), the heiress of the fortune of James Buchanan Duke (1856–1925) who founded the American Tobacco Company and Duke Energy and who underwrote Duke University. JSB's implication that she is to the Scribner empire what Doris Duke is to the Duke empire is, at least, partly in jest.

I'm so sorry about Pat, I know how you must miss him because he was very much of a person and certainly made himself <u>felt</u>. My poor dog I hardly notice – she is so neutral that except when she is being a damn nuisance I don't even know she is around. I cannot give the smallest approval to your plan to get a cocker. I have always thought they were damn fools and Minnie has not changed my mind. I never have seen one yet that wasn't a sissy compared to a terrier, compared to anything! But I must admit my aversion is probably prejudiced. I don't really like to have a dog that's complex and sensitive. I think a dog should be a relief from the difficulties of human nature and not another creature who is easily hurt and whom one must treat with constant tact. But that is doubtless an indication that I have a vile and domineering nature. I must admit that when I am in a bad humor I often take it out on Tinker Bell,[1] but it doesn't seem to disturb her simple devotion and it ^doesn't^ prey on my conscience a bit. It just relieves my temper and Tink takes it quite as a matter of course. However as you got on admirably for years with touchy Pat maybe you had better get a touchy cocker. Only beware of the scary ones (and they are legion). Pat was certainly brave as could be and I'm sure you would be disgusted with a dog that runs shrieking with fright every time someone laughed out loud. I advise a terrier myself. Of course, if you want a dog that will own you completely and demand affection day and night (I have never seen one that wasn't spoiled) get a Dachshund. They are too much trouble for my impatient and selfish nature – I expect the dog adore me, not vice versa – but they certainly are smart little fellows.

I wish I could come down to see you. I do miss you, and heaven knows when I will be able to get down or when you will stray up this way again after the thorough freezing you got in the White Mts. (Do you shudder at the thought of the "N.E. School"?).[2] I have got myself really trapped for the time being and this is as close as I can get to you. Yellow paper and airmail envelopes and a paper and pencil message of Love,

Julia

---

1   Julia's dog, presumably named for Tinker Bell, a fictional character in the play *Peter Pan* (1904) by J. M. Barrie (1860–1937).

2   JSB is referring to the trip she and MKR took through New Hampshire after MKR's discharge from Harkness Pavilion on 13 October 1941. "N[ew]. E[ngland]. School" is not identified.

MKR to JSB, 7 April 1942. TLS, 5 pp. PM: SAINT AUGUSTINE |
APR 19 | 9 PM | FLA. AD: Miss Julia Scribner | 9 East 66th St. | New
York City.

Cross Creek

April 7, 1942[1]

Dearest Julia:

I'm back at the Creek on the most divine April day you can imagine, and
how I wish you were here to enjoy it with me. The orange grove is in full
bloom, and while you might claim that it reeks like Vera deep in Chanel,[2]
I think that in a natural state it must smell better than Heaven. There are
four pairs of red-birds and several of the West Indian ground doves in the
feed-basket and bird-bath, and red-birds are busting a gut to out-sing one
another. When Idella[3] and I drove over yesterday we stopped and gathered
iris and wood-lilies, so all is elegant indoors, too. I had soft-boiled Mallard
duck eggs for breakfast and Dora's cream fell into the coffee in thick blobs,
and I don't see how I can return to the swank of Castle Warden, where the
cream is thin. Don't ever get yourself torn between love of a man and love of
a place, though I don't know how to stop it once it's happened.

I adored the Twelve Months[4] that you sent me. The man's mingled venom
and love of nature reminded me of you.

I had a terrific delight that I wished I might have shared with you. Sigrid
Undset[5] spent almost a week with me. There is a woman. I felt like a small
wave washing against a piece of mediaeval architecture. At first she seemed
like one drained of all emotion but a cold hate, and the empty shell frozen.
What she has been through is incredible, and when a rich bitch at Norton's
hotel moans about leaving behind her personal treasures in Paris, I wish I
could take the creature by the scruff of the neck and hold her in front of
Undset just to be looked at.

---

1   The twelve-day period between writing and mailing the letter is not explained. Perhaps MKR
meant to write "17" for "7," but that is speculation.

2   Vera Scribner, JSB's mother, whom MKR saw as her competition for JSB's affection. Chanel, a
moderately expensive perfume.

3   Idella Parker.

4   Llewelyn Powys (1884–1939), English essayist and novelist, *The Twelve Months* (London: Bodley
Head, 1936).

5   Sigrid Undset (1882–1949), Norwegian novelist, awarded the Nobel Prize for Literature in 1928.

Undset had two sons. The elder was killed in the first two weeks of fighting. The younger escaped to America with her, but is now back with the Norwegian forces, wherever they are, waiting for the return attack, and his chances are not bright. She was the first Norwegian writer banned by the Nazis. She said she had "that honor". It was desirable for her to get out, for the Germans used prominent people as hostages and held them over the heads of others to get things done to suit them. She had twenty minutes to get out of her home, and must have escaped with no more than the clothes on her back. The Germans are in her home---it dates back to 1,000, and is furnished with Scandinavian and Norse antiques older than the house. She says that if and when the Germans are driven out, they will burn everything behind them. She lives alone in a small one-room apartment in Brooklyn and cooks her own breakfast and supper.

After she got over her first terrific reserve, she proved to be one of the warmest, most lovable people I have ever known in my life. She has a beautiful deep rich speaking voice. I felt I had won a major battle when I got a hearty laugh out of her, and another, when, after a grand day spent in the Scrub, lunch by the edge of the sink-hole, a trip on Orange Lake at sunset to see the birds, we had highballs when we came in and both got rather high, mostly from fatigue and excitement. She laughed that rich laugh and said, "I feel so goot!"

When I see you, I'll tell you some of the wonderful Norwegian folk tales she told me.

Isn't there any chance of your coming down? You can't do twenty-four duty forever. Whitney Darrow and his bride[1] came to St. Augustine for luncheon and he said you had had a little spell of illness. You should have seized it to come down here to recuperate. If a chance comes, please hurry down, on the shortest notice. Any time at all would always be all right.

Whitney wants me to do a book called "Cross Creek Cookery",[2] and I plan to do it. I'll have to spend time in the kitchen checking recipes for exact proportions, and need someone to eat the products.

Our apartment is almost ready at Castle Warden and it should be very attractive. Norton threatens to lock me in it.

Loads of love,

Marjorie

---

1 Charles Whitney Darrow (1881–1970), sales manager and later vice president of Scribners, and founder of the Princeton University Press. Darrow married Alice Waring Dunham (1889–1977) on 28 March 1942.

2 *Cross Creek Cookery* (New York: Scribners, 1942). See Tarr, *Bibliography*, A6.1.

. . .

JSB to MKR, [13 July 1942]. ALS, 4 pp. PM: FAR HILLS | 9 A.M. |
JULY 14 | 1942 | N.J. AD: Mrs. Norton Baskin | Castle Warden Hotel |
St. Augustine | Florida. VIA AIR MAIL envelope.

Monday [13 July 1942][1]

Dear Mrs. Baskin:[2]

I surely to god hope that you aren't sore at me for mentioning you in the
same sentence as Edna Ferber![3] Of course I know all along that you belong
right up with America's Cook Book[4] – in fact you even have an edge on it
as you undoubtedly call a capon a spade, and none of this namby-pamby
'young rooster' stuff. Anyway I can tell you I have hurt feelings. After the
countless times I have pleaded with you in person and by mail for your waffle receipt ^receipe [sic]^ I have to wait until you publish a book to get it.[5]

I have been missing you very much lately. Reading about cheese grits
and Salt Spring[6] crabs and peppermint ice cream brings back many meals
in Crescent Beach. When you think of what a caraway seed, or was it a bun,
did to Proust[7] you can imagine the intensity of my nostalgia. I hardly dare
expose myself to the whole book (I've only seen the little pamphlet, or I suppose it should be called horrid word brochure).

My life is so dull and Red Crossy[8] these days that I have lots of time for
brooding. Of course I also spend a lot of time thinking up and out new ideas
(to me), theories, etc. Most people seem to stop doing that about seventeen or
eighteen, but I go right on getting worse with the years I think, and it's still my

---

1   The postmark is, in part, blurred and obscured.

2   After the initial letters, when JSB wants to upbraid humorously MKR, she addresses her as
"Mrs. Baskin."

3   Edna Ferber (1887–1968), known for her epic novels about American life, such as *So Big* (New
York: Doubleday, Page, 1924), and *Show Boat* (New York: Doubleday, Page, 1926), the latter earning
her a Pulitzer Prize.

4   "America's Cook Book," likely Fanny Farmer (1857–1915), *Boston Cooking-School Cook Book*
(Boston: Little, Brown, 1896), which was immensely popular and went through myriad printings.

5   See JSB's first appeal for the recipe on 1 April 1941. The "book" is *Cross Creek Cookery*.

6   Salt Springs, a natural mineral spring, approximately thirty-five miles east of Ocala.

7   Marcel Proust (1871–1922), French novelist, author of the seven-volume *À la recherche du temps
perdu* [*In Search of Lost Time*] (1913–1927). At one point, he tastes a traditional small French cake
known as a *petite madeleine* and has an intense sense of pleasure that he recalls repeatedly in the
novel. This metaphor for the difference between voluntary and involuntary memory has become
familiarly known as the "madeleine episode."

8   JSB is referring to her many charitable endeavors, including her volunteer work for the War
Department.

favorite occupation. I hope it's not a sign of retarded development or something. The ideas all get expounded to a dear, simple, I mean uncomplicated – earnest friend of mine.[1] By that process they completely cease to bother me if they ever have, and I usually forget them but poor Cath takes these wanton words quite to heart, and I find weeks afterward that she has been wrestling with some cracked theory that I can hardly remember. I trust that she will soon learn not to believe everything someone tells her – even if it is her old friend Scribner, and I'll feel I've really done her a good turn. Well, enough of the life of the mind, though as I say it's the only amusing life I have at the moment.

The life of the body is entirely deadly—a round of 'trail disasters', Motor Mechanics classes, First Aid drills, Airplane spotting, etc. On account of gas I stick close to home. Unfortunately the golf club (my one form of exercise) is 8 miles away so I've only had 3 games this year, but that doesn't break my heart. I occasionally trim trees or something instead. One form of exertion is pretty much as bad as another.

The worst thing now is that if I haven't had my phonograph for about a month. It had to go to NYC to be fixed and so far no way of getting it out has developed. I can easily do without gas, tires, and any kind of food or clothing they want to ration, but I simply must have music: the silver lining of the situation is that I have more time for reading. I've read <u>The Dreamer</u> of Green.[2] Remember, you read it when I was in Fla., but I never got around to till now. I liked it. I think he is a really good writer. I think shortly his first novel in Eng. is going to be published. (It seems I am thinking in translation). Also Nancy Hale's book[3] (in galleys) which Max has probably mentioned to you. It's good and good reading and very conversationable, though not exactly world shaking and here and there not 'true'. I think it ought to do a pretty bit of selling but who knows. Now I am reading a book, <u>Let Us Now Praise Famous Men</u>.[4] It's very slow reading but in parts so good that the effort is more than worthwhile. It's supposed to be written from an entirely new angle – got quite a lot of talk when it came out some said it was the road of the future, and some said it was a blind alley. Probably you've read it. I also

---

1   Catherine Gilpin.

2   Julien Green (1900–1998), American writer who wrote primarily in French, *Le Visionnaire* [*The Dreamer*] (Paris: Libraire générale française, 1934). Trans. Vyvyan Holland (London: Heinemann; New York: Harper, 1934).

3   Nancy Hale (1908–1988), American novelist and short fiction writer, *The Prodigal Woman* (New York: Scribners, 1942). Perkins mentions that he sent the novel to MKR on 9 September (*Max and Marjorie* 533).

4   James Agee (1909–1955), American novelist, poet, and film critic, *Let Us Now Praise Famous Men* (Boston: Houghton, Mifflin, 1941), a portrait of three sharecropper families in Alabama. Photographs by Walker Evans (1903–1975).

read a book called <u>The Spirit of Paris</u>[1] which has given me a terrific desire to go and live there a couple of months. I <u>love</u> living and traveling in foreign places, very impractical.

I wonder if you've been getting advertisements as I have from all the places we stayed in New England.[2] I'll never get over my disappointment in the weather on that trip. That snowstorm in the White Mts. and all those ghastly closed hotels. I was so counting on showing you idyllic N.E. and all we saw was rain and snow and fog – like the background of a psychological melodrama. I'll never be happy till you see it at its best – summer, I think.

The bug situation is getting acute – there must be a hole in the screen, and so I must get out of here – can't concentrate[3] with moths and whatnots fluttering around me. Do drop me a line or paragraph in between [naps]. I do miss you and wonder how you are and how's Norton and where's Bob and has Cecil[4] still got his job? I feel as if I hadn't seen you in years. Couldn't you argue with Daddy[5] about the contract or something and come up? I promise you wouldn't freeze up here now. It's almost as warm as Fla.

Ever so much love,

Julia.

. . .

MKR to JSB, 16 July 1942. TLS, 3 pp. PM: SAINT AUGUSTINE | JUL 16 | 6 PM | 1942 | FLA. AD: Miss Julia Scribner | Far Hills | New Jersey. [in MKR's hand circled at the top] Air Mail. Envelope stamped: VIA AIR MAIL. LH: Marjorie Kinnan Rawlings | \<Hawthorn,\> Florida.

Castle Warden

St. Augustine

July 16, 1942[6]

---

1 Paul Cohen-Portheim (1880–1832), Austrian freelance travel writer, *The Spirit of Paris*. Trans. Alan Harris (London: Batsford, 1937).

2 JSB is referring to the trip they took after MKR's discharge from Harkness Pavilion on 13 October 1941.

3 At the bottom of the page, JSB draws an arrow up the right side, across the top, and then finishes the letter in the left margin.

4 Robert Camp Jr. and Cecil Clarke, the latter was the assistant manager at the Ponte Vedra Innlet Hotel. See MKR's letter on 16 July 1942.

5 Charles Scribner III.

6 MKR strikes through Hawthorn, and writes in the St. Augustine address. She again uses a

Dearest Julia:

    2 cups flour, sifted with

    1 tablespoon sugar

    1 teaspoon salt

    4 teaspoons baking powder

    Stir in 3/4 cup sweet milk slowly and beat until smooth.

    2/3 cup melted Crisco (melted, but not too hot) Measurement <u>after</u>
        melting

    Last,

    2 well beaten eggs

Don't ever say again that you had to buy the cook-book to get the waffle recipe.[1] The trick is in the large quantity of melted fat. Most waffles are tough and leathery from not using enough shortening. The waffle iron should of course be smoking hot before putting in the batter, which I pour from a pitcher. Also, waffles are best made at table. They must not stand in the kitchen with a cover, before serving, or they soften and toughen.

I am staying at the cottage for a couple of weeks to get the cook-book done. This time it is Whitney instead of Max[2] who is on my tail, for the book is definitely a "product". Whitney threatens "disaster" if I don't meet the deadline. I find that I simply cannot work at Castle Warden. I hurt Norton's feelings by telling him that I associated him and Castle Warden with fun. I said, "Good God, man, would you want me to associate you with the wash-tubs?" and he said he wouldn't. He comes down about every other night and I shall go in tonight for dinner. The beach roads are closed at sunset,[3] but when necessary we can detour by Highway 1, crossing the Crescent Beach bridge with parking lights only. I have black-out shades all over the cottage, but usually prefer just to go to bed when it is dark, about nine o'clock.

Idella is still with me, thank Heaven, and I have a new pointer puppy, brown and white, named Moe, as I think he will always be a rough country fellow. He is four months old and engaging in a coltish way. There will never be another Pat. Norton still has the very handsome red, marcelled cocker

---

capital "I" for "1," which irritated JSB.

1   JSB had asked for MKR's waffle recipe the previous year; see JSB's letter dated [31 March 1941]. MKR encloses the first four lines of the recipe on the left with a large brace.

2   Whitney Darrow and Maxwell Perkins.

3   The beach road (A1A) was closed and then patrolled at night in anticipation that the Germans would land personnel on the beach.

spaniel that adopted him, Topper. Fortunately the hotel chef and his wife,[1] who managed the waitresses, linens, etc., are mad about dogs and Topper and Moe sleep in the tenant house with them and their own three cockers. The hotel inspector rated Castle Warden at 96 instead of 100, because when he came, there were five dogs milling around in the kitchen. The chef serves an enormous steak, solely, I am sure, because few can eat it all and the dogs get the rest.

Verle Pope got itchy and is a lieutenant with the army air corps at Keesler Field, Biloxi, Miss.[2] Edith rented their apartment—her wicked old father who went through the fortune that was Edith's mother's own and should have come to her, had the grace to die---in debt---Edith managed to sell his house---and has joined Verle in Biloxi.[3] We miss them both very much.

Bob Camp came down Sunday with two aviation cadet friends and we had a jolly time. He heard from the Navy that his papers were acceptable but there was no opening. So the draft is likely to pounce. Cecil tried to get in the Army on his own terms, but could not, so is still Assistant Manager at the Ponte Vedra Innlet.[4] His sight is so bad without glasses that I doubt if he is useable material.

The swimming has been grand. I certainly wish you were here. You could do airplane spotting here just as well as in New Jersey. Norton and I spot and love it. He is also a fire warden.

You might know I would wait to write you when I should be deep in work on the product---. So back to the menus. Seriously, can't you come down?

Loads of love,

<u>Marjorie</u>

. . .

JSB to MKR, 19 August 1942. ALS, 3 pp. PM: FAR HILLS | 12 [pm] | AUG | 1942 | N. J. AD: Mrs. Norton Baskin | Castle Warden Hotel | St. Augustine | Florida. VIA AIR MAIL envelope.

---

1 Clarence M. Huston was the chef at the Castle Warden Hotel. Audrey, his wife, ran the dining room. Their son, Robert, did odd jobs.

2 Keesler Air Force Base, Biloxi, Mississippi, activated in June 1941.

3 Lorena Florence Tugby Taylor (1864–1932) and Abraham Morris Taylor (1862–1942), Edith Taylor Pope's parents. He served in the Florida State Senate from 1925 to 1931.

4 Ponte Vedra Innlet Hotel, associated with the prestigious Ponte Vedra Inn and Club, was a separate hotel on the beach, offering 32 guest rooms, open on a seasonal basis, at a modest price.

[19 August 1942]¹

Dearest Marge –

This letter may be even more incoherent than usual as I am at work guarding the eastern seaboard alone – and I am sure I'm am going to miss whole flights of bombers. Our OP² has been moved from a marvelous lovely hill miles from everywhere to a hill over the village of Peapack.³ Right beneath us is a lime factory or kiln or whatever, the village road, a main highway, and the railroad tracks. As you can imagine the extraneous noises are awful. Every truck that goes up the highway sounds like a plane, and I'm afraid the planes may sound like trucks.

Marge, to hell with defense etc. – I can't resist your invitation any longer. It seems years since I have seen you, and it is almost one! Could I come around the 15ᵗʰ of Sept.?⁴ I'm depending on you to say "no" if that is a bad time, and I can come just as well any other time. So treat me quite frankly and don't you dare be polite as I have seen you be with the Bergs!⁵

I have the most enraptured accounts of the cook book from Max and Daddy.⁶ It seems Max can't believe anyone, even you, could write a cook book that is wonderful reading. I can't wait to see it. Daddy is awfully pleased with Bob's drawings⁷ – says they are really swell, but I haven't seen them either – except the few that were in its 'brochure' and I loved those.

There are two training planes that keep appearing in all directions and are driving me nuts – also buzzards. Very confusing!

I saw in the Publishers Weekly that in Nov. Knopf is going to publish another volume of Isak Dinesen's stories.⁸ I wish it was going to be the novel I saw announced a couple of years ago. I have often wondered if some horrible thing had happened to it – sunk in the Atlantic for instance.

---

1 Written in a second hand at the top of p 1: [Aug 1942].

2 OP, Observation Post.

3 Peapack, a village just north of Far Hills.

4 JSB was in Florida by 18 September; see Maxwell Perkins's comment to MKR in a letter on 18 September 1942: "Tell Julia her brother is now an Ensign in the U.S. Navy" (*Max and Marjorie* 534). JSB's brother is Charles Scribner IV (aka Jr.). By 30 September MKR and JSB were in Atlanta to continue their trip with the U.S. Forest Service and were in North Carolina on 2 October (*Love Letters* 70).

5 Norman and Julie Berg of Atlanta, who repeatedly took advantage of MKR's hospitality, were not favorites of JSB.

6 Maxwell Perkins and Charles Scribner III.

7 Robert Camp Jr. did the "drawings" for *Cross Creek Cookery*.

8 Isak Dinesen, *Winter's Tales: 11 Short Stories* (New York: Random House, 1942). Dinesen's only novel, *The Angelic Avengers* (London: Putnam, 1946), was published under the pseudonym Pierre Andrézel.

Life continues to be increasingly quiet here. We haven't even had a trial disaster for months. The Motor Corps[1] is not what it used to be before gas rationing. I haven't been farther away than Long Island. This is the first summer that I haven't gone up to New Marlboro[2] for a couple of weeks at least, and I really miss it. I've never had a great fondness for N.J. and now I'm truly homesick for New England air and flora and hills. I may get up there in Oct. and do a little shooting.

(In addition to planes I'm having a strenuous time watching my dog. The last time I had her up here she got into the Ladies privvy [sic] and if that happens again I think I will have to get rid of my car.)

This last week we have had the worst floods here that anyone can remember. For the first time in history the train service collapsed. I hear that a house was washed onto the tracks between F.H. and Bernardsville,[3] but that seems too good to be true and I suspect that it was only embankment trouble. Our house came through all right – no floods in the cellar but most people suffered badly from that. The garden is rather a wreck, and I'm afraid that many of the orchids that I walked miles to get and brought home from New M.[4] were washed away.

My watch is about over, so I'll wind up – Promise you won't let me be a bother, and you won't moan and say 'Oh, God, why did[5] she have to pick that date! Just tell me when you want me – or don't want me. Love to Norton and lots to you,

Julia

. . .

MKR to JSB, 21 August 1942. TLS, 6 pp. PM: SAINT AUGUSTINE | AUG 22 | 9 AM | 1942 | FLA. AD: Miss Julia Scribner | Far Hills | New Jersey. LH: Marjorie Kinnan Rawlings | Hawthorn. Florida.

Box 550
St. Augustine

---

1   The Motor Corps of the American Red Cross, founded in 1917, aided the troops in myriad ways, one of them transportation.

2   New Marlborough, Massachusetts, in the Berkshires.

3   Far Hills and Bernardsville, New Jersey.

4   New Marlborough.

5   JSB writes "UP" in the next line to direct MKR to the top margin of the page, where she finishes the letter.

August 21 [1942]

Dearest Julia:

I want you to do me a great favor, yet I believe that it may turn out to be a kindness to you, too.

I have been in correspondence for about two months with a young man,[1] 23 years old, who was born in South Carolina, his father American, his mother English, lived there as a boy then moved to England. He said that since his mother was English, the family way of life had always been British. He wrote me from a military hospital in Quebec, Canada, when he was waiting for an operation that would determine whether he ever walked again. He was writing me about "Cross Creek" and about "The Yearling". He wrote that he had read "The Yearling" while being bombed in London, in an air raid shelter. He read it aloud to the people in the shelter. He said that a little Cockney boy listened with big eyes to the accounts of Jody and cried out, "I wish I was him, oh, I wish I was!"

He said that the book "brought a warm glow into that crowded shelter". Naturally, my heart melted at once. He wrote that he felt sure he would walk again, "as I want once more to walk barefooted down a red clay road." He said that he just wanted me to know what my books meant to people like him, and that they had "helped him to forget a little what he saw at Dunkirk."[2]

I wrote him air mail at once, and it seemed that my letter reached him as he had come out of the ether after his operation. Other details about him have come out casually in our correspondence. All his family has been killed in the war. I asked him about his branch of the service, and in what capacity he served at Dunkirk, and he wrote me the story, briefly and casually, that is one of the most heart-breaking I have ever heard. It was evidently very difficult for him to write about it at all, and if you do meet him, please do not indicate that I have told you anything. He might tell you something of it

---

1   Here begins the saga of Perry Patterson, who duped not only MKR but also JSB and the Scribner family. Allegedly, he stole both money and influence from MKR and JSB, and even had the temerity to appropriate without return JSB's typewriter. There is even a hint that he tried to become romantically involved with the vulnerable JSB. Truth and fiction collide as the Patterson caper unfolds.

2   The Battle of Dunkirk, 26 May–4 June 1940, the greatest naval rescue of World War II. With the British Expeditionary Force and its Belgian, Dutch, French, and Polish allies surrounded by the Germans at the French coastal town of Dunkirk, nearly 1,000 military and civilian vessels sailed from England in what many thought would be an impossible effort to save the troops. In spite of vicious aerial and artillery bombardment, during the course of the nine days, over 300,000 troops were evacuated, including nearly 85 percent of the British forces then mustered. Although Allied losses were heavy in terms of both men and materiel, the success at Dunkirk became a rallying point for the otherwise much beleaguered British and their allies.

himself, but I feel I should not violate his confidence, since he plainly does not care to talk about it.

He had a twin brother who was unusually close to him. The brother was a pilot in the R.A.F. Perry was in camouflage (evidently an artist originally) and trained as a gunner. At Dunkirk, he and his brother were sent out to identify enemy camouflaged bases. They went through a hell [hail] of gunfire, his brother was wounded and the plane shot down. His brother, wounded, motioned to him to jump with his parachute. He refused. The plane crashed. His brother was dead. He said that he was unhurt, yet that does not seem literally possible. He carried his dead brother three miles to the coast, where the evacuation was in progress. Three times he was turned back because he was carrying a dead man. At last he found an old Scotch fisherman who said, "I don't care what the orders is. I'll take you and him. I've got two meself."

He said that one of the first people he saw when they reached the English coast, was their old nurse. He said that he.felt safe in leaving his brother's body with her. Then he went into the regular army, and has never told me how or where he received his serious wound.

The operation <u>was</u> a success. He is now in New York City, engaged in camouflage work again. He is likely to be sent to the New Orleans shipyards to do work, and if so, hopes to stop off and see me. He still wears a brace and says he limps a little, but will eventually be able to discard the brace.

He wrote me lately that he is ordered to England to receive the Distinguished Service <Cross> ^Order.^[1] He said that he had no one to share the news with, but me, and felt I would understand. Said he must [illegible excision] be receiving it "for being scared to death"---no intimation as to what he did, to receive it. Hardly for bringing out his brother's dead body, since that was taboo. Don't mention this, either, although he might speak of it, though I doubt it.

Anyway, in one of his letters he wrote of what a treat New York was, that for fifty cents he could sit in a balcony and hear divine music, and that there was a wonderful radio station in New York that played symphonies before breakfast.[2] At one time that he wrote, he said the radio was playing some lovely Slovac dances, I thought, my Heavens, with the few people in the world who have a passion for music, Julia and this chap ought to at least meet.

---

1   Distinguished Service Order (DSO), a metal for gallantry awarded officers in World War II. MKR excises "Cross" and inserts "Order" above the line by hand.

2   Perhaps the Blue Network (ABC) that began to broadcast the Metropolitan Opera in the early 1940s. The network tried to counter the soap operas broadcast by NBC and CBS with a variety of broadcasts devoted to music.

Now, as a person, he may prove perfectly impossible. He writes a beautiful, simple letter---in speech, he may be tongue-tied. He may be a wizened little person with freckles and sparse, sandy hair. But the inmost core of him is fine and lovely, so I'm risking my request that you contact him. His name is Perry Patterson, his address 38 West 12th, N.Y.C. – oddly, he has <Tomas> Thomas Wolfe's old room.[1]

I don't know the etiquette of such meetings, but I'm writing him that I'm asking you to contact him. I don't know if he's fixed for money, but he probably has at least enough to take you to tea, so if he insists on that, better agree. Or, if you care to ask him to go to tea some place where you have a charge account, that would be all right, I know.

If you find him worth knowing as a person, you'll thank me. If not, try to find the things he has revealed in his letters, for I know it's there, and forgive me.

Lots of love,

Marjorie

. . .

MKR to JSB, 22 August 1942. TLS, 1 p. PM: SAINT AUGUSTINE | AUG 22 | 7 PM | 1942 | FLA. AD: Miss Julia Scribner | Far Hills | New Jersey. LH: Marjorie Kinnan Rawlings | Hawthorn, Florida.

[22 August 1942]

In case you can't make this out (the ribbon won't reverse) am trying to say Sept. 15 is fine and I'm thrilled to death![2]

Dearest Julia:

I can't tell you how thrilled I am that you are really coming for a visit. September 15 will be grand, or any date earlier or later.[3] I hadn't planned to

---

1   Thomas Wolfe (1900–1938), American novelist. The claim by Patterson that he lived at an address where Wolfe once lived has not been confirmed.

2   Written in MKR's hand at the top of p. 1.

3   JSB was in Cross Creek near 18 September. Maxwell Perkins writes to MKR on 18 September, "Tell Julia her brother [Charles Scribner IV] is now an Ensign in the U.S. Navy" (*Max and Marjorie* 534). MKR and JSB left Cross Creek the third week, most likely on 21 September (see MKR's letter dated [7 September 1942]). The purpose of the trip, guided by a member of the U.S. Forest Service, was to allow MKR to collect material for her ecological article "Trees for Tomorrow," *Collier's Magazine* 117 (8 May 1943): 14–15, 23–25 (see Tarr, *Bibliography*, C626). MKR and JSB were in Biloxi, Mississippi, on 24 September (unpublished letter to Ida Tarrant on 23 September, Special Collections, University of Florida Library). They were in Atlanta by 25 September and in Jackson, Mississippi,

go away at all, and it will be like a vacation to have you come. (Am using a rented typewriter and can't make the ribbon reverse).

Don't worry about your defense work---you can go right on with your spotting with me! Either Norton or I takes the 12 to 2 (noon) shift at Crescent Beach.

This ribbon condition is awful! Hope you can at least make out that I'm thrilled you're coming!

Love,

Marjorie

. . .

MKR to JSB, 29 August 1942. TLS, 3 pp. PM: SAINT AUGUSTINE | AUG 29 | 3 PM | 1942 | FLA. AD: Miss Julia Scribner | Far Hills | New Jersey. LH: Marjorie Kinnan Rawlings | Hawthorn, Florida.

[29 August 1942]

Castle Warden
St. Augustine

Dearest Julia:

Do you have an identification card from the Coast Guard or Army? We have to have them here, to cross the bridges to and from the beach. I thought we would probably be at the cottage a good part of the time you are here, and asked the Coast Guard about a guest. They said you would have to have an identification card. Since everyone is likely to need one sooner or later, suggest you get one before you come.

Don't know through what authorities you would proceed, but here we need a birth certificate, 3 photographs of the passport type, and finger-prints are taken. The card issued should get one in and out of everything but jail.

And please do write Bob (The Innlet, Ponte Vedra, Fla.)[1] that you are coming. He would never forgive either of us if you did not.

My half-English friend, Perry Patterson, of whom I wrote, is going back to

---

by 27 September (unpublished letters from NSB to MKR and MKR to Ida Tarrant, Special Collections, University of Florida Library). On 2 October, MKR sent a postcard from Murphy, North Carolina, to NSB saying they are in the "beautiful mountain country" (*Love Letters* 70). MKR was back in St. Augustine by 8 October, when she sent a wire to Perkins assuring him that she would be returning the proof of *Cross Creek Cookery* shortly (*Max and Marjorie* 536–37).

1   See MKR's letter on 16 July 1942.

England to do his work, but if you have time to contact him before he goes, it would be nice.

Have just had a typically Whitney Darrow lament and request. In the preface to my cook book, I said that while some of my recipes might sound outlandish, they were all extremely palatable, and the reader could either believe me or "fall back in cowardly safety on Fannie Farmer."[1] Whitney wrote, aggrieved, that it would be hard for his salesmen to sell my cook book, with such a reference, since "America's Cook Book"[2] competed with Fannie Farmer's "Boston Cook Book". I wrote him that it made no difference to me, but that Fannie Farmer was still THE Authority, and that America's Cook Book "competing" with the Boston Cook Book was like saying that Pollyanna,[3] the Glad Girl, competed with the Bible as a source of spiritual comfort. It will probably end friendly relations between Whitney and me---.

It will be so grand to see you. Just can't wait.

Love,

Marjorie

.   .   .

JSB to MKR, [31 August 1942]. ALS. 2 pp. PM: FAR HILLS | 8 AM | SEP 1 | 1942 | N.J. AD: Mrs. Norton Baskin | Castle Warden Hotel | St. Augustine | Florida. RA: J. Scribner | Far Hills, N.J. VIA AIR MAIL envelope.

Monday PM [31 August 1942][4]

Dearest Marjorie –

I haven't time to write you a complete report on Perry – It would take hours and I have to get up at the crack of dawn tomorrow. However, we are very much "in contact" – He has just left here this AM having come on Thurs.[5]

Thank God you wrote me as we rescued him almost literally from starvation. He is a most remarkable person and when you think what he has been

---

1   See JSB's letter dated [13 July 1942], 126, n. 4.

2   *America's Cook Book.* Compiled New York Herald Home Institute (New York: Scribners, 1937).

3   Reference to Eleanor H. Porter (1863–1920), who created in her novel *Pollyanna* (1913), an unusually optimistic character named Pollyanna.

4   Written in an unknown hand on p. 1: [9-1-42], which is the mailing date, not the composition date.

5   Perry Patterson arrived on Thursday, 27 August 1942.

through and how sound and natural he is I think he deserves admiration more than anyone I have known. Daddy[1] has bought an option on a children's book he is writing which should take care of him for a week or so and if all goes well with the book he will get an advance which will enable him to get down to see you – his great ambition – and take him safely to Canada. I think he expects to go back to Can about Sept 12th but he changes his mind several times a day so we can't really keep up with him. I think the book may be quite good – about a donkey mascot with the British in Egypt & Libya – that's where he was wounded – Anyway he's probably told you about it.

The whole affair would be less complicated if he hadn't decided to fall in love with me! Natural effect I guess of not having seen a girl of his sort since the war began. Anyway so I distract him so he can't write here and had to return to Tom Wolfe's room to work on 'Zubu'.[2] If it weren't for that we'll make him stay with us till he goes to Can and no one in the family would care how long it was. Everyone including Buzz[3] (whom he is continually advising on his perplexed love life and who calls him 'The Voice of Experience['])) is crazy about him.

I am having lunch with him on Wed.[4] and I'll see if I can't get him out again. I think the food etc. is good for him[.] He looks like a bean pole, but when the food is around he certainly can eat.

Anyway, never fear, we'll take care of him and I tell you all about him when I see you if you don't see him first. He's probably written you all about coming out etc, but I just wanted you to know that we won't let the poor guy get lost in N.Y.C. again. Will write very soon. and thanks for wanting me down so much,

Julia

. . .

MKR to JSB, [7 September 1942]. ALS, 4 pp. PM: SAINT A[UGUSTINE] | SEP[T] | 7 [AM or PM?] | 19[42] | FLA. AD [in MKR's hand]: Miss Julia Scribner | Far Hills | New Jersey. Air Mail. Envelope stamped VIA AIR MAIL.

Monday [7 September 1942][5]

---

1 Charles Scribner III.

2 Thomas Wolfe's room in New York City. See MKR's letter on 22 August 1942. "Zubu" is apparently the proposed title for Patterson's book.

3 Buzz, the nickname for Charles Scribner IV (aka Jr.), JSB's brother.

4 2 September 1942.

5 Part of the postmark has been torn away. Written in a second hand on the envelope: Sept 7, 1942.

Dearest Julia:—

It was such fun to talk with you and Perry. What a nice voice he has. But he should be spanked for spending so much of his money to chat, 1000 miles away.[1]

I think it is wonderful of you and the family to take him under your wing. It must have put him back on his feet. His whole story is somehow fabulous, and it seems like a "happy ending", regardless of whether you feel toward him as he does toward you.[2]

I felt terribly sure that you spoke the same language, and that makes for a good friendship, whatever else happens.[3]

Think I will be through with the Cookery proof <u>before</u> Sept. 15, so if you can and want to come earlier, fine. They don't take much time or mental energy in any case. Could finish while you were here, perfectly OK.

My trip to gather material for the forestry article (which the Sat. Eve. Post wants)[4] will take me at a lovely time of year through the Appalachians and the Tennessee and Carolina mountains, so I deliberately named Sept. 21 as the starting date, intending to persuade you to make a week or ten days of the trip with me. If this is selfish of me, and you'd rather spend all your time in Florida, just say so, and I can start the trip later just as well. But I thought we would really enjoy it. I am going in a forestry car, with a "guide" who is the public relations man[5] from Atlanta, very nice, but again I am selfish in not wanting to be alone with him that long. But the country should be gorgeous then.

Let me know, and I hope it appeals to you, for it's what I'd like to do. And come any time you can get away.

Love,
Marjorie

The date is the first Monday in September.

1   Unlike at Cross Creek, MKR had a telephone at Crescent Beach.

2   MKR is referring to JSB's comment that she had to reject Patterson's overtures while he was at Far Hills. See JSB's letter dated [31 August 1942].

3   MKR clearly has more in mind than finding a "good friendship" for JSB. She had already tried to match her with Robert Camp Jr. and Perry Patterson is yet another candidate.

4   About the article, MKR writes to Perkins in a letter dated [October 1942], "I have been deep in finishing my article presumably for the Saturday Evening Post on the matter of our American forests. I guess I wrote you that I took a two-weeks' trip with the U.S. Forest Service, covering nearly 5,000 miles through the south-east, to gather material" (*Max and Marjorie* 540). See "Trees for Tomorrow." *Collier's Magazine* 117 (8 May 1943), 14–15, 24–25. See Tarr, *Bibliography*, 233, C626 and *Uncollected Writings*, 289–95. For the itinerary, see MKR's letter on 22 August 1942, 135, n. 3.

5   Joseph Hessel; see the next letter.

. . .

JSB to MKR, 9 September 1942. ALS, 2 pp. PM: torn away, except:
FAR [HILLS] . . . N.J. AD: Mrs. Norton Baskin | Castle Warden | St.
Augustine | Florida. [At top of envelope in JSB's hand]: <u>AIR MAIL</u>.
LH: FAR HILLS, NEW JERSEY.

Sept. 9. [1942]

Dearest Marjorie:

I can't very well come before the 15th so just before that is a certain time of
month[1] when I usually spend several days of headaches – and I don't want to
come down and waste precious days with you taking pills and powders (the
sensational cure I started on our motor trip last fall was temporary in the
extreme. The vitamin B seemed to scare the headaches for a couple of weeks,
but my system soon got in stride again and I became absolutely impervious
to the stuff.)

The trip sounds divine, but you say I should take a week or ten days with
you. <u>How</u> <u>long</u> are you going off with this man?[2] Are you going to winter in
the wilds with him? Anyway, if I came down on the 15th I would have till the
21st in Florida and I could chaperone for a while on the trip. Is that OK? So
instruct me to do exactly what you want, as I don't care much what State I
am in as long as I get to see you and I can come any time <u>after</u> the 15th. If you
decide you want me to come then, do let me know what they are wearing this
year in the forest primeval![3]

Perry left for Canada yesterday[4] after signing his contract. It was all ter-
rifically exhausting and I feel quite limp today which I suppose is only the
half of what he feels.[5] Only a fiction writer would think that my "not feeling
toward him as he feels toward me" makes ^room^ "for a grand friendship."
Oh, well, I'll give you all the dope when I see you.

I bought this writing paper last fall specially to impress you and Bob
Camp. The only trouble is that my writing takes away from its impeccability.
It looks better with my typewriter but Perry has that. He is so overcome by

---

1   JSB apparently suffered from menstrual headaches.

2   MKR was to be accompanied by a U.S. Forest agent, Joseph Hessel; see JSB's letter dated [13?]
October 1942.

3   An allusion to the first line of the epic poem by Henry Wadsworth Longfellow (1807–1882),
Evangeline: A Tale of Acadie (Boston: Ticknor, 1847).

4   Tuesday, 8 September. Perry Patterson, who claimed to be a Canadian citizen.

5   JSB's double entendre on "limp" would not be lost on MKR.

his contract that he is planning an autobiographical novel, some fairy stories, a poetic cycle, and maybe another novel – on the level.

Tell me when you want me –

Lots of love,
Julia.

. . .

JSB to MKR, [13?] October 1942. ALS, 8 pp. PM: partially torn away: NEW YO[RK N.Y.] | OCT 1[3?] | 130 PM | 1942 | GRAND CENTRAL STATION. AD: Mrs Norton Baskin | Castle Warden Hotel | St. Augustine | Florida. VIA AIR MAIL envelope.

I have your sunglasses which I am returning and will you send my sugar card before the family throws me out[1]

[13?] October 1942[2]

Dearest Marge –

I got this far {up}[3] three days ago or more and have been finishing it since then – only not on paper. As Racine said of Phèdre, "c'est prêt il me reste qu'a l'écrire."[4] It gives me quite a lift of morale to think that in composition I have something in common with Racine.

I have been torn between reveling in my beloved northern, Yankee cold, raw countryside and thinking with regret of what an ass I was to leave when you were not yet at the point of throwing me out, I try to console myself with the thought that you are battling to the death with the forests of the south-eastern U.S. and therefore somewhat preoccupied – And if I were there I would undoubtedly quote a bit of Joyce Kilmer at you which might not strike you a bit funny, no perhaps it's just as well I aint.[5]

The mystery of "L'affaire Patterson" is still deepening. Daddy had a letter from him, in which he said he was leaving for Eng. (and we had a note from

---

1   JSB inserts her postscript at the top of the p. 1. The "sugar card" refers to rationing, which began for sugar on 5 May 1942.

2   Written in a second hand at the top of p. 1: [Oct. (13?) 1942].

3   JSB inserts an arrow pointing at the dash in the salutation.

4   Jean-Baptiste Racine (1639–1699), French dramatist, author of the tragedy *Phèdre* (1677): Ma pièce est terminée il me reste à lécrire [My piece is finished, I still have to write it].

5   Joyce Kilmer (1886–1918), American poet, killed by a sniper at the Second Battle of the Marne. His poem "Trees" (1913), for which he is most often remembered, begins with the lines "I think that I shall never see / A poem lovely as a tree."

the "Harrison"[1] of his address saying he had heard from Perry's C.O. that he had arrived safely) that he was bringing his little niece[2] (you know that story don't you? If not let me know and I will tell you) back with him, and that in the early part of December he was going home for good where he would "sit in Scotland and write sad laments." If he is in the army how can he be going back to Scotland and if he isn't how is he doing all this running back and forth across the Atlantic. I am utterly unable to figure the whole thing out. Oh, and my God! after I thought I had coped successfully with the dedication question he sent Daddy directions to dedicate it to me. I'll have to tell him that juveniles don't have dedication pages.[3]

(Another slight interruption – of about 36 hours had to have lunch, take a British Commodore riding, do up two horses, drive to Princeton for dinner and bring Buzzie home, play golf with Buzz because of the absence of his girl, and bid Sandy farewell – he has suddenly become an officer and is off to a training center.)[4] (At this point I noticed that I was almost numb with cold so I set off to find my electric heater which I found in Muddy's[5] orchid room. I plugged it in and the damned thing blew out the fuse and damn near blew out me! Then I had to hunt up fuses and replace the blown one – ^and^ analyze the heater, whose trouble was beyond my repairing skill. So off I went to find another heater. Found two – blew one more fuse, and the other wouldn't work at all. In desperation I searched the attic, and there I found a two plate electric stove,[6] which I am now sitting almost on top of. I think it is quite obvious that anyone with a talent for distractions like mine should just forego writing completely, but in the few moments I have before the roof falls in or one of the horses breaks loose I try to write a couple more pages.)

Speaking of letters, I had a ponderous two-pager from Joe.[7] I must quote part of a paragraph. "The next three paragraphs should be devoted to an ecstatic portrayal of my feeling concerning our journey and adventures in the land of trees, chiggers, rattlesnakes, broken springs and cotton. I might add balconies, except that I wonder if they were always so goddamn Platonic. Forgive me if I am like that. Just a hangover from having spent too many of

---

1   Harrison is unidentified; see JSB's letter dated [7? November 1942].

2   Not identified.

3   Apparently a reference to *Zubu*, the children's book Patterson was claiming to write.

4   Sandy Dillon.

5   Muddy, JSB's nickname for her mother Vera Scribner.

6   That is, an electric cooking plate with two burners.

7   Joseph Hessel, the U.S. Forest Service agent who took MJR and JSB through the Deep South in order that MKR could observe the forests for her *Collier's* article "Trees for Tomorrow." See MKR's letter on 22 August 1942, 135, n. 3.

my early years above in the big woods." Thanks again Marge, for your watchful eye. Not that I have any great horror of being attacked – I might even say, quite the reverse, but I don't want the protagonist to have a wife and three little children – no future in that as Granny[1] would say – and above all I don't want him to be Joe Hessel.

The quinces are going to be difficult, but never fear – I'll get them if I have to advertise in the Times. Granny's trees have all died, and I haven't yet discovered anyone else with a tree or trees. I am going to try a big farmer's market near here. You'ld think they were the apples Freia grew near Walhalla (remember) for their damn scarcity.[2] It's just the sort of riskless challenge I enjoy and I'll love every step of the search. So don't think of me cursing you in one market after another. I'll be having a lovely time.

The Russian novel[3] I was telling you about seems fascinating, although I've only managed to read about 20 galleys.

What I would like to do right now is spend about a week in bed with some painless disease, just a temperature would be OK, so that I could get a lot of reading done, and then spend another week in my eyrie here on the third floor luxuriously hearing my record library. I'd be like a miser in his attic counting over his precious gold pieces. But – instead – within an hour I have to be the gracious daughter of the house at a large and boring dinner of the family's friends and tomorrow I have to go out to lunch and dinner.

Just when I am in my most hermitlike mood – why do we let life be such a damned nuisance to us – I would so <u>enjoy</u> being Above and not speaking a word and no one would be the worse off for my doing so. I think maybe I will be an eccentric old maid and live as I damn well please. And anyone who says one wouldn't enjoy doing as one damned well pleased (provided of course no one <was> ^is^ trampled in the process) is a damned lousy hypocrite and a puritanical killjoy. Or so I feel at 7 PM of this Saturday evening. And now, goddamn it, I have to go and get dressed in evening clothes which I loathe, and I'll have to take at least two drinks in order to be pleasant and genial, and that will give me indigestion tomorrow. It's not

---

1 Granny, Louise Flagg Scribner.
2 Freia, the Norse goddess of love, war, and death. Valhalla is the paradisiac mead hall of Odin, king of the Norse gods. When warriors were killed in battle, half were said to have gone to the scared fields of Freyja and half to Odin at Valhalla. In his opera cycle *Der Ring des Nibelungen*, Richard Wagner (1813–1883) combined Freia with the goddess Iðunn, a Norse goddess associated with apples. In the opera, Freia supplies the gods with golden apples that keep them young.
3 Perhaps Mark Aldanov, *The Fifth Seal*; see JSB's letter dated late May 1943, 185, n. 3.

logical – And I don't think I'll fit into the evening clothes because I seem to be <u>much</u> fatter than I was last year.

The end to all the above raving should be of course, that the dinner was lots of fun and I had a lovely time. But it wasn't, and the dress <u>was</u> tight so I had to suffer the confinement of a girdle.

Now that I have head and all back into my musical and various other preoccupations the pangs of my unfortunate amours are pushed into the background again. Not so fun as usual as I had a most upsetting conversation with one of my two best friends who is a former victim. She had had a visitation while I was away from one of his later victims. I have realized that he is extremely selfish, quite bitter and unsure of what he wants and his ability for getting it, but they are convinced that beneath what I assure you is an unbelievably charming exterior there is something dark and almost pathological and quite repellant in him. I never felt that of course, but I can't deny their conviction and evidence, and it gives me a queer feeling to be in love with someone who may be like that. Well, the whole situation is much to[o] complex for me to try to write it.[1]

Again I must go and dress for dinner, and this time I think I'd better put an end to this thing while it will still fit into the envelope. I haven't tried to say what fun – well, more than fun – it was to be with you. There's no point in messing up the paper with emotional prose a la Scribner, but just thanks like before for wanting me to come. You liking to have me around is one of the nicest things I have.

Lots of Love and do come up to New York, you and Norton. We'ld have real fun.

Julia

Love to Norton

. . .

MKR to JSB, [26 October 1942]. ALS, 3 pp. PM: SAINT AUGUSTINE | OCT 28 | 5 AM | 1942 | FLA. AD: [in MKR's hand]: Miss Julia Scribner | Far Hills | New Jersey. LH: Mrs. Norton Baskin | Castle Warden | St. Augustine, Florida.

Monday [26 October 1942]

---

1 JSB's love interest here has not been identified.

Dearest Julia:

Am here for short one minute between two damn trips. Just back from Tallahassee, where the governor's wife[1] roped me in to hold her hand while she gave a book review of "Cross Creek"--- and headed out now to the Creek with a new photographer who is doing pictures of my peculiar foods for an article somebody is doing on my outlandish habits for the Saturday Post.[2] Max,[3] of all people, urged me to do it, as valuable publicity for the damn cook book. I talked Norton and Cecil[4] into going with us and they'll probably curse me heartily before we're through.

The photographer had orders particularly to get me cooking alligator tail steak. He was so upset when I told him you just couldn't wander around my back yard and pick up an alligator, that I set out to borrow one, and the Alligator Farm[5] made me a present of one, which goes with us to the Creek, too!

Your most welcome letter came and am hurrying to get this off with the sugar card[6] before the time is up. Will write you when I get back.

The next article[7] is begun, but all this stuff is raising Hob[8] with it.

Loads of love,

Marjorie

. . .

MKR to JSB, [2? November 1942]. ANS, 1 p. Envelope is missing. LH: MARJORIE KINNAN RAWLINGS | HAWTHORN, FLORIDA.

Monday [2? November 1942][9]

---

1 Mary Groover Holland (1896–1975), wife of Spessard Holland.

2 See "Marjorie Kinnan Rawlings Hunts for Her Supper." *Saturday Evening Post* (30 January 1943): 26.

3 Maxwell Perkins.

4 NSB and Cecil Clarke.

5 The Alligator Farm has been open since 1893 and is on Anastasia Island, north of St. Augustine.

6 A sugar ration card.

7 The dating of this letter suggests that it might be "Christmas at Cross Creek." *American Cookery* 47 (December 1942): 168, 184. See Tarr, *Bibliography*, C625, and *Uncollected Writings* 285–88.

8 Raising Hob, slang for unwanted disruptions. "Hob" is a truncation from "Hobgoblin," known for being mischievous.

9 Tentative date based upon sugar coupon reference. In her letter dated [26 October] 1942, MKR says that she intends to get the coupon off to JSB shortly. In this letter, she reports that the coupon is gone, cashed in by Clarence Huston, the chef at the Castle Warden. Thus, this letter is placed after 26 October. The first Monday after it is 2 November.

Dearest Julia---

Just a hurried line to say you are a wizard to get the quinces! Was I thrilled! Have made a year's supply of the most beautiful jelly and had some quinces left over to give to Aunt Ida and Mrs. White.[1]

Found Norton's chef had cashed your October ticket (sugar) so had him send you 5 lbs![2] Didn't want to run any risk of your Mother[3] not letting you come again!

Am still sweating, over the Forestry article,[4] and is it a mess! Will write when I finish the damn thing for better or for worse.

Love,

Marjorie

. . .

JSB to MKR, [7? November 1942]. ALS, 9 pp. Envelope is missing.

Saturday [7? November 1942][5]

Dearest Marjorie –

So much water has passed under the bridge since I last wrote that it's a wonder the bridge hasn't collapsed and gone along too.

To dispense with trivial things – I am glad the quinces arrived safely. I was afraid they would be a rotten mess or mass by the time they reached Fla. as they seemed quite over-ripe to me. It was the tailend of the quince season, and I couldn't get any that were less ripe. Of course maybe they were all rotten and you just wrote me a horrible polite lie out of the goodness of your heart – even so – there are no more quinces this year! But I have found a beautiful – and I

---

1   Elizabeth Frazier (Mrs. Reginald) White 1899?–1964), Aunt Ida Tarrant's landlady in St. Augustine.

2   MKR had intended to send JSB a Ration Card for sugar. See MKR's letter dated [26 October 1942], 145, n. 6.

3   Vera Scribner.

4   "Trees for Tomorrow." In an undated letter to Maxwell Perkins, mostly likely sent in late October or early November, MKR reports, "I have been deep in finishing my article presumably for the Saturday Evening Post on the matter of our American forests. I wrote you that I took a two-weeks' trip with the U.S. Forest Service, covering nearly 5,000 miles through the south-east, to gather material. I don't think I am the person to do such an article, but have done the best I could" (*Max and Marjorie* 540).

5   Written in a second hand at the top of p. 1: [1942 or 3?]. 1942 is correct. The tentative date is based upon the references to the quinces. In her letter tentatively dated 2 November, MKR acknowledges that the quinces have arrived and she has made the "most beautiful jelly." In this letter, JSB refers to this expression and then thanks MKR for the 5 lbs. of sugar she had sent through chef Huston. The first Saturday after MKR's letter is 7 November, the date assigned this letter.

think <u>free</u> – source of supply for next year. And if that "most beautiful jelly" in your letter is a noble fiction I can get you some of the next most beautiful jelly.

I am awfully embarrassed about the sugar. (And I assure you that I am not regarding 5 lbs of sugar as a triviality). Surely Mr. – I can't remember his name[1] – didn't get 5 lbs for one of my tickets! I feel I should at least send you back the correct change. You can't make 5 lb gestures like that. It's unpatriotic and probably liable to prosecution. Let me know and I will make amends – I owe you 4 lbs, don't I? By the way it is not patriotism that brings me to the back of this page. Wait till you see all I have to tell you – and I do want to get it all in one envelope!

Alors[2] – we plunge into an extremely fascinating tale: You remember in my last letter I said the mystery of l'affaire Patterson was deepening? Well <they're> ^it's^ un-deepened a bit. L'affaire Patterson is more than a mystery it's deception – in the 'grand style fleuri et romantique.'[3] I am not sure yet of all that is fake or any that is true, but I'll tell you all I know. Remember also that I said in my last letter Daddy[4] had a note from R. Harrison enclosed with Perry's manuscript and letter, saying P. had arrived safely in his beloved Scotland? Being a polite man, Daddy wrote Harrison thanking him for the note and expressing relief that P. gotten over OK. A few days later Daddy had an outraged letter from R. Harrison saying he couldn't understand D's letter – that he had never sent any manuscript <u>or</u> letter and that P. had never left Canada. He said that he had met P. ^(in a drugstore)^ while he (H) was on leave in N.Y.C. and they had gotten talking. When P. said he was going to Can. to enlist H asked him to look him up. Our good P. did that all right and stayed a week at H's house in Ottawa before he enlisted and still visits there two or three times a week. H. says his house is right near P's barracks. We have had a couple more letters back and forth with H. (incidentally [h]is signature in no way resembles the writing of 'H' who wrote first) but nothing new has turned up except it is almost certain P. never left Can.

When that letter appeared I felt the time had come to look up some of P's illustrious antecedents. I spent a long afternoon in the Public Library.[5] First I looked through several editions of Br. Who's Who for Dr. Sir John P. No such

---

1   Chef Clarence Huston at the Castle Warden.

2   *Alors* is French for "So."

3   *Fleuri et romantique*: French for "flowery and romantic," a reference to the Art Nouveau movement that was popular from approximately 1890 to 1910, characterized by its natural, flowerlike forms.

4   Charles Scribner III. R. Harrison: Not identified.

5   New York Public Library.

P.—nor any Dr P. who conformed in any way to P's data. Then I looked in the London Telephone Book. None again. Nor any Dr. P who lived on Barclay Sq. I picked up a 1937 book as P said they had lived there for some time tried '38 too. I also looked in the London directory of [Peerage and Sovereign] but no Dr Sir J.P. no Dr. J.P. Then I thought I'd have a look for P's maternal grandmother the one with the Mary Stuart title Duchess of Carlisle.[1] If there was such a title, word hadn't got round to Burke's Peerage.[2] I looked back as far as '36 though she must have been alive (?) during or just before the war as P. described her reactions to air raid drill. But I think the title was impossible anyway as there is an Eng. title earl of Carlisle and there couldn't be a Duchy & an Earldom in the same name. As to his paternal great aunt Lady Argyll – we had many an anecdote about her both in and out of court. She was at one time lady in waiting to Victoria according to P.[3] Well the former D. of A. was rather <closely> close to V. She was one of her daughters![4] But she died a <u>long</u> time ago. The Duke's 3rd wife was a secretary to the Queen but she died in '24,[5] so she hardly fits into the picture either.

About a week later when P. should still have been away I should think Daddy received another manuscript from him, a Scottish fairy story—very nice too, just a bit overwritten in spots. There was no letter with it, only a short effusive note on the excellence of Daddy, his liquor and his hospitality.

We were all in a great dither over the thing. Muddy took it very hard [and] refused to believe that P. could deceive or that she could <u>be</u> deceived. I was intrigued with the thing and overcome with curiosity. So was Granny[6] who said "Oh, wouldn't it be wonderful if the Scribners had lots of money! We could hire a private detective and find out all about him!" She also thinks you should write a story about him. I must say I also heaved many a sigh of relief that I had not fallen [for] any of his lies or advances. I thought at first that the whole affair was quite harmless. After all, even though he had gotten money out of us the book was good. (Though perhaps already written & published) And P's elaborate stories had not actually hurt anyone. But

---

1   Mary Stuart (1547–1587), also known as "Queen of Scots," executed by her cousin Elizabeth I (1533–1603), Queen of England, for allegedly plotting against her.

2   Burke's Peerage.

3   Victoria (1819–1901), Queen of the United Kingdom, Great Britain, and Ireland from 1837 and also Empress of India from 1876.

4   JSB confuses Lady Elizabeth Leveson-Gower (1824–1878), first wife of George Campbell, 8th Duke of Argyll (1823–1900), with their son John Campbell, 9th Duke of Argyll (1845–1914), who married Victoria's daughter Louise (1848–1939) in 1871.

5   George Campbell's third marriage, on 30 July 1895, was to Ina Erskine (d. 1925), who was private secretary to Victoria when she was married to Campbell.

6   Louise Flagg Scribner.

the more I imagined how I would feel if I had fallen in love with him and perhaps even become engaged to him! The more I felt that his actions were not exactly honorable. And speaking of horror, I don't think I told you but at one point in our heated affair he asked me to go to Canada when he got there and spend a weekend with him. Doubtless my refusal was what made him decide I was cool and spiritual – and not the type for a "soldier of fortune" like himself. — And we thought there was more poetry than truth in that phrase!!

I had a long letter from him mailed the 23rd of October starting off with a poetic description of the clouds <about> above which the plane flew into and the soft Scottish rain etc. etc. Not a word about the niece who was to be brought to the security of the U.S., but a list of the musical activities that had taken place in Ottawa while he was away! (By the way, I have a feeling much could be learnt from this Mrs. Patterson who lives in Richmond – if she exists. Haven't you a friend there who could nose around some). Otherwise the letter was very nice and typical Perry. He said he was coming down soon to see us before he returned to Eng. for good. I hope to God he does as he has my typewriter – irreplaceable now – and if he doesn't I shall die with curiosity.

There are only two proved points in his story. He must have been in or around the hospital as he used the stationary [sic] and got letters from you there. He definitely <u>can</u> do Chinese dances, I saw him, and they must have established considerable study whether they are authentic or not.

I wrote him gossip about my trip etc. and said I hoped he was coming as we were all anxious to see him again, which certainly ain't no lie. As far as I know Harrison hasn't said anything to P. about the forged letter etc. Of course if he has we'll never see our fair P again, but if not I shouldn't be surprised if he appeared. Even if he does come perhaps we shall never get the truth, but I am certainly going to sit him down with a glass of whisky and have a try.

Boy how we Scribners bit! You <had> ^have^ a good excuse. That beautiful soul that shone forth in his letters after all was only a beautiful imagination but you didn't know at first that P. was a writer. I'm not saying that <u>all</u> writers' beautiful souls are just beautiful imaginations. I'm just saying that anyone with a beautiful imagination can have a beautiful soul at least on paper. And so the matter stands at the moment. I'll let you know if anything new turns up. Let me know if he writes you anything pertinent. He's mentioned that you told him off for calling us c. and s.[1]

---

1   C: Charles; S: Scribner.

In this momentous period Perry was not the only interest. In fact something has happened which drove P. quite out of my mind and has kept him in the background since. Cath,[1] the pillar on whom I lean in my dark moments, got engaged and married in two days. It came as a great shock to everyone including Cath. Not there was anything 'shotgunning' about it.[2] Her husband instead of leaving for overseas as he expected was transferred to another "Fort" and given seven days leave. This obviously was Providence in Opportunity knocking at the door or something,[3] and it wouldn't do to pass it up, so they didn't.

I had been preparing myself all summer for the eventuality, but not too intensely because I never thought it would occur till "after the duration," and I must confess I spent a couple of the blackest nights and days I can remember. Not that I'm not immensely pleased with her husband and happy that she is happy. But when one's friends marry much of the closeness of the friendship is lost. <Of course> And for the one who is not married it is a lovely feeling. You got married quite young so perhaps you didn't go through the business. It amounts almost [to] the end of a certain phase of my life, perhaps the end of growing up. Cath was the best of my friends who was 'single' and by far the dearest of any of them. My life in Far Hills has an alarmingly different aspect. So you see it made one of those awful emotional paradoxes. The more I loved Cath the more happy I was at her happiness, and the more miserable at my loss.

Fortunately these inevitable finishes don't ache for long. They are reasonable to the mind and natural to the heart. I feel now only the way I feel when I see places that were wonderful to me as a child and whose wonder I want to feel again but cannot. It is sad in a way, but railing against it only takes one farther from it – and you get old lots faster.

I have more dirt about Joe,[4] but I haven't a minute to write it down – must meet Daddy. Will send another installment soon.

Much love

Julia

---

1   Catherine Mellick Gilpin. Husband: McGhee Tyson Gilpin (1919–2000).

2   Allusion to a shotgun marriage, where pregnancy leads angry parents to force the woman and the man to marry.

3   An allusion to Christ (Providence) knocking at the door in Revelation 3:20.

4   Perhaps Joseph Hessel of the U.S. Forest Service.

. . .

MKR to JSB, 11 November 1942. TLS, 4 pp. PM: SAINT
AUGUSTINE | NOV 13 | 1 PM | 1942 | FLA. AD: Miss Julia Scribner |
Far Hills | New Jersey. Enclosure: 2 magazine clippings.

Nov. 11, 1942

Dearest Julia:

Time out, on manuscript paper,[1] in the midst of the typing of the goddamn
forest article,[2] to answer your revelation just received. IT IS UNCANNY---
out of a clear sky <u>yesterday</u> I said to Norton that there was something so darn
queer about Perry Patterson that I was having fits. I said that I questioned
whether he had ever left Canada. And Norton said, "Well, just thank Heaven
Julia didn't fall for him" Then comes your letter.

As you say, the one thing we know is that he received letters from me at St.
Anne's Military Hospital, Quebec.[3] He could even just have been an orderly
there. It isn't reasonable that he could have walked and ridden horseback
as he did with you, with the type of injury he described, and after so recent
an operation. He could have been a psychopathic case at the hospital---but
why at a military hospital, then? Does your father[4] have a contact with some
bookstore in Quebec, of whom he could ask (for purposes of protecting
himself if Perry has simply passed on an already-published thing) that they
send someone in person to the hospital to inquire of Perry's case and history
there? If I wrote, or even if your father wrote, the hospital would be likely to
be noncommittal.

It is queer that, being a psychopathic liar, and being broke, he didn't try
to wrangle money out of me, after I poured my heart out in sympathy. It is
all utterly weird. If he gets an inkling of what you have found out, through
Harrison[5]---and why would he go on using the Harrison address for his mail
(I had a letter from him about ten days ago, using that address) if he is in
barracks nearby? The barracks address would carry out his "theme" much
better.---if he finds out, or if he shows up in New York again and you try to
pin him down, he will of course just fade from the picture. But don't let's rest

1   That is, MKR is typing on the paper she uses to submit manuscripts.
2   "Trees for Tomorrow."
3   Ste. Anne's Hospital, founded in 1917 to treat World War I troops, is in Sainte-Anne-de-Bel-
levue, Quebec, Canada.
4   Charles Scribner III.
5   R. Harrison, through whom Charles Scribner III communicated about Patterson's alleged manuscript. See JSB's letter dated [7? November 1942], 147, n. 4.

until we track down as much as we can. The Military Hospital seems the best bet for finding out something about him. What an imagination! Norton asked why anybody with an imagination like that would NEED to plagiarize or pass on somebody else's manuscript or book, and I said that it is one thing to let the imagination run riot in a lot of very personal lies, and quite another to sit down and do an OBJECTIVE piece of creative writing. It is completely intriguing. And again, thank God you didn't fall for him, for he evidently has all the charm and brains in the world. I have known liars, but never in my life such a superb or complex one. And to think I wished him off on you![1] With his beautiful soul! Tell Charlie to charge off whatever he paid him against my account! But my God, I never expected him to be a charmer who would take EVERYBODY into camp.

Joe Hessel[2] sent me a hand-made silver pin, and I thought he probably sent you a diamond brooch---. The shape I was in that night, it's God's mercy I am fat and forty and just didn't appeal to him. But something told me to keep him away from you. Write me all the dirt.

I told you the truth about the beautiful quince jelly. Some of the quinces had gone, some were going, but if the whole bushel had been perfect, I didn't have enough sugar for more than the 21 glasses. I gave away about a half-peck to Aunt Ida's landlady,[3] who preserved them, had to throw away perhaps a fourth that were decayed, and just had to let about the last peck ruin, for lack of sugar. But jelly does not keep more than a year in this climate, and 21 glasses make a glass about every other week, so I have a year's supply. Just come down this winter and eat some for yourself. Started to drop you a postcard this week while working at the cottage on the article, to mention again how grand the glasses look on the shelves, and to speak of the loveliest bouquet I had in the blue and mauve bowl.[4] I had small chrysanthemums of the most exquisite pinking mauve in it.

Now my dear, I am depressed about your feeling about this disappearing-into-the-void-of-marriage business. You may or may not have known it, but one reason you were not too happy here and wanted to get back, was that you felt the old closeness between us was broken. If you had stayed longer and been at the cottage or the Creek, you would have gotten over that. And as you grow older, you will learn what is perhaps the greatest tragedy of human life: that we are each of us unutterably lonely, and no friendship, no passion, no marriage, ever joins any one of us so completely

---

1 A clear indication that MKR was looking for a husband for JSB.
2 Joseph Hessel of the U.S. Forest Service. See JSB's letter dated [13?] October 1942, 142, n. 7.
3 Elizabeth White.
4 The bowl JSB gave MKR as a wedding present.

and permanently to another human being that we can avoid that loneliness. The stupid never feel it to begin with. Those of us cursed with the search for perfection do---and we never find it. I don't say that the perfect union of one sort or another is impossible. I still believe in it! Presumably, the Brownings had it---yet I wonder.[1] One finds it temporarily in a passionate attachment. I myself have hoped that I would find it in a quieter sort of thing with Norton, if I was patient enough. At the moment, the horror of his life makes it impossible.[2] Yet I feel that if I stick it out, there may be a sort of twilight peace, for Heaven knows he is the loveliest human being I have ever known. I have had much more than my share of love in my life, more men who loved me than is really decent, and looking back on them it seems that if I could combine this from one, that from another, this from one way of life, something else from another way of life, I would have that completion that all of us who are sensitive long for. I have never found it. I am forced to the conclusion that we must accept the loneliness and learn to take from life what is good and right for each of us, and to be very grateful for moments of completion, and for anything that approximates it. If and when you marry, you will find that it does not cut you off from the need of other kinds of friends. And when Cath[3] or I or any others of your friends marry, they still need you, if they have loved and needed you to begin with. Fortunately, we can love many very different sorts of people, and need them in many very different ways. I wish I could tell you that marriage answers all needs, or that a great love between a man and a woman, regardless of marriage, and I have known that, too, answers all needs, but as far as I know, it does not. Some rather stupid women, and some rather dull men, seem to find all they need in marriage, but they are people who do not ask very much.

I have been sorry to see that you are a perfectionist, as I am. It makes life much more difficult and complicated. But without exactly compromising, it is possible to find and accept much that is satisfying. The ultimate satisfaction seems to be in the realm of poetry, with the exception of brief moments. When I am much older than now, I expect to add up those brief moments and find them a formidable total.

I myself need you as a dear friend as much now as I ever did, and after

---

1   Robert Browning (1812–1889) and Elizabeth Barrett Browning (1806–1861), Victorian poets, whose love affair has become legend. MKR would have known well their celebrated declarations of love for each other, perhaps most beautifully articulated in EBB's *Sonnets from the Portuguese* (1850).

2   MKR is referring to the work necessary to get the hotel on stable footing.

3   Catherine Mellick Gilpin.

Cath gets over the first flush of enthusiasm for her new life, she will, unless she is one of the stupid women (and I can't imagine a close friend of yours being that) need you as much as ever. And for yourself, you must take friendship and love and passion and marriage as they come---without expecting either Nirvana or Olympus out of any of it.[1]

I don't know anyone else to whom I could write this way. I make a great front of being a woman who "has everything". But in my way, having had everything, I am as lonely as you are.

Well, I didn't start out to write like this, but just to say that though I am appalled at the P.P.[2] revelations, I am not surprised. And do see what Charlie thinks about contacting the hospital to find out something definite.

Love,

Marjorie

The enclosed, in a magazine Norton takes called "Hotel Management", was what set me off about Perry, for I said to Norton that with the exception of the height, it sounded like Perry![3]

Transcription of the enclosed clippings from *Hotel Management* article "Wartime Tricks of Hotel Crooks"

Not so long ago a warrant was issued by the Putnam County, Tennessee, police for the arrest of a hotel sneak thief known as Eddie Dutch (pronounced "Dootch"), alias Johnnie Vanderbilt. He is about 21 years old; 5 feet, 8 inches tall; has mouse colored hair, neither blond nor brunette; dark eyes; and sometimes wears glasses. He allegedly stole $35.50 worth of clothing from a guest in a hotel in Monterey, Tennessee, skipping his hotel bill besides.

The engaging Eddie is an exceedingly fast talker. His stories vary in detail, but generally he represents himself as a Canadian flyer who is on his way to Florida for further training with the U.S. forces. He does not, however, wear a uniform. He has a Southern rather than a Canadian accent, and one of his favorite articles of apparel is a brown sweater with a white

---

1 Nirvana, Sanskrit, to indicate the highest form of existence, that beyond the bodily state. Olympus, the home of Zeus, the most powerful god in Greek mythology.

2 Perry Patterson.

3 For the enclosed magazine clippings, originally published in *Hotel Management* (New York: Ahrens, 1942–1945), see Figure 3, 314.

"B" on the chest. Eddie likes girls and asks to be introduced to them. He also talks to two pals of Italian descent who are planning to meet him in a Buick coupe, but who never quite seem to catch up with him. Nervous and fidgety, he will talk your arm off if given half a chance. When confronted with the guest whose clothes he had allegedly stolen, Eddie's powers of persuasion were such that he not only talked the guest out of preferring charges, but almost succeeded in selling him the nebulous Buick coupe for $300! Moral: *Beware of men in mufti*[1] *who represent themselves as being in the armed forces*. Many swindlers of this kind are on the road today. In addition, a number of genuine soldiers and sailors are hiding out, A.W.O.L., and probably broke, in hotels.

★ Morals ★

- Photograph and fingerprint new employees.
- Never let a new, uninvestigated employee get access to your check book.
- Before you invest in new help, investigate.
- Beware of guests who let the boys handle some, but not all, of their luggage.
- Don't let convincing conversationalists talk you into letting them off.
- Don't let fast talkers rush you into cashing company checks.
- Beware of men in mufti who represent themselves as being in the armed forces.
- Watch for soldiers and sailors who hide out, A.W.O.L., and probably broke, in hotels.

---

1   Mufti: civvies—that is, civilian clothes worn by military personnel.

War and Peace

1943–1944

Your rage about the sins of man and the sins against man is a good and

righteous rage. Use that, too. It is part of the best of you.

[MKR to JSB, 26 March 1943]

At the moment I'm enjoying a small breakdown. Unfortunately I can only

devote half a day to it as I have to go out

for dinner, the opera, and dancing with a R.N. Lieut.

[JSB to MKR, late May 1943]

JSB to MKR, [Early January 1943]. ALS, 4 pp. Envelope is missing.

[Early January 1943][1]

Dearest Marjorie –

You know after I sent off my last letter to you I felt there was something generous about it. I was stricken with 'Malaise,' and then I realized that I had indulged in one of our worst family faults – extoling the beauty, worth, uniqueness, hard to getness, nothing like-itness of our gifts. Beware of the Scribners bearing gifts.[2] Christmas at our house is really something when the whole family arrives and we start opening presents. Muddy feels Aunt Louise[3] isn't raving enough <of> over her Chinese bowl (and who can rave <u>more</u> than Aunt L.?) so she snatches it from her, and holding it to the light <u>manages</u> to rave harder than Aunt L. Granny[4] explains to me in words that would make even the manufacturer blush the supremacy of the fountain pen she has bought – the pen she [????] herself is marvelous but this is [????] that. And Aunt L. disclaims or [????][5] virtues of a pair of gloves — better, more useful by far than anything I've ever heard. I will say that Aunt L's gentleness of nature always prompts her to say that I must take them back if there is something I need more, whereas Muddy would see you dead first — or often — if the word 'exchange' were ever mentioned. And I am right in there butting. I'm always annoyed when I'm on the receiving end—I always feel like saying "if it's so damned good, and you took so goddamned much trouble why don't you keep it" — but I always am just as bad. I hereby apologize for taking out on you something which should be kept strictly a secret family vice. Apology is good for the soul and soothing to the conscience—or are they the same thing? I hereby declare that there is nothing extraordinary about what I sent you, <u>nor</u> did I take any spectacular trouble about it, <u>and</u> not only do you not have to appreciate it, but I think it would be quite a refreshing and relieving gesture if you flung it out <one> ^or^ gave it to the next person you have to give a wedding present to. That

---

1 Written in a second hand at the top of p. 1: During War. JSB's claim that her Christmas gift was "nothing extraordinary" anticipates MKR's statement of gratitude in the next letter, 14 January 1953.

2 An oblique reference to the adage "Beware of Greeks bearing gifts," referring to the Trojan horse that helped the Greeks to defeat Troy in Homer's *The Iliad*.

3 Louise Scribner Schieffelin (1883–1963), JSB's paternal aunt.

4 Louise Flagg Scribner, JSB's paternal grandmother.

5 The ink and even the lines of the notebook paper in this rectangular section of the letter have been erased.

would be the most useful solution. If I don't control myself, I shall be telling you again what a unique gift it is — not only do you have the pleasure of receiving it, but you have the stupendous pleasure of not having to buy <u>one</u> wedding present!

I'm having a horrible time. I go out every night and I'm exhausted and rushed every day and don't have time even to read a light novel. Also my conscience is troubling me because I am not yet installed in the volunteer job I intend to take at the OPA.[1] But things are so thick — in fact (<that> things being mostly the Navy, British & American) that I am usually within having a headache or quivering on the brink of one. I <u>long</u> for a few days at the Public Library[2] – or a quiet morning strolling through a few art galleries on 57th St and lounging around in the lobby of Carnegie or Town Hall looking at the programs of the various recitalists.[3] My ideal life is outrageously lazy, contemplative and dillettantish [*sic*] — in other words quite in keeping with my character and potentialities. Quite sensible of one to <u>want</u> to do what I am capable of doing. But, of course, I'll never achieve even that mode[st] goal — my conscience will land me with petty responsibilities, or I'll get married — or I'll have to work for my living. Sometimes I get so exhausted with the endless and hopeless injustices in this and the horrors of our rampant capitalism, the talk of whose leaders it is my unhappy lot to have to hear, choking down argument, I think that after the war I would like to go to some nice socialist country like New Zealand or Sweden – not expecting Utopia, but just comparative peace. But in a socialist country I'd have to work for my living and then where would my contemplative leisure be? Working for one's daily bread is something everyone can do if they have to, but some only then. But this was only going to be a short apologetic note and now look where I am – and it's getting interesting too – to me, that is. I'm almost to my favorite subject – the struggle between my social and private conscience and my character – man and mouse and the mouse always wins – I'll stop at once.

Much love,

Julia

I think I'll play a little of that Schubert to lift me out of my favorite subject into a loftier objectivity. Schubert's the boy for greatness <and> ^in^ sim-

---

1   The Office of Price Administration (OPA) was the government agency that controlled the pricing of goods and rationing during World War II.

2   New York Public Library.

3   Carnegie Hall, a concert space in Manhattan located on Seventh Avenue between West 56th and 57th streets, opened in 1891. The Town Hall, a performance space in Manhattan on West 43rd street, opened in January 1921.

plicity, Mozart for greatness in elegance, Beethoven for greatness in emotion and struggle.[1] Wow – don't <u>ever</u> remind me of those! In fact, don't remember them. This is all the[2] exuberance of being alone for an evening. The family has gone to NYC and I have stayed just for the joy of have the house to myself – or rather to have <u>myself</u> to myself.

. . .

MKR to JSB, 14 January 1943. TLS, 5 pp. PM: SAINT AUGUSTINE | JAN 14 | 3³⁰ PM | 1943 | FLA. AD: Miss Julia Scribner | c/o Charles Scribner | 597 Fifth Avenue | New York City. LH: Mrs. Norton Baskin | Castle Warden Hotel | Saint Augustine, Florida.

Jan. 14, 1943

Dearest Julia:

An absolutely superlative, superb, breath-taking and obviously rare old print, plainly discovered for my delight after untold agonies of search and turmoil and expense, reached me two days ago in a wooden crate, which W.D.[3] unboxed downstairs for me. He found no card in it, and the address was something Lexington Avenue---but I knew at once, even before your letter arrived today,[4] that so extraordinary, magnificent and munificent a gift could have come only from you.

Now if you will file the above under "Satisfaction Received" I'll tell you what I really think of it.

It is one of the most fascinating things I have ever possessed, and I am itching all over until I can corral a real Florida historian to talk it over with me. I pore over every catalogue from the Old Print Shop,[5] watching for Floridiana, and have now and then seen minor items listed, at terrific prices, have longed for them a moment, then decided that after all they were unexceptional. I did pick up two old St. Augustine prints, very small and not awfully old, 1800 or something like that.

---

1   Franz Schubert (1797–1828), Austrian composer of the late Classical and early Romantic periods; Wolfgang Amadeus Mozart (1756–1791), Austrian composer of the Classical period; and Ludwig van Beethoven (1770–1827), German pianist and composer of the late Classical and early Romantic periods.

2   JSB inserts the remainder of her postscript horizontally in the left margin.

3   W. D. Williams, who worked as a porter at the Castle Warden Hotel.

4   JSB's letter dated [early January 1943].

5   Old Print Shop, the renowned business on Lexington Avenue in New York, New York.

The Spanish period in Florida is naturally the least rewarding in this type of material, and any genuine Spanish items are the most highly prized by historians and collectors. Both the Florida and the St. Augustine Historical Societies will be green with envy when they see this. I shall arrange to "leave" it to one of them.

The matter I can't wait to go into with a historian, is whether the print is more or less factual, or one of those delightful Middle Age myths, done from report and imagination. You remember the maps before Columbus' time, showing the world ending a little east of Egypt, and populated with sea serpents and hell fire. 1671, the date of the engraving, is <u>awfully</u> old for Florida material, as there was such a long gap between the first actual landings in the 1500's, and actual colonization.

This engraving seems definitely to pre-date the building of the old fort in St. Augustine.[1] Neither watch tower in it is anything like the tower on the present fort. Also, in the history of the present fort, there was never a community of houses inside the fort. I have a dim memory of a very early stockade at St. Augustine, inside of which the residents had houses. The stockade was much earlier than Hernandez,[2] the founder of St. Augustine proper, if I remember correctly, and may have been Jean Ribault's stockade. Jean Ribault[3] was the leader of the French whom ^the Catholic^[4] Hernandez massacred, somewhere near my cottage, "not as to Frenchmen, but as to Huguenots".[5]

The stockade and town in the engraving could not possibly be on the site of St. Augustine itself, for there is no water west of the fort, and the distance

---

1   Castillo de San Marcos is the oldest and only seventeenth-century fort in America. It was built and rebuilt between 1672 and 1695, owing to the constant raids carried out by various Colonial Powers. It is on the north end of St. Augustine and was originally the gateway to the city. The Castle Warden Hotel, sold by NSB in 1946 and since December 1950 a Ripley's Believe It or Not! Museum, is located several blocks to the north of the Castillo.

2   MKR is likely confusing Joseph Marion Hernández (1788–1857), influential plantation and slave owner and first delegate to the House of Representatives from Florida, with the Spanish Admiral, Pedro Menéndez de Avilés (1519–1574), who is credited with founding St. Augustine on 8 September 1565.

3   Jean Ribault (1520–1565), French naval captain and explorer, helped to explore and then to colonize much of the area in the southeast from St. Augustine, Florida, to Port Royal Sound, South Carolina. In the name of the French Huguenots he reinforced Fort Caroline on the St. Johns River (Jacksonville), founded Charlesfort near Port Royal Sound in South Carolina (Parris Island), but he and his troop were then surprised and massacred by the Spanish led by Pedro Menéndez de Avilés south of St. Augustine, at a place subsequently known as Mantanzas [Spanish for "slaughter"] Inlet, hence MKR's claim that the massacre took place near her cottage at Crescent Beach.

4   Inserted above the line in MKR's hand.

5   Menéndez de Avilés led the massacre.

between the cortege of the Spanish lady in the foreground and the stockade is apparently only a stone's throw, while the actual distance between the north tip of Anastasia Island and the old fort it considerable. I am wondering if there was ever a stockade on Anastasia Island itself, and in the engraving the observer is looking across the bay <u>from</u> St. Augustine. None of this can be resolved until I catch a historian.

If the engraving is fanciful, it is all the more valuable. The Spaniards did not bring their ladies to Florida, as indicated in the engraving, but Norton suggested that the elegant lady might be an Indian princess, with whom the Spaniards "took up" whenever feasible. I shall have to check further, but the negroes in the picture would appear to be an engaging anachronism. Also, what appear to be negroes may really be Indians. The Spaniards under the very early de Soto[1] enslaved the Indians. De Soto had an Indian princess for a temporary lady friend, then betrayed her, in the name of God. I'll give you a report later.

Anyway, I am simply enchanted to have the engraving, an extremely valuable one, whether fact or fiction.

You will never be happy until you leave capitalism and its haunts behind you and strike out on your own. I would have <o>urged, coerced and <bBillied> ^bullied^ you into it long ago if it were not for those damn headaches that lay you so low. I am torn between thinking that they come from some mechanical pressure from the various physical accidents you have had, and thinking that they come from an emotional and frustrating pressure. I long so often to be a combination of God and a good doctor. But whatever the state of your health, happiness for you can come through only one of two channels---making your own living and doing some sort of work that you are equipped to do---or a happy marriage, for in marriage any woman who is not tormented by being definitely a creative worker, can find content and a sense of accomplishment. This is especially true if the man is doing something that the woman considers at least worthwhile. But you are too sensitive a person to be living the life you are living. It is probable that in your case, as it was in mine, only your mother's death[2] will liberate you, and that is a price one would not wish to pay for liberation. I

---

1   Hernando de Soto (1500–1542), Spanish explorer and conquistador, is said to have first landed near present-day Daytona Beach. After plundering the area and enslaving the indigenous people, he moved west, finally dying on the banks of the Mississippi River.

2   Vera Scribner. MKR's relationship with her own mother was banal at times and tumultuous at times. MKR much preferred to be at her father's farm in Maryland than in her mother's kitchen in Washington, DC. In 1928, and now married to Charles A. Rawlings Jr., MKR reviewed and ruminated, seldom sparing hyperbole, on her relationship with her mother in a lengthy manuscript en-

hope and pray that you may find some compromise. Do make a supreme effort to stop the silly things you are doing and get into something that you like and understand and in which you can be useful. And don't feel that your training and qualifications are limited. Limitations are only a challenge. With your magnificent mind and sensitivity, you can find or make a place for yourself. How I wish you were my daughter! You are exactly what I should choose if I could have a daughter, and I would be the right sort of mother for one like you.

I imagine that Charlie[1] (your esteemed father) had mentioned to you that I am being sued for libel---$100,000---which I don't have---by "my friend Zelma" of chapter 5 in "Cross Creek". I was really amazed, as she knows perfectly well that I had no unkind motive in writing about her. My lawyer[2] thinks the case will be great fun and that she doesn't have a chance.

Scribner pere may also have mentioned that I am coming to New York for an operation in early February.[3] The operation is not at all dangerous, involving only the removal of several small tumors in the uterus, but it seems that three weeks in the hospital are required and the convalescence is slow. I am being deliberately rather pitiful about it, to lure Norton to take me up so that we may have a few days in New York seeing shows etc. Then I plan to come back alone by plane, as much more comfortable in a wobbly state. I shall be at Medical Center, and hope subway connections are not too bad between there and your east side New York address, so that you may come up to the hospital now and then and hold my hand.

With love,

I am sending this c/o Monsieur Scribner, as I don't know whether you're in town or country---[4]

---

titled *Blood of My Blood*, published posthumously (Gainesville: University Press of Florida, 2002), edited by Anne Blythe Meriwether.

1   Charles Scribner III.

2   Philip S. May Sr.

3   MKR was in Harkness Pavilion for nearly a month. She arrived by plane on or about 16 February and was dismissed from the hospital on or about 13 March. She went there to be treated for her acute diverticulosis, but the doctors quickly discovered that she had abscesses on her uterus. Dr. Virgil Damon performed a hysterectomy. The recovery, which included psychiatric counseling, was lengthy and exacerbated by her persistent longing for NSB, whose owner/management duties at the Castle Warden Hotel made it impossible for him to leave Florida for any length of time. JSB was her companion of choice during the ordeal. MKR came home by train on 17 March.

4   The postscript is in MKR's hand. That is, New York City or Far Hills, New Jersey.

MKR to JSB, 30 January 1943. TLS, 2 pp. PM: Saint Augustine | JAN
30 | 9 PM | 1943 | FLA. PM2: New York, N.Y. | FEB 1 | 9 - PM | 1943.
AD: Miss Julia Schribner [*sic*] | c/o <Charles Schribner> | <597 Fifth
Avenue> | <New York City>. [Written in second hand and underlined
in blue pencil] Opened by | Mistake. [To the right in a second hand
in pencil] 39 East 79th St | N.Y.C. LH: MARJORIE KINNAN RAWLINGS |
HAWTHORNE, FLORIDA.[1]

January 30, 1943

Dearest Julia:

The artist of the Florida scene was Montanus.[2] My lawyer, Phil May, a
pretty good historian, saw the print and immediately exclaimed, "This is
something almost priceless." He thinks it is probably reasonably accurate, as
there was a stockade and settlement a hundred years or so before the present
Fort.[3] Most of such things were done by artists who worked only from the reports of the old explorers, and so they were likely to add fanciful details. Phil
does think it is likely that there were negro slaves here that early. Anyway he
assures me the print is exceptionally choice and valuable.

I really don't see why you should feel called upon to traipse up and
down the wilderness, disillusioning people about me.[4] That follows soon
enough. Do give me a break and allow a new friend to become attached to
me before the disillusionment settles in. Then, as with you, it is too late for
serious damage. Also, I am not a slave to the stomach. If you would bother
to read my cook book you would come across the item where I mention
the frugal meals that I eat when I am alone. The sherried kidneys I give you
for breakfast are for your pleasure, you ungrateful little wretch, not mine.

---

1 MKR mailed this letter from St. Augustine on 30 January (PM 1) to the wrong address. It was
opened at Scribners (blue pencil), then readdressed (pencil), then rerouted on 1 February (PM 2).
2 Arnoldus Montanus (c. 1625–1683), Dutch author and cartographer. MKR's print is from his *De
Nieuwe en Onbekende Weereld: of Beschryving van America en't Zuid-Land* [*The New and Unknown
World, and the Southland*] (1671). Pbd. in Amsterdam by Jacob van Meurs (1619/20–c.1680), Dutch
engraver and publisher. In the same year, the work was also trans. and pbd. in England by John
Ogilby (1600–1676), Scottish translator and cartographer, as *America, Being an Accurate Description of the New World*.
3 Although the depiction of the fort in St. Augustine, Florida, is somewhat accurate, the mountains in the background of the print are not.
4 The "new friend" alluded to has not been identified.

Expect to be along the end of this coming week. Will let you know. Norton may come up with me.

Lots of love,

Marjorie

Send me your apartment address, so I can send tangerines.[1]

. . .

JSB to MKR, [2 or 3? February 1943]. ALS, 3 pp. PM: envelope is missing.[2]

[2 or 3? February 1943]

My god, Marge, you really must be sore at me! You must be raging. What else could explain the horrible mutilation of my name – not once, but twice –

---

1 MKR inserts this typewritten postscript, underlined in her hand, above the LH on p. 2. JSB's address is 39 East 79th St.

2 The exact date of this letter has been difficult to establish. It is clearly in response to MKR's letter written on 30 January. On the envelope, Scribner is spelled "Schribner" twice. In the letter itself, MKR refers to the mailing of tangerines and to JSB as an "ungrateful little wretch." What revelation precipitated such a slur, if it is one, is not clear. JSB could not have received this letter before 1 February, when it was redirected by the New York post office (see header above). In a letter to her attorney Philip May on 5 February, MKR says that she will be leaving for New York by "train or plane" on "Tuesday or Wednesday" (10 or 11 February, *Selected Letters* 235). She apparently went by plane and was met at the airport by Charles Scribner III and JSB (Silverthorne 218). Based upon her letter to Aunt Ida Tarrant on 12 February, MKR was to be operated on 18 February (see 167, n. 5). Further, we know that NSB came by train to be with her (see 165, n. 5), and then writes to her on 22 February that he was safely home in St. Augustine, but "hated" to have left her. On 24 February, he writes to express his happiness that she is doing so well (unpublished letters, Special Collections, University of Florida Library). Nevertheless, JSB's reference to MKR "being spent" over the operation would seem to indicate that this letter was written after 18 November, which is in contradiction to the emotional and physical facts. For example, the "blizzard" referenced would almost certainly be to the snowstorm that engulfed New York City on 28 January (see 165, n. 7), which is referred to as "last week" when the snow was "kneedeep." And, if the snowstorm reference is correct, when JSB says she had lunch with Edith Pope, then this letter would have to have been written during or after the first week of February, which seems unlikely because of the suggestion that MKR is "spent" as a result of the operation on 18 February. The reference to the "blizzard" could be to a substantial snowstorm of 4 inches on 27 February. But, if this storm is "last week," then this letter was written during the first week of March. Yet JSB's anger here is in contradiction to MKR's letter on 6 March to Aunt Ida saying JSB comes to the hospital every day (unpublished letter, Special Collections, University of Florida Library). Finally, it does not seem reasonable that JSB would write such a sharp letter of retort while at the same time visiting MKR every day in the hospital. Therefore, current evidence suggests that the letter was written sometime before it was received on 1 February, and almost certainly before MKR arrived in New York on 10 or 11 February, when she was met by the Scribners (see 166, n. 4).

Julia Schribner, c/o Chas. Schribner's Sons. Dies irae, dies illae.[1] I can't figure what has set you off so. Whether it is my disillusioning M.O.[2] or my remarks about your prandial[3] preoccupation. Tsk, mere molehills. Nothing so venomous as that dart you aim at me – about letting the friend get attached first and then 'as with me' it is too late for 'serious damage.' Any illusions you had about me were of your own optimistic making – not mine! Also I have read your cookbook and I know all about the frugal meals you eat when you're alone – I've eaten them with you.

I had lunch with Edith today,[4] and was telling her how maligned I was (by you) and she was so soothing – told me you were really very fond of me and you must be spent over your operation[5] – that I suddenly thought maybe it wasn't so light and humorous after all. She was quite like Mr. Alves.[6] If <I> ^you^ really are sore do let me know and I will refrain from irritating you further, but I was looking forward to a nice bout of name calling by mail. I had lunch with Edith last week too. She wanted to go to this certain super French place which she said was terribly crowded. She told me to be there at twelve sharp and she would have already fastened on a table. The soul of Yankee promptness, I arrived there at about 11:50. Edith arrived at 1:30. – And I didn't even have a timetable to read. She had a pretty good excuse though, she'd been to the doctor's. We had a fine time at lunch and bucking the blizzard afterward.[7] We both kept saying how you would have died if you'd been here. The snow was in places kneedeep and everywhere over the top of galoshes. The wind was such that at one point, battling into it with my umbrella a gust pushed me back several feet – me absolutely stiff-legged, with Edith hauling away on my arm trying to keep me on the sidewalk.

On Sunday E. went to see Carson McCullers in Brooklyn.[8] It must have

---

1 Latin: *Dies iraes, dies illae*: "That day is a day of wrath," as in the first line of the Requiem Mass found in the Roman Missal of the Catholic church.

2 Latin: *modus operandi*, method of operation.

3 Prandial (i.e., during lunch), often used humorously.

4 Edith Pope.

5 MKR's operation, a hysterectomy, was to be performed, subject to physician approval, on 18 February at Harkness Pavilion (see MKR's unpublished letter to Aunt Ida Tarrant on 12 February, Special Collections, University of Florida Library). The date of 18 February is consistent with NSB's letter to MKR on 22 February, reporting that he arrived back on the train in Florida on 22 February, with the assurance that he hated to leave her. On 24 February, NSB writes that he is glad to know she is doing so well. On 13 March arrangements are made for MKR's return to Florida (unpublished correspondence, Special Collections, University of Florida Library).

6 Carl Alves, see JSB's letter dated [24 February 1941].

7 NYC had a major snowstorm of 7 inches on 28 January.

8 Carson McCullers [born: Lula Carson Smith] (1917–1967), American novelist and writer, married Reeves McCullers in 1937, divorced him in 1940, and moved into a brownstone at 7 Middagh

been a horrible experience, and loses nothing, of course, in Edith's telling. It seems she lives in the depths of dirt and degeneracy – lesbians and pansies on every hand and an awful air of 20's Dadaism.[1] Erika Mann & Auden and Richard Wright & his white wife (I think they are rather less depraved than the rest) Harpers ^Bazaar^ Editors, a lesbian novelist from Ga. writing a novel about <lepracy> leprosy etc.[2] C MacC. read some of her "work in progress" & E said it was awful much worse than Reflections –.[3] I'll tell you more fascinating & repelling details when you arrive.[4]

I had just a minute today to dash into the P.L.[5] and I <says> ^saw^ that they have a lot of cards on Montanus in the file – he wrote books about several far off places – so I'm sure I can pin down your print.[6]

It seems awful I look forward so much to seeing you and counting the days till you arrive when it will not be such an unmixed pleasure for you. You must make Norton come up. It will be lovely to see you – even if you are lying pale and listless on an adjustable bed. But you must leave a few days for New York City before you dash up to the Bronx.

I hesitate to give you my address – the tangerines may be lightly brushed over with cyanide – well I shall fling myself on the remnants of your friendship – 39 East <79> ^79^.

St., Brooklyn, owned by George Davis (1906–1957), formerly a fiction editor for *Harper's Bazaar* (1936–1941) and at this time an editor at *Mademoiselle*. By 1943, McCullers was already made famous by *The Heart Is a Lonely Hunter* (Boston: Houghton, Mifflin, 1940). "The Ballad of the Sad Café," likely the subject of this reading, was published in *Harper's Bazaar* 77 (August, 1943): 72–75, 140–61, and created a sensation because of its articulation of female dominance. See also n. 3 below.

1 Dadaism, avant-garde movement that became prominent in 1917 and ended in 1923, although its influence on later movements, such a Surrealism, was profound. Dada aimed at the destruction of aesthetic principle, and in art and poetry moved toward depicting the moment through absurdist rhetoric and dissembling form.

2 McCullers and Davis shared "February House" (named by the diarist Anaïs Nin [1903–1977] because she noticed the large number of residents with birthdays in February) with several other writers and artists, including the English-American poet W. H. Auden (1907–1973), the striptease artist Gypsy Rose Lee (1911–1970), and others, including émigrés escaping Nazi Europe such as Thomas Mann (1875–1955) and his family, including his eldest daughter, the novelist Erika Mann (1905–1969). Richard Wright (1908–1960), American novelist and writer who frequented February House, married, on 12 March 1942, Ellen Poplar (b. Frieda Poplowitz; 1912–2004), a Communist organizer in Brooklyn. The "lesbian Georgia novelist" is unidentified.

3 *Reflections in a Golden Eye* (Boston: Houghton Mifflin, 1941), a novel that focuses on repressed sexuality, voyeurism, and murder. McCullers was working on "The Ballad of the Sad Café," which involves a sexual triangle and was published by *Harper's Bazaar* in August 1943. She also was at work on *The Member of the Wedding* (Boston: Houghton Mifflin, 1946), which focused on sexuality and race.

4 JSB's comment "when you arrive" suggests that this letter was written before MKR's arrival in New York on 10 or 11 February.

5 New York Public Library.

6 Montanus, the artist. See MKR's letter on 30 January 1943.

Much love from

"the ungrateful little wretch".

.   .   .

MKR to JSB, 4? February 1943. ALS, 5 pp. PM: Saint Augustine
| FEB 4 | 6³⁰ PM | 1943 | FLA. AD: Miss Julia Scribner | 39 E 79ᵗʰ |
New York City. [In the left margin of the envelope in MKR's hand]:
Air Mail Special. Stamped in red on the envelope over the address:
Pec[1] Claimed by Office | On First Address. PM: torn away. LH:
MARJORIE KINNAN RAWLINGS | HAWTHORN, FLORIDA.

Thursday [4? February 1943][2]

Dearest Julia:—

The horrible truth must out- I dictated my last letter to you, and never
thought to look at the envelope!!!

My so-called fan mail has been heavy, and I have used a stenographer[3]
about once a month to help me catch up. I had her in to try to finish up
everything before I came north. I never have used her for personal letters
before, but I had so damn much to do to get away –- and have bad flu and
bronchitis, too –- that I thought I'd better have her do a note to you, or it just
might not get done. I dashed from my session with her to the Creek, to meet
my income tax man,[4] as I didn't want to have to torment myself with that
when I came home weak and wobbly.

My apology is not so much for her error, strange as it is, as for doing a
very personal letter through a stenographer, as a matter of fact, I have about
2 dozen letters from friends, unanswered as far back as last June, just because
I wanted to do them personally.

You know I could never be seriously sore with you under any conditions
and was joking about everything.[5]

I'd have been leaving about today if it weren't for the damn bronchitis. I
don't dare go into a colder climate with it, also know a surgeon wouldn't cut

---

1   "Pec," acronym of the Italian *posta elettronica certificata*—that is, Certified Mail.

2   This date is predicated on the assumption that JSB received MKR's letter of 30 January on 1
February, which would then give JSB time to respond and for MKR to write this letter on Thursday,
4 February. If not, then the Thursday of this letter would have to be 11 February. The tentative date
here assumes the first possibility, even though the time line is very tight.

3   Not identified.

4   Cecil Bryant.

5   See MKR's extended comment in letter on 30 January 1943 about being perturbed with JSB.

a darn thing while I had a cough. If I can get over the worst of it, will try to leave Monday if I can get a reservation by train or plane.

Can't take many days for fun before going to the hospital, as I have to hit it between "periods",[1] but would love to take 2 or 3 and would rather hear some good music than anything else. Want to see "Skin of our Teeth" and "Three Sisters."[2]

Will wire when I know plans definitely.

Much love,

Marjorie

Also meant, apropos of disillusionment etc., that <u>you</u> had become fond of <u>ME</u> before it set in, too late for serious damage!

. . .

MKR to JSB, 22 March 1943. ALS, 4 pp. PM: torn away, leaving only: HA[WTHORN] ... FL[A.]. AD: Miss Julia Scribner | 39 East 79ᵗʰ St. | New York City. LH: Marjorie Kinnan Rawlings | Hawthorn, Florida.

March 22 [1943][3]

At the Creek

Dearest Julia:—

Reached St. Augustine safely, Siamese and all, but didn't have quite energy enough to write you. Idella was waiting for me, and drove me here Saturday.[4] Was immediately embroiled in a new war at the Creek, between two rival

---

1   Menstrual cycle.

2   Thornton Wilder (1897–1975), American dramatist and fiction writer, *Skin of Our Teeth* (1942), a dramatic allegory about humankind, was awarded the Pulitzer Prize. Anton Chekov (1860–1904), Russian dramatist and fiction writer, *Three Sisters* (1901), a drama about the dire circumstances of four children of a dead Russian military officer.

3   Written in a second hand on the envelope: Mar 22 / 1943.

4   MKR arrived back by train from New York, but according to this account was in St. Augustine before proceeding on to Cross Creek on Saturday 20 March, being driven there by Idella Parker, hence the Hawthorn PM for this letter. Her Siamese cat, Smoky, and the pointer dog, Moe, must certainly have joined her in St. Augustine. However, this account conflicts with what she writes to NSB on 17 March, in which she describes the horror of the train ride from Jacksonville to Gainesville because of "washed-out" tracks "15 miles north of Gainesville" (*Love Letters* 82–83). According to this account Parker met her in Gainesville and brought her to Cross Creek. Further, on 22 March, the date of this letter to JSB, MKR writes NSB that she "Drove in to see the young grove apparently ruined" by the freeze and then describes in detail the "new war on at the Creek" (*Love*

fishing Czars. One of them came in yesterday when he saw me lying on the day-bed on the porch, to get in his side first.[1]

"Now I don't want to worry you, but---."

My young grove was badly damaged by the freeze. They were late oranges and so unpicked, and they are ruined for anything but juice---canning or pulp.

Norton, to his surprise and some horror at himself, fell in love with the kitten, who adopted him and ignored me. He began calling him "Smoky", and the name has stuck and the kitten answers to it.

Moe did not leave me, except to eat, after I arrived. He and Smoky are only beginning to make tentative overtures. This morning Smoky went so far as to begin to play with Moe's tail. It suddenly dawned on him that he was playing with a bit of TNT and he made a jump for the bed.[2]

I suppose the trip tired me, for I didn't feel very well in St. Augustine. I am feeling infinitely better now. Probably a fishermen's war is just what I need.

Strangely, my flower garden came out of the freeze very well. It would look like a wretched little patch to you, but I have two lovely bouquets of baby's breath, stork and delphinium.

The orange trees are beginning to bloom, but the bloom will be light. Will be here a month.

Loads of love,

Marjorie

. . .

JSB to MKR, [23? March 1943]. ALS, 4 pp. PM: Far Hills [illegible]. AD: Marjorie K. Rawlings | Cross Creek | Hawthorn | Florida. VIA AIR MAIL envelope.

Letters 83) referenced in her letter to JSB (see the next note). Which account is precise has not been determined.

1   The clandestine war was between Tom Glisson (1897–1950) and William "Old Boss" Brice (1861–1945), rivals for the fishing trade at Cross Creek. The declared war was between Brice's son-in-law, the "unpleasant" Hugh Williams, who bought a piece of grove between Glisson and MKR. Glisson believed that Brice through Williams was in cahoots with his "rival as fishing Czar," O. E. Martin, whose interest was in blocking Glisson's access to the Creek. The humor of the situation was not lost on MKR. But still recovering from surgery, she was understandably perturbed by this "most complicated matter" (*Love Letters* 83–84).

2   MKR's description to NSB of the antics of Smoky, the cat, and Moe, the bird dog, are nearly identical. See *Love Letters* 83.

Tues. [23? March 1943][1]

Dear Marjorie –

Probably you won't even recognize me on this paper, but I have been re-formed by the patriotic posters telling me to lighten the Air Mail load.[2]

I'll send this to Cross Creek as I imagine you must be there by now.[3] Basking in the sun under orange blossoms, no doubt. We have blue birds, robins, snow drops etc. but it's been definitely cold this weekend.

I'm in the country[4] still – and will be most all week, I guess. Shirley Morgan[5] came to stay with us and immediately got a high temp. and terrific cold. Muddy has gone to town & left me in charge. I'd welcome a few days in the country alone, but this is a bit different. If I sit down at my desk to read over a few old love letters or contemplate a symphony or a song recital, my conscience bites me and says <u>no</u>, you must go down and sit with her. This is sort of irritating seeing as at the time I am always wanting to do something else. You know my base nature – <u>and,</u> I think if I sit with her I'll undoubtedly get her cold – which is an awful one. If only she would take a nap in the PM so I could play some of my new records.

I've seen Dr. A[6] since you left and I just now talked to him on the phone. He keeps asking me frantically if I haven't heard from you. Do drop one of us a line to calm him down – just "arrived safely near collapse" or something like that. Dr. A and I have gotten nowhere as yet. I'm still telling him my history and as we have quite short sessions, a week apart, this could go on for a month. However, I haven't had a headache since you left (despite some really tough days). This is so extraordinary I am wondering in spite of myself if that worm capsule of Dr. Burbank's[7] could <really>have had something to do with it.

I miss you very much, and I'm haunted by flower shop windows where I'm always seeing just the flowers to bring you. I didn't see nearly as many that were 'just right' while you were here. I kick myself also because there you were lying helplessly[8] in my power and I never got around to talking all

---

1   Written in a second hand at the top of p. 1 below Tues.: [illegible]. See JSB's apologia on 1 April, which seems to reference this letter, making this letter the earlier of the two. Dated by the next letter, in which MKR discusses the terms of the birthday present sent to JSB.

2   This letter, in small hand, is written on watermarked, onion-skin paper.

3   MKR arrived back at Cross Creek on 23 March 1943.

4   Far Hills, New Jersey.

5   Perhaps Eleanor Shirley Morgan (1918–1981).

6   Dr. Atchley.

7   Reference to a remedy developed by Luther Burbank (1849-1926).

8   JSB is referring to MKR's stay at Harkness Pavilion in February–March 1943 (*Love Letters* 72–

the things I had been saving to talk to you, and here am I still stuck with them festering in my brain. But that's just as well, I guess. They'll keep – in fact they'll spread and multiply, I'm afraid. Sometime – after the war, when doing nothing is less bad on the conscience – you must let me come to Cross Creek for a couple of weeks. That sounds now somewhat like my plan to visit Paris with Cath[1] – by the time the war is over I might be married,[2] or, worse yet, working – in any case unable to do <u>what</u> I want, <u>when</u> I want, but it is pleasant to contemplate while it is feasible.

I am very much excited by a book I have now The Writings (in small part) of Péguy.[3] He was a French philosopher & poet, socialist and free thinker turned ardent Catholic, killed in last war. Julian Green's biographical preface should be printed in the Atlantic or some such. It is wonderfully done and tells the story of one of the most interesting men I have ever read about. I'm afraid it won't be widely read otherwise, theological books unless they are written by Harry Emerson Fosdick or Emmett Fox don't get around very far.[4] If it turns out to be as marvelous as I think (I haven't read far beyond the Preface) I'll send it down to you.

Oh, I was about to close without telling you about my birthday present. It seems there was a little misunderstanding somewhere – principally between Mr. Randall & me. One tern[5] was $95, and the other $85. They suggested (in the Rare Book dept.) that I could chalk you up for $25 & pay the rest myself, but I took the idea quite coolly and suddenly lost all desire for the dern terns. I think through your generous thought & noble gesture you are

---

82), at which time JSB visited her almost daily.

1   Catherine Ginna Mellick Gilpin.

2   This is likely a fanciful projection, partly sarcastic, rather than a pending announcement. The actual announcement of JSB's engagement to Thomas Bigham was in the *New York Times* (6 March 1945), Sect. S: 26. They were married on 24 May 1945 (*New York Times* [25 May 1945]: 13). See Figure 6, 316. MKR was not in attendance, most likely because of her implicit disapproval of Bigham and because of her strained relationship with Vera Scribner, whom MKR referred to as "the bitch" in a letter to JSB on 5 March (*Love Letters* 78).

3   Charles Péguy (1873–1914), French Catholic socialist who argued for the infusion of faith into every aspect of life, often at the objection of the hierarchy of the church. He was killed in World War I at the Battle of Marne (6–12 September 1914). JSB's reference here is most likely to *Basic Verities: Prose and Poetry* (London: Kegan Paul; New York: Pantheon, 1943), a translation by Ann and Julian Green.

4   Harry Emerson Fosdick (1878–1969), Baptist minister who during the 1920s was a popular radio personality, advocating for Fundamentalism. Emmett Fox (1886–1951) championed the New Thought Movement that argued that we are what we think, which in turn led to the Power of Positive Thinking crusade.

5   JSB is referring to two prints of terns. David A. Randall (1905–1955), legendary manager of the Scribner Rare Book Department, 1925–1955, and later head of rare books at the Lilly Library, Indiana University, 1956–1975.

now shed of all further effort – except perhaps a good wish and a nugget of wisdom to help me through my next quarter century. And don't tell me it won't be so bad! All that would mean was that the bright edge of conscience would be dulled, perception and identification would comfortably shrink, every ethical sensibility deadened, turned to a blind dishonest optimism. I've seen enough young liberals turned old conservatives, socialists turned Republicans and I had rather flagellate myself with the sins of man and the sins against man every day of my life, than try to forget what I have known. So if you want to wish something, wish that it will be harder – that I shall see more clearly, feel more sharply, know more deeply – and that sometime in the next 25 years I will <u>do</u> <u>something</u>. For that I will need a little more physical strength and a lot more moral strength. Enough of strife – you are not well enough yet for me to take unfair advantage [of] you by air mail and pin you down and force you to read such turmoils.

Much love,

Julia

PS: You will be overcome with confusion probably, as I was, by the end of this letter. I was writing away and quite blithely, and just where I told you not to say it wouldn't be so bad, I stopped – and started on a train of thought so violent that I seethed and boiled for a good half hour before the end came out – with a rush and certainly in a different mood. But who would know – unless I put a red light there or write in red pencil "think with anguish on this for half an hour before you continue." It makes me think of something by my new friend Péguy wrote – "A word is not the same with every writer. One man tears it from his guts, and another takes it out of his overcoat pocket[.]"[1] One moment I was taking words from one pocket after the other, and the next moment, almost, I was tearing them from deeper than my guts, but the words are the same and who can tell the difference. How can you tell feelings in words without long explanations for every word and explanations of explanations.[2] How can you change the kind of words and have someone know they are changed. How much they are changed, the overcoat kind are the safest. I am always telling myself to stick to them – and spread them around through the others so no one will notice them – because they won't understand them, so hide the bloody words (they must come out), flank

---

1 *Basic Verities* 47.

2 JSB alludes to the satiric remarks in *Don Juan* (1819–1824) by George Gordon, Lord Byron (1788–1824), who describes Samuel Taylor Coleridge (1772–1834) as a "hawk encumber'd with his hood / Explaining Metaphysics to the nation— / I wish he would explain his Explanation" (Dedication, Section II, ll. 13–16).

them with funny words and no one will hear them. But sometimes I must be heard, sometimes I cannot keep betraying the words that betray me, and so although I said I wouldn't make you suffer, I make you suffer this winding struggling attempt at communication. No matter what I feel at the beginning it comes through frustration to this dreary finish of the lonely ego whining that no one understands it. So it is true. I should conceal the bloody words. When I feel something of truth, of strength, of resolve, I reach for the word and when I wrench it hurts and it is truly torn but it is not good enough, it belies its meaning, it will not be understood. It should be hidden, be brushed by quickly, not lingered over, explained, moaned over, till what I felt is debased, worse belied by ends than by the word, in writhing attempts to arouse pity for inarticulacy. I know. I won't do it again. I won't revel in my shortcomings, but pass over them. Leave the good bloody words to the poets. It's the old problem – that comes between man and God so often – and man and man – man aspires and, as it must always be to something beyond him, fails. The failure directs his attention from the high purpose to himself. Once his gaze is shifted from the heights he can see many reasons why he could not make it – it was too high, too hard, no one else he knew made it – you can think them up yourself – (All preoccupation with self is food to the devil or could easily be.) The separation is lost in the shuffle, the vision that inspired it is lost too. If I were a preacher, (and had not these limitations) couldn't I preach a great sermon? Seriously, in the smallest sin within ourselves, if we see it truly, we can see the pattern of the greatest evil. God, I should burn this, not think of sending it. But that would not be honest – and only because I would be afraid you would laugh. No, if you shall say 'My God, is this Julia' you shall say it. I am feeling in an honest mood.

. . .

MKR to JSB, 26 March 1943. ALS, 8 pp. PM: CITRA | MAR | 27 | AM | 1943 | FLA. AD: Miss Julia Scribner | 39 E 79th St. | New York City. RA: [holograph] Rawlings | Hawthorn | [printed] FLORIDA.

Cross Creek

March 26 [1943]

Dearest Julia:—

There is so much I want to say, and I am handicapped by two things— I am forbidden the typewriter, on which I have been accustomed to think for more than twenty-five years—and Smoky will not get off the bed tray on which I am writing. A small paw thrust out now and then to intercept the intriguing scratch of the pen is no help, either.

How could I possibly laugh at you?[1] For one thing, I know what you mean. For another, you have expressed with great luminosity the torment that afflicts not only the artist, but the truly sensitive mind and spirit. For you are an artist, and probably the key to your torment lies in the fact that so far you have found no valid or even satisfactory outlet for that artistry. You are probably suffering at this moment for having let pass beyond your control an expression of your agony. If you will look up again Thomas Wolfe's "The Story of a Novel"[2] you will find his admission of this same suffering—actually, a sense of nakedness, of shame, that overwhelms one who has torn the works from his guts and then cruelly sent them out into an irrevocable daylight where they are doomed to wander for any dolt to observe their pitiableness, their inadequacy and the embarrassing blood with which they drip. The one compensation is that those who are not dolts see beyond the blood and tatters and take the wanderers to their hearts, for the sake of the breath of life that is in them.

One point on which I want to scold your "ego" just a little, is on your masochistic desire to feel that your torment is unique. It is unique, of course, in the sense that each individual, fortunately, is unique. Otherwise there would be no excuse for any book, any poem, any painting, any composition of music—any producing, even, of a human child. So the agonized groping of the sensitive individual to make sense out of a totally inexplicable universe is unique. And because it is unique, as the individual is unique, he is doomed to loneliness. I think I have quoted to you before James Boyd's "Loneliness is the terrible discovery of maturity."[3] That maturity comes sometimes early, as with you, sometimes late, and sometimes never.

But there is truly comfort in the willingness to admit that there are a hell of a lot of these uniquely suffering souls in the same boat. The loneliness is mitigated when contact is made between or among them. The contact may come—and never permanently, only in flashes that tide one over, just as the appeasement of thirst or hunger is temporary and only tides one over, and must be repeated—the contact may come through hu-

---

1 See the previous letter.

2 Thomas Wolfe, *The Story of the Novel* (New York: Scribners, 1936) was intended, in part, as a compliment to the renowned editor Maxwell E. Perkins, who guided Wolfe through the immensity of his language and metaphor, but in the end it became a self-absorbed confessional on his fictional sins and literary conflicts.

3 MKR was reading James Boyd (1888–1944), famous for his novels about the frontier (*Max and Marjorie* 167, n. 1).

man love or companionship; for the creative worker, through being able at brief moments to fulfill Conrad's requirements of the artist (in the Preface to "The Nigger of the Narcissus") "to make you feel, to make you understand, above all, to make you see;"[1] for the receptive and sensitive mind, whether creative or not, through those lightening-like bursts of revelation that come from good writing, good painting, good music, and from moments of truth and beauty in human life and in nature. Those who are or pretend to be completely confident in a religious faith claim to hold the key to it all, apparently an unquestioning belief that "God's in his heaven, all's right with the world."[2] I do not believe any of them tells the truth. Those most vociferous in their "faith" are likely to be the pettiest in daily life. Even the great Sigrid Undset, who had given herself willfully to the Church and to God, has a cynicism that shocks me. She believes that human nature has never changed, will never change, is incapable of change. The individual can only make his own direct contact with God and so save his own soul. She said this to me in those words. All these people unfairly leave too much to God. If there is any alibi at all for human existence, it is in mankind's latent capacity for approaching godhood and for an ultimate union with and understanding of godhood. If one denies this capacity, no matter how deep-buried, how wracked and smothered by human evil, one can only wipe off humanity as a mistake and a total loss—and something in us knows better.

My dear, in making any effort to "soothe" you as to the future, your future, I should be the last in the world to want you to drug yourself with the syrup of indifference and complacency. You yourself have indicated the answer— a greater awareness, even greater suffering. And above all, an _effort_ which only you yourself can make to turn your agony into some constructive channel. You cannot continue to let it burn you up from within. It will always consume you to a large extent, and _should_, but it is required of you, as the kind of person you are, that you should let it out of its cage and _use_ it. How you do this is again something only you can know. You may eventually do creative writing of some sort, perhaps critical writing, which when good is also creative. And as to your writhings over inarticulacy, you have had only a taste of the Hell in which live those who have the audacity to make a public profession of articulacy, and who tear the words from their guts instead of taking them out of their overcoat pockets.

---

1   Joseph Conrad, _The Nigger of the Narcissus_ (London: Heinemann, 1897). Conrad's preface, to which MKR almost precisely alludes, was suppressed until 1914. Conrad's exact words are "to make you hear, to make you feel—it is, before all, to make you _see_" (New York: Doubleday, 1914, x).

2   Robert Browning, _Pippa Passes_ (1841), a drama in verse, ll. 7–8.

Anyway, get your headaches under control (knowing Dr. Atchley, I should guess that he is working slowly and periodically on purpose) then make some sort, any sort, of constructive decision and go on from there. The original decision may prove to be not the right one. That won't matter. You will have established the habit of work and of making constructive decisions. Any new channel you take will be traveled with greater knowledge and greater assurance. And don't use the war as an alibi for putting it off. Your "work" dancing with officers etc.[1] is not as valuable as making a useful human being of yourself, a coordinated human being, so that you will be able in all humility, to give something back to life.

Also, any limitations, real or imagined, are unimportant. We can each only do the best we can with whatever we have to work with. But we are obligated to do that best, and you are not doing it.

Your rage about the sins of man and the sins against man is a good and righteous rage. Use that, too. It is part of the best of you. Every such individual rage is a vital part of the great sweep of human hope. The slow spreading of that rage is the yeast in the cosmic bread.

What I have tried to say is also inarticulate. It has also a touch of hypocrisy, for my own rage and despair so often overwhelm me, and I have to fight constantly to keep my balance. But I do fight, and I do believe what I have said.

All my love,

Marjorie

. . .

JSB to MKR, 1 April 1943. ALS, 1 p. PM: New York, N.Y. | APR 2 | 4:30 PM. AD: Marjorie K. Rawlings | Cross Creek | Hawthorn | Florida. VIA AIR MAIL envelope. Stamped in red on envelope: VIA AIR MAIL.

April 1 [1943]

Dearest Marjorie –
How can I thank you for your birthday present to me.[2] Ever since I had sent the letter I had felt ill that you knew I would and I planned to write you

---

1 JSB volunteered to dance with the troops, as in the United Services Organization (USO), to boost morale.
2 JSB's birthday was 26 March.

a bright extroverted letter to sort of "cover up" the other. Then, when I got back to town Monday AM[1] there was your letter. And I was so full of shame and embarrassed that I didn't dare open it. There was a letter from Roger[2] too and I read my way through its ten long pages all the time wanting to throw it away and read yours, and yet also wanting to pretend yours wasn't even there. I knew I had to face it sometime, and I tore it open. I wasn't afraid you'd laugh, not when I wrote that. I was afraid you'd be – well, I guess repelled is what I meant. If I could tell you how I felt about the time I reached the second page I really would be an artist – an unfrustrated one. But I can only say I felt as if you had taken my hand and I felt so grateful – I can't ever say how much. It was the finest birthday present I have had ever. And I had some fine birthday presents, this year and every year. I had the affectionate memory of my two aunts[3] who, come hell and high water, would never forget that unimportant date. You don't expect that of aunts. And Granny,[4] who come <u>more</u> than hell and high water wouldn't forget, and my parents, who are so generous with everything they can give. What you gave me is what they cannot give.[5]

Your letter wants a long reply (at least I want to give one) and I am full of it. Don't worry, it won't be frenzied or frantic and every word will be precooled and preshrunk before it gets on paper. But I just haven't had time to get it on paper yet and won't for a couple of days, and I couldn't let another day pass without saying this much of thanks. I hope you are glowing with health and strength. You may have a pint or even two of my blood anytime.

Julia

. . .

MKR to JSB, 5 April 1943. ALS, 2 pp. PM: HAWTHORN | APL 7 | 1943 | FLA. AD: Miss Julia Scribner | 39 E 79th St. | New York City.

Hawthorn, Fla.

----

1 Monday AM—that is, 29 March.
2 Roger: Not identified.
3 JSB's aunts Louise and Gladys Augusta Casey Willets (1889–1978), her mother Vera's sister.
4 Louise Flagg Scribner.
5 This extraordinary confession, that JSB's parents could not give what MKR has given, is the raison d'être for this volume of letters. MKR gave an unconditional love and sisterly understanding, including requisite admonishment, that Charles Scribner III and Vera Scribner could not possibly approach as parents. MKR was JSB's confidante. In turn, JSB, with requisite blemishes, was the daughter MKR, with equal if not more pronounced blemishes, longed to have.

April 5, 1943

Dearest Julia:—

I was so glad to hear from you today[1] and to know that the things I wanted so much to say to you didn't register as just an assortment of platitudes. And please don't write me pre-coded and pre-shrunk[2] letters! I much prefer a dash of frenzy.

I'm passing on to you a book I've just read, "The Choice",[3] sent me in advance of publication by Norman Berg. It has some very obvious and immature faults, but it still has something to say, and some of it is along the lines of your own distress. I don't need to point out the faults—you will gnash your teeth over them yourself. But I think it will interest you anyway, for the very things the writer is groping for.

Alas, the terns! Far from feeling that the search is ended, I am trying to decide whether to pay $85 or to find something else at $27.50. I don't know why the arbitrary figure, as $85 would be nothing to bring you joy. I just look at my old Print Shop Catalogue and see if they have lower prices on terns.[4] I suppose you wouldn't settle for a wren or something.

I am finally sending Charles Junior[5] the erudite "Lucretius,"[6] autographed by the author. I used the Far Hills address.

Norton is coming over tomorrow, and probably needs rest more than I do. His wonderful W.D.[7] is in New York, presumably at the bedside of a very ill mother, but possibly looking up a defense job, so Norton has had his nose to the grindstone and his ear to the hotel telephone. My ever more wonderful Idella is making me too comfortable for my own good.

Love,

Marjorie

---

1   MKR is referring to JSB's letter on 1 April 1943.

2   JSB's words, as in minimal or truncated.

3   Charles Mills (1914–1975), *The Choice* (New York: Macmillan, 1934), a novel about a young man rebelling against the shallow life of a small Georgia town.

4   Terns, sea birds related to gulls. MKR is referring to a print. See JSB's letter dated [23? March 1943].

5   Charles Scribner IV (aka Jr.), JSB's brother.

6   Titus Lucretius Carus (c. 95–55 bce), Roman poet and philosopher, whose only known work is *De rerum natura* [*On Nature of Things*], a treatise on atomism, all things are made up of irregular shaped atoms. MKR is, of course, joking when she says the work is "autographed by the author."

7   W. D. Williams, NSB's porter and bartender, who came with him to the Castle Warden Hotel from the Marion Hotel in Ocala (*Idella* 95, 101). When W. D. left, MKR wrote to NSB on 2 April 1943, "My Lord, life without W.D.!! even for a while. May I be the first to extend my heart-felt sympathy" (*Love Letters* 87).

MKR to JSB, 28 April 1943. TLS, 6 pp., holograph postscript on the verso of p. 6. PM: Hawthorn | APR 29 | 1943 | FLA. AD: Miss Julia Scribner | <39 E. 79th> | New York City. [In MKR's hand below the typed AD]: Far Hills N J. LH: Marjorie Kinnan Rawlings | Hawthorn, Florida.

April 28, 1943

Dearest Julia:

The letter, obviously written by Perry[1] himself---I, too, recognized the machine type---is incredible. Receiving the typewriter (from Washington, where he seems to hang out, for some reason) does appear more hopeful. I had considered trying to steal a typewriter for your birthday present, as I felt I was responsible for your losing yours. What strikes me as so strange, is that Perry would be so crooked about things that even crooks are often honorable about, and yet did not take <davna> advantage of our joint gullability [*sic*] to get money---aside from taking the "advance" from your father[2]. He could easily have hit me for a couple of hundred.

I don't believe it would do you a bit of good to write to either address given, though it would be fun to try the Washington one, saying what you mentioned. I do not see how he gets by with the uniform, to say nothing of the medals (easily picked up in any pawn shop).[3]

The tangerines were plucked by the tie-tongued and half-witted George Fairbanks (see the chapter Residue in Cross Creek).[4] I packed them with my lily white hands and toted them to the express office, hoping they would arrive in edible condition. I found by accident that one tree still had edible tangerines on it. You should see me wolf a tangerine, ignoring the bland diet. You paint an appalling picture of picking off the harmless threads. You are such a precisionist!

I don't know whether to be surprised by the Dean's demanding a rake-off

---

1 Perry Patterson was using JSB's typewriter, which he had "borrowed" but not returned.
2 The working title of Patterson's children's book was *Zubu*. See JSB's letter dated [13?] October 1942.
3 If Patterson fraudulently wore a uniform and displayed medals, he would be breaking the law.
4 George Fairbanks (1897–1972), the "last of a proud and prosperous line" who once owned valuable hammock and grove land at Cross Creek. But in his later years he had to be looked after by "Old Boss" Brice and Feldon Snow Slater, for if left to himself he would forego clothes and groceries when "liquor might be bought instead" (*Cross Creek* 125–28).

or not.[1] When I met him, I tried futilely to reconcile his elegant clothes, his obvious earthiness, his dirty stories, with his indubitable spirituality. Perhaps it is after all the ideal combination. I rather fancy myself as going in for the same thing (without the elegant clothes). He sent me through Scribner's (unsigned) two of his religious books, and I have been totally unable to write and thank the man, as they are written in so puerile a style (dictated, probably, since he told me he worked that way) that what he had to say seemed invalidated by the moronic viewpoint. What he had to say was true and good, but I for one, and I know you feel the same way, can never accept anything that possesses no style. I do think he is truly a man of God. And I know damn well he has more sex appeal than any man I have ever known, except a present Brigadier-General[2] with whom I was frightfully in love. He also had a wife and four children, and couldn't "jeopardize his career" for a trifle like love. It has been a source of considerable satisfaction to me that I have been able to put him totally out of my heart and find great happiness in marriage, while he continues to write desperately unhappy letters.

I saw what must have been excerpts from Julian Green's "Personal Record"[3] in the Atlantic Monthly, and have not been so thrilled with anything since Tom Wolfe's "Story of a Novel". Have you read Wolfe's "Letters to his Mother"? (Scribner)[4] Wonderful. But what a Nasty family. To save my writing a business letter, which I loathe, the next time you're in Scribner's will you ask them to send me all the books of Julian Green (charge to author's account). Did you pay for "When the Whip" for Pardue?[5] He hasn't thanked me, either! Perhaps same reason.

---

1   Harry Austin Pardue (1899–1981), served as dean of St. Paul's Cathedral, an Episcopal church in Buffalo, New York, from 1932 to 1943, when he moved to Pittsburgh, Pennsylvania. There, he was consecrated as the fourth bishop of the Episcopal Diocese of Pittsburgh, a role in which he served from 1944 to 1968. Pardue wrote religious books for Scribners, most notably *Bold to Say* (New York: Scribners, 1940) and *Your Morale and How to Build It* (New York: Scribners, 1942). In what might be considered a curious historical irony, JSB's future father-in-law, the Rev. Canon Thomas James Bigham (1875–1949), also served in the Pittsburgh diocese.

2   Almost certainly Brigadier-General Otto Frederick Lange (1891–1965), assistant commanding general of the 36th Infantry Division during World War II, and recipient of the Silver Star. He was promoted to the rank of brigadier general in 1941, reclassified to the rank of colonel at the end of the war, and promoted again to brigadier general in 1948. MKR knew then Major Lange as early as 1935 when he was a professor of military science at the University of Florida. Lange became a close friend and hunting companion of MKR (see *Max and Marjorie* 189–90, Silverthorne 109–10, 114–15, 138–39). In her will MKR left her desk from the front porch of Cross Creek to Lange.

3   Julian (Julien) Green (1900–1998), American author and translator, *Personal Record, 1928–1939* (New York: Harper, 1939).

4   Thomas Wolfe, *Letters to His Mother* (New York: Scribners, 1939).

5   *When the Whippoorwill—* (New York: Scribners, 1940). See Tarr, *Bibliography*, A4. See also 179, n. 4.

Love,

Marjorie

Don't know whether to be happy or not that your troubles are traceable to migraines. Just plain neuroticism (which I share) is more simply cured when the patient has what is known as a "clear area" (mentally). But if I can accept a perpetual diet, you can accept periodic hypos. And since you have the headaches only now and then, not, like Mrs. Atchley,[1] all the time, who has to take the stuff every day of her life, you should be able to manage. And since a lot of the trouble is subsidiary to the migraine, it seems possible and plausible that as time goes on, you will need fewer hypos. Have you taken up with Dr. Atchley the possibility that much of your pain and distress could be mechanical, after the horse accident? Pressure on nerves, etc. Good osteopaths are wonderful and have done lots for me.

(over)[2]

Bird feed basket.[3] Should have a narrow rim, so the birds can light there but the chickens can't. Some have a central container for a mixture of suet and seed, but I don't want that as too difficult to replace. I want the kind that has a central container for loose grain, that drops down into the rim, like a self-stoking furnace. about $2.

. . .

JSB to MKR, 25 May 1943. ALS, 4 pp. PM: NEW YORK, N.Y. | MAY 25 | 1230 AM | 1943 | GRAND CENTRAL A[NNEX]. AD: Mrs. Norton Baskin | Castle Warden Hotel | St Augustine | Florida. Envelope air mail stationery: THE COPLEY-PLAZA | BOSTON. LH: THE COPLEY-PLAZA | BOSTON, MASSACHUSETTS | CHAUNCEY DEPEW STEELE | GENERAL MANAGER.

Monday the 24[th4]

Dearest Marjorie –

The reason you haven't heard from me in so long, (as if it hadn't happened before), is that I am at work on a colossal letter to you in answer to yours

---

1   Mary Cornelia Phister Atchley (1889–1982), wife of Dr. Dana Atchley.

2   In MKR's hand.

3   MKR draws a bird feeder at the top of the page, then inserts her handwritten postscript to the letter. See Figure 1, 310.

4   Written in a second hand on the envelope: May 25 / 1943.

of the twenty-sixth – of March.[1] There is a good <chanc> chance you will never see it, but I rather enjoy writing it although it is the toughest job I have tackled since the days when I was imperially told to hand in a short story. I have hope too that it will be of some help in my "integration" as Dr. Atchley puts it. Anyway – it <it> is miles or rather hours from completion so I think I'd better send you this news report.

I finally got the Bird Feeder – rather a struggle. It seems they are out of season. Interesting I think that there is definite "bird feeder season." I have sent you also the Green books.[2] The only books of his in print, are a recent, and I believe, poor, novel Then Shall the Dust Return (approx.)[3] The Péguy trans. and the 2 autobiogs.[4] I sent you the letter too. If you want the novel, let me know. I felt that if as you say every writer should be allowed one bad book, it is also only fair that his critical admirers should not read it.

I hear you have had the Davenports & Willkie staying with you.[5] It must have been fun. I suppose you are now an ardent Republican – one of the new non-revolutionist liberal Republicans, of course. Well, I must say I think Willkie has grown up a good deal since '40. However I can't forget whose side he is on and who is on his side – and just what those 100% Americans mean by "the American Way of Life" and "Free Enterprise" etc. etc.

If my writing seems more godawful than ever, I have a legitimate excuse. I'm on the fast Boston NY train and it's about an hour late. We have been up to see Buzz[6] who is now in the Navy & taking a short course at Harvard.

I hadn't been to New E. since our famous trip, and I can't tell you how good it looked to me even if it was only shore New E which isn't a patch or mountain New E. I knew I had missed it but I was surprised by how much I felt when I saw the houses and the stone walls and the lovely villages. It's the only place that seems home to me. I love everything about it. The trees – elms in every town and lilacs around every farm house, and the big maples and white pine, and the kinds of wild flowers that grow there, the

---

1   MKR's letter on 26 March 1943 addresses in detail the lonely but provocative life of the artist and its application to the trials of identification that JSB was experiencing.

2   MKR had requested that JSB send her any books by Julian (Julien) Green. See MKR's letter on 28 April 1943.

3   Julian Green, Then Shall the Dust Return (New York: Harper, 1941), transports the reader from past to present to observe culture and to discover self.

4   JSB also sent books by the French philosopher Charles Péguy. See JSB's letter dated [23? March 1943].

5   Russell Davenport (1889–1954), American publisher and writer and campaign manager for Wendell Willkie (1892–1944), unsuccessful candidate for president in 1940. Marcia Davenport (1903–1996), American novelist. Edith Willkie (1890–1978), wife of Wendell Willkie.

6   Charles Scribner IV (aka Jr.), JSB's brother.

rocky and up and down fields, there's only one flat field in all of the New Marlboro farms, the clean cold brooks, I hate the warm brown bedded streams in N.J., and the white house and church – really everything including the way the rain falls and the sun sets. I still plan to have a house on that hill above New M. village, I'm sure I showed you the spot, even though the land has been sold! I have planned gardens and planting and of course the house. That has changed this week, because of the passion roused in my breast by the cottages I saw from the train windows. It was going to be field stone, sort of semi-modern, but now it is going to be a white New En farm house – with lilacs and green shutters. It will be rather harder to do, I think. Difficult to preserve the exact character and still have all modern conveniences.

I had a lovely time in Boston. As you know I am an ardent city lover, becoming more and more so. I look forward to spending a week or so there alone sometime. I managed to get to the Museum of Fine Arts and the Fogg Museum of Cambridge.[1] The latter is the most attractive museum I have ever seen. Unfortunately both had all their first string paintings put away, but some of the second team were well worth seeing. Also went to the Public library & the Widener Library[2] at Harvard. This last is really swell, and all around the University Harvard Yard is lovely and has lots of red brick and elm atmosphere. Went to see the world famous Ware Collection of glass flowers at the Agassiz Museum.[3] You must see them some time. They are really breathtaking – I would like to spend a couple of weeks studying them.

My headaches are coming along OK. I take shots everyday – sometimes I have to take two, but I am hoping that things may improve and I have great confidence in Gynergen and Dr. A.[4] Otherwise my health is ghastly. I had flu 3 weeks ago and I have had a sore throat & sinus trouble ever since. This is really the longest siege of that sort of thing I've ever had. Tonight I'm afraid the whole thing is blossoming into a terrible cold. It's most annoying to have my headaches under some control for the first time in my life and be plagued

---

1 Fogg Museum, the oldest of the Harvard University art museums, has especially strong collections of Italian Renaissance, British Pre-Raphaelites, and twentieth-century French artists in addition to nineteenth- and twentieth-century American works.

2 Widener Memorial Library, Harvard University, built to honor Harry Elkins Widener (1885–1912), who perished in the sinking of the RMS *Titanic* in 1912.

3 Ware Collection of Glass Flowers, made by Leopold Blaschka (1822–1895) and Rudolf Blaschka (1857–1939), comprise more than 4,300 glass plants, housed in the Agassiz Museum of Comparative Zoology, Harvard University.

4 Gynergen, a preparation of ergotamine tartrate used to treat migraine headaches, and Dr. Atchley.

with this completely unusual ill health. However I dare say I'll recover before it goes into TB.

Granny[1] has sold her house and rented an unfurnished apt. for two years – just across the Ave. from where we were this winter. I wish you could have seen the house. It had a great big paneled library which was one of the most magnificent rooms I have ever seen. Not too terribly large in size and marvelous proportions & Grandpa's[2] beautiful books. Moving out – and in is going to be pandemonium, and will probably give Granny a stroke and Aunt L. & I nervous breakdowns.

We are approaching NYC so must end.

Much love,

Julia

. . .

JSB to MKR, late May 1943.[3] ALS, 10 pp. Envelope is missing.

[Late May 1943]

Dearest Marjorie –

It is always such weeks before I answer your letters. The main reason, passing over such facts as a great talent for distraction and a genius for procrastination, is that there is always so much to say that I feel I must have a great gap of time to write at all. And lately the only gaps I seem to have are half an hour to collapse on the bed or take a bath before I dash on to something else. I'm thoroughly sick of being a one woman USO[4] camp. I came to N.Y. full of plans for tremendous study at the Public Library[5] etc. and all I've done is seen the interior of several night clubs – and most of the stores in the city. I do waste endless time shopping. I spend a whole afternoon in Macy's and a morning in about 4 other stores and end up exhausted not having

---

1   Louise Flagg Scribner.

2   Charles Scribner II (1854–1930).

3   This letter is dated by the previous one, 25 May 1943, in which JSB tells MKR she is working on a "colossal letter." In addition to its qualifying length (10 pages), JSB also tells MKR that she will send Niebuhr's *Man and Immoral Society* (see 185, n. 5). In MKR's letter on 17 June 1943, she asks JSB, "Was it you or Max who sent me Moral Man and Immoral Society?" So, JSB had begun drafting this "colossal letter" prior to sending the one on 25 May, and she sent it to MKR in time for her to be "enraged" by Niebuhr on 17 June, which makes late May a logical sending date.

4   USO: United Service Organizations, founded by Franklin D. Roosevelt, whose main purpose is to entertain the troops overseas.

5   New York Public Library.

scratched <u>one</u> name off the Xmas list. At the moment I'm enjoying a small breakdown. Unfortunately I can only devote half a day to it as I have to go out for dinner, the opera, and dancing with a R.N. Lieut.[1]

I spent this AM reading the book you sent me.[2] I think it is fascinating and I'm very grateful for it. I'd never heard of it. It's just the sort of meditation on morals, civilization etc. that I love – by the way have you read <u>The Fifth Seal</u>?[3] I think I wrote you about it. Make Max send it to you if you haven't – it is really a brilliant book, and will probably sell under 1000 copies. Speaking of brilliant I have just finished the Pearson biography of Shaw,[4] who, as you know is one of my favorite people. I enjoyed the book and am more in love with GBS than before. Which is evidently just as it should be – endless women seem to have fallen for him – this one even had her hair turn white because of his fatal charm.

But on quite another level is the book I'm in the middle of at the moment – I don't think any book has ever made such an impression on me. I feel it is a turning point in my life or rather my concept of life – or philosophy. I never know the right word to tack on to that area. And it's not really a turning point, either but more like an opening up and illumination of the way I was already going – though slowly and hesitatingly. (Though I'm inclined to believe no one but myself, I'm still quite sceptical of myself.) Anyway this book to end all books in my life is <u>Moral Man and Immoral Society</u> by Niebuhr. I haven't read any of The Nature & Destiny of Man series.[5] It was one of those you read and disagreed with wasn't it? I'm going to send you MM&IS. Perhaps you will not admit all of it. You say you still believe in the perfect companionship or love affair. I confess I am a perfectionist and I crave the perfect state and the perfect human relationship, and I will not call something less than that "perfect", but I certainly do not expect to find either. They are impossible, all literature and wishful thinking of that ilk to the contrary. Niebuhr's straight thinking and integrity are a breath of air – sometimes it blows rather cold but it is a relief from the endless

---

1 The Royal Navy lieutenant is not identified.

2 Not identified.

3 Mark Aldanov (1886–1957), Russian novelist and critic, *The Fifth Seal*. Trans. Nicholas Wreden [1901–1955] (New York: Scribners, 1943), a novel about the dissolution of pre–World War I civilization and the anticipation of political, hence moral revolution.

4 Hesketh Pearson (1887–1964), *George Bernhard Shaw: His Life and Personality* (New York: Collins, 1942).

5 Reinhold Niebuhr (1892–1971), *Moral Man and Immoral Society* (New York: Scribners, 1932), which argues that humans are more likely to sin when part of a social group. Perkins later sent MKR *The Nature and Destiny of Man* (New York: Scribners, 1941) by Niebuhr (*Max and Marjorie* 489–90). See MKR's letter on 17 June 1843, 197, n. 2, for her opinion of Niebuhr.

sentimental rationalization and platitude and panaceas. "If we do this or that everything will be perfect." This is not the sort of thing I can discuss in writing – or even in conversation. My mind has been boiling rapidly for about 20 minutes without a single coherent statement floating to the top, so I better move on before I develope [*sic*] a headache. I sometimes forget how poor my education is until I come against such an impasse. Reading Niebuhr too is a terrific struggle, even though I am eager as a birddog and can understand it all. Buzz[1] can read that sort of thing like a novel, and I stagger along, after literally sweating and taking minutes to every paragraph. I think if I work more on that sort of thing I will improve, my brain muscle is just terribly untrained and undeveloped. Probably I will become able to express myself better too.

I certainly did a poor job of expressing myself on the marriage question. I never <intended> ^<meant>^ thought that my friends "disappeared into the void of marriage." My life is pleasantly full of pleasant proofs to the contrary. I spent an average of two nights a week all fall in Rossie's apt along with her two children & husband[2] and we call up or see each other almost every day. And you were hardly in a "void." I will admit that I felt that perhaps you liked to have me around because you were so alone and it was good to have someone who didn't "irritate" you for companionship. I thought that since you had married you wouldn't need my companionship to such an extent. I was happy and grateful to see that your feeling toward me wasn't just based on your being alone. You made me feel one friendship was not changed at all for which happiness I thank you with all my heart.

What I was mourning was not the loss of Cath's[3] affection, but the end of a special kind of friendship. The kind that begins when you decide "to be best friends" with somebody. It is an inevitable victim of grownup responsibilities. Even though Cath and I are more fond of each other than ever and even if we[4]

Well, the gap was not long enough – Now it's two days later. I must do something about that poor thought up there; What I was trying to say is that we can never again be as we were – wise and (or) foolish virgins with not a responsibility except to ourselves, speculating on love and life, planning great things abroad and a fine time in Paris or Budapest, or even a week in Vermont. Now Cath (and others) is full of domestic and wifely responsibility,

---

1   Charles Scribner IV (aka Jr.).

2   Perhaps Allia Nora Rossie. See Scribner Archive, Firestone Library, Princeton University.

3   Catherine Ginna Mellick Gilpin. See JSB's reactions to Mellick's impending marriage in JSB's letters on 11 November 1942 and 26 March 1943.

4   The reason for JSB's pause in mid-sentence here is unidentified.

and where before our lives were all open to each other, as far as possible, now there is a great part of her life that I do <u>not</u> share. Of course I don't resent that or consider it anything but healthy wealthy & wise.[1] The sad part is that I am the last rose left blooming alone, all my friends being now in someone's buttonhole. So there is no one to plan a gay spinsterhood with, (Cath and I had often considered that contingency), and there is an end to girlhood friendship, to put a pleasant thing in sickening words. I got the greatest hurt I've ever had from it, but also the most joy – not the greatest, but the most. And friendship becomes adult – firmer founded, but not so exciting and full of adventurous possibilities – and <u>don't</u> for <u>Godsake</u> bring the vulgar side of your mind to bear on that innocent phrase.

Now that that point is clear as mud, I must say I am stricken with horror at the earlier parts of this epistle. How can you bear it? How can you encourage it with your wonderfully prompt answers? As soon as I get serious I cease to make sense, as there is about a 15 minute interval between every sentence at the end of the 15 mins I am arrived at a quite different point than where I left off and then emotion makes me Edgar Guesty and enthusiasm unnerves me completely.[2] The end result leaves me so sickened I feel I should never write you or just send humorous postcards. I am embarrassed beyond words (unhappily not literally true) by my expression of gratitude. It looks horrible and sounds horrible, glib, and pseudo-religious, but I do mean it most truly and "with all my heart"! The betrayal of my efforts at communication will sometimes get me down completely and I shall give up. Only then I'd probably burst. I can't be facetious all the time. If all this mess of inner frenzy and its sad communicatory gasps is taken out on you, it's somewhat your fault because you live in Florida and because I keep remembering your sympathetic nature.

Marge, you old analyzer, I am ashamed of you at one point in <u>your</u> letter. You must have forgotten I'm not as young as I look – or as I <u>am</u>, if you think I must grow older to learn the facts of inner life – the unremedied loneliness. It's the cold truth I've known by heart for quite some time. I can remember when I didn't know but that "me" seems years ago and very young. I must have been aware of the loneliness in the early teens. I'll tell you a lovely ironical story about it. When my famous unrequiting lover first told me he loved me, I was not yet very deep in myself, the coup de grace was yet to come. But I can remember more clearly than what he said

---

1   JSB uses part of this same expression, "healthy, wealthy, and wise," in her letter on 9 August.

2   JSB is referring to Edward Guest (1881–1959), American poet, known for his sentimental and optimistic verse, often referred to as "The People's Poet."

what I said to myself as I went down to the cabin to bed – not "this is love", or "how wonderful to have such a marvelous person in love with me", but over and over out loud in my mind I said "I'll never be lonely again." Just to say that over now I can almost be again as I was then. God what a mocking irony and how damned blind innocent we are to begin with. Perhaps it is good to believe though, even if only for a couple of days. I know I have never gone to sleep so happy and so sure. Or with less reason to be so. Well, at least I got out of it a thorough education on the subject of loneliness starting from this absolute "scratch".

I don't think I can give you any news on the P.P.[1] situation. Daddy has sent you all.[2] Didn't you nearly <u>scream</u> and tear out hair over the Arlington Cemetery story? God knows how much will ever find out. When the doctor so persistently refused to tell what was wrong with Perry I had a few gruesome conjectures – but no symptoms. What I regret most is my typewriter and my <u>terrific</u> compassion.

I suppose by now you are finished with forests.[3] Clint sent me a bunch of pictures.[4] Mostly awful ego-shattering shots of me astride an engine, or a pile of cotton or having burrs removed. One I enjoyed – maybe he didn't send it to you – it's slightly libelous looking – you with a most pixilated expression (though it was pumpkin not apple night, I see) creating a pie and me watching with a perfect blend of skepticism and admiration, just the sort of blend I'm always looking for. Of course I do look something like Tallulah B.[5] before she went on the wagon.

You can't think how <u>delighted</u> I was to hear Joe[6] sent you a silver leaf too. Mine came with such an un-father-of-3-children like note[.] I was quite upset, and toyed (for the first time in my life) with the melodramatic idea of sending it back.

---

1 Perry Patterson.

2 The material that Charles Scribner III sent to MKR on Patterson has not been located.

3 MKR had been touring the forests of the southeast with the U.S. Forest Service in September–October 1942. JSB went on part of the trip (*Love Letters* 70, n. 1). See also "Trees for Tomorrow."

4 Perhaps Clint Davis (1909–1971), who took and published many photographs in his role as the director of information and education for the southern district of the U.S. Forest Service. In 1946, Davis would be promoted to Washington, DC, where as the information specialist in charge, he played the central role in making Smokey Bear the Forest Service's primary symbol for fire prevention awareness.

5 Tallulah Bankhead (1902–1968), American actor, known for her raspy voice, dry wit, and droopy eyes.

6 Perhaps Joseph Hessel of the U.S. Forest Service. See JSB's letter dated [7? November 1942], 150, n. 4, and see also Figure 7, 314, in which two men, possibly "Joe" Hessel and "Clint" Davis are removing burrs from MKR's and JSB's clothing after their visit to a cotton field.

I must quit it's the small hours of the AM and I have to go to town this AM.

Lots of love,
Julia

. . .

JSB to MKR, 10, 11, and 30 May 1943. This letter remains in the possession of JSB's daughter Hildreth. It is likely that JSB never sent it to MKR.

May 10 (1943?)

Dearest Marjorie:

Here is the answer to your birthday letter, which had to come.[1] Even if I had decided to spare you I would have had to answer to myself and it seems that the only way I have to explain myself to myself is to explain myself to you; or rather to make an attempt at explanation. The hugeness, the complexity of what I must say almost unnerves me and even at this moment <tends to> persuades me to give up, but I have also a feeling that I must go on, that I must get some of this confusion on paper in front of me so that perhaps I may understand it better. I shall have to say things I have never said before, and which I always have been and am even more afraid to say. Not that they are shameful but that they are of my very core, (soul, I almost said), and they are so vulnerable and the wound would be so deep. I hope to God this doesn't end by your wishing never to see me again, or my wishing never to see you again. I'm sure I will not – I have so much faith in your understanding, and I think you will be able to bear up. I shall try to keep frenzy out, <and> though certainly this cannot be exactly passionless, and I shall be honest even if it kills me. To that end ^first^ I shall hang the devil that stands behind me whispering "this must be well done, must be moving. You must make an impression of the size of your soul and the depth of your pain and the number of your virtues." It seems practically impossible ever to be rid of this little Lucifer. No matter how humble one becomes he can creep in with a pride in the extent of one's humility through all the stages of charity and humility, the most unprideful virtues, this subtle sin is at hand <to betray>[.] Perhaps the most one can do is to recognize him. So I don't hang him, I recognize him. And I, who am thinking almost all of

---

1 See MKR's letter on 26 March 1943.

the time on what sort of impression I am making, shall try not to impress, but to explain.

I have been thinking hard about this 'answer' for six weeks now, but it is different every time I think of it. It is so multiple, so diffuse, so many fragments of 'answers' that I scarcely know how to go about setting it down. Much of it appears impossible of coordination. That is I think, rather a characteristic of life as opposed to art. You hear of objections to certain philosophies because of dualism – Well, here is not just dualism but quatrilism, centesimalism. What I believe, what I am, what I do or may do all should be approximately the same, I suppose, but they seem to be in me woefully separate. I shall see now just how separate.

You said in your letter that those who use or pretend to be completely confident in a religious faith claim to hold the key to it all, apparently in unquestioning belief that "God's in His Heaven, all's right with the world" and you don't believe them. You are quite right. Of course these are people, I'm sure, who go through life without a shadow of doubt to darken their paths. Brains are necessary to doubt, but also doubt is necessary with brains. Periods of doubt and despair are almost a part of faith and they are mentioned in many of the writings of the saints. The religious books I have read are quite open about it and these sessions of doubt are technically called 'periods of dryness' or <of blackness> ^"dark night of the soul."^ Perfect faith is more than men are capable of, and the key does not always unlock the door, but I believe it is the right key although I have not got it. Then you accuse Sigrid Undset of pettiness & cynicism, and you are shocked that she is so because of or despite religion. I believe as she does that human nature never has changed, never will change, and is incapable of change, but I cannot honestly feel that such a belief is petty or cynical. I know the first is true and I think the other two are reasonable deductions from that. Did human nature change from the dawn of history to the time of Christ? And has it changed from this time till now, despite the inspiration supposedly 'officially endorsed' by millions of men, of the perfect man and the perfect life? You might say that we have more painless means of capital punishment than crucifixion, but if you think a moment you will remember that we soak men in kerosene and set them afire and hang them from a tree. It is not exactly official, but there are plenty of people capable of it. The slaughter of the innocents, the inquisition are not dead horrors of history – they are <u>now</u>, <u>today</u>. Certain cruel practices have been outlawed by Reason, but if Reason is overthrown human nature proves itself to be as capable of cruelty as ever. I believe that the only hope of improving not human nature but human life is through Reason. Reason is of the mind and the mind is of the body and so capable of improvement and growth. I think it is necessary to recognize & admit the evil in men and to try by the only means we have, Reason, to create it. I think that denying the evil, or hoping that improvement is just around the corner, or trusting to overthrow it by education or religion are futile and probably always will be. This is not very well explained I know, but all of what I would like to say is in Niebuhr's <u>Moral Man and Immoral Society</u>, which I shall send you and which I think will redeem the poor impression you got from <u>Nature & Destiny</u>.[1] <Niebuhr> I hold this belief not through cynicism and certainly not through pettiness born of a blind faith, but because I cannot bear to be resigned to the injustices of the world and because honesty will not let me see any easier way to improve them. This does not mean to me "wiping off humanity as a mistake and a total loss." How could we even if we wanted to? I don't see why we should expect humanity to be a successful or unsuccessful experiment in terms of our world. If there is God, why would he work in ways of our conceptions? I don't know how to explain all of creation in terms of God or 'not God' – who does – and if we cannot understand the fact how can we understand the reason behind it? It doesn't upset me somehow. I am upset by living not by the reason for life, just as I am upset by the thought of dying and not of death itself. Why should existence need an alibi if we exist? One thing we have unshakeable, which men share with every living thing, even the worm, even with the living thing the worm feeds on even the grass, ^the will^ to live and to create life. And so, success or failure, we will go on, and we cannot be resigned to a bad life because it will not end in our times or in our children's time or their children's or on and on beyond. If we have one thing sure, that life cannot end, then there is a certain strength (perhaps a strength of desperation?) to be got from that. At least there is for me. Other people may need other strength. I do not insist that everyone drink at my well.

When S. U.[2] told you that "the individual can only make his direct contact with God, and so save his own soul," I think she expressed in a very succinct way what is wrong with a large part of religion as practiced today – or as a matter of fact, not particularly today but since Christianity began; this idea of having a direct contact with God and any kind of contact or lack of contact you please with the world. Christ said <"No man cometh unto the Father except by Me."> To be exact, "I am the way, and the truth, and the life: no man cometh unto the Father but by me."[3] And certainly

---

1 See JSB's letter dated late May 1943.
2 Sigrid Undset.
3 John 14:6.

the way and the truth and the life are set forth clearly, absolutely in his teachings, and certainly they are not a 'direct contact with God' and saving one's own soul.' I believe it, for they are all one, is "Thou shall love the Lord thy God with all thy heart, and with all thy soul, and with all thy mind. This is the first and great commandment. And a second like unto it is this. Thou shalt love thy neighbor as thyself." and "A new commandment I give unto you: that ye shall love one another"[1] and the same through as many teachings and parables and stories. Perhaps no where more clearly than in the story of the good Samaritan.[2] This is not really meant to be a righteous condemnation of Sigrid Undset, but an explanation of why I cannot find what I want and need to find in religion or churches. Surely the man by the side of the road is not just an individual. He is the black man, the jew, everyone who is oppressed or persecuted. And where has one more reason to expect to find the good Samaritan <and> than in the Christian church where they <preach> ^read^ over and over this lesson and others like it. But they pass by on the other side of the road. They even avert their eyes. "This people honor me with their lips, but their heart is far from me. But in vain do they worship me, teaching as their doctrine the precepts of men." The most spiritual man of the church I have met is Dean Pardue,[3] and he is a 'man of good will' but not a man of God, a disciple of Christ. I cannot say why I who am so reasonable in every thing also cannot accept a compromise on this subject. I do not expect perfect justice, or perfect government – but in none of these things have we got perfection to guide us, but if a man professes to be a priest and a follower of Christ how, if his belief is true, can he attempt less than to follow truly. I see the man lying beside the road, and I do not pass by but I stand and stare and my heart burns to help him, and I am sick with shame because I see him and desire to help but do nothing, and I do nothing. The love of the world and reason are so strong in me, they make me so well-balanced. Balance is not quiet and peacefulness, it is two weights striving against each other and pain. And it is purposeless, static. Only when it is so overthrown, for good or evil, can one get anywhere, I have in me the seed that was flung among the weeds, and the weeds cannot completely choke it, but neither can it rise above the weeds.[4] My eye offends me and I have not the strength to pluck it out, my hand offends me but I have not truly the will to cut it off. I am weak for I have no faith and very little hope, only charity. If you say, how

---

1 Lev. 19:18 and John 13:34.
2 Luke 10:25–37.
3 Austin Pardue. See MKR's letter on 28 April 1943, 180, n. 1.
4 Matt: 13:3–8.

can I believe so in Christ and not in his Father I don't know. If you say how can I feel that this way is the way and yet have no faith in the resurrection or the life everlasting I don't know.[1] And if you ask why do I believe that I should forego the treasures of this world as He taught, but not believe that I am storing up treasures in Heaven I don't know. I only know that I do believe these things. Someday I may know, or I may not need to know but shall have found faith. Now I am tortured because I know the truth but do not live it. I am ashamed of my weakness, and because of the weight of this guilt and my despair of ever having the strength and courage to do what I believe I should do, I am afraid I may deny the truth.[2]

Believe me, Marjorie, I know all the reasonable, comfortable, sensible advices to cure what is to the world my 'mental sickness,' religious delusions, 'guilt complexes.' Do you think they are not all on the other side of the scale? I know them all. But they are petty when they are face to face with what they would destroy. And if, as it sometimes seems, I must choose between health and wealth in a figurative worldly sense and the Truth of the Life of Christ and whatever it ^may^ make of me, then, when they are brought together, health and wealth seems much the lesser. If I will not leave go what I have of them, at least I will not leave go, not a grain of the truth for more of them. I believe "What profiteth it a man if he gain the whole world and lose his soul."[3] I don't know why. I don't really believe that it would mean heaven or hell, that I must do it for some ultimate eternal reason. But what I have I must keep; it may yet be better. And I hope I would be willing to suffer a good deal for the miserable worthless prideful crumb of pain it is now. That too is far more hope than certainty.

All of the above was written May 10 and 11. It is now May 30. Although I have not added a word to this in that time I have thought about it, and while in some respects I think I understand farther the situation does not resolve or become simpler. That is hardly the nature of such a situation, to be simple or clear. The more ^one^ considers oneself, that is, self including all the complexities of Reason and Life or Civilization whatever you want to call it, the more rather than the less appears to be considered. It is like a gothic façade to which is almost endlessly added a saint here, a devil there, a scroll, a flower, building a richer and richer complexity without actually changing the design – or changing the form perhaps, but not destroying it. Sometimes I think what shall I not find if I keep on searching. That is what

---

1   As in the last two lines of the Apostles' Creed.
2   As in the Apostle Peter's denial of Christ in the Gospels: Matt. 26:33–35, Mark 14:29–31, Luke 22:33–34, and John 18:15–27.
3   Matt. 16:26 and Mark 8:36.

makes the pursuit so fascinating – and dangerous. Certain <the> virtues and certain vices I am sure I would not find in my design. But this is a digression.

I'm afraid the four pages above are not only complex, but confused. None of it, however, was set down for effect, but only because it was so. In places it gets rather forced and biblical sounding. That is because I had been reading the bible to find just what I wanted to say and the words just came out that way in the heat of the moment. I could go back and write it in plainer words that might affect you as more genuine, but that would be a self conscious effort, and <in> this is mostly, and perhaps only, for me, and for me the effort would only distract me from the content. There was a point I intended to make when I started out on the subject of the individual making his own contact with God and which got lost. I think it is very important and to me it is even crucial. If only I believed otherwise my conscience would be far less painful and my life much easier. That is: That it is not enough not to do anyone harm. That one must do 'anyone' good. As I understand the teaching of Christ it is not possible to express Christianity in a personal communion with God and a passive attitude toward mankind no matter how sinless and full of good will that attitude may be. I think that is the pattern of most of the Christian religion. Sometimes they even leave out the good will. They are all from, the Pillars of Fire's[1] to the Catholics, violently concerned with the saving of souls and the purifying of hearts, and the souls are not expected to help the helpless, to give comfort rather than judgment, they are expected to eat the right food, and wear the right clothes and refrain from polluting their minds with certain books and plays and movies, and give the right amount of money to the church and above all to believe the right beliefs and never to put the word of Christ above the word of the church. There is much food for thought in that last – think how vital it is to many churches. There are some churches, Protestants, which are not even concerned much with the saving of souls. Their <beliefs are> ^point is^ limp and far gone with compromise with the world. They preach good will more perhaps than the others, but only so far as it is safe and will not outrage their richer members, and that is still so far short of Christ and Christian honesty that it has no strength. They seem to be violently concerned about nothing; except the maintenance of their finicky little differences from other Protestant churches. I cannot see that this "personal" salvation has any basis in the life of Christ. He was anything

---

1   Anti-Catholic Methodist sect named after the Pillar of Fire (Exod. 13:21–22), known as the "Holy Rollers," infamous because of their zeal and support of the Ku Klux Klan.

but a meditative hermit. I believe that the foundation of Christianity is the active expression of charity toward every man. As I look on what I wrote there I see I have just succeeded in transposing into dry and stilted words "Thou shalt love thy neighbor as thyself." To interpret a "neighbor" as a member of one's social class, or religion, or race, or color is to perpetuate the agony and crucifixion of Christ. I was going to say here that of his true followers Christ asked more than just the obedience to this commandment. I was thinking of "For I have come to set a man at variances with his father, and the daughter against her mother, and the daughter in law against her mother in law. And a man's foes shall be they of his own household. He that loveth father or mother more than me is not worthy of me and he that loveth son or daughter more than me, is not worthy of me. And he that taketh not his cross and followeth after me, is not worthy of me. He that findeth his life shall lose it: and he that loseth his life for my sake shall find it."[1]

. . .

MKR to JSB, 17 June 1943. TLS, 4 pp. PM: SAINT AUGUSTINE | JUN 17 | 2^PM | 1943 | FLA. AD: Miss Julia Scribner | Far Hills | New Jersey. LH: MARJORIE KINNAN RAWLINGS | HAWTHORN, FLORIDA.

June I7, 1943

Dearest Julia:

Just a word to let you know that I'm in the land of the living. Have been looking forward to your long epistle. Don't get cold feet about sending it. Nothing but the primer achieves complete articulacy, you know.[2]

Sight unseen, I ordered you an old flower print from the Dr. Thornton series, 1812,[3] I think <they were> ^was the date.^ Of those the Old Print Shop[4] had, only three seemed of the type of American wild flowers in which you are particularly interested, and of those one was sold, one out on approval,

---

1   Matt. 10:35–39.

2   Primer, the first school book, as in the *New England Primer* (c. 1690), iterations of which were used well into the twentieth century.

3   Robert John Thornton (1768–1937), *Temple of Flora, or Garden of the Botanist, Poet, Painter, and Philosopher* (London: Printed for Thornton, 1812). The original book, approximately 800 copies printed, contained 31 plates. MKR was buying only one print, most likely from a disbound copy of the book.

4   Old Print Shop, New York City, founded in 1898.

and the shop thought the remaining one the most attractive. Turn it in for something else if they gave me a bum steer.

Well, Norton has signed up with the American Field Service,[1] begins his appalling series of shots today, and is scheduled to leave for overseas inside a month. I feel as though God's old steam roller had passed over me. I didn't know a thing about it until he was practically in. He had gone on suffering in his quiet way until he came to his decision---which after all only he could make. I loathe it but I wouldn't lift a finger to stop him. In the last war their casualties were twice the ration of regular Army casualties. They operate with their ambulance right in the front line of battle. It is an altruistic service, for they pay their own expenses, draw only $20 a month, and in case of death or injury have no claim on any government. They are under British officers. They were also the most decorated branch of service, and as Fred Francis[2] said cheerfully to Norton, "You'll come home either a hero or a corpse."

The time of embarkation is a military secret, but I think they always sail from New York. If so, I'll go to New York and be with him while he waits for final orders, so will see you.

Today he gets shots for cholera, typhoid and typhus, then one shot a day of various things for sixteen days. They give them the final shots en route. He has a very nice chap coming to run the hotel, whom you may remember---Doug Thompson,[3] a tall dark fellow who was his assistant at the hotel in Ocala. I will rent or close the hotel apartment and live at the cottage in the summer and at the Creek in the winter. My next book seems to have taken shape in my mind,[4] and I hope it isn't a false alarm, as work will save my sanity. It's no harder for me than for any other woman, except that Norton is really a rare soul and I am not alone in feeling that the world without him wouldn't be half as nice a place.

---

1   In May 1943, NSB signed up with the American Field Service as an ambulance driver, and in July he was told to report. He was sent by Liberty Ship to the India-Burma theater as a part of the British Army to be trained. Because of the perilous situation and because of the secrecy of his location, his letters to MKR were sporadic and often edited by the War Department (Silverthorne 220–21). He eventually contracted malaria and severe dysentery and was flown home to Miami, arriving on 29 October 1944, and then taken to Harkness Pavilion in New York in November, all by arrangement of MKR (*Love Letters* 436–38).

2   Frederick Gomer "Fred" Francis (1899–1962) and his ex-wife Jean D. Goode Francis (1896–1981), from St. Augustine, were favorite bridge partners of MKR and NSB.

3   Douglas C. Thompson, who after NSB sold the Castle Warden, became the St. Augustine City treasurer and tax collector. He and Chef Clarence Huston were often in conflict (*Love Letters* 117).

4   *The Sojourner* (New York, Scribners, 1953) took MKR nearly ten years to complete. See Tarr, *Bibliography*, A8.

Probably see you soon.

Much love,

Marjorie

Will talk to you about the Julian Green books when I see you.[1] Was so thrilled to have them. Was it you or Max who sent me Moral Man and Immoral Society?[2] Niebuhr enrages me. He calmly takes as premises the most <u>debatable</u> statements. I was fuming about it and Norton said, "You just stick to your moral man and leave immoral society alone."

. . .

JSB to MKR, [27? June 1943]. ALS, 4 pp. Envelope is missing.[3]

Sunday [27? June 1943]

Dearest Marjorie:

It was good to hear that you are OK. I was afraid perhaps you might have had some sort of relapse, though Lord knows I have seen enough evidence of your unpoetically stalwart constitution. I can imagine easily how blue you are about Norton's going, but you must be awfully proud of him, too. I can't see how he will survive the preparations for overseas – one shot a day for 16 day[s][4] – and then more! It sounds like a survival of the fittest contest. Buzz[5] thought they treated him royally in the Navy, but it was nothing like that. Incidentally, a very great friend of the family's, Mrs. Moore,[6] whom we all stayed with in Palm Beach, is a bosom friend of the head of the A.F.S., Steve Galatti.[7] Nowadays you never know when such roundabout connections

---

1 Per MKR's earlier request, JSB sent her the works of the novelist Julian (Julien) Green.

2 In *Moral Man and Immoral Society*, Niebuhr argues that humans are more likely to sin when part of a social group. See JSB's letter dated late May 1943, 184, n. 3.

3 Letter dated by the mention of NSB leaving for India, which MKR mentions in the previous letter

4 As in the vaccines that NSB was required to receive before going overseas. See MKR's letter on 17 June 1943.

5 Buzz, Charles Scribner IV (aka Jr.), JSB's brother.

6 Fanny Mann Moore. See JSB's letter dated [24 February 1941], 84, n. 4.

7 Stephen Galatti (1888–1964), decorated director general, American Field Service, New York, who was to help with NSB's removal from India. On 27 July 1944, MKR writes to NSB, who is still in India, that she is in contact with Galatti, whose communication to her she quotes, "'I regret very much but there is no way of letting you know regarding Norton's arrival here. I will be able to let you know when I receive word that he has left the other side. I know you will realize that all matters pertaining to shipping are entirely secret'" (*Love Letters* 427). Clearly, MKR had already used JSB's influence to initiate contact with Galatti.

may come in handy. I know in the Navy nothing seems to happen unless you have a friend who has a friend in the Navy dept in Wash, who will pick your papers out of the scrap basket or the "don't look at for six months" file and place them on the proper desk.

I have your present.[1] Daddy[2] just brought it out from town (this is Monday PM now). It is really lovely and already hanging in a conspicuous spot in my bedroom. My only worry is that it is something terribly superior and extravagant – it does look it! – in which case, Marjorie, you should not have done it. As you once said to me, "think of the gasoline and tires you could be buying for your car!" (Doesn't that lend a lovely pre-war tone to our friendship?). I must say – seeing as how you spent a whole letter picking historical holes in the print I sent you[3] – that the flower, Dodecatheon meadia, otherwise known as American Cowslip or shooting Star, is an inhabitor [sic] of the mid-western & western plains, and it is here imaginatively pictured on a rocky seashore with two galleons or whatnot in the background. All of which makes a much nicer picture than plains.

As to the long epistle – In the first place its nowhere near finished.[4] In the second what is worrying me is not lack of articulacy, but too damn much. I'm not sure that it ever will be finished, though I suppose I should complete it just for the sake of completing at least one thing in my life. The initial thought was that it would make things simpler or clearer, and I started out, though I was not oblivious of certain of my shortcomings, with the feeling that I had here and there a noble spot in my character. I have become instead twice as confused – the conflicting motives which seemed difficult when dragged all the way out into the open seem insuperable, and I am so repelled by the flaccid and exhausted something that in my character that I have not much heart for poking around it any more. Merely to think about this dreary subject, and of course I do think about it even if I don't write about it, send me off into a dreary state. "Zehrt er heimlich auf Seinen eig[e]nen Wert In ung'nügender Selbstrucht" (if you can stand a little Goethe – I remember you know German)[.][5] To climax properly this unhappy discovery the whole of my situation was revealed sharply focused

1   The print MKR had sent to JSB from the Old Print shop. See MKR's letter on 17 June 1943.

2   Charles Scribner III.

3   The print of the old fort at St. Augustine that JSB sent to MKR as a Christmas present. See MKR's letter on 30 January 1943.

4   JSB is referring to her letter on 31? March 1943 in which she tells MKR that she had a long letter to write, partly on the subject of inarticulacy.

5   Translation: He secretly feeds on / his own merit, / in unsatisfying egotism. JSB quotes lines 40–42 of "Harzreise im Winter [Winter Journey in the Harz]" (1789), a poem by Johann Wolfgang

in a book I was reading the other day. A girl, very young and beautiful, is given to constant nibbling of chocolates and bonbons. The inevitable effect upon her figure ensues. Her beauty begins to coarsen and she sees her husband, whom she worships, begin to lose interest in her. Although she knows it is because she is becoming gross, she is quite unable to cease indulging herself, and day by day she swells and swells and is more miserable as she sees her husband's love turn to disgust. Finally he leaves her and her life is ruined. She does nothing all day but think of him and eat chocolates. That is most of the painful pages I have written expressed in a few lines. It's not a very nice story. I despise it almost to the point of doing something about it. But is there a point where weakness becomes strength?

In the more superficial and immediate problems I am in a hell of a stew. Particularly as Dr. A.[1] is returning from his vacation in a few days and I fear is expecting me to come in with my personality (?) neatly integrated, and a lovely detailed set of "plans for the future" in my hand. If only I had a somewhat better body, I could be a WAAC[2] or make airplanes, but as it is a take the hypos everyday (<u>not</u> occasionally) and still have headaches certain days of the month (and, charmingly, almost <u>every</u> time I forget to take the dose) and I still feel exhausted a good part of the time. Otherwise I'm fine.

Well, enough gloom for the present. I will write you shortly about the many literary "bonbons" I have enjoyed lately. There are quite a few I would like to discuss with you – or it will be more expounding, won't it? One of the advantages and disadvantages of long distance communication.

Thanks again for the print. It is truly lovely. By the way I'm sure your new book[3] inspiration is due to the dream I told you when you were in the hospital – As I remember it was definitely going to be your masterpiece so far. Much love, Julia

Love and admiration – lots of it – to Norton

---

von Goethe (1749–1832), German poet, essayist, and philosopher. Johannes Brahms (1833–1897), German composer, pianist, and conductor, incorporated these lines into his *Alto Rhapsody* (1869).

1   Dr. Atchley.

2   Women's Army Auxiliary Corps (WAAC) was created on 15 May 1942, and converted to active duty status on 1 July 1943, as Women's Army Corps (WAC).

3   JSB is referring to MKR's comment that she had the subject of a new novel in mind, which eventually became *The Sojourner*. See MKR's letter on 17 June 1943, 196, n. 4.

. . .

MKR to JSB, 20 July 1943. ALS, 6 pp. PM: DETROIT, MICH. 2 | JUL
20 | 3-PM | 1943. BUY WAR BONDS AND STAMPS. AD: Miss Julia
Scribner | Far Hills | New Jersey.

Detroit

Tuesday [20 July 1943][1]

Dearest Julia:—

Of all Christ-forsaken places to get stuck for a whole day, Detroit is it!
Arrived at 9 this morning and can't get a train out to my village[2] until 5 this
afternoon. No bus at all. Have walked until my feet hurt and it is still too
early to begin drinking, even for me! Am using the Book-Cadillac hotel[3] for
headquarters and will try to find a movie this afternoon. It also takes a hell
of a long time to get to Florida from here—two nights and a day. Henceforth,
I shall limit my travels to New York only, until I get my helicopter.

This place is a madhouse. I had forgotten how big it is. The phone book is
almost as thick as the Manhattan one. The defense work[4] has finished things.
I stood in line at the hotel for breakfast. Lots of negroes on the streets.

The one bright spot is that I feel perfectly O.K. Had a nice quiet week-end
with Marcia.[5]

The Toscanini broadcast would have infuriated you as it did Marcia, as it

---

1 NSB departed on a Liberty Ship for the India-Burma theater on 7 July 1943, and soon after MKR
checked into the Harkness Pavilion where Dr. Atchley treated her once again for diverticulosis, this
time prescribing belladonna and luminol. As she writes to Edith Pope on 14 July 1941, the "dos-
age . . . works divinely" (*Selected Letters* 240). MKR then went to Michigan to visit her Traphagen
relatives, who were to be the subjects of her planned novel, arriving in Detroit on 20 July.
2 Most likely Holly, Michigan, the ancestral home of Frances Osmun Traphagen (1847–1925)
and Abraham Traphagen (1842–1925), MKR's maternal grandparents. MKR's Aunt Ethel Traphagen
Riggs (1879–1954), who now lived on the family farm, proved to be a rich source for family lore.
3 The Book-Cadillac Hotel, built in 1924, is on Washington Avenue in Detroit.
4 Detroit's contribution to the war effort cannot be overestimated. The major automobile companies retooled. At Ford's nearby Willow Run plant, B-24 bombers came off the assembly line at a
rate of nearly one per hour. Chrysler built the M3 and then the more powerful M4 tanks. General
Motors built landing vehicles and provided munitions. Willys and Ford built jeeps. In spite of racial
tension that resulted in a 1943 race riot, Blacks worked with Whites in the factories. Thousands of
Black people had migrated from the segregated South to find economic opportunity, emboldened
by President Roosevelt's "Double V Campaign," Victory in Europe and Victory over Racism.
5 Marcia Davenport, the novelist. The experiences MKR describes here and in the rest of the
letter took place in New York City, not Detroit.

was a "light" program, beginning with the Poet & Peasant Overture!![1] Even I should have been grateful for a somewhat stronger dose.

Sunday night Marcia and I went to the Hemingway movie.[2] We were mad about it, especially that terrific Greek actress who did Pilar. Ingrid Bergman made me sick at my stomach. She was the weakest part of the show.

Had a grand visit Saturday afternoon with Sigrid Undset.[3] She is doing some secret pre-invasion work for the War Dept. Finances are not too good for her. She said she had to drop her war work now and then to do an article "to keep the pot boiling". She could get her Swedish royalties, but she has a sister in Sweden collect them and distribute them among relatives and other needy Norwegians.

Picked up mail at the Gotham[4] and there was a most welcome note from Norton, which the Field Service held about a week before mailing. He said he felt all right, and Dr. Atchley was a wizard. I was so relieved.

It was grand to see you. I would have blown up Medical Center if it hadn't been for your coming up.

Will reach home July 28, thank God.

Lots of love,

Marjorie

---

1   Arturo Toscanini (1867–1957), Italian conductor, and principal conductor of the NBC Symphony Orchestra, which was created for him and which performed weekly from 1937 to 1954. Franz von Suppé (1819–1895), Austrian composer of operettas and overtures, included among them *Poet and Peasant* (1846). MKR and Davenport went to the actual performance (*Love Letters* 99).

2   *For Whom the Bell Tolls* (1943), by Ernest Hemingway (1899–1961), starring Gary Cooper (1901–1961) and Ingrid Bergman (1915–1982). Katina Paxinou (1897–1973) played Pilar and won the Academy Award for Best Supporting Actress. Writing to NSB on 29 July, MKR concedes that the film was "superb," but is less charitable about Cooper and Bergman, calling them the "weaker parts." The film is "stolen" by Paxinou, whose performance takes "your breath away" (*Love Letters* 99).

3   Sigrid Undset (1882–1949), Norwegian novelist, was awarded the Nobel Prize in Literature 1928. According to MKR, Undset, who was living in desperation in a walk-up in Brooklyn, was at this time "doing a secret job for the American government" (*Love Letters* 98).

4   Gotham Hotel, which MKR did not particularly like. In a letter to NSB dated [17 February 1943], she writes, "The Gotham is nothing extra, but is all right (*Love Letters* 72), and later on 24 July 1944, she concedes that the view of Fifth Avenue is good, but "I don't like the Gotham itself" (*Love Letters* 426).

. . .

MKR to JSB, 29 July 1943. ALS, 9 pp. PM: HAWTHORN | JUL | 30
| 1943 | FLA. AD: Miss Julia Scribner | Far Hills | New Jersey. LH:
Marjorie Kinnan Rawlings | Hawthorn, Florida.

Forgot to ask—how much was the bird feeder? Will remit![1]

Thursday [29 July 1943]

Dearest Julia:—

Were Norton's letters a thrill! Came to St. A. yesterday to a stack of mail literally a foot high,[2] saved the best for last, your envelope last of all—and know under the circumstances you don't mind my being happier than if it had been a letter from you.

He said he put in 36 hours in his bunk, while the leader wondered if he had drawn a neurasthenic or a doper. Then he felt all right, and is enjoying the trip immensely. Failure of passports to arrive in time held out some of the unit— Norton's arrived when he was on the pier—so there are only 7 aboard. Each has a cabin to himself and an individual cabin boy. They eat with the captain and the food is wonderful.

Certainly a de luxe way to go to war. Norton said the first night he knew he heard 3 torpedoes swish by, just missing the boat—then later realized it was someone flushing the John! He is crazy about all the men but one, and he is a stinker that they all despise in unison. He says he himself is the oldest but they show him no respect. He said, "We all talk like Hemingway characters. Now and then an eight-letter word creeps in but you realize it is formed of two four-letter words."[3]

My Michigan trip was pleasant in many ways, spoiled a bit by the intrusion of two cousins (daughters of my aunt-hostess!) that I have no use for.[4]

---

1 MKR inserts her postscript at the top of p. 1. JSB had purchased a birdhouse for her. See JSB's letter on 25 May 1943.

2 The postal service from overseas during the war was erratic at best. A good deal of the mail coming to the United States via the APO (Army Postal Service) was censored, taking out names and places, anything that the enemy could use. MKR is repeating to JSB what NSB's letters said about his trip to the war zone.

3 See NSB letters to MKR written while still at sea on 20 July (unpublished letters, Special Collections, University of Florida Library).

4 Aunt Ethel Traphagen Riggs now owned the former Traphagen farm (*Love Letters* 100–01). She married Lauren A. Riggs (1875–1956) in 1907. The two daughters, MKR's cousins, are Isabel A. Riggs (1911–2001) and Marion Gertrude Riggs (1915–2001).

My aunt had some wonderful family letters dating back as far as 1822. It was fascinating to re-create the people from their correspondence. Most of the letters were entirely unstilted. Was shocked to find that my great-grand-mother[1] wrote a great deal of poetry—very religious in nature, and, shall we say, uneven in quality. Now and then she used a quite telling phrase. "The Savior's heart and hands were weary, too." And she wrote to a grieving sister, "Do not let your sorrow drink your blood."

A great-great aunt[2] in 1869 asked a sister how she felt on the subject of woman's suffrage. The first convention for it was held that year. She wrote, "I myself am much in favor of it, and mean to exercise every privilege given me."

I had a day with a great-aunt[3] who is a riot. Some years a widow, she married an old guy when she was nearly 70, and he proved an awful flop. He is alive, but she has not lived with him for some years. She showed me a picture of him and I said, "I don't like his face." "Well," said Aunt Effie (84 years old) "You wouldn't like his hind end, either."

Came to the Creek last night and Martha and I got high together and swore undying fealty.[4] Moe and Smoky[5] were fine, but a few days ago Moe hadn't been able to stand it any longer, and was found by a friend on the road half-way to Hawthorn, headed for St. Augustine, to find me. He loves me the most of any dog I ever had.

Will go to the cottage tomorrow to stay until October.[6] Had a good visit with Sigrid Undset.[7]

Love,

Marjorie

---

1   MKR's paternal great-grandmother was Bridget McCabe Traphagen (1820–1842), who married Wessel Traphagen (1810–1862), the parents of Abram Traphagen, MKR's grandfather. Her maternal great-grandmother was Catherine Beardsley (1825–1908), who married William Nelson Osmun (1824–1901), the parents of Frances M. "Fannie" Traphagen, MKR's grandmother.

2   Not identified.

3   Effie Ceal Osmun Mabie (1877–1953), sister of MKR's grandmother Frances Traphagen, lived in Pontiac, Michigan. MKR's description of Aunt Effie is very similar to that in a letter to NSB on 29 July 1943, except she adds the following details, "Aunt Effie's first husband committed suicide because of ill health, and the old gal came to life after years of frustration. [She] married an old codger when she was nearly 70, who proved an awful flop. She hasn't lived with him for 8 years" (*Love Letters* 101–02). Aunt Effie married Raymond Jay Mabie (1870–1952) in 1916.

4   In a letter to NSB on 29 July, MKR recounts the episode, "When I got in last night, I invited Martha to have a drink with me. We got high as kites and swore undying loyalty" (*Love Letters* 102).

5   Moe, the pointer dog, and Smoky, the cat.

6   MKR's next letter to NSB, from Crescent Beach, is on 1 August.

7   MKR visited Undset in Brooklyn before going to Michigan. See MKR's letter on 20 July 1943.

. . .

JSB to MKR, 8 August 1943. ALS, 2 pp. PM: NEW YORK, N.Y. |
AUG 9 | 11-PM | 1943. AD: Mrs. Norton Baskin | Crescent Beach |
Star Route | St. Augustine, Florida. RA: J. Scribner | Far Hills, N.J.
VIA AIR MAIL envelope.

Sunday [8 August 1943]

Dearest Marjorie:

Here I am just slipping under the wire (at this end) in time to say "Many
Happy Returns"[1] and all of them healthy and, to a reasonable degree, wealthy
and wise.[2] I remembered your birthday <u>last</u> week and was all prepared to
shower you with cards, letters, gifts and maybe even a contraband telegram,
all to arrive correctly on the proper day. But somehow I forgot it <u>this</u> week
until now, and so here I am in my usual scramble.

(As a slight indicator of my present lack of orientation in time; yesterday I
went to the movies in Morristown with Granny[3] & an elderly friend. The village green was all cluttered up with grandstands flags etc. When G. & friend
wondered "what for?", I rather startled them by saying "Oh, for the Fourth
of July, of course.")

I am sending you Saki[4] and from town shall send you something slightly
more substantial, though less enduring.

I have also sent (lend-lease) Aragon & Bloch.[5] Hope they arrived safely.

Any day now I shall toss together a letter to you, but as everything in my
life at the moment seems problematic & doleful (except the "Fairie Queene")[6]

---

1   JSB is referring to MKR's birthday on 8 August.

2   "Healthy, wealthy, and wise" is widely attributed to Benjamin Franklin (1706–1790).

3   Morristown, New Jersey, is thirteen miles from Far Hills, New Jersey, the location of the Scribner estate.

4   Saki, pseud. Hector Hugh Munroe (1870–1916), wrote political satires, but is especially known
for his witty, cynical short stories. Munroe was killed in France in World War I. JSB might be sending MKR a Saki print. The "less enduring" gift is likely alcohol.

5   Louis Aragon (1897–1982), considered one of the founders of Surrealism, author of eclectic
novels, poetry, and political tracts and a major proponent of Communism in the West. His novel
The Bells of Basel (1934, trans. 1941), concerning humankind's social responsibility, was popular in
the West. Jean-Richard Bloch (1884–1947), French critic and member of the French Communist
Party, "— & Co." [1918], trans. C. K. Scott-Moncrief (New York: Simon & Schuster, 1929), a novel in
which a Jewish family named Simler move their cloth-making business from Alsace to Vendeuvre,
a small town west of Paris, where they open a factory. See MKR's positive response to Bloch in her
letter on 12 August 1943.

6   Edmund Spenser (1552?–1599), English poet, best known for his allegory *The Fairie Queene*
(1596), dedicated to Queen Elizabeth I, in which he examines, among other things, One True Faith

it wouldn't do at all for a birthday letter, and so it will have to wait until that crisis is past.

As a birthday thought for you, I would like to say that since hearing of the venerable – nay, positively biblical – ages of your relations, I am going over in my mind which of my cherished possessions I shall leave to you in my will. You might let me know if there's anything that has caught your fancy.

Much love – I wish I would be with you and have a real celebration. We might – you and I – try getting drunk and swearing undying fealty.[1] But we really don't have to, do we –

Julia

. . .

MKR to JSB, 12 August 1943. TLS, 5 pp. PM: SAINT AUGUSTINE | AUG 13 | 6 PM | 1943 | FLA. AD: Miss Julia Scribner | Far Hills | New Jersey. LH: MRS. NORTON S. BASKIN | CRESCENT BEACH, STAR ROUTE | ST. AUGUSTINE, FLORIDA.

Aug I2, 1943

Dearest Julia:

The shrimp boats are dotted over a very calm ocean and a large tropical freighter is on the horizon. A school of fish was jumping in about three feet of water close to shore, and I didn't enjoy my swimming too much, thinking that sharks might be coming in after them. I have just had breakfast in the midst of an appalling mess.

The maid problem seemed insuperable---two different ones promised to come, and then got cold feet at the thought of the isolation.[2] I kept house

---

(Una) and Untested Faith (Red Crosse Knight). The influence of Spenser's epic, both in concept and in form, upon subsequent poetry cannot be overstated.

1   JSB is playfully referring to MKR's report in the previous letter that she and Old Martha Mickens got drunk and swore fealty to each other. See Figure 2, 313.

2   Idella Parker had left MKR for a new life in New York City. MKR simply could not function without a maid. It especially became a crisis at Crescent Beach. MKR became desperate. She writes to Perkins on 11 August that she has a "good" maid coming, Zamilla Mickens "Sissie" Fountain, the daughter of Martha Mickens (*Max and Marjorie* 551). On 3 August she complains to NSB, "The glamorous colored girl couldn't come, as her mother didn't care to have her alone at the beach. . . . But a gray-haired colored woman . . . says she will give it a try." On 11 August MKR returns to the subject, "Jean Francis' good maid Ruby . . . says she will come, and I think means it. I offered high wages, but it will be worthwhile. . . . She is probably just as good as Idella." On 15 August MKR reports, Ruby is "too good to be true." On 25 August she despairs, "The pluperfect Ruby couldn't take the nights alone in the bottom-of-the-sand dune apartment" where the rattlesnakes gathered. On

in fits and starts, mostly fits. When there was no longer a clean teaspoon, I would drop work and wash the dishes. When Moe and Smoky[1] and I would get all tangled up in papers on the floor, I would stop and sweep. I have been trying to catch up on correspondence and there is no hope of getting to work on the book before the first of September. I have to stop anyway and battle with Norton's and my income tax.

A very good maid, as good as Idella, whom I have known before, has just returned to St. Augustine and says she will come, and I think she means it, as she has lived at the beach and likes it.[2] She also brought back with her a mongrel black puppy that she wants to take with her, and it isn't everybody, even in these help-less days, who would let her do that. She is to come tomorrow.

How depressed you sounded. I am so sorry you have the black curse, too. I have to fight it so much of the time, and it seems to me no one has less reason to be depressed than I, ordinarily.

I have already devoured the Bloch,[3] and it is magnificent. I thought that artistically it went to pieces at the end with a terrific crash, as though the old Simler factory building had suddenly caved in. It simply is not good objective art to end a book with a flood of preaching and analysis, especially coming from a character who has practically not appeared in the book before. The characters themselves must work out and express whatever the artist is trying to say. Until the end, though, I thought the book was one of the most sensitive and revealing and moving I had read in a long day.[4]

I shall be up against that same problem in the book[5] I shall be doing---working out more or less abstract ideas through character and action. I am appalled sometimes at the difficulty of it. My hope of salvation is that I am deeply in love with two of the characters, greatly amused by a third, and loathe a fourth.

I haven't heard from Norton again since the letter from at sea that I wrote you about.

---

26 August MKR opines, "Ruby agreed to come back, but only if she could work 9 am to 6 pm" (*Love Letters* 105, 108, 110, 115, 118). MKR needed Idella to return, which she finally did. Idella proved to be MKR's "perfect maid" (*Idella* 37). "I feel perfectly sure that the Lord sent me Idella" (*Cross Creek* 203).

1 Moe, the pointer dog, and Smoky, the cat.

2 Ruby.

3 Bloch's "— & Co.". See JSB's letter on 8 August 1943.

4 In the epilogue to "— & Co.", Benjamin Simler, who has spent the majority of the novel in the United States, returns in time to offer his cousin Louis Simler a series of sermon-like pronouncements on life, America, divine justice, the workers, and the fate of the Simler family.

5 *The Sojourner.*

Did your father[1] tell you that the Gainesville judge dismissed the lawsuit? The enemy can make an amended declaration if they choose, which my lawyer thinks will automatically be dismissed again. They then can ask for trial before the Florida Supreme Court, and if that is denied, the thing is ended.[2]

I have not gone back to the airplane spotting, through sheer cowardice over learning the types of planes. Will go at it again next week.

Bob Camp is now stationed at Pensacola, Fla., taking advanced gunnery and also doing some instructing. He signed himself Trigger Camp.

Verle Pope got his captaincy and will be moved soon, he hopes overseas. Edith has been here but joins him tomorrow.

Lots of love,

Marjorie

. . .

JSB to MKR, 16 August 1943. ALS, 4 pp. PM: NEW YORK, N.Y. |
AUG 18 | 2 – PM | 1943. AD: Mrs. Norton Baskin | Crescent Beach |
Star Route | St. Augustine, Florida. RA: J. Scribner | Far Hills, N.J.
VIA AIR MAIL envelope.

Monday – [16 August 1943][3]

Dearest Marjorie:

That's a hell of a thing, that I sounded depressed in your birthday note[4] – when I thought I had tossed it (depression) off as lightly. Well, for godsake don't let it worry you, because the chances are you will never receive anything but depressing letters from me. You are about the only person – why qualify for appearance's sake – the only person I can be depressed with, and I get exhausted being depressed by myself. I realize that is another weakness of mine, and for your sake I hope it may mend. The other

<hr>

1 Charles Scribner III.

2 The lawsuit brought by Zelma Cason, claiming she was libeled in *Cross Creek*. MKR reports in a letter to NSB on 11 August, "The Gainesville judge threw out the suit," but Cason's lawyers "can ask for a hearing before the Florida Supreme Court" (*Love Letters* 108). The lawyers did and the Court reversed the decision, found MKR guilty of "Invasion of Privacy," and fined her $1. For a complete history of the case, see Patricia Nassif Acton, *Invasion of Privacy: The "Cross Creek" Trial of Marjorie Kinnan Rawlings* (Gainesville: University Press of Florida, 1988).

3 Written in a second hand at the top of p. 1: [Aug 2? 1943].

4 JSB's letter on 8 August 1943.

possible cure would be falling in love, which if somewhat more reciprocal than the last time,[1] would produce a marvelous, though passing <u>uplift</u>. Until either self-discipline or self-preoccupation set in, I warn you, things will be dreary, and you must keep an image of my kindness & innocent face before (and wholesome!?) so as not to begin to think of me as a Julian Greene[2] character.

I'm glad you liked the Bloch.[3] You know, I don't remember the end at all, except that I got very bored there – just at the finish. I think <u>many</u> books – not unnaturally – must fall apart at the winding up places because there are so many that I can remember the beginning and or through – but not the end. Just the other day Muddy spoke of the end of Malaisie[4] which you sent me only a few months ago. I would recall scene after scene vividly, but the end not at all, and it seems it was very dramatic – running amuck, double murders etc. She said she thought it was overdone, and I had to admit I had forgotten it completely. One's aesthetic memory, mine anyway, seems to be very charitable. If there is anything really <u>good</u> in a book I remember it and all the parts that are dull, over – or underdone just fade. Finally the book, in a sense, becomes transfigured and exists only in the better parts. What I remember most clearly is the quality of enjoyment I got from it. I can remember this "feel" when I have lost the plot and most of the characters. I think most books, after a long unchecked-upon stay in the mind, become overrated. Of course some are so dependably wonderful almost as the seasons.

I am reading Peguy[5] again. It is quite beyond me to say how good he is. He is as solid and uncompromising as a rock and yet he is gentle too – He is like no one I have ever read or read of. He can't be attached to any school and I don't think any school can be attached to him. He is usually called "a great Catholic philosopher" or "a great C. poet", (How I hate the distinction between Catholic & Protestant philosophers & poets. Why can't they just be Christian?) but he seems too plain and simple to fit comfortably into either of those exalted niches. He is too unintellectual and too easy to understand to be a regular philosopher and too unfanciful to be a

---

1   JSB seems to be referring to an actual person: not identified.

2   Julian Green, the novelist whom JSB especially liked. MKR shared her enthusiasm; see her letter on 28 April, asking JSB to instruct Scribners to send her "all the books" by Green.

3   Bloch's, "— & Co.", which MKR deemed "magnificent," except for the ending. See her letter on 12 August.

4   Henri Fauconnier (1879–1973), French novelist, *Malaisie* (New York: Macmillan, 1931).

5   Charles Péguy, French socialist.

poet. I have tried to think of other plain poets – Bobby Burns, Whitman,[1] but Peguy is much plainer. Yet what he writes is, I think, undeniably great philosophy & poetry. You must read him. Unfortunately the only book in Eng. contains just short selections from his works, but it is arranged with the French on one side of the page,[2] and a translation on the other, and so by the time I have finished the book I think I ought to be able to cope with the French alone. I don't know if one can buy any of his books here but the Public Library[3] has them all.

When I wrote the last note I was expecting to send you some ancient rye, but on the way to buy some, I stopped in at the Argosy Bookstore and they had a new Montanus[4] that I thought was very attractive & would make a nice pair with the one you already have. Old rye is not an entirely unmixed blessing anyway, as it faces you with the dreary problem about having your rye and drinking it too.[5] I couldn't remember just how I had framed the other picture so thought it was safer I send it nude. I'm sure St. Aug. is up to framing.

I was so glad to know about the case.[6] That was a good birthday present, wasn't it.

I have just loaded myself down with a flock of non-fiction books, which I despise! (Unless they're like Journey Among Warriors, and they usually ain't.) Falange about Nazism & Fascism in South A. & Undercover about same in U.S.A. Roi Ottley's book New World Acoming about the negro question, Spanish Labyrinth supposedly the best book to date about recent (100 years or so) Spain which you know is one of my pet problems. And that rather frightening looking novel The Conspiracy of the Carpenters, which

---

1   Robert Burns (1759–1796), Scottish poet, a champion of the poor. Walt Whitman (1819–1892), American poet, a champion of Democracy. The theoretical distinction between "plain" and "ornate" styles, delineated by Yvor Winters (1900–1968) in his influential essay "The Sixteenth-Century Lyric in England" (Poetry 53 [1939]: 258–72; 54 [1939]: 35–51), can be defined roughly as the difference between simple yet thematically significant poetry versus that which is decoratively focused on "the pleasures of rhetoric for its own sake" (262).

2   JSB is referring to the translation by Ann and Julian Green, Basic Verities, where the French text and the English translation are facing each other. See JSB's letter dated [23? March 1943], 171, n. 3, and 172, n. 1.

3   New York Public Library.

4   See MKR's comments on Montanus in her letter on 30 January 1943.

5   JSB is playing with the conundrum in language of the English proverb: "having your cake and eating it too."

6   In her letter on 12 August 1943, MKR informed JSB that the judge ruled in her favor in the "Cross Creek" libel trial (see 207, n. 2). The Florida Supreme Court, upon appeal, reversed this decision.

from the outside I would guess to be difficult but important. I bet you know if any of them are imperative![1] Above.[2]

Bad news I'm afraid about my headaches. No time to give you the dreary details now. I am fascinated by your relations with your new characters![3] Please don't worry about keeping up your correspondence with me. I am always happy to sacrifice myself for art, as Mr. Alves[4] would say.

Much love.

Julia.

. . .

MKR to JSB, 28 August 1943. ALS, 6 pp. PM: HAWTHORN | AUG 30 | 2 PM | 1943 | FLA. AD: Miss Julia Scribner | Far Hills | New Jersey

Aug. 28, 1943

Dearest Julia:—

Here I am at the Creek for the week-end, and hot as hell. Finally plugged in the elegant D.C. fan Norton gave me, though I feel guilty about using gas for the Kohler.[5] But have the colored boy watering things while the motor runs and filling the tank, so it's not too extravagant. The crepe myrtle blossoms are dropping into the bird-bath and the red-birds are eating from the feeder you sent—and you have not said how much I owe you for it.

---

1 Eve Currie (1904–2007), French-American writer, *Journey Among Warriors* (New York: Doubleday, Doran, 1943); John Roy Carlson [Arthur Derounian] (1909–1991), Armenian-American writer, *Falange: The Axis Secret Army in the Americas* (New York: Putnam, 1943); Allan Chase (1913–1993), *Under Cover: My Four Years in the Nazi Underworld of the Americas* (New York: Dutton, 1943); Vincent L. "Roi" Ottley (1906–1960), African American journalist, *New World a-Coming* (New York: Houghton, Mifflin, 1943); Edward FitzGerald "Gerald" Brenan (1894–1987), British writer, *The Spanish Labyrinth: An Account of the Social and Political Background of the Civil War* (Cambridge: Cambridge UP, 1943); Hermann Borchardt (1888–1951), German writer, *The Conspiracy of the Carpenters: Historical Accounting of a Ruling Class*. Trans. [June] Barrows Mussey (New York: Simon & Schuster, 1943).

2 JSB places an arrow symbol pointing up after "Above."

3 JSB is referring to MKR's preliminary work on what finally becomes *The Sojourner*. See MKR's letter on 29 July 1943.

4 Carl Alves, see JSB's letter dated [24 February 1941].

5 D.C. fan, a direct current cooling fan. Kohler, a generator. MKR is concerned about using gasoline, especially since it was being rationed.

All my thanks for the delightful <u>Saki</u>[1]—and the Thorntons[2] print is <u>elegant</u>. I can get it framed almost like the other one, and they will make a stunning pair. Some day Norton and I will have a home, instead of a hotel, a beach cottage and a farmhouse, and what lovely walls we shall have, with your prints and the Audubons and Bob's paintings.

I am getting along better than I expected to, but the most <u>awful</u> <u>waves</u> come over me of missing Norton, usually at the most awkward times, such as in the middle of a bridge game, when I think how much more fun it would be if he were my partner.

I am practically paying ransom money to keep a maid at the cottage, and even so she arrives by bus at 9:15 A.M. and leaves at 6 P.M.,[3] but it is worth it to keep things straight behind me while I work. I am only making notes on the book, but it is as definitely work as the actual writing. Just as soon as the weather turns cool I shall come to the Creek, I hope about October first.

I do want you to come to the Creek for some of the winter hunting. The place is large and rambling enough so that I should be able to work while you are here. I'll lay in a supply of reading matter to keep you occupied when I'm at the typewriter—which is not too many hours a day.

One of Martha's daughters is going to help me this winter. She has never done my kind of cooking but is young and willing and it will work nicely. She is the wife of Henry, the colored man in "Cross Creek" who shot Adrenna's husband Samson.[4]

---

1 Saki [Hector H. Munro] (1870–1916), British writer of witty, sarcastic, and often macabre stories. The closest Saki title to the date of this letter is *The Short Stories of Saki* (New York: Viking, 1943).

2 Robert John Thornton, the artist. See MKR's letter on 17 June 1943, 195, n. 3.

3 MKR is speaking of Ruby Dillard, the maid whose services were obtained from Jean Francis.

4 Zamilla "Sissie" Mickens, married Henry Fountain who subsequently shot Adrenna Mickens's husband Samson in a quarrel, the subject of which was never made clear. "Old Boss" Brice and Tom Glisson were on Henry's side, and MKR would have been until she found out that Brice had bribed the judge who then ruled in Henry's favor. MKR was appalled at the injustice done Samson, whose belly was full of No. 5 shot, yet Henry had been released. MKR threatened to go to the governor, but settled for a warrant for Henry's arrest. Samson, whose sole skill was growing roses, was terrified and very soon thereafter left the Creek upon MKR's gentle persuasion, with a month's pay. Henry's trial was a farce, and after some clear abuses of the truth on both sides, the judge dismissed the case against Henry. MKR was held in contempt for abusing the judge's discretion. She refused to pay and warned everyone from the Creek that if there were another shooting, she would be the one doing it. Later, as a gesture of goodwill, all participants made up. Henry went back to working in Brice's grove, Samson was gone but enriched, and MKR was able to get back to her writing, until Adrenna, her valued but easily impassioned maid, suddenly left with yet another man in tow. MKR was not yet aware that Idella would soon return (*Cross Creek* 192–203).

Poor Henry died yesterday in the Veteran's Hospital. The hospital wired his wife at once, informing her, and asking for permission for an autopsy (for they never found out what was wrong) and asking if she wished burial at government expense in the national cemetery at St. Augustine etc. The wire was addressed to Zamilla Fountain, <u>Colored</u>, Route 1, Hawthorn, and just because it was only another dead nigger, the Western Union operator at Hawthorn made <u>no</u> <u>effort</u> to have it delivered, and just dropped it in the mail—which arrived at noon today. The wire said "Deliver and check charges with gov't. Hospital" but the white-trash bastard thought it didn't matter. Actually, it messed up everybody, the Hospital (by the time I 'phoned them it was too late for an autopsy), the family (the wife, knowing he was in serious condition, had hitch-hiked early this morning to go to see him) and me. The burial had to be held up until Tuesday, and of course I have to take the family over for it, and had to wire cancelling my Monday spotting. The hospital was as upset as I, and I think the Western Union Southern gentleman will find he was a little careless with government orders. If it had been a white woman's husband, the sheriff himself would have delivered that wire, if necessary.[1]

Don't just write "Bad news about the headaches" and then not another word! Doesn't the medicine work, or what???

The Aragon book was <u>grand</u>. I loved it. Will return it and the Bloch soon.[2]

Write me about the headaches. The Mountbatten[3] appointment to S.E. Asia, with the hint of a Burmese attack at the end of the monsoon season about Oct. 1st, means that Norton will arrive just in time to pick up the first wounded.

Love,

<u>Marjorie</u>

· · ·

MKR to JSB, 5 September 1943. TLS 1 p. PM: Saint Augustine | Sep 8 | 11 AM | 1943 | FLA. AD: Miss Julia Scribner | Far Hills | New Jersey. LH: Mrs. Norton S. Baskin | Crescent Beach, Star Route | St. Augustine, Florida

1   MKR repeats the story, in more detail, to NSB in a letter on 28 August (*Love Letters* 116–19).

2   Louis Aragon, *The Bells of Basel*, and Jean-Richard Bloch, "— & Co.". See JSB's letter on 8 August 1943, 204, n. 5.

3   Louis Francis Albert Victor Nicholas, Lord Mountbatten (1900–1979), head of the Southeast Asia Command, commanded the Allied operations against the Japanese in Burma. See MKR's letter to NSB on 28 August 1943 (*Love Letters* 116, n. 1).

Sept. 5, 1943

Dearest Julia:

Just a line to say that I had a cable from Norton this morning announcing his arrival at his destination, "perfectly fit". The cable had at the top "Sans origine"---and I'll bet anything he is in the Middle East, where French is used, and not in India.[1]

I feel at least a temporary relief.

Have been listening to the N.Y. Philharmonic. A Chilean pianist did a Liszt piano concerto very much to my taste.[2]

Marjorie

. . .

JSB to MKR, 13 September 1943. ALS, 6 pp. PM: NEW YORK, N.Y. | SEP 16 | 130 PM | 1943 | STA. G. AD: Mrs. Norton Baskin | Crescent Beach | Star Route | St. Augustine, Florida. RA: J. Scribner | Far Hills, N.J. VIA AIR MAIL envelope.

[start of p. 1]

Sept. 13. [1943][3]

Dearest Marjorie:

I was so glad to hear that Norton has arrived safely. Probably you will have a letter from him pretty soon. Of course mail is awfully slow. Though I think it is much slower going <u>out</u> than it is coming home. I get letters from Sandy[4] (Air Mail) from New Guinea & Australia in about 10 days and sometimes less! Air Mail letters to him take about 3 weeks or a month, and if he is off somewhere on his little boat, much worse. A funny thing is that I get Air Mail letters much quicker from him than V Mail.[5] This is probably a Pacific pe-

---

1 NSB was, in fact, in India.

2 Claudio Arrau (1903–1991) is considered one of the most celebrated pianists of the twentieth century and is especially known for his wide array of interpretations. He performed Piano Concerto No. 2 by Franz Liszt (1811–1886), accompanied by the New York Philharmonic Orchestra, conducted by Dimitri Mitropoulos (1896–1960), broadcast by the Columbia Radio Network, beginning at 3 pm on 5 September.

3 Written in a second hand after the date on p. 1: [43].

4 Sandy Dillon, a beau of JSB.

5 V Mail, Victory Mail, was inaugurated on 15 June 1942 in an effort to reduce the weight of mail sent overseas to servicepeople. The process of the system, developed by Eastman Kodak, was to

culiarity as N. African V Mail gets here in a week. And Air Mail to England frequently goes by <u>very</u> slow boat. So much for the U.S. Post Office. Which incidentally is the object of a whispering attack at the moment by frightened capitalists. It is held up as a gruesome example of mismanagement & inefficiency of Gov. controlled system. The punch line is "Just imagine if the telephone & telegraph were run by the Gov. you wouldn't phone or receive a wire on Sundays." It doesn't help much to point out that in the Scandinavians, England, France and god knows how many other countries where T&T is Gov. owned this is hardly the case – and as far as I know Post Offices are closed everywhere on Sundays.

These rumors that Daddy[1] brings home with him from bank meetings and from the big shots on the club car are pretty depressing some of them and if you could hear and see panicky way in which they are delivered and received you'ld think you were seeing a couple of Southern women whispering about Eleanor Clubs the same mixture of fear and rage.[2] One of the most vicious I have heard was about rationing. It seems that is a terrible New Deal plot to kill off capitalism or should I say "free enterprise." The N.D. unable to kill off said F.E.[3] by frontal attacks initiated rationing so that the rich would be able to get no more food than the poor. We would all be reduced permanently to a poor standard of living. The rich being unable to buy more with their money – money would lose its value. And phtt!! F.E. would be dead. Thank god this nightmare seems to have died down somewhat. If it doesn't die down completely it may easily hamstring what must be done after the war.

While on the dreary subject of rumors, I must tell you that I regret to say that I think <u>Under Cover</u> is an "imperative book" to use an unhappy phrase.[4] I regret because it isn't going to cheer you up much to read it – particularly as almost every day in the papers you can find a continuation of some chapter of the book – and also because it is quite repetitious and dull reading. The first objection only makes it <u>more</u> imperative and the second

---

write the letter, then photograph it, and then to put it on microfilm. One microfilm, approximately 1,600 letters, was the size of a pack of cigarettes, and this could easily be shipped. When the microfilm arrived overseas, it was reproduced in the original letter form and delivered to the addressee.

1   Charles Scribner III.

2   Eleanor Clubs, named after Eleanor Roosevelt, an outspoken advocate of Black Rights, were rumored to have been formed throughout the South at the beginning of the war in order to organize for fair wages and labor practices and to displace their White bosses. Later investigations by the FBI demonstrated that the rumors were false.

3   That is, the "New Deal" and "Free Enterprise."

4   John Roy Carlson [Arthur Derounian], *Under Cover: My Four Years in the Nazi Underworld of America* (New York: Dutton, 1943).

you must just bear – and as one who read it from cover to cover I'll advise that you can skip a bit – though you read so damned fast that hardly seems worthwhile. I'm not sending it now in case you have it already – just let me know.

I have two more Julien Green's <u>The Dark Journey</u> and <u>Christine</u> which contains his first book The Pilgrim on the Earth[1]. I shall not be able to get around to them for some time, so if you'd like to read them, I'd be glad to send them along. I don't know whether reading distracts you from your work or not. That leaves only two books that I haven't got of his.[2] <u>Midnight</u> and <u>The Strange River</u>. I think I can get ahold of both of them, OK – oh and I see there's <u>Suite Anglaise</u> which I have an idea is sissy, then there's <u>Varouna</u>. I saw a copy of that in the Librairie Francaise but I don't think it's been translated yet.[3] Let me know if you want those too. I have a ton of stuff to get through yet so you can have them for as long as you like.

I had a pleasant experience of ars longa[4] – or something like that the other day. Daddy got the London Times Lit. supplement, which I always read and often I see a book I would like to have reviewed there. I used to just curse the war, but this time I tried a very nice but <u>very</u> highbrow book store that I had visited in ne Aragon [sic].[5] I found that despite war, submarines, shipping difficulties etc. etc. they imported books regularly and had on hand about every new "literary" book that came out in Eng. The book I wanted was right there on the table: (A book of Garcia Lorca's poems translated by J. L. Gili and Stephen Spender)[.][6]

It seems as though it must be about futile to translate a poet so violently lyrical as Lorca, and yet even if what I know must be a deformation (if not something worse) of the original I find more enjoyment than in most contemporary poetry. I try to imagine Keats or Byron done into Spanish.[7] I should think it would be a mess. But somehow Lorca or anyway something

---

1 Julien Green (1900–1998), American writer who wrote primarily in French, *The Dark Journey* (*Léviathan*, 1929), *Christine, The Pilgrim on the Earth* (*Le voyageur sur la terre*, 1927). His debut novel was *Mont-Cinère* (1926), or *Avarice House* (New York: Harper, 1927).

2 *Midnight* (*Minuit*, 1936) and *The Strange River* (*Épaves*, 1932).

3 *Suite Anglaise*, Les Cahiers de Paris, 1927. *Varouna*. Librairie Francaise (*Then Shall the Dust Return*, 1940).

4 As in the Latin phrase "*ars longa, vita brevis*" ("art is long, life is short").

5 In the holograph, JSB writes "ne Aragon," a region in northeast Spain. Given the impossibility of a visit to Spain in 1943, and her recent fascination with Louis Aragon, she may have meant "Argosy," an antiquarian bookstore founded in 1925, located at 116 E. 59th Street, New York City.

6 Federico García Lorca (1898–1936), Spanish poet, playwright, and director, assassinated by Nationalist forces at the beginning of the Spanish Civil War. *Poems of F. Garcia Lorca*, trans. by J. I. Gili (1907–1998) and Stephen Spender (1909–1995 [Oxford: Oxford UP, 1939]).

7 John Keats (1795–1821), George Gordon, Lord Byron (1788–1824), English Romantic poets.

very swell comes through. There is one marvelous poem in the book, "Lament for Ignacio Sancho Mejias" (a famous toreador).[1]

It is rather fun comparing translations – there are a few bits from the plays that are in the book we published and there are two poems which Rolfe Humphries translated also – in his "Out of the Jewel."[2] They are often surprisingly different, even when they say the same thing (which they <u>don't</u> always). Here are the first two lines of one of the monologues in "Yerma"

Graham & O'Connell:[3]
"Oh, what a field of sorrows!
Oh, this is a door to beauty closed!"

Gili & Spender:
Alas, what a meadow of sorrow!
Alas, what a door shut on beauty!"

I think the first would sound much the better spoken on the stage (or read to oneself for that matter). It has a smoother line. The second chops itself up. In some other places I prefer G&S.

The most drastically different conceptions are of a poem called "The Faithless Wife." G&S have it in blank verse with very irregular verse divisions – paragraphs really, while Humphries has made a regular jingle of it. <u>What</u> the hell was it to begin with?

Listen to this little passage:

G&S
In the farthest street corners
I touched her sleeping breasts,
and they opened to me suddenly
like spikes of hyacinth

H:
I roused her sleeping bosom
Right early on our walk;
Her heart for me unfolded
Like jacinth on the stalk.

---

1 Ignacio Sancho Mejias (1894–1934), bullfighter, gored to death in the ring at Manzaneres, in western Spain, 13 August 1934.

2 Humphries, *Out of the Jewel* (New York: Scribners, 1942). Lorca's "Yerma" (1934), a drama is three acts about a childless woman in rural Spain who desperately wants to conceive. "The Faithless Wife," a poem about a married woman who deceives a man into thinking she is a virgin.

3 Richard L. O'Connell and James Graham-Luján, translators.

Most of the time Rolfe is clever as hell in using almost ten same words and fitting them into relentless meter and rhyme,[1] but what I want to know is, did Lorca use that meter and rhyme? Here is a complete N. verse[2]

Not nard nor snail had ever	Nor nard nor mother-o'-pearl
Texture of skin so fine,	have skin so fine
Nor crystal in the moonlight	Nor did crystals lit by moon
Glimmered with purer shine:	shine with such brilliance,
Her thighs slipped from beneath me	Her thighs slipped away from me
Like little trout in fright,	like startled fish,
Half chilly (but not frigid),	half full of fire,
Half full of shining light	half full of cold.[3]

The words are practically the same but the rhythm makes the effect quite different.

<u>Sept. 14</u>

You asked for more information on the headaches. The fact is I'm afraid that the Gynergen[4] isn't much help. As Dr. A.[5] told me that was the only hope he could hold out to me, that puts me just about where I was when I started. It's just damn good luck that, so far, I don't have to earn my living, and can afford to go to bed when I'm laid out – and do nothing when I'm tired.

Quite a bit of interest has happened lately in my life, amatorily speaking. My one love[6] has finally gotten himself married. And so now there is a legal end to that affair which has already had so many endings I can't even remember all of them. Except for two days that's all it consisted of – endings and beginnings – in exhausting and pitiless succession. The last ending had been so final, as you know. I haven't seen or heard from him for about three years, that you might [think] this would be quite painless. It was not, and I have still to wait for the ending, whether gradual or sudden, which will be completely final. I think it's a bit naïve to expect it at all. It is really extraordinary this affair, because of its terrific uniqueness. Before

---

1 Rolfe Humphries (1884–1969), trans. *The Poet in New York and Other Poems of Federico Garcia Lorca* (New York: Norton, 1940).

2 Letter verses are a tool for memorization, especially of passages in the Bible.

3 JSB compares translations by Humphries of Lorca's "The Unfaithful Married Woman" (ll. 29–36) and then by Gili and Spender of "The Faithless Wife" (ll. 28–35).

4 First marketed in 1921 and commonly used to suppress the effects of migraine headaches.

5 Dr. Atchley.

6 Not identified.

it, through all the most susceptible adolescent years, I had never even the smallest degree of feeling – I had almost decided I was completely sexless and would never fall in love. Then this, which god knows was serious enough from every angle – and again, so far, although I have occasionally felt physically or companionably attached to someone, I have felt not even the slightest bit of love.

Well, to return to events I passed a dreary couple of nights going over the past. Thinking if I had said this or done that, if I had taken that course instead of the one I did take, would things have been different? I agonized again over the horrible mistakes I made in my bewildered innocence. Boy, I really was innocent and bewildered. I should think there is nothing more wonderful than first love when it goes well. I don't mean of course the average half based meaningless affair, but when it was as it was with me. I know that when it does not go it is the sharpest of pain, because you are not yet used to being hurt and you haven't yet come to expect the pain which is at the other side of every joy. I know you never get <u>used</u> to being hurt, but somehow though it may not be more intense, it seems heavier when it is first so uncomprehendingly and so unexpectedly experienced. Injured innocence has more than a poetic claim for sympathy. It is a truly pitiful thing. I'm not just bemoaning my own fate. It is long enough ago to have become rather objective, and more a feeling I have for all suffering innocents, not just myself.

<u>Again</u> I shall try to go back to events. After these couple of nights of fruitless wrestling with the past, something occurred which quite took my mind off my troubles. One afternoon while I was hostessing at the Eng. Speaking Union,[1] three Belgian R.A.F. officers came in. They had quite a dash to them and all the little Royal Navy officers sitting around were woefully eclipsed. Of course I immediately asked them if they knew my Belgian cousin (in the Bel. Army in Eng.) They all knew him well. One was even a cousin of his wife, and as they all came from Brussels, we were soon embarked on a session of did you know so and so? Brussels is a small city and everyone knows or at least knows of everyone else, so that our session was very successful. (The whole affair is quite lengthy. I should be telling it to you, but to avoid complete collapse from writer's cramp I'll have to cut it ruthlessly.) The plot in brief is that we had two gala days, and the point is that Cupid came nearer with one of those arrows than he has in many years. A little time more and I think he would have gotten the range. Just

---

1   English Speaking Union, international educational charity founded in London (1918), had a New York branch established in 1920 that was located at 30 Rockefeller Plaza.

my damn luck to meet him at the end of his leave when he had already been here a week. I suppose if I don't tell you a bit more you'll curse me from here to St. Aug. Well, two of them were small & blonds. Typical Belgians. And one was tall & dark and also handsome as hell. Need I go into which one it was? I fear that this proves to me that I definitely go for something so super attractive and with such high powered sex appeal that everyone else wants it too. Of course I take into account quality of mind & spirit, but it seems to take the other to get me at all interested. Andre is the type that people, women that is, turn around to look at on the street. I realize this makes him sound somewhat repellant. When I added to Cath & Rossie[1] that he has a small black moustache they almost expired with horror. I hope you will be a little more sophisticated about it. And also have more confidence on my discretion. I've never been known to go for smoothness and I can assure you I'm not starting now. They had all had quite a bad time in the war, Andre worst of all because he was captured by the Germans in the invasion of Belgium. He has been in 14 prisons and concentration camps, mostly G. but some were Spanish. I never found out how he escaped, because we were always having too good a time to discuss such subjects. He told me quite a few stories of the Spanish prisons – some humorous – and some not so humorous about the nightly torturing of a Republican whose cell he shared for a while. None of this seems to have put the slightest dent in his spirits. He is the gayest person I have ever met. He just infects every member of a party and you find yourself and everyone else having the best time you've ever had. We had one marvelous lunch, just the four of us, at the Brussels Restaurant which is super de luxe and they, naturally, were treated like princes.[2] We had cocktails, bottles of wine, a "fines"[3] on the house to end up. As we thoroughly nourished our bodies and spirits we told dirty jokes in three different languages argued whether Bruegel the Younger was any good as a painter and whether Goya had ever left Spain after his youth and I had a couple of serious discussions about food.[4] Andre & I discovered we had had the same practical joke tricks in our youth (they must have a Johnson, Smith & Co in Belgium)[5] which practically made us soulmates.

---

1 Catherine Ginna Mellick Gilpin, one of JSB's best friends, and Allia Nora Rossie.

2 The Brussels Restaurant was located at 28 E. 63rd St., New York.

3 Fines is a generic term for high-quality French brandy, including cognac and armagnac.

4 Pieter Bruegel (1564–1638), the "Younger," son of Pieter Bruegel (c. 1525–1569), the "Elder"; both were Flemish painters. Francisco Goya (1746–1828), Spanish painter and printmaker.

5 Johnson, Smith, & Co., mail order company established in 1914, which sold novelty and gag gift items.

Just my luck, as Mr. Alves[1] would say, that when my blood pressure was really starting to rise & the world was beginning to look rosy despite all the worries that daily besiege me – Andre & Bobby had to leave. However the future is not entirely black, they expect to get another leave before they go back to Eng. (They are training in Can.) Guy didn't have to go so soon so he spent the weekend with us in the country. Really they were the sweetest, most attractive and natural people we have met during the war. And that's saying a hell of a lot. Must go now. Much love per usual.

Julia

P.S. I forgot to say he gave me his wings and also a magnificent compact with two Belgium & U.S. flags in enamel.

. . .

MKR to JSB, [13?] September 1943. ALS, 1 p., with enclosed type-scripts of parodies to Emily Post,[2] 3 pp. PM: SAINT AUGUSTINE | SEP 17 | 5[30] PM | 1943 | FLA. AD: Miss Julia Scribner | Far Hills | New Jersey.

Emily Post[3] is the most humorous writer in modern American literature. Her column the other day was a riot, so I sent it, with the enclosed to Norton, and did a copy for you.

Marjorie

Sept. 13, 1943[4]

---

1 Carl Alves, see JSB's letter dated [24 February 1941].

2 These parodies are mentioned in MKR's letter to NSB, 20 Oct. 1943: "I sent Julia a copy of the shandy-gaff take-off that I wrote for your amusement, and she was disgusted. She said she is a vomitophobe, and often sits miserably through lunch or dinner in a restaurant, in fear that some nearby drunk will be ill. I don't think being ill is funny, either, but nausea seemed to me the only satisfactory answer to Emily Post" (*Love Letters* 152). These parodies were not among those found in the MKR-Baskin correspondence; see Brent E. Kinser, "'The Least Touch of Butter': Marge and Emily on Manners," *Journal of Florida Literature* 10 (2001): 1–9. See also "Parodies of Emily Post," *The Uncollected Writings of Marjorie Kinnan Rawlings*, ed. Rodger L. Tarr and Brent E. Kinser (Gainesville: University Press of Florida, 2007): 298–302.

3 Emily Post (1873–1960), a widely published syndicated columnist on the subject of manners. Her book, *Etiquette* (New York: Funk and Wagnalls,1922), was considered the authority on social behavior.

4 This date is related to the MS of the Post parodies by MKR, not the date of MKR's forward to JSB. It is more likely that the date of this letter is closer to the postmark date.

TRY A DASHING MANNER WHEN ORDERING SOFT DRINKS

That anyone should feel self-conscious about ordering a non-alcoholic drink in a cocktail lounge is without reason! And yet, it is very curious that when a teetotaler orders his pet drink in a cocktail lounge, he (sometimes, even she) is likely to be seized with shyness and weakly whispers—"Tomato juice." This attitude is quite evident in the wording of this letter:

"I don't care for anything in the line of alcohol, and yet I like very much to go with my friends to cocktail lounges for the same of sociability. I must say, though, that most of my friends (as well as their friends) do not look upon something cooling to drink as coming in the non-alcoholic category. Can you tell me what is the least conspicuous drink for me to order at such a time?"

As I have already noted, "least conspicuous" is the one thought to avoid. The way to "carry off" a soft drink order when all others order strong ones, is to say with the manner of demanding particular attention---"Bring me an orange and ginger-ale shandy-gaff with maraschino cherries and plenty of mint leaves at the top." If you say it with the manner of a Southern Colonel ordering a double strength mint julep, this can be most effective.

Dear Mrs. Post:

May I trouble you again? I know I did something wrong, but I don't know what it could have been, unless I just didn't look far enough ahead. It is so hard, Mrs. Post, to know what is good manners when the unexpected happens. I did just as you told me about ordering the non-alcoholic drink, and oh my God, Mrs. Post.

I went into the Waldorf bar with my friends, as usual. Most of them ordered Manhattans but there were two Scotch and sodas. I could see my turn coming and I began to tremble. I repeated over and over to myself, "Least conspicuous is the one thought to avoid." It took all my will power, Mrs. Post, but when the waiter turned to me, I stood by the table, pulled up my skirt and fixed my garters and said, "Bring me an orange and ginger-ale shandy-gaff with maraschino cherries and plenty of mint leaves at the top."

The waiter said, "Sorry, Miss, we're out of mint leaves."

I thought, "What would Mrs. Post tell me to do now?" and decided you would say to carry it off in a dashing manner by avoiding being inconspicuous. So I beat my fist on the table and I shouted, "Then damn it, go out and GET some mint leaves! Go and borrow some from the Ritz!" It seemed to me that was about what a Southern Colonel would have done. The waiter bowed and went away and everybody stared at me. I heard a man at the next table say, "Jesus, is she tight!"

But I still felt all right about everything, because if you follow Emily Post, you just can't go wrong. My Mama done tol' me.

Well, it was the longest time before our drinks were served, and my friends said, "Why the hell didn't you stick to your tomato juice?" Finally the drinks came and my orange and ginger-ale shandy-gaff was half full of maraschino cherries and there was practically a basket of mint leaves at the top and I have always been allergic to maraschino cherries and anything like mint reminds me of grass that dogs eat when they feel sick. One of my friends said, "Well now I know how to get what you want at the Waldorf. Just forget you're a lady." So I drank my orange and ginger-ale shandy-gaff and I ate all the maraschino cherries and I ate all the mint leaves.

And then, Mrs. Post, the most awful feeling came over me and I got to thinking about dogs and grass and all of a sudden I woopsed and there were maraschino cherries and mint leaves all over the Waldorf bar. I have never been less inconspicuous in my life. I could dimly hear people complaining and a great big man came in and took me by the shoulders and pushed me out of the door and I heard him say to my friends, "The management will call the police if any of you appears at the Waldorf again," and they said, "We had no idea she was so far gone." I screamed, "Ask Emily Post! Ask Emily Post!" and my friends said, "Take it easy. It could happen to anybody."

They walked me up and down and I began to forget the mint leaves and somebody said, "Your mistake was in ordering that mixture, the shape you were already in. What you need is a good stiff straight drink". I was seized with shyness and wanted to weakly whisper, "Tomato juice", but my strength was gone. They took me into a bar on a side street and gave me a glass with whiskey in it, and it was delicious and made me feel better than I ever had in my life before. So I drank another, and since then I have had no more trouble, with shyness or tomato juice or mint leaves.

But what is worrying me is this question of etiquette:

Should I have gone back to the Waldorf and cleaned up where I woopsed the orange and ginger-ale shandy-gaff with maraschino cherries and plenty of mint leaves at the top, or did I do right to leave the waiter to do it?

ANXIOUS

· · ·

MKR to JSB, 28 September 1943. TLS, 9 pp. PM: HAWTHORN |
OCT 5 | 1943 | 8 [AM?] | FLA. AD: Miss Julia Scribner | Far Hills
| New Jersey. LH: MARJORIE KINNAN RAWLINGS | HAWTHORN,
FLORIDA.

Sept. 28, 1943

Dearest Julia:

I am moving to the Creek tomorrow, for the winter.[1] I have never been
able to settle down to work on my book, probably because of the uncertain-
ties that have hung over me like a Damoclean sword,[2] from Norton to my
maid![3] But I shall go at it there, whether I feel like it or not.

It is on my mind that there is something I must thank you for, and I can't
place it. You are always doing so many lovely things for me, that this is probably chronic. Anyway, whatever it is that you have sent me, I enjoyed it! I'll
return the two French books shortly.

About the Julian Green. I have read "The Dark Journey",[4] but the others I
do not know, and should be glad to borrow them.

Norton is definitely in India. He wrote of going to a race and watching the Maharajas, and of sharing a man servant with two other men, each
paying the poor bastard a rupee a week (30 cents), and of leaving soon for
A.F.S.[5] headquarters in the hills, where the English send their families in hot
weather, and India is certainly the only place where you get that combination. I am not too happy about it, as he will evidently go into action following
Mountbatten's push against the Japs to re-take the Burma Road,[6] and I am
afraid the Japanese campaign will take longer than the German. Yet the first

---

1   MKR did not leave Crescent Beach until 1 October 1943, reporting in a letter to NSB on 30 September that she was about to begin "packing and sorting. It is simply gorgeous today and it seems
inane to leave" (*Love Letters* 135).
2   Damocles, allegedly a courtier in the Court of Dionysius II in fourth-century bce Syracuse, is
the subject of a parable: He was accorded the opportunity to sit on the throne to experience the trials and the tribulations of wealth and power. When he looked above his head, he saw a sword hanging precariously by a single thread, ready to break at any moment, hence the Sword of Damocles.
3   At the time, MKR was trying to get Idella to return from New York.
4   Julian Green, *The Dark Journey* (New York: Harper, 1929).
5   American Field Service.
6   Louis Francis Albert Victor Nicholas, Lord Mountbatten (1900–1979), head of the Southeast
Asia Command, commanded the Allied operations against the Japanese in Burma. The Burma
Road, approximately 720 miles, was built to link Burma with southwest China.

German bomb could get him and his ambulance just as neatly as the last Japanese bomb.

Your Belgian officer[1] sounds fascinating. I should be glad to have you have an <u>Affaire</u> with him, yet I should hate to see you become engaged to, and marry him, for the reason that all those Continental men are such bastards about women. No matter how complete and lovely and satisfying a wife they have, they take it for granted that there will be other women, and we American women, with plenty of sex appeal on our own account, able to have all the lovers <u>we</u> wanted, still have the feeling of All or Nothing at All, and we just can't take male philandering. Of course, if you put this up to a continental male, he would assure you suavely that you were the One Woman. I may be doing Andre a grave injustice.

Norton, as was to be expected, wrote the most engaging account of his sea trip, which he said discreetly was "not uneventful". I feel sure he was in the convoy that was attacked at the entrance to the Mediterranean, for two days after the Germans claimed they sunk several of our ships there, I had a wire from A.F.S. headquarters saying they had had a cable from the unit that they were safe.

Norton evidently became buddies with the ship's captain, saying modestly that he thought it was because the only other older man in the unit was a bastard. The captain had him in his cabin for drinks etc., and Norton wrote such a funny story of the last day on board of their daily calisthenics. The last exercise of the hour was the push-up, and while they were supposed to do it six times, Norton said that by the end of the hour he was always only good for two, whereupon he collapsed upon the deck in hysterics, and the British officer in command reluctantly in hysterics with him. The last day Norton collapsed as usual, and the Captain had the stage set. He shouted "Stretcher!" and two sailors dashed up (the Captain had them waiting) and rolled Norton on a stretcher and bore him off to the Captain's cabin, where he was "revived" with brandy.

About a week later, and I see I used the word "bastard" three times in as many pages. Must have been in a disagreeable mood.[2]

Am at the Creek and still not too good a mood. A combination of anxiety about Norton, about not getting down to work, and the despair at setting in to train Sissy, Martha's daughter, who doesn't know a dinner napkin from a sanitary one. Of course, I'm darn lucky to have someone to train and should be ashamed to mind. Am probably just using it as an alibi for not working.

---

1 Andre: last name not identified.

2 If one week later, this letter would have been continued from here around 5 October. MKR was back at Cross Creek on 1 October (*Love Letters* 136–37).

But Idella did have me spoiled. Had a letter from her today and she said she hated it there and thought about the Creek all the time. Said her husband in the service had just been moved and didn't want her to leave New York until he knew more about his future whereabouts. She was just off a job for 3 weeks to pick up a little pin-money---$35 a week! She'll probably show up just about the time I've taught Sissie to make Crab Newburg. [1]

Smoky has become perfectly adorable and looks at me occasionally with reluctant affection. He and Moe together are most ingratiating. I suggest that any place you go this fall, you steal a box of shotgun shells. We are having an awful time getting any. My gun is a 20,[2] in case you can steal any for me. This against the day when you come down during the hunting season. Quail are abundant. The squirrels are stripping my trees of the huge pecan crop, and I set out yesterday with my .22 rifle and hoarded box of cartridges, only to have nothing happen when I pulled the trigger on an unmissable shot. I was stuck with .22 shorts instead of .22 longs.

We have an awfully nice invitation for this spring, if we could both make it. A friend of ours, Capt. Henry Heyl, was one of the group of Boston doctors I may have mentioned who were stuck in Florida so long. They were torpedoed on their way to Africa, and evidently went through severe exposure. They were in time for the Tunisian campaign,[3] and no more into action than it was found Henry had developed T.B. in one lung, and he was sent back to Walter Reed.[4] He is young, as good doctors go, in his very early thirties, but has already made a distinguished reputation as a brain surgeon. Half an hour before he took the 'plane for home, he took 2 (50-millimetre) bullets out of a man's brain, in what one of the other doctors wrote me was an exquisite operation. He is now at Fitzsimmons General Hospital in Denver, and being terribly philosophical about it all, though his heart must have been broken. He does very nice sketching, and to keep busy, began writing---and sold a short thing to the Atlantic

---

1   MKR used the same language about Sissie and Idella in a letter to NSB in early October (*Love Letters* 139).

2   That is, a 20–gauge shotgun. Because of rationing, any ammunition was difficult to obtain.

3   Henry L. Heyl (1906–1975), a prominent Boston neurosurgeon, served in the Army Medical Corps, and later was an instructor in surgery at Dartmouth Medical School. MKR was promoting as a love interest for JSB. In a letter to NSB on 28 September, MKR opines, "I wrote him among other things about Julia, with the usual effect. I have always wished I had had a chance at the one man she cared for" (*Love Letters* 134–35). As part of the North Africa Campaign, the offensive to retake Tunisia began on 5 January 1943, with U.S. and British forces collapsing on the German Forces led by General Erwin Rommel (1891–1944). The Germans surrendered on 13 May, having lost 40,000 men in Tunisia alone. The campaign was a decisive defeat for the Germans, and paved the way for the Allied invasion of Italy.

4   Walter Reed Hospital, Washington, DC.

Monthly[1] right off the bat. and the Atlantic Press asked to see any book he might do. He wrote that he will be well enough to leave in the Spring, and he has bought a house and 200-acre farm somewhere near the Vermont-New Hampshire line, near Manchester, I think, and will go there about April to live quietly until he can go back to his surgery. I wrote him that you and I had promised ourselves a wild-flower spring in that section, and he invited us to come and stay with him as long as we would! He said that if pressed, he would even go with us on our hunts, as New England wild-flowers and birds were the only things he <u>knew</u>---anything else he had only learned. He is a bachelor,[2] and terribly nice. He wasn't as spectacular as some of the older doctors, but as I saw more and more of him, and they all spent a weekend at the Creek, he wore so well, and had an adaptability and consideration for others that was most endearing. I am not cooking up any romantic scheme, as I don't think you would be interested in him that way, but you couldn't help liking him as a friend. Anyway, I wrote him that if my work went either well enough or badly enough, the visit appealed to me, and when Vermont or New Hampshire entered into it, you were easily sold.

Lots of love,

Marjorie

I didn't mean what I said about recommending an affair with Andre, or anyone. You would hate it. As you said once yourself, it is most desirable, when embarking on something perilous at best, to be able to see the other shore. I meant only that an American woman's relation with a Continental can be unusually dangerous, just from the difference in ideas for a scheme of living. God knows there are enough predatory and ramble-footed American husbands, and I suppose there are single-standard Europeans!

Was able to get the new print framed almost exactly like the other one.[3]

---

1   Heyl's "Bottle Hunt in North Africa," *Atlantic Monthly* 172.5 (November 1943): 107–10.

2   Heyl married Katherine Agate (1914–1998) in 1944.

3   The postscript is typed at the top of p. 1. The reference is to the Robert John Thornton print that JSB sent to MKR. See MKR's letter on 28 August 1943, 211, n. 2.

. . .

MKR to JSB, 7 October 1943. TNS, 1 p. Enclosed photograph of
Henry Heyl's farm in Vermont with his description on the verso.
PM: Hawthorn | Oct 7 | 2 PM | 1943 | FLA. AD: Miss Julia Scribner
| Far Hills | New Jersey. LH: Mrs. Norton S. Baskin | Crescent
Beach, Star Route | St. Augustine, Florida

[Heyl's description]:
Taken last spring (April) looking East.
The buildings occupy the North East portions of the 200 acre hill top ^farm^.
No other neighbors visible – or nearer than ¼ mile. Conn. Valley just beyond
with N.H hills in background
Farm is 1½ miles west of Norwich, Vt.

[7 October 1943].

The place Capt. Heyl[1] invited us to. Looks as though it would be most attractive when the leaves are out.
Heard from Norton again, and he is in the hills for a couple of months of
training.
   Says it is beautiful country with gorgeous flowers and vegetation.[2]

. . .

JSB to MKR, 18 October 1943. ALS, 6 pp. PM: NEW YORK, N.Y.
| OCT 19 | 2 PM | 1943 | STA. [illegible]. AD: Mrs. Norton Baskin |
Cross Creek | Hawthorn | Florida. VIA AIR MAIL envelope. LH:
Marjorie Kinnan Rawlings | Hawthorn, Florida.

Oct 18 '43

Dearest Marjorie:
   What an awful correspondent I am! All the various correspondences up
are like a necklace of millstones to me and keep me from enjoying the only
one I would carry on of free will. As it is now I contemplate a letter to you
– and I think no, I must write so and so first. And I don't feel like writing to

---

1   MKR relates the story of the farm in Vermont to Baskin in a letter on 15 August 1943, and asks,
"What about Henry Heyl for Julia?" (*Love Letters* 110–11). For the enclosure, see Figure 4, 315.
2   NSB was in India with the American Field Service.

either so <u>or</u> so – so, I don't write to anybody! Then, too, I have one failing that will undoubtedly keep me from the hazards of a literary career. I write mentally, and I find that the thought is a perfectly satisfying outlet and quite obviates the bother of the deed. I write you letters almost everyday, all starting quite properly "Dearest Marjorie:" – or under extenuating circumstances "Marjorie!" They are composed in "letter writing style", I mean not just as one thinks, and usually are rather lengthy. That's one of the greatest things about these letters, I can be so comprehensive without getting writer's cramp, and the little things don't bother me like how many times the word "quite" has been used on that page (or "things"!) Whatever is written in this way, whether a letter to you or to Lotte Lehmann or Tommy Beecham,[1] or a scintillating page for my journal, ever I have planned it to my satisfaction, I'm through with it, and any further traffic with the idea I find exhausting and boring. Often writing is rather dull because of this. There may be something I have to tell you or a review I force myself to write, and having told you or written it several times, it is a dreary anticlimax to get it on paper. Definitely I will never be a writer. Ideas to me are a delight – and their communication in the abstract – but my fancy is a newborn bird that doesn't care much for sitting, and the lengthy work of translation I find a headache – neither fascinating nor necessary. My medium would be a thought machine that could be shut off – even I, innocent, fairly young virgin that I am, have thoughts that I should keep to myself.

There now, I've wasted a whole page of your & my time. Too bad I didn't take care of that by V mail.[2] So much factual matter to be got through too. I'll begin at the beginning:[3]

I received your Emily Post outrage and enjoyed it greatly up to about what my course in creative writing would spot as this point[4]. There she was sick and right there you lost a customer. Because the way your heroine felt about the grass dogs eat, only about ten times more so, I feel about people being sick. I am a vomitophobe of pathological intensity. And my greatest nightmare is drunks in restaurants who look as if they might be sick. God, many's the good meal almost lost myself just watching them with dreadful

---

1 Charlotte "Lotte" Lehmann (1888–1976), German soprano, also a poet, novelist, and painter. Thomas Beecham (1879–1961), English conductor and founder of the Royal Philharmonic Orchestra and the London Philharmonic Orchestra.

2 JSB means that her words should be compressed, as in V Mail, so not to waste time or space.

3 JSB is alluding to Lord Byron, *Don Juan* (1819), Canto I, Stanzas 6–7, where Byron trivializes epic poets who always begin "*in medias res.*" As Byron avers, "My way is to begin with the beginning."

4 JSB inserts a drawing of two peaks what looks to be a plot mountain chart, pointing specifically to the top of the second peak.

fascination and fearing the worst. I think I'll get off this subject <u>right</u> <u>now</u>. You'll forgive me if I don't cherish that particular spread. I'll make up for it on the next one.

Now, Marjorie, you are working yourself into an awful sweat over my love life and the first thing you know it's going to be upsetting you more than it is me – that is unless I closely follow your advice in which case it would probably take a psychiatrist months to untangle the knots. First you tell me to have an "affaire" but don't marry Andre.[1] Then maybe he's OK. Then you have practically tucked me in bed with a young brain surgeon,[2] telling me this, while that I musn't imagine there is any romantic scheme to it at all (now where is that letter about Perry?).[3] Marjorie, what must Henry think?! I suppose you have written him that I am about 26 and lovely and need nothing so much as a husband & children "but this is not any romantic scheme because I don't think you would be interested in her that way, but you wouldn't help liking her as a friend." Tsk, tsk. Well, I guess you're bound to hit on something good sometime, but what do you think about the TB? Well anyway, I arrive at the end of the letter wondering whether to marry Andre or have an "affaire" with him – or both, when suddenly you tell me I can't have this "affaire" with A or anyone, and there I am all frustrated again – and then you shrug your shoulders, verbally. Eh, friend the fact is Andre left just a little too soon, I think. Anyway he has sunk into past. I may say I was planning not marriage, but a perfectly delightful affair – after the war, of course. I figured on a sort of touring affair – around France. I'm sure A. would be the perfect companion for such a venture. The only thing that worried me was that I might get too attached to him – but one way or another it might work out nicely. The question, anyway, is safely academic though you never know what might happen if he appears again.

The picture you sent of Dr. Heyl's farm has become a sort of icon. About everyday I pull it out and look at it. I suppose to you it looks somewhat cold, bleak, but to me it looks like Vermont--inland New England. I don't understand why N.E. should mean so much to me. Despite all my talks of being a Yankee, I am overwhelmingly New York by breeding and much more southern than N.E. Not only do I have a terrific predilection for N.E. &, of course, my beloved home town (and I <u>don't</u> mean Far Hills) but I have a positive aversion to the thought of living anywhere else in the U.S.A. I

---

1   Andre, the Belgian Army lieutenant. The last name is not identified.
2   Henry Heyl.
3   Perry Patterson.

think I'd rather live abroad than in the south or west. Something in me has stubbornly decided on a house. Perhaps I shall never live there, but my house is where I showed you, maybe you remember, on top of that hill over the village in New M.[1] It is all planned, the garden, which trees shall be cut down, what shall be planted where, the house changes occasionally, but in the main it has been the same since I first discovered home in 1937 and this year I found a place I could dam up a stream & have a swimming pool. You know, although we have fastened on practically the opposite end of the USA, I think it may be we are more the same than different because of that. Most people take over a place, but with us it was the other way round – and quite apart from such sentimental ties as ancestral lands or place of birth – or growing up or "lovely" people for neighbors. It's impossible to figure out. Aunt G. or Aunt L.[2] try to sell me on more convenient locations and Muddy tries to sell me on more beautiful views all not more than a mile or two away and although I can appreciate the superior convenience & beauty, unshakably, that place is home and everyplace else is just a nice place.

I shall of course ^tsk^ love ^tsk^ to go to Vermont, romance or no romance.[3] I couldn't think of missing a chance to go to New Eng. One thing only could deter me, and that would be a lack of plumbing. Is that lovely N.E. farmhouse modernized? I suppose a doctor is apt to have plumbing, but you never can tell some people have queer notions. They like to "camp out." I regret to expose this vulgar unromantic streak which threads through my every dream, but I figure you know it anyway, and are not unsympathetic.

I am going to try to get some shells this week, but I may only get my eye spat in. Speaking of getting, I did mean to get you some quinces this year but I kept forgetting at all the proper times. I'll send some next year.

Glad to hear Norton has gone up to the hills of India. It shouldn't be bad there. Do his letters take ages to get to you? I still get Sandy's[4] from N. Australia in about 10 days. He gets my letters, but doesn't get a darn thing else sent him. His mother sends him books almost every week & I send him the New Yorker, but I don't think he has ever gotten books or mag.

No news on the headache front. Poor Dr. Atchley almost goes into a decline every time I appear. He said he had never before had such a bad result with syringes. I had to have a full length picture taken of my interior which

1 New Marlborough, Massachusetts.
2 JSB's aunts Gladys and Louise.
3 JSB circles "of course" and inserts "tsk" above the line. She then draws an arrow after "love" pointing to another "tsk" above the line, with a small circle and another arrow pointing to after "go."
4 Sandy Dillon, a beau of JSB.

cost the family 100 bucks & gave me a blasting headache – not a bit to eat till 4:30 PM. Nothing of interest was revealed. This week I have another horrible test. No breakfast again. They stick a qt. of glucose into a vein and then every hour for 4 hours they extract a pint or so of my hard earned blood. Couldn't say what that might reveal, but I can guess. Dr. A. wants me to go back to a guy I used to go to who gives very subtle scientific exercises. I always thought it was about the best of many "cures". Also he wants me to go to some very famous psychiatrist (?). I have absolutely no enthusiasm for this idea. Not that I have any prejudice against p's – good ones – but it's just like lots of things – you think they're OK for the guy that wants them but you'd just as soon leave 'em alone yourself. I think a good deal of my spiritual privacy. I don't much care what physical nooks & crannies they poke into, but I think my immortal soul is my own business and a darn sight more important than my headaches. But I suppose it must be done, and perhaps whether or not he can deduce whether or not I am a malade imaginaire[1] by my intellectual processes with venturing into deeper realms. Frankly my idea for a cure now is to try to be hypnotized and told I will not have a headache. Do you read the Readers Digest?[2]

I wish you were here now to go to the Ballet with me. I think I shall go Wed. if I survive the glucose & blood ordeal. There are a couple of good new ballets this is a much better company than the one you saw.

I am just finishing New World A'Coming.[3] Very interesting – lots of information and a little bit dryer than I expected. Incidentally I think it's one of the most attractive jobs of bookmaking I've seen in a long time. For many books are in make up either dull or positively lousy, lots of Scribners I regret to say. There's one question I've meant to ask you for ages – why did you think I wouldn't like Winesburg, Ohio?[4] Don't you? I'm reading Leaves of Grass[5] now – poetry takes me a long time. You have to have a quiet

1   The phrase *malade imaginaire* is French for "imaginary invalid"—that is, a hypochondriac.

2   *Reader's Digest*, founded in 1922, a widely read general interest family magazine.

3   Roi Ottley (1906–1960), American journalist and social historian, *New World A-Coming: Inside Black America* (Boston: Houghton, Mifflin, 1943). MKR praised the book, writing to NSB on 2 November 1943, "I spent the whole morning reading a new book by a Negro, 'New World A-Coming'. . . . It is a well-balanced book, and covers almost every angle of the situation, and it really lays the cards on the table. It comes down to the simple fact that Democracy is a farce if we hold a race as a subjected people, segregated, denied self-respect, kept from participation in civic matters, and all the rest of it. The Negro who wrote the book agrees that it is up to the individual Negro to make himself an acceptable citizen---but it is undeniable that artificial barriers should not be put in his way" (*Love Letters* 164).

4   Sherwood Anderson (1876–1941), American novelist and short fiction writer, *Winesburg, Ohio* (New York: Heubsch, 1919), a collection of stories about life in small-town Ohio.

5   Walt Whitman (1819–1892), American poet and essayist, *Leaves of Grass* (Brooklyn: Privately

time to read it. I am also struggling with two <u>marvelous</u> books of poems by Aragon – the struggle is not with Aragon but with the French. You will have them sooner or later.[1] There was one from <u>Le Creve-Coeur</u>[2] in the back of the novel you had perhaps you didn't see it. Aragon's poetry really sings. It's the damndest thing – I can read some of it only understanding every third word and get a hell of a bang out of it. It's too late now to start writing about it.

In fact it's <u>very</u> late. I hope you are in good health and not too much bothered by things. I would rather be talking to you than writing to you – not just because of the way I feel about writing, but because of the way I feel about you,

Much love,

Julia.

P.S. In case, by some horrible mixup which only Edith Pope could imagine, you got the <u>utterly</u> <u>mistaken</u> impression that I don't enjoy your fussing around with my "affaires" and marriages – Well, hell, if I hadn't had a note from Edith today I never would have thought up such an impossible misunderstanding. I positively depend on your advices – or more accurately the interest which prompts it. I feel that what I need now in this period of my life is one of your inspired teacup seances.

. . .

MKR to JSB, [24?] October 1943. TLS, 7 pp. PM: HAWTHORN | OCT 23 | 2 PM 1943 | FLA. AD: Miss Julia Scribner | Far Hills | New Jersey. LH: Marjorie Kinnan Rawlings | Hawthorn, Florida

Oct. 24, 1943[3]

Printed, 1855), a collection of diverse and radically different poems, both in style and in content, that celebrate sensual pleasure and the birth of America, a central work of American poetry.

1 Louis Aragon, *The Bells of Basel* (1941) and Jean-Richard Bloch, "*— & Co.*" (1929). See JSB's letter on 8 August 1943, 204, n. 5.

2 Louis Aragon, *Le crève-coeur* [*The Dying Heart*] (London: Curwen/Horizon, 1942).

3 MKR's date on this letter is 24 October. The postmark is 23 October. It is possible, although not likely, that the envelope does not go with this letter. More likely, MKR has misdated the day she wrote the letter. However, in the absence of evidence, the editors have retained MKR's date. At the same time period, MKR also got confused about dates in a letter to NSB: "Oct. 25? Monday, anyway" (*Love Letters* 156). 25 October was, in fact, a Monday. The date she puts on this letter, 24 October, was a Sunday. Another possibility, very unlikely, is that the small, rural Hawthorne post office neglected to move forward its hand-stamped postmark, and the postmark, therefore, should be 25 October.

Dearest Julia:

I have just finished reading "Under Cover" on your recommendation, and it is really an eye-opener. It makes you so damn mad, especially at people like Wheeler and Nye and Fish and Reynolds, who of all people should know better, and are in a position to do so much damage. It is an outrage for Reynolds to be on the Military Affairs Committee---I felt that always.[1]

Several weeks ago I received an anonymous typewritten letter mailed from New York, using the very line that Carlson traced, damning both Willkie and Roosevelt, and blaming the Jews and Communists for everything; it was supposed to be a chain letter, and was to be signed and sent to ten other people---bad luck if you did not etc. I started to toss it out as just the work of a fool and a crank, then got to wondering if it could possibly be part of an organized effort to appeal to ignorant people---so mailed it off to the FBI. I was amazed to have a personal letter from J. Edgar Hoover,[2] thanking me, and giving me an address to use if I got any information. After reading Carlson's book, I understood that it was really part of that vicious network, still operating.

The book certainly teaches you how to recognize the source of all the griping and defeatist rumors that get around, and each of us can make himself a one-man committee to combat them wherever found.

I had qualms about the Emily Post parody after I sent it off to you and Norton. I agree that nausea is not amusing---but it seemed the only satisfactory answer to Emily Post's asininity![3]

I am so distressed about the migraine situation, and feel I should apologize to both you and Dr. Atchley---and to your bill-paying family!---for encouraging you to make another futile try. It does begin to look as though the thing were psychic---as my intestinal trouble is most of the time---though it does seem as though there must always be some physical complication,

1 For Carlson's *Under Cover*, see MKR's letter dated [13?] September 1943. Burton Kendall Wheeler (1882–1975), Democratic senator from Montana, broke with Roosevelt over the politics of the New Deal. Gerald Prentice Nye (1892–1971), Republican senator from North Dakota, an isolationist. Hamilton Fish Jr. (1888–1991), Republican representative from New York, frequent critic of Roosevelt. Robert Rice Reynolds (1884–1945), Democratic senator from North Carolina, strident isolationist and alleged apologist for Nazi aggression.

2 John Edgar Hoover (1895–1972), the director of the FBI from 1924 to 1972. Controversial, demanding, and uncompromising, Hoover was largely responsible for creating the aura of the FBI. For a discussion of the chain letter MKR mentions, including a copy of MKR's letter to Hoover, dated 25 September 1943, and Hoover's reply, dated 7 October 1943, encouraging her to report anything untoward, see Rodger L. Tarr, "MKR and the FBI," *Rawlings Society Newsletter* 11 (June 1998): 2–5. MKR was impressed that Hoover would even reply (see *Love Letters* 144, 154).

3 See JSB's letter on 13 September 1943.

or the neurosis would not express itself in some particular part of the body. Just as emotional or neurotic stress in me, goes to my physically weak point, the diverticulated insides! One does have a horror of laying all one's most spiritually intimate reactions on a laboratory table. I should never urge you to do it. You will just have to decide for yourself how far you object to the migraine! In your secret soul, you may possibly cherish it, as a valid escape from contact with an unsatisfactory world. Lots of terribly painful intestinal attacks, I am sure, are caused by being fed up with doing things I didn't want to and seeing people I didn't want to see. When you're in bed with pain, you're safe!

I was really just thinking aloud about Andre.[1] I feel that you need physical love very much---as what normal woman does not?---yet that alone is not the answer. We are so complicated, we just need too much! Norton wrote me, "Don't dispose of Julia too precipitously. I have several splendid specimens I should like to enter in the Scribner Handicap". (I had written him about Henry Heyl's invitation, and he was as suspicious as you. But I really do not think Henry is what you want. His way of life, his tastes, his intellect, yes--- but just something about him personally that I should not choose for myself or for you. Yet he is a dear. And as cagey about women as you are about men. He wrote me that he should only care to marry if loyalty between the two was so implicit that it could never be questioned. I think that perhaps I feel that he would ask and expect a little too much of a woman, in small ways. But I may be mistaken.)

One wonderful thing about Norton is that he asks nothing of me, demands nothing, is outraged only when I show unreasonable temper, and then is outraged in a generous and kindly way. I wrote him one ugly letter--- not about him---but just being in an evil mood, I snapped around about this and that---and the next day before mailing, added a note that I probably shouldn't send it, but that he knew damn well I wasn't sweetness and light[2] all the time. He wrote back that he should be terribly suspicious if I wrote nothing but sweetness and light, in fact, would think I was only giving him Service Men's Correspondence Form No. 2.[3]

My intrusion on your most intimate affairs comes only from my admiration and love of you, and my desire to have you get what you deserve---the best.

Your writing letters etc. in your head, then losing the desire to make them

---

1 Andre, the Belgian soldier JSB met in New York City. His last name is not identified.

2 Sweetness and light, the cornerstone definition of culture articulated by Matthew Arnold (1822–1888) in *Culture and Anarchy* (London: Smith, Elder, 1869). Arnold borrowed the phrase from Jonathan Swift (1667-1745) who popularized the expression in *The Battle of the Books* (1704).

3 Most likely, NSB means a "Dear John" letter.

articulate, is typical of the day-dreamer and the escapist. I fought that battle for years and years. When I was working on my first book,[1] I would leave the typewriter and go and lie down on the couch and go into dreams so much more satisfactory than work or reality---then kick myself up and off and back to the typewriter for a few more lines. I won the long battle then. Without the definite creative urge, which you evidently do not have, it would be a much harder job. It takes a powerful impetus to snap out of it. And all or more accurately <u>because your way of life</u>, while not the right one for you, tends to make it easy for you to just think and dream and listen to music and read other people's books. It is all most understandable, yet I long for the day when, through love or work or both, you will participate more actively in living, and so, more satisfactorily for you, my dear and lovely Julia.

I had a wonderful batch of letters from Norton about three weeks ago and nothing since.

His unit has moved up into the hills of India where the scenery is magnificent and the insects are terrific. He said that if a tsetse fly had not bitten him, it was only because it could not find space. He said that he had been obliged to let the alcohol get out of his system, as on their rare leaves to go to a nearby city, dreadful whiskey costs fearfully for a thimbleful. He said that he had hoped the Army would strengthen his character, but it had only tightened his morals and loosened his bowels.

I hope you will write to him---he would love it. Vol[unteer]. Norton S. Baskin, American Field Service, A.P.O. 886, c/o Postmaster, N.Y.C.

I have been unable to get to work on my book.[2] It is probably being mulled over in my subconscious and is not ready, for I wake up with ideas and titles, so I am not letting it bother me.

When would be a good time for you to come down?

All my love,

Marjorie

. . .

JSB to MKR, 5–6 November 1943. ALS, 6 pp. PM: FAR HILLS | 930 AM | NOV 8 | 1943 | N.J. AD: Mrs. Norton Baskin | Cross Creek | Hawthorn | Florida. VIA AIR MAIL envelope.

Friday

---

1   *South Moon Under* (New York: Scribners, 1933). See Tarr, *Bibliography,* A1.
2   *The Sojourner* (New York: Scribners, 1953). See Tarr, *Bibliography,* A8.

Nov. 5. [1943][1]

Dearest Marjorie:

I certainly did a lousy job of tempering my facetiousness if you had to explain your motives taking such an interest in my love life. Your interest is about the only bright spot in that desert waste and also one of the brightest spots in my life and for godsake don't let any foolish remarks of mine persuade you otherwise. Facetiousness is a family weakness.

At the moment I am languishing in bed with a head cold. Not a very bad one, but I always take colds very seriously and imagine terrible consequences of sinus abcesses [sic] etc. in a rather Abstemious manner. Tomorrow I fear I have to go to Baltimore to christen a ship named after my great or great great grandfather[2] I'm not sure which the idea gives me no pleasure. All that stuff of champagne bottles & bouquets of roses & standing on a huge platform in front of a crowd really goes against my grain. Perhaps if I had earned notoriety I might enjoy it, but the unearned show I find painfully embarrassing – at least in prospect. Of course I might take an awful fancy to it. The other day I met a woman[3] who is a sort of intellectual artistic cosmopolitan & was evidently a very good violinist – played in ensemble with many of the great musicians & was, or is, intimate with practically all of them, lived in such places as Germany, France, & China and also is pals with writers, painters, actors etc. etc. She's quite an entertaining old girl – you would enjoy her I'm sure. She's not a bit the precious type, in fact she's almost tough – comes from Portland Ore. & has a strong western accent and flavor. Anyway, the point of this is that she decided the moment she saw me that I was an actress, and, when she found I was not, she told me with western frankness that I would be wasting my time until I was! So maybe she detected a hidden hankering for the public eye.

Which reminds me – I saw Othello this week.[4] What a marvelous play it is. In the final scene ever the hard-to-move I was almost collapsed. It is a

---

1   Written in a second hand on p. 1: [43].

2   Most likely great grandfather, Charles Scribner I (1821–1871), the founder of Charles Scribner's Sons. JSB's great-great-grandfather was Uriah Rogers Scribner (1778–1853). The Liberty Ship was christened SS *Charles Scribner*, was launched on 6 November 1943, was sold in 1947, and was scrapped in 1973.

3   Not identified.

4   JSB is referring to the Theatre Guild production by Margaret Webster (1905–1972) of *Othello*, starring Paul Robeson (1898–1976), Jose Ferrer (1912–1992), and Uta Hagen (1919–2004), which opened at the Shubert Theatre on 19 October 1943 and closed on 1 July 1944. This was the first play by William Shakespeare (1564–1616) produced in America in which the leading actor was Black. Robeson was an internationally known singer, actor, and activist. Robeson played Othello; Ferrer, Iago; Hagen, Desdemona; and Webster, Emilia.

fine production, but not, I think, a great one. At least I found many parts of the acting that I would not have done that way. (And this was before my [career?] was announced to me). No one is particularly bad and no one struck me as more than good. Robeson's beautiful voice and magnificent stature and his color are all assets and so is Uta Hagen's beauty – but Desdemona has to be beautiful. I liked Margaret Webster's (who directed) Emilia very much, though she would have been a bit more frenzied in the last scene. Her voice was far better than any except Robeson's and her speech was far better than any of them at all.

Next day

Well, all the public appearance surmise was a waste of time, for this morning I was too ill to go, and I have had a not unpleasant day in bed. Since I have gotten over the headache I woke up with I haven't felt badly – in fact most people wouldn't be in bed with such a minor ailing, but I am so glad to get any somewhat legitimate excuse to stay in bed – that I am firmly settled and would happily stay here until some very special musical event routed me out. It so happens that today I am missing just such an event, a recital by one of the two, Lotte Lehmann and Wanda Landowska,[1] for whose recitals I never fail to buy tickets. Occasionally, as now, I don't get to use them.

Mr. Darrow showed me a poem that Norton had sent you from India.[2] I thought it was a gem! Do send me a copy – I think Dr. Atcheley [sic] would appreciate it.

Let me know the dates of the birds season and any dates that are good or bad for you and I will try to figure when I can escape my jobs. One thing that worries me somewhat is that my hunting boots are only 9" high – come hardly half way to my knees – should I have high boots on account of the snakes? I haven't had a chance to try for shells yet, but I think I can get some, all else failing, from a friend of Aunt Louise's – and mine – chairman of the board of Remington.

Yesterday, I read Green's The Dark Journey. It was awfully good but I still didn't like it as much as The Closed Garden.[3] I'm beginning to think

---

1   Charlotte "Lotte" Lehmann, German soprano. Wanda Landowska (1879–1959), Polish pianist and harpsichordist, who gave a recital at Town Hall on 7 November 1943 (New York Times 7 November 1943: 53).

2   Whitney Darrow, then sales manager at Scribners. NSB's poem is reproduced by MKR in her letter on 10 November 1943, where she also relates what shotgun shells she requires.

3   Julian Green (1900–1998), American novelist, playwright, and essayist, The Dark Journey (New York: Harper, 1929). The Closed Garden (New York: Harper, 1928). See also JSB's letter on 13 September 1943 and MKR's letter on 28 September 1943, 223, n. 4.

that this is perhaps not entirely that the CG is his best book but somewhat that it is the first one I read. To me the mental anguish becomes a bit surfeiting with repetition. I got positively annoyed with these characters at times. I felt if they didn't climb down off their racks for a few minutes and enjoy a meal or <u>something</u> I would throw the book across the room. His books are so inward too that there is never a moment's relief from the torment. No objective description of scenes or actions etc. in fact not a damn thing but tortured emotions. His skill in that field is marvelous, but I think the field is so limited as to limit also his stature as a writer, compared to Aragon, Malraux, or Bloch[1] there is rather a gamble as I have only seen one of the long list of his works.

Incidentally did you ever read a book called <u>Diary of a Country Priest</u> by George Bernanos?[2] It is very very good. I must try to get ahold of another copy, mine was lent I forget to whom and disappeared. He recently wrote a book called <u>Lettre aux Anglais</u> which is soon to be published in English.[3] I have read a lot about it. It has been called one of the most important books of our time. I'm not sure whether it should be called religious or philosophical or what, but I am eagerly watching for it. Mr. Wheelock[4] told me he tried to get it for us, but unhappily failed. I think it might be a good counterbalance for the Franco loving Spellman.[5] Today I reread the first book Ward Dorrance[6] wrote and the first I saw of his I had been wondering for sometime if I would still think it as good as I did when I first read

---

1   Louis Aragon and Jean-Richard Bloch: See JSB's letter on 8 August 1943, 204, n. 5, and MKR's letter on 28 August 1943, 215, n. 2. André Malraux (1901–1976), French novelist, theorist, and statesman, perhaps best known for his novel *Le condition Humaine* (Paris: NRF, 1933), trans. Haakon M. Chevalier (1901–1985), *Man's Fate* (New York: Harrison, Smith, & Hass, 1934).

2   Georges Bernanos (1888–1948), French critic of the elite, *Diary of a Country Priest* (New York: Macmillan, 1937).

3   *Lettre aux Anglais,* translated into English by Harry L. Ossorio as *Plea for Liberty: Letters to the English, the Americans, the Europeans* (New York: Pantheon, 1944).

4   John Hall Wheelock (1886–1978), poet and editor at Scribners. JSB means by "us" that Wheelock tried to acquire the rights for Scribners.

5   Francis Joseph, Cardinal Spellman (1889–1967), was the titular head of the Catholic Church in America. Through his influence at the Vatican, Spellman helped Franklin Roosevelt in his determination to support the Nationalist dictator Francisco Franco (1892–1975) during the Spanish Civil War (1936–1939) against the Republicans, the result of which was the overthrow of Democracy in Spain. Franco, who was also supported by the Nazi Party through Adolph Hitler (1889–1945), remained dictator of Spain from 1939 to 1975. Ernest Hemingway, *For Whom the Bell Tolls* (New York: Scribners, 1940), records this victory of Fascism, to which Cardinal Spellman through his machinations lent support.

6   Ward Dorrance (1904–1996), American teacher and novelist. Perhaps JSB is referring to *We're from Missouri* (Richmond Hill, NY: Missourian Press, 1938). Scribners published two of his novels, *Where the Rivers Meet* (1939) and *The Sundowners* (1942).

it in '38. I thought it even better. He is one writer whose career upsets me, and I'm afraid it doesn't upset anybody <else> around Scribners except me. When I think of the collared editorial pains taken over some books which don't have a damn thing except possible sales appeal and the disinterest in a guy that has the stuff I'm sure Dorrance has I get irritated as hell. That last book of his The Sundowners, I don't know if you read it, had wonderful satisfying parts, but such acute plot trouble that it was awful to print in the shape it was in. He murdered his beautiful description of the country by a misfit episode in a city and a horrible Hollywood Hurricane. I feel certain that he can write a hell of a book and I keep hoping.

I have just started Goodbye West Country by Henry Williamson the Eng. naturalist. It is a diary or a journal and quite fascinating but I [find?] him so painfully pro Nazi that I can't really relax and enjoy it. By the by, I think you are being unnecessarily charitable or naïve to opine that our dear patriots Fish, Wheeler, Reynolds etc. ought to know better. I think they know damn good and well what they are doing—just as well as McWilliams, Dennis, Coughlin and Patterson.[1] Though I do think Fish & Patterson are as dumb as they are malicious – which is plenty. The others are a damn sight more evil than dumb.

Have you heard that our pal Pardue[2] has been made a bishop? I suppose that means he can't go dancing in Café Society[3] anymore.

I have been a few times to the ballet. They have had the misfortune of losing their two greatest stars—Markova and Baronova.[4] They are both irreplaceable and I hope they will come back for their absence is very no-ticeable. Everything seems just a little flat and of course their best roles fall very flat. Maybe they will be back for the spring season in which case you'd better come up and confer about your book or see Dr. Atcheley [sic]. You haven't seen Markova and Dolin in Giselle and as a ballet.[5] Even you

---

1   Senators Burton Wheeler, Gerald Nye, and Representative Hamilton Fish. See MKR's letter dated [24?] October 1943, 233, n. 1. Republican Representative from Connecticut John D. McWil-liams (1891–1975); Democratic Senator from New Mexico Dennis Chávez (1888–1962); Monsignor Charles E. Coughlin (1891–1978), anti-Roosevelt, anti-democratic, and anti-Semite, who had a very wide radio audience during World War II; and Robert D. Patterson Sr. (1891–1952), distinguished serviceman in World War I, was Roosevelt's under secretary of war (1940–1945).

2   Austin Pardue. See MKR's letter on 28 April 1943, 180, n. 1.

3   Café Society, an upscale nightclub in New York (1938–1948). Cafe society is also a term for a trendy lifestyle. It was also the title for a popular film by Paramount Picture in 1939, starring Mad-eleine Carroll (1906–1987) and Fred MacMurray (1908–1991).

4   Alicia Markova (1910–2004), English-born ballerina; Irina Baronova (1919–2009), Russian-born ballerina and actor.

5   Anton Dolin (1904–1983) danced with Markova in Giselle at the Metropolitan Opera House in 1943. Markova either became ill or was hurt and was replaced by Alicia Alonso (1920–2019), the

haven't lived until you've seen that. I have a terrible fear she may not come back as she left for an operation to repair some "muscular strains" the papers said. It sounds so vague as to be suspicious. I also saw twice the show that the Negro dancer Katherine Dunham and her troupe have been playing with immense success. I guess you'd call it a dance revue.[1] I would see it gladly twice a week! You'ld love it I know. Muddy adored it and she has always been as anti-Negro as a Miss'ian.[2] It is completely attractive and charming and fun-wonderful dancing as you may well imagine, and though every dance dealt with sex and some none too subtly, she loudly proclaimed that she had never seen a show done with such infallibly good taste. Marjorie, couldn't you get ahold right now of that helicopter you're going to have after the war. Then you could pop up on days when you are unable to work. There are so many things I want to take you to now. There has been a colossal Van Gogh[3] show going, the biggest & best since the historic 1935 show at the Mus. Of Mod. Art and there are lots of other good things about. I shall never be happy, of course, till I take you to the opera. Not any opera, but certain ones with certain casts. You will have to submit to a long preparation, I'm warning you in advance as that you will realize it is inescapable and submit gracefully.

Two or three weeks ago I had a long weekend with no guests to entertain, and, though I did have letters to write, I skirted duty. With this leisure I started a project I had been rolling around in my brain for some time. I had been very much offended by the scenery and costumes for Aida[4] at the Met. I studied all the Egyptian pictures I had, and drew several costumes and sketched ideas for sets. I dabbled in water color for the first time since my coloring book days, and became quite intoxicated with it. I painted a couple of autumn leaves which came out much better than I dared hope. I also did a couple of abstracts (and let me tell you they are fiendishly difficult I found) and a lot of experimenting. Unfortunately I haven't had any time since to paint. I have studied more at the Public Library[5] and am fast becoming an expert on Egyptian costume. I am dying for time to get back

Cuban ballerina, whose interpretation of Giselle, the peasant girl, was so impressive that her name became forever linked to the role.

1   Katherine Dunham (1909–2006), choreographer, dancer, and anthropologist, who through her troupe made modern dance and music of the African diaspora popular.

2   As in Mississippian.

3   Vincent Van Gogh (1843–1890), the Dutch post-Impressionist. There were a number of Van Gogh exhibitions in New York, including at the Museum of Modern Art, in 1943.

4   Aida, an opera in four acts by the Italian composer Giuseppe Verdi (1813–1901), opened at the Metropolitan Opera House on 6 March 1943.

5   New York Public Library.

to my colors – bed is a poor place. The trouble with all my creative efforts is that if I have to do anything else I am too tired to do them. At any rate, I still enjoy my studies at the library. There is no place, not even a concert hall, that thrills me as much as a library. I feel completely happy and alive the moment I get into the big file room. I keep saying to myself, "Imagine, all those books and anyone can have any of them for nothing." It seems hardly credible. I think a library is the noblest institution that exists. And the attendants are all so nice and absolutely panting to go to all kinds of trouble even for me, just as though I were some important person or about to produce a world famous book. And for nothing! Even the check room is free. Museums are wonderful too, but much more impersonal. There's something so companionable about sitting on the bench waiting for your number to flash up and then settling comfortably at one of the lovely big tables with people all around comfortably settled too. I feel as cozy as a cat by a stove. I shall have to manage to spend more time there. I think really I'd make a very happy book worm.

I'm sorry to hear that you haven't been able to get started on your book.[1] It must make you sort of nervous. Have you been reading much? I hope you have been able to teach your maid[2] to distinguish various types of napkins! How have your insides been doing? I have been subjected to horrible tests by Dr. A. They have found one slightly abnormal thing. I don't handle sugar properly in my blood (I have <u>not</u> got diabetes) so I am on a diet of lots of proteins and not much starch or sugar. Eat all the meat & cheese you can get says Dr. A. Ha! Ha! What the hell does he think I've been doing. Also I have to eat 2 eggs for breakfast. As you know my stomach is very sensitive in the morning and I find that the highly scented N.Y.C. eggs put me off, ruin my morning almost as much as the syringes did. Well, stay away from headaches & take care of yourself.

Much love,

Julia

---

1   *The Sojourner.*

2   Zamilla Mickens "Sissie" Fountain. As this juncture MKR was trying to get Idella Parker to come back to Cross Creek, for, as she wrote NSB on 6 November 1943, "It would take 2 or 3 years to make anything of Sissie, and even then I am not sure it could be done" (*Love Letters* 167).

MKR to JSB, 10 November 1943. TLS, 3 pp. PM: HAWTHORN |
NOV 12 | 2 PM | 1943 | FLA. AD: Miss Julia Scribner | Far Hills | New
Jersey. LH: Marjorie Kinnan Rawlings | Hawthorn, Florida.

Nov. 10, 1943

Dearest Julia:

Will answer your letter later. This is just to send you Norton's verse as you
asked.[1]

And to say that our hunting season opens Nov. 20 and lasts until Feb.
something, but early in the season would probably be better than late, for
several reasons, one being that God knows I should be into the book later on.

I can get you a two-weeks' hunting license at a reasonable figure, which is
probably as much hunting as we would care to do anyway, while an out-of-
state seasonal license costs very high.

In shells, I myself need .20's, while the man[2] who would take us and who
handles the dogs needs .12's preferably but could use .16's. He has no shells
either. So come any time that suits you best.

Much love,

Marjorie

Will probably forget it when I really write you, so just must pass on an
angle of Norton's hospitalization. A British Colonel came through the hospital, inspecting, followed by three nurses, (Majors) two Captains and three
Sergeants. He stopped at each bed and asked a question. At Norton's he said,
"And where is your pain, young man?" Before Norton could tell him in basic
English, his eye caught sight of the chart, "Complaint: hemorrhoids", and he
turned as red as a beet and said, "Ah yes, clearing up, no doubt," and beat a
hasty retreat.

Also, when Norton was ready to leave the hospital, the bluff British
sergeant told him he was to "parade" before the Colonel before dismissal.
So Norton went into the storeroom and got into his uniform. He arrived
at the Colonel's office on the dot, and the Sergeant almost tore the place
down---he was supposed to "parade" in his hospital garb. The Sergeant

---

1 MKR reproduces NSB's poem at the bottom of this letter. See also JSB's letter on 5–6 November
1943, 237, n. 2.

2 Most likely, James Chester "Chet" Crosby (1905–1980), MKR's hunting companion and grove
manager.

said he would have to go on in, "But the Old Man will be furious." The Colonel asked Norton questions, and whether he had any comments, and Norton apologized for his misunderstanding about garb. The Colonel said, "Oh, I think you can get by in here, but the Sergeant will be mad as the devil."

> Lament from Norton Baskin:
> Of uncooked foods be ever wary---
> Avoid exhausting dysentery.
> By night stay in your netted area
> And thus combat the dread malaria.
> Stay off the jungle paths unbeaten---
> By India's snakes you'll not be eaten.
> These lessons taught and duly learned,
> I hoped for perfect health, well-earned---
> But no one taught how to avoid
> The ignominious hemorrhoid.

. . .

MKR to JSB, 20 December 1943. TLS, 3 pp. PM: HAWTHORN | DEC 20 | 2 PM | 1943 | FLA. AD: Miss Julia Scribner | Far Hills | New Jersey. LH: Marjorie Kinnan Rawlings | Hawthorn, Florida

Please send me your grandmother's address---would like to send her oranges or tangerines (if the latter are not frozen by 3 nights at 32 degrees).[1]

Dec. 20, 1943

Dearest Julia:

A check is a horrid present (unless it is a large one!) but when I send it to someone else to buy records for you, I know there is needless scurrying-around---so please consider this small item enclosed as already-bought re-cords---perhaps you'd like some of the Budapest String Quartet,[2] if they meet your fanatical taste.

Any time that suits you to come, is swell with me. Come either to Gaines-ville, Ocala or St. Augustine, wherever you can make the best connections.

---

1   MKR inserts this postscript at the top of p. 1.
2   Budapest String Quartet, whose emphasis was Classical music, was in existence in various itera-tions from 1917 to 1963, and in 1943 the quartet was recording for Columbia Record Co.

Don't try that awful Hawthorn train again—the difference in distance is not worth it. My wonderful Idella is coming back the day after New Year's,[1] and as a guest, you'll never know how damn lucky you are. I am paying her fabulous wages for the deep South, but I decided money wouldn't do me a bit of good in the insane asylum, whither Martha's depressing daughter Sissie has been fast driving me. It would take pages and put you into hysterics if I tried to give a list of Sissie's sins of omission and commission.[2] Just for instance: (she does nothing that she is not told specifically to do, and even then the results are usually weird) discarded New York papers lay for some 24 hours on the couch on the veranda. I finally told her to remove them. Just before I dropped them there, I had used the spray gun on a colony of flying ants that appeared in the roof directly overhead, and a large pile of dead flying ants lay under the N.Y. newspapers. Sissie removed the papers, as told. She did not disturb the ants. I hadn't told her.

You are going to be rather late for good quail shooting, for as the season goes on and hunters disturb the coveys, the birds are harder to find. But we'll enjoy going out anyway. Am hoping my Christmas present will be a box of .20 shells for me and one of .12's or .16's for my hunting friend![3]

When you come, if you have any extra room and can get it, please bring, as my order, not a gift, as much Bourbon or rye or a blend as you can get or carry. We just can't get it. I know it is scarce there, too, but would appreciate your trying.[4] And you know how you love a difficult and exasperating search, so that you can complain bitterly for weeks.

A merry Christmas---mine will be lousy, but I plan to get drunk to get through the day.[5] Norton sent me a cable and a new A.P.O. address. His old

---

1 Idella returned to Cross Creek on 3 January 1944, to replace the "dirt and stupidity" of Old Martha and Sissie, as MKR reports in a letter to NSB on the same day, "She pitched in on the awful kitchen and in a couple of hours turned it into a rural model for *Good Housekeeping*. She said, 'I'm getting sorry for you,' and when she hit my bedroom, I think she was really rueful" (*Love Letters* 226).

2 MKR is alluding to the Catholic teaching about the Sin of Omission (Venial Sin) and the Sin of Commission (Mortal Sin). Zamilla Mickens "Sissie" Fountain, was the daughter of Martha "Old Martha" Mickens, the Cross Creek matriarch.

3 James "Chet" Crosby.

4 Prohibition, lifted in 1933, had a major impact on the quantity of alcohol produced. Just as the distilleries were reaching full production, the United States entered World War II in 1941. The sale of alcohol to make spirits was discouraged because alcohol was needed for the war effort to make rubber and munitions, among other essentials. As a result, the supply of alcohol for drinking was curtailed dramatically. Distilleries did not return to full production until after the war in 1946.

5 MKR went to Crescent Beach for Christmas, and as she admits to NSB in a letter on 26 December, "I was damned if I was going to be a sissy, so I drank like a fish and made myself have a good

one in India was 885. The new one is 465. Since the S. Pacific A.P.O.'s are the 900's, and N. Africa is the 300's, I am afraid 465 is Italy or the Balkans, and that he is being sent where there is action and ambulance service is needed, since the Burmese push[1] has not begun. These are the times that try men's souls[2] and have women biting their finger nails.

Much love,

Marjorie

. . .

JSB to MKR, 26 January 1944. ALS, 2 pp. PM: NEW YORK N.Y. | JAN 26 | 3³⁰ PM | 1944. AD: Mrs. Norton Baskin | Cross Creek | Hawthorn | Florida. VIA AIR MAIL envelope. Stamped: VIA AIR MAIL.

Jan 26, 1944[3]

Dearest Marjorie:

The date I am coming down is the 4th.[4] I am coming by the Seaboard,[5] so I will see if they will let me off at Island Grove. I will go in there today in fact, and will write again in a day or so and let you know the result.

I haven't had a bit of luck with the barbecue cloth errand. McCutcheon's had never heard of such a thing and Mosse very vaguely thought that perhaps they might have had such a thing once, but certainly no longer. I am going to try Abercrombies' and Lewis & Conger.[6] I can't think of any place else that might have it. (It sounds to me as if you were trying to outdo Fred's Pulitzer Prize tea-cloth.)[7]

Have been seeing quite a bit of Edith.[8] She had a thrilling weekend in Far

---

time. I had fought off some bad moments, with success, but just before Christmas dinner yesterday it hit me too hard and too unexpectedly and I burst out crying" (*Love Letters* 214).

1   To oust the Japanese from Burma under the direction of Lord Mountbatten.

2   "These are the times that try men's souls," declared Thomas Paine (1737–1809) in *The Crisis* (1776–1783), a series of patriotic pamphlets that inspired the Continental Army and the efforts toward independence from Great Britain.

3   In JSB's hand at the top of p. 1: 31 EAST 79 ST., the address of her grandmother Louise Flagg Scribner.

4   JSB arrived on 5 February 1944, as MKR writes to NSB on 4 February, "My dear Julia arrives tomorrow morning" (*Love Letters* 258).

5   Atlantic Seaboard Railroad.

6   McCutcheon's, Mosse Linen, Abercrombie & Fitch, and Lewis & Conger, department stores in New York City. See MKR's letter on 29 January 1944.

7   Fred Francis of St. Augustine. See MKR's letter on 17 June 1943, 196, n. 2.

8   Edith Pope.

Hills. She caught a terrible cold and Daddy broke two ribs,[1] but probably you know all about it already as she told me she had written you. At the moment she is away – went off to see Verle,[2] but she gets back tomorrow and I hope to get her to come to the opera with me on Saturday. It is especially good – The Marriage of Figaro.[3]

Could you drop me just a line or a postcard telling me if you have a reasonably large French-English dictionary? If you do it would save me about 2 lbs, which is very much to be considered when one is laden with guns, shells, whisky, hunting boots etc.[4] I am not planning to bring anything in the way of evening clothes, so if you are thinking of going to any large & formal parties let me know!!

Poor Norton does seem to have gotten himself put in a horribly uncomfortable spot. I have one slight clue which seems to bear out your idea of where he is. In Scribner's I saw a small Xmas card from Eugene O'Connor who was Mrs. Weber's assistant in the ad. dept.[5] His address was also APO 405 – the Xmas card was something about how to say Merry Xmas in Burmese, Chinese & some Indian tongue – so he must be <some> where boundaries of all three countries meet. O'Connor has something to do with the Red Cross.[6] If I can find any more about it I'll let you know.

There is a possibility that I should be engaged on a literary effort myself, though not of a creative nature. I have to see Daddy about it today. If so you won't have to worry about me disturbing your work. In fact you'll have to work frantically to set up a stimulating <excp> example. I need a terrific atmosphere of work about me to keep up my morale – that's why I've been in collapse ever since I left school.

If there are any other N.Y. errands you want done – write me quickly –

1 Perkins writes to MKR on 19 January 1944, "Charlie Scribner had a bad fall, and broke a rib and maybe broke something else too. But he makes light of it on the telephone, and expects soon to leave on a vacation" (Max and Marjorie 560).

2 Verle Pope, Edith Pope's husband.

3 Mozart's opera The Marriage of Figaro (1786), performed on 29 January 1944 at the Old Met, 1411 Broadway, home of the Metropolitan Opera in New York City, conducted by Bruno Walter (1876–1962).

4 Earlier MKR reports to NSB on 5 January 1944, "Julia, bless her heart, sent me 2 boxes of 20 gauge shells and 2 of 12's, and I shall pass on the 12's to Chet, who has given me quail three times" (Love Letters 227). Because of the war, ammunition was in short supply, so this was an especially welcomed gift. Chet Crosby served as their hunting guide and was MKR's grove manager.

5 Eugene O'Connor and Dorothy Weber (1900–1956) of Scribners' Publicity Department.

6 JSB may be confused here. The O'Connor associated with the Red Cross is Daniel Basil O'Connor (1892–1973), who from 1944 until 1949 was the chair and president of the American Red Cross.

though I don't seem to be very successful. It's going to be wonderful to be with you again – I can't wait now to get to Cross Creek.

Much love,

Julia

. . .

MKR to JSB, 29 January 1944. TLS, 1 p. PM: HAWTHORN | JAN 29 | 5 PM | 1944 | FLA. AD: Miss Julia Scribner | 31 East 79th St. | New York City. RA: Mrs. Norton Baskin | Hawthorn, Florida. Air mail envelope with integral stamp.

The Creek

Jan. 29, 1944

Dearest Julia:

The mail just brought your letter, and when you say you are "coming down" the 4th, I don't know whether you mean you are leaving New York the 4th or arriving here the 4th---but your next letter will make all clear.[1]

I'll answer your questions hurriedly. The barbecue cloth was definitely at Mosse or McCutcheon's,[2] so since they don't have it, don't bother. I believe now it was Mosse who advertised it just once, a couple of months ago.

Now do not bother with any whiskey. I am on the wagon and hope to stay on until I lose 20 lbs., and I have plenty of whiskey for guests.

I have no French-English dictionary at all. I had wonderful Heath dictionaries, French, German, etc., and they simply disappeared.

I'm so terribly sorry about your father's accident.[3] Give him my love and sympathy.

It will be so grand to see you.

Much love,

Marjorie

---

1   JSB arrived on 5 February. MKR writes to NSB on 4 February, "My dear Julia arrives tomorrow morning. Idella has the back bedroom and bath spick and span . . ." (*Love Letters* 258). The train was 10½ hours late, arriving in Island Grove at 9 pm on Saturday, as MKR reports to NSB on 7 February. On Sunday they went quail hunting with Chet Crosby (*Love Letters* 258, 260).

2   Mosse Linen, specialty store located at 659 W. 5th Avenue, New York. McCutcheon's Department store, located on 5th Avenue at 49th Street, New York.

3   Charles Scribner III had fallen and had broken a rib. See JSB's letter on 26 January 1944, 246, n. 1.

MKR to JSB, 31 January 1944. ALS, 2 pp. PM: Saint Augustine | Jan
31 | 2 PM | 1944 | FLA. [In MKR's hand] <u>Special</u> <u>Delivery</u> | Miss Julia
Scribner | 31 East 79th St. | New York City. RA: Mrs. Norton Baskin |
Hawthorn, Florida.

Monday

Jan. 31, 1944

Dearest Julia:—

A hurried note—

I forgot to say that you had better bring one dinner or evening dress. Bob
Camp wants us to spend a week-end at the Naval Air Station at Pensacola
while you are here, and if it suits you I'd love to go. We will stay at the hotel, but have most meals except breakfast out at the Officers' Club. Saturday
nights are always more or less formal, usually with a dance, so you'll need
one long frock.

We will go by 'plane between Jacksonville & Pensacola, both ways. There
are several flights a day and it is only a couple of hours that way.

If your train doesn't stop at Island Grove it is perfectly O.K., as I have an
errand to be done some time in Ocala anyway.

Just suit yourself, and <u>don't</u> bother with whiskey.

Love

<u>Marjorie</u>

Am at the cottage for two days only. Don't let the postmark upset you.

. . .

JSB to MKR, 16 March 1944. AL, 4 pp. PM: NEW YORK, N.Y.
| MAR 17 | 7³⁰ PM | 1944. AD: Mrs. Norton Baskin | Hawthorn |
Florida.[1]

March 16 [1944][2]

Dearest Marjorie:

---

1 Written in a second hand on the envelope: March 17, 1944.
2 Written in a second hand after JSB's date on p. 1: [1944].

Finally made home after a not very pleasant trip.[1] The train wasn't at all overcrowded, in fact I had my section all to myself so didn't have to get into an argument as to who had the legal right to the forward-riding seat, and the dining car was never more than half full. But the second day I developed a hell of a headache and so spent the day suffering and feeling ill and taking pills. Happily we were only 1 hr. late. I also had to fight off a fat rich young man from Pittsburgh who told me he had inherited god knows how many businesses. He has a 128,000 acre cattle ranch in Fla. I was not feeling at all friendly. Also on the train were three of the most horrible drunken young Southerners. Just the type who push negroes off sidewalks, and talk happily about "killing off some of the black s.o.b.s[.]" They sat across from me at breakfast revoltingly drunk and consuming more liquor, and they cursed the waiter constantly. They sat in my car and generally raised hell. Every time I passed by there was a chorus of lewd remarks. I was so furious that they certainly would have regretted any further advances, and drunk as they were I think they would sense it. The porter was also cursed out, but he seemed to bear up under it quite calmly. It was all quite gruesome. Thank god I expressed the big bag. I just don't know what I would have done if I had to carry it. When I got on at Ocala I had to walk back about 8 cars, and with papers, book, purse etc slipping it was a hell of a job. After about 4 cars I collapsed, but a porter appeared and took the bags for me. Then at Penn Station[2] there wasn't a single porter, so supporting myself with sniffs of smelling salts I had to carry the bags & go on to the taxi platform. What a nightmare if I had had the big one.[3]

Marjorie: I have something very much on my conscience. There is something I must tell you which I meant to tell you before I left, but from sheer cowardice of hating to say something disagreeable and not wanting to irritate you I didn't. I fear it makes this an unpleasant letter to receive from a departed guest, but I have nice grateful letters to write you and I don't want to mix them up with this. I shall write them as soon as I have this off my chest.

When you have one of your nervous spells and a few drinks, (and the two seem to go together), something serious happens to your coordination or reflexes or both. I don't believe I have ever been so scared in a car as I was on two days with you. I don't think you realize this change in your reactions and that's why I must tell you. I don't mean the night of the blowup

---

1 JSB left Cross Creek on 13 March 1944 (see *Love Letters* 298).

2 Pennsylvania Railroad Station in Manhattan, built in 1910, a Beaux-Arts masterpiece, destroyed in 1963.

3 That is, the big bag JSB decided to send express.

in Ocala.[1] Of course I was nervous then, and you were in no condition for safe driving, but I think you realized it that night and tried to be careful – Anyway that was an exceptional occasion. The days I am talking of are the first day Moe ran away and the day you killed the mule. The first day we set out for Citra at terrific speed. You asked me if the speed made me nervous, and I, not having noticed yet the oddness of your driving, said "No" Do you remember? I can't explain exactly what you do, but your judgment seems all wrong and you drive with very untypical carelessness. Ordinarily I feel completely safe when you are driving and never have a qualm. But that day every time you turned a corner or passed a car I felt it was sheer accident that nothing happened. I can tell you I was really frightened, so much so that I was madder at you then I ever hope to be again, because I really thought you were going to land me in the hospital with a broken something for no damn reason but you wearing off your nervous mood. The day of the mule I could see you were in the same condition and that's why I wasn't so enthusiastic about Gainesville and kept being hopeful about the weather. The way you backed the car out of the shelter I knew I was in for another bad ride and as soon as you <backed> turned onto the road I could feel that lack of control. I tried to make myself relax because I had given myself a hell of a headache before, and I told myself that the chances were we would <u>not</u> have an accident. You may not have been frightened after the mule but I can tell you I was. Not because of what had happened but because of what I knew might have happened – not to us but to someone else. All that day and the next, and even now I had and have a picture of J.T.[2] He was bareback and if his seat had loosened and he had lost control of the pony, the pony might have turned into us just as easily as the mule. And that day you would have hit him just as surely as you hit the mule, and if you had been driving your usual careful way you certainly wouldn't have hit either. If you wonder why I didn't backseat-drive – well, I don't do it automatically, you know. I have trained myself not to in reaction from the <u>terrible</u> back seat driving that I have heard all my life. And I didn't really

---

1 The so-called blowup took place at a cocktail party given by Robert Camp Sr. and his wife, Rebecca, at their home in Ocala. MKR, who had been struggling with her own racism and issues of race, was offended by the "Fascist platitudes" about blacks she was hearing that evening of 14 February. She describes the volatile scene, fueled by alcohol, in a letter to NSB on 16 February 1944, reporting that when "someone made a typical southern and ugly anti-Negro remark, I found myself expounding moral principles. . . . Julia said yesterday that everything I said was true and right and needed saying, but I went at it the wrong way---she feels as I do, and has for a long time" (*Love Letters* 268–69).

2 J. T. "Jake" Glisson (1927–2019), perhaps the prototype for Fodder-wing in *The Yearling*, the son of Tom and Pearlee Glisson, regularly rode his pony on the road where the accident took place.

think you were that vague at the moment. When I saw the mule trotting so fast and aimlessly up the road I thought you would put on the brakes and slow down because you are usually so careful about cows on the side of the road. Every moment I thought you would stop, and then I saw it was too late to say anything and I just prayed the mule would go the other way. I finally yelled at you and even then you didn't put on the brakes for what seemed like a minute (fraction of a second, of course) I think actually not until we had hit the mule.[1]

Of course I realize that a good many people would have hit the mule just in the same way when they are driving entirely normally – that is, expecting everything to get out of their way. I have seen quite a few driving in and out of NYC. Often I have seen [an] accident going to happen sometime before it actually did. But those people always do have accidents and they kill a good many people. You are a long way from that kind of a driver, in fact you are almost exaggeratedly safe, (not that one really can be that in a car.)

I'm worried, of course, about your cracking yourself up, but what worries me most is the other side of the accident. I know that if you ever seriously crippled or killed someone you would never get over it. And terribly seriously, I think you easily might when you are in that mood and condition.

There is an incident that made a terrible impression on me. A girl I know slightly, a wild type rather, driving home from a party weekend ran into two little boys on bicycles, and killed one and hurt the other so badly that he had to have one leg amputated. When something like that happens to someone you know it seems a lot more real than a hundred newspaper stories. And on rare occasions when I feel I have to let off steam and flirt with danger or explode, thank God I always have remembered it and taken my foot off the accelerator. The plain bad fact is that when you start taking risks with a car you are playing not with suicide but with murder. There is no eternity of

---

1   JSB is referring to Sunday, 12 March, when MKR ran into a "runaway" mule (or the mule ran into MKR, depending upon whose story one wants to believe) on the way to Gainesville to see a movie. MKR reports to NSB that she was "doing no more than twenty-five an hour" when one of Old Boss Brice's mules came "galloping toward me in the middle of the road." MKR claims she veered to the right, but the mule "swerved into my path." MKR vows that she "slammed on the brakes, but mule and car met with utterly disastrous results to both." MKR and JSB were bruised, but not seriously injured; the car was a wreck; and the "poor mule was killed almost instantly" (*Love Letters* 299–300). Although clearly JSB would disagree, both George Williams, who was driving the mule home, and J. T. "Jake" Glisson, who was passing by on his pony, confirm MKR's story. MKR often drove at high speeds, often under the influence of alcohol, and she suffered a number of accidents as a result.

personal pain which justifies endangering momentarily or in the smallest possibility another human being.

It should go without saying, but perhaps it is better said, that I do not believe you are the sort of person who takes risks like that. If I did I wouldn't be writing this letter. What I said above I said to myself as much as to you, because I want never to forget it. Maybe it doesn't seem important compared to the negro problem or war or peace, but it is part of the same truth that concerns them: that one is responsible not just to oneself, and not just to the people around one, but properly to every human being in the world. I have gotten beyond what I set out to say.

What I believe is that you are unaware of the definite blurring of your reactions on occasions such as I have told you of, and so I had to tell you of it. And beg you to be careful.

Try to remember even if you are sore that I wouldn't have said this unless I really cared very much about what happens to you. That's not just an empty phrase. I mean it truly.

. . .

MKR to JSB, 21 March 1944. TLS, 7 pp. Envelope is missing. LH: Marjorie Kinnan Rawlings | Hawthorn, Florida.

March 21, 1944

Dearest Julia:

For your special benefit, I am struggling to remember to use an l for a one, instead of I. Then if I can remember not to forget things you tell me, of course I shall be perfect, and what will you do for grievances?

After writing Edith[1] to St. Augustine telling her to wire me on arrival, and to make it sound important, so that the Island Grove agent wouldn't put it in the rural mail a day or two later, I received a wire from her, "Leaving Florida Saturday. Absolutely urgent see you. Come at once. Edith." Mr. Neal[2] was not impressed and J.T. Glisson brought the wire out many hours later. Having totally forgotten my own message, I went into a dither, had a hasty supper, piled the battered farm truck full of myself, Moe, Idella, suitcases, cream, eggs, butter, vegetables, meats and a washtub of flowers and two pans of bread set for the last rising. Half-way to St. Augustine I remembered---.

---

1 Edith Pope and Verle Pope.
2 Mr. Neal [Neil], husband of the postmistress at Island Grove.

This was Wednesday, and we reached the cottage at 10:30 at night, and as a matter of fact I am glad that I did come at once, for Edith and Verle really were leaving Florida Saturday. Edith spent Thursday afternoon with me, and Verle joined us for dinner and the evening. St. Augustine being famous for its literary teas, it seems dreadful not to have one for Edith's real success, so I approached her on the idea, prepared to lose her friend-ship at the mere suggestion, but she was pleased and touched. I got on the 'phone and arranged for a cocktail party for Friday afternoon at the Castle Warden. We had about sixty people, and the Hustons put on a very nice affair for me. The hors d'oeuvres table was in the center of the second floor lounge and I have never seen a lovelier table of its sort. Mrs. Huston used a lace cloth, and a huge but low arrangement of lemon-yellow iris and cande-labra with tall yellow candles, and the most gorgeous array of canapes etc. etc. I managed to get an orchid from Jacksonville for Edith, and someone else had one for her, so she dripped properly. Others of her friends told me afterward that it had seemed dreadful not [to] have a brawl for her, but it was such short notice, and only the wonderful and terrible Hustons could have managed it.

People were still there at nine o'clock, and I went to the bathroom in the room Doug had set aside for the party to use---and the bed looked SO invit-ing, and I lay down for JUST A MOMENT---and the next I knew dawn was showing through perfectly strange windows and I didn't know where the hell I was and the party was over and Edith and Verle had gone to Colorado.[1]

I left the truck door open so that Moe could go in and out, and he slept in the truck all night, and was nice about it, but awfully reproachful the next day, much more so, I am sure, than Edith.

Incidentally, I have read "Colcorton"[2] and think it is a beautiful job, com-pletely satisfying.

I have been playing around in St. Augustine since, dashing to elegant last-of-the-season parties in the dilapidated truck---with Moe. At a cocktail party Sunday a man said, "We'll see you at dinner." I said, "Indeed? When?" "Why, tonight." His wife had asked me, at Edith's party, and I had accepted with pleasure and that was the end of it. Fortunately, I was free to go, as it proved to be one of those formal squab dinners where throwing out a place at the

---

1   MKR is a bit more frank in her letter to NSB on 18 March 1944, "I gave a party for Edith to celebrate her new book. . . . Well, I might as well tell all---. I had had two or three highballs" before the party, and "through my party I tossed off Manhattans like water" and "walked in a trance" and "calmly went to bed" (*Love Letters* 303).

2   Edith Pope's bestselling novel, *Colcorton* (New York: Scribners, 1944).

last minute raises the devil. I had told Aunt Ida[1] I would pick her up that evening to bring her to the cottage, and I had a guilty conscience at arriving so late---only to find that she thought it was the next day I was coming for her---.

I am terribly fond of Aunt Ida, but she is one of the duties Life has imposed on me, and I suffered through the day she spent with me, until she came out with something that recompensed me for all. She has for a friend a most depressing old lady named Mrs. Palethorpe, and Aunt Ida said, "Oh, I must tell you. I have found out something from Mrs. Palethorpe about the cultivation of roses. Mrs. Palethorpe has wonderful roses. If you possibly can, save your urine. Mrs. Palethorpe says there is nothing better for rose-bushes. Just lately, Mrs. Palethorpe hasn't been able to. She has gotten so stiff and sore, she just can't manipulate it."

The horticultural advice floored me from beginning to end. In the first place, I struggled so to achieve two bathrooms at the Creek, just so no one would have to save their urine, that it seemed like a waste of good plumbing, even for one's rose-bushes. I assumed of course that Mrs. Palethorpe saved her urine in a pot-pot, if she possibly could---then at the end of the dissertation I was faced with the appalling picture of Mrs. Palethorpe attending each rose bush individually, personally and with necessary accuracy. I could well see that if one became stiff and sore, manipulation would be difficult if not impossible.

We return to the Creek tomorrow. I am hoping to find word waiting of a good buy in a car.[2] Moe and Idella and flowers and bread ready to be baked, and I, can only travel socially in a farm truck about so long without being put down as eccentric.

I have missed you dreadfully, and shall continue to miss you. Chet[3] came out to see if we managed the towing trip without incident. He thinks you are wonderful, and adores you, but alas, his saying that you didn't bother him as most women do, was even more "wholesome" than we feared. He said I didn't bother him, either, and you and I are the only women who don't, and he means particularly that he felt with us no embarrassment at asking to be put out on a tussock.[4] To give you a blow more deadly than my description

---

1   Aunt Ida Tarrant.

2   MKR's Oldsmobile was destroyed when she hit the mule. See JSB's letter on 16 March 1944, 251, n. 1.

3   Chester "Chet" Crosby.

4   That is, a hunting coat. MKR is referring to the hunting incident when JSB fell off a pier into water up to her "arm-pits." Completely soaked, she had to take off her clothes to dry, and while they dried she and MKR ate fire-roasted fresh quail, JSB temporarily dressed in Crosby's windbreaker.

of you as wholesome, Chet said, in his raptures about you, "She has a good clean face." Sorry, Pal----.

Lots of love,

<u>Marjorie</u>

. . .

JSB to MKR, 21 March 1944. ALS, 6 pp. PM: NEW YORK, N.Y. | MAR 21 | 7-PM | 1944. AD: Mrs. Norton Baskin | Hawthorn | Florida. [In JSB's hand in block letters at top of page 1]: 31 EAST 79.

Tuesday. [21 March 1944]

Dearest Marjorie:

I guess I was asking for winter, and I certainly got it. We have had a fine healthy blizzard <though> though it has come appropriately to a sad end today, the first day of Spring.[1] Yesterday I wandered all over town with an inch deep layer of snow on me. I really didn't mind any of it – even the snow going down the back of my neck and over the top of my galoshes. Gosh, but you would have been miserable! Everyone was huddled up with the anguished expression on their faces which comes as a result of snow down the back of the neck, and I repulsed those who noticed me <but> by whistling & singing my way through the drifts. In the evening I ventured forth again to go to a pious recital at Carnegie Hall. It was rather disappointing and I got as far as boredom now and then. I had a moment of amusement in the intermission, however. I had wended my way per usual to the Ladies retiring room, and while trying to push my way back into the hall I got in line of fire of a conversation – "I don't see any of our New Rochelle friends here" was the phrase I picked up. I thought to myself 'tsk, what an unworthy thought for the intermission of a Schnabel recital.'[2] Then, practically in the hall, somebody bellowed in my ear "I don't see any Riverdalers here tonight." I wondered for some time just what reflection it was of the state of mind to hear such – not at the opera or the Philharmonic

---

He was asked to stand a short distance away. MKR is also teasing JSB about her seeming inability to impress a man, even while half-dressed. See MKR's letter to NSB on 7 February 1944 (*Love Letters* 260).

1   The first day of spring in 1944 was 20 March.

2   Artur Schnabel (1882–1951), Austrian Classical pianist known for his performances of works by Beethoven and Schubert.

– but at <the> an all Beethoven sonata evening with the echt[1] Beethoven sonata interpreter of our time!

I wish I could send you a transcript of my first conversation with Mr. Alves.[2] After allowing myself a day to recover from the headache I developed on the train, I girded my morale and called him up. As typical 'Alves' the phone call was better even than the letter. First of all he was delighted to say that he had not yet recovered from the sad episode of martinis, clams and strained groin. Not at all. Then after a few polite questions about my trip he said with macabre relish "A most tragic thing happened the other day." And I was told of the death in a plane crash of an ex-pupil – he had been married just nine months and his wife was going to have a baby. I tried to get the conversation off this subject by asking about Mary Friedman.[3] "Oh" says Mr. A. "You've heard about what happened to Friedman?" I led him on with confessed ignorance – fascinating tale – it seems Mary was singing Nedda in Pagliacci in San Fran.[4] when, to her horror, after the "Vesti la giubba"[5] the Pagliacci fell <u>dead</u>! Such a thing could only happen to a pupil of Mr. Alves.

Thursday I am having lunch with him, and he tells me he has lots he is saving to talk to me about. I am prepared for a morbid meal. Oh, my god, Marge, that reminds me. I don't think I ever told you about the time I took <u>him</u> to lunch at Schraffts.[6] He had taken me several times and I said it was my turn – to square things. He had a whole lunch, soup, and for the main course corned beef hash and vegetables. As he was plowing through (an appetite almost equal to yours) I spied a bit of steel wool – a hair of steel wool to be exact – in his hash, and thinking that if <u>Mr. A.</u> swallowed it he would undoubtedly die of a punctured gut, I pointed it out to him in a nonchalant manner. He examined it carefully and layed [*sic*] [it] on the edge of his plate. Then he proceeded to finish the hash. When the plate was polished and bare except for the wisp of steel, he caught the eye of the hostess and called her over. (Mr. A. has been eating at Schraffts regularly for about 30 years so he was up to this feat. For amateurs it is recommended they do not

---

1   *Echt*, German for "genuine" or "real."

2   Carl Waldemar Alves, JSB's voice teacher.

3   Mary Friedman: Perhaps Miriam Friedman (1897?–2001), the San Francisco opera singer.

4   *Pagliacci* (1892), literally the Italian word for "Clowns," an opera by the Italian composer Ruggero Leoncavallo (1857–1919). Nedda is the wife of the leader of the troupe of clowns, Canio (who plays Pagliaccio in the frame tale of the opera), who murders her and her alleged lover Silvio at the end of the opera.

5   "Put on the costume," an aria sung at the end of act 1 of *Pagliacci*.

6   A chain of restaurants, candy and gift shops primarily located in the New York metropolitan area.

even <u>try</u> to catch the eye of a S. hostess. People have worked up nervous breakdowns on problems less knotty than this.) She stalked over with <tr> a condescending dignity worthy of Pallas Athena,[1] and Waldemar[2] said in a conversational tone "Look what was in my corned beef hash." Never have you seen such an awful collapse of grandeur. The hostess wilted, turned pale and then red, and gave forth incoherent cries of horror and apology. Mr. A., to my great relief, was quite pleasant and said he didn't wish to complain and he had eaten his meal. "I just thought you should know," said he, and then delivered the coup de grace, "For a moment I wasn't sure I was in Childs or Schrafft's"[3] At this Athena looked so undone that I started to reach in my purse for my smelling salts. More horror, more abject apologies – she snatched up a menu and begged Mr. A. to order another dish, as he had had a good lunch he wasn't up to another entrée, and so he decided just to have dessert and coffee. The hostess thanked him profusely and dashed off with the practically empty plate at arms length. She came back in no time bringing a waitress in tow with the dessert and coffee, and snatching the check from my side scratched off Mr. A's entire lunch! I have never yet been able to figure whether this squared Mr. A. and I or not, but I told him I'd take him to lunch anytime provided he brought the steel wool along.

I sent you some books yesterday. The Sender novel[4] and another which I figured should slow you down a bit. I won't be able to get around to either for a month or two so take your time. I also returned the Koestler – a marvelous book[5] just my meat although at moments I felt his theories of history and self were going beyond me. I recommended it to Buzz.[6] I think he will love it, and in telling him about it I evidently piqued Daddy's[7] curiosity about it, because two days later he asked me for the title.

I dragged down to the office the day after I got home to make out my

---

1   Pallas Athena, Greek goddess of fertility, born from the head of Zeus.

2   As in Carl Waldemar Alves.

3   Childs' a New York chain of restaurants founded in 1889. Childs' lost much of its value when one of the founders, William Childs, imposed his vegetarian diet on the menu. The backlash led to a steady decline until meat and alcohol were restored to the menu in the late 1930s. But the chain would declare bankruptcy in August 1943.

4   Unidentified novel by the Spanish writer Ramón José Sender (1902–1982). See 258, n. 12.

5   Arthur Koestler (1905–1983), *Arrival and Departure* (New York: Macmillan, 1943) was sent to MKR by Norman Berg. MKR writes to NSB on 27 November 1943 that the book is a "knock-out" (*Love Letters* 186).

6   Charles Scribner IV, JSB's brother.

7   Charles Scribner III.

income tax, and I told Max to send you at once 2 copies of Edith's book.[1] The mix up was that he thought <u>Edith</u> would have sent you a copy. Probably you saw the rave reviews in the Times.[2] I haven't been able to find any other reviews. I'll go down to the office again in the next couple of days and find out if there are any more.

Ever since I have been home I have been seeing books which because of their superior length recommend themselves for you. Did you ever read "The Pasq^u^ier Chronicles" by Georges Duhamel,[3] "The Thibaults" Roger Martin du Gard[4] or "The Men of Good Will" series of Romains?[5] All works of Proustean or better than Proustean length.[6] Then how about Fielding, Richardson, <Stene> Sterne and Smollett to go old English?[7] I have never read any of these as their vastness has always sort of put me off. I can't put down a vision of you thirsting for more and bigger and longer books. It's quite shocking the way you consume them. I cannot read them slowly enough (if they are good). The longer I take with a book the deeper it goes into me and the more I can remember of it. "The Brothers Karamazov"[8] took me most of the summer – "Kirsten Lavransdetter"[9] part of another summer – and I spent all of last summer on "The Faerie Queen."[10] Of course I fling other current books around at the same time. I wish now I hadn't read the Péguy play so fast[11] – also the Sender book. I read his other "Counter Attack in Spain"[12]

---

1 MKR and Maxwell Perkins had an extended discussion on Edith Pope's *Colcorton* (New York: Scribners, 1944), which proved to be a critical success. Perkins was at first "puzzled" when he read it in manuscript. On 13 November 1943, MKR acknowledges how important it was that Perkins was willing to work "intensively" with Pope who has "real genius" (*Max and Marjorie* 556).

2 Orville Prescott (1907–1996), "Books of the Times," *New York Times* (13 March 1944): 13; William du Bois (1903–1997), "Colcorton's Secret," *New York Times Book Review* (26 March 1944): 3.

3 Georges Duhamel (1884–1966), French author of *Des Chroniques Pasquier* [*The Pasquier Chronicles*] 10 vols. (1933–45).

4 Roger Martin du Gard (1881–1958), French novelist, author of *The Thibaults*. 8 vols. (1922–29, 1936, 1940).

5 Jules Romains (1885–1972), French writer, author of the novel cycle *Les Hommes de bonne volonté* [*Men of Good Will*] 27 vols. (1932–46).

6 As in Marcel Proust.

7 Henry Fielding (1707–1754), Samuel Richardson (1689–1761), Laurence Sterne (1713–1768), and Tobias Smollett (1721–1771), all early developers of the English novel, which by modern standards would be considered of immense length.

8 Fyodor Dostoevsky (1821–1881), Russian novelist, author of *The Brothers Karamazov* (1880).

9 Sigrid Undset (1882–1949), Norwegian novelist, Nobel Prize winner (1928), and Rawlings's friend, author of the trilogy of historical novels *Kristin Lavransdetter* (1920–22).

10 Edmund Spenser (1552/53–1599), English poet, author of the epic allegory *The Faerie Queene* (1590, 1596).

11 One of Péguy's three plays: *Jeanne d'Arc* (1897), *Le Mystère de la Charité de Jeanne d'Arc* (1910), or *Le Mystère des Saints Innocents* (1912).

12 Ramón José Sender, *Contraataque* [*Counter-attack in Spain*]. Trans. Peter C. Mitchell (Boston:

over two or three months. When I read little bits at a time and gnaw over each chapter as I go I do better – but it is a great handicap to my ambition to be widely read.

Saturday and Sunday evenings in Far Hills I helped Daddy go over a dozen or two cases of Grandpa's books.[1] It is at once a fascinating and tedious job. Old novels, old histories, old travel books and books of poems, and as we flung them to one side I kept feeling there was a nugget somewhere in each one of them, "wrapped in layers of wool" as your pal Samuel Johnson said."[2] I salvaged an Eng. Fr. Dictionary, a lovely edition of "Robinson Crusoe"[3] with lots of pictures and which seems to go on beyond the edition I believe, and a <u>large</u> "History of Spanish Islam." Why the latter I don't know, except it looked marvelously scholarly and interesting at the same time. When I looked at the introduction I found that at one time anyway it was considered a 'classic' of history – written originally in French by a Dutchman named Douzy.[4] I found a "Natural History of Shelbourne" with all the plates that were in yours and in the back a whole lot of plates I don't remember seeing in the 'first'[5] – pictures of the buildings etc. of the village. Does yours have these? If not remind me to show these to you sometime. There is enough reading in the house now for a lifetime, but lots of it is terrifyingly rare and valuable and finely bound. <with> My habits of reading in the bathtub and over the basin, not to speak of our toilet, won't be just the thing for most of them.

You would enjoy going over the books, I know. I wish you could sit in on our dusty sessions. I am so used to being around you I keep seeing things I want to show you and thinking things I want to say to you. Chet[6] would say it would take me at least a week to get over it, but <it's> it is a week and I'm not over it yet.

I have turned "R. under A."[7] over to Daddy. I wonder if anything will come of it? In two ways it would mean a great deal to me. Well, I shall wait and see,

---

Houghton, Mifflin, 1937).

1   Charles Scribner II (1854–1930).

2   See Samuel Johnson (1709–1784), English essayist, poet, biographer, *A Dictionary of the English Language* (London: Strahan & Knapton, 1755) on the manufacture of wool into thicker layers.

3   Daniel Defoe (1660–1731), English writer who popularized the art form of the Romance, *The Adventures of Robinson Crusoe*. 3 vols. (London: Taylor, 1719–20).

4   Reinhart Dozy (1820–1883), Dutch historian, *Spanish Islam: A History of the Moslems in Spain*. Trans. Francis G. Stokes (London: Chatto & Windus, 1913).

5   Gilbert White (1720–1793), English naturalist and ornithologist, *The Natural History and Antiquities of Selborne* (London: Bensley, 1789).

6   Chet Crosby.

7   Thomas A. Browne, *Robbery Under Arms*. See JSB's letter on 18 April 1944, 261, n. 3.

and then I'll write you – if something comes I shall tell you the two things with a sigh and if nothing comes of it I shall tell you with another variety of <agh> sigh – So the difference between success and failure is merely the quality of a sigh. With this delicately profound thought I shall go out and <u>breathe</u> some of the air of the first day of spring. Appropriately Northern it is too. Warm and sunny with lots of slush underfoot.

Lots of love,

Julia

P.S. I have sent you something which will bear out your definition of me as "half-batty." I am not, of course, half-batty, and I bear <out> you out only in a spirit of noble generosity.

. . .

JSB to MKR, 18 April 1944. ALS, 4 pp. PM: NEW YORK, N.Y. | Apr 19 | 5³⁰ PM | 1944. 2nd PM: Hawthorn | June [rest of PM illegible]. AD: Mrs. Norton Baskin | <Cross Creek> St. Augustine | <Hawthorn> Star Route to Crescent Beach | Florida.[1] RA: J. Scribner | Fall Hills, N.J. VIA AIR MAIL envelope.

April 18. [1944][2]

Dearest Marjorie:

You have heard of my ignominious illness – (Serious though, fraught with possibilities of infirmities.) I have managed to recover without heart trouble, deafness, blindness and not even a touch pneumonia to the disappointment of the doctor and my friends and relations. They positively hovered over me like a flock of vultures, waiting for some awful aftereffect to arrive. But I was not feeling in the mood for dramatics, and I got well and feel actually better than before. I look quite glowing. Granny shook me some this evening by telling that my complexion looked marvelous and adding that she thought I had looked rather bilious all winter! My only comfort was that Chet[3] didn't notice it. Incidentally I think that having a clean face is not quite so bad as being wholesome. It has a sort of athletic flavor, whereas 'wholesome' always

---

1   The second postmark indicates that this letter was forwarded from Hawthorne to Crescent Beach. The forwarding information that replaces the original address is in a second hand.

2   Written in a second hand and inserted after the date: [1944].

3   Crosby grew attached to JSB, as MKR writes in a letter to NSB on 8 March 1944, "Chet is grieving over Julia's leaving, and is taking us fishing in the morning and again on Sunday" (*Love Letters* 294).

brings to my mind the horrible word 'nutritive.' Just my odd mind, I suppose. And that reminds me that Granny has a pleasant way of describing a sensible meal – she never calls it 'well-balanced' or 'wholesome' but 'hygenic'[1] (Why did I start that – I can't spell it – so much so that I can't find it in the diction-ary!!!<)> oh, hell, you recognize the word anyway, and you must admit it is an interesting choice of word. Now I am going to have to spend days look-ing through magazines for a message on feminine h – so's to find out how it's spelled. Can't understand why I can't locate it in the dictionary. I've tried every combination of letters I can think of. Do mention it in your next letter in case I am still struggling.)

I started a letter to you in the early stages of my measles, 2nd or 3rd day, but after a page felt too exhausted to continue and the next day worse and the next day worse etc. Then when I felt better I was kept in grotto-like dark-ness, which affected my morale very much. You will recall my feelings about brooding in the dark! I wanted to thank you for the really swell birthday present – this is half of it.[2] Do you think it improves my writing? I feel that it makes it rather worse as it slips along so fast it enables me to leave out a few more letters here and there. Anyway it's very comfortable and you can blame yourself if it's worse to read.

I have such lots of things to tell you it depresses me terribly – I mean the thought of having to write so much. I think the only putting of pen or pencil to paper I really physically enjoyed was the writing out of <u>pages</u> of <u>Robbery Under Arms</u>.[3] Of course, that's just how I feel <u>physically</u> about writing, noth-ing to do with how I feel about writers. No more word about R.U.A., but I think it's pretty sure that no matter how lovely anyone thinks it is it won't be published at least for the present on account of the paper situation which is acute. Have you ever heard a publisher purring with delight over the fact that there is <u>nothing</u> big or important on the fall list. That's what Scribner's is doing now. I am casting about in my head for another editorial job,[4] but am slightly cooled off by the thought that no matter how fascinating the

---

1   JSB means "hygienic."

2   For her birthday, 26 March, MKR gifted JSB a Parker pen, more than likely the new "Parker Vacumatic Major Fountain Pen." Later MKR was to do an ad for Parker. See her letter on 21 Febru-ary 1948.

3   Rolf Boldrewood [Thomas A. Browne] (1826–1915), *Robbery Under Arms: A Story of Life and Adventure in the Bush and In The Goldfields of Australia*. 3 vols. (London: Macmillan, 1888).

4   From this passage, it seems likely that JSB had been invited to bring projects to Scribners. Her comment that their list is suffering from war restrictions on paper suggests not only her frustration in this role but also her concern for what the lack of new titles meant for the future of Scribners. *Robbery Under Arms* was not republished by Scribners, and she would not serve in an editorial capacity until she did so as MKR's literary executor.

morsel I dish up nothing will come of it. Still I have vague notions about an anthology I know Daddy[1] has been having vague notions about for some time. I shall broach it to him, I think. I refuse to tell you about it. You would be unsympathetic – not for purely literary reasons.

I met a man whom I like more than about anyone who has appeared in my life so far (Relax, he is married with children and at least one grand-child.) If our love at first sight ripens, for he professes himself very taken too, I think he may have a profound influence on my life. That sounds melodramatic but I felt a real recognition of someone I wanted to learn from and I think he wanted to teach me. He is a professor (D.D.) at General Seminary here in N.Y.C. He is a terrific scholar who is at the same time acutely and practically aware of the 'actual' world. A <u>much</u> bigger man mentally and spiritually than Pardue,[2] no comparison. If he doesn't get ahold of me as he promised, his is one person I shall get around to hunting down myself.[3]

I am sending you a couple of things from the New Republic – one is a stupid review of Lillian Smith (Isn't it wonderful how she is selling?) I don't know why I send it except to express to you how dull I think Malcolm Cowley is.[4] I was horrified to find he was doing the Perkins articles.[5] He lacks the NYer verve completely. I think he has no more sense of humor than a seasick cat. The articles reflected the lack quite clearly in my opin-ion. One of the few things about the New R. that depresses me is his lead review every week. Also Edmund Wilson[6] is getting me down – another drip. I curse every week with disgust – I now take 10 minutes out to recurse all such horrors as Russian dictionaries. The only thing I am obliged to him for is his unmasking of translations. I thought I should reach out and buy that Augustine book (forget title)[7] but I am so horrified at the thought that

1   Charles Scribner III.

2   Austin Pardue. See MKR's letter on 28 April 1943, 180, n. 1.

3   The person here is almost certainly another clergyman she met before she knew Thomas Big-ham, her future husband.

4   Malcolm Cowley (1898–1989), rev. of Lillian Smith (1897–1997), *Strange Fruit* (New York: Rey-nal & Hitchcock, 1944) in *New Republic* 100.10 (March 1944): 320.

5   Malcolm Cowley, "Unshaken Friend I–II." *New Yorker* 20.7–8 (1 April 1944): 28–32, 35–36; (8 April 1944): 30–34, 36, 39–40. Rpt. *Unshaken Friend: A Profile of Maxwell Perkins* (Boulder: Rine-hart, 1985).

6   Edmund Wilson (1895–1972), one of the paramount critical journalists of the time and the fore-most leader of Freudian-Marxist literary criticism. He was the associate editor of the *New Republic* (1926–1931) and the book reviewer for the *New Yorker* (1944–1948). JSB's critique is somewhat surprising, for one of Wilson's most famous books, *Axel's Castle,* was published by Scribners in 1931. Curiously, MKR makes no mention of Wilson in her letters to Maxwell Perkins.

7   Frank J. Sheed [Francis Joseph Sheed] (1897–1981), trans. *Confessions of St. Augustine* (New

half of it is cut out I don't know what to do except to learn Spanish. How about <u>Canape Vert?</u>[1] Should I read it? There was a marvelous review of the Brazilian book <u>Rebellion in the Backlands</u> by Ralph Bates in the New R.[2] (that I must buy, 8.00 not withstanding.) Only I am alternately satisfied and enraged by a sentence in the beginning. "It stands aside and above the foothills of Brazilian literature (whatever the hell they may be J.B.S.)[3] as say, <u>Don Quixote</u>[4] dominates its own landscape; or as Jean-Richard Bloch's <u>And Company</u> stands firm as a granite axis above the sliding detritus of contemporary French literature." And perhaps you can enlighten me on the next sentence: "And to compare it to a book that sums up a mental process that is the polar opposite. Cunha's <u>Os Sertoes</u> is as lovely above its Amazonian verdure as the Parnassian <u>Les Trophées</u> on its marble slopes." Never heard of Les T. – please tell me what it is – you've been to college. Well, from here on the review stops throwing weight around and gets interesting. But to get back to the first sentence – I enjoy the high opinion, shared by me, of Bloch, however I am outraged to have Aragon referred to as "sliding detritus" – not to mention Malraux, Bernanos[5] and I'm sure others I could rally if it weren't so late. Have you read any of the poems yet? Read Misery and Poverty in Péguy.[6] I shall write you this periodically till you give in. The "St Joan" has grown on me more and more.[7] It is an amazing feeling I keep understanding more and more of it, though I haven't so much as opened the book since I've been home. It seems I didn't realize while I read how much I was actually getting. I have tried in all the French

---

York: Sheed & Ward, 1944).

1   Philippe Thoby-Marcelin (1904–1975) and Pierre Marcelin (b. 1908) *Canapé-Vert*. Trans. Edward L. Tinker (1881–1968) (New York: Farrar-Rinehart, 1944), a novel about the lives of Black peasants in Haiti.

2   Euclides da Cunha (1866–1909), *Rebellion in the Backlands* [*Os Sertões*] (1902), trans. Samuel Putnam (1892–1950), rev. by Ralph Bates (1899–2000), *New Republic* (21 February 1944), 250–52, recounting the horror of poverty in rural Brazil. JSB goes on to quote Bates's review, 250..

3   J.B.S.—that is, "just bull shitting."

4   Miguel de Cervantes (1547–1616), Spanish novelist and playwright, *Don Quixote* (1605, 1615).

5   Jean-Richard Bloch, see JSB's letter on 8 August 1943, 204, n. 5; José María Heredia y Heredia (1842–1905), Cuban-born poet, author of *Les Trophées* (1893), a series of 118 sonnets written in the French "Parnassian" style, a reaction against Romantic sentimentalism; Louis Aragon, see JSB's letter on 8 August 1943, 204, n.5; André Malraux, see JSB's letter on 5–6 November 1943, 238, n. 1; and Georges Bernanos, see JSB's letter on 5–6 November 1943, 238, n. 2.

6   "Misery and Poverty," a reference to Péguy's distinction in "De Jean Coste" between misery, where economic life is not assured, and poverty, where it is.

7   Péguy was born in the French town of Orléans, also the birthplace of St. Joan of Arc (c. 1412–1431), burned at the stake by the English, declared a martyr in 1456, and canonized in 1920. JSB is referring to one of Péguy plays, *Jeanne d'Arc* (1897) or *Le Mystère de la charité de la Jeanne d'Arc* [*The Mystery of the Charity of Joan of Arc*] (1910).

book shops I know to get the 2nd & 3rd "St. Joans" but no luck. If I could organize my life a little I could read them at the library.

I have been looking at papers for news of the Burma affair,[1] and feeling for you. Have you heard lately from Norton – his letters now must be <u>since</u> the push started. I take comfort from his letter about the ability of the hospital to leave in 1 hour. At least they shouldn't get caught anywhere as a stationary hospital might. Today the news from there seems better at last.

I do hope you are OK and wish you were around where I could harangue you for a couple of hours, and ask you all sorts of questions. Has Moe re-formed? Were you able to get a good car? Prices for 2nd hand cars are <u>awful</u> up here. I could get about $1000 <u>more</u> for my car than I paid, so you can imagine what the purchaser would have to dig out. Love to Chet, Moe, Martha, Idella, etc. And to you ever so many thanks for the inspirational present (I needed a pen <u>badly</u>) and ever so much love,

Julia.

. . .

JSB to MKR, 25 April 1944. ALS, 2 pp. PM: NEW Y[ORK, NY] | APR 26 [1944] | 1 PM | STA[TION illegible]. AD: Mrs. Norton Baskin | Cross Creek | Hawthorn | Florida. VIA AIR MAIL envelope.

April 25. [1944][2]

Dearest Marjorie:

From Max via Daddy I hear that you have heard from Norton since the Burma business[3] started and also that you have found a new approach to your book and are about to start work. I can't tell you how happy I was to have such good news from you. I do hope that you can get news from Norton regularly. I suppose it's difficult as both Norton and whoever carries

---

1   The Allied invasion of Burma to repulse the Japanese began in January and had intensified in its brutality by April 1944. See JSB's letter on 25 April 1944, 264, n. 3.

2   Written in a second hand on the envelope: APR. / 26 / 1: PM / 1944, and after April 25 on p. 1: [1944].

3   Maxwell Perkins and Charles Scribner III. The "Burma business" JSB alludes to was among the most savage since Japan had conquered Burma in 1942. Begun in January 1944, the newest incursion into Burma was led by the Allied Commander Lt. General Joseph Stilwell (1888–1946), known as "Vinegar Joe" because of his caustic personality. The Allied objective was to open the borders between China and Burma and between India and Burma. The victory went to the Allies, but not before over 20,000 Allies were killed and over 40,000 Japanese. JSB was driving an ambulance in the India theater. Stilwell was born in Palatka, Florida, 45 miles east of Cross Creek.

the mail must be awfully busy. I also hope that this will be the right track for your book.[1] I'm sure it will be a tremendous relief to have something to think about beside the news that one has to read in the papers. Even R. U. A.[2] was a good rest though I groaned a good deal about its boresomeness, and I am eager to do something else. Of course I realize there is a lot of suffering connected to writing (I can imagine it with terrifying clearness!) whereas chopping and hauling things around is mere mental exercise. But, what the hell, at least it's suffering that gets you somewhere.[3]

I sent you some asparagus. I hope it arrived before you left for the cottage – if you <u>have</u> left as I hear you intending. If you got it OK, let me know if it was in good condition. It is still coming from Calif. so I am worried that so much travel may be too much for it – But if it was OK, I'll send you some every week while the season lasts. It's perfectly easy – I just get it across the street and use up some of Granny's[4] accumulated boxes & wrapping paper.

I saw a fascinating sight today. Ernest Hemingway with a long and practically white beard – also a pot belly which I should think would be rather a liability when combined with a young and possibly restless wife.[5] He asked after you and sent you his best.

Last weekend, mostly to make you feel better about men and somewhat because I wanted to, I sallied forth to greet the first wildflower. I found the bloody little thing (bloodroot it was too) and in the doing ruined one complete pair of Bendel stockings <u>never</u> before worn![6] One more of these semifatal incidents which attend my showing any interest in botany and I'm going to take the hint and leave Nature to her own devices. Anyway, I took the flower home and started to draw and paint it. Again it did me dirt. I carefully and agonizingly drew it and started in on the painting when it <u>opened wide</u> for no good reason, having been up to then a tight bud. It quite shattered my composition, leaving it at a crucial moment without a model. It was

---

1   *The Sojourner.*

2   *Robbery Under Arms* by Thomas A. Browne. See JSB's letter on 18 April 1944, 261, n. 3.

3   Perhaps an allusion to John Keats (1795–1821), English Romantic poet, and his well-known description of human experience as a "Vale of Soul-Making." In a letter to his brother George and sister-in-law Georgiana Keats, 14 February–3 May 1819, Keats writes, "Do you not see how necessary a World of Pains and troubles is to school an Intelligence and make it a soul. A Place where a heart must feel and suffer in a thousand diverse ways!" (*John Keats: Selected Letters*, ed. Robert Gittings [Oxford: Oxford UP, 2010]: 233).

4   Louise Flagg Scribner.

5   Hemingway and Martha Gellhorn were married in 1940 and divorced in 1945.

6   Henri Bendel, fashionable women's accessory store on Fifth Avenue in New York, established in 1895.

too late to start all over (light gone) and anyway I was exhausted creatively. It just goes to show you should never trust a wildflower. In fact, leave the damn things strictly alone – if you escape near-drowning, poison ivy and decimated nylons there are other sub[t]le disasters waiting for you – not to mention hayfever.

The ballet has been wonderful – and popular to an amazing degree. Two companies playing at the same time and both regularly sold out. I went at the last minute to the Ballet Theatre playing at the <u>Met</u>![1] and was able to get only the 9th seat in a box practically on the stage. From my near seat I had <and> ^an^ excellent view of the prompter's box the first fiddler and the double basses – also the dancers when they took their curtain calls. Must go to bed –

Much love,

Julia.

. . .

MKR to JSB, 19 May 1944. TLS, 9 pp. PM: CITRA | MAY | 19 | P.M. | 1944 | FLA. AD: Miss Julia Scribner | Far Hills | New Jersey. LH: MARJORIE KINNAN RAWLINGS | HAWTHORN, FLORIDA.

May 19, 1944

Dearest Julia:

You left Florida in the nick of time.[2] When Edith Pope spent a week here, I found her with her near-sighted eyes peering practically into the puss of a real coral snake---. Moe[3] and I spend half the nights chasing varmints, and one night of a big haul, I shot a huge possum under the bedroom window, devouring the eggs of a setting duck, and corraled a large turtle. Martha's family, according to Idella's report,[4] was up by dawn the next morning, and

---

1 *Fancy Free*, presented by the American Ballet Theatre, choreographer Jerome Robbins (1918–1998) and composer Leonard Bernstein (1918–1990), premiered at the Metropolitan Opera House on 18 April 1944.

2 JSB left on 13 March, having arrived on 5 February at Cross Creek (see *Love Letters* 258). MKR writes to NSB on 13 March 1944, "Well, my beloved and half-batty Julia leaves me today. I don't know what I shall do without hearing 'Oh, God damn it!' a hundred times a day, rushing to see what catastrophe has occurred, and finding that perhaps she has put her elbow in the whipped cream" (*Love Letters* 299).

3 Moe, MKR's pointer dog.

4 Martha Mickens and Idella Parker.

by the time Idella came to get my breakfast, the Mickenses had cooked and eaten the turtle, washed the pot and had the possum cooking. Now three panthers are reported living a couple of miles away, a male and a female and a young one. I feel sure they are only large wild-cats, however. The summer heat has begun, and I shall soon think of moving to the cool cottage. If transportation were not so awful, I should take Moe and Idella to the mountains somewhere for the summer.

I'm so sorry you had the measles, but thank god you got them in New York---.

You did not keep your promise about the asparagus, for which I thank you deeply---I mean for sending it. You were only going to send me some when it began coming in at a low price from your own territory. That California box must have set you back the price of a whole record album. But it was much enjoyed---but don't play false like that again.

Also, many thanks for the books, which I have just finished and shall return shortly. I enjoyed particularly the Sender "Counter-Attack in Spain",[1] and it seemed to me to be "For Whom the Bell Tolls" without love in a sleeping-bag. I am intrigued by news of Hemingway's beard. I am wondering if it may be a defense against Martha---.[2]

I have been plodding through three heavy but fascinating books; the 2-vol. Myrdal "An American Dilemma"; "Rebellion in the Backlands", a Brazilian classic; and "As We Go Marching", by one John Flynn, an obvious Roosevelt-hater. The latter makes out a very good case for the fact, or fear, that we are taking exactly the same course that led in Italy and Germany to fascism.[3]

There are many fallacies, however, some of them being in Flynn's own basic assumptions. One is evidently that idealistic dreaming is folly, and that the only answer is practical common sense. Another is that he offers no choice between a return to the old capitalism, and fascism. Fascism, and a totally

1   Ramón Sender, *Counter-attack in Spain*. See JSB's letter on 21 March 1944, 258, n. 12.

2   Martha Gellhorn. See MKR's letter on 1 January 1941, 80, n. 3.

3   Gunnar Myrdal (1898–1987), Swedish economist and sociologist, author of *An American Dilemma: The Negro Problem and Modern Democracy* (New York: Harper, 1944). Myrdal argues that segregation will no longer be viable in post-war America. See MKR's elaboration in her letter to NSB on 17 April 1944 (*Love Letters* 332–34). Euclides da Cunha, *Rebellion in the Backlands*. See JSB's letter on 18 April 1944, 263, n. 2. John Flynn (1882–1964), American political operative, author of *As We Go Marching* (New York: Doubleday, 1944). Flynn claims that poor post-war planning by the Roosevelt Administration would lead to Fascism in America. Flynn formed the America First Committee to oppose militarism and intervention by the United States in world affairs. He is the source for the contention that Roosevelt knew beforehand that the Japanese were going to attack Pearl Harbor, a theory that was later dismissed.

bureaucratic and centralized federal government, are certainly not desirable, but neither is capitalism. The book was sent me by a plump plutocrat,[1] and I shall write him that I have never read a more convincing argument for out-and-out Communism!

I have really been through the mill since you left. I did not know whether Norton was dead or alive, or a Jap prisoner. As it proved, he got out his ambulance just ahead of the Jap near-encirclement, and had to abandon all his person belongings, including a Tibetan lama's brocaded robe he had bought for an evening wrap for me, when he was on furlough up near Mt. Everest. He got out, with a load of wounded, with only what he had on his back.

I had no sooner got my breath after a cable that he was safe, when a disastrous fire, of which you may have heard (the N.Y. Tribune carried a story about it just under a concert item!) struck the Castle Warden, and the woman in whose room the fire started, evidently from her falling alsep <asleep>[2] with a lighted cigarette, and our dear friend Mrs. Pickering in the pent-house apartment, lost their lives. I have never been so knocked out.[3]

Incidentally, the Hotel Commission wrote the hotel manager that they had always felt dubious about the safety of the apartment, and would not give again a permit for anyone to live there.

Just before this happened, and just after Edith was here, I was ready to begin work again on my book.[4] I was thrown off my stride, naturally, but still expect to settle down to work after two or three other friends make brief visits. Meantime, I have been doing some work for the Office of War Information, perfectly futile stuff, I am sure, but one cannot refuse.[5]

---

1 Not identified.

2 MKR excises and inserts the correction in pencil above the line.

3 The fire at the Castle Warden took place on 23 April. Ruth Hopkins Pickering (1900–1944), a close friend of MKR and NSB, perished. As MKR writes to NSB on 25 April, "There was nothing in the Jacksonville paper about Ruth's death or the fire. The woman who started the fire proved to be a Jacksonville beauty parlor operator, and her family proved to have considerable influence and kept the whole thing out of the Times-Union. They evidently did not want it known she was in St. Augustine, where she had no business. I am wondering . . . if she set the fire deliberately to commit suicide that way" (*Love Letters* 347–48). The original determination by the police was that the fire was caused by a lit cigarette, but rumors abound. In these accounts, the other woman was Elizabeth "Betty" Norvelle Richeson (1914–1944), who was there to meet her lover "Mr. X." The hotel is now the Ripley's Believe It or Not! Museum, which encourages the legend that the ghosts of Pickering and Richeson can be heard screaming out at night. In several accounts of this paranormal guise, Mr. X, who is alleged to have killed Richeson and then set the fire, can be heard as well.

4 *The Sojourner.*

5 MKR is referring to her article "Florida: A Land of Contrasts," *Transatlantic* no. 14 (October 1944): 12–17, which she did for the Office of War Information for the British magazine "for the

I am sorry that you got frightened about the mule accident after it was all over and you returned home. With all due admission that I drink too much, I do not believe that I am a menace on the public highways, for I have been driving, drunk and sober, for twenty-five years, and if my reflexes were too unreliable, I should have had some sort of accident long before this---and have not. As you noticed when we left Ocala after the Negro dispute, I drove with deliberate slowness when I have had a good many drinks.[1] The day we hit the mule, or the mule hit us, I had had two drinks before dinner, and was certainly not in any dangerous condition. The time element is impossible to gauge in such an event, and as I look now at the curve where the accident happened, it could only have been a matter of split seconds. I myself felt the accident approaching, but told myself that a horse or mule never wavered as do the hogs and cattle which I always stop for, and that the mule would certainly continue down the middle of the road. I looked, two days later, at the road, and it still held my wheel-marks where I had drawn far to the side. And Mr. Williams himself said that I put on the brakes before the mule swerved and climbed into the car.[2]

When I first talked to Dr. Atchley about you, he warned me not to mix psychiatry with friendship, and I shall not do so now---but my dear, for some obscure reason, you are afraid, mentally and physically. I could give you my thesis about it, but it is dangerous ground. I used to think that simple sex frustration was all that was wrong, but there is something far beyond that.

When you wrote that you considered my dangerous driving "brought on" one of your migraine headaches, you were admitting that the headaches are psychic. The hell with Dr. Atchley---I am going to say what I think. I think that after a happy and sheltered childhood, you found maturity unpleasant, for several reasons: sexual frustration and sexual guilt (but you should feel none, as masturbation is the medically accepted substitute for the desirable sex relation); the realization in maturity that you were at odds with your environment, and had liberal ideas that are anathema to those with whom you associate. My theory is, that while you recognize these factors, you are clinging to the safety of childhood and refusing to enter adult life, with its responsibilities and disagreeableness. I think you are subconsciously using the migraines as an alibi. This was almost proved by the fact that for your

purpose of giving Britishers an understanding of the U.S.A. and its mental workings." (*Love Letters* 361, 395). See also Tarr, *Bibliography*, C628.

1   MKR is referring to the argument she got into at the Camp cocktail party over the racial slurs of the partygoers. See JSB's letter on 16 March 1944, 250, n. 1.

2   See JSB's letter on 16 March 1944, 251, n. 1.

first three weeks here, when you were happy and occupied, you had no headache. Then the boredom of the backwoods life over-took you, you became restless and unhappy, and became antagonistic to me, and to the unfamiliar milieu---which would happen to me, and does happen, after too long a time in an urban atmosphere.

I had a part in your sudden unhappiness, and without meaning to make you feel that you were ever unwanted, it was this: being addicted to so-called creative work, I can go only so long without doing something along that line. These things go in nervous cycles. I wanted you here very much, and hoped that a quiet atmosphere in which you were thoroughly approved, would do you good. But the time was actually too long for <u>both</u> of us. I became tense from not working---you became tense from staying too long in an environment that did not satisfy you. You became subconsciously conscious of my tenseness, as I did of yours. So until we are both psychoanalyzed, and able to live with those dreadful normal people, which God forbid, it seems to me to come down / ^to^ the fact that neither of us should stay longer than two or three weeks in a place that does not harmonize with our natures! Do you agree?

<It has turned> Capt. Heyl[1] is about ready to move to his New Hampshire place, and I do hope we can join him there, perhaps, with Norton, in the fall. He seems to have licked the germ, and his troubles now are with local contractors who can't understand why anyone is in a hurry about bathrooms.

Much love,

<u>Marjorie</u>

---

1   MKR was encouraging a relationship between Heyl and JSB as late as March 1944 (see *Love Letters* 290), but by this juncture she had second thoughts, which she expresses to NSB in a letter on 11 May 1944, "I wrote Henry Heyl, and decided to warn him that Julia was a problem child. He can't help falling for her, and I felt he should know she was a neurotic of the first order. It may be just a challenge to his medical knowledge, but he is certain to like her, and so---." JSB's letter on 16 March 1944, critical of MKR's drinking and driving, may have precipitated this warning to Heyl. But MKR ends her letter to NSB by relaying that JSB had "almost walked out of the family home in protest against their lack of liberalism. This has melted me, and I shall write to her tenderly" (*Love Letters* 360). MKR's report here that Heyl "seems to have licked the germ" is unfortunately inaccurate. Heyl developed a neurologic disease that eventually took his life.

· · ·

JSB to MKR, 14 June 1944. ALS, 2 pp. PM: New York, N.Y. | Jun
14 | 2³⁰ PM | [1944]. AD: Mrs. Norton Baskin | <Cross Creek> |
<Hawthorn> | Florida. [written in a second hand] St. Augustine |
Star Route to | Crescent Beach. RA: J. Scribner | Far Hills, N.J. VIA
AIR MAIL envelope.

June 14.[1944][1]

Dearest Marjorie:

Somewhere I have half of a letter to you, but it seems to have completely
disappeared. No doubt it will turn up and I will finish it and send it along,
but in the meantime I must send along this small "promissory ^(?)^ note." I
have been awfully busy and we have had <u>large</u> house parties every weekend
for a month or more. Weekends are the only time I get to writing letters so
my correspondence has reached a new low.

This last weekend we had Buzz, Aunt Gladys, Mr. Leirens (my Belgian
friend) and Jimmie Reynolds (a pansy artist), Edith and another prospective minister[2] – Needless to say they came in shifts, as we just don't have
that many beds. Even so I had to spend one night on the sofa in my sitting
room which caused me some pains at such an upsetting of my ordered life
and a sleepless night. Edith looked very well and pretty and chic, and was
an enormous success with everybody. We hope to have her with us at least
once more as she doesn't leave <th> till the <middle> first of July. (I'm so
sleepy I just can't write straight – weekend hangover no doubt plus the fact
I have been taking more exercise of late and also I have had a sore throat for
a week and I am occasionally downing a sulfa pill. That always undermines
me). After all that you can see this can't go on much longer – particularly

---

1   Written in a second hand below date on p. 1: [1944].

2   Buzz: Charles Scribner IV, JSB's brother; Aunt Gladys: Gladys Augusta Bloodgood Casey Willets, sister of Vera Gordon Scribner, JSB's mother; Charles Leirens (1888–1963), Belgian photographer and musician; James Russel "Jimmy" Reynolds (1904–1963), American jazz pianist whose ensemble played at the Hollywood Cafe in New York; Edith Pope; and "another prospective minister":
perhaps Thomas Bigham. Previously, JSB had expressed serious interest in "another" minister (see
her letter on 18 April 1944, 262, n. 3), If that minister was not Bigham, then it is entirely possible
that this minister is. If so, this "prospective minster" she apparently views as a candidate for her
affection, especially since the earlier candidate was married. However, JSB's comments here might
just be sarcastic humor, born out of her exasperation that everyone, and especially MKR, was intent
on finding her a husband. And this would then be the first mention to MKR of Bigham, whom she
married eleven months later.

as I have not yet got over the "hump" of the week – that is my Tues, Wed. & Thurs. stint.

I hope to go up to New Marlboro[1] Thurs. afternoon – My Penn station shift is early from 8 AM till M or N or whatever they call noon. I am longing to get some New England air. New York of course never calls but New Jersey does.

Well, I <u>must</u> go to bed. . . . This is just to break the silence on my end of the line – I'll write you a real letter soon –

Love –

Julia

P.S. I enclose a map I cut from PM[2] a couple of weeks ago. It is the most detailed one I have ever seen of the Burma area. Edith tells me you hear regularly from Norton and he is doing OK. I hope the possibilities of having to make such close escapes as he did is quite a thing of the past there now. As far as I can make out things are pretty much under control there at the moment.

. . .

MKR to JSB, 18 June 1944. TLS, 3 pp. PM: SAINT AUGUSTINE | JUNE 19 | 10 AM | 1944 | FLA. AD: Miss Julia Scribner | Far Hills | New Jersey.

Crescent Beach
St. Augustine, Fla.

June 18, 1944

Dearest Julia:

I was glad to have even a sleepy note[3] from you. I envy you New Marlboro, as it is hot as hell just now even at the beach, where we moved last week. If transportation by car were possible, I should move my large family to the mountains somewhere, or even to Maine, but it isn't worth while coping with buses or trains, especially as we have been warned that if we leave home now we may not be able to get back.[4] The family has been increased by little

---

1 New Marlborough, Massachusetts.
2 *PM* was a liberal newspaper published in New York City from June 1940 to June 1948. The editor was Ralph Ingersoll (1900–1985).
3 That is, JSB's previous letter on 14 June.
4 War time restrictions discouraged travel by train or plane.

black Martha,[1] the cute one of Sissie's children. Sissie let us take her for the summer, and in the fall she will decide whether we can keep her. I think she will agree by that time. The little thing is amazingly smart and Idella is very happy. When we set out, Idella said, "Mr. Baskin better hurry home, or there won't be room in the car for him." We can always get a trailer for Moe and Martha---.

I had been here just two days when I had a wire from old Martha, "My baby Hettie (who was all of 50) died in Salisbury Maryland.[2] Please return at once." I could not see what good I could do at Cross Creek with baby Hettie dead in Maryland, so just wired the faithful Chet[3] asking him to check and lend Martha money if necessary for anything that made sense. Actually, I could not possibly have gone, as I have been finishing a 2500-word article for the War Board that had to be in New York by Tuesday. Will go in to St. Augustine to mail it today.[4]

Mail has been coming through from Norton a bit more reliably. He keeps insisting that he is perfectly safe, but the road has been blocked behind them many times again, and each morning the British clean out night-laid land mines and snipers, then smoke screens are laid down for the ambulances to make an afternoon run to gather the wounded. Norton said the Japs keep popping up so steadily that they think they must be breeding in their fox-holes. One of his friends was wounded on a run, and a patient killed. Some-times he is down at the base hospital on the Manipur plain,[5] sometimes up on a mountain---between the British and Jap artillery fire --- where they have two dug-in rooms, one a First Aid post, the other their living quarters. Sometimes there are four men there, sometimes two. One man is cook and Norton is dish washer. He wrote, "Here I am under shot and shell, and all I will get will be dish pan hands."

The news of Ruth Pickering's death in the fire[6] took the wise-cracks out

---

1   Martha "Little Martha" Fountain (1939–1993), daughter of Zamilla Mickens "Sissie" Fountain (1907–1998) and Henry Fountain (b. 1895?).

2   Hettie Lou Mickens (1910–1944), daughter of Martha "Mattie" Jackson "Old Martha" Mickens (1878–1963) and William "Old Will" Mickens (1866?–1966?). MKR repeats here almost verbatim what she wrote to NSB on 17 June. On 30 June, MKR informs NSB that "they brought Hettie's body to Florida and buried her at Macintosh" (*Love Letters* 396, 409).

3   Chet Crosby.

4   The article solicited by the Writer's War Board could be "The Southern Soldier and the Negro" (untraced), which MKR writes about to NSB on 23 June 1944. The article was rejected, says MKR, because it was deemed "'too controversial'" (*Love Letters* 403–04).

5   Manipur Plain, the central plain of Manipur, a state in northeastern India.

6   The fire at the Castle Warden Hotel. Pickering was a friend of the Baskins and was staying in their apartment on the top floor when she died.

of him, which the war did not seem to be able to do, but I am hoping he will recover his usual rare spirits before long. He has also had dysentery for more than two weeks, which he attributed to the diet (everything is flown in, so their food is rudimentary) and I only hope it is that and not the tropical dysentery that comes from a bug, for that has life-long effects, I understand. He is hoping for leave which is due him and if he gets it, will go to Kashmir.[1] He is also trying to contact a friend[2] of ours who is a flier on the China route, to see if from the inside he can wangle a plane ride any part of the way home.

Dr. Henry Heyl has recovered from his germ, is married, and had moved to the Vermont place.[3] He said our invitation to visit there is more cordial than ever. I think I met his wife, at Ponte Vedra, where she was still numb from the death of her first husband, a flier, in 1941. She seemed very nice, and must have something to her, for last summer she volunteered for farm work and did the work of a hired man on a New England farm. She is a painter and sculptor. I had mentioned your migraine to him and he said he would like to talk with you about it, as he has done a good deal of specialized work along that line. He is one of the finest brain surgeons, so I hope his work is not entirely operational! I don't know whether it would be beyond the pale for three strangers to descend on a bride, but you and Norton and I would certainly enjoy a little jaunt up there in the fall. I don't know how much of a hurry Norton will be in when he returns. He may want to head straight for Florida. But I will certainly be in New York a couple of weeks anyway, waiting for him, as I won't know exactly when he will arrive.

I spent last week-end, just before coming here, at the Naval Air Base at Lake City, with Dr. (Lt.) and Mrs. Lyons.[4] I saw a good deal of Bert Cooper,[5] the Lt. chaplain who came to the Creek, and he is really an exceptional person. He got your address from me as he said he wanted to write you. I

---

1   Kashmir, region in northwestern India.

2   Not identified.

3   Henry Heyl (1906–1975), Katharine Agate Heyl (1914–1998). Heyl, who was to become a famed neurosurgeon, was assigned at the outset of World War II to a medical unit at Fort Blanding when MKR met him. He was then sent to England, where his skills saved the lives of the most gravely wounded troops. The "germ" was actually lymphoma, which was misdiagnosed, and which led to debilitating spinal complications. After he could no longer practice, the Heyls moved to a farm in Vermont.

4   Clifford Lyons and Gladys Lyons. See MKR's letter on 8 September 1944, 294, n. 1.

5   Lt. Bertram Cleveland Cooper (1918–1998), Navy chaplain, who before his enlistment served as assistant rector at the Church of the Advent in Birmingham, Alabama. Clearly, MKR has identified him as a potential suitor for JSB.

really had an awfully good time, my first real outing in many months. The Commandant and his wife[1] had us over for dinner on Sunday, and Bert was there, also a perfectly charming protégé of his, Philip Harris, son of a writer (I think Scribner) I never heard of, Cyril Harris.[2] Lt. Harris brought some wonderful records, and is as music-mad as you. He won't do for you, as he is only 21 or 22! But he was born old, and I liked him so much. We also went to a dance at the Officers' Club, and Bert Cooper is a <u>wonderful</u> dancer.

Cliff Lyons took me one night into the amazing Celestial Navigation Trainer and had some of the men put on the show for me. The trainer duplicates the cock-pit of a bombing plane, and all the elements of flight are reproduced by instrument. Underneath, charts are moved slowly under some sort of lighted glass, as though the plane were at an elevation of 10,000 feet. The students can even see where their mimic bombs land, and so make corrections. Overhead is a huge steel dome, set with a replica of the stellar Heavens, and the students learn their celestial navigation there. It has saved many lives since it began to be used in 1942, as the men don't have to make their mistakes in actual flight. It used to be very hush-hush, but is no longer secret. You would have loved it, but the higher mathematics were beyond me, and I was polite to Cliff Lyons for almost 24 hours, for he teaches the stuff. The young pilot who handled the controls for us said that flying was a cinch; it was only navigation that was difficult. In the Navy, pilots have to be navigators, too, which makes sense. Cliff said they were showing the trainer to Eric Johnson[3] / ^(Johnston?)^, and something went wrong so that the plane tilted, and the whole effect of flight at high altitudes was so realistic that Johnson tried to climb out in a panic! (Just another frightened capitalist.)

Much love,

<u>Marjorie</u>

---

1 Not identified. Lake City, Florida, Naval Air Station was commissioned in December 1942 and disbanded in March 1948.

2 Cyril Harris (1891–1968), American writer of historical fiction, *Trumpets at Dawn: A Novel of the American Revolution* (New York: Scribners, 1938); *Richard Payne* (New York: Scribners, 1941); and *One Brave Thing* (New York: Scribners, 1942). His son, Phillip Loma Harris (1921–1950), who attended Bard College where his father was an associate professor of English, lived in Cambridge, Massachusetts, at the time of Cooper's wedding; see MKR's letter on 14 June 1946.

3 Perhaps Eric Johnston (1896–1963), a venture capitalist, who was president of the U.S. Chamber of Commerce, president of the Motion Picture Association of America, and private envoy for Franklin D. Roosevelt to Joseph Stalin (1879–1953).

MKR to JSB, 8 July 1944. TLS, 6 pp. PM: SAINT AUGUSTINE |
JUL 28 | 1944 | FLA. AD: Miss Julia Scribner | <Far Hills> | <New
Jersey>. AD inserted in another hand: c/o Mrs. Scribner Schieffelin
/ Eastway / Saunderstown / R.I. LH: MRS. NORTON S. BASKIN |
CRESCENT BEACH, STAR ROUTE | ST. AUGUSTINE, FLORIDA[1]

July 8, 1944[2]

Dearest Julia:

The asparagus arrived---but alas, it is probably impossible to transport it
this far in hot weather, except in refrigerated cars. I noticed in TIME that it
has been discovered that asparagus butts are perfect for growing penicillin
mould. Well, there must have been enough to save the lives of a regiment---.
I hate to tell you, but was afraid if I did not, you might try sending another
box. I do appreciate your bothering and I am terribly regretful not to have
had the asparagus.

I don't know whether you like mangoes or not. I prefer them to any except
the finest peaches, but while some people have a passion for them, others
do not, and you might dislike them because they don't taste like Vermont
apples!!!! But if you do happen to like them, I am having them sent regularly
from a woman in Miami and will have her send you a box the next time I
order. She also handles very choice avocados.

Edith wrote from MacDowell[3] and is delighted with it. The studio by itself
in the woods sounds fine, but I could not stand sleeping in the Florida room
in the "big house" and having to eat with people three times a day. She says
that Verle[4] assures her he is in no danger from the robot bombs, but nobody
in the world is safe from anything any more. Of course, we never were, but
the natural catastrophes don't seem quite so insulting.

I am reading a book that I think you would enjoy---Peter Domanig, by
Victor White.[5] I avoided it because it was on the best-seller lists, but finally
ordered it and am finding it fascinating.

---

1 The letter is redirected to Mrs. Scribner Schieffelin, who was Louise Scribner Schieffelin (1883–
1963), the daughter of Charles Scribner II (1854–1930) and the spouse of George Richard Schieffelin
(1884–1950), chairman of the board of Scribners.

2 The letter is dated 8 July and the postmark 28 July, which might indicate that the envelope does
not belong with this letter.

3 Edith Pope was on a fellowship to the prestigious MacDowell Colony for the arts.

4 Verle Pope, husband of Edith Pope.

5 Victor White (1902–1960), *Peter Domanig: Morning in Vienna* (Indianapolis, IN: Bobbs-Merrill,
1944).

I made a third beginning on my book[1] that seemed a little more promising and thought I could go ahead. I got a good stenographer[2] whom I had used before and got caught up on correspondence. I even dictated letters to men in the Service, which I usually write personally, and for "material" alternated between describing finding a sea-turtle nest (for the more moronic-sounding correspondents) and passing on some of Norton's choicer bits for those I thought would appreciate them. One of the latter is a lieutenant flying the Hump,[3] and he is trying to contact Norton, and just missed him twice. Norton was able to <tumb> thumb a ride on a plane out of the Manipur plain to Calcutta when he went on leave, by running into a pilot who was a friend of Lt. Huish,[4] and hopes to meet Huish on the chance that he can wangle him a plane ride for at least part of his long trip home.

I heard from him from Calcutta, where he was hoping to get to the Vale of Kashmir,[5] and since a cable came, saying he would not be able to get mail out for a time, and I have not heard from him in over three weeks, I am sure he made it.

I am glad to report that I have lost ten pounds, and I think the other ten (or fifteen---I'll see how the fanny looks) will come off with a little less struggle. Being able to walk on the beach helps a lot, for Moe and I do four miles at a fast clip. I haven't done much swimming, as the water has been rough, and I am uneasy entirely alone, for the undertow has drowned two or three people lately. Also, a commercial fisherman reported seeing a good many sharks in front of my cottage--- waiting for the ten pounds, no doubt. If I could count on them to nip off neat slices in the right places, it would be all right, but I'd hate to lose an arm or a bosom.

Oh, I didn't finish my story about getting to work. I was all set, when ev-

---

1 *The Sojourner.*

2 Marjorie Glisson (1921–2000), daughter of Tom Glisson (1897–1950) and Pearlee Glisson, and sister of J. T. "Jake" Glisson of Cross Creek. On 30 March 1944, MKR wrote to NSB that she was trying to get on the "nightmare of unanswered correspondence, which has now reached two or three hundred letters" and is hoping that Marjorie Glisson "will be just what the doctor ordered." On 5 April, she observes in spite of "weird" mistakes, Marjorie was "better than I dared hope for" in spite of the fact, she opines on 19 November, that her husband had been away at war for two years and she was "six months pregnant when he walked in last week" (*Love Letters* 310, 316, 451). Many of the war letters of which MKR speaks are now housed in Special Collections, University of Florida Library.

3 The Hump was the area on the eastern end of the Himalayan Mountains over which Allied pilots flew to get supplies from India to China.

4 Lt. Huish is not identified. See MKR's letter on 24 July 1944, 281, n. 4.

5 Vale of Kashmir, a large valley in the Himalayan Mountains.

erything was turned upside down for Aunt Ida[1] and I had to bring her here to the cottage. Mrs. White suddenly announced that she wanted to close her house for the summer and since she is not feeling well, did not know what her fall plans would be. There was nothing for it but to pack Aunt Ida and bring her here. The housing situation is all but impossible. By the grace of God, I found a small apartment that is exactly right for her, and I was able to have her trunks, desk and a whole van-load of old-lady's junk that looked as though a squirrel had been collecting it down the ages, moved to the apartment instead of having to store them and move them again. Some repairs are being made and it will probably be a couple of weeks before she can move in, perhaps longer, so I am stymied again.

I think I wrote you that Idella and I have taken little black Martha.[2] Idella keeps her out of my way and the little thing is as bright and teachable as can be. Moe[3] has not done any running away over here.

I haven't heard from Bob or Cecil in a long time.

Norman Berg has completed his training in the Marines and expects to go overseas shortly, doing personnel work, that is, picking out men according to their aptitudes, as replacements for killed and wounded men. He is such an impeccable judge of men, I am sure he will not make a single mistake!!!!

Did I remember to write you that when Bob came to see me at the Creek two or three months ago, he too jumped on me for being the worst judge of people he'd ever known? I asked where I had erred, and he said, "Norman Berg, for instance". I almost had hysterics but of course could not explain why![4]

---

1 Aunt Ida Tarrant, who was eighty-four, was staying at the home of Mrs. Reginald White of St. Augustine, and was asked to leave because of the burden of taking care of her. On 6 July 1944, MKR's message to NSB was blunt, "Well, Mrs. White is kicking Aunt Ida out, just that. That is certainly her privilege, as there is no reason for her to run a charitable institution, and Aunt Ida is not her responsibility, but the way she did it is needlessly cruel. She should have told me she did not want her, and I could have cooked up something in such a way as to spare Aunt Ida's feelings . . . (*Love Letters* 412–13).

2 Idella Parker and "Little Martha" Fountain. See MKR's letter on 18 June 1944.

3 MKR's pointer dog, who had been running away at Cross Creek in search of female companionship.

4 MKR is referring to the row she had with Camp who thought her view of the "Negro question" was patronizing. He then turned on JSB and insisted that her "liberalism was meaningless, as she did nothing about it, and did not intend to disrupt her easy and parasitical life to do anything helpful to mankind---a conclusion I had come to about her since her revelation of herself in the long weeks she spent here!" Camp went on to say that MKR was the "poorest judge of human nature he had ever known . . . remembering Norman Berg's accusation of the same thing." MKR confesses to NSB, "I was speechless!" (*Love Letters* 317). Camp's attack on JSB may be connected to MKR's failed attempts to promote him as JSB's suitor.

Much love,

Marjorie

. . .

MKR to JSB, 24 July 1944. TLS, 5 pp. PM: ST. AUGUSTINE | JUL
| [24?] | 1944 | FLA. AD: Miss Julia Scribner | Far Hills | New Jersey.
LH: Mrs. Norton S. Baskin | Crescent Beach, Star Route | St.
Augustine, Florida

July 24, 1944

Dearest Julia:

I think, if it is feasible, I'll ask you to go on a leisurely treasure hunt for me. Off and on, when you're in New York, how about prowling around and finding a hotel that you know I'd like? Somewhere in that vast metropolis there must be a hotel that I should really enjoy.

Correspondence with Norton is utterly frustrating, and we are trying now to find out if he can give me any notice of his time of arrival.[1] I don't have the faintest idea whether he will want to spend some time in New York or not. If he plans to be there just two or three days, the hotel doesn't matter, but for a week or ten days, it is a different matter. I despise the St. Regis,[2] am not too keen about the Plaza,[3] the St. Moritz[4] is not bad but is rather out of the way. When Norton went to New York alone he went to the Barbizon Plaza,[5] but I get claustrophobia there. I thought the big corner room we had on the 19th floor of the Gotham[6] was attractive and was certainly reasonable, $12, I think, for two, but I don't like the rest of the hotel, though if we are not going to be there very long it is probably our best bet, as it is so central. When in New York, I love being high up, with a good skyline view. Without putting yourself through the punishment of a search for the Golden Fleece or the Holy Grail,[7] you might, when you're in different neighborhoods, drop in on different hostelries and look at their high up rooms and price them (a suite

---

1 MKR is now planning for NSB's return from the India-Burma theater.

2 St. Regis at 2 East 55th St.

3 Plaza at 769 5th Ave.

4 St. Moritz at 50 Central Park South.

5 Barbizon Plaza at 140 East 63rd St., until 1981 a hotel for women. How NSB was able to book rooms there is a mystery.

6 Gotham at 5th Ave and 55th St.

7 Golden Fleece, in Greek mythology, the story of Jason and the Argonauts' quest for the fleece of a golden ram to secure Jason's authority as king. Holy Grail, the cup that Jesus drank from at the

would be nice, if not <u>too</u> expensive, no more than $15, I should say) and decide whether they would cheer or depress me. Norton will be so happy to be there that he won't care about anything.

He did get to the Vale of Kashmir but spent most of his leave in the hospital. His dysentery was the bacillic [*sic*] type and just did not clear up. The doctor finally gave him relief with one of the sulfas and Kaolin.[1] Kaolin is also used as a beauty clay and Norton said he had taken so much that he would be known as the man with the beautiful bowels.

He said there could not possibly be a place on earth more beautiful than Kashmir.

He returned to his base about July 6, and has since been acting as assistant to the AFS executive in charge of the unit who has the courtesy title of lieutenant, which gives Norton a courtesy title of sergeant. An old lady in Union Springs[2] said she would like to write dear Norton and asked his mother[3] for his address, She gave it, beginning with the Vol. (for volunteer) Norton S. Baskin. The old lady was puzzled and decided that it must surely be Col.---so a letter arrived for Colonel Baskin. He thanked her and told he 'twa'n't so, and she wrote back loyally that she was sure, by the time his year was up, he <u>would</u> be a colonel. He said that being a courtesy sergeant with only fifty days more to go, he doubted whether he could make it.

He finally made contact, or had contact made, with another of my unknown correspondents who had sounded so nice. He was interested in meeting the chap, who was a lieutenant flying the Hump, in the hope of wangling a plane ride part-way home. The man ran him down in New Delhi and Norton invited him for drinks and said he looked forward to two good hours of talking about Lt. Huish.[4] Another wash-out. It would upset me, except that it bears out my theory that one's social personality bears no relation to one's creative ability. All these impossible pick-ups of mine have written the most wonderful letters. The moral is, read 'em, don't live with 'em.

I have been stuck with Aunt Ida[5] for two weeks, as her landlady wanted to close her house. I found (seems to me I have written you this) a rather weird little apartment for her that is just right, and she moves in tomorrow. Idella

---

last supper, part of the quest motif in Arthurian literature, hence the most sought after object in medieval lore.

1   Kaolin, made from clay, a medicine to treat severe dysentery and cholera.
2   Union Springs, Alabama, where NSB was born and raised.
3   Florida Binney Sanford Baskin (1869–1958).
4   Lt. Huish is not identified.
5   Aunt Ida Tarrant.

and I have worked like dogs getting things in shape for her. She is blissfully happy about it.

When I travel these days, my car is beyond belief, containing me, Aunt Ida, Idella, a nigger baby[1] and a bird-dog, and they all have to go when I go. I did ditch them to go into town to play bridge the other afternoon, and when I returned four hours later they greeted me with cheers and barks as though I had been gone a month. I think they had suspected that I was tempted just not to come back---.

The nigger baby is not so goddam cute day after day. It is really not her fault, but that of her lazy and dirty mother,[2] but we are having a time making a human being of her instead of a little black animal I turned her over my knee the other day, when she deliberately disobeyed me about something that was really important, and spanked her as naturally as though I were the mother of ten. And I had always sworn that force was not only unnecessary, but the sign of a moron. Well----!

Now don't take the hotel hunt too seriously. If I know within two or three weeks when Norton is likely to arrive, I'll just come up to New York to be on hand. That would be some time in October.[3] Unless he had the great luck of flying home. And of course it is possible he might land on the west coast!

This is a Lt. Huish---all about me.[4] And how are you?

Love,

Marjorie

.   .   .

JSB to MKR, 3 August 1944. ALS, 6 pp. PM: Saun[derstown] | [illegible] | R.I. Written on envelope in another hand: [Aug 1944]. AD: Mrs. Norton Baskin | Crescent Beach | Star Route | St. Augustine | Florida. RA: J. Scribner | Far Hills, N.J. VIA AIR MAIL envelope.

August 3 [1994][5]

---

1 Martha "Little Martha" Fountain.
2 Zamilla Mickens "Sissie" Fountain.
3 NSB arrived in Miami, Florida, on 29 October and was immediately put on a plane to New York.
4 MKR may have intended to type "There" instead of "This." Lt. Huish is the pilot from whom NSB hoped for help in getting a flight home from India. See MKR's letter on 8 July 1944, 277, n. 4.
5 Written in a second hand after the date: [1944].

Saunderstown, Rhode Island

Dearest Marjorie:

Here I am, looking out on the same Atlantic you are. I am staying here with Aunt Louise[1] for about 2 weeks. It is a lovely place – all'round as nice – just as I have been on the Atlantic coast. I think Maine is more beautiful, but there are the awful fogs and it is much harder to get to from N.Y. I have been swimming usually twice a day. The water is bracingly cold, but not freezing. I bicycle miles, 15 at least, and I eat such huge meals that I am beginning to worry about my waistline despite all the exercise. I brought along a two vol. set of the complete Greek drama[2] and was determined to fill in that awful gap in my reading. However I fear I will not manage to finish more than one of the vols. I was put off for a while by "Rome Hanks"[3] which I think has magnificent spots. I think the form was a bit tough, somehow I just couldn't feel right about the Christ episodes. Nonetheless, the guy can certainly write in a big way. I have also a terrific amount of correspondence that must be done at the expense of the Greek drama. Lately I have been so busy in N.Y. what with more hostessing, more Penn. Station Lounge,[4] a new "cure"[5] etc, that I have fallen almost hopelessly behind. I blush to think of how many letters I owe you! The trouble is that the first one I owe you is rather difficult, but I guess that it must be did otherwise the ghost of that letter will bother all my subsequent answers.

I'm afraid that I let my conscience lead me into hot water as it undoubtedly will most of the time I listen to it. I am sorry to have you think me so very much of a fool and a coward. I own up to being a good deal of both, but I'm not so much of a fool as to warn you of reactions that I thought were the same as they had been for 25 years, nor such a coward that I succumb to nerves every time I go out in a car. – But let's forget about the whole damn thing.[6]

As to my physical cowardice generally, it is something I was born with;

---

1   Louise Scribner Schieffelin. See MKR's letter on 8 July 1944, 276, n. 1.

2   Perhaps *The Complete Greek Drama*. Ed. Whitney J. Oates (1904–1973) and Eugene O'Neill Jr. (1910–1950), 2 vols. (New York: Random House, 1938).

3   Joseph S. Pennell (1908–1963), *The History of Rome Hanks and Kindred Matters* (New York: Scribners, 1944), a historical novel about the Civil War and Reconstruction.

4   The Pennsylvania Railroad set up lounges at its various stations to provide services via the USO (United Service Organizations) for the troops passing through. JSB volunteered as a hostess at Penn Station in New York.

5   JSB is likely referring to the various treatments she was taking for her migraine headaches.

6   JSB lectured MKR about her dangerous driving, especially when under the influence. MKR did not appreciate the lecture and related her displeasure in a letter on 19 May 1944.

the reverse side, I think, of my active imagination. When I was very small I refrained from beating my brother[1] to a pulp not due to any charity, but because I plainly could foresee the dire consequences. I just have the sort of mind that sees ahead always – and that adds up to cowardice. Though I hope that when I see things that can't in any way be avoided I face them as well as the average. To wish to be braver is to wish that I should have less imagination – and to wish that life should be less painful, but less vivid. Perhaps it is a tiny victory over cowardice that I don't often wish it.

Mutual cowardice is something a good deal more difficult to put one's finger on and analyse. I cannot decide what it is exactly. I don't think honestly that I refuse to face any fact or idea no matter how bitter or cruel, just because it is bitter or cruel. That is, I don't since I have come mentally of age. Everything I think up as an example of my mental fear turns out to be actual <u>physical</u> fear. So I can't say anything on this as I can't seem to isolate it.

Often I think, when the old accusation comes up of refusing to face adult responsibilities, if I had married one of my suitors, and had had a couple of children and was now struggling with an unsuccessful marriage, no one would suggest for a moment that I was refusing said responsibilities – though I might be on poor terms with domestic ones. Yet because I had the good fortune to escape that unhappiness, and in the light of my inner evolution it would be that certainly, I am clinging to childhood. If I decided tomorrow to marry Sandy[2] you would think probably "at least Julia is becoming an adult". But actually I should be running away from what is most "adult" in my life. I own that I have not yet found strength to go forward, but I feel, now at least, that I shall never [be] so weaker that I try to go back. Because I have said to you that I would like always to stay a child, you musn't think that I ever dream of trying to be one <u>again</u> – or <u>still</u>. And if I say that I would like to die as quickly and painlessly as possible, it doesn't mean that I contemplate suicide – or even that I brood on death. I am convinced truly that childhood, given the modest securities that a child needs, is the happiest time of life. You will find my reason in Peguy's "Misery & Poverty."[3] Roughly: pain qualifies joy, but joy does not qualify pain. Once one has realized the pain of the world one can never forget it, no matter how great the joy of the moment. It doesn't seem to me unnatural occasionally to sigh and wish that one were safe in innocence

---

1 Charles Scribner IV (aka Jr., aka "Buzz").

2 Sandy Dillon.

3 Péguy, the French philosopher and poet and a favorite of JSB. See her letter dated [23? March 1943].

again where joy was whole: Or through with the present pain sooner than later. That is all that lies behind my tired wishes. Not futile brooding, but just – passing fancy. I suppose they would sound shocking and cynical to someone less aware of pain and less frank in talk, but they shouldn't to you. – The reasons that I lack this strength to go forward (and I admit the speciousness of the unhappy marriage answer) are as you said, much deeper than plain sexual frustration. And they are certainly much deeper than those you found.

I have never denied being sexually frustrated (though I can't see that it is the one mover and shaker of the world as true Freudians[1] hold it to be). But where you found symptoms of sexual guilt I can't imagine. The fact is that I have never masturbated medically approved or otherwise. Oh, perhaps as an infant – I read somewhere most infants do, but I am certainly not bowed down by that hypothetical guilt.

As to my shock at my family's cool reception to my liberal ideas, can you think that suddenly they sprang, fully armed, from my head like Pallas Athena?[2] I grew up with the same ideas as my parents. When I began to look again at certain ideas that I had despised, and to find some – or much – truth in them, I knew as I changed my own mind toward them how my parents would feel, for we had condemned them together. I had no shock or surprise, except in the fallibility of my inherited ideas, and that was not deeply wounding because I had not lived by them long, or embraced them with any passion warmer than preordained acceptance. I knew I would be opposed, called a fool, a parlour pink[3] and worst all (!) a traitor to my class. I had used the terms often enough myself to know damn well that they would now apply to me.

I do take refuge in my headaches. I willingly admit that they are an excuse for not doing a good many things that I don't want to do. If I didn't have them I probably should find other excuses – or I might feel so much better that I <u>would</u> want to do some of the things. For I don't believe they are just something I dreamed up to get out of "adult responsibilities." In the first place they started years before I needed excuses, and in the second place – well, you should try one sometime. They don't just come when I am bored either. Many a concert or whatnot that I've been dying to go to I've missed with great disappointment and cursing. And because I got one when I was

1 Sigmund Freud (1856–1939), Austrian neurologist and psychiatrist, who argued, among other things, that sexual impulses were the triggers for neuroses.

2 Pallas Athena, virgin god of the ancient Greeks, who sprang forth fully armed from the head of her father Zeus.

3 "Pink" and "pinko" are derisive terms, coined in the United States in 1925, for a Communist.

nervous in the car with you doesn't seem to me to prove that they are just imagination – a nervous affliction.

Whenever you get nervously upset or overtired you get an attack too, but that doesn't mean that your diverticula (?) are mere nervous manifestations. I don't imagine that my headaches are anything that can't be overcome. Other people have overcome things hundreds of times worse. Nor do I give up hope that they may be helped.

There are still your two letters which have just been forwarded to me to be answered and lots of news to tell you, but this letter doesn't seem to be the place. It's too long already and too somber. I'll write you again before I leave here. I am thrilled about Norton's imminent homecoming. And double thrilled by your loss of ten pounds for the occasion. Now, Marjorie, do take off at least 15 more. You must be an absolute [illegible] to welcome Norton.

Much love,
Julia

. . .

MKR to JSB, 9 August 1944. TLS, 5 pp. PM: Envelope is missing. LH: Mrs. Norton S. Baskin | Crescent Beach, Star Route St. Augustine, Florida.

Aug. 9, 1944

Julia my dear:

I am crushed, for I feel that my amateur attempt to find out why you are unhappy, against Dr. Atchley's specific warning, has only added to your confusion. And your letter has added to mine, for you insist that you are subject to a chronic physical fear, and I should have thought it was just the opposite.

I should certainly never urge you to go to a psychiatrist, for to me they savor only of ancient witchcraft---although Dr. Atchley's very mild psychiatry (he insists he is not one, but only uses it in connection with diagnosis, on which he is a world expert) did help me a great deal. But it just is not natural for an attractive girl as young as you,[1] to be subject to such despair and depression, especially since you insist that the sexual angle is a minor one---as of course it is.

---

1   JSB was twenty-six years old.

You and I have a great deal in common, but we diverge on one point that may or may not be important: while my mother could have afforded to keep me on as a parasite, somehow it never occurred to me to do anything but plan to <u>work</u> after I left college. My marriage was only incidental,[1] and I kept on with a job, and I still feel that I only justify my existence when I am producing, in one way or another. The urge is something beyond the feeling of wanting to make one's own living, for I could now live on earned increment. And Norton's[2] income is more than sufficient for us both. But I still feel I must justify myself by <u>work</u>. You seem not to have this feeling. How far the migraines are to blame, I wouldn't know, but I feel that you are missing a profound <u>satisfaction</u>. Married to a man whose work a woman considers useful enough so that she can give herself to his life, is probably the best female life, but after that, doing a type of work for which she is fitted, and which she loves, is next best. I have never had the former---the one man I was in love with, whose work seemed valuable to me, was married, and conditions were such that I was the first to admit that he could not become un-married, to marry me---.[3] And without work of my own, I don't know what I should have done. Of course I have the advantage over you (apparently) of having the so-called creative urge, so that expression of my thoughts and emotions is vital to me. But I still think that you will be miserable as long as you are not married to a man whose work you respect and/or as long as you live a parasitic existence. You simply have too much on the ball, to dilly-dally around, hostessing and going to concerts. One has to use the utmost one's faculties and capabilities, and you just are not doing that. Again, the migraines enter in---.

I cannot for the life of me see why you do not take more interest in the house of Scribner. Your darling Father[4] is highly-keyed and not too strong, and I can see the day coming when you and Charles Jr.[5] will be at the head of the house. If you marry a man worth marrying, well and good, but if you do not, it seems to me that you and your brother together contribute spectacular help to the publishing business, with your taste, your scholarship, your understanding of what is important in literature and what is not. And of all the places where the migraines would fit in, if they prove intractable,

---

1   MKR's first marriage to Charles A. Rawlings Jr. They were married in May 1919 in New York and divorced on 10 May 1933 in Florida.

2   NSB, MKR's second husband. MKR and NSB were married on 27 October 1941 in St. Augustine, Florida.

3   Most likely, MKR is referring to Major General Otto Lange (1891–1965), then Major Lange, professor of military science at the University of Florida (*Max and Marjorie* 190).

4   Charles Scribner III.

5   Charles Scribner IV.

the Scribner business would be it, for you could take off any time necessary to recuperate, without the fear of the ordinary job-holder of losing the job. Believe me, you must use your great gifts in some way. You have the gifts, and you cannot drop them by the wayside.

By all means let us forget my drunken driving and your reaction thereto, and let us forget your sexual difficulties, and remember only that we love each other and would each go a long way to help the other.

Marjorie

.   .   .

JSB to MKR, 15 August 1944. ALS, 8 pp. PM: NEW YORK, [N.Y.] | AUG16 | 8 - PM | 1944. AD: Mrs. Norton Baskin | Crescent Beach | Star Route | St. Augustine | Florida. [In faint pencil on the back of the envelope] Rebellion in | the Backlands | Winesburg, O. | Berlin Diary | Nest of Simple Folk | Life & Times of Spanish Town | Holy Otto | Richard Wagner | Guy de Pourtales | Little Hotel | Norton | Heat / R. Bert.[1]

Tuesday. [15 August 1944][2]

Dearest Marjorie:

To my horror I see that in my violent concentration on getting a tan, I let the "ides of August"[3] slip past without my noticing them. I had been working on a suitable remembrance a month or so before with no results, but I want to go back to work on it so please forgive if it doesn't arrive till the ides of Sept. And most of all please forgive my temporary forgetting of the date.

As you will notice this didn't get written while I was in Saunderstown.[4] The first week up there went at a normal pace, but the second week went so fast that before I had time even to get a step further in the Greek drama I had to take the train home. It was really lovely there. Perfect swimming and

---

1   *Rebellion in the Backlands* by Euclides da Cunha; *Winesburg, Ohio* by Sherwood Anderson; *Berlin Diary* by William L. Shirer; *A Nest of Simple Folk* by Seán O'Faoláin; *The Idea of the Holy* by Rudolf Otto; *Richard Wagner: The Story of the Artist* by Guy de Pourtalès; *Little Hotel* by James Flora; Norton Baskin; *Heat* by James M. Cook; Albertus R. "Bert" Strabbing (1865–1943), Holland, Michigan.

2   Written in a second hand at the top of the letter is [1941?]. This date is incorrect.

3   MKR's birthday on 8 August. Interestingly, MKR's letter on 9 August 1944 makes no mention that JSB missed her birthday.

4   JSB had been visiting her Aunt Louise.

as R.I. is almost as flat as Fla, I was able to wander off for miles every day on my bike and explore towns (which are very frequent) and all the nice farming country that lies just back of the coast. Then Aunt L. is blessed with a marvelous cook and what with the brisk sea air and more exercise then I've had since I was a kid, I had a terrific appetite, so that made a happy combination.

I have a cousin who lives up there in the summers on a fascinating farm which has been in the family (Muddy's mother's) since about 1715.[1] The house was built in 1702 and has been almost unchanged since then. There have been some new things added in various periods (and one bathroom) but all the old things are still there. I think it's the most interesting house I've ever seen in this country. I do wish you could have seen it. It is incredible that it has remained so completely in its original state. There are even bullet holes in two of the doors from the Revolution. It was at that time a billet for a number of American soldiers and it was attacked by a party from an English man o war which came up Narragansett Bay to Saunderstown. Even the spikes in the upstairs bedroom driven into the corners of the walls by the soldiers to hang their uniforms on are still there! I found the doors themselves rather more interesting than the bullet holes in them. They have been painted so many times that the surfaces are deeply cracked and wrinkled – like old, old faces. And the floors all have profound dips in them from the strain of carrying people and furniture for so long. They are all worn down and the knots stand up in little bumps. I don't see myself why they don't collapse. There must be some limit to the life of a board. But everything seems to live on and on. The hinges too and even the little nubbles of wood that hold the cupboards closed and the archaic looking screws that hold the nubbles. The house looks very respectable and in excellent state of repair and neatness as every good New England house must. The only things that look much the worse for time are the elms on the lawn. They are still magnificent, but beginning to die and some were knocked down by the hurricane in '38.[2] After this cousin dies the house and the farm go to the N.E. Society for the Preservation of Antiquities[3] as a museum park sort of thing, which I think is a very good idea. Aunt Gladys[4] at one point, (in the past) made huge efforts to buy it, but happily failed.

---

1   Hildreth Kennedy Bloodgood (1861–1918), JSB's maternal grandfather and later the namesake of her first child.

2   The so-called Great New England Hurricane (aka Long Island Express, Yankee Clipper) came ashore on 21 September 1938, as a Category 3.

3   Society for the Preservation of New England Antiquities.

4   Gladys Augusta Bloodgood Casey Willets (1889–1978), sister of Vera Gordon Bloodgood Scrib-

Now, Marjorie, I have just gotten your letter and you mustn't be upset about adding to my confusion because you really haven't. You mustn't be in such a dither about my fears – and I didn't flatly deny psychic or emotional fear I just said I couldn't put my hands on them. When you speak of my physical fear as "chronic" you make it sound like an acute pathological condition which I think is overplaying it a bit.

According to Freud everything is due to sex and according to someone I forget the name[1] everything is due to fear and according to Pavlov[2] (whose theories I rather fancy) everything is due to conditional reflexes. Surely they all exaggerate, like the doctors who blame all ills on vitamin deficiency, or vertebrae, or allergy. I should think chronic physical heroism would be even more of a pathological condition than chronic physical cowardice because it's more unreasonable – and it's certainly a much more dangerous disease! I think you are right about the work angle, and unquestionably much of my <u>personal</u> depression is due to my un-useful existence and unused potentialities. I also agree that the logical place for me would be in CSS.[3] The only trouble is that I haven't the faintest desire to work there. Over and over I try to convert myself painting rosy pictures of myself acquiring a pleasant degree of fame, making a pleasant amount of money, messing around with manuscripts, typography, designs for jackets, meeting fascinating authors etc etc. And I think "wouldn't I love to do all those things" and I think back "no." I am not unaware that that sounds rather childish. I could go on for pages of analysis of motives, rationalization, revelation and all that sort of thing, but what's the point. I am one who has no objections to conducting tours of my inner life to reasonable depths. All the vagaries of my limited sexual and emotional life are quite free to be examined by the interested and sympathetic. But these levels are hardly the essential. And to go over and over them always avoiding the essential is to talk a great deal and say nothing very important. I am almost that fond of talking but definitely not of writing. So I heartily second your motion to forget my rather ordinary fears, complexes and sexual difficulties (and for gsake don't think up anything more colorful in the latter. I assure you I am concealing no peculiarities, and being of a fairly conservative nature, I

---

1 JSB may be thinking of Carl Jung (1875–1961), Swiss psychiatrist, once a disciple of Sigmund Freud, who writes in his *Psychology and Religion* (New Haven: Yale UP, 1938), "Our world is permeated by waves of restlessness and fear" (59).

2 Ivan Pavlov (1849–1936), Russian physiologist, pioneered the concept of "conditioned reflex," which he achieved through an experiment popularly known as "Pavlov's Dogs."

3 Charles Scribner's Sons, the publisher.

should blush every time you looked at me if I thought you were going on from masturbation to bigger and better preoccupations). But I don't want to drop the business before saying that I deeply appreciate the affection that prompted you to pick it up.

I have been having quite a correspondence with Bert Cooper.[1] We have started an argument on C. S. Lewis.[2] He says he expects he may be up in NYC on a leave sometime soon. Ahem, may I mention that I seemed to detect a faint murmur of the grinding gears of the M.K.R. Matrimonial Machine. Model J.B.S. in the background?

I have read a lot of interesting things lately. Aside from R Hanks[3] & the Greek drama, Berlin Diary[4] which I simply couldn't put down. It seemed much more interesting now than when it was published. A Life of Mozart and some of his letters – one of the most human of all geniuses. If you are around a library I advise you to borrow a copy of W. J. Turner's "Mozart," or Emily Anderson's trans. "The Letters of Mozart & his family."[5] (I belong to the N.Y. Public Library, and I consider it the best club in N.Y. I read madly now that I don't have to buy the books) I also read a life of Aphra Behn[6] (remember the poetess with the extraordinary career in Untermeyer's Anthology.[7] She was the pioneer of women writers. I think you would have loved your ancestress.) Then a couple of books of Beethoven criti-

---

1   Cooper also had begun a significant correspondence with MKR. See Brent E. Kinser, "'I'd Much Rather Write You Instead': The Letters of Marjorie K. Rawlings to Bertram C. Cooper," *Journal of Florida Literature* 13 (2004): 1–33.

2   Clive Staples Lewis (1898–1963), Irish-born critic, novelist, and theologian, known especially for his Christian apologetics. In his parallel correspondence, Cooper sent MKR Lewis's epistolary novel *The Screwtape Letters* (1942), in which the demon Screwtape writes to his nephew Wormwood with advice on tempting a British man called "the Patient" away from Christianity. Wormwood fails. MKR writes to Cooper on 17 July 1944: "'Screwtape' was hard but delicious" but that she was "much more interested in the psychic approach to Divinity than in the rationalistic" (Kinser, "I'd Much Rather Write You Instead" 3–4).

3   Joseph Stanley Pennell (1857–1926), American artist and author, *The History of Rome Hanks* (New York: Scribners 1944), a historical novel set during and after the Civil War.

4   William L. Shirer (1904–1993), American journalist, *Berlin Diary: Journal of a Foreign Correspondent, 1934–1941* (New York: Knopf, 1941). Shirer is best known for *The Rise and Fall of the Third Reich* (New York: Simon & Schuster, 1960), an unparalleled retrospective on Adolph Hitler (1889–1945) and the Nazis.

5   William James Turner (1889–1946), Australian-born poet and biographer, *Mozart: The Man and His Works* (New York: Knopf, 1938). Emily Anderson, ed. (1891–1962), *The Letters of Mozart and His Family*. 2 vols. (London: Macmillan, 1938).

6   Aphra Johnson Behn (1640–1689), English Restoration playwright. novelist, and poet, said to be the first woman to earn income from her writing.

7   Louis Untermeyer (1885–1977), American poet, editor, and critic, *A Treasury of Great Poems* (New York: Simon & Schuster, 1942), who excluded Behn from his earlier anthologies, but who later became her champion.

cism. And for about the best criticism I have ever read try John Middleton Murry's <u>Shakespeare</u>.[1] Did I already tell you that? I was put onto it by Dr. Simpson, my pal at General Seminary.[2] Did you ever read anything by a Dane called Martin Andersen Nexo?[3] I read an article about him by J. R. Bloch ("And Co.")[4] in a French newspaper and I'm searching for some of his books. You didn't say much about "Os Sertões".[5] I have it and am preparing to read it. Have you read "Winesburg Ohio" yet?[6] Remember I will never stop bothering you until you do. Also what did you think of "A Nest of Simple Folk"?[7] I think it is a wonderful picture of Ireland. I have just started "Life and Death of a Spanish Town"[8] I seem always to be reading one book on my special subject, Spain. Actually I have three other books – no four – on the same subject lined up waiting to be opened. There are lots of other literary matters which I must discuss with you, but this is getting to be overwhelmingly "listy."

I will write at length about hotels when I have done a little more research on the subject. I think you are hoping for the impossible, though. If the St. Moritz is somewhat out of bounds that makes "bounds" very limited and you are not apt to find anything with all the charm of a Dickensian Inn and Mother's country cooking in midtown Manhattan. There may be something of the sort around the village, but that would be neither central nor high with view. However I will look. I have heard of a small hotel which overlooks the garden of the Mus. Of Mod. Art.[9] I fear that you and I are both too prone to be depressed by hotels – <u>you're</u> even <u>worse</u> than I am. Remember the frantic changes on the forestry trip?[10]

The heat here has been beyond words ghastly. Every AM the papers are full of news of deaths caused by it in the city. I keep longing to be back at

---

1   John Middleton Murry (1889–1957), English writer, *Shakespeare* (London: Cape, 1936).
2   The Very Reverend Cuthbert Simpson (1892–1969) was a fellow at the General Theological Seminary, New York. Later he was Regius Professor of Hebrew and then Dean of Christ Church, Oxford University.
3   Martin Andersen Nexø (1869–1954), Danish socialist who encouraged social revolution.
4   See JSB's letter on 8 August 1943.
5   Euclides da Cunha, *Os Sertões* (1902) [*Rebellion in the Backlands*].
6   Sherwood Anderson (1876–1941), American fiction writer, *Winesburg, Ohio, A Group of Tales of Ohio Small Town Life* (New York: Heubsch, 1919).
7   Seán O'Faoláin (1900–1991), *A Nest of Simple Folk* (London: Cape, 1933), a novel of peasant life in anticipation of the Republic of Ireland.
8   Elliot Paul (1891–1958), American journalist, *Life and Death of a Spanish Town* (New York: Random House, 1937). See JSB's letter on 9 September 1944.
9   Museum of Modern Art at 11 West 53 St., New York.
10 The trip through the forests of the South that led to MKR's "Trees for Tomorrow."

Aunt L's[1] lying in a wet bathing suit on the beach. We had one really boiling day there before I left and I spent the entire day AM & PM on the beach soaking up sun. Everytime I got hot I went into the lovely cold water till I was almost gooseflesh – then I went back and lay in the sun some more. I think it was the most luxuriously and sensuously leisurely day I have ever spent. I didn't even think. I just enjoyed heat and cold and rest of a delicious sun and air variety.

Now all I do all day is sweat. Not a particularly delicious occupation. I do hope it is not relatively hotter where you are. Must go to bed.

Much love,

Julia

. . .

MKR to JSB, 8 September 1944. TLS, 4 pp. PM: SAINT AUGUSTINE | SEP 8 | 1 PM | 1944 | FLA. AD: Miss Julia Scribner | Far Hills | New Jersey. LH: Mrs. Norton S. Baskin | Crescent Beach, Star Route | St. Augustine, Florida.

Sept. 8, 1944

Dearest Julia:

I was trying just to slur over my birthday and was glad when you didn't remember it, so don't go on one of your terrific hunts for a gift! And don't break your neck over finding the perfect hotel, either, as you are right about my never finding the qualifications that would please me. The Central Park area is not "out", and I might try the Sherry-Netherlands[2] this time, though the fact that Fred Francis[3] always goes there should be enough to steer me away.

My last letter from Norton was dated Aug. 22 and he was in Calcutta, having fits because his headquarters was being dilatory and incompetent about getting him passage home. He said that a nigger whore-house would be run with more system---.

My reducing was going along surely but so very slowly, so I began going four or five times a week to an old masseur here who is a wonder, and we are really getting results. I can get into dresses that I couldn't zip up a year ago.

---

1 Aunt Louise.

2 Sherry-Netherlands Hotel at 5th Ave. and 59th St.

3 MKR is having fun with the reputation of her St. Augustine friend Fred Francis, whom she believed was a philanderer.

We are confident we can reach the goal I have set by the time I leave for New York. Dr. Berry[1] is a little bitty lean man seventy-four or more, and used to work under the famous Muldoon,[2] and took care of some of the old-timers such as Chauncey Depew, Arthur Brisbane and W. R. Hearst,[3] and has more strength and vim than any younger man I have ever been to. He has thrown his heart into the stint I have set him and is making the damndest saga of it. He had me black and blue until I hardened up, and once he asked if he was hurting me, and I said yes, but I knew it was necessary. He said, "Yes, love taps ain't going to do <u>you</u> no good, Mrs. Baskin."

"Never give up the ship," he says every time, and then pounds like hell. He phones his wife every time when he finishes, and reports the progress. "I'll do it if it can be done, Mother. You know me, Mother, never say die." It makes me feel like an almost insuperable challenge.

Idella[4] is happy about it, and unselfish enough not to grieve that now she won't get my best clothes!

When I receive my next cable from Norton, which will mean that he is leaving, or will have left (for our cables have been taking seven or eight days) I think I can figure five weeks for his return, so am planning roughly to come up between Oct. 1 and 8.

I gave up the <u>fourth</u> attempt on my book,[5] but have done several short stories.[6] I'm working four afternoons a week at the Red Cross. Have also done several articles for the Writers' War Board.[7] Feel sure I can settle down

---

1 Mr. and Mrs. George Berry, owners of the Berry Health Institute, located at 86 Charlotte St., who often advertised a "Scientific Body Massage" delivered by "Expert Masseurs" (*St. Augustine Record* [4 July 1937]: A-6).

2 Perhaps John Muldoon (1896–1944), American rugby player who won a gold medal in the 1920 Olympics.

3 Chauncey M. Depew (1834–1928), American lawyer, president of New York Central Railroad, and U.S. senator 1899–1911. Arthur Brisbane (1864–1936), American journalist and newspaper editor. William Randolph Hearst (1863–1951), American businessman who at the time controlled the most powerful newspaper chain in the world.

4 Idella Parker.

5 *The Sojourner.*

6 "The Shell," *New Yorker* 20 (9 December 1944): 29–31; "Black Secret," *New Yorker* 21 (8 September 1945): 20–23; "Miriam's Houses," *New Yorker* 21 (24 November 1945): 29–31. See Tarr, *Bibliography*, C629, C631, C632. On 11 October 1944, MKR writes to Maxwell Perkins, "My book will have to wait for some sort of security of my personal life before I go ahead with it. I have done some short stories, one of which will be in the *New Yorker* soon" (*Max and Marjorie* 574).

7 MKR had an off-again, on-again relationship with the Writer's War Board, a brainchild of the literary raconteur Clifton Fadiman (1904–1999), book editor at the *New Yorker* and moderator of the popular radio program *Information, Please*. Fadiman oversaw the scheme to have noted writers comment on subjects of his choosing and for outlets of his choosing. MKR was always uncomfortable with Fadiman's control over content and venue. Nevertheless, as part of the war effort she tried

happily on the book after Norton is home and life begins to be reasonably normal.

I feel perfectly grand. Haven't had a drink in more than a month.

Bob Camp is now a full lieutenant and is at Quonset, R.I., and hopes and expects to go to sea when he finishes his course there.

Dr. (Lt.) and Mrs. Lyons[1] are coming over for the week-end. Did Bert Cooper get to New York? I am innocent of any designs on Bert, and you do not detect any trace of my fine Italian hand in his contacting you. He asked for your address when I visited in Lake City.[2]

Went to Ponte Vedra[3] last Saturday night and had a lousy time, most of the party strangers and all drinking while I didn't.

Much love,

Marjorie

. . .

JSB to MKR, 9 September 1944. ALS, 4 pp. PM: SAUNDERSTOWN [Rest of the PM is obliterated by the removal of the stamp]. AD: Mrs. Norton Baskin | Crescent Beach | St. Augustine | Florida. VIA AIR MAIL sticker on envelope.

c/o Mrs. Scribner Schieffelin | "Eastaway" | Saunderstown, Rhode Island.[4]

Sept. 9 [1944]

Dearest Marge –

---

to oblige. Her most noted article was "Florida: A Land of Contrasts," *Transatlantic* no. 14 (October 1944): 12–17 (see Tarr, *Bibliography*, C628), and her most controversial offering, "The Southern Soldier and the Negro" (MS not located), which was to be published via the newspaper syndicate Newspaper Enterprise Association (NEA), but which was rejected by the editors because of its pro-Black content (see *Love Letters* 119n, 361, 397, 403, 404, 404n).

1   Clifford P. Lyons and Gladys Lyons, the former chair of the English Department at the University of Florida before becoming a lieutenant in the Navy, stationed at the Naval Air Base in Lake City, Florida. Lyons was at one point designated MKR's literary executor. After the war, Lyons became a department head and then dean at the University of North Carolina, and in this capacity rejected Bertram Cooper's overtures for compassion. In a letter to NSB on 10 February 1953, MKR says that she informed Cooper that she was aware of Lyons's "pomposity," and that "I myself was through with him" (*Love Letters* 665).

2   For JSB's account of the visit, see her letter on 9 September [1944].

3   Ponte Vedra, Florida, an ocean community, east of Jacksonville and 26 miles north of St. Augustine.

4   Written in JSB's hand at the top of p 1.

I'm up here on the N.E. seacoast again, but my major occupation of my last visit, acquiring a tan, is out of season now, so I'm doing more reading and more bicycling. I took off rather suddenly. Aunt L.[1] was very anxious to have me here again, and although miraculously she seems better, I couldn't refuse.

I had quite an active time while I was in NYC. Of course <u>both</u>[2] my Florida men had to arrive in NY on the same day! I dropped in to Daddy's[3] office after meeting up with Bert & lunching with him, and there, right in the office was Bob. His whole family are in NY at the Barb. Plaza[4] so he couldn't come out for the weekend which was just as well, because we didn't have a bed – an <u>empty</u> bed, that is – in the house. I came into town Mon. and went out with Bob that evening, somewhat to Bert's chagrin I think. But, what the hell, I certainly had to go out with Bob <u>once</u> and he was leaving Tues. We had a delightful evening. We discussed painting solidly from 7 PM till midnight which is my idea of a marvelous time. Then we moved on to general subjects and Bob's life in the Navy in particular. The only drawback to the evening was that Bob insisted on going to a couple of nightclubs and I found staying up till 2 AM on 1 sherry and 2 coca colas rather exhausting. Bob was in wonderful form and looked leaner than ever and very hard and brown – just like an old seadog I told him.

I hope Bert had a good time. He was quite tired I <shall> think, and in a very depressed and confused state. He started to talk one evening when we were alone, but I was very dull and obtuse, and firmly pursued irrelevant parts of his conversation, because I thought he would say something that he would wish the next day <when> that he hadn't said. I think when one ^is^ wavering on the edge of a difficult decision, particularly a decision where one may go the way that conscience says is the wrong way though reason holds out for it, that just by admitting in a weak moment that one way may take that "reasonable" defeat vaguely commits one to it. Of course this is just intuition not experience. I do hope that Bert manages to get the active duty he was going to struggle for in Wash., for I think he will feel much better about things if he does. He was full of apology for his moods of the weekend, which was unnecessary, as they weren't that generally obvious at all. I must admit he is an enigma to me, because I keep wanting to put him in the "big, friendly, earnest, enthusiastic" category, and he won't stay in it at all. Also

---

1   Aunt Louise.
2   Bertram Cooper and Robert Camp Jr. The former acknowledged that he was smitten by JSB, the latter claimed that he was not.
3   Charles Scribner III.
4   Barbizon Plaza Hotel.

he makes me feel I must be awfully repressed, <bec>[.] He is very liable to burst into song or poetry in a loud and serious way, and I always react with horror and embarrassment – New England, I guess. We got on very well though, despite the ups and downs, but I don't think there is a great future for our friendship – he was very dramatically 'Who knows if we shall ever meet again' at our parting.[1]

I was reading a book he presented to me which I hear you liked very much and wrote great essays about – epistolatory essays – "The Idea of the Holy."[2] I had rather a struggle with the first 50 pages, the Deutsche style, but I'm used to it now and it's going rapidly. I am still enjoying the quotations more than the book, however.

I have just finished two tremendously interesting autobiographies of Spanish women – Constancia de la Mora's and Isabel Palencia's.[3] The former, "In Place of Splendour"[4] I just loved and I heartily recommend it to you. I am also reading Elliot Paul's, "Life & Death of a Spanish Town"[5] in my less numinous[6] moments. Pretty soon I expect I'll be able to give lectures on modern Spain!

The other night I had the most realistic dream about you. I met you in NYC where you had come as per schedule to meet Norton, and you were so slim and svelte that I was bowled over and couldn't take my eyes off you. I

---

1   MKR responds to a missing letter from a clearly disappointed Cooper on 12 September 1944, and in a way that reveals both her identity and her disappointment as a matchmaker: "I am extremely interested in your report on the Scribner menage and Julia's relation to it. I am afraid that you saw and felt the truth with distressing clarity. I too rather wish you had fallen in love with each other, for I think she could follow a man with strong and noble convictions and be saved. As it is, I have almost come to the reluctant conclusion that she is a damned soul. She is not actually selfish, for when her affections are involved, she is capable of great effort and generosity—yet perhaps it is selfish after all, for a limited devotion is only a minor extension of one's own self-love. . . . I think you are correct about the hold her mother has over her, despite a deep-seated antagonism and mutual disapproval. . . . Her father is tense and not happy, drinks too much, lives a high-life, and will snap out like a light. . . . She has been a heart-breaking disappointment to me, for I love her dearly, and it is wicked to waste a mind and sensitivity like hers" (Kinser, "I'd Much Rather Write You Instead" 8–10).

2   Rudolf Otto (1869–1937), German theologian, *Das Heilige* [*The Idea of the Holy*] (1917). Trans. John W. Harvey (Harmondsworth: Penguin, 1923), a depiction of the non-rational aspects of religious experience.

3   Isabel de Oyarzábal de Palencia (1878–1974), *I Must Have Liberty* (New York: Longmans, Green, 1940).

4   Constancia de la Mora (1906–1950), Spanish activist, *In Place of Splendour: The Autobiography of a Spanish Woman* (London: Joseph, 1940).

5   JSB is repeating herself. She has already informed MKR a number of times about her reading of Paul in previous letters. See Index.

6   JSB is alluding to the *Idea of the Holy*, in which Otto develops the concept of "the numinous" as an expression of the nonrational aspects of the divine; see above, n. 2.

could draw a picture of you – if I could draw. I saw you so exactly – wearing a black dress. We had a long and dull conversation, Most of which I could write down but won't because of its dullness – the fee per visit of various doctors was one of the subjects!

I had a much more glamorous (for me) dream or rather two dreams, the previous night. In the course of a single night I wrote a brilliant passage semi-stream of consciousness, semi evocative word patterns on love, of which I can't remember one damn word, and I painted a crude but impressive and very "sultry" sunset. The latter doesn't look so good in the daylight, but of course it may be that I remember it imperfectly!

I am staying here till the 19th, because on that date I have to travel to NYC with Aunt L. She can't travel alone and her daughter-in-law[1] can't go with her then so that leaves me. I'm worried about the hotel situation for you. I talked with quite a few people without getting any good suggestions, and I just didn't have time to go to the ten different places myself. I don't know just when you are coming up, but you shouldn't make the reservation too late as the city is awfully jammed up. If you won't be coming for a couple of weeks after the 20th, I'll go to work that date and line up something, but if you're coming sooner I think you'd better reserve now. – The Gotham again or the St. Moritz I guess, are the best. Don't try the Plaza- it's very run down and gloomy. I visited people there several times last winter. There is nothing around the Gotham that I know of that is better than it is, except the St. Regis which you don't like and which is also more expensive. Just drop me a line up here when you are coming to N.Y.C. (address on top of page one)

Much love,

Julia

. . .

JSB to MKR, 14 September 1944. ALS, 8 pp. PM: [SAUNDERSTOWN] | SE[P] | illegible] | R.I. AD: Mrs. Norton Baskin | Crescent Beach | St. Augustine | Florida. VIA AIR MAIL sticker on envelope.

Sept 14. [1944][2]

---

1   Aunt Louise. Her son was George McKay Schieffelin (1905–1988); her daughter-in-law was Louise Winterbotham Schieffelin (1907–1979).

2   Since the hurricane described in this letter did not come ashore until 14 September, and since

8:00 PM

Dearest Marjorie:

This will be – is – a letter from the midst of a hurricane.[1] I'm not sure just how much more will get written. We still have lights, but we are already getting deep puddles of water in the living room. The center of the storm is not due for 3 or 4 hours, so I guess this prelude is later going to seem quite mild. It's severe enough now to make me prefer to have something to do instead of just sitting and gauging each tremor of the house. The radio has been quite dramatic all day, but somehow it just didn't seem any worse than "thrilling" to me until it really started to blow. Now they have become brutally frank and say we may expect something at least as bad as 1938.[2] All the houses we can see have been evacuated – of course the hell of it is we can't see anything now but wet blackness – (the lights are going down, I hope they will find new strength – OK) We are higher up than our neighbors, about 30 ft I should say from the shore (lights going again) – (candles lit) perhaps as much as 40 ft. It doesn't seem possible that any tidal wave would be that high, so we weren't warned to leave. We are on a little cove about one mile in from the entrance of Narragansett Bay –[3] A bit north therefore of where they figure the storm center will pass. However the papers comfortingly say that it is worse at the outer edges of the storm than in the center. This house stood up in 1938. I'm just wondering how much it has weakened since then. There are Aunt Louise, myself and two Scottish maids here. The lights are now down to a faint glow, and the house is shaking with deep awful thuds. It feels like an earthquake, but it hardly seems likely that there could be that in addition to the other horrible manifestations of nature. The "numinous" is so damned thick you could cut it with a knife – although this is a bit more "tremendous" than "mysterious."[4] The howling of the wind and battering of the rain are very loud, of course, but they seem pleasantly normal in contrast to these thuds. I don't know whether it is the crashing of the

---

the letter is continued on 15 September, and since postal services were most assuredly interrupted, it seems very likely that this letter was not mailed for a number of days after the hurricane.

1 The "Great Atlantic Hurricane" made land fall at Pt. Judith, Rhode Island, on 14 September, a Category 3, with maximum sustained winds of 145 mph.

2 The "Great New England Hurricane" made land fall on Long Island, New York, on 21 September 1938, a Category 3 storm, with maximum sustained winds of 120 mph.

3 Narragansett Bay, a bay and estuary on the east side of Rhode Island.

4 JSB is alluding to a significant phrase in *The Idea of the Holy*, "*mysterium tremendum et fascinans*," by which Otto theorizes that the experience of religion, the numinous, can be broken down into the components of *mysterium* [mysterious], complete unlikeness; *tremendum* [tremendous], awesome unapproachability; and *fascinans*, fascination in spite of fear. See JSB's letter on 9 September 1944, 296, n. 2.

sea – dreadful thought, or the house literally being rocked to and fro on its foundations – somehow that doesn't seem quite so bad. The water has come down the chimney so that our cheerful logfire has been put out except for a couple of red embers. They won't last long. The lights are still on but so low that we can't listen to the radio. It's now 9 PM. The worst thought – it seems incredible – is that this must get steadily worse for 2 or 3 hours. I don't see how the house will possibly stand it. We are sitting in a big living room that is the whole center part of the house. There are 3 big windows and two French doors which open out to a shallow porch which overlooks the sea. We are momentarily waiting for these doors and windows to blow in. Then I guess we will move into my bedroom which is on the cliff side of the house. The doors are sort of bulging in with each gust so I guess it won't be very long now. I do wish I could look out a window and see where the ocean is. It would be comforting to see it approximately in its place. High tide is not for an hour now, (I just jumped up and banged one of the door locks back into place with a log) as I was saying, of course the tidal waves if any won't come in until the peak of the storm or a little after. Earlier one of the spookiest sounds was the drip of a roof leak into a large tin basin. It kept reminding me of a story I had read where someone was driven nuts by the sound of dripping water. Now the tap, tap, tap is such a comparatively little noise that we only hear it in occasional lulls. A few minutes ago the lights went off completely, which gave a very lonely isolated feeling. Our radio link has been out and the lights seemed our last connection with civilization. Then miraculously they came on again in almost normal strength. Now they are gone again, and not apt to return. It is impossible that the vines and poles could stand much more of this wind. The doors just gave an awful creak. They will break in with a horrible crash, and we will both give a yell of terror. It's very black in here with just the 2 candles. Unbelievably the wind is stronger now. The tremors seem less terrifying for being less few and far between. Aunt L. is sitting on a sofa eating campfire marshmallows. She says "it doesn't seem natural for anything on land to toss about as much as this house." The imminent breaking in of the doors is becoming a complex. Our nerves are on edge waiting for it.

A few minutes ago I went upstairs and looked out to sea. At that time the lighthouse was still going out on the point and a few lights could be seen. No use looking for them now. There was not enough lightning for me to be able to see the beach.

One thing I have always wanted to see was a barometer falling at a dramatic rate. That wish has been granted. It can't fall very much further. The needle even goes down of its own accord without being tapped.

This house has recently been sold, and Aunt Louise was inspired just now to make the unfortunate remark that "it would be too bad if after the man had payed his $14,000 the whole house should blow away." I reminded her that it would be incomparably worse for us – so much so that to hell with him.

Moment by moment new leaks are appearing. But the walls and roof are still with us. And it only has to get worse for about 2 hours more.

In the midst of this turmoil, what do you think I have – a headache![1] Ain't it marvelous how persistent are the little symptoms. I've had one for 3 days, and I so hoped that the excitement of the hurricane would cure it. But no, it's just as petty and nagging as if I had nothing else to think of.

For the moment there doesn't seem, to be anything more to write. Just more and more wind gradually building up – louder and louder – more and more rain – inside and out – louder still – more shaking, trembling – the candles are waving ominously. In ten minutes it will be high tide.[2] I'm going up there to try to look out and see the ocean. It is <u>literally</u> getting every minute louder. I don't feel nearly so frightened as an hour ago. I'm just amazed. I don't understand how such a wind can be – much less increase. Aunt L. has just come up with another cheery saying – She says – "at least neither of us is having a baby tonight." She thinks "it's terrible to have a baby in a storm." She is a post mistress of the far fetched cheery saying.

I just thought I have never written a letter so painlessly in my life.

Just went upstairs and looked out again. No more lightning so I couldn't see the ocean except very indistinctly. I think it is way over the beach and the road back of it. The lighthouse is still going – a heartening sight. And there is a glow at an Army station[3] on an island across from us.

The storm is still on the increase. But, do you know, I'm amazed myself – but right now, I'm sleepy. All the frightened feeling up and down my back and in my stomach has gone. I have become really accustomed to the howling, battering, shaking, vibrating and all the other damned symptoms of this storm. (Just as I write these blasphemous words, it is suddenly much worse, and I feel again that I am quite close to danger.) Well, so it goes. I don't suppose I could actually get to sleep. The house would keep giving me profound nudges. Hell, I'm going to try anyway. The barometer[4] is still

---

1   In JSB's case, headache almost certainly means migraine, for which she was under medical treatment.

2   The high tide during the Great Atlantic Hurricane was 9 feet above mean sea level. Witnesses reported waves of 25–30 feet.

3   Fort Varnum, a defensive fort intended to protect the west passage of Narragansett Bay.

4   The lower the barometer goes the more intense the storm is.

going down and still has a little way to go. From that angle I have no complaints. It is behaving according to my desires completely and willingly – Boy, you should feel the way this house is pitching now!! Can it possibly remain in one piece? – Do you know what the barometer says? Delightful conversation—"Stormy". Well, the next 1/2 hour to 2 hours will decide whether this letter gets mailed – and other more important things about my immediate future. I shall try to nap until the light of dawn makes visible the devastation.

11:30. The storm seems to have passed by. The house is terribly quiet and still. The wind is still roaring, but the rain has stopped – outside at least. In here the drips and trickles sound very loud in the new silence.

I didn't do very well on the napping. At the peak of the storm (about 11) the wind shifted, happily for the porch doors, but the shift brought a new noise. The wind started removing the shingles from the roof (I guess). The noise was alternately like tapping and like dozens of people shuffling around up there. Occasionally a window blew in somewhere so all in all I never got to sleep. Well, it's not so very late now. I have just had a hearty snack and expect to sleep very well from now on.

The stillness in the house is really oppressive. I am conditioned to wind at this point. Outside I can hear crickets! Definitely the hurricane has passed. I'll look at the barometer – It went up a fraction of an inch when I tapped. If there were only more light I'd go look down at the beach. But it's foggy and very dark so I'll go to bed instead.

Next day – Things aren't really so bad as they might be. The beach is a mess, and the big public bathing club is just kindling wood, but most of the houses are OK. I just drove the 3 miles to Saunderstown. The houses all have an unkempt look, with patches of shingles missing and screens dangling. Quite a few trees are broken and the leaves on all of them have either been blown off altogether or are terribly frayed.

The thing that worries us now is when we can get electricity again. To hell with the lights, but we can't get a drop of water because the pump goes by electricity! There is no open well or stream or pond, and a very steep climb down the cliff to the ocean.

I don't feel in a very good humor about the whole thing, because, although I woke this AM feeling fine, I now have a headache again. I thought surely the terrific change in barometric pressure would cure it.

I'll close with a few bits of news. Bob is up here at Quonset[1] on a course,

---

1 Robert Camp Jr. was at the naval air station, built in 1941, on Quonset Point, a small peninsula in Narragansett Bay.

you know. He called me, and was coming the night before last for dinner, but he never appeared, and we haven't heard a word. Of course, our phone is out of order now.

Then yesterday I got a very cheerful note from Bert.[1] He has got his sea duty and expects to leave very soon. I am delighted about that.

I suppose Norton has left for home by now.[2] It's wonderful to think I will see you both before very long.

Greetings from the path of the hurricane!

Much love,

Julia

. . .

MKR to JSB, 20 September 1944. TLS, 6 pp. PM: SAINT AUGUSTINE | SEP 26 | 4 PM | 1944 | FLA. AD: Miss Julia Scribner | Far Hills | New Jersey. LH: Mrs. Norton Baskin | Crescent Beach, Star Route | St. Augustine, Florida.

Sept. 20, 1944[3]

Dearest Julia:

The blow-by-blow saga of the hurricane[4] really had me hanging on the ropes. In the middle of it, I thought, what the hell, she got out all right or I wouldn't have received the letter! But until I reminded myself of that, I could picture "came the dawn", with your pale body floating on the receding sea---and Aunt Louise still eating marshmallows. I can understand grabbing the Scotch, but I should never choose marshmallows for stimulation under such circumstances. And I'm awfully glad neither of you had a baby.

Well, those are the risks when you live in dangerous places like Rhode Island. Now in safe Florida---. I was actually sorry we didn't get just a bit more of the blow, for I love that sort of weather, with the seas over the lower

---

1 Bertram Cooper, whom MKR describes in a letter to NSB on 5 October 1944 as a "delightful Episcopal minister who is now a Navy chaplain. He leaves shortly for duty in Hawaii" (*Love Letters* 434).

2 NSB did not leave Calcutta until 28 October 1944.

3 Written in MKR's hand in pencil at the top of p. 1: "I read half of Peguy again when I was at the Creek."

4 Called the Great Atlantic Hurricane, the storm reached Category 4 when it brushed the Outer Banks and then weakened slightly when it hit the New Jersey/New York coastline on 14 September 1944.

dunes. We did have high seas, and the cottage screens were damp with spray, but it was not spectacular and my terrace awning didn't even break loose, as it has done in several storms.

Unless his cable has been held up, Norton is still stuck in Calcutta. I can stand anything but uncertainty, and am about nuts. Unless he has left and I have just haven't had the word, he could not reach N.Y. now before the end of October.[1] I think I shall come up about the middle of October anyway, as I'd like to catch the short ballet season then. I love that time of year in the North, though I understand that because of the drought there will be or is no lovely autumn foliage this year. I'll probably hit the first nasty cold weather, and shall rage as you do about spiders. Tommy Sabin and his wife, and Cecil[2] stopped by for dinner last night, and Tommy said that there are very few ships going to India now, and everything is being sent to the European front. He also said Norton didn't have a prayer to fly home, as the AFS, for some reason, having something to do with the British, all but forbids it. Tommy said he could have flown, but they made such a stew about it, that he dropped it. (He was with the AFS in Africa and Italy.) He reassured me about Norton's dysentery, saying the bacillic [*sic*] is not the same as the amoebic, and while it is more painful while you have it, you do get over it.

What a trick for Bob to pull. They were probably all working very hard battening down against the impending hurricane, but my God, he could have phoned you. When we thought the storm might hit here, great squadrons of planes flew over, evidently moving from the Key West base to inland bases.

I have not heard from Edith Pope in six weeks or more, and yesterday in came a 1942 book on Greece, signed by the author, from Edith to me. I hope she hasn't got involved with a writer in Greece. I haven't finished the book, but so far it doesn't seem good enough to warrant her sending it as literature, so I suspect an interest in the author.[3]

I'm glad you like L. and D. of a Spanish Town.[4] I was mad about it. I've read so many books lately that seemed promising but let me down dread-

---

1   NSB reached home from India on 29 October.

2   Tommy Sabin, son of Cecil and Dossie Sabin. MKR reports on Tommy Sabin's war experiences in a letter to NSB on 21 November 1943: Sabin was "bored to death for several months in Syria and Africa, then went into the Italian campaign, where he is now." He says that "things now are too horrible for words." MKR adds, "The basic stupidity of the human race, in allowing war, crushes me. I think that is why the work I am doing now is bad" (*Love Letters* 183).

3   Perhaps James Aldridge (1918–2015), Australian novelist, *Signed with Their Honour* (Boston: Little, Brown, 1942), about a British squadron in Greece during World War II.

4   Elliot Paul (1891–1958), American journalist, *The Life and Death of a Spanish Town* (New York: Random House, 1937), about Fascism in the Spanish Civil War.

fully. Rome Hanks[1] was so exciting at first, and I thought, God, he can write, then it turned into a meaningless mess. They just don't know how to make a coordinated work of art. The Razor's Edge and Huxley's Time Must Have a Stop did the same thing. Also Lebanon.[2]

I was impressed with Sumner Welles' book, and wish to Heaven he was in the State Dept. instead of that trouble-making ass of a Hull.[3] I also liked Harry Brown's A Walk in the Sun[4] very much. Anna and the King of Siam[5] was of course not literature, but it was most engaging reading.

The New Yorker bought one of the stories[6] I did this summer, but I think Carl Brandt[7] is stuck with the other one[8] I sent him. It is definitely queer, and if I were an editor, I don't think I would buy it. I rather liked it myself, and Carl wrote that he was "breathless" when he finished it, but I see no good reason for printing it.

Although I had lost 14 pounds, my weight suddenly got stubborn and would not budge one ounce. The old masseur[9] and I battled for a week, I starving and walking and exercising, and he pummeling every day, and we

---

1   Joseph Stanley Pennell (1903–1963), American novelist and short fiction writer, *The History of Roman Hanks and Kindred Matters* (New York: Scribners, 1944), about the Civil War and Reconstruction.

2   W. Somerset Maugham (1874–1965), British novelist, *The Razor's Edge* (New York: Doubleday, Doran, 1944), about a young man's search for spiritual fulfillment; Aldous Huxley (1894–1963), British novelist, *Time Must Have a Stop* (London: Chatto & Windus, 1944), about mysticism in a hedonistic world; Caroline Miller (1903–1992), American novelist, *Lebanon* (New York: Doubleday, Doran, 1944), about a child of nature who confronts human betrayal.

3   Sumner Welles (1892–1961), American politician, *The Time for Decision* (New York: Harper, 1944), proposed that Germany be divided into three parts after the war. His concept was based upon the "Good Neighbor Policy" he had earlier proposed for South America while he was Under Secretary of State from 1937 to 1943. A confidant of Franklin Roosevelt, Welles was in constant conflict with Cordell Hull (1871–1955), the Secretary of State (1933–1944), who in effect conceded foreign affairs to Welles, who in turn was eventually forced to resign because of a homosexual encounter. In spite of his forced resignation, Welles continued to advise Roosevelt and continued to be a thorn in Hull's side.

4   Harry Brown Jr. (1917–1986), American poet and novelist, *A Walk in the Sun* (New York: Knopf, 1944), about combat in Italy during World War II.

5   Margaret Landon (1903–1993), American writer, *Anna and the King of Siam* (New York: Day, 1944), sold over one million copies, was made into a hit film in 1946, and into the hit Broadway musical *The King and I* in 1951, composed by Richard Rodgers (1902–1979) and Oscar Hammerstein II (1895–1960).

6   "The Shell," *New Yorker* 20 (9 December 1944): 29–31. See Tarr, *Bibliography*, C629.

7   Carl Brandt, MKR's literary agent.

8   Most likely "Donnie, Get Your Gun" (unpublished), a Quincy Dover story, which MKR claimed was about her good friend Dessie Smith Vinson Prescott (1906–2002), whom MKR immortalized in "Hyacinth Drift" (1933), a largely nonfictional account of their trip up the St. Johns River. See Tarr, *Bibliography*, A5, B6, C595.

9   Dr. Berry, MKR's St. Augustine masseur.

didn't get off a bit, so I went to the hospital for a metabolism test, and was gratified to have it minus 14, enough to account for it. My doctor[1] put me on thyroid and said there was no reason why I shouldn't be able to finish the stint I have set myself. I feel marvelous, but the thyroid does make me very nervous. I have to check with the doctor every week or so to be sure it is doing no harm.

Have to go to town.[2]

Love,

Marjorie

. . .

JSB to MKR, 27 September 1944. ALS, 2 pp. PM: NEW YORK, N.Y. | SEP 28 | 930 AM | [Gray?]. AD: Mrs. Norton Baskin | Crescent Beach | St. Augustine | Florida.

Sept. 27 [1944]

Dearest Marge –

No time for a real letter – I must get to bed quickly to prepare for Penn Station tomorrow AM and the apt is littered with chores for me to do before that! But I must tell you that if you haven't made your hotel reservations do so at once. The hotels are crowded and getting worse all the time. It is hell to get a room.

I am thrilled by your reducing saga. My dreams of you, svelte in black, seems about to come true! I saw Dr. Atchley yesterday and he asked after you fondly, and was delighted at your shrinkage. Had lunch yesterday with Edith.[3] She looks really swell. She's gained about as much as you lost – says she weighs more than she has since she was 15. It's most becoming to her. She told me all about life at MacDowell.[4] It seems the musical angle was the best

---

1 Likely Riverside Hospital, Jacksonville, Florida, but unlikely Dr. T. Z. [Turner Zeigler] Cason (1886–1968), who was for a long time MKR's physician in Jacksonville. In 1943, Dr. Cason's sister, Zelma Cason (1890–1963) filed a lawsuit against MKR for "invasion of privacy" because of MKR's depiction of her in *Cross Creek*. Dr. Cason helped his sister gain evidence against MKR. As MKR points out in a letter on 12 January 1944 to her attorney Philip May, "I was forced to question the good wishes of her family" (*Selected Letters* 244), most notable of whom was T. Z. Cason.

2 MKR inserts the last line in pencil.

3 Edith Pope.

4 MacDowell Colony, Peterborough, New Hampshire, founded in 1907, an artist colony that supports and promotes the arts, but especially the interdisciplinary relationship of the arts. MKR was not charitable about Pope's selection to attend the colony, writing in a letter to NSB on 23 May 1944,

(Incidentally I don't think the back situation is as acute as you surmised). She is coming out for the weekend, so I may be going to "Harriet"[1] with her tomorrow night.

Another note from Bert[2] – He's off to report to the Com[mand]. of the Pacific Fleet, so I guess there's no point in writing till I get another address.

Do hope Norton has managed to get off by now. It seems <u>awful</u> that he has to hang around there for no good reason. Looking forward so much to seeing you – There should be <u>two</u> ballets going by the time you come up.

Much love – will write something decent soon (but maybe not time this weekend with Edith and I think Mr. Leirens[3] (Belgian) to keep happy).

Julia

. . .

JSB to MKR, 8 October 1944. ALS, 4 pp. PM: NEW YORK | OCT 9 | [10?] PM | 1944. AD: Mrs. Norton Baskin | Crescent Beach | St. Augustine | Florida. RA: J. Scribner | Far Hills | N.J. VIA AIR MAIL envelope.

Sunday [8 October 1944][4]

Dearest Marjorie:

I was awfully upset to hear all the complications about Norton – but from what I['ve] gotten from Daddy[5] his (N's) postdates all the previous reports and he did seem to be better. I do hope you have heard more good

---

"She was 'accepted' for the MacDowell Colony in New Hampshire---where I would not be caught dead" (*Love Letters* 372).

1   *Harriet* (1943), a play about Harriet Beecher Stowe (1811–1896), starring Helen Hayes (1900–1993), written by Colin Clements (1894–1948) and Florence Ryerson (1892–1965), opened at the City Center on 27 September 1944.

2   Bert Cooper: MKR had openly promoted Cooper to JSB. She did not mince words in a letter to Norman Berg on 18 July 1945, "I don't know, of course, where you are, but if you ever run into a Chaplain. Lt. Bertram Cooper, on the U.S.S. Bountiful, in Pacific waters, he is a good friend of mine, a scholar, a profound thinker. He was in love, in a soul-saving way, with Julia Scribner, wanting to make her happy and take her out of her dreadful environment. Julia has recently married [24 May 1945] another Episcopalian minister [Thomas Bigham], assigned, fortunately for her, to a professorship at the Union Theological Seminary in New York. Her last letter to me does not sound too happy. Bert Cooper and I have agreed to axe her husband if he does not please her" (*Selected Letters* 268).

3   Charles Leirens (1888–1963), Belgian photographer and musician. See JSB's letter on 8 October 1944.

4   Written in a second hand at the top of p. 1: [10-8-44].

5   Charles Scribner III.

news from him by now. I shall stop into Scribners tomorrow to see if there is new word from you. I feel that Norton's comment on the efficiency of the AFS[1] must be quite accurate. But they must have some good doctors out there![2]

I expect you have seen Edith[3] by now. Poor thing, she got her usual "staying with the Scribners'" cold. A dash of Florida air will fix her up, I guess. I'm delighted she is planning to spend this winter here. I hope to see lots of her. Incidentally, I met Greece[4] and perhaps you are not so far off after all, as I am sure he is smitten with Edith. However, she doesn't seem to be any more involved with him than she is with practically every member of the MacDowell Col[ony]. She is guiding all their troubled lives so far as I can see, and she was continually surrounded by painters, musicians and poets while in N.Y. Her main problem child is a female poet,[5] awfully queer and awfully troubled. But you have probably heard all.

I feel most dreadfully about the death of Wilkie.[6] I can't think of a worse loss except FDR. It seems to leave the better elements of the Republican party with^out^ a <voice> leader (though it was awful here for<ever> ardent Willkie-ites swarmed to Dewey<)>[7] and the poor guy didn't seem to be leading anybody much). Although I was against him in '40, I think the '44 Willkie was the outstanding spokesman for democracy in this coun-

---

1   American Field Service.

2   NSB was in a hospital in Calcutta, India, suffering from, among other things, acute dysentery. MKR used every influence possible to get him flown home. She contacted Stephen Galatti, the director general of the American Field Service (AFS), New York, who in turn contacted the authorities in Calcutta, but could promise little because of the secrecy involved. She then contacted General Brehon Somervell, commanding general of the Army Services Forces, who cabled the "commanding general of the China, Burma, India theatre," asking that he make inquiries about NSB who was in "47 British General Hospital, Calcutta." Somervell was advised that NSB could travel "after Oct. 14." Still the word on NSB's condition and transfer was murky. MKR at one point threatened to contact Eleanor Roosevelt, "my ex-hostess," for "she loves to meddle in such things" (*Love Letters* 433). MKR was also in contact with Somervell's wife, Louise, a friend, who brought further pressure to bear. MKR wanted NSB to be flown directly to New York and then admitted to Harkness Pavilion under the care of Dr. Atchley. Her wish was not granted. NSB was flown to Miami, then to New York, arriving on 30? October. It took him months to recover fully from his harrowing experiences.

3   Edith Pope.

4   The man who wrote a book on Greece and who MKR and JSB once thought was having an affair with Edith.

5   Not identified.

6   Wendell Willkie, who was defeated by Franklin D. Roosevelt in the 1940 presidential election, died on 8 October 1944.

7   Thomas E. Dewey (1902–1971), twice the Republican nominee for president, was defeated by Roosevelt in 1944 and by Harry S. Truman (1884–1972) in 1948, the last considered one of the greatest political upsets in history.

try. His Herald Tribune articles were magnificent. I didn't agree with the economic ones – but as far as I can see no one has come near his stand on foreign <policl> policy, social legislation, state vs federal gov't and the negro problem.[1]

I suppose in all the hullabaloo over that old politician, Al Smith's death (35,000 people outside St. Patrick's, etc) they'll hardly notice Willkie.[2]

I must say I think Dewey and the present Republican hysteria are enough to kill anybody. The more godawful [sic], stupid, farfetched Dewey's speeches are the better people seem to like them. And what irritates me beyond words is the way he keeps referring to the "detailed" programs he has set forth and which all the R's have taken to blathering about ("He's so constructive")[.] I search and search through his speeches but have never found one yet! I do feel that he will be defeated, but he is deserving of so much a bigger defeat than it seems he will get. We, and our agents, congress & senate, are certainly in a terribly divided state to try and make a peace.

Tomorrow I am embarking on what might turn out to be a career. I start a course in photography at the New School for Social Research[3] under Berenice Abbott,[4] a photographer I admire most passionately. That New School is a wonderful place. When I looked through the catalogue I saw dozens of courses I was dying to take (you know how I love education). Unfortunately most of them coincide with the photography but I see a couple in the spring term which I shall take – one under Leirens.[5]

Am also about to plunge head first into the music and ballet season. Daddy said you expected to come up anyway around the first week in Nov.[6] Trust you will stay to vote despite the ballet.

No word from Bert.[7] Wish he would send me an address as I would like

1 Willkie was an interventionist, believing that the United States should enter the war to protect its Allies. He was a civil rights activist, opposing the racial politics of the Deep South. And at the end he was a trusted adviser to Roosevelt. For copies of Willkie's articles for the *New York Herald Tribune*, see the Irita Van Doren papers at the Library of Congress. Van Doren was the editor of the *Herald Tribune Sunday Book Review* section and allegedly had a longtime affair with Willkie.

2 Alfred E. Smith (1873–1944), four-term governor of New York and presidential candidate in 1928, died on 4 October 1944.

3 The New School for Social Research, New York, New York, founded in 1919 to promote the work of progressive thinkers and teachers, especially for adult learners.

4 Berenice Alice Abbott (1898–1991), American photographer, considered one of the foremost documentary photographers, especially of portraits and of architecture.

5 Charles Leirens.

6 The presidential election was held on 7 November 1944.

7 Bertram Cooper.

to send him a Schraffts[1] box or some such for Xmas. If you have his address would you send it to me?

Haven't read anything fascinating of late – mostly newspapers[,] magazines and photography books.

Oh, great excitement I forgot to mention - Sandy Dillon[2] got engaged to a girl from Maine – very nice. I felt rather stumped at first as to how to act as the former woman in his life at such intimate occasions as the family dinner celebrating the engagement. However I made out finely and became a bosom friend of the fiancée's and have been support at all the lunches, teas, cocktails etc. that the poor thing had given in her honor. I'm not sure that I should be happy to have inspired such confidence in her. I don't know what the complicated feminine reaction should be. I'm not so good at com. fem. rea. anyway simple ones are more in my line, so I just felt quite friendly – and in a lovely burst of generosity gave her my favorite record album, a tribute which I fear she could not sufficiently appreciate. The only dark aspect of the whole thing is Granny's – She refuses to allow Sandy's name to be mentioned as she thinks my life has been permanently and hopelessly blighted by him in the most dastardly fashion! Muddy & Daddy & Aunt L try to assure her that I hadn't faintest notion of marrying him etc etc. but she just thinks they are all fools. Have you noticed that it is impossible to change the mind of anyone who is convinced you are a fool and incapable of seeing their point of view.

Well, I must go to bed! Have to get up at 6:30.

Much love, and I do hope you have now got good news of Norton.

Julia

The pen which writes so illegibly but so comfortably is the one you gave me.[3]

. . .

MKR to JSB, 27 November 1944. TLS, 2 pp. AD: Miss Julia Scribner | 31 East 79th St. | New York City. PM: HAWTHORN | NOV 27 | 2 PM | 1944 | FLA. 8¢ Air Mail stamp. LH: MARJORIE KINNAN RAWLINGS | HAWTHORN, FLORIDA.

Nov. 27, 1944

---

1   Schrafft's, New York candy and gift store.
2   Sandy Dillon, one of JSB's former beaux.
3   The Parker pen MKR gifted to JSB. See JSB's letter on 18 April 1944.

Dearest Julia:

We managed the trip home very well, though it did set Norton back a little. Smoky wet my bed on the train but aside from that has behaved beautifully.[1]

I had such a welcome home that I have been as gloomy as you. We walked into the hotel[2] to spend the night and here was a note from Idella that she was not returning;[3] and a note to call my lawyer,[4] his cheery word being that we have got to go through with the law suit. The Florida Supreme Court ruled that Zelma has a reasonable case for invasion of privacy, for "nominal" damages, unless it can be proved that publication of the book was "in the public interest." Of course I hope to prove hell out of that, but I do dread the whole nasty business.

I decided to come on to the Creek anyway, as Doug[5] was depressing Norton to death. He couldn't wait to show him pictures of the fire! When Idella didn't show up, old Martha of her own accord pitched ^in^[6] and cleaned house quite acceptably, the black bitch Idella having left both places filthy. Martha will stand by to clean up after me and I don't mind the cooking, though it worries Norton to have the stirring around all the time. Idella <u>knew</u> she was not coming back, for she had taken everything of hers from the cottage, and in her farewell note said hypocritically "I just don't know how I am going to get my things from the cottage---when she didn't have so much as

---

1   NSB was in Harkness Pavilion for nearly a month. He and MKR returned to Florida by train c. 25 November. His recovery was arduous, fraught with setbacks, but within two months he was able to travel to see his family in Union Springs, Alabama. Smoky, the cat.

2   Castle Warden Hotel in St. Augustine, then owned by the Baskins.

3   Idella Parker suffered MKR's racist outbursts on a number of occasions. See Parker, *Idella*, *passim*. For an overview of MKR's conflicting attitudes toward race, see C. Anita Tarr, "'The Evolution of a Southern Liberal': Marjorie Kinnan Rawlings and Race," *Journal of Florida Literature* 15 (2007): 141–62.

4   Philip May Sr., who, as MKR's lead attorney, filed an appeal of the Florida Supreme Court decision. MKR had been found not guilty in the original trial, whereupon Zelma Cason's lawyers filed an appeal before the Florida Supreme Court. On 23 May 1947, the Supreme Court reversed the lower court decision and found MKR guilty of "invasion of privacy." May filed an appeal. It was rejected. MKR was fined $1. Maxwell Perkins wrote immediately to MKR on 29 May 1947, "This is just to say how deeply I sympathize with you in the outcome of the appeal. It all seems utterly mysterious to me." To which MKR responded on 7 June, "The ruling is truly idiotic, but it means that while I have not injured Zelma in any way whatsoever, the Florida Supreme Court is backing up some strange law on the Florida books, whereby I have automatically invaded Zelma's privacy" (*Max and Marjorie* 610–11). This was the last letter Perkins wrote to MKR. He died suddenly on 17 June. For a complete hearing of the case, see Patricia Nassif Acton, *Invasion of Privacy: The "Cross Creek" Trial of Marjorie Kinnan Rawlings* (Gainesville, University Press of Florida, 1988).

5   Douglas Carlton Thompson (1912–2001) managed the Castle Warden Hotel while NSB served with the American Field Service in India.

6   Inserted in MKR's hand above the line.

a shoe-string there. If she had told me earlier, I should have stayed in New York longer, until Norton had more strength. And Chet[1] could have found me someone to help if I^'^d[2] had any notice. It was a typical nigger trick and is most discouraging anent my theories of opening the gates wide to the black brothers. You would think Idella had had enough education and sense not to have done such a thing.

Chet regrets that you won't be down, but he says the hunting is poor, as the foxes have been eating the quail. He says the coveys only have two to five birds.

Moe[3] was wild with joy at my return, and is a bit hurt about my showing up with another damn cat, but is being a gentleman about it.

The weather is wonderful.

Much love,

Marjorie

---

1   Chet Crosby, MKR's grove manager.
2   The apostrophe is inserted in MKR's hand.
3   Moe, MKR's pointer dog.

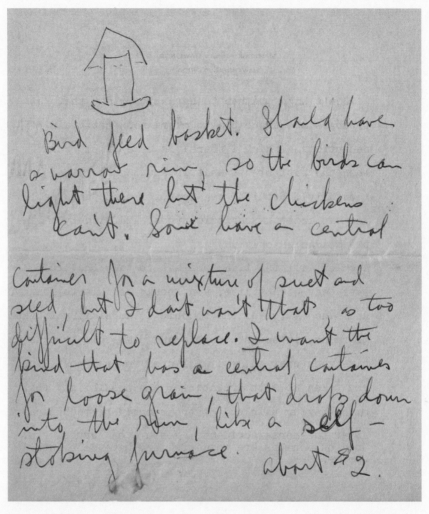

Bird feed basket. Should have a narrow rim, so the birds can light there but the chickens can't. Some have a central container for a mixture of suet and seed, but I don't want that, is too difficult to replace. I want the kind that has a central container for loose grain, that drops down into the rim, like a self-stoking furnace. about $2.

Figure 1. MKR's letter on 28 April 1943. Courtesy of the Department of Special and Area Studies Collections, George A. Smathers Libraries, University of Florida.

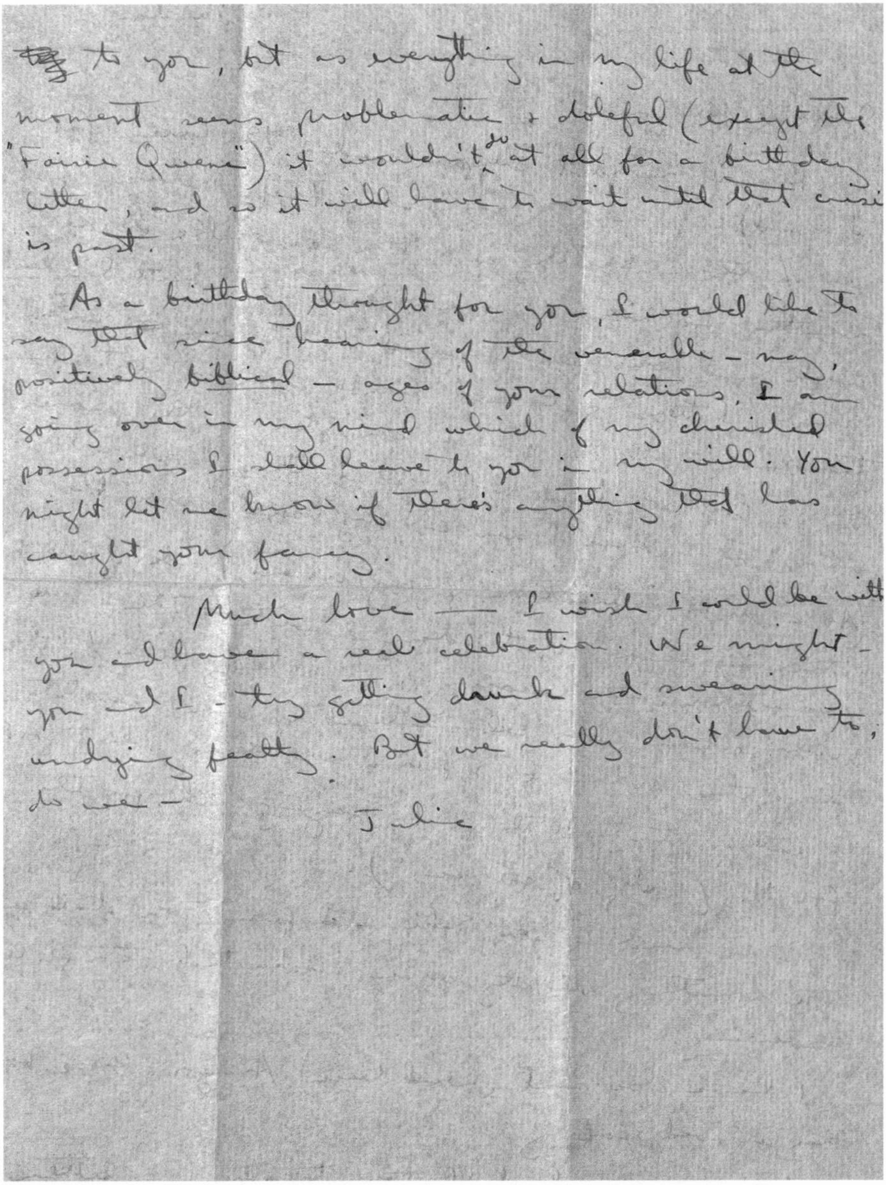

...to you, but as everything in my life at the moment seems problematic & doleful (except the "Fairie Queene") it wouldn't do at all for a birthday letter, and so it will have to wait until that crisis is past.

As a birthday thought for you, I would like to say that since hearing of the venerable — nay, positively biblical — ages of your relations, I am going over in my mind which of my cherished possessions I shall leave to you in my will. You might let me know if there's anything that has caught your fancy.

Much love —— I wish I could be with you and have a real celebration. We might — you and I — try getting drunk and swearing undying fealty. But we really don't have to, do we —

Julia

Figure 2. JSB's letter on 8 August 1943. Courtesy of the Department of Special and Area Studies Collections, George A. Smathers Libraries, University of Florida.

might be termed t.
. Shortly before dawn this
. room of a sleeping guest, apparen
keleton key, and rifled his clothes. The gue
woke and spotted him, but he managed to get away
and to take with him the guest's billfold containing
$24.

Not so long ago a warrant was issued by the Putnam County, Tennessee, police for the arrest of a
hotel sneak thief known as Eddie Dutch (pronounced "Dootch"), alias Johnnie Vanderbilt. He
is about 21 years old; 5 feet, 8 inches tall; has mouse
colored hair, neither blond nor brunette; dark eyes;
and sometimes wears glasses. He allegedly stole
$35.50 worth of clothing from a guest in a hotel in
Monterey, Tennessee, skipping his hotel bill besides.

The engaging Eddie is an exceedingly fast talker.
His stories vary in detail, but generally he represents himself as a Canadian flyer who is on his way

(Please turn to page 74)

HOTEL MANAGEMENT

● WARTIME TRICKS OF HOTEL CROOKS

to Florida for further training with the U. S. forces.
He does not, however, wear a uniform. He has a
Southern rather than a Canadian accent, and one of
his favorite articles of apparel is a brown sweater
with a white "B" on the chest. Eddie likes girls and
asks to be introduced to them. He also talks of two
pals of Italian descent who are planning to meet
him in a Buick coupe, but who never quite seem to
catch up with him. Nervous and fidgety, he will talk
your arm off if given half a chance.

When confronted with
the guest whose clothes he
had allegedly stolen, Ed-
die's powers of persuasion
were such that he not only
talked the guest out of
preferring charges, but almost succeeded in selling
him the nebulous Buick
coupe for $300! Moral:
*Beware of men in mufti
who represent themselves
as being in the armed
forces.* Many swindlers of
this kind are on the road
today. In addition, a number of genuine soldiers
and sailors are hiding out,
A. W. O. L., and probably
broke, in hotels.

Minor variations mark
the met...

keep reminding
lookout for the m
descriptions are
tive Bulletins. T
types of hotel cr
have proved this to
these menaces to ho

Never Accept Restit
Finally, a word abou

★	MORALS	★
★ Photograph and fingerprint new employees.		
★ Never let a new, uninvestigated employee get access to your check book.		
★ Before you invest in new help, investigate.		
★ Beware of guests who let the boys handle some, but not all, of their luggage.		
★ Don't let convincing conversationalists talk you into letting them off.		
★ Don't let fast talkers rush you into cashing company checks.		
★ Beware of men in mufti who represent themselves as being in the armed forces.		
★ Watch for soldiers and sailors who hide out, A.W.O.L. and probably broke, in hotels.		

Figure 3. Enclosures to MKR's letter on 11 November 1942.
Courtesy of the Department of Special and Area Studies
Collections, George A. Smathers Libraries, University of Florida.

Figure 4. Henry Heyl's farm. Courtesy of the Department of Special and Area Studies Collections, George A. Smathers Libraries, University of Florida.

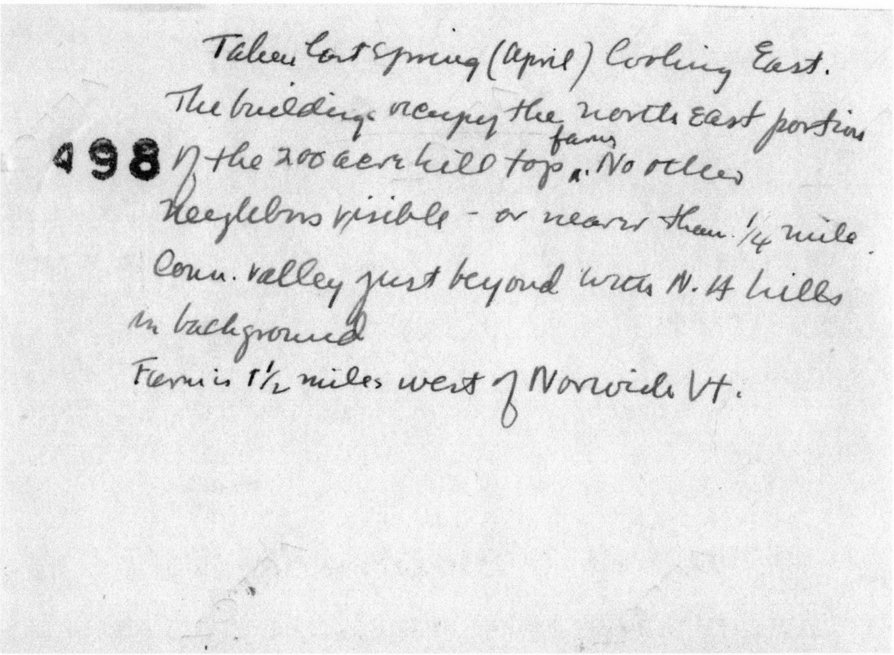

Taken last spring (April) looking East.
The building occupy the north East portion
498 of the 200 acre hill top. No other
farm
Heyldoms visible - or nearer than ¼ mile.
Conn. valley just beyond with N. H. hills
in background
Farm is 1½ miles west of Norwich Vt.

Figure 5. Description of Henry Heyl's farm, MKR's letter on 7 October 1943. Courtesy of the Department of Special and Area Studies Collections, George A. Smathers Libraries, University of Florida.

Figure 6. The wedding of Julia Scribner and Thomas Bigham, 24 May 1945. Courtesy of Hildreth Bigham Mc-Carthy.

Figure 7. JSB and MKR visit a cotton field, September–October 1942. Courtesy of Hildreth Bigham McCarthy.

Figure 8. (*above*) Young Julia Scribner riding at Mepal Manor, the estate of her namesake and grandfather Hildreth Kennedy Bloodgood, in New Marlborough, Massachusetts. Courtesy of Hildreth Bigham McCarthy.

Figure 9. (*left*) MKR with her Siamese cats at Van Hornesville. Courtesy of the Department of Special and Area Studies Collections, George A. Smathers Libraries, University of Florida.

The Height of Friendship

1945–1947

I cannot tell you how happy it makes me to find you as gloomy as ever.
As I think I wrote you once before, I was SO afraid that marriage might make
you cheerful, and so, not yourself.

[MKR to JSB, 14 June 1946]

Nothing would make me happier than if I could be
useful as well as ornamental as a friend.

[JSB to MKR, (21) August 1947]

. . .

MKR to JSB, 10 January 1945. TLS, 2 pp. PM: HAWTHORN | JAN 10
| 8 AM | FLA. AD: Miss Julia Scribner | 31 East 79th St. | New York
City. LH: Marjorie Kinnan Rawlings | Hawthorn, Florida.

Jan. 10, 1945

Dearest Julia:

I just cannot <u>trust</u> you. I send you out on a minor errand, to pick up a little
old small teapot, and you show up with a Spode, circa 1790.[1] I shall never
again dare murmur of my needs. If I asked you to hunt me up some hairpins,
you would probably prowl around until you found some little gold numbers
hammered out by Cellini.[2] Needless to say, I am <u>thrilled</u> by the Spode. It is
altogether lovely, and should have a niche of its own, to be viewed and not
used. However, I shall use it, threatening death to anyone who breaks or
chips it. As a matter of fact, I shall probably have to wash it myself. It was a
wonderful thing for you to do, but of course it means the special lens or the
enlarger[3] will be gone without---.

I had two other gifts that also floored me. Norton gave me the Encyclope-
dia Britannica,[4] somehow a rather formidable token of affection---. And A. J.
Cronin sent me one of the more expensive Havell Audubons, a white heron
at Key West.[5] Allah[6] is good, but these three things quite overcame me.

Things collapsed at the Creek in true Creek fashion. Martha[7] developed a
dangerous infection in a finger and I sent her home to keep it in hot Epsom
salts water. Her daughter Sissie[8] helped out for one day, then was snatched

---

1 Spode, English pottery company founded in 1770 by Josiah Spode (1733–1790), who developed
a method for creating fine bone china around 1790.
2 Cellini, a prominent and expensive jewelry story in New York.
3 That is, a camera lens and enlarger.
4 The "New 14th Edition" of the *Encyclopaedia Britannica* was published in 1933.
5 Archibald Joseph Cronin (1896–1981), Scottish novelist and physician, best known for his novel
The Citadel (London: Gollancz, 1937). MKR is referring to the so-called Havell engravings of John
James Audubon's *Birds of America*, done by the master engraver Robert Havell Sr. (1793–1878)
between 1826 and 1838. The "double-elephant" folio, the largest of the engravings, is 39.5" × 26.5",
was very rare, even in 1944. The Great White Heron at Key West is Plate 281. MKR quickly learned
that she did not have an original, and laments to NSB in a letter dated [4 May 1945]: " I put up the
Audubon, and noticed . . . that it is not a genuine one, only a chromolithograph done in 1860. . . .
It is not valuable at all, and I am much relieved, as I didn't want A. J. sending anything as expensive
as the original would have been. The picture simply dwarfs the dining room . . ." (*Love Letters* 448).
6 Allah, Islamic name for God.
7 Martha "Old Martha" Mickens.
8 Zamilla Mickens Fountain.

across the state where old Boss Brice[1] was dying. I took over for a day, even doing the milking. Then a cold I had been fighting went into bronchitis and I had to go to bed. Then Norton took over! He was most amusing about it, and almost competent. He brought me breakfast, the tray decorated with the only flowers in my garden, narcisi, cut off with about one inch of stem so that they were useless for any other decorative purpose. He churned butter and washed dishes. Martha milked with one hand. When I found that I was in for some days of bed, we said What the hell, and drove into Ocala to the hotel,[2] where I went to bed and had the doctor.[3] We left Moe at the vet's and took Smoky with us.[4] It took Smoky just one meal to realize that a bell-boy bringing a covered tray was bringing his private rations, and now he <u>loves</u> bell-boys. We spent ten days there and are home again. Everyone has recovered.

The new Smoky is adorable. He and Moe are fast friends, so much so that Moe, who is deeply in love, sometimes becomes a little confused. Norton is supposed to stay in bed rather late, so all four of us have breakfast together. One morning Norton and I were working on our trays, Smoky was smacking his lips over his dish of scrambled eggs on the coverlet, and Moe was draped over my side on the bed looking pitiful and smelling to Heaven and being given bits of my crunchy toast. It seemed very cozy and homey to me, but Norton remarked, "Breakfast with the Joad family---."[5]

Norton is improving every day, but it is slow business.

One night Smoky slept with us, between our faces. Norton turned out the bed light and I said, "Let me move the cat so you can kiss me good-night." He said, "Yes, I'd hate to have you tell me I'd missed."

Loads of love and swooning

Thanks,

<u>Marjorie</u>

---

1 William H. Brice.

2 The Marion Hotel, once managed by NSB.

3 Not identified. See MKR's letter to Ida Tarrant on 18 January 1945, in which she discusses the stay at the Marion Hotel (unpublished manuscript, Special Collections, University of Florida Library).

4 Moe, the pointer dog, and Smoky, the cat.

5 John Steinbeck (1902–1968), *The Grapes of Wrath* (New York: Viking, 1939), in which the poverty-stricken Joad family is forced to migrate from Oklahoma to California as a result of the Dustbowl. The novel was awarded the Pulitzer Prize in 1940, and remains one of the stellar examples of dystopian fiction.

···

JSB to MKR, 16 February 1945. ALS, 4 pp. PM: NEW YORK, N.Y. |
GR[AND CENTRAL STATION] | FEB 16 | 9 - PM | 1945. AD: Mrs.
Norton Baskin | Cross Creek | Hawthorn | Florida. RA: J. Scribner |
31 E. 79 St. N.Y.C. VIA AIR MAIL envelope.[1]

Friday – [16 February 1945]

Dearest Marjorie –

First off, let me thank you for the tangerines. I enjoyed them hugely, and
in a Proustian poppy-seed manner[2] felt myself back in Cross Creek occupied
with quail and Robbery Under Arms[3] and Moe's fleas and vagrancy. Thanks.

I seem to have such newsy letters to write you lately – first the job, and
now, the fact that I am planning to be married. This letter really should be
1000 pages long to give you all the ins and outs of this fact, but the pressure of
events is so terrific at the moment that I can only give you the barest outline
and save the rest for other letters or better yet for a five hour chat. This darn
note has to be finished in 25 minutes.

The bare outer facts are that he is Tom Bigham,[4] the minister who stayed
with us so much last year. Though he is a parson we will not have a moving
life from one parish and Ladies Auxiliary to another because he expects
to hold a proffessorship ∧(?)∧[5] at the General Seminary right here in NYC
until the retirement age of 70. G.S. is like a little university with a campus
and everything right in the middle of the city (9ᵗʰ Ave & 20ᵗʰ St). We will
live in the seminary looking out on lawns & trees etc. I think university

---

1   Written in a second hand at the top of p. 1: [2-16-45].
2   JSB is alluding to Marcel Proust, "In the shadow of young girls in flower," Part II of *A la recher-che du temps perdu* [*In Search of Lost Time*], where Proust compares the act of human kindness to a poppy field breaking into flower.
3   *Robbery Under Arms*, the triple-decker novel by Thomas A. Browne [pseudo. Rolf Boldre-wood]. See JSB's letter on 18 April 1944. JSB continues the recurring joke of the novel's length, when she saw it in manuscript at Scribners—that is, when she has nothing else to do, she can get back to reading the triple-decker novel.
4   Bigham was an Episcopal priest and professor of ethics and moral philosophy at the General Theological Seminary in New York, from which he was graduated, joining the faculty after his ordination in 1936. He continued his studies at Columbia University. He was named a full profes-sor in 1959 and retired in 1970. After his retirement, he became a clinical counselor at the Gould Farm, a psychiatric rehabilitation center in Monterey, Massachusetts. He died from pneumonia on 28 April 1990 in New Orleans, Louisiana, the residence of his daughter Hildreth Bigham McCarthy, MD (*New York Times*, 5 May 1990: 31).
5   JSB inserts the question mark above the line, indicating a lack of confidence in the spelling of "professorship."

life shall suit me very well. We shall be, for several years anyway, exactly as poor as church mice, but I see no fear of starvation (except due to my cooking). We cannot be married until the middle of May (end of term), a fact which becomes daily more irksome. (Couldn't you have some vital business in NYC at that time?) (Though really some other time than the actual wedding would probably be better as I would be so busy I wouldn't get a chance at the 5 hour chat then) Muddy,[1] who took the news of the job very well, has taken this very badly. I think she really doesn't like him and considers him a totally unsuitable husband. Daddy[2] is noncommittal, of course. Granny is thrilled – loves clergymen, thinks we are ideally suited and is very fond of Tom though she barely knows him. I have run out of pictures sending them off to my aunts, but as soon as I get a chance to print 20 more I will send you one.

The bare inner facts, and they are so gloriously unbare that I can hardly approach them by that, or any other phrase, are that I love him more than I ever hoped or believed it possible for me to love someone again.[3]

And he understands me more truly than ever in my most hopeful, lonely moments I ever imagined anyone would. I hardly believed, even in theory, that two people could know and trust each other so completely. It is the completeness and unreservedness of our knowledge, trust & understanding of each other that seems to me so extraordinary and wonderful. One reason for it perhaps is that I think under the surface we are very much alike. Sometimes, long before there was anything definite between us, when I would see him acting or reacting a certain way I would feel as if I was looking in a mirror.

I think you will like him, Marge, though maybe not at once. He is terribly reserved and wears a slightly formidable moustache. The first time I met him I thought he was awful then the second time I must have said to myself there is a man I could marry. And you know, I had not been able to say that to myself for about 8 years.

I will tell [Granny] tonight and she will [inform] you all about him, as she has been with him several weekends. She can give you an objective, but I hope personal report.

I find you can have a picture after all, just located another one. Unfortunately he doesn't like it, but it looks very much like one aspect of him.

---

1 The "job" is JSB's new found career in photography.

2 Charles Scribner III.

3 JSB seems to be referring to a former beau in her comment "love someone again." The person in question has not been identified, but it might be the clergyman she describes in her letter on 18 April 1944 (see 262, n. 3), the one who was married, had children, and a grandchild. JSB repeatedly parried MKR's suggestions that she might consider an affair. See JSB's letter on 18 October 1943.

Granny thinks he is better looking than the picture, but I'm not so sure – different, but he is not handsome from any aspect, the spots on his face are freckles, which don't show nearly as much in real life than on the film. His age is 33. Must close.

Much love

Julia

Love to Norton

. . .

MKR to JSB, 21 February 1945. TLS, 3 pp. PM: CITRA | FEB | 22 | P.M. | 1945 | FLA. AD: Miss Julia Scribner | 31 East 79th. St., | New York City. LH: Marjorie Kinnan Rawlings | Hawthorn, Florida VIA AIR MAIL envelope.

Feb. 21, 1945

Dearest Julia:

Your news bowled me over, for I did not know there was anything in the air. I can't tell you how happy I am about it, for from the things you say, Tom[1] is certainly the right man. You have something rare together, and it is the sort of thing that never lets you down. I almost wired you, "Delighted that you are committing Bighamy", but I knew / ^the^ local agent would take out the "h" and you would have the FBI on your trail.

Everything seems so right. I have included a clergyman in my mind, along with an artist or a musician, as one of the few types of men that would not disappoint you. You are such an incurable idealist that a man who aimed at anything lower than the stars, would enrage you. And the fact that you will live in your beloved New York is wonderful.

I think I shall have to ask Granny[2] about the matter of a wedding gift. I imagine the family will give you your silver, china and linens, perhaps furniture. Of course, you will get an autographed copy of "Cross Creek Cookery", and, if you will keep it secret from Whitney Darrow, Fanny Farmer's "Boston Cook Book",[3] which has always been my Bible. But I want to add something to the menage other than silver bon-bon dishes.

---

1   Thomas Bigham.

2   Louise Flagg Scribner.

3   Whitney Darrow (1881–1970), business manager and later executive vice president of Scribners. MKR's joke is that she should be trying to sell her own cookbook, not that of Fannie Farmer (1857–1915), *Boston Cooking-School Cook Book* (1896). See MKR's letter on 29 August 1942.

I should love to be at the wedding, but as you say, I would see less of you than / ^in any^ other conceivable circumstances. Perhaps next fall or winter Norton and I will come to New York for the fun we missed when he was in the hospital.

I don't think I need to say that I should adore to have you and Tom use the cottage for your honeymoon if you would like it, and would even provide a maid, but I imagine that you will prefer to be in New York or New England. New England must be divine in May. But if by any chance you'd like the cottage, just say so.

I can imagine that your mother[1] would be disturbed by anything except an extremely worldly marriage, but I consider you a brand snatched from that particular burning.[2] You could accidentally have cared for a man with entirely material standards, and then been miserable. Applause for Granny---.

Well, my dear, I feel that you will be in wonderful hands---and Tom will, too.[3] I look forward to knowing him. I hope you will take the wedding preparations in your stride and not let people upset you with trivial details.

All my love,

Marjorie

. . .

MKR to JSB, 7 March 1945. ALS, 5 pp. PM: HAWTHORN | MAR 15 | 2 PM | 1945. AD: Miss Julia Scribner | 31 East 79th St. | New York City.

March 7, 1945

Dearest Julia:—

I had a letter from Edith[4] that I don't understand—she said neither of you had heard from me—and I wrote you both long letters—yours, of course, on

---

1 Vera Scribner.

2 MKR is echoing *Amos* 4:11, where God warns the sinners of Israel: "I have overthrown some of you . . . and ye were as a firebrand plucked out of the burning." It is more likely, however, that MKR is thinking of John Wesley (1703–1791), the founder of Methodism, who believed that he was, as a child, a "burning brand snatched from the fire," a sign of Divine intervention that led him to the path of righteousness.

3 MKR is putting the best light on what for her was a disappointment. She knew nothing of Bigham until JSB's letter, and she also had hoped that JSB would marry Bertram Cooper. JSB's language of qualification, almost apology, in the previous letter also kindles the flame of disappointment. Finally, JSB's declaration that MKR not come to the wedding because JSB would not have time for her no doubt added to the wound. Hurt feelings would be assuaged over time, but at this very moment, in this very letter, MKR, in her own words, was "bowled over" by the announcement.

4 Edith Pope.

the subject of your marriage, of which I approved whole-heartedly. I mailed yours to 31 E. 79th.[1]

I do so want to add something to your menage that you really want. I did think of sending you a credit slip on Sloane or McCutcheon[2] for instance, but decided it was best to send you for wedding present a check to be used for some specific thing that you want. This is a terribly unglamorous way to make a gift, but it is safer, since you will receive so many gifts—many of them totally unusable.

I am at the cottage, getting it ready for spring and summer use. (Incidentally, I wrote you that while you probably would prefer to spend your honeymoon in New York City or New England, if by any chance using the cottage for that purpose appealed to you and Tom, I should love to have you use it, and would provide a maid-service as part of my wedding gift.)

Idella left everything in very bad shape.[3] I had two women working yesterday, and a man and woman working today, and will be lucky if they finish today.[4]

My Kentucky friend, Lois Hardy, whose husband is a colonel over-seas,[5] arrives this afternoon to spend a couple of weeks with us. We will go to

---

1 MKR is referring to her letter on 21 February congratulating JSB on her pending marriage. MKR was more circumspect in a letter to Maxwell Perkins on 11 April 1945: "I gather that Julia's approaching marriage to the young clergyman has been a bomb shell in the family. I know it has to Vera, who is selfishly putting Julia through a big formal wedding, which she hates. Edith Pope [see *Selected Letters* 261–62] did not care for the man, and neither did a most attractive friend of mine of whom I had hopes for a romance with Julia, also an Episcopal clergyman, but a lieutenant-chaplain in the Navy now. They felt he was a bit of a stuffed shirt and had his eye on the main chance. However, I do trust Julia's judgment, for she has been cold to so many suitors, and she is very much in love and says that she and the man have a rare understanding (*Max and Marjorie* 577). The "attractive friend" is Bertram Cooper.

2 W. J. Sloane Department Store on 5th Ave., founded in 1843 and closed in 1985, known especially for its fine linens and home furnishings. McCutcheon's Department Store on 5th Ave., founded in 1925 and sold in 1965, known for its fine linens and women's furnishings.

3 Idella Parker left MKR in the late fall of 1944, one of the many times she departed, often without notice. However, Parker's view of their volatile relationship is somewhat different. In retrospect, she felt that MKR was too often alone and too dependent on alcohol. Parker felt that MKR depended upon her: "I felt sorry for Mrs. Rawlings, and my love for her grew because it seemed she had only me and her dogs to depend on. This is maybe one of the reasons I kept leaving and coming back, for she depended on me. . . . I did my best to protect her and help her as much as I could. I loved her then, and I love her still" (Parker 85). MKR's dependence on Parker never waned, even after her marriage to NSB, Parker remained an integral part of the family. In this instance, Parker came back to MKR on 1 August, concluding "we were meant to be together" (*Max and Marjorie* 580).

4 MKR employed a Mr. Bowen to do carpenter work, but he was not dependable and was drunk most of the time (*Love Letters* 439–40). She hired two "fly-by-nights," who apparently lasted only a day (*Selected Letters* 262). She had a maid for Crescent Beach, Dorothy May, but she also proved not dependable. Martha Mickens continued at Cross Creek, like Parker now a member of the family.

5 Lois Clark Hardy and James Edward Hardy.

the Creek, but if the weather is warm, will come to the cottage for at least a week-end.

The Creek is simply heavenly. The orange trees are in full bloom, and my flower garden will soon provide flowers to fill the house. I put in new rose-bushes and have had my first dozen roses. I have calendulas, baby's breath, pinks, snapdragon, delphinium, lark-spur, bachelor-buttons, and stock.

We have gotten along very well with only old Martha for help, but I have rounded up another colored woman to help while Lois is there. Martha said the perfidious Idella wanted to come back, so Norton and I saw her and she said she would let me know, but no word has come.

Norton begins to look better, especially as he has picked up a little tan. He has begun taking his highballs again, and I must say they seem to do him good.

We've been down to Rollins College, where they had to call mostly on home-folks for their Animated Magazine.[1] I read my story that was in the Dec. 9 "New Yorker", "The Shell".[2] Col. Scott[3] was on the program and we saw a good deal of him and his attractive wife at parties before and after. We liked them very much.

Then a few days ago I went alone to Tallahassee, to speak at the colored State college, Florida A.&M.,[4] where Mary McLeod Bethune was being honored.[5]

It was most interesting and I was awfully glad I did it. Some of the Teach-ers and visiting educators and newspaper people were really delightful—and some of them much blonder than any of our friends!

I had a wonderful letter from Bert Cooper from the U.S.S. Bountiful. He

---

1 *Animated Magazine* was not a traditional magazine. The name was used as a fundraiser, the brainchild of Hamilton Holt, the president of Rollins College. Holt would invite famous people, who would give readings or lectures, which were then only reported in the magazine. The presence of these celebrities helped to raise funds for the college. MKR, a favorite of President Holt, gave several readings over the years.

2 "The Shell," *New Yorker* 20 (9 December 1944): 29–31. See Tarr, *Bibliography*, C629.

3 Col Robert L. Scott Jr. (1908–2005), famed American ace over the China-Burma theater, said to have shot down as many as 13 Japanese aircraft, flying the P-40N fighter, made famous by the Flying Tigers. Scott flew "The Hump" over the Himalayas during the same time that NSB drove an ambulance for the American Field Service. There is no evidence that they ever met until their meeting at Rollins College. During the war Scott wrote two famous books about his experiences, *God Is My Co-Pilot* (New York: Scribners, 1943) and *Damned to Glory* (New York: Scribners, 1944). He retired as a brigadier general. His wife was Catherine "Kitty" Green Scott (d. 1972).

4 Florida A&M University, Tallahassee, Florida.

5 Mary McLeod Bethune (1875–1955), educator and civil rights advocate, founder of what is now Bethune-Cookman University in Daytona Beach, Florida.

said he hoped he would hear from you again, and I must write him that you will probably have very little time for other clergymen.[1]

I do hope you received my other letter. Mail is often peculiarly delayed these days.

Much love,

Marjorie

. . .

JSB to MKR, [26 March 1945]. ALS, 5 pp. PM: NEW YORK, NY | MAR 27 | 7³⁰ PM | 1945. AD: Mrs. Norton Baskin | Cross Creek | Hawthorn | Florida. RA: [CHARLES SCRI]BNER'S SONS | PUBLISHERS | [597] FIFTH AVENUE, NEW YORK 17, N.Y.[2] V[IA AIR MAIL] stamped on envelope.

\<Sunday\>

Monday[3] [26 March 1945]

Dearest Marjorie –

I am completely overwhelmed by your present! And I am bursting with gratitude – and also with an awful sense of how many words you have sweated out of your brains to make that amount.[4] Heavens, in the "high-class" "low circulation" magazines it must amount to practically a whole short story! Knowing how hopelessly generous you are I should have been better prepared for such a tremendous gift, but it still came as a great surprise. You are a darling, and I do appreciate that fact and the gift quite beyond the Scribner ability with words! We shall put great and serious thought to the spending of it. Probably it will be some piece of furniture for our (still hypothetical) home.

---

1 Aboard the Navy hospital ship USS *Bountiful*, Cooper was comforting physically and psychologically wounded Marines from the Battle of Iwo Jima, 19 February–26 March 1945, one of the fiercest encounters in the Pacific theater during World War II. MKR writes to a war-shattered Cooper on 11 April: "I am afraid that you will not be hearing from Julia for some time. I have what will probably seem bad news for you. She is marrying . . . the clergyman you did not approve of, Tom Bigham. . . . She is very much in love with him, and since she does not fall in love at all lightly, it may be all right. I take cheer from the fact that Vera, the bitch-of-a-mother, is crushed by it" (Kinser, "'I'd Much Rather Write You'" 10–12).
2 Written in a second hand on the envelope: Mar. 27 / 1945.
3 Written in a second hand at the top of p. 1: [3-27-45].
4 MKR sent as a wedding gift a check to be used for something the Bighams could use for their new home. See MKR's letter on 7 March 1945.

It seems so awful not to have you somewhere at hand – to rejoice <and> ^or^ groan with me, depending on the situation at hand. And particularly awful that you haven't met Tom. You won't be up until next fall?!?!

Thank you too, for the sweet offer of the cottage. I regret to say we could afford neither the time nor the fare. We will only have a week, and Tom has to cut a couple of classes to take that. Aunt Gladys[1] is giving us her house in New M.,[2] and I am hoarding gas in order to be able to drive up and back.[3] It should be beautiful then (the wedding date is now May 24), but, of course, it will probably rain from the 24th to the 1st of June![4]

How perceptive you were to warn me against being upset by the material mundane side of the wedding, I thought I would just let that side roll off my back, but I must say that very side is not rolling off but <u>resting on</u> my back and wearing hell out of me. Muddy took the news even worse than I had expected, and is not becoming as resigned as I thought she would. So she is taking out all her disappointment and resentment over this unsocial marriage I am making, but having a wedding to end all weddings. To make up for the fact that I am not marrying a Vanderbilt or a future Master of Foxhounds, I am being subjected to a Vanderbilt wedding.[5]

Marjorie, you know how I hate such affairs. They are the very apotheosis of everything I loathe in the life I have led, and now this event in my life which means so much and so deeply has to be made into a sort of garish nightmare. I can assure you that on no point have I been asked what I would like, and when I fail to show proper enthusiasm (which is frequently) I am "impossible" "ungrateful" etc. etc. What with this and the continued sniping at Tom, and endless references to this or that person who is "so in love" meaning of course that I'm not, I get pretty worn down. Muddy has seen Tom just once since we've been engaged, at which point with icy smile and an edgy voice she said "Well, I never thought I'd have <u>you</u> for a son-in-law[.]" That sort of slowed up conversation and shortly afterward she left!

Aside from all this gloom, everything is fine. We both have our sinking spells of feeling maybe this is all an awful mistake, but then we confess all our

---

1 Gladys Augusta Bloodgood Casey Willets (1889–1978), sister of Vera Scribner.

2 New Marlborough, Massachusetts.

3 World War II gas rationing was still in effect.

4 "Julia B. Scribner New Jersey Bride," *New York Times* (25 May 1945): 13. The marriage took place at noon on 24 May at the St. Luke's Episcopal Church, Gladstone, New Jersey. The ceremony was performed by the bridegroom's father, the Rev. Canon Thomas Bigham, and the bride was given in marriage by her father, Charles Scribner III. She wore the bridal gown of her mother, Vera Gordon Scribner.

5 JSB is speaking of the fabulously wealthy Cornelius Vanderbilt (1794–1877) and his descendants.

misgivings and feel quite comfortable and sure that everything is OK. I must say that being engaged for 4 months is a dreary mistake though – <Both> for the leisure it gives Muddy to keep enlarging the wedding, for the time we waste when we might be together, and for the great strain of keeping apart! The only consolation is that perhaps it will be like my awful diet of last summer which gave me a new and thrilling appreciation of food! Tom is terribly busy, so that I hardly ever see him more than 2 evenings a week, and then perhaps not till after dinner one of those evenings. I could stay in and see him weekends, but he has two masters theses ^(?)^ to write, and I know they'll never get done if I'm hanging around.

I'm very busy myself. I still go to Stillman[1] almost everyday. Steve now has a very good man helping him so there isn't much for me to do. I am trying now to get back to my own work. And also I am helping Miss Abbott[2] organize an exhibition of photography. This work has the most future in it (aside from my own). I feel it a great privilege to be able to work with her, and I have hopes that there may be several of the exhibitions yet to come.

We are now approaching Hoboken[3] – no more spare hours until I take the train next Friday. This, being Holy Week,[4] is Bach Week,[5] The B Minor, 2 St. Matthew Passions. Right from this train I go to the New School[6] for a meeting on the exhib. And then classes <for> until 10:30 PM. Tomorrow I have to work for Steve & Miss A. and get my hair done, lunch with Cath,[7] go to the B Minor, and to a ^musical^ party afterward. Wed. Stillman, Abbott, dentist and a session on the wedding entailing the second meeting between Muddy, Tom, etc. All through this I try to take some pictures myself and keep ahead of engagement presents and flower thank you letters. You can see I'm well occupied.

I'm so glad to hear Norton is on the mend. You've certainly had a siege of domestic trouble – I hope that is OK now so you can enjoy your friends visit.

---

1   Photographer and operator of Stillman Studios, see JSB's letter on 14 May 1945.
2   Berenice A. Abbott [Bernice Alice Abbott], American photographer known for her emphasis on realism. Her photographs of New York City in the 1930s are among her most famous.
3   JSB is riding in a train approaching Hoboken, New Jersey, a major terminal in the 1940s.
4   Holy Week began on Palm Sunday, 25 March, and extended to Easter Sunday, 1 April.
5   Bach Week, choral music by Johann Sebastian Bach (1685–1750). *St. Matthew Passion*, a sacred oratorio, was composed by Bach for St. Thomas Church, Leipzig, first performed in 1727, where he was choral director.
6   New School, founded in 1919, is a university in New York devoted to the liberal and performing arts.
7   Catherine Ginna Mellick Gilpin (1918–1966), one of JSB's best friends, was one of two attendants at JSB's wedding. In 1942, she married McGhee Tyson Gilpin (1919–2000), thoroughbred horse breeder, Far Hills, New Jersey.

Have you & N done any fishing with Chet?[1] And did the latter ever mention if he got my Xmas present?

With so many, many thanks, and fervent wish you were here's without number and much love,

Julia

. . .

MKR to JSB, 6 April 1945. TLS, 6 pp. PM: HAWTHORN | APR 7 | 2 PM | 1945 | FLA. AD: Miss Julia Scribner | 31 East 79th St. | New York City. LH: MARJORIE KINNAN RAWLINGS | HAWTHORN, FLORIDA.

April 6, 1945

Dearest Julia:

I am just sick that you are being put through the inane hell of a big formal wedding. It is a combination of primitive hang-over from the days when a daughter was literally sold, (or in some tribes, bought!) and the most materialistic sort of showing-off. It violates all the sacred privacy of a man and woman joining their lives, for better or for worse. If it were not that you would have to live so long with the unpleasant aftermath, I should urge you and Tom to chuck the whole thing and slip off to the private chapel of some clergyman friend---but you would pay more than it would be worth. I hope the wedding will prove the last gesture you have to make to a conventional life for which you were never fitted, and which I hope you are leaving forever behind.

I am just back from Atlanta,[2] where Norton and I went when I was a guest on "Information, Please,"[3] for Red Cross benefit. It was really lots of fun, and thank God, they asked questions about snakes and lizards, so that I did not need to give away my ignorance on more literary questions. The governor of Georgia,[4] also a guest, proved himself a scholar and took care of the most difficult questions. He is a relation-in-law of Norton, being a nephew of the husband of Norton's oldest sister.[5]

---

1 Chet Crosby.

2 MKR numbers the pages but gets them out of order, and she writes at the top of the page numbered 2: "(I took quite a jump on page nos!)." She corrects the page numbers in pencil.

3 *Information, Please*, a radio quiz program that aired from 1938 to 1951 before it shifted to television, was created by Dan Golenpaul (1900–1974). The radio show had three regulars and one guest star, whose challenge it was to answer submitted questions. See 331, n. 1.

4 Ellis Arnall (1907–1992), governor of Georgia from 1943 to 1947.

5 NSB's oldest sister, Janise Adilon Baskin Ellis (1893–1981) was married to Joseph Dalby Ellis

The morning after the program, Fadiman, Adams, Kieran[1] and I went out to Lawson Hospital,[2] where the wounded veterans are mostly amputees. Before we spoke informally in the auditorium, we were asked to go through the officers' ward, and it made me and Fadiman almost literally ill. What killed us was the indomitable spirit of the men, some with no legs or arms at all, some with one or the other missing. They wise-cracked with us and were completely gay.

You should be here now---three sows that I have been trying futilely to sell, produced young, and instead of being rid of hogs altogether, I now have thirty-eight---. The piglets are adorable and you would love them.

Yesterday Old Will announced to me that the tires on the farm truck were not my own, and that a drunken carpenter[3] I had had building duck pens, had undoubtedly switched his tires for mine. Well, I had the serial numbers of the tires on the inspection card, so I lay down under the truck to check the numbers, all of them being on the inside of the tires. We have had no rain, and there is nothing dirtier than pure dust. Also, Martha had handed me an egg from a nest, which I put in my pocket---. When I finished, hot, dirty and spattered, I found, as I might have known, that they were all my tires---. Life has been a bit dull at the Creek, and I am sure Will hoped that I would go out shooting.

Max Perkins sent me the second volume in Santayana's personal history, "The Middle Span,"[4] and while I could never be as cynical as he, no matter how life betrayed me, it is one of the most delightful things I have ever read. Santayana is a strange mixture. He cannot get away from Catholicism, yet he denies the power of the spirit over the material.

After having written me from India that he could not return to the trivialities of hotel life, Norton has become intrigued again with the Castle Warden and is taking over the management. He is so gregarious, so truly loves people en masse, that it is truly his métier. People who frequent pub-

---

(1891–1969).

1   Clifton P. Fadiman (1904–1999), author, editor, radio and television guru; Franklin P. Adams (1881–1960), journalist and wit; John F. Kieran (1882–1981), journalist and later television personality. Fadiman was the moderator of *Information, Please*.

2   Lawson General Hospital, Chamblee, Georgia, was opened in 1941 and was intended, but not exclusively, for the treatment of amputees coming home from World War II.

3   "Old Will" Mickens. Mr. Bowen, a local carpenter. MKR later came to the rescue of the destitute Bowens, feeding them, then contacting the County Welfare Board on their behalf. See letter dated [21 February 1950] (*Love Letters* 561).

4   George Santayana (1863–1952), Spanish ex-patriot philosopher, *The Middle Span* (New York: Scribners, 1945), the second volume of his autobiography. Influenced by nineteenth-century existentialism, Santayana became an avowed atheist, but paradoxically continued to value the teachings of the Roman Catholic church while asserting reason as the avenue to understanding.

lic places love him for it, and I suppose he does have a great deal to give to the transient and the sociable. His return to the hotel leaves my private life more confused than ever. I am moving soon to the cottage, and he plans to make his headquarters there, but I am afraid it will not be conducive to work. There is no need for him to be at the hotel early in the morning, and I think he will be likely to sleep late and drift in to town in the early afternoon---raising hob with my working habits, which are to have coffee in bed quite early in the morning, then work hard from 9 to 12, and from 2 to 4. What I want is a husband who will get the hell out about seven o'clock in the morning, and not appear again until the cocktail hour, having home dinner with me and either spending the evening, or going out with me. As you know, Norton is everything lovely, and I love him dearly, but while I have no illusions about my work, and certainly do not think that I am writing for the ages, still I HAVE TO WRITE, and as Thomas Wolfe wrote in "The Story of a Novel",[1] a born writer decays inside when he is deterred from writing.

It seems to me most fortunate that you and Tom have almost precisely the same interests, and will have the same way of life, and any divergency of interest will be minor, and all to the good, for as Kahlil Gibran[2] says, there must not be too much together-ness in being together. We are individuals after all.

Don't try to write me.

Much love,

Marjorie

. . .

MKR to JSB, 5 May 1945. TLS, 4 pp. PM: HAWTHORN | MAY 7 | 2 PM | 1945 | FLA. AD: Miss Julia Scribner | 31 East 79th St. | New York City. LH: MARJORIE KINNAN RAWLINGS | HAWTHORN, FLORIDA.

May 5, 1945

Dearest Julia:

Having just written by hand a conventional note of regret (well, more or less conventional) to your esteemed parents, at my inability to be present

---

1   Thomas Clayton Wolfe (1900–1938), *The Story of a Novel* (New York: Scribners, 1936).

2   Kahlil Gibran (1883–1931), Lebanese-American popular philosopher, best known for *The Prophet* (New York, Knopf, 1923), MKR is referring to Gibran's poem "On Marriage": "But let there be spaces in your togetherness, / And let the winds of the heavens dance between you."

at your marriage and reception, I can now say to you in my more familiar medium that I really am damned sorry not to be there. If you have wedding dress pictures taken, may I have one?

With the reception at one, you won't be able to get away before two---but guess you will still reach New Marlboro[1] before dark. I'm afraid you'll be worn out with the hullabaloo, but I think all that will drop from your shoulders the minute you get in your car and head out for <u>freedom</u>.

I hope Norton and I can get to New York some time in the fall. We were certainly gypped out of <your> ^our^ last fall, and have something coming. My two Kashmir wool dresses from Bonwit Teller's Salon de Couture[2] came out very well indeed, and I want some of the evening materials made up. I can guarantee that I'll be north in the fall, anyway. Can come up with very little expense, too, as the "Information, Please" people gave me a standing invitation to be on the program again any time I was in New York. I was on the program in Atlanta, for Red Cross benefit, and turned my remuneration in to the Red Cross there, but should pocket it another time. $250 is high pay for having fun.[3]

I am moving to the cottage Monday for the summer. A very nice middle-aged colored woman, well educated, drives a car etc., is to keep house for me--if nothing niggerish happens! She has just postponed her coming a week, which is always a bad sign.[4] However, it was she who asked for the job, and I am paying her $5 a week more than the wages she herself suggested, and I took her to the cottage and showed her the maid's apartment and she seemed pleased, so I'm keeping my fingers crossed. I shall simply die if I don't settle down to work on a book.

I get my new "B" gas coupons the 12th of May and shall send you two, which will give you 10 gallons of gas to take an extra jaunt or two while you and Tom are in New England. You will probably enjoy walking rather than riding, but I thought it would be nice to be able to go some place lovely too far away for walking. Don't forget when you turn them in that B's are worth 5

---

1   New Marlborough, Massachusetts, where the Bighams were going for their honeymoon at Me-pal Manor, her grandfather Hildreth's estate.

2   Bonwit Teller's Salon de Couture—that is, a dress made at Bonwit Teller, one of the most fashionable department stores in New York. The art deco building was destroyed in 1980 to build Trump Tower.

3   See MKR's letter on 6 April 1945 about her first appearance on *Information, Please* in Atlanta, Georgia.

4   Annie Carter. MKR writes to NSB about the situation in a letter dated 6 May 1945, "I don't believe Annie Carter's tale for a moment. Husbands appear from Oklahoma, without notice, at the crucial moment, only in nigger women's alibis. I learned that lesson from Idella [Parker]" (*Love Letters* 448).

gallons each. Don't feel Black-Marketish about it, as it only means I eliminate one trip back and forth to the Creek.[1]

Much love, and don't let things get you down.

Marjorie

Oh, forgot to tell you that Bob Camp was home on leave and came out to see me. He was on two aircraft carriers in the Pacific and both had Hell bombed out of them! The second was by one of those Jap suicide attacks and the damage stopped just short of where Bob was, and they could not get out, smoke and flames, and he opened an absolutely forbidden hatch and got out. They were just 27 miles off Japan. His job has been Air Intelligence, briefing etc., but he was assigned in addition to making drawings of the damage to the carrier, so that they could be flown to the Seattle shipyard that would do the repairs. One of the Admirals commended him and later the shipyard said the accuracy of the sketches made it possible to do the repairs in just a third of the usual time. He was not bragging, just "telling". He looked ten years older and his beautiful black hair is thin and receding. He said the reason was that he was so scared the hair stood up and then broke off!

He was very gay about it all and not at all mentally damaged.[2]

· · ·

JSB to MKR, 14 May 1945. ALS, 4 pp. No envelope.

Monday –[3]

Dearest Marge –

This will be probably quite tough to read as I am on the train – But you

---

1   The rationing system, overseen by the Office of Price Administration (OPA), during World War II was complex and often abused. "A" coupons meant that the bearers were of "low priority" and thus entitled to about 4 gallons of gasoline per week, "B" coupons entitled the bearer to roughly double that amount per week and were given to farmers and commercial enterprises "deemed necessary" to the war effort, a designation given wide latitude. Local rationing boards set exact amounts. MKR would have been given such coupons as a farmer, not as a writer. And NSB would have been given "B" coupons as owner of the Castle Warden, a commercial enterprise. It was illegal, however, to tear coupons from the booklet and give them to other people, a rule impossible to enforce. Hence coupons were used as a form of barter, in effect a form of money.

2   MKR inserts this line in pen vertically in the left margin.

3   Inserted at the top of the page: [Late 40's, early 50's?]. The letter is dated by JSB's allusions to MKR's letters on 5 May and 21 May 1945 (see below), making 14 May 1945 the only possible "Monday."

must be used to it. I <u>always</u> seem to write to you on the train. It's my only hour of leisure while awake, I guess.

I am overcome by the offer of your 2 B coupons.[1] It doesn't make me feel blackmarketish, but it makes me feel I'd be an awful heel if I took them. I know [how] essential your trips to the Creek are particularly in view of Martha's shortcomings as a business & ^(?)^person^n^el[2] manager. I figure we can safely get up & back, and will probably have some left over. I'll be able to figure that better after I see what we use going up, but I'm sure there'll be a reasonable margin – So it will be OK, Marge, – really you'ld better keep that trip to the Creek.

I hope by this time you have figured out some schedule whereby you can write. I know you'll be miserable if you don't. Surely you can figure some way – Change your usual hours, or make Norton go in to the hotel for lunch, or both. I have done just enough of work I <u>belong</u> to do, to realize how frustrated, bored, and positively unhealthy one feels when unable to work. I imagine I shall have a great struggle finding time to work while at the same time learning to cook & housekeep. However, I'm sure I can find some way, particularly as Tom is anxious for <the> me to keep on with it. He seems to be able to organize his life so that he does about 3 men's work and yet has free time to[o], so I'll let him go to work & organize me!

We both think your phrase – "the inane hell of a fashionable wedding"[3] is beautifully accurate. It has been exhausting and probably will <u>be</u> ever more so. I have already had pictures taken in my "costume" and will be glad to send you one.[4] I hope they'll be half way decent. Photographically I know they are going to curdle my esthetic stomach. I bore up with fortitude under all the photographer's directions until he put me into a couple of poses so trite that even the cover editor's of the Woman's Companion would scorn them.[5] I came out of my 'attitude' and said to him, "I sure wish I had the piece of 5X7 film you're wasting on this pose." This actually did some good.

<u>Do</u> come up this fall without fail. I just cannot go on too long being married to a man you've never see[n]. The Info Please is a lovely way to pay the hotel bill isn't it?[6] I want to figure some method whereby Tom gives lectures or sermons in England or thereabouts so that we can get abroad on some of

---

1   See MKR's letter on 21 May 1945, where she reports that she sent the B coupons in spite of JSB's protest.

2   JSB inserts the (?) and "n" above the line indicating her insecurity about the spelling.

3   See MKR's letter on 5 May 1945.

4   See MKR's letter on 5 May 1945 and Figure 6, 316.

5   Woman's Home Companion, founded in 1873, popular monthly magazine with a circulation of more than 3,000,000 readers at the time.

6   See MKR's letter on 5 May 1945.

those 4 month summer vacations. Perhaps I can go on a photographic job if I will keep my nose to the film. Berenice Abbott is most encouraging about my work.[1] I fume terribly at my amateurishness and have to keep reminding myself that 6 mos ago I had never even made a print. I may work with B. A. on some photographic books. This would certainly be good for my <th> technique. Steve Stillman turned out to be so sloppy technically that he did me more harm than good.[2] Too much emphasis on technique is the fatal disease of most photographers in this country, but a fluent technique is almost essential for esthetically serious work. Just as in writing or any other art, no matter how important what you have to say is, to say it most effectively you must say it beautifully. I must say I can think of a couple of photographers who have something so true and original to say in their pictures and whose sense of composition is so good that they are truly great photographers despite mediocre or worse techniques. I can't think of any technicians who are artistically of any importance.

Marjorie, you mustn't be perturbed if you don't hear from me for weeks to come. The amount of letters I have to write staggers my imagination – At the moment only about 75, but I suppose it will end up close to 200. You <u>know</u> what acute pain writing causes me!

How is Norton? I trust in almost 100% shape. Edith is fine.[3] She was out at F H two weeks ago.[4] I looked forward so much to her being up here and then I got so damn busy & involved in matrimony that I've hardly seen her. Do give my love to Bob Camp if he is still around.

Well, I must get to bed to prepare for another hectic day tomorrow. (This letter got off the train somewhere in the middle of the esthetics monologue.) How I wish I could have you around for just 24 hours. It would take about that long of straight talking (I don't mean "from the shoulder" but uninterrupted) to get you right up to date.

Much love,

Julia

---

1   See JSB's letter dated [26 March 1945].
2   Stephen Lewis Stillman (b. 1904), photographer, operated Stillman Studios at 159 E. 48th St., Manhattan; see JSB's letter dated [26 March 1945].
3   Edith Pope.
4   F H: the Scribners' home in Far Hills, New Jersey.

MKR to JSB, 21 May 1945. TLS, 1 p. PM: SAINT AUGUSTINE |
MAY 21 | 4 PM | 1945 | FLA. AD: Miss Julia Scribner | Far Hills |
New Jersey. LH: Mrs. Norton S. Baskin | crescent beach, star
route | st. augustine, florida

May 21, 1945

Dearest Julia:

How strange it seems that I shall never again address a letter to Miss Julia
Scribner.

I enclose the B coupons,[1] in spite of your protests, as I really think you
may want to take a drive while you are in New Marlboro[ugh].

Well, my dear, needless to say that I wish you all possible happiness and
contentment. There is something so peculiarly right, in spite of one's essential loneliness, in a man and a woman working out a scheme of life together.
And I think you will make a very good wife. But for God's sake don't try to be
a perfectionist about housekeeping and cooking! It can get you, and it doesn't
leave you a minute for anything else.

Good luck and have a wonderful time[.]

All love, Marjorie[2]

. . .

MKR to JSB, 26 June 1945. TLS, 3 pp. PM: [illegible]. AD: Mrs.
Thomas Bigham | c/o Mr. Charles Scribner | 597 Fifth Avenue |
New York City. LH: Mrs. Norton S. Baskin | Crescent Beach,
Star Route | St. Augustine, Florida.[3]

June 26, 1945

Dearest Julia:

You've been back about three weeks, and I'll bet you aren't half-way
through the Thank-you notes. I hope the loot is worth the trouble. Of
course, you have to be just as polite over a combination aluminum vinegar

---

1   MKR enclosed two gas rationing coupons, See MKR's letter on 5 May 1945.
2   Both parting and signature in MKR's hand.
3   Written in a second hand on the envelope: 26 June / 1945.

and mustard stand as over a sterling silver tea set---or didn't you get either one.

I never fared very well on wedding gifts, since both my marriages were rather casual. The blue and Parma-violet bowl[1] you gave me was the nicest.

I haven't sent the cook-books I promised.[2] Thought I'd wait and see whether you felt there was any hope. Of course, you will do well anything you decide to do. Chet Crosby[3] insists he could have made a crack quail shot out of you if he'd had you a couple of weeks longer.

I am having a peculiar servant problem. I acquired a colored woman whose husband and son are both in the Army.[4] She is always pleasant, is immaculate and could not be more anxious to please—and I think would stay happily for the duration. There are two things against her: she cannot cook; and she gets on my nerves terribly, for no reason at all. Now Idella writes that she is ready to come back.[5] I don't know what to do. If I dismiss Annie and Idella clears out again in a few months, I would be worse off than before, for Annie would be gone forever, as I hate to think of the people ready to snap her up, cook or no cook. A bird in the hand, you know, especially a blackbird---.[6]

Edith Pope is expecting Verle home soon. I heard he got his Majority, and the Air Medal to boot. I don't know whether he will go to the Pacific or not. Edith moved from the Lafayette to a friend's apartment on Gracie Square, but I don't have the address.[7]

Norton has been unable to move to the cottage, because of the steady stream of help coming---and going. As fast as he hires them, the Chef[8] runs them off. I have a suspicion that the Chef does it, perhaps only subcon-

---

1   That is, made in Italy. See MKR's letter on 13 December 1941, 117, n. 2.

2   Fannie Farmer's *Boston Cook Book* and MKR's *Cross Creek Cookery*. See MKR's letter on 21 February 1945, 323, n. 3.

3   James Chet Crosby.

4   Annie Carter.

5   MKR always preferred Idella Parker, who was more a family member than a maid. In a letter to NSB on 25 April 1945, MKR quotes from a letter from Parker: "'I can never say that I do not want to work for you again and tell the truth . . . but it's just, I can't, not now anyway. I do hope you get one of those persons and even though they are not what you want, try and use them until the way is clearer for me'" (*Love Letters* 446). From the context of these remarks, it is clear that MKR had written Parker to come "home." The whole situation was complicated by the fact that Edward "E.M." Thompson, Parker's brother, had recently been killed in action in World War II.

6   MKR is combining the seventeenth-century English proverb, "A bird in the hand is worth two in the bush," with the children's rime "Four and twenty blackbirds baked in a pie." MKR's racial insensitivity continues in spite of her public protestations about the treatment of Blacks.

7   Verle Allyn Pope, a member of the U.S. Army Air Corps in World War II, subsequently was elected to the Florida House and later the Florida Senate, in all serving thirty-eight years, two as president of the Senate. The Popes were among the closest friends of the Baskins.

8   Clarence Huston.

sciously, to make sure that Norton stays around. Norton spent one Saturday night, arriving very late, and Sunday, and when we went in Sunday evening for supper, the Chef came out and said reproachfully to him, quite ignoring me, "Good evening, stranger." And it was the first time Norton had been away. If I ever divorce him, I shall name the chef as co-respandant [*sic*]. He is reasonably well, but gets exhausted easily.

Write me when you finish the notes, or when you can't stand them any longer.[1]

Love,

Marjorie

. . .

JSB to MKR, 7 July 1945. ALS, 5 pp. PM is missing. AD: Mrs. Norton Baskin | Crescent Beach | St. Augustine | Florida. LH (embossed): 6 Chelsea Square | New York, N.Y. VIA AIR MAIL envelope.[2]

July <4> 7

Dear Marge –

As I have about 125 letters to write, I can't even foresee when the job [will] be finished and as I was tired of them even before I began, I guess this is as good a time as any to dash off some news to you. I feel as if I hadn't had time to draw a slow breath since about a month before the wedding. Except on the honeymoon and then we were both too exhausted to do much. Do you remember what the weather was like on our trip through New E.?[3] Well, it was just like that on the honeymoon. It rained for all but about 2 days and we had 2 nights of frost – in June! I don't know what we'd have done without your 10 gl. of gas.[4] With that we went to the movies about 1/2 doz times and saw a horrible succession of musicals. We didn't have <u>one</u> picnic. That rather devastated me as I had seen a series of beautiful days spent out in the open with that wonderful country all abloom with Spring. We only went fishing once and then it was raining and we caught

---

1 MKR finishes the note in pen after the word "when."

2 Written in a second hand on the envelope: Jul. 3 / 1945.

3 JSB is referring to their trip through New England in October 1941, after MKR had been dismissed from the Harkness Pavilion (see JSB's letter dated [13 July 1942], 128, n. 2, and *Love Letters* 64).

4 The gas bought with the two rationing coupons MKR sent JSB (see MKR's letter on 5 May 1945).

only two miserable baby trout. To top the whole thing off I got a terrible cold two days before we went home.

Despite this dismal sounding saga I had a perfectly happy time. I know so many people who look back with horror on their honeymoons. I feel very grateful that mine was so peaceful and, figuratively, sunny.

We did very well in the present line.[1] The no. is now 314 with at least a dozen or so to come. Very few lemons, some of which we were able to return so that we now have several large credits in several stores.

It is just desperate having all those letters to write plus many other friends who should be written to, right at a time when we are trying to fix up the apt. Things are so hard to get now that for instance I have already spent most of 3 days trying to get a particular paper for the dining room. One really should be able to give full time to that for a couple of weeks and get it underway. We have such a large apt – 9 rooms all but 2 of which we have to fix up. The rooms are big too – The living room 20' × 20', bedroom same, study about as big, dining room 20' × 14', hall about 50 ft long! Our ceilings are about 11 ft high. Edith[2] has probably written you a description. She was here for dinner the other night.

I have for the summer a maid who belongs to one of the other profs. We pay her almost more than we have between us – $35 a week. This is current NY wages for a "live out" maid. She is black. Fairly clean, fairly good cook – not very active. Day before yesterday she just didn't come in because she had "important business". At $6 a day, that causes me no uncertain pain.

Still if I didn't have Annie[3] I don't know when I'd do anything but house-work. As it is I haven't taken one picture or made one print since I've been married, a fact which increasingly makes me nervous. When I get the wedding and the house under control I'll set up at least one day a week as photographic day, and really do some work. Organization is, I think, the main necessity.

Well, I must go back to work. I can't wait to have you come up and see the Seminary[4] and the apt [apartment] which will surely be finished by the time you come. Don't come in Sept!! (We'll be away the whole month as that is Tom's vacation.)

Much love to you and Norton and do write again. I love to hear your news.

Julia

---

1   That is, wedding presents.

2   Edith Pope.

3   Annie, JSB's housekeeper.

4   General Theological Seminary of New York, where Thomas Bigham was a member of the faculty.

MKR to JSB, 8 July 1945. 4 pp. Envelope is missing. LH: Mrs.
Norton S. Baskin | Crescent Beach, Star Route | St.
Augustine, Florida.

I am suffering horribly because of the N.Y. truck strike. Haven't had my
Herald-Tribune or Sunday Times for 10 days.[1]

July 8, 1945

Dearest Julia:

This does not call for any answer, poor creature. I wish I could help you
with the letters. I know how depressing it is to have them piled up.[2] Norton
helped me with my accumulation when we were at the Creek, but you know,
someone else always says just some little, insignificant thing that you would
never say, and you get a funny feeling. All you can do is stick with it, making
a stint of a certain number a day.

I'm glad you have a maid, even at those awful wages. I am appalled at the
size of your apartment. The Seminary[3] must expect you to fill it with children. You certainly couldn't afford to fill it with guests, after you've paid the
maid. On second thought, children would cost even more.

Life is looking a little brighter for me, for Idella[4] is coming back the first of
August. She said she guessed we were meant to be together. I don't know how
I'll stand the rest of the month with the Annie[5] I have. She drives me crazy.

I have made a new beginning on my book,[6] which suits me a little better
than the six previous starts, though it is still not right. But I'm going ahead
anyway, as once I get the proper swing, I can go back and rewrite the first
part again. I've done a good many short stories lately, all of which have been

---

1   MKR inserts her postscript above the letterhead. On 30 June 1945 (p. 1), the *New York Times*
reported that a trucking strike for better wages and benefits had been called by members of the
Newspaper and Mail Deliverers Union in New York. According to the report, eleven metropolitan
papers, including the *Times* and the *Herald Tribune*, were affected. The strike ended on 17 July,
when the union accepted the authority of the War Labor Board and returned to work under the
terms of their old contract pending arbitration (*New York Times* 1 July: 1; 18 July: 1).
2   MKR is referring to the correspondence she was receiving from the troops, mainly from overseas, and often just before they went into battle. A number of these letters are in the Rawlings
Archive, Special Collections, at the University of Florida Library
3   The General Theological Seminary, New York.
4   Idella Parker.
5   Annie Carter.
6   The manuscript of *The Sojourner*.

rejected. The New Yorker told Carl Brandt they felt what I was doing was "terribly experimental", which gives me the private hope that it may be good! I have almost enough for a book, and I may let Max see them, with that in mind. It would tide me over until I finish the novel.[1]

I had an amusing experience at the hotel[2] Saturday night. Norton introduced to me a young pianist, now at Camp Blanding, a private, who is a friend of Philip Barry's son.[3] They come to the Castle every week-end they can get a pass. With this very nice chap was a girl. How she got on the subject, I'll never know, but she announced that she had never been so disappointed in a book as in "Cross Creek". She said it was about a kind of life and people she just wasn't interested in and didn't care to read about. She said, "It was just so queer," She turned to me and said, "Didn't you think so?" I was about to pop, and the boy was squirming, and Norton was having a wonderful time. She said to Norton, "I understand the author has an interest in this establishment." Norton spoiled it all by saying, "She is the author." Later he asked me what I thought of the girl, and I asked him if I could possibly be a little prejudiced---.

Max, of all people, probably because Whitney[4] is away, sent me a full-page ad put out by the Wine Advisory Board, this particular one to be in Collier's and Life, and featuring Marjorie K.R., with picture, references to Yearling, Cross Creek and C.C. Cookery, and giving an alleged recipe from

---

1   MKR writes to Maxwell Perkins on 18 July 1945 that Carl Brandt and Bernice Baumgarten, her New York agents, were "enthusiastic" but unable to sell "one of them" because in the words of the New Yorker they were "'terribly experimental." The New Yorker had already published three of the stories ("The Pelican's Shadow," "Jessamine Springs," and "The Shell") and was about to publish a fourth, "Dark Secret" (Max and Marjorie 580). Later, in a letter to Perkins on 17 August 1945, MKR refers to them as her "'queer' stories," another of which, "Miriam's Houses," Brandt managed to sell to the New Yorker. Another, "Donnie, Get Your Gun" was rejected by the Saturday Evening Post and remains unpublished (Max and Marjorie 580). And another, "Miss Mofatt Steps Out" was later sold to Liberty Magazine. "The Friendship," published by the Saturday Evening Post in 1949, may also be one of the so-called queer stories. Add to this list "The Enemy," published by the Saturday Evening Post in 1940, "In the Heart," published also in 1940 by Collier's Magazine, and "The Provider," published by Woman's Home Companion in 1941, and the list of MKR's experimental fiction swells. See Tarr, Bibliography, C611, C612, C614, C615, C617, C629, C631, C632, and C633. See also Short Stories.
2   Castle Warden Hotel.
3   Philip Barry (1896–1949), American playwright, best known for his play The Philadelphia Story (1939). The son mentioned is likely Philip Barry Jr. (1923–1998), eventually a producer, who was in the Navy in World War II.
4   Maxwell Perkins alerts MKR about the ad in a letter on 5 July 1945, "I am sending you an ad which . . . will run in one issue of Collier's and one of Life. It seems to me that it is a good ad for three of your books and no more objectionable than any ad." MKR responds on 18 July, "I never heard of anyone's rushing out to buy a book after seeing it mentioned in a wine ad, but if you think it's a good idea, why, all right" (Max and Marjorie 579–80). Whitney Darrow (1881–1970) was the sales manager at Scribners and later a vice president in the firm.

said M.K.R. To my amazement, Max thought it was a good idea, because of the free advertising for the books. I'm sure I've never run out and bought a book after reading a wine ad---. Max also said Edith is working, and it is going easily.[1] Did I tell you Verle is a Major and has about six medals and citations? No, Edith hasn't written me yet. I need her to give me a full description of your vast suite.

Your honeymoon sounds ghastly, but I suppose you were both so glad to be away from confusion that you didn't mind the rain and the movies.

As I said, don't try to answer this. I just felt like chatting with you.

Much love,

Marjorie

.   .   .

JSB to MKR, 5 September 1945. ALS, 2 pp. PM: MARION | SEP 6 | 4 PM | 1945 | MASS. AD: Mrs. Norton Baskin | Crescent Beach R.F.D. | St. Augustine | Florida. LH (embossed): 175 Ninth Avenue | New York City. VIA AIR MAIL envelope.[2]

This is the Seminary's address, but do use 6 Chelsea Sq. for me – it's so much more elegant![3]

Sept <6> 5

Dearest Marge:

We are at present on vacation and about time too. I never put in such a three weeks as the preceding ones what with moving, housekeeping in two apts at once and a mass of interior decorating struggles. Tom had his thesis and 6 term papers to write. He worked all through the night until time to set off on the day's work at least 2 nights a week. I still can't take time to do much more than tell you that I haven't time to write as we are now in the process of polishing the thesis and it runs to some 250 pages. It must be finished by tomorrow afternoon so that tomorrow night Tom can prepare the paper he has to read at the religious congress we have to attend the 7th, 8th, & 9th. Peaceful as hell, isn't it?

But we are managing to sandwich in a little rest & repose. We are with

---

1   In a letter to MKR on 5 July 1945, Perkins writes of Pope, "The only good news I know is that Edith Pope has begun to write, and has found it goes easily" (*Max and Marjorie* 579).

2   Written in a second hand on the envelope: Sep. 6.

3   JSB inserts this postscript above the embossed letterhead on p. 1.

Cath[1] now in Marion Mass on Buzzards Bay. After the Boston congress we go to Aunt L's[2] in R.I. for a week. That should be quieter with the paper out of the way and the thesis out of reach being typed. After that we hope to motor around the Green Mts.[3] Some. I do hope we have better weather than on the trip you & I had there. I am so anxious to get back into those mts now that we have gas again.

Edith[4] gave me your news – including the ghastly snake story.[5] I find it hard to feel the same about Cross Creek since hearing it – I used to think CC was so homelike. I'm sorry to hear that Norton has to work so hard. I do hope that doesn't mean that you won't take your N.Y. trip. I'll be so disappointed if you don't get up here.

Your present has materialized into a very handsome blonde modern bureau and 5/6's of a matching chest of drawers for our bedroom. We had a terrific search to find just what we wanted and that not in a suite including a bed or beds which we didn't need. We are absolutely delighted with what we got and I feel it was well worth the search and looks like a $400 suite.[6]

Sometime next winter, if I manage to get a maid upon my return, life may be peaceful enough that I can write you long contemplative epistles all about my recent reading. Since May as far as I can recall I haven't read a single book. Till then I guess it will just be these hurried gasps –

Much love,

Julia.

P.S. I have now just 12 wedding present letters to write. Late arrivals

---

1   Catherine Gilpin.

2   Louise Scribner Schieffelin.

3   Green Mountains in Vermont, where JSB and MKR visited in 1941.

4   Edith Pope.

5   JSB is referring to one of the more celebrated snake adventures that took place at Cross Creek. On 17 August 1945, quoting in part from Martha Mickens, MKR writes to Maxwell Perkins: "The toilet would not flush. I used it for about eighteen hours, and Martha went to the bathroom to clean. She called out, 'There's something in the toilet.' I said, yes, I knew, it wouldn't flush, and did she have any idea what it might be. 'Yessum. Cottonmouth moccasin.' It stuck its head up when she sifted in the Dutch cleanser, and stuck it up again when I peered it. I slammed down the lid and blocked the crevices with bath towels and went to Ocala on business. . . . When I reached home, my good friend Leonard [Fiddia] . . . had speared the moccasin with an ice pick, hauled it out and killed it outside. It was four feet long and thick enough in the middle to have blocked the toilet. He found a break in the drainage tile where it had gotten in, and fixed that" (*Max and Marjorie* 582–83).

6   JSB is referring to the check the Bighams received from MKR as a wedding present. Perhaps the mention of the "$400 suite" is the amount of the gift. If so, the purchasing power of the gift in 2022 would be $6,400.

. . .

MKR to JSB, 22 September 1945. TLS, 3 pp. Envelope is missing.
LH: Mrs. Norton Baskin | St. Augustine, Florida.

Sept. 22, 1945

Dearest Julia:

Well, I have missed all the hurricanes at the beach, and was disappointed to find that I was going to miss the one last week.[1] I had arranged to go to the Creek for the week-end and had promised Idella[2] to take her home, so went ahead. Sunday afternoon I picked up Idella and we headed for the cottage. The storm had begun in our section, but I thought I could beat it to the coast. It was moving at 18 miles an hour and I expected to be moving at 40 or 45. I didn't take into consideration the fact that it was moving in a circular fashion and also did not know that it was to go out to sea AT St. Augustine. I still have not seen a hurricane from the cottage, but I have seen all there is to see, and it is quite enough. We drove right through the very worst of the damn thing. The last hour was almost literally out of this world. I got stalled in a <u>lake</u> on the road <it> $5 and three boys got me pushed out. With full lights on, most of the time I couldn't see the road at all. It was like driving down the middle of a river. The driving rain looked like snow, a blizzard. Now and then a gust would knock the car a couple of feet to one side. It seemed as though I should have to park and sleep in the car. Idella chose the back seat with Moe, and I was to take the front seat with Tony the cat. We were going to make our supper from the farm butter I was taking back. But we did make it, and I got Idella to a colored boarding house and went on to the hotel.[3] I dashed from the car to the lobby with the puss in my arms and Moe slinking with his tail between his legs, and we were drenched, disreputable-looking outfit. And there stood Verle and Edith.[4] You might know Edith would come home to a hurricane. Verle had <u>flown</u> in the day before from San Francisco, where he had gone to receive the Croix de Guerre. Planes were grounded at Tampa, but his pilot was an overseas one of high enough rank not to be subject to orders, so the

---

1 Hurricane Nine of the 1945 hurricane season made landfall at Homestead, Florida, on 15 September as a Category 4 storm. It moved up the center of the state back into the Atlantic Ocean near St. Augustine and made a second landfall near Savannah, Georgia. Nearly thirty people were killed and more than 1,600 homes were destroyed in addition to other significant damage.
2 Idella Parker.
3 Castle Warden Hotel.
4 Verle Pope and Edith Pope.

fools flew on to Jacksonville. I got into a pair of Norton's pajamas and they brought up drinks and supper to the room, where Moe ate everybody's crackers and pie-crust. The next morning was gorgeous and we came on to the cottage, though water was still deep on parts of the road. Power had been off in town, and didn't come on at the beach until Monday night [17 September].

When I got to the Creek, I found that Little Will, Martha's son who had worked for me before, was back and was anxious to stay. He has a new wife[1] of whom Martha approves and she was willing to stay, too. Little Will professed to be shocked at the way things had run down and already had the yard in wonderful order and the garden ready for planting. The comfort of the Creek, with Idella and a good man both there, is irresistible, so I shall think up some excuse for moving over for the winter. I may have written you that Norton has a charming nephew[2] who has been in the Pacific several years and who is on his way home and will go into the hotel as manager. That should mean freedom for Norton.

I also may have written you that I have an architect working on enlarging the cottage, so that I can stay in the winter if I want to. I am buying another 100 feet to the north, to protect me, and may put a large studio work-room and another bathroom there, or I am turning the terrace into a glassed-in dining-room, and I may put a new room and bath on the south end of that. I have plenty of land in that direction, and the architect thinks he can do more that way in making the exterior attractive, instead of being just a long narrow yellow box. He may use some other material, coquina perhaps.

I don't know yet whether I can make it to New York this fall or winter. It depends partly on whether Norton can go, and partly on my finances. Doing the cottage will be expensive, and I am having to pay Little Will high wages, I am building a new tenant house with bathroom etc. (we expect to get an electric line at the Creek this winter) and I am probably buying a house for Aunt Ida,[3] so with nothing coming in except occasional light royalties, I may want to economize. If I do go to New York I shall buy a fur coat and have Bonwit Teller's Salon de Couture[4] make up some of the

---

1   Perhaps Bettyrene, although no evidence has been found that she was married to "Little Will" Mickens (see *Love Letters* 455).

2   MKR is referring to George Baskin Jr., a veteran of World War II and the son of NSB's elder brother George (1896–1927). NSB also considered hiring his sister, Sara Pauline Baskin (1898–1984), as temporary help (see *Selected Letters* 274.).

3   Aunt Ida Tarrant.

4   Bonwit Teller: See MKR's letter on 5 May 1945.

evening dress materials Norton brought me from India, and it might be I'd find I had to live in the fur coat and evening dresses, which isn't awfully practical. Will let you know later.

Hope you got into the mountains with good weather.

Much love,

Marjorie

. . .

MKR to JSB, 20 October 1945. TLS, 4 pp. PM: OCT 22 [Rest of PM is torn away or illegible]. AD: Mrs. Thomas Bigham | 6 Chelsea Square | New York City 11. LH: MRS. NORTON BASKIN | ST. AUGUSTINE, FLORIDA.[1]

Angel, without combing the town, will you see if you can find me some quinces? Not too many, about 20 lbs.? Check enclosed. Use Castle Warden for express address if you find them.[2]

Crescent Beach

October 20, 1945

Dearest Julia:

I am <u>charmed</u> to have the wedding picture, and pleased that it is an informal rather than a studio one, both because the expression on your face is a true expression and not a fixation in aspic, and because it is apparently so good of Tom. Many thanks, and thanks, too, for the little pine pillow. It made me homesick for those mountains in the fall. The photo of yours seems to me as fine a study in light and shadow and pattern as any I have seen.

It looks now as though I sha'n't get to New York this fall. Norton is so tormented with the help problem in his hostelry that he can't leave, and I'd hate to leave him. He looks quite peaked. The latter catastrophe was when the sister of his very good female day clerk[3] went suddenly stark raving mad and was found lying in the middle of San Marco Avenue spitting at passing and puzzled autos. The mother has collapsed and Mrs. Wagner has had to leave the hotel and take over. So until a substitute can be found, Norton has to be

---

1 Written in a second hand on the envelope: Oct. 22, 1945.
2 MKR types this postscript above and to the right of the letterhead on p. 1. She also encircles the dates and letterhead to indicate she is at Crescent Beach, not St. Augustine.
3 Mrs. Wagner: First name: Not identified.

on the job 12 hours a day and 24 hours when Mr. Rawlins,[1] who has ceased to be a joke, just doesn't arrive for night duty. But things are improving and as of half an hour ago, he had adequate help in the kitchen and bar etc.

I decided that the book,[2] which was about a quarter along, was only a mill-stone around my neck, so one evening I tore it in shreds so small I couldn't change my mind and piece it together the next morning, and I feel definitely liberated. I have made a new start that is not quite so off-key. I've done endless short stories of a peculiar almost sadistic sort, most of them being refused by one and all, but one selling now and then, one to be in Town and Country and one in The New Yorker.[3] I think both of them might interest you.

Last week I "spoke" at a little country school near the Scrub country, the ages of the pupils ranging from 6 to 18, and with the addition of the village folk, up to 80. The Battle Hymn of the Republic was sung, the 23d Psalm read, the Lord's Prayer recited, the salute to the flag given, a hymn sung by the glee club, then MKR, then two little girls marched up to the platform in stiff terror and one thrust at me a bouquet of yellow wild flowers and said, "A gift from the school to friend and neighbor", and the other thrust at me a small wrapped package and said, "A gift from the speech club to the guest", and when I opened the package at home, it was a box of Daredevil Dusting Powder.[4]

Edith and Verle had Norton and me for dinner at the cottage at Ocean Manor.[5] When we arrived, rather late, we had a drink, and chatted, another drink, and with a sudden surprise, Edie said, "Oh, how long does it take to bake potatoes?" I asked how long had they already been in the oven, and it seemed they hadn't gone in yet. I said it took from 45 to 60 minutes according to size, she murmured that they were on the small side, so I said 45 would do. When they appeared on the table an hour later, they had originally been the size of golf balls and were now the size of walnuts, and were nothing but shell. The tomato aspic had a good flavor but was a bit fluid, and Edie said that she had made it that morning, and that afternoon she looked, and it hadn't set, and then she remembered she had forgotten to put in the gelatin. So she stirred the gelatin in and she guessed it hadn't had time enough to become solid. For dessert, she put on the table a large platter of brownies, supposed to last several days, and they were very good and we sat and ate them all. She was so pleased they were good, as they'd

---

1   Mr. Rawlins: First name: Not identified.

2   The manuscript of *The Sojourner*.

3   See MKR's letter on 8 July 1945, 342, n. 1. "Miss Moffatt Steps Out" was published in the *Liberty Magazine*, not in *Town and Country*. The one in the *New Yorker* is most likely "Miriam's Houses."

4   Dorothy Gray Dusting Powder, fragrance "Daredevil."

5   Ocean Manor, St. Augustine Beach, was owned by Verle Pope.

been in the oven about ten minutes when she remembered she hadn't put in the vanilla and the nuts, so she took the pans out and added the vanilla and the nuts and put them back. "It's surprising, too," she said, "because I noticed afterward that I'd mixed up two recipes on the Baker's chocolate[1] wrapper, and had part of the Brownie recipe and part of the chocolate cake recipe. Oh boy, I love to cook."

Norton remarked to me later that he could understand her new enthusiasm, as every dish must simply <u>amaze</u> Edie.

I think I wrote you that Little Will is back at the Creek, and with that encouragement I am having the farm-house painted. I think I wrote you too that I am adding to the cottage, another bathroom and dressing room beyond the big bedroom, turning the terrace into an all-glass dining-room, and beyond that a large studio work-room with fireplace and bathroom and high enough to have a useable over-hanging balcony on the ocean side. I'm using the native coquina rock for the additions, to try to take away from the yellow shoe-box effect of the cottage.

In the mail with your welcome gift, there came an <u>appalling</u> one; two immense scrap-books, bound in fine brown leather, with Marjorie Kinnan Rawlings in gilt letters an inch high---scrap-books about MKR.[2] One has a sequence of pictures of me, from the age of 4½ mos. to the 40's. Two of the old maid aunts[3] had spent years getting them together---. The one bright spot is that they included that Christian Science Monitor Interview, "Today's Woman",[4] and I shall certainly insert beside ^it^ my own "Yesterday's Woman", for my own satisfaction. The books are so bulky that I don't know where I can hide them where no one will come across them. Norton insists I should keep them on a table in the living room spread with Fred Francis' Pulitzer Prize Edition luncheon cloth.[5]

Do wish I could see you.

Much love,

<u>Marjorie</u>

---

1 Baker's Chocolate Company was founded in Dorchester, Massachusetts, in 1764, and purchased in 1927 by the Postum Cereal Company, which became General Foods in 1929.

2 The scrapbooks are now held in the MKR Collection at Smathers Library, University of Florida.

3 Grace Kinnan and Wilmer Kinnan, MKR's aunts who lived in Phoenix, Arizona.

4 Sarah Pfeiffer, "Only One Road to Success—says Marjorie Kinnan Rawlings." *Christian Science Monitor* (4 September 1940).

5 Fred Francis, together with his ex-wife Jean Francis who was a good friend of MKR, was an off-again, on-again friend whom MKR tolerated.

. . .

MKR to JSB, 20–21 November 1945. TLS, 2 pp. PM: HAWTHORN | NOV 20 | 2 PM | 1945 | FLA. AD: Mrs. Thomas Bigham | 6 Chelsea Square | New York City 11. LH: MARJORIE KINNAN RAWLINGS | HAWTHORN, FLORIDA.

Nov. 20, 1945

Dearest Julia:

A thousand thanks for bothering with the quinces. They arrived in perfect shape for jellying and I have a beautiful array of solidified rubies. Someone en route had ripped off part of the top and taken out perhaps six. I had enough for my purpose so didn't go to bat over it. But I am sure the thief thought they were choice apples, and how I'd have loved to have seen his face when he bit into one! Virtue is its own reward, and his sin was properly punished.

I have been in one of my jolly jams, so awful that I have howled with laughter. Idella had a serious operation a month ago and is out of the picture for another month.[1] I had a painter[2] coming to the Creek farmhouse, and we had to house-clean thoroughly ahead of him. Little Will is back with a young new wife[3] willing to work, and I expected to use her. She has had some sort of flu for two weeks. Old Martha and I have been doing it <u>all alone</u>. In the midst of it, the painter went away for ten days. Tomorrow the painter is bringing his wife to help me, not so much because he is touched by my unwonted activity, but because he suspects a man of courting his wife while he is away.[4]

My Oldsmobile has been giving all sorts of trouble, so that I have to be pushed two out of three starts. But I am supposed to have the first new Olds to reach Ocala.

Bert Cooper is seriously considering giving up the ministry. He is staying

---

1 Idella Parker.

2 Wilson, a painter and carpenter MKR employed, largely with regret because of his perpetual tardiness and absenteeism, "fretting and stewing all day," as she reports to NSB in a letter dated [19 November 1945], "as to whether the black painter of white walls would return at all" (*Love Letters* 450).

3 Fanny Mickens, whom MKR hoped would be a "stabilizing influence" on the otherwise wayward "Little Will" (*Love Letters* 466).

4 On (15? January 1946), MKR writes in exasperation to NSB: "Wilson, the painter and carpenter announced firmly to the Mickens that he would not return until after the holidays. It seems the sheriff for whom he is working now gave him permission to shoot the man hanging around his (Wilson's) wife, so Wilson can't pass up a chance like that . . ." (*Love Letters* 455).

in the Navy another year, and will reach Tokyo soon, and may possibly take up teaching as a career.

Next morning.

The painter's wife did not come. Oh well.

Chet Crosby's good country bird-dog, Buddy, was stolen a week ago. Chet is simply ill over it. And hunting season began yesterday. I want him to use Moe, quite selfishly wanting Moe's training completed, but Chet says he is always afraid of accidents when using someone else's dog.

I should be upset by the non-progress, to use a euphemism, of the book,[1] but somehow am not. There is some strange barrier between me and it, and one morning I'll wake up and it will be gone. The barrier, I mean and hope.

This sounds like one of your gloomy letters of old. Quinces and dogs stolen, car not running, book not being written, help not arriving, and pig won't jump over the stile and we won't get home <until> ^before^ morning. But just wait until the fire begins to burn the stick and the stick begins to beat the pig![2] The New Yorker took another story, and Liberty took one.[3] You will like the N.Y.-er one but not the other.

Bright spots in the blackness: three Pinocchio rosebushes are producing. How I have loved them, and thank you for introducing us. Turk's-cap and angel's-trumpet gorgeous. Well, can't leave Martha to hold the fort alone, so must go. So many thanks for sending us the quinces.

Lots of love,

Marjorie

. . .

JSB to MKR, 31 December 1945. ALS, 6 pp. PM: NEW YORK, N.Y. | JAN 1 | 10-PM. | 1946. AD: Mrs. Norton Baskin | Crescent Beach | St. Augustine | Florida. RA: J. Bigham | 6 Chelsea Sq. N.Y.C. 11. VIA AIR MAIL envelope.

---

1 The manuscript of *The Sojourner*.

2 MKR is alluding to a chain-folk tale, "The Old Woman and Her Pig," in which one event becomes the cause of the another until the situation is resolved. In this case, the Old Woman could not get her "pig to jump over the stile" until she unlocked a sequence of forces that eventually caused the pig to jump over the stile and settle in the sty.

3 "Miriam's Houses," *New Yorker* and "Miss Moffatt Steps Out," *Liberty Magazine*. See Tarr, *Bibliography*, C632 and C633. See also *Short Stories* 352–58, 359–67.

New Year's Eve[2]

Dearest Marge:

All the wonderful fruit arrived – and thanks ever so much from us both. Just as I was lamenting the lack of tangerines in the box of oranges a whole crate of tangerines arrived. And since then I think I have eaten even more tangerines than I did the last time I was at Cross Creek.

We sent you and Norton for Christmas a subscription to our favorite magazine which I hope you will enjoy as much as we do – also hope to hell you don't already have it! The best thing about it is it puts you on the track of many fascinating books that seem to have dropped out of sight. (And which are hard as hell to get, incidentally!)

I am also sending you a couple of my pictures.[3] I'm not enough of an artist to escape embarrassment at this gesture, but I feel you'd be interested to see them and I want very much to have you see them. Then although they don't represent much material value they represent a hell of a lot of work. I'm having an awful time deciding what to send you. One I am sure of – the picture of the old man which I took (with, I feel, no small amount of skill & cunning) while riding in the 3rd Ave. El.[4]

I've enjoyed your NYer stories very much, particularly the one about the little boy.[5] An amazing thing happened apropos an earlier story of yours the other day. T.[6] & I were talking about the recognizability of some clergymen ever without their round collars, and he said he had read a wonderful story <about> on the subject once, which he had always remembered and then proceeded to recite your story of the traveling preacher.[7] I knew it at once because I loved that story myself. He is now more than ever anxious to see you. Really, Marge, this separation is terrible – can't I begin to hope that you & N.[8] may come up in the Spring?

---

1   JSB inserts this postscript at the top of p 1. Edith Pope and Verle Pope.

2   Written in another hand below New Year's Eve: [12–31–45].

3   Not identified.

4   Third Avenue Elevated (aka Third Avenue EL or the Bronx EL), ran from Manhattan to the Bronx in various iterations from 1878 to 1975.

5   "Black Secret" involves a boy named "Dickie" who overhears a startling conversation between his mother and the town gossip that concludes that "all men are beasts." and prone to miscegenation (*Short Stories* 346).

6   Thomas Bigham.

7   "Jessamine Springs," a Freudian-laced story of the Reverend Pressiker, who is looking for male companionship, only to be rejected by a man who recognizes him as a preacher. Pressiker wonders aloud, "Now, how could he possibly know I was a preacher?" (*Short Stories* 325).

8   NSB.

I wish you would write me Bert Cooper's address. I have an awful guilty conscience about him. I wrote him when I became engaged. Thereafter got a couple of really bad letters from him about how awful T. was & how I was flinging pearls (JBS)[1] to a swine (TJB). I never did write him again – not out of fury, because I'm sure he was not in good shape at the time & no doubt regrets his lack of control, but just because I didn't get around to it at the time and then didn't have his address. I would like to tell him that my silence doesn't mean I never wish to speak to him again or hear his name mentioned as certainly must appear to be the case.

I hope you and N. are well. Your life must be quite hectic & exciting what with building additions to two homes. We live in a frenzied whirl. Tom has classes several nights a week and we tear our hair trying to fit social responsibilities into the other nights. To show the state I'm in I merely skip through the NYer & The New Republic. You know I used to read each from cover to cover – When you write I wish you'ld put in a sentence or two on how Henry James[2] strikes you. I've been reading a lot of his short novels & I don't know what to think. Most impressive critics say he's the greatest Am. writer. Of course he does write wonderfully well – so that until you think about it you don't notice how he writes at all. But I get so damned bored with his boring "half alive" upper class characters. Someone, I forget who, said that Daisy Miller[3] was the greatest – Well now wait & I'll see what the hell he <u>did</u> say – William Dean Howells said – "Never was any civilization offered a more precious tribute than that which a great artist paid ours in the character of Daisy Miller"[4] Ye gods! I may be having a blind spot, but the impression I get from James is the mediocrity of his view of life. His characters seem to live & die for awfully small potatoes and cold ones at that. "The Beast in the Jungle"[5] seems to be all of James in a nutshell. Is that sort of thing major? I got a fascinating little book for Christmas which celebrates this same tiny, vacuum-like, suffocating weltanschauung[6] – but

1 (JBS)—that is, Julia Bloodgood Scribner, JSB's maiden name.

2 Henry James (1843–1916), American ex-patriot novelist and critic, who celebrated the nuances between sophisticated Europe and innocent America.

3 James's novella, *Daisy Miller* (New York: Harper, 1879), a story of a coquettishly sly, but thoroughly American innocent Daisy Miller, whose world is brought into relief by her companion, the sophisticated European Frederick Winterbourne.

4 William Dean Howells (1837–1920), American novelist, editor, and critic.

5 James's short story, "The Beast in the Jungle" (1903), a psychological study of a self-despairing, self-indulgent, self-absorbed man who rejects passion, love, and marriage because he believes there is a "beast in the jungle," a revelatory event that will confirm his self-anointed "passion" that life is meaningless. Years of experiences prove him wrong, and he is left to emote on the grave of the woman he so artfully rejected.

6 Weltanschauung, a particular philosophy or view of the world held by an individual or group

so differently done. Perhaps in this case I lean from the purist to the sur-realist. But if I have to look at a dish of cold grey porrige ^(?)^ [*sic*] I rather like a bright red lobster claw stuck in the middle of it. This wonderful book is "The Metamorphosis" by Kafka.[1] Have you ever read any Kafka? Do get this if you can – if you can't I'll send it to you. T. & I are going to get his novel "The Castle".[2] But we were so done in by "The M." we're almost afraid to read it.

I must stop. Much love to you & N. & thanks a million for the fruit. Write me about James. Isn't my friend Aragon[3] getting recognition?

Love,

Julia

I expect to be dead by morning. We're eating a leg of venison for dinner & I'm sure it's bad!

. . .

MKR to JSB, 4 January 1946. TLS, 5 pp. PM: SAINT AUGUSTINE | JAN 8 | 3 PM | 1946 | FLA. AD: Mrs. Thomas Bigham | 6 Chelsea Square | New York City 11. LH: Marjorie Kinnan Rawlings | Hawthorn, Florida.

I do hope you have noticed that now I ALWAYS use the l.c. "l" for a one.[4]

Jan. 4, 1946

Dearest Julia:

My God, "What is your opinion of Henry James"!!! On second thought,

---

of individuals.

1 Franz Kafka (1883–1924), a German-speaking Bohemian novelist, who lived a life of loneliness and despair that was manifested in his writings, but with no more spectacular effect than in the novella *Die Verwandlung* [*The Metamorphosis*] (Leipzig: Wolff, 1915). Fraught with the language of disease and decay, the story spins a tale of a salesman Gregor Samsa who awakens to find himself transformed into a horrible bug. The reader is left to observe the bug scurrying through a life of Freudian denial and Marxist depersonalization, as he tries to survive in a world of homo sapiens determined to crush him, at least figuratively.

2 Kafka's *Das Schloss* [*The Castle*] (Munich: Wolff, 1926), a story about "K" who is first intrigued, then obsessed, then maddened by his efforts to get inside a castle, where he believes the "legislators of the town" reside in secret, determined to keep him at bay.

3 Louis Aragon, the Spanish novelist, who caught JSB's fancy. See JSB's letter on 8 August 1943, 204, n. 5.

4 Typed above the letterhead on p. 1. That MKR used the capital I for 1, as in I940 instead of 1940, was a source of irritation for JSB; see MKR's dating of her letters on 1 January 1941 and 16 July 1942.

a completely reasonable question. I haven't read him in years, but will try something of his again and give you an answer! At the moment, I have two distinct memories: one of involved and unattractive sentences and general stuffiness, the other of an utterly fascinating long story[1] whose title I have forgotten, but real people chased a ghost or <vie> ^vice^ versa through a house in some stage of construction or destruction. A room, or a door, that wasn't there, had something to do with it, and the long sentences used for this material had an enchanting impact.

We had a card from "Encore"[2] saying that the first copies would be delayed but would all eventually come. We look forward to having it, and many thanks.

In speaking of sending me some of your pictures, what do you mean, you're "not enough of an artist to escape embarrassment at this gesture"?? Count me out as an artist then, too.

I have visualized your coming across my New Yorker stories, knowing how thoroughly you usually read it, and thought, dear Heaven, Julia is going to pan this or that one. Much relieved that you have liked them. "Town and Country" is printing an awfully queer one in their March issue.[3] Would like to know what you think of it. (Embarrassment.)

I'm glad Bert Cooper's tirades didn't disturb you. He had every intention of offering you best wishes etc. I feel there is nothing really personal in his objections to Tom, that it is purely an unadmitted jealousy, as is quite natural. I thought I convinced him that being so far away, he had built you up into the dream-girl that every man overseas longs for (not meaning to imply that anybody is nuts who makes you his dream-girl) and that he wasn't as smitten as he later claimed. He had a chip on his shoulder about your family's way of life and general viewpoint, and told me after he last saw you, that he felt you had a touch of the taint of snobbery. I knew he was wrong about that, but I reminded him later, for his own peace of mind, that he had not thoroughly approved of you and yours, and was crazy to begin suddenly to

---

1   MKR's characterization of "long story" suggests she is referring to *The Turn of the Screw* (New York: Macmillan, 1898). However, there are other candidates, such as "The Ghostly Rental," *Scribner's Monthly* 12.5 (September 1876), where the presence or absence or illusion of doors is key to the frame-plot.

2   *Encore Magazine*, a compendium of old and new literary material "*Edited by the Staff of* The Saturday Review of literature." The January 1946 issue featured a diverse range of contributions that included, among several others, a short story by the contemporary American writer William Faulkner (1897–1962), "Dry September" (1931), and excerpts from a review by the Scottish biographer, historian, and essayist Thomas Carlyle (1795–1881), "Boswell's Life of Johnson" (1832), entitled "Boswell and His Book."

3   "Miss Moffatt Steps Out," appeared in *Liberty Magazine*, not in *Town and Country*.

grieve for you. I reminded him that he made no attempt to "make time" with you, before Tom entered the picture seriously.

Bert is a terribly lonely soul, understandably frustrated by the ascetic life, for which he is not fitted by temperament. I never knew a man more desperately in need of love and affection. God is theoretically enough, but unless a man is a St. Francis or a Paul,[1] he needs the manifestation of divine love in an earthly form. Bert, being sensitive, was shocked to his roots by the horrors of war, and especially, I think, by seeing human pettiness rampant in the midst of stark tragedy. All of these elements were back of his outbursts against your marriage. Do write him a kindly note, ignoring everything, for I think in the end he will prove a good friend to you and Tom both. He has a great gift for friendship. His address is just U.S.S. BOUNTIFUL, c/o Fleet Post Office, San Francisco. He was headed for Japan at last reports.

I am happy to note that marriage hasn't changed you at all. Your anxiety that the venison might be bad, sure, almost hoping, it was bad, was so typical. I presume as usual all was well, or I should have had a wire from your father,[2] or seen a sad item in the TIMES and TRIBUNE.[3]

Prospects for our getting to New York are poor. In desperation, I may come up alone, especially after the law-suit, which comes off the middle of February.[4]

I may have written you that Norton has taken a contract on running all of MARINELAND except the <qua> aquarium, expects to make a mint of money, and will be more tied down than ever. Douglas Burden, who heads the thing along with "Sonny" Whitney,[5] was at the Castle Warden and was terribly impressed with the atmosphere, good taste and good food, and

---

1 St. Francis of Assisi (1181?–1225), Founder of the Franciscan Order, known for his humility. St. Paul (4 bce?–c. 64–67 ad), leader of the first generation Christians, primarily through his preaching and his Epistles. Theologians argue that St. Paul is the most important figure in Christianity after Christ.

2 Charles Scribner III.

3 *New York Times* and *New York Herald Tribune.*

4 The lawsuit filed by Zelma Cason against MKR for invasion of privacy in *Cross Creek.*

5 Cornelius Vanderbilt "Sonny" Whitney (1899–1992), a businessman and investor, under secretary of commerce (1949–1950) in the Truman Administration, a principal founder of Marineland in 1938. William Douglas Burden 1898–1978), a naturalist, also a principal founder of Marineland, largely responsible for making it the world's first oceanarium. Whitney and Burden are further responsible for making Marineland, south of St Augustine, one of Florida's largest tourist attractions, made most famous by its dolphin shows and rental properties. NSB sold the Castle Warden Hotel and became the operator and the manager of the Dolphin Restaurant and Moby Dick Lounge. It was at the Dolphin Restaurant that MKR first encountered Ernest Hemingway and Martha Gellhorn together, in September 1940, when she invited them to her Crescent Beach home. MKR "liked

talked Norton into the Marineland thing. At any rate, when my books stop selling altogether, it will be nice to have a rich husband.

Edith[1] is working hard on her book.

I am still doing nothing but short stories, but will have to get into a long sustained job soon. Another book idea is tempting me, much more pleasing (to me) to do, than the ambitious project, and it is possible that it is the right thing after all.

Much love, and I shall give you a definitive estimate on James at any time---.

Marjorie

. . .

MKR to JSB, 22 February 1946. TLS, 2 pp. PM: CITRA | FEB | 24 | P.M. | 1946 | FLA. AD: Mrs. Thomas Bigham | 6 Chelsea Square /| New York City. LH: Marjorie Kinnan Rawlings | Hawthorn, Florida. Envelope stamped VIA AIR MAIL.

Cross Creek

Feb. 22, 1946

Dearest Julia:

I think your photographic studies are superb. The old man reading the newspaper, in that wonderful light, I like the best, the tree in the court-yard next, again with marvelous light and shade, and the building entrance---- down near Wall Street, isn't it---last; last only because the other two are so supremely good.

Also, Norton and I are enchanted with "Encore", of which we have had two issues.[2] The only thing as good that I have seen lately is the February "Atlantic Monthly", to which I hope you subscribe, and if you do not, I'll have it sent you.

Your esteemed parents[3] are stopping in St. Augustine at my husband's hostelry next Monday and Tuesday, and I have wired them asking them to arrive in time Monday for buffet supper at the cottage with the Popes,

---

Martha immensely" (*Max and Marjorie* 469). See Rodger L. Tarr, "Hemingway's Lost Friend: Norton S. Baskin," *Hemingway Review* 25.2 (Spring 2008): 136–39.

1   Edith Pope, *The Biggety Chameleon* (New York: Scribners, 1946), a children's book on manners.

2   See MKR's letter on 4 January 1946, thanking JSB for sending *Encore Magazine*.

3   Charles Scribner III and Vera Scribner stayed at the Castle Warden.

James Branch Cabells and the Owen D. Youngs.[1] At the time I wired them I didn't know whether the Youngs could be there, as they had a tentative date with that old bastard, Herbert Hoover,[2] but I said that surely they could spend one evening with all Democrats if necessary---and have had no answer. The Youngs WILL be there, informing me to that effect yesterday when they spent the day here at the Creek with me. Owen is that rare combination, a capitalist and an idealist, and when he showed me Herbie's last letter to him, between us we tore Herbie to pieces, agreeing on his lack of integrity.

A dreadful thing happened, which Owen thought most amusing, and Louise Young did not. They brought their young female police dog with them, in heat, and Moe got in through four open inches in the car window, and we heard the virgin's screams, and found Moe assailing her---whether successfully or not, only some weeks will tell. Owen said that if the worst had happened, they would wire me to come for the puppies, though he would like to keep one, as he was sure the combination would be brilliant.

Dr. Atchley was due to arrive in St. Augustine tomorrow, then Norton was to drive him to the Creek for the week-end, but a wire from Mrs. Atchley said he has pneumonia. He was to be on his way for a week or so with the Philip Barrys[3] at Hobe Sound.

Bob Camp has been by several times, is working on some murals he was supposed to have done before the war. Hope he will have his one-man show in New York soon, as he has some gorgeous stuff to exhibit.

The Creek is at its best, I have Idella[4] and also a good man on the place, orange trees in full bloom and do wish you were here. When do you and Tom take your vacation? Any chance of your coming now?

---

1   Edith Pope and Verle Pope. James Branch Cabell (1879–1958), American novelist, who later was instrumental in bringing MKR and Ellen Glasgow together, best known for *Jurgen* (New York: McBride, 1919), a provocative foray into fantasy and love in the Middle Ages, and Priscilla Shepherd Cabell (1879–1949). Owen D. Young and Louise Powis Young owned "Washington Oaks," once a plantation, now a state park, three miles south of Marineland. The Youngs were among MKR's best friends and were responsible for bringing her to Van Hornesville, New York, where she bought a home and spent the summers from 1947. Young was one of the most influential businessmen in the country, serving as chairman of the board of General Electric (GE), founder of Radio Corporation of America (RCA), and a diplomat for the U.S. government.

2   Herbert Hoover (1874–1964), conservative Republican president of the United States from 1929 to 1933, who was caught in the maelstrom of the Great Depression (1929) and its aftermath, and who was soundly defeated by the liberal Democratic candidate for president in 1932, Franklin D. Roosevelt.

3   Philip Barry, the dramatist. See MKR's letter on 8 July 1945. Hobe Sound, St. Martin County, Florida.

4   Idella Parker.

Love, and many thanks for the pictures and for "Encore".

Marjorie

. . .

MKR to JSB, 14 June 1946. TLS, 4 pp. Envelope is missing. LH:
MARJORIE KINNAN RAWLINGS | CROSS CREEK | HAWTHORN,
FLORIDA.

June 14, 1946

Dearest Julia:

I cannot tell you how happy it makes me to find you as gloomy as ever. As I think I wrote you once before, I was SO afraid that marriage might make you cheerful, and so, not yourself. Let me hasten to assure you that I won't be arriving at the time of your other guests, though I was sore tempted to announce that I should.[1]

I hope to God, now that the law suit is <u>apparently</u> through its worst stage, that I can forget it and get down to work on my book.[2] I am at Crescent Beach, and enjoying being here. There is no valid reason why I should not work.

You evidently have been out of touch with the suit, or you would have mentioned it. There was evidently almost nothing about ^it^ in papers outside of Florida, which amazed and dismayed me, for I thought they would get the implications, whereby if I lost this case, no writer would be safe from this old English common law charge of "invasion of privacy". Anyway, the suit, or trial, lasted all one week and two days of the next, and I was on the witness stand two solid days and parts of others. In case you have forgotten, or thought it had been settled, this was Zelma's suit for $100,000 for invasion of privacy. Her lawyers threw everything at me but the kitchen sink, and they ran the gamut of dirt and prejudice, from Jews, Yankees, "niggers", to Progress and Poverty,[3] and the sex life of my Mallards. I'll take that up point by point. They mis-quoted the Dreyfuss case ("Gentlem[en] of the jury, Dreyfuss was a Jew".)[4] Nothing would

---

1   From the context of this letter, there seems to be a JSB letter missing.

2   The manuscript of *The Sojourner*.

3   Perhaps a reference to Henry George (1839–1897), American economist, *Progress and Poverty* (San Francisco, CA: Hinton, 1879), an immensely popular work on the distribution of wealth that exerted an enormous influence on economic theory in the Twentieth Century.

4   The Dreyfus Case (*l'affaire Dreyfus*) brought into glaring light anti-Semitism in France at the end of the 19th and the beginning of the 20th centuries. Alfred Dreyfus (1859–1936), a Jew and a

do but that I was not only a Yankee, in spite of my two Kentucky slave-owning great-grandmothers and my Grandfather Kinnan's having been a Methodist preacher in South Carolina,[1] but a carpet-bagger, who "came down here" for the express purpose of being disagreeable. As to "niggers", "Gentlemen of the jury, it is exactly as though Joe Louis[2] had stalked into Gainesville and knocked down a private citizen, without provocation. He may have done it with great finesse, as we admit that this woman handles language beautifully, but is that any reason for the public to applaud such a malicious attack?" As to Progress and Poverty, "Gentlemen of the jury, is there to be one law for the rich and famous, and another law for the poor and humble?" As to the sex-life of my Mallards, and other breeding habits of animals noted by me, and as to colored Adrenna's being "shingle-butted"[3] and having a fatal appeal, that all meant that I had deliberately interpolated "lewd, vulgar, lascivious and salacious" passages for the sole purpose of assuring a wide sale for "Cross Creek".

On the other side of it, we kept the thing on as high a plane as possible, and it was not wasted on the jury. Zelma not only lied like hell on the stand, as did her only three witnesses, but she was belligerent, and made it clear that if there was any "malice" in this, it was all on her side. They were suing for "punitive" damages, for "malice", in addition to the $100,000 for invasion of privacy. (I was obliged to tell her from the witness stand my net worth, which Norton and my lawyer and I finally figured out to be $124,000, which includes my grove, everything of any sort that I have.) Since there were 121 named characters in "Cross Creek", many of whom occupied infinitely more space in the book than Zelma, and were named by their full names to boot, as against her first name only, I could easily have been left owing more money than is in the Florida State Treasury.

I'll have to see you to give you all the details. One amusing thing happened. I soon realized, under cross-examination, that I could not possibly

---

captain in the French Army, was convicted of selling secrets to the German government. He was committed to prison at Devil's Island, French Guiana, in 1894. Five years later new evidence was discovered that would exonerate Dreyfus. A retrial was ordered, but once again he was convicted. In 1906 he was pardoned and restored to the rank of major in the French Army. He served in World War I.

1   Asahel Simeon Kinnan (1832–1882) was a minister, but according to the *U.S. Civil War Draft Records: 1863–1865*, he was living in Ohio when he was drafted into the Army of the North on 1 July 1863.

2   Joe Lewis Barrow (1914–1981), the celebrated boxer and Heavy Weight Champion from 1937 to 1949.

3   In *Cross Creek*, MKR describes Adrenna Mickens as a "lean angular creature" who was "shingle-butted, but what there was of butt stuck out sharply. She was a *femme fatale*" (22).

be hurt, and I began to enjoy it and to more or less "take over". Zelma's law-yer[1] asked me some idiotic question, and I said, "Now do you mean so and so, in which case the answer would be one thing, or do you mean this and that, in which case the answer would be something quite different", and so on. He floundered around, and finally my lawyer jumped up, and perfectly dead-pan, said, "Mr. Walton, what are you doing?" Zelma's lawyer said most plaintively, "I'm answering her question." And my lawyer[2] said soothingly, "Mr. Walton, you don't have to answer her question. She has no right to ask you questions." The Judge[3] almost had hysterics.

Well anyway, the jury rendered a verdict for me of "Not Guilty" in very short order. Now Zelma's lawyers have filed a motion for a new trial. We think the Judge will deny this, and the opposition will probably appeal to the Florida Supreme Court. My lawyer thinks everything is all right. He had only been afraid of having an illiterate jury. The motion for the new trial is based on 66 charges of error in the Judge's rulings, and my lawyer wrote me anent this, "When I showed the motion to my partner, I said that it was in-conceivable that even the most incompetent judge should make 66 mistakes sufficient to cause a new trial, and the zeal of Zelma's lawyers reminds me of Santayana's definition of a fanatic, 'a person who re-doubles his efforts after he has lost sight of his purpose.'"[4]

Bert Cooper has just married a girl he had cared for a long time ago.[5] She comes of an extremely wealthy family, and that is the one thing that worries him. He is just back from Japan, as a matter of fact walked into the trial and when I ran to embrace him roared out, "Marge, what are these sons of bitches doing to you?" and insisted on being called to testify, to the effect that he had prescribed "Cross Creek" as a cure for homesickness for Southern men. Some of his Navy friends in Hawaii sent him by plane 100 orchids, in time for the florist to make them up for the wedding, and Bert wrote me, "Here I am with a black-Susan capital and a milk-weed

---

1   Zelma Cason's principal lawyers were J. V. [Joseph Vertrees] Walton (1884–1963) from Palatka, Florida, and his daughter, Kate Walton (1913–1985) who was graduated from the University of Florida Law School in 1936.

2   Philip Stockton May Sr. (1891–1975).

3   John A. H. Murphree (1904–1987), appointed Florida circuit judge in 1943.

4   George Santayana, *The Life of Reason* (New York: Scribners, 1906): 13, asserts, fanaticism is "redoubling your effort when you have forgotten your aim" (13).

5   Bertram Cooper and Constance Lang (1919–2009) were married on 7 June 1946 at St. Bar-tholomew's Church in New York. Her parents, Robert Lang (1892–1958) and Clara Batterman Lang (1892–1993), lived in Southold, Long Island, New York. The source of the family's money is uniden-tified. Cooper had performed the marriage ceremony for Connie's sister Mary in September 1945 in the same church.

income---and a hundred orchids." He is retiring from the ministry and will get his Ph.D. at Columbia, to go into teaching. He and Constance (I forget her last name) may come down some time this summer. They are honeymooning at Nantucket.

I shall certainly get to New York within the year, perhaps in the fall, preferably after the ballet opens. God, I'd love to have seen the Old Vic repertoire.[1]

Please send me copies of any of your prints that you like especially.

Much love, and when are you and Tom coming to Florida???????

Marjorie

. . .

JSB to MKR [Late July–Early August 1946]. ALS, 3 pp. PM: FAR [HILLS] | [envelope torn] | N.[J.]. AD: Mrs. Norton Baskin | Crescent Beach | St Augustine | Florida.[2]

[Late July–Early August 1946][3]

Dearest Marjorie –

I acknowledge with shame that my lapse of correspondence is even worse than usual. But not entirely without reason this time. The fact is that I am with child,[4] (though by no means 'great' as yet), and am in an acute state of mal de mer[5] all my waking hours and spend most of my sleeping hours dreaming about how sick I am! The depths & heights and breadth[6] of my nausea are quite beyond description, and I certainly would never wish you might feel them, so better leave it uncomprehended. Fortunately for womankind it seems comparatively few get in for it on this scale.

You can well imagine then an effort of will such as writing a letter is almost beyond me. I try to persuade myself that if I don't occasionally add a link to the bonds of friendship my friends will all slip away, but this

---

1   London's Old Vic Theatre brought Shakespeare's *Henry IV*, starring Ralph Richardson (1902–1983) as Falstaff, to New York in May for six weeks.

2   Written in a second hand on the envelope: [during trial].

3   This dating is based on MKR's response to the news of the pregnancy in the letter dated 8 August 1946.

4   Hildreth Bigham (McCarthy, MD), the Bighams' daughter, was born on 1 April 1947.

5   *Mal de mere*: French for "seasickness."

6   JSB is echoing the words of Elizabeth Barrett Browning (1806–1861) from Sonnet 43, "How Do I Love Thee?" from *Sonnets from the Portuguese* (1850): "I love thee to the depth and breadth and height / My soul can reach" (ll. 2–3).

argument is not too effective because I'm so apt to find myself in a mood of not caring if my friends slip away to hell and back. So Marjorie dear, if you find me not caring about you with the old fervor you will understand, I trust, that it is a purely physiological state. For the time being those noble organisms of mind and spirit are quite subdued by that ignoble organ, the stomach.

I was most interested in your account of the trial,[1] and when Edith[2] was with us I made her tell several times over all she knew. Also I read all the articles in the Miami Herald. I am most anxious to see the SRL[3] writeup [*sic*]. I don't get the SRL so I must call Scribners to find out if it has or when it will come out.

I was most distressed to learn from Edith that you had had a bit of the old gut trouble. I hope it was just the strain of the trial and that you are entirely ok now. Have you been able to settle down to work yet? Needless to say the very thought of work is quite beyond me at the moment.

Have you ever read a book of stories by Steen Steensen Blicher?[4] It was very quietly put out by the Princeton Press for the Am. Scandinavian Foundation or some such,[5] but it has a long forward by Sigrid Undset and I thought she might have sent it to you. If not I would like to lend it to you and I also would like to lend you "Speak to the Earth" by Vivienne de Watteville.[6] The latter is impossible to get in this country. It is full of wonderful things about animals and living out in the wilds of Africa.

I must try to eat now – Love to Norton and very much of same to yourself.

Julia

---

1   The "Cross Creek" libel trial, which MKR recounts in detail in her letter on 14 June 1946.
2   Edith Pope.
3   SRL: *Saturday Review of Literature*.
4   Steen Steensen Blitcher (1782–1848), Danish poet and short fiction writer, *Twelve Stories*. Trans. Hanna Astrup Larsen (1873–1945), and editor of the *American-Scandinavian Review*. Intro. Sigrid Undset (Princeton: Princeton UP, 1945).
5   The American-Scandinavian Foundation, founded in 1910 to promote cultural and educational exchanges between the United States and Denmark, Finland, Iceland, Norway, and Sweden, was located at 116 E. 64th St., New York City.
6   Vivienne de Watteville (1900–1957), British travel writer, *Speak to the Earth: Wanderings and Reflections Among Elephants and Mountains*. Preface by Edith Wharton (1862–1937), published (London: Methuen, 1936), a book about East Africa.

. . .

MKR to JSB, 8 August 1946. TLS, 3 pp. PM is torn:
HAW[THORN] | A[UG] | 2 [P.M.] | F[LA.]. AD: Mrs. Thomas
Bigham | <General Theological Seminary> / <6 Chelsea Square>
/ <New York City>. Redirect AD in second hand: c/o Mr.
Charles Scribner | Far Hills | N.J. MKR writes at top of envelope:
Air Mail. LH: MARJORIE KINNAN RAWLINGS | CROSS CREEK |
HAWTHORN, FLORIDA[1]

Crescent Beach
St. Augustine

Aug. 8, 1946

Dearest Julia:

I am torn between joy about the baby, and distress that it is taking so
much out of you.[2] Literally, I presume. I am surprised that your doctor cannot control the nausea, as a Doctor uncle[3] of mine, years ago, told me that
no woman need be unduly nauseated by pregnancy. To cheer you up, a niece
of Norton's[4] was dreadfully nauseated the first three months, then came out
of it nicely and has had no trouble since. I do think that as the weeks go by,
you will settle down.

It is too late for me to attempt motherhood, as the removal of my uterus at
Medical Center[5] in 1943 ended all hope of it. So save your prayers. However,
a Greek youth of 20 wrote me from Athens, having decided, idiotically, from
reading "Cross Creek", that I was a sympathetic and kind person, and asked
me to take him on.[6] I inquired of Idella[7] whether we should accept a Greek,
twenty years old, and she said, "How old?"-----------!!!!!

I am so excited about the baby. Will it be a boy or a girl? Will it be an aesthete, an intellectual, a scientist, or, God forbid, a business man or woman?
Will it derive from your father or your mother,[8] from you or from Tom, or

---

1   Written in a second hand on the envelope: Aug. 12 / 1946. This mailing date is speculation.
2   See JSB's letter on her pregnancy, dated [late July–early August 1946].
3   Perhaps Clarence A. Traphagen (1871–1925).
4   NSB's niece is not identified.
5   Harkness Pavilion.
6   Not identified.
7   Idella Parker.
8   Charles Scribner III; Vera Scribner.

from long forgotten chromosomes and genes far back in our past? You must be pondering endlessly about the potentialities.

Bert Cooper and his bride have been spending two weeks in Florida with Norton and me, and we have enjoyed them to no end. Connie's family is a wealthy one, from some place on Long Island, I forget where---oh now I remember---at Southold, at or near Orient Point. Connie is perfectly darling.[1]

Well, today I pass the half-century mark, as James Branch Cabell reminded me, in dedicating his new book to me, "There Were Two Pirates".[2] When Norton said "Happy Birthday" to me this morning, I said, "I don't think I can stand <another> another fifty years, I think it would kill me."

Now please keep me in touch with Bigham Jr., whether she or he, for I understand that after a certain period, sex and so on can be determined. And may I be Godmother?[3]

Don't worry about losing friends and influencing doctors. Just write me when you feel you can, for you know how much I love you.

Marjorie

.   .   .

MKR to JSB, 22 September 1946. TLS, 5 pp. PM: BLOWING ROCK | SEP23 | 2 PM | 1946 | N.C. LH: Marjorie Kinnan Rawlings | Cross Creek | Hawthorn, Florida.

Give my love to Dr. Atchley![4]

Box 335
Blowing Rock, N.C.

Sept. 22, 1946

Dearest Julia:

---

1   See MKR's letter on 14 June 1946.

2   James Branch Cabell, *There Were Two Pirates* (New York: Farrar, Straus, 1946).

3   In a missing letter, confirmed within the context of MKR's letters, JSB apparently wrote that she was "thrilled" that MKR wanted to be a godmother. Previously, on 24 September MKR writes to NSB the following: "She [JSB] simply floored me by saying that she was thrilled that I wanted to be godmother. I had said no such thing, in fact, it had never occurred to me! But I wrote back that it would please me to no end, and would probably save hard feelings among all her many friends and relatives up there. She begged me to come to New York this fall" (*Love Letters* 478). The letter above confirms that MKR asked JSB. Just why MKR is being disingenuous with NSB is not so apparent.

4   MKR writes this message at the top of p. 1. Dr. Atchley was treating JSB during her pregnancy.

Norton forwarded your letter to me here.[1]

I can't tell you how sorry I am that you are going through such torment. The least you could do is produce a genius. Nothing else will be worth while---. If Dr. Damon[2] has given up on the hope of relief, all you can do is take it like a little man. I offer this one bright ray: Norton's niece-in-law went through a similar hell. The doctors said they had seldom had such a case of protracted and <u>continuous</u> nausea in pregnancy. It lasted four months, then cleared up entirely, and she is going through the last months in complete comfort.[3]

I am afraid that this experience, on top of your normal gloomy outlook, will make you the most cynical of mothers---. I feel guilty at being god-mother, when you have so many relatives and friends who will want to be, but it may save you an argument among them!

I hadn't heard a word about Edith's illness.[4] Norton hasn't seen them lately. She was working awfully hard, and probably over-did it.

I am not exactly "writing a movie", but it is dangerously close. M.G.M. bought my already-published story "A Mother in Mannville".[5] They wanted me to do a story for their damned dog, Lassie, and I refused, then it oc-curred to me how easily that particular story could be enlarged for the purpose. Pat[6] could just as well be a collie. They also wanted to use the boy who plays Jody[7] in the Yearling film, and the story seemed made to order. They agreed, and the first idea was that I do them a 50-page outline of what I had in mind, for $10,000. The producer came on from Hollywood to talk it over with me, and as we talked, I realized I might as well go the whole way and give them a complete story, in narrative form. It is to be at least 150 pages, and I get $30,000, whatever the results, if I finish within the

---

1 JSB's letter mentioned here seems to be missing. Note also that in the second paragraph MKR refers to being a godmother, which indicates that JSB has confirmed or has asked her in the missing letter. MKR refers to the letter in a letter to NSB on 24 September 1946, "I had a cheery letter from Julia, in spite of depressing news. Her nausea continues so extreme . . . [S]he becomes dehydrated and literally starved, and has to go to the hospital in an ambulance for intravenous feedings" (*Love Letters* 478).

2 Virgil Damon, MD, Harkness Pavilion.

3 Regarding nausea, MKR essentially repeats what she had written in her letter on 8 August 1946.

4 Edith Pope, another indication that a letter from JSB is missing.

5 "A Mother in Mannville," *Saturday Evening Post* 209 (12 December 1936): 7, 33. The story was adapted for film, *The Sun Comes Up* (1949), a musical starring Jeanette MacDonald and Lassie, produced by Robert Sisk (1903–1964). See Tarr, *Bibliography*, C602 and Appendix 2.2. MKR was hired by MGM to do the adaptation, but had little to do with the actual script, although she was given screen credit.

6 Pat, the pointer dog in the story.

7 Claude Jarman Jr. (b. 1934).

required time, and another $30,000 if and when they begin production. I also had to agree to give them two weeks more of time for revisions, either out there, or with the producer hanging around in Florida. I don't know which I will do. Carl Brandt[1] would prefer that I make them come to me, just for the sake of being high-hat. I am tempted to go out there, <for> so that I can see my brother,[2] and also my dearest college friend,[3] who lost her husband this summer. They were terribly in love and it was dreadful. That's just my Scotch blood popping up. It wouldn't kill me to pay my own expenses.

I thought at first the story might do to publish, as a juvenile, but it is utter trash, from a literary standpoint.[4]

Since the original story had a mountain setting, and I hadn't been here for ten years, I wanted to refresh my memory. Norton drove me up, with Moe and the cat, with no idea of where we would light. We were only on the road over-night, fortunately, for we found the only place within two hundred miles where we could have stayed with the animals. The tourist courts gave out when we hit South Carolina, and the hotels would not consider a dog AND a cat. About 7 o'clock at night, the hotel in Chester, S.C., remembered it had an apartment at the back of the hotel, ground floor, with a separate entrance, and they let us have that.

Blowing Rock is a sickening summer resort, but I knew the season would be about over, and we found just the right place immediately. The house is a mile out of town and has the most breath-taking view over miles and miles of valleys and mountains. It has all modern conveniences, electric stove, big Frigidaire, big fireplace, etc., and a bedroom and bathroom downstairs, which I assigned to Idella, and two bedrooms and bathroom upstairs. I use the bedroom with the same mountain view. Norton stayed three days and Idella arrived the day he had to leave. I hope he can come up another week when I am ready to come home. No one else can make out his pay-roll, be-

---

1   Carl Brandt, MKR's New York literary agent.

2   Arthur Kinnan Jr., MKR's brother, whom she was devoted to, but whose debts and personal problems she had to settle on a regular basis.

3   Beatrice Humiston "Bee" McNeil (1896–1982), a close friend and a classmate of MKR's at the University of Wisconsin, whose spouse, William Grant McNeil (1900–1946), had just died.

4   MKR expanded "A Mother in Mannville" and gave it the new title "Mountain Prelude," which was published as a serial in the *Saturday Evening Post* (April–May 1947). At another juncture, with the encouragement of her agents Brandt and Brandt, the story was retitled *A Family for Jock* and offered with assurances of expansion to Scribners for publication as a novel. In a letter to MKR on 7 November 1946, Maxwell Perkins is blunt: "I do not think A Family for Jock should be published as a book. It isn't written as you would have written it had you intended it to be a book" (*Max and Marjorie* 599).

cause of the social security deductions etc., so he can only be away between a Monday and a Monday.

I would love to come to New York this fall, but don't know how it will work out. I understand the hotel situation is beyond the pale, and I wouldn't dream of staying with you, in your condition. It would scare me to death to have you faint on me![1]

I do hope the nausea wears itself out, and it may.

I'll be here until the story is finished, at least three weeks, possibly longer.

The foliage is beginning to turn and it is beautiful, and the weather wonderful, even when it rains.

Much love,

Marjorie

. . .

MKR to JSB, 9 November 1946. TLS, 1 p. PM: SAINT AUGUSTINE | NOV 9 | 2³⁰ PM | 1946 | FLA. AD: Mrs. Thomas Bigham | 6 Chelsea Square | New York City. LH: MARJORIE KINNAN RAWLINGS | <CROSS CREEK> | <HAWTHORN,> FLORIDA.

Crescent Beach
St. Augustine[2]

Nov. 9, 1946.

Dearest Julia:

A hurried note to say that it does seem likely that I shall be coming to New York, and shortly.[3]

I finished the story for MGM,[4] and Carl Brandt and MGM are starry-eyed

---

1   MKR did go to New York in late November and stayed at the Waldorf-Astoria Hotel, where she met MGM producers, perhaps with Robert Sisk, the producer, although that is not clear. On 1 December 1946, she writes to NSB that she "must bathe and dress to go to Mrs. Scribner's," which would be JSB's grandmother, Louise Flagg Scribner, who lived in the city. She then adds, "Am having dinner Thursday [5 December] with Charlie and Vera," JSB's parents (*Love Letters* 483). Curiously, JSB is not mentioned, although it is entirely possible that she came to Mrs. Scribner's to meet with MKR and/or attended the dinner with her parents.

2   MKR types to the right of the letterhead the Crescent Beach address on p. 1.

3   MKR arrived in New York in the last week of November. See unpublished letters, Special Collections, University of Florida and *Love Letters* 482–83.

4   The adaptation of "A Mother in Mannville" and "Mountain Prelude," finally entitled by MGM *The Sun Comes Up* (1949), a drama/musical, starring Jeanette MacDonald, Lloyd Nolan, Claude Jarman Jr., and Lassie. The film was a huge success, grossing nearly $2 million. MKR is given film

over it, which is sufficient guarantee that it has no literary quality at all, and that Max Perkins will agree with me that it cannot possibly be published in book form.[1]

I think I wrote you that I promised two weeks of revision, with a choice between going to Hollywood and having the producer come here again. He phoned me from California last night, and gave me the alternative of meeting him in New York for the work, and I said that off-hand, I believed I preferred that. They want very few changes, nothing important, and with all expenses paid, and probably being put up in style, it seems a fine chance to see you, meet Tom, see Dr. Atchley, and perhaps get in some ballet and theatre. By seeing Dr. Atchley, I mean only socially and personally, for I am very well indeed.

He [Dr. Atchley] wrote me how distressed he was about your nausea, but did say that it was nothing beyond the normal. I know that you are certain that no one has ever suffered as you have, so this probably will not please you. I'm hoping you are feeling more comfortable now.

I'll let you know if and when this is definite, and where I'll be.[2]

Much love,

Marjorie

. . .

MKR to JSB, 6 January 1947. TLS, 4pp. PM is missing. AD: Mrs. Thomas Bigham | 6 Chelsea Square | New York City 11.[3] LH: Marjorie Kinnan Rawlings | cross creek | hawthorn, florida.

Jan. 6, 1947

Dearest Julia:

That <u>marvelous</u> mince-meat! Your shopping proclivities really get results. I never had any so good. Many thanks indeed.

We celebrated our Christmas with dinner on Christmas Eve, as Norton

---

credit, but the plot is changed dramatically to suit MacDonald's musical talents. See Tarr, *Bibliography*, 268. Carl Brandt: MKR's literary agent. See also MKR's letter on 22 September 1946, 366, n. 5.

1 Perkins did agree and she subsequently abandoned the project. See MKR's letter on 22 September 1946 for Perkins's evaluation, 367–68, n. 8.

2 MKR stayed at the Waldorf-Astoria Hotel at MGM's expense.

3 There is no PM or stamp on the envelope. Written in a second hand on the envelope: Jan - 47.

had to go back Christmas.[1] I took Aunt Ida[2] over with me, and invited Bob Camp's mother and grandmother.[3] We had a quiet but pleasant time, Aunt Ida getting more kick out of her glass of sherry than I would <????> ^out^ of a magnum of champagne.

We've been having the weirdest time with the animals at the beach cottage. Moe had been going out several times in the night, just to get attention. Norton or I would groan and let him out, then just as we were dozing off again, he'd yip to come in, and one of us would groan and get up and let the bastard in. Also, a mother raccoon and two half-grown young ones have been coming each night to the rubbish pit to prowl, and I've had Idella put food for them. So when Moe can't think of anything else to do, he goes out to do some token barking at them. As Moe would go out, the cat[4] would come in, and as Moe would come in, the cat would go out---. Norton and I wondered why we felt dizzy in the morning---. A while ago, Moe fell in love, on a most temporary basis, with a horrible little female mongrel dog, with the head of a Skye terrier and the body of a rat. He would spend the nights out, then want to come back in about 5 in the morning.

I came back to the cottage from a few days at the Creek, and Norton announced that he had solved the problem. Each night he left the front door partly open, and propped open the screen door with a log of wood, so the procession could go in and out as it damn well chose. I asked what we'd do in the summer, because of mosquitoes, and he asked gloomily if I <u>had</u> to figure so far ahead, that sufficient unto the day was the relief thereof. I said OK, but God knew what else we could expect to come in the house, with his open door policy. Sure enough, this morning Moe's ghastly girl friend was asleep on a rug in the hall, and the raccoons had been on the porch just outside the front door. A few more nights, and I'm sure they'll come in, too. Norton says he doesn't even care, as long as he can catch up on his sleep.

The packing house didn't have tangerines at Christmas, but they were to pick mine last week, and I ordered a box sent you. I'm going to the Creek tomorrow for a week, and I'll try to pack myself a basket of the pale yellow ones you liked.

Had the architect in again to work on new plans for enlarging the cottage, but guess I'll end up with almost the original plans, though it's more money

---

1   NSB had to go back to Marineland to oversee the restaurant and the bar.
2   Aunt Ida Tarrant.
3   The maternal grandmother of Robert Camp Jr., Mary Jane Smith Anderson (1862–1953).
4   Benny, the cat.

than I wanted to put in. But I am too desperate for a dining-room, at least one more bathroom, and especially a studio work-room for me.

I enjoyed the Isabel Bolton book[1] and loaned it to Edith.[2] She said she'd mail it back to you, and I said I'd ask you first if you wanted it back. I wasn't sure whether you loaned or gave it to me. She is lending it meantime to James Branch Cabell, as she and I agree he needs to know more about women. A fascinating book, that couldn't help but interest you, is Anais Nin's "Ladders to Fire".[3]

I do hope you're feeling well and that the young Bigham is behaving.

Much love,

Marjorie

.   .   .

MKR to JSB, 15 February 1947. TLS, 2 pp. PM: SAINT AUGUSTINE | FEB 17 | 4 PM | 1947 | FLA. AD: Mrs. Thomas Bigham | 6 Chelsea Square | New York City 11. LH: MARJORIE KINNAN RAWLINGS | CROSS CREEK | HAWTHORN, FLORIDA.

Feb. 15, 1947

Dearest Julia:

I think of you so much these days, and must admit that I picture you as preceding yourself by a good two or three feet. I do hope you are feeling well. I can't wait to come up for the christening, and imagine you are a bit impatient, yourself!

I have been having my usual weird times, the latest being the entertaining at the Creek of THREE old maid aunts.[4] I was a nervous wreck when they left. They are bigoted, insensitive, and certain that they are omniscient. They know nothing of life, have no genuine human sympathy, and when they make what they consider profound remarks on international affairs, it is like three gnomes popping out from their holes under tree-roots to comment on the state of the human world.

---

1   Isabel Bolton [Mary Britton Miller] (1883–1973), *Do I Wake or Sleep* (New York: Scribners, 1946), an impressionistic style story of secret love set against the social intrigues of New York society.

2   Edith Pope.

3   Anaïs Nin [Angela Anaïs Nin y Culmell] (1903–1977), French-Cuban essayist, novelist, and short fiction writer, *Ladders to Fire* (New York: Dutton, 1946), a feminist view of living in a man's world.

4   Grace Kinnan, Marjorie Kinnan, and Wilmer Kinnan.

Have you ever read Alain Fournier's "The Wanderer"?[1] If not, you would probably not be interested at this moment in your life, for you are living in a state of complete reality, where the Fournier book deals with the hazy realm between reality and dreams. Fournier was a great admirer of Peguy,[2] a friend, too, I think.

I am moving to the Creek this week to get down to hard work. I have dilly-dallied long enough.

I see Edith Pope more often than anyone around St. Augustine, and she is well and just a little smug, being "the lady author" just enough to alarm me about the quality of her work-in-progress. Yet I do expect her to come up with a very fine book.

This is just to say Hello, and with all my love.

Marjorie

. . .

JSB to MKR, ALS, 4 pp. 26 February 1947. PM: NEW YORK, N.Y. | FEB 26 | 5³⁰ PM | 1947. AD: Mrs Norton Baskin | Cross Creek | Hawthorn | Florida. VIA AIR MAIL envelope.[3]

Dearest Marjorie –

Despite all the silence I have been thinking of you a great deal too, and intend daily to write. But this is a dreadfully vegetative condition and what little energy I have seems to devote itself to thinking up distractions to keep me from doing what I should do, I have even taken up crossword puzzles & crostics and you know what a poor opinion I used to have of them.

It's disgracefully late to even bring the subject up, but thanks so much for the wonderful oranges and tangerines. We both enjoyed them very much. Though I hid most I think. Tangerines make me very nostalgic, and I think of Cross Creek and quail shooting with Chet & Buddy,[4] and all my futile editorial work on "Robbery Under Arms"[5] and trying to keep Moe and his fleas home, etc and so on.

---

1 Alain-Fournier [Henri-Alban Fournier] (1886–1914), French writer killed in World War I near Verdun in 1914, *Le Grand Meaulnes* (1913), *The Wanderer*. Trans. Francoise Delisle (1886–1974 [Boston: Houghton Mifflin, 1928]), a novel about the machinations of a Romantic searching for the ever elusive ideal.

2 Charles Péguy, one of JSB's favorite philosophers.

3 Written in a second hand on the envelope: Scribner / Julia

4 Chet Crosby; Buddy, his bird dog.

5 Rolf Boldrewood, *Robbery Under Arms*, the work on the Australian bush. See JSB's letter on 18 April 1944, 261, n. 3.

My size at the moment would really impress you. I weigh 147 stripped or a good 35 lbs more than the normal. And it's all baby, as I am pleased to say I have not taken up swelling in the ankles or hands or any such. The discomfort at this point is formidable, though I guess one should be happy that one's insides operate so well when you consider how shoved around in a pile and generally mashed up they are. And all the joints in one's back and pelvis from the waist down are coming apart and they are very creaky and groany. Well it won't be long now, in theory just a bit more than 2 weeks.[1]

I am so delighted to know that you really will come up for the baptism.[2] We must find a time convenient for you. Isn't there something about that awful case[3] coming up again? The family are going away the first week in April for 18 days. Therefore we can't plan to have it before the very end of April or the beginning of May. I'm afraid if I've planned it before the family's trip I might be late in delivery and still unable to go up & down stairs or something dull like that. The Bighams[4] are coming in from Pittsburgh & Mr. B will officiate but they can come anytime at all as long as they know a couple of weeks in advance. So let me know how things stand with you as soon as you know. I suppose if the miserable case comes up there's no telling how long it will take. Well, we can just wait till its [sic] over and <that> then set a date a couple of weeks from then. By the way, I completely forgot to ask you when you were here – you have been baptized yourself, haven't you?

I am horrified by what you say about Edith.[5] I never noticed the slightest "lady-authorism" in her before, did you? I trust it is just a passing whim. All that she writes north about her book <was> is groans of agony, despair & defeat. Maybe you caught her in the throes of a reaction.

I am carefully saving all your recommendations of reading matter. Perhaps up in the hospital I'll feed my old intellectual self. At the moment I really can't concentrate on reading at all. I start a Dostoyevsky[6] novel and think

---

1   Hildreth Bigham was born on 1 April 1947.

2   MKR saw JSB when she came to New York to meet with Robert Sisk of MGM in late November 1946. Since there is no mention in the letters about coming to the baptism before this letter and in the context of JSB's query about MKR's own baptism in this letter, it is clear that the subject was brought up during MKR's visit.

3   The *Cross Creek* defamation lawsuit was now in appeal before the Florida Supreme Court.

4   Bigham's father, the Rev. Canon Thomas Bigham, was married to Ida Newell Bigham (1871–1955).

5   Edith Pope, whom MKR suggests in her letter on 15 February might be suffering from hubris because of her recent literary successes, which means that MKR is suffering from a slight case of envy.

6   Fyodor Dostoyevsky (1821–1881), Russian novelist essayist, journalist, part of the so-called Realist Movement.

it is simply superb & then never get around to finishing it. It's the damndest feeling. At this point I don't even finish detective stories if I drop them at all. I do hope this vegetablism[1] is just a temporary thing.

I am so glad to hear that you are at Cross Creek writing with both hands, so to speak. I guess it will be difficult to get into the old grind, but immensely satisfactory I should think.

I'm full of vague plans and efforts at plans for my future – besides being a mother. If only we have a little time when you're up here I shall tell you about them. If I only had a Cross Creek to take you to, but damn it, here you'll be in N.Y.C. surrounded by all your glamorous literary friends not fiends, friends![2]

Tom and I have had long and exhausting session of thought over the name for our offspring. It is now fairly settled that if a boy, he will be called Joel Kirkpatrick, a Bigham family name. The real rubs are if it is a girl. I would like to call her Louise after Granny & also Aunt Louise, but Muddy is so set that she should be named after her that that would cause an awful stink. I don't like the name Vera anyway, and that amount of pressure arouses every ounce of my resistance so that I just can't – won't. I am seriously considering Hildreth[3] which was Muddy's father's name and which I have always liked very much. How does it strike you? Of course the one thing which can never cause any argument is naming it after either Tom or me, but T. strongly disbelieves in naming children after parents. Oh dear, aren't families difficult, and now we're about to become one!

Much love,
Julia

P.S. Love to Norton. Is there any chance of him coming up too?
P.P.S. Of course you will be notified at once of any event. Should it be to Cross Creek?

· · ·

MKR to JSB, 2–4 March 1947. ALS-TLS, 3 pp. (pp. 1–2 holograph, p. 3 typed). PM: CITRA | MAR 5 | 10 AM | 1947 | FLA. AD: Mrs. Thomas Bigham | 6 Chelsea Square | New York City 11.

---

1   That is, living in a vegetative state, not the act of eating vegetables alone, hence "vegetablism."
2   JSB inserts an arrow pointing back before "not" because she fears from her penmanship that MKR might misread her first attempt at "friends."
3   Hildreth Kennedy Bloodgood (1861–1918), husband of Julia Clifford Casey (1865–1894) and father of Vera Gordon Bloodgood Scribner, mother of Julia Bloodgood Scribner Bigham.

At the cottage

March 2, 1947

Dearest Julia:—

This is a pretty kettle of fish. I have <u>not</u> been baptized.[1] My father[2] had an over-dose of Methodism, being the off-spring of several generations of fire-and-brimstone preachers, and left all formal church relations up to the later decisions of his son[3] and daughter, who took up no such relations.

Norton, who has been twice a god-father but never a father, says <yo> ^a god-parent^ promises all sorts of spiritual guarantees, and that I am automatically a pariah. I have never felt so crushed.

However, this impasse will make it possible for you to solve one more step among your friends, and to choose another god-mother in my place.

I can only say that I shall still think of myself as godmother, spiritual and in every way, to your child. If the House of Scribner should fall, and I should still have an orange grove; if the formal god-mothers should enter whore-houses, presumably disqualifying themselves; if anything in this uncertain world should ever give your child any need of me in any possible fashion, I should nurture it to the best of my ability with sustenance, with spiritual comfort and a passing on of the deep love I feel for you.

Now if Tom[4] suggests that it would still be possible for me to be baptized,

Back at the Creek[5]

March 4

continued

it would be impossible for me to decide quickly what formal affiliations I would want to make. So ask another friend instead, with my regrets and blessings.

I am surprised that Vera[6] should insist that a girl be named for her. It is Tom's and your child, so stand firm. I think "Hildreth" would be an enchanting name.

I do hope that your doctors have told you that being vegetative is the

---

1 See JSB's letter on 26 February 1947.
2 Arthur Frank Kinnan (1859–1913), husband of Ida May Traphagen (1868–1923); father and mother of MKR.
3 Arthur Houston Kinnan (1900–1961).
4 Bigham presumably would know as an Episcopal priest and Bible scholar.
5 MKR finishes the letter on her typewriter.
6 Vera Scribner, JSB's mother.

normal biological reaction to advanced pregnancy, designed as a protection to both mother and child. It is wonderful that with all that extra weight, you have not had any swelling of ankles etc. But what are you going to do, labor and bring forth a <u>mountain</u>?

I am writing your father,[1] and will ask him to wire me the arrival of the new Scribner-Bigham, with especial emphasis on <u>weight</u>.

And even though I am suddenly a leper, I shall come to see you as soon as possible.

I think I wrote you that Bert Cooper's extremely nice wife Connie is well along in pregnancy, and was in one of those Long Island wrecks. She had a brain concussion, but she and the child are all right.[2] Bert is now in their house at Chapel Hill, and she may have joined him by now.

I didn't have a chance to send you any of the pale yellow tangerines, as the first cold spell ruined them. The thicker-skinned oranges show some damage in my groves, but it is not extensive.

Much love, and I'll be thinking of you.

<u>Marjorie</u>

. . .

JSB to MKR, 23 March 1947. ALS, 6 pp. PM: NEW YORK, N.Y. | MAR25 | 2—AM | 1947. AD: Mrs. Norton Baskin | Crescent Beach | St. Augustine | Florida. VIA AIR MAIL envelope.[3]

Sunday [23 March 1947]

Dearest Marjorie –

You are no more disappointed than I am. I was looking forward so much to having you officially part of my family. But that is life, I suppose, and laws. I cannot say that the requirement that baptismal sponsors be baptized members of a church is really unjust or unreasonable, and yet in a broader sense I cannot feel myself that you would be any different if forces quite beyond your control, and if you were <u>very</u> little – perhaps outside your consciousness, had had you baptized at a tender age. But just such a technicality <yo> would make you legally eligible. That is part of the blindfolded quality of all laws, I guess. Even if you are not officially godmother I shall always think of you so. And I know my child will not receive any other christening gift to

---

1 Charles Scribner III.

2 Bertram Cleveland Cooper III was born on 15 June 1947.

3 Written in a second hand at the top of p.1: [3-25-47].

compare with your promise of moral and material support. I hope we will not have to take advantage of it, and equally that we will never forget to be deeply grateful for it.[1]

Another thing I am most disappointed about is that now you have no reason to come up. Marjorie, won't you, and Norton too, come up and visit us soon? It is such years since I have seen you and your movie visit[2] was so unsatisfactory. Why you only saw Tom <u>once</u> and then with a whole roomful of people. I wish you would come and stay right here. You really wouldn't be uncomfortable. And I don't think it would be too noisy as the baby will reside way down the hall. I shall pester you on this subject till I get a satisfactory answer.

Yesterday I had a phone call from Edith.[3] She says you are all getting discouraged. All I can say is just imagine how you would feel if you were carrying it! I now weigh 150[.][4] As this will be the 3rd week I really feel something will happen.[5] I am betting on my birthday on Wednesday![6]

Edith tells me Dr. Atchley is going to be staying with you this coming week. I am in despair to hear that he will be away. I was counting on him to come and celebrate with me if I feel fine and condole with me if I feel awful. Tell him to be sure to get back before I leave![7]

You wouldn't know me, Marge, I have become such a vegetable. And if I can nurse the child I guess I will be for as long as that continues. It is a most disconcerting feeling. I said to Tom the other night "It makes me <u>terribly</u> nervous to feel so relaxed!" He looked rather amused and said <he> he thought it would be quite fascinating to be my analyst! He has really been

---

1 Philosophically, much less practically, MKR was caught in the vise of Episcopal Canonical Law—that is, to be a godparent one must have acknowledged formally, through baptism, that Christ is the Redeemer, the Son of God. Not being baptized permanently excluded MKR, unless she were first to be baptized, from undertaking the responsibilities of a godparent, most important of which is to see that the child is raised a Christian. The hypocrisy of this canonical edict was not lost on JSB, hence her comment about the "blindfolded quality" of all laws, canonical law notwithstanding. What made this all the more hurtful to MKR was that she had already announced that she was to be the godmother, as in a letter to Maxwell Perkins on 13 February: "I have long tales to tell you, when I see you, which will probably be in April, if that is when Julia's baby is christened, when I will be a god-mother" (*Max and Marjorie* 603).

2 That is, when MKR visited with the MGM hierarchy in New York in November 1946 about the script of what finally became the film, *The Sun Comes Up*.

3 Edith Pope.

4 JSB underlines "150" three times.

5 JSB believed that she was already three weeks overdue. As it turned out, she had another week to wait. Baby Hildreth was born on 1 April.

6 26 March.

7 That is, leave the hospital after having given birth.

a rock in a weary land[1] through all the trials of pregnancy. I feel more and more selfcongratulatory [*sic*] about marrying him.

Well, I must drag my spread bones and my stretched skin off to bed, where I spend the night not exactly tossing, that's too light a word, but <u>heaving</u> to and fro, applying heat pads to various portions of my anatomy, downing bisodols[2] by the handful, rising and pacing the floor, reading detective stories, listening to all night radios shows and emiting [*sic*] groans of discomfort. Through all this T. sleeps like a top occassionally [*sic*] giving forth a few sympathetic noises in his sleep which is not so annoying as it sounds. It is rather a comfort to see <u>someone</u> asleep when the baby and myself are so wide awake and kicking.

I hope you will have a telegram from Tom <u>soon</u>.

And Marjorie, don't forget to plan to come and see us. Love to Norton and ever so much to yourself.

Julia

P.S. What's happened about the law suit?[3]

· · ·

MKR to JSB, 9 April 1947. TLS, 4 pp. PM: HAW[THORN] | [illegible] | 1947 | FLA. AD: Mrs. Thomas Bigham | 6 Chelsea Square | New York City 11. [MKR inserts above the AD]: <u>Air Mail</u>. LH: Mrs, Norton Baskin | <st. augustine,> Florida.[4]

Cross Creek
Hawthorn

April 9, 1947

Dearest Julia:

I've been hoping for a note from Dr. Atchley[5] before writing you, to know whether to toast your complete health or condole with you if you are not entirely recovered. Tom's wire said that you and the baby[6] were both doing

---

1 An allusion to Isaiah 32:2: "a man shall be . . . as the shadow of a great rock in a weary land."

2 Bisodol, a tablet to relieve stomach acid and dyspepsia.

3 The appeal of the *Cross Creek* lawsuit verdict, then before the Florida Supreme Court.

4 Written in a second hand on the envelope: April 9, / 1947. MKR excises St. Augustine and replaces it with the Cross Creek address and date on p 1.

5 Atchley had just returned from Florida after visiting with MKR.

6 Hildreth Bigham who was born on 1 April 1947.

well, but that was just a few hours after the birth. Dr. Atchley promised to write me all the details, but I can just see the poor little man <u>trotting</u> up and down those corridors on his return from Florida.

Eight pounds and eight ounces make "a mighty big chile", as Martha[1] remarked, but what I want to know, is what did you do with the other thirty pounds?

I went to the cottage[2] over the Easter week-end, and without Idella,[3] as she wanted to be at her home. Norton lately has just been having a large glass of orange juice for breakfast, but the first morning, catching me on my own, he allowed as how he'd eat breakfast with me. Well, the coffee was strong as lye, and when I tried to poach eggs, I made the most awful mess of it. Norton said, "Why, love, you can't cook, can you?" I decided I should have published the cook-book[4] under a pseudonym!

Verle was away, so I asked Edith[5] down for overnight, and we talked about eight solid hours. She is looking wonderfully, but agonizing over her book. The week before, she and I had gone to a revival of the Spanish Fiesta in St. Augustine. It was held on that charming little old narrow Aviles Street, and was all most engaging. The Spanish and Minorcan residents appeared in lovely old costumes, the children sang old Spanish songs and danced quaint little dances, and the booths along the street had such things as flowers, fromajardies,[6] fried shrimp, etc. Edith and I went to the children's puppet show, "Don Quixote",[7] and laughed ourselves sick. You would have loved it.

I finished the first draft of the child's story[8] for which Bob Camp has

---

1   Martha Mickens.

2   Crescent Beach, Florida.

3   Idella Parker.

4   *Cross Creek Cookery* (1942).

5   Verle Pope and Edith Pope.

6   From the French *fromageries*, "cheese shops."

7   Cervantes, *Don Quixote*. See JSB's letter on 18 April 1944, 263, n. 4.

8   *The Secret River* (New York: Scribners, 1955), published posthumously under the editorship of JSB. See Tarr, *Bibliography*, A9. The illustrations were not done by Robert Camp Jr., but by Leonard Weisgard (1916–2000), award-winning American book illustrator. MKR writes to Maxwell Perkins on 13 February 1947 about not using the Camp illustrations, "But if I do a book about a negro child in a creative way, that leaves out entirely the child's book for which Robert Camp has already done all the paintings and drawings, and I hate to let him down." Perkins then assures MKR in a letter on 25 February that "I believe you could write a sad and lovely story of a negro child. I don't see either why Robert Camp's pictures might not be adjusted to such a book." MKR sent the first draft to Perkins on 18 March. Perkins responded briefly on 28 March, finding it a "little story of great charm and delicacy," but in need of "considerable changes." On 31 March Perkins sent a long letter of evaluation saying that he liked the "quality of enchantment, the magical quality," but that the story should be "more realistic," the kind of "wild logic" found in *Alice and Wonderland*." In yet

already done lots of paintings and drawings. Max gave me one of his wonderful letters of criticism, and I am going at it again. I had done it halfway between reality and pure fantasy, and Max said to throw the emphasis on the realism, and to develop the whole story more. It's a job I'm really enjoying. Bob's stuff for it is stunning.

Chet Crosby sends his congratulations and kind regards. For three years he has said he was going to write you a letter. This, for him, is about the same sort of project as though you set out to pick my entire orange crop single-handed.

I wish I could walk in on you this beautiful morning with a bouquet from my country garden. The shabby little plot, more raggedy than ever, with only old Will[1] to take care of it, is producing tall snapdragon, fine stock, delphinium and larkspur, and a few roses. I'll soon have Pinnochios,[2] and then I'll be perfectly happy.

I'm sending you flowers when you get home. I know that your room must have been so filled that you yelled at the nurse to get the darn things <u>out</u>.

Hope you have a good nurse to take home with you for Hildreth.

I'll certainly come up to see you before too many months.

Meantime, all my love.

<u>Marjorie</u>

Give my love to Dr. Atchley.

.   .   .

MKR to JSB, 25 April 1947. ALS, 8 pp. PM: GAINESVILLE | APR 29 | 1947 | 3³⁰ PM | FLA. AD: Mrs. Thomas Bigham | 6 Chelsea Square | New York City 11. LH: Mrs. Norton S. Baskin | crescent beach, star route | st. augustine, florida.

April 25, 1947

Dearest Julia:—

---

another letter on 16 April, Perkins writes to say that Camp's picture of Calpurnia, the black child, was "wonderful, and others are very promising though some of them do run too far toward the grotesque." (*Max and Marjorie* 603–10). As always, MKR accepted Perkins's criticisms with aplomb. She had long revered him as an editor and as a man. These editorial insights on the manuscript were his last. Perkins died suddenly on 17 June 1947. MKR tried, but could never again work effectively on *The Secret River* without him. Fortunately, nearly a decade later, the ever-loyal JSB rescued the manuscript from the Scribner files and set forth to finish a project MKR could not.

1   William "Old Will" Mickens, husband of Martha Mickens.
2   Pinocchio, a type of tulip.

There may be a note from you at the Creek— I do hope so, though I don't see how you'll find time these days to write any letters. I have been at the cottage for ten days, as I wrecked my car.[1] I was not tight, but I was driving too fast under the circumstances, as it turned out. It was raining, and the road to the Creek had been <u>oiled</u> that morning, which I did not know, and could not have noticed because of the rain. Around a curve, we skidded, and turned over twice. Idella has two ribs cracked, I have nothing broken, but one side of my face, one hip and ankle and various other spots look like an artist's palette. Moe wasn't hurt at all.

One side of the car is nicely mashed in, but the Oldsmobile Co. in Ocala is going to let us have a new car by the middle of May. My insurance covers everything, even Idella's and my doctor and X-ray bills. We have agreed never to drive over 50 again. I had set her a bad example, and when she drove, she was hitting it up as fast as I had been doing.

Norton drove over and brought me here, though at the time I didn't think I was hurt at all, and I'm glad he did, as the next morning I couldn't <u>move</u>. The doctor said, "Well, the Lord just wasn't ready for you."

I have had a nice colored woman[2] helping me here. I am going back to the Creek next week, to Norton's utter disgust.

Two of my old maid aunts[3] were at Marineland for two days this week, leaving yesterday, and I am so depressed. (Not because they left, but because they came!) They consider themselves so spiritual and noble, and their standards are entirely worldly and revolting. One of them was lamenting the fact

---

1   MKR describes the accident in a letter to Norman Berg on 1 May 1947: "I went and wrecked my car, and Idella and I didn't miss the Grand March [Death March] by much. I'll hasten to add that I was only gloriously bruised and shaken up, while poor Idella, equally bruised, broke two ribs." MKR goes on to blame the road department for putting oil on the gravel and continues, "I owe somebody about forty feet of fencing and posts. And oh man, you should see the car!" (*Selected Letters* 294–95). Idella Parker's remembrance is considerably different. "When she had too much to drink, Mrs. Rawlings sometimes got it into her head that she wanted to drive somewhere." According to Parker, MKR "got mad at me and started cussing and storming about how I always had to be going to Reddick and so on. I could tell it was whiskey talking. . . . She grabbed the keys and stomped out to the car, shouting to me and Pat [the bird dog] to come on." Parker goes on to describe how "we careened along the sandy road toward Island Grove. . . . She was driving too fast, swerving all over because of the whiskey in her." On a curve the Oldsmobile flipped over twice. Parker then gives a blow-by-blow account of the wreck, followed by: ". . . I was hurt worse than she was." Dr. James Lawson Strange, the doctor in McIntosh, "patched up my broken ribs and said I was lucky my back wasn't broken. . . . 'You stay with that woman long enough,' he warned me, 'and she'll kill you'" (Parker 76–78). See JSB's very frank admonition about drinking and driving in her letter to MKR on 16 March 1944.

2   Annie Carter.

3   Grace Kinnan and Wilmer Kinnan, MKR's so-called Phoenix aunts.

that my brother has no son,[1] but said the name would not disappear, as she had located male Kinnan distant cousins. She said, "This nice part of it is, they are all extremely well-to-do."

I had them to lunch at the Cottage yesterday, and asked Edith Pope and Aunt Ida.[2] Edith saved my life, as they high-hatted Aunt Ida leaving her dumb, and I was too paralyzed with horror to say a word. Edith chatted gaily and kept things going.

When you stir out of the vegetative state, do read the new abridgment of Arnold J. Toynbee's "A Study of History."[3] It is hard, slow reading, and absolutely exciting and stimulating. It gives me a completely new perspective on the rise and fall of civilizations.

I did a stupid thing—sent an order to Constance Spry[4] for you, and asked them to phone to find out when you would be home—forgetting all about the strike.[5] But maybe you both have dial phones.

We are allowed to make any calls we want from Crescent Beach, as we are so far from town.

Hope all goes well with you and Hildreth.

Much love,

Marjorie

. . .

JSB to MKR, 6 May 1947. ALS, 6 pp. PM: NEW YORK, N.Y. | MAY 8. | 12 [P]M | 1947. AD: Mrs Norton Baskin | Cross Creek | Hawthorn | Florida. VIA AIR MAIL envelope.[6]

Love to Norton &
to Edith[7]

---

1   Arthur Houston Kinnan, MKR's endlessly struggling brother, had a son named Arthur Jeffrey Kinnan (1951–), and when her brother's financial situation later reached a nadir, the Baskins considered adopting Jeffrey, a plan that MKR finally considered unwise, not only for Jeffrey, but also for Arthur and his estranged wife, Grace Campbell Kinnan, not to mention MKR herself (see *Love Letters* 606–10).

2   Aunt Ida Tarrant.

3   Arnold Toynbee (1889–1975), *A Study of History*. 6 vols. (London: Oxford UP, 1934). Divides twenty-six civilizations and ranks their rise and fall upon what he calls challenge and response.

4   Creator of floral decorations.

5   The National Federation of Telephone Workers (NFTW), made up mostly of telephone operators, began a nationwide strike on 7 April 1947 over wages and working conditions. The strike lasted five weeks. However, some nonunion workers in NYC settled after twenty-three days.

6   Written in a second hand at the top of p. 1: [5-8-47].

7   Edith Pope.

Tuesday. [6 May 1947]

Dearest Marjorie –

The reason that you haven't heard from me lately is not that I haven't been writing letters, but that I've been writing so many I'm worn to a frazzle. Having a baby is almost as strenuous as getting married in the amount of correspondence it involves. I did get a most beautiful bunch of flowers from you when I returned home – white stock and pink carnations & blue iris. We called C. Spry[1] several times to find out who it was from and they finally dug up your letter. Many many thanks. It was wonderful having them after I got home instead of at the hospital where I was about buried in flowers.

Hildie[2] and I are doing OK. I am in despair over my weight! I am 15 lb. heavier than at the start of this adventure and can't get into a single of my old dresses! I am now undergoing the humiliation of having to wear a maternity dress. A week from today I see Damon[3] for the final time & I think I shall have to ask him to recommend a diet. An agonizing thought when I am enjoying food for the first time in nine months! Our daughter is as good as a baby could be. Her appetite & digestion are still perfect so she is very easy to take care of. She is really a fascinating little person – something new every day – they change so fast at this stage of their lives they make an adult feel awfully stuffy and static.

When do you think you would be able to come up and see us! I am all impatience to see you and show you what I've produced! Tom's entire family, mother, father, sister, brother-in-law & their baby[4] are coming on from Pittsburgh for Memorial Day weekend – but any time other than that would suit us fine.

I haven't started any work yet. Everyone told me I would feel rather peaked for a couple of months & I guess they are right. Also you would be surprised what a psychic shake up the whole affair is. Not that I have any strenuous post-natal depression or indeed any outward manifestations, but I dream lucid dreams and feel-well, just unable to get started at work or even at planning work.

I cannot say that I feel a bit like a parent. I feel just the same Julia and find it very hard to believe that I am responsible for the baby in the back room!

At first I felt just satisfaction that I had produced such a splendid healthy

---

1   Constance Spry, the floral decorator.
2   Hildreth, the baby girl.
3   Virgil Damon, MD.
4   In addition to his parents Ida and Thomas are Bigham's sister Mary Bigham Porter (1902–1991) and her husband George DeVore Porter (1905–1976). The baby is Marydee Porter (1945–).

specimen – then pride that she was such a <u>good</u> baby and so much admired & commended. It really wasn't till this last week or so that I began to feel affection for her as <u>herself</u> rather than just the general emotional response to the cuteness of babies – when they are cute. There has been no occasion to arouse my fierce protective mother instinct so I can't really tell you anything about that.

I have been so busy writing that I haven't done any reading except for Kilvert's <u>Diary</u>.[1] I am sure you haven't missed it, but if by any chance you have, do get it.

I must be off to bed – am still supposed to be up only 12 hrs a day.

How is <u>your</u> creative life? I am vastly relieved that you are completely whole physically – When I opened your letter and saw something about "car turned over" I galloped my eyes around the page to see what part of you was in plaster or stitched up! Hope Idella is feeling OK now.

You certainly have terrible "aunt trouble". I'ld like to see some of them sometime – how many are there anyway or are they the same ones that keep coming back?

Much love,

Julia

· · ·

MKR to JSB, 10 June 1947. TLS, 2 pp. PM: SAINT AUGUSTINE | JUN 10 | 4 PM | 1947 | FLA. AD: Mrs. Thomas Bigham | 6 Chelsea Square | New York City 11. LH: Marjorie Kinnan Rawlings | Cross Creek | Hawthorn, Florida.

June 10, 1947

Dearest Julia:

I tried to think of something useful or attractive for Hildreth,[2] and picturing your apartment piled high with bassinets, English perambulators, rattles, silver cups and lace bonnets, I gave up in despair and am sending a War bond, for you to use for her as you wish.

I am rushing around these days, so will make my news snappy. Idella never came back, as she got married.[3] She doesn't even like the man very

---

1   Robert Francis Kilvert (1840–1879), Herefordshire clergyman, famous for his *Diary* of life in the Wye Valley. See *Kilvert's Diary*. 3 vols. (London: Cape, 1938).

2   Hildreth Bigham, JSB's baby girl and first child.

3   Bernard Young. As Idella Parker later reports, Bernard said he would "take care of me, and that

well. I think she just wanted a go at being the lady of the house. I decided to kill a whole covey of birds with one stone, and am having the beach cottage enlarged--- a studio work-room and two more bathrooms. While that is being done, and probably for the whole summer, I am going to Van Hornesville, N.Y. Mr. and Mrs. Owen D. Young[1] insist on lending me one of their houses there,[2] near their own summer home. I plan to settle down to hard work on my book. The place will be ideal, just isolated enough, an attractive, small, old house, but modernized, and Mrs. Young is engaging a white woman[3] to come in every day and take care of me. I am really thrilled about it. Having the Youngs, <whome> to whom I am devoted, near by, will keep me from being too lonely while I work, for when the day's job is done, I often long for companionship.

Poor Norton is the goat. He will work with the architect, and when things get too tough at the cottage, will stay at Marineland. He has to be there anyway, as he has a new Chef[4] coming in a couple of weeks. He will drive me to Van Hornesville, and come back by train or 'plane. We could not stop in New York coming or going, as I will have Moe and Benny the cat with me.

However, I see no reason why I cannot either drive to New York, or take a train, while I am at Van H., if Bessie the white woman will take care of the animals while I am away. I shall settle down to buttering up Bessie. Then I can have a day or two with you, see Dr. Atchley, / ^(socially)^[5] and so on, see your mother and father and Max.[6]

I really expect to stay up there until October at least, especially if my work goes well.

I wouldn't have to work for 'that old woman' [MKR] any more, and his promises sounded wonderful to me" Parker adds, "I stuck it out and stayed with Bernard for seven long years, but it was never an ideal marriage. Knowing that I could never depend on Bernard, I went back to work for Mrs. Rawlings only a few weeks after I married him" (Parker 99, 101). In fact, after moving to Van Hornesville, New York, in June, MKR comments in a letter on 11 July to NSB, "I had a nice letter from Idella, and she said she longed to be here with me" (Love Letters 491).

1   Owen D. Young and Louise Young had a home in Van Hornesville, New York.

2   Brown's Hollow, a small farmhouse restored by Louise Young and occupied by MKR for the first two summers she spent in Van Hornesville.

3   Bessie, last name not identified.

4   NSB apparently fired Clarence M. Huston, his chef at the Castle Warden, who had moved with him to Marineland when he took over the management of the Dolphin restaurant. In a letter on 2 April 1946, MKR had already warned NSB that the food at the Dolphin is "not right. . . . Besides the poor quality, it is not served attractively. . . . It is the same old Castle Warden menu, of even lower quality, at a higher price." On 9 July 1947, MKR confirms her judgment, "I think it is grand that you are liberated from Mr. Huston. I know how painful the break was for you, but he had bullied and harassed you too long" (Love Letters 465, 490).

5   MKR inserts "(socially)" above "Dr. Atchley."

6   Dana Atchley, Charles Scribner III and Vera Scribner, and Maxwell Perkins.

Idella <talked to> called me on the 'phone last night (she is now living in St. Augustine---I am writing from Crescent Beach) and when I told her where I was going, she said she surely hated to have me leave her behind. She said "When you come back in the fall, perhaps I'll be settled." I shouldn't be at all surprised to have her rejoin me then.[1]

I'll keep you informed, and we can certainly get together somehow.

Much love,

<u>Marjorie</u>

We plan to leave next Monday June 16.[2]

. . .

JSB to MKR, 1 July 1947. ALS, 4 pp. PM: NEW YORK, N.Y. | JUL 3 | 8 - PM | 1947. AD: Mrs. Norton Baskin | c/o Owen D. Young | Van Hornesville | New York. LH (embossed): FAR HILLS. NEW JERSEY.

July 1 [1947]

Dearest Marjorie –

I am sitting in semi-darkness on the porch enjoying a wonderful storm. The air is so deliciously cool and wet after the past few days that I can't miss a moment of it. It reminds me of the time I wrote you during the 1944 hurricane though the elements are now merely sportive.[3]

There are so many things to write you – I know how awfully you must be feeling about Mr. Perkins death.[4] I have thought of you often since it happened. It was so sudden and shocking, but I thought it must be particularly cruel the way you got the news at the end of your long trip.[5] I really didn't know him at all – I talked with him very little – Mostly, in fact, about "How is Marjorie?" and "What have you heard from Marjorie?" I do wish I had

---

1   MKR left for Van Hornesville in mid-June of 1947. She return to Cross Creek in October. In a letter to Norman Berg on 4 November, MKR reports, "Idella [Parker] has come back to me, only because an opening for her husband [Bernard] unexpectedly came up at Norton's bar [at Marineland]. They will both live in the new nice garage apartment at the cottage [at Crescent Beach]" (*Selected Letters* 307).

2   The postscript is in MKR's hand.

3   See JSB's letter on 14 September 1944.

4   Maxwell Perkins died on 17 June 1947.

5   Charles Scribner III sent a telegram to MKR on 17 June 1947 informing her of the death of Perkins: "MAX DIED OF PNEUMONIA EARLY THIS MORNING AFTER TWO DAYS ILLNESS." The telegram was sent to Island Grove, Florida, and was resent on the same day: c/o of Mr. and Mrs. Owen D. Young | Van Hornesville, New York (*Max and Marjorie* 611).

known him, because I can't think of anyone who was more loved by all who did. I know Daddy is quite crushed by his loss. I think Mr. Perkins was really his dearest friend. It must seem hard to write now without his helpful and encouraging criticism to look forward to – but surely much of what he wrote you in the past was not just for the moment, and is continuingly inspiring as only he could be.

You are such a darling to send Hildie[1] that wonderful present. I shall put it away in her own special fund along with a present from her great-grandmother.[2] I now have a picture of her going off to Paris to study art or some such glamorous thing. What a vivid imagination mothers have! If I do say so myself she is a perfectly beguiling baby – I think you will be delighted with her.

Marjorie – please don't go home without spending a few unfrenzied days with us. I do want to see you for more than an hour at a time, and to have you really meet Tom. And, of course, you must have leisure to dandle Hildie on your knee and succumb to her subtle charms. We still have an unoccupied guestroom – the baby has not curtailed our hospitality – the next child will do that.

I hear through Daddy that you have a lovely place complete with trout stream. It sounds wonderful – I haven't been near a mountain for ages. I hope they will inspire you as they do me. The Youngs[3] must be awfully nice. I do wish you a happy and profitable summer. I can imagine how hard it has been settling into work with the damned lawsuit coming right on top of the war[4] and I hope this change of air will make the painful business of work easier. I am very tender-hearted and sympathetic about the difficulties of work now as I am trying myself to get onto the straight & narrow path which I found so happily back in '44 and strayed away from shortly before I got married. There are so many psychic complications that if I tried to write you about them I'd probably end up a writer instead of a photographer. I wouldn't be able to anyway as I am still pretty much in the midst of them – I hope by the time I see you I will be able to talk of some of the struggle in the past tense. There is no dodging the fact that this is one of the crucial battles of my life so far – if not the crucial one. And there is quite a gathering of neuroses to be worked through – old old ones – before I can free the energy that goes into them for satisfying creative work. Well, enough of the battleground of

---

1   Hildreth Bigham.
2   Louise Flagg Scribner.
3   Owen D. Young and Louise Young.
4   In May 1947, the Florida Supreme Court reversed a lower court ruling and found MKR guilty of "invasion of privacy." She was fined $1 and court costs on 14 August.

JSB – though as you know the typography pretty well you may be interested! As you can imagine, it is literally as well as figuratively a headache!

I have read two good books lately. One – <u>Christ Stopped at Eboli</u>[1] you shouldn't miss. The other, also about Italy, is <u>The Gallery</u> by John Horne Burns.[2] It is a war book – but practically no shooting – A really good book which has no need of the qualificative that it is a first novel. Martha Gelhorn[3] wrote Daddy about it – said it was a wonderful book why hadn't he published it? and he brought it home one night – That's how I happened on it, though I had read a very good review of it and did want to read it. I hope to have very little time for reading from now on, but I do want to read the book you told me of – by Alan Fournier (?).[4]

Tom is away at the moment reading a paper at a very learned and esoteric theological conference. I wanted to go because it promises to be interesting but what with the high cost of eating and of bearing and bringing up children it seemed economically sounder for me to stay here with the family. Marjorie, does it ever seem as incredible to you as it sometimes does to me that I have a daughter? Being married doesn't seem strange at all, but being a mother does – Maybe after a couple of years it will seem equally normal though perhaps always more complicated. Life would seem to prove that it is easier to treat a spouse as an individual than it is to accord the same right to a child.

Do take care of yourself – and drop me a line between chapters if you have the strength. Ever so many thanks to you from Hildreth & me –

Much love –

Julia

. . .

MKR to JSB, 17 July 1947. TLS, 1 p. Envelope is missing.

Van Hornesville, N.Y.

July 17, 1947

Dearest Julia:

---

1   Levi Carlo (1902–1975), Italian painter, writer, and activist, *Christ Stopped at Eboli* [*Cristo si è fermato a Eboli* (1945)], trans. Frances Frenaye ([1908–1996] New York: Farrar, Straus, 1947).

2   John Horne Burns (1916–1953), American writer, *The Gallery* (New York: Harper, 1947), about the Allied occupation of North Africa and Naples.

3   Martha Gellhorn, war correspondent and former wife of Ernest Hemingway.

4   Alain-Fournier, *The Wanderer*. See MKR's letter and 15 February 1947.

I have just bought the most enchanting old house up here,[1] circa 1800, exquisite lines, butternut-wood paneling, about eight acres of land, a magnificent view (on clear days you see one end of Otsego Lake,[2] James Fenimore Cooper's "Glimmer Glass"),[3] peonies, lilies of the valley, raspberry, currant, gooseberry bushes, apple orchard and so on.

I feel more at home here than at Cross Creek, and the second time I saw this place, I told Mr. and Mrs. Young I had to have it. They have managed to have it set aside when a nice young farming and dairy couple[4] bought the farms adjoining. The Young's have bought and restored many lovely old places around here. I also bought yesterday from the couple some old stuff in my house, antique beds, spinning wheel, etc.

I am afraid Norton is going to be rather upset, as he will picture me living here for the six summer months and at Cross Creek the six winter months! He is having the beach cottage enlarged while I am [a]way.

I plan to come to New York in September, but meantime, would you like to leave your cares and neuroses behind you and come up here for a week or so? I have an extra bedroom, all modern conveniences, a maid as often as I need her, and there are your sort of woods to walk in. How about it?[5]

---

1   MKR's fear is how will NSB react. In a letter on 24 July 1947, she approaches the purchase with certain trepidation: "I have bought a place up here! Now wait, now wait, until you hear about it." She then describes in detail the footprint of the house and points out, "I paid $1250 for the whole thing." (*Love Letters* 492). The legal purchase of the property took place on 10 July (*Selected Letters* 300).

2   Otsego Lake is the source of the Susquehanna River. Cooperstown, New York, is located on its southern end.

3   James Fenimore Cooper (1789–1851), noted for his historical romances of frontier life in America, referred to Otsego Lake as "Glimmerglass" in *The Deerslayer* (Philadelphia: Lea and Blanchard, 1841) .

4   Ellis Frederick and Lilian Frederick. MKR writes to NSB on 16 July, "The Fredericks and I are buddies already" (*Love Letters* 493).

5   MKR's invitation did not include JSB's husband, Tom, as she confesses to NSB in a letter on 2 August 1947: "I had written Julia Scribner 'to visit' and 'to my utter horror she replied, asking if by 'You' I meant her alone, or herself and Tom, if the latter, they could come from Aug. 8 to 13 inclusive." MKR admits, "I am terribly disappointed, and hope it still works out that Julia will come alone. It is hard for me to think of her as a pair" (*Love Letters* 497). Tom did, indeed, come with JSB, the two arriving later than expected on 11 August, but he returned by himself to New York on 14 August, when MKR writes to NSB: "Tom is really just as nice as can be, and I like him, and think he is really all right for Julia" (*Love Letters* 499). However, her impressions are different when she opines to Norman Berg on 22 August: "Julia Scribner and her husband spent a week with me. I like him, but am afraid I did your trick of arguing too vociferously . . . that if I were going to be a man of God, or give myself to the Church, I should go all out on it. His position is that 'the Church needs administrators as much as it needs saints.' This left me cold and I said so, and I don't think he likes me any more." He is "so High Church as to be almost Catholic, and it seems silly to me when he is not at all a mystic" (*Selected Letters* 302).

Love,

Marjorie

. . .

JSB to MKR, ALS 2 pp. [22 or 29 July 1947].[1] Envelope is missing.
Notebook paper is torn and severely browned.

Tuesday[2]

\<Monday>

Dearest Marjorie –

I am delighted to hear that you have become half-way a Yankee again.
The place sounds too good to be true! Like the "dream cottage" in a "woman's["] novel! Of course I am dying to see it. I can't be sure in your letter
whether 'you' is the 2nd person singular or second person plural, so will
you kindly be your frank self and tell me. If you mean me and Tom we
could come up between Thursdays – say arrive Fri the 8th of Aug and leave
Wed the 13th – if you mean me I could arrange to come up sometime when
Tom is away – he has to be away for 5 days sometime or another before
the [first?] of Sept – maybe he could work it for [that] same time. Now,
Marjorie, please don't have any qualms about being polite or wounding
our feelings to the core – if you don't want Tom just say so. We will both
understand quite comfortably if for either whimsical or practical reasons
you want me solo. In any case, if you are working (and Daddy[3] tells me you
are) I we will not speak to you between breakfast and the cocktail hour [il-
legible, MS torn]

We are leading a very quiet life and I can't think of any fascinating news
to tell you. This last weekend we visited Rossie Havemeyer[4] in Long Island.
This was our only social event of the summer and wasn't very interesting as
we had to go to several very large and very dull parties. I have always thought
Long Island was rather "stale flat and unprofitable" in every sense.

Both of us are mainly engaged with trying to get some work done – results

---

1 This undated letter is clearly written in response to MKR's letter on 17 July 1947, in which she
informs JSB that she has purchased a home in Van Hornesville, New York. JSB dates her letter
Tuesday, which means this letter was written on 22 or 29 July.
2 Written in a second hand at the top of p. 1: [c. 1947] / [Van Hornesville].
3 Charles Scribner III.
4 Rosalind Havemeyer (1917–2017) was graduated from Foxcroft School, and was at this time on
the board of Union Theological Seminary of New York.

so far most un-noteworthy. T. has two books to be put into shape for publication and two articles ditto, and a doctor's paper to write or at least plan and a certain amount of studying to do also.

I must be off now & develope [*sic*] a roll of film! Write me at Far Hills as we will be here for a couple of weeks more anyway.

I shall hope to see you soon –

Much love,

Julia

. . .

MKR to JSB, 1 August 1947. TLS, 2 pp. PM: origin is blurred | 142-159 | AUG 2 | 1947 | R.P.O. AD: Mrs. Thomas Bigham | c/o Charles Scribner | Far Hills / New Jersey.

Van Hornesville, N.Y.

August 1, 1947

Dearest Julia:

The "you" was second person singular, for the simple reason that it never occurred to me that Tom could get away for a week.[1] I pictured him as terribly busy day after day, and you longing for country walks and trees, day after day, and thought you might like to shed domesticity for a bit.

Now the invitation certainly holds good for both of you, or for you alone, just according to what appeals to you (plural). There is no "mystical" reason for not including Tom, though there is one most practical aspect of which it is only fair to warn you. I have hot water and all that sort of thing, but the bath-tub is a Sitz bath! I wrote a nasty little essay entitled "The History and Use of the Sitz Bath", for a most exclusive publication put out (by hand) twice a year by one of Mr. Young's sons.[2] In case you have never seen a sitz bath, it is only about two feet square, very shallow, so that when you sitzen sie dich[3] in it, the water overflows to hell and gone. I usually sit

---

1   MKR is responding to JSB's query if "you" meant her husband Tom Bigham as well. See JSB's letter dated [22 or 29 July 1947]. MKR is being disingenuous. She meant JSB alone, as she writes to NSB on 2 August. See MKR's letter on 17 July 1947, 389, n. 5.

2   "The Use of the Sitz-Bath: A Study Based on Experiments in the Brown's Hollow Laboratory," *Dumpling Magazine* 2 (6 July 1947): 3–7. The magazine was privately published by the family of Owen D. Young. Its publication was overseen by Richard Young, the son of Owen D. and Louise Young. See Tarr, *Bibliography*, C636.

3   Compare "setzen Sie sich," German for "sit down."

on the side and dabble---. You could manage it nicely, but Tom is a right big man, and his rear would have a terrific displacement---. The one night Norton was here, he used the Yogi method, and recommended it highly. I tried it, and thought I never WOULD get my legs untangled.

There is an alternative to the Sitz bath. Down the road a piece, two elderly maiden ladies, the Misses Tiers,[1] in reduced circumstances, have just turned their home into a sort of boarding house, and you and Tom could have the whole upstairs, and bathroom with regular tub. Whether you singular or plural come up, we would be taking some of our meals there, and getting chicken pie and cherry pie etc. for other meals as they are superb old-fashioned cooks.

A white woman[2] (who goes to the local beauty parlor three times to my one) comes in every day to clean up, and she will come and get breakfast.

Now there is no entertainment here. This is a country village, and nothing happens. We did have a big morning today, as the 4-H Clubs had a cattle judging contest at Mr. Young's dairy farm. There are grand walks to be taken, gorgeous views etc., but no High Life. You-all (Southern plural) will have to decide for yourselves whether it appeals to you.

I did begin my book,[3] and it was horrible again, so I am not working now---.

If you, singular, were in a peaceful mood, I know you'd love a few days up here. I don't know Tom's tastes well enough to know whether he'd like it or not. I think Mr. Young[4] will be here between the 8th and the 13th, and if so, I can promise an evening with him, which is always a rare treat.

You-all let me know, and if you both come, let me know whether you'd rather use the Sitz bath or sleep and bathe at the Misses Tiers.

I presume you'd be driving. Van Hornesville is not on all the maps. It's on Route 80, and is 15 miles from Cooperstown. Mrs. Young[5] calls it a 5-hour drive from N.Y. City, but Mrs. Ambrose Clark[6] does it in 3 hours (with chauffeur and Packard). Leaving from Far Hills would probably save a lot of time.

Much love,

Marjorie

---

1 Not identified.

2 Not identified.

3 The manuscript of *The Sojourner*.

4 Owen D. Young.

5 Louise Young.

6 Florence Lockwood Stokes Clark (1875–1950), was married to the sportsman and horse breeder Frederick Ambrose Clark (1880–1964), heir to the Singer Sewing Machine fortune.

. . .

JSB to MKR, [21] August 1947. ALS, 3 pp. PM: FAR HILLS | 10³⁰ AM | AUG 25 | 1947 | N.J. AD: Mrs. Norton Baskin | Van Hornesville | New York.[1]

Thursday [21] August 1947[2]

Dearest Marjorie –

I made the trip safely and in very good time, although in places the traffic was very bad. Your lunch was a very good idea – I ate it on the wing and then stopped and had a couple of cups of coffee.[3]

I hope to move back to Chelsea[4] next week, probably Wed. I long to get home again. And there are so many physical difficulties to working at photography being away from all my equipment conspires with all the weakness of my character.

I got Hildie all dressed up Monday [18 August] and went to work on her with the big camera. I was limp with physical and psychical exhaustion at the end of the "exposing." Last night I developed the films. The films turned out to be fogged with age and the front end of the bellows had come loose from the lens end <of t> so they were light-streaked as well!! All this after having spent over an hour just getting the bathroom dark enough to develop in with lord knows what all pinned over the window[.] Nothing but the most <u>complete</u> sablest [blackest] darkness will do. It took me another hour to get the solutions to the right temperatures. You see what I mean about only needing a pencil & paper for poetry!? Nonetheless I shall have a fine portrait of our girl to show you when I come up again or die in the attempt.

Tom hasn't figured yet just when he will go away, but I'll let you know as

---

1 Written in a second hand on the envelope: [1947?]. The letter is dated by the first Thursday before the PM.

2 Written in a second hand above Thursday on p. 1: [8-25-47].

3 Thomas Bigham and JSB arrived for a visit with MKR on 11 August. He left on 14 August, returning to New York by train. JSB left on 16 August and drove to the Scribner estate at Far Hills, New Jersey. MKR changed her reserved opinion about Bigham, as she confesses to NSB in a letter on 14 August, "Tom is really just as nice as can be, and I like him, and think he is really all right for Julia." On 16 August she laments to NSB, "Julia left this morning, and we both grieved. . . . [Tom] is so High Church that he is almost Catholic" (*Love Letters* 499–50).

4 As in Chelsea Square, or the campus of the General Theological Seminary, where Bigham was a member of the faculty. The Seminary is situated on the full city block between 9th and 10th Avenues and 20th and 21st Streets in the Chelsea district of Manhattan. The Bighams lived at 6 Chelsea Square, one of the faculty residences on campus.

soon as he decides. Probably <when> it will be earliesh [*sic*] in Sept. If for any reason you want me at any <u>particular</u> time, let me know and I'll come.

My heart is with you in all your troubles – and I'm keenly aware that that isn't awfully helpful. Nothing would make me happier than if I could be useful as well as ornamental as a friend, and I count on your friendship to let me know if I ever can.[1]

Much love,

Julia

Just now, reading this letter, I suddenly recalled several years ago – maybe five or so – writing you a letter. It was on my birthday and I was very unhappy and upset – it took me a whole afternoon to write it.[2] Now I can't remember at all what it said. But after I sent it I felt embarrassed and frightened too. I thought "you fool, there you've sent out a piece of yourself." I can feel this moment the anxiety that I was in for days. I shall never forget the morning your answer came – the understanding and warmth of your response to my inarticulate pain and self-revelation. I remember it vividly now and I want to tell you so. It was one of the really good things that have happened to me in this life.

· · ·

MKR to JSB, 2 September 1947. TLS, 1 p. PM: VAN HORNESVILLE | SEP | 3 | A.M. | 1947 | N.Y. AD: Mrs. Thomas Bigham | 6 Chelsea Square | New York City 11

Sept. 2, 1947

Dearest Julia:

I am recovering today from giving a picnic yesterday for the whole Young family, 21, I think it was.[3] Fortunately, it was a divine day, and people spread

---

1   What JSB means by "all your troubles" is difficult to parse. At this juncture MKR was upset by the slow progress on her manuscript of *The Sojourner* and also upset about her recurring health problems, partly brought on by the lengthy *Cross Creek* trial and appeal. The death of Maxwell Perkins in June was to her an "unspeakable tragedy." Yet MKR was also thrilled by the purchase of the home in Van Hornesville, and her relationship with NSB seemed to be on an even keel.

2   See, for example, JSB's confessional dated [27? June] 1943, one of the most introspective of her letters.

3   The family of Owen D. and Louise Young, which would have included the families of Phillip Young, Richard Young, Charles Young, and Josephine Young Case, the children of the Youngs.

out on the terrace. Mary[1] helped me from 10 to 5:30 and the Misses Tiers[2] made baked beans, rolls, cakes etc. Benny[3] did not come to the party, and last night would hardly speak to me. He likes his company one or two at a time, so that he can think up ways of bothering them.

There was the most terrific crash of lightning this morning. Moe and Benny were terrified. It broke a light in Mary's kitchen into <u>powder</u>, and blew out all the Young lights and fused an outlet altogether.

This is just a note to say that any time you can come will be grand.[4] It doesn't seem to appear on the time table I have, but there is a train that leaves New York about 10:30 A.M. and reaches Fort Plain, (just 10 miles from here) about 3:30 P.M. It has a diner. I know there is such a train, as Mrs. Young's daughter Virginia[5] arrived on it a few days ago.

I have just written Norton that I expect to stay until the middle of October---. He hopes to come for ten days, and fell in with my suggestion that he meet me in New York and have a couple of days there before coming here. But there are things I want to do and people I want to see, that will take more than two days, and it might be a good idea for me to drive you home when you leave here, and get my personal stuff done, to be free to play with Norton later.

Please don't worry about me. Like you, I probably just ask too much of life. But if you don't try for it, you sure as hell won't get it. And what seem like mistakes often turn out all right. Anyway, we all need a shoulder to cry on. Thanks for yours.

Love,

<u>Marjorie</u>

. . .

MKR to JSB, 15 September 1947. TLS, 2 pp. Envelope is missing.

Sept. 15, 1947

Dearest Julia:

---

1 Mary Bronner Sickler (1916–2007), MKR's maid, recommended to her by the Youngs.

2 Misses Tiers, MKR's neighbors who were unmarried sisters. First names of the Tiers: Not identified.

3 Benny, MKR's cat, whom JSB especially did not like (*Love Letters* 499).

4 JSB came on 18 September and left on 25 September (see MKR's letters to NSB on 16 September and 24 September 1947; *Love Letters* 503–4).

5 Virginia Brown, daughter of Louise Powis Young and Elwood S. Brown (1883–1924), Louise's first husband.

A grand morning---your letter saying you are really coming[1]---and we hit water a couple of hours ago. It seems to be a fine vein, and the water is like ice. They will pump out all afternoon to check on the speed of the flow.[2] The two dreary burrowing earth-worms came to life and actually seemed like men. Louise Young was with me, and she picked up a handful of the gray marly clay and modeled a face of me with my pleased expression---.

No, I have not begun the book again yet, but it is pushing harder for birth every minute. If it breaks the sack[3] while you are here, it won't matter, for you could take the car and prowl around for camera subjects. If not, I'd like to go with you while you prowl, if it wouldn't bother you. We were at Little Falls[4] again last week, hunting "diamonds", and I think you will find some striking subject matter there.

When I decided on two trips to New York, I thought, or hoped, you would be here earlier. I talked with Norton on the 'phone last night (I put in a person to person call at Marineland, operator said, "We are ready with your party", I cried out, "Hello, darling!"---and it was the colored bar-boy[5]---) and he is meeting me in New York Oct. 5. So, the two trips would come too close together. I hope you don't mind, and I will plan to drive to New York Oct. 3. Or probably to Far Hills. I agreed to speak at Colgate Oct. 2.[6]

Mr. and Mrs. Young will be pleased that you are coming now, as they have to be away for about ten days, and were afraid I'd be too lonesome. Mrs. Powis[7] is leaving for Florida tomorrow, so I won't be stuck with having to play cards with her. We do have to watch the Young's dog, Vic, as they are afraid she is coming into heat, but have to leave her behind. We can take her in the car with us, and with Moe.

Now unless I hear from you to the contrary, I'll meet the afternoon train

---

1   This letter is missing See JSB's letter dated [21] August 1947, where JSB says she will let MKR know the date she can come. MKR's comment, "No, I have not yet begun the book again," also indicates that she is responding to a specific question by JSB.

2   On 16 September MKR writes in a letter to NSB, "We got water yesterday, at 207 feet . . . and it is a fine steady flow of 8 gallons a minute, well above the average, they say" (*Love Letters* 503).

3   That is, begins to be born.

4   Little Falls, New York, approximately fourteen miles north of Van Hornesville, is known for its diamond hunting.

5   Perhaps Bernard Young, who was married to Idella Parker at this time and whom NSB had to fire in 1950 after he was caught "watering" drinks at Marineland (see *Love Letters* 581).

6   MKR's nerves were "shattered" at the prospect of giving a lecture at Colgate University, especially since it was President Everett Case who invited her. It "went off all right. The chapel was full, a thousand or more, and it was a grand audience, mostly G.I.'s," as she reports to NSB in letters on 1 October and 3 October (*Love Letters* 506).

7   Owen D. and Louise Young, and Julia Powis, Louise Young's mother.

at Fort Plain Thursday the 18th.[1] If there is any change in your plans, you can wire me in care of Owen D. Young, or phone the house, as the maids will be there, and the wire and 'phone number is Richfield Springs 23 J 2. There is no Western Union in Van Hornesville.

<Unl> Much love to you, and my best to Tom. I hope you told him how much I liked him.

<u>Marjorie</u>

. . .

MKR to JSB, 30 September 1947. TLS, 1 pp. PM: NEW YORK, N.Y. | NOV 4 | 6 - PM | 1947. AD: [Mrs.] Norton Baskin | [Cresc]ent Beach R.F.D. | [St.] Augustine | Florida. PO Stamp: Missent to Sanford Fl[a.][2] VIA AIR MAIL envelope.

Sept. 30, 1947

Dearest Julia:

Just a note to say that Norton is coming a week or two later than we thought. Principally because of the storms[3]---they had <u>three</u>---the workmen won't be through with the cottage, and after that, Norton writes that there is a terrific clean-up job to be done before he'll let me walk in. This suits me to a T. It is just as likely to be pleasant weather later as now, and it will probably mean in any case that we'll spend more time in New York City.

For three mornings, Moe has been going out at 6 A.M. and not returning until 8 or 8:30. Yesterday morning Halvor[4] brought him home. Vicky[5] is definitely "that way", and it seems Moe had been paying formal calls. Louise

---

1   MKR writes to NSB on 16 September, "Julia is coming this Thursday to spend a week" (*Love Letters* 503). The train from New York stopped at Fort Plain, approximately twelve miles from Van Hornesville.

2   The envelope is largely illegible because it is mangled. The PM could be a resent (second) postmark, since the letter was first sent to the wrong city in Florida.

3   Hurricane George (aka Fort Lauderdale Hurricane) came ashore as a Category 4 with wind gusts in excess of 155 mph. The storm did widespread damage to southeast Florida and then crossed Florida, exiting at Tampa, and finally coming ashore again near New Orleans. MKR writes in a letter to NSB on 23 September, "Was so glad to have your letter yesterday about the hurricane. I can't help wishing I'd been there, to see the real thing on the coast. Too bad the cottage wasn't ready, so that all the Baskins could have gone there. It is so darned <u>low</u> at Marineland, that I was afraid of a tidal wave" (*Love Letters* 504).

4   Halvor Sandvold (1905–1983), the Norway-born caretaker for the Youngs' houses and grounds, who also took care of MKR's gardens.

5   Vicky, the Youngs' dog, who was in heat.

said that yesterday morning she thought she heard a dog's steps on the stairs when she was in her bedroom. She looked around to make sure Vicky was in the room with her. There came a scratching on the door---I'm sure it was a rapping[1]---and there was Moe, doing the courtly romantic thing by going straight to his lady's bedroom---.

Then Louise infuriated me by saying, "I was afraid SHE would get run over on the highway if SHE started back to Brown's Hollow, so I told Halvor to put HER in the station wagon and take HER back to you." God damn--- I felt like using your substitutional expression for cussing---.

HE is menstruating like mad---.

I'll let you know when our plans are definite.

Much love,

Marjorie

.   .   .

MKR to JSB, 6 October 1947. TLS, 2 pp. PM: VAN HORNESVILLE | OCT | 6 | A.M. | 1947 | N.Y. AD: Mrs. Thomas J. Bigham, Jr. | 6 Chelsea Square | New York City 11.

Oct. 6, 1947

Dearest Julia:

All your latent nobility gathered itself together when you invited Norton AND Benny[2] AND me to stay with you and Tom.[3] I cannot, of course, accept such hospitality for any of us, but you are wonderful.

Norton can always get us in a hotel. It is likely to be the Barbizon-Plaza, which is the least of my favorites, but he knows the manager quite well. Also, he doesn't mind New York traffic, and will probably want to keep the car in town, and the B.-P. has a parking lot less than a block away.

I have written Marcia Davenport,[4] asking her if she is in a position to keep Benny for a week. She is so mad about cats that it would not be a chore for her, unless she has recently acquired cats of her own, which makes a tabby of another color. We could also go by New Hartford, Conn., and leave Benny

---

1   A reference to "The Raven" (1845) by Edgar Allan Poe (1809–1849): "As of someone gently rapping, rapping at my chamber door" (1. 4).

2   Benny, MKR's cat.

3   If the invitation was by letter, then JSB's letter is missing. It is always possible that the invitation was given over the telephone.

4   Marcia Davenport (1903–1996), American novelist.

with Bernice Gilkyson,[1] who is a catophile and at present has no cats of her own. It just occurred to me that the Barbizon Plaza might let me keep Benny there. We have been allowed to take him into lots of hotels that wouldn't consider the bulky and unattractive Moe.

I should be afraid of three things if you tried to keep Benny in your apartment. He might jump into the baby's crib with all friendly intentions of investigating or playing with her, and if the baby flailed her arms and feet around, Benny might play in his usual rough fashion and scratch her, which would be ghastly. And Benny is so slick about making a get-away, that it would take someone's full time to keep him from slipping out the service entrance, or out of the front door when the Bishop walked in, and finding Benny in Old Chelsea would take most of the winter---. And finally, you would be so worn out between these two contingencies that it might cause a great strain on our friendship. Please don't worry, I'll find some place for Benny.

I have a long wild tale to tell about Moe when I see you. He was stolen yesterday, and so on, but is now home safely.

Norton just happened to get me on the 'phone at the Young's [sic] late yesterday afternoon, and I am to be there at 6 this evening for another call. We have practically agreed that he is to come up right away, while the weather is so gorgeous, and then if the cottage isn't habitable when we get back, I really should spend a week with Martha[2] at Cross Creek anyway, and he can finish up then.

I have even been brushing my teeth at the Young's [sic], to save water here, and this morning the well has much more water in it, so I think we can manage for the few days he'll be here.

I'll let you know by wire or phone when he'll be here and when and where we'll be in New York. How would it suit you if I came down for lunch with you some day, spent the afternoon, and Norton joined us in the evening? I do want to get acquainted with Hildreth and have some time with you. I almost hope I have diarrhea, so that I can use your bathroom----.

Much love,

Marjorie

---

1 Bernice Lesbia Kenyon Gilkyson (1897–1982), American poet and editor at Scribners, who wrote under the name Bernice Kenyon.
2 Martha Mickens.

. . .

JSB to MKR, ALS, 2 pp. [Early November 1947] Envelope is missing.[1]

[Early November 1947]

Dearest Marjorie –

I trust that you & Norton & Mopey & Benny had a safe trip home. I hear that you made Moe & Benny sleep in the car at Far Hills which I think displays a quite unwarranted lack of confidence in their manners.

I have sent you the picture of your view, but not a print of the white house as I am not satisfied with the one I have and haven't gotten to making another. I have been at a rather low photographic ebb again. I must pull myself together.[2]

There isn't any news of interest here except that Hildie has been making great strides at growing up, due no doubt to the tremendous stimulation she got from Norton. She now stands up by herself in her little chair and is passing through a canine speech period – she says "Ba-wow-wow-wow."

The only point of this letter really is to tell you that you are constantly in my thoughts and prayers, I have a good feeling that everything will turn out well. But in the mean time it must be tough as hell – this interim of inaction. If there is anything at all I can do for you here you will let me know, won't you?

Much love,
Julia

. . .

MKR to JSB, 6 November 1947. TLS, 2 pp. PM: SAINT AUGUSTINE | NOV 6 | 4 PM | 1947 | FLA. AD: Mrs. Thomas J. Bigham | 6 Chelsea Square | New York City 11. LH: MARJORIE KINNAN RAWLINGS | HAWTHORN, FLORIDA.

Crescent Beach
St. Augustine

---

1   This undated letter was likely written early November (perhaps very late October) of 1947. In the third week of October NSB was in Van Hornesville, New York, visiting MKR, as was JSB. MKR, JSB, and NSB then departed for a week in New York. While in New York, NSB spent meaningful time with JSB's baby daughter Hildreth, who particularly loved his attention. JSB had given birth to her just months earlier on 1 April 1947. The context suggests that MKR and NSB stayed, at least one night, at Far Hills, New Jersey, the location of the Scribner estate. MKR's letter on 6 November 1947 responds to JSB's tease about Moe and Benny sleeping in the car at Far Hills.

2   JSB is speaking of her photographs of MKR's new home in Van Hornesville, and the views from that home.

Nov. 6, 1947

Dearest Julia:

It is not that I <u>made</u> Moe and Benny sleep in the car at Far Hills,[1] but that I successfully resisted Vera's insistence that they sleep in the house---. Their sleeping at Cross Creek, at the beach cottage, at Brown's Hollow,[2] at tourist cabins on the way to Florida, involved a certain amount of sleeplessness on Norton's part and mine, and since they cause no trouble at all together in the car, I kept them there our jolly night at Far Hills.

We stayed up until about 3 A.M., Norton the drunkest and the most engaging of any of us.

I am working against time so will make my story short. I leave day after tomorrow, Saturday, for New York, spending Sunday and Monday nights with Marcia Davenport before going into Harkness[3] Tuesday afternoon. Operation probably Thursday or Friday. The cancer-tester's report said "probably no malignancy, but very unusual cells," so I go to Dr. Damon's[4] office early Monday morning for more slides to be made for another test.

It is a pity that Norton and Hildie can't see more of each other---. They stimulated each other no end.

If my operation is as simple as believed, ten days in the hospital will be enough, or two weeks at the most. If I don't feel quite up to travel after that, I'll try for a hotel, and if I can't get in one, think I should really rather ask you to put me up a couple of days, than impose on Marcia[5] again. Much as I like and admire her, there is always a debit and credit relation there---.

Will 'phone you Monday [10 November].

My love to all,

<u>Marjorie</u>

---

1   Far Hills, New Jersey, the home of Charles Scribner III and Vera Scribner. The Baskins visited the Scribners on their way back to Florida in late October at which time, as MKR reveals to Norman Berg in a letter on 4 November, a "routine check-up . . . revealed a condition that will probably prove simple to take care of, but that should not wait for attention, almost certainly <u>not</u> a malignancy . . ." (*Selected Letters* 306). After a brief stay in Florida, MKR returned to New York on 8 November for the operation.

2   Brown's Hollow, New York, the farmhouse restored by Owen D. and Louise Young, where MKR stayed.

3   MKR was admitted to Harkness Pavilion on 11 November and discharged in early December. Two procedures were performed, one the repairing of diverticulum and the other the removal of cysts from each breast. See *Love Letters* 507–10.

4   Virgil Damon, MD.

5   Marcia Davenport.

. . .

JSB to MKR, 27 December 1947. ALS, 4 pp. PM: NEW YORK,
N.Y. | DEC 29 | 10³⁰ AM | 1947. AD: Mrs. Norton Baskin | Crescent
Beach R.F.D. | St. Augustine | Florida. VIA AIR MAIL envelope.

Dec 27. [1947] [1]

Dearest Marjorie –

I have received an avalanche of crates from Florida – wonderful pre-
serves and now oranges. There is a small "falling rock" coming your way,
but it hasn't even gotten this far yet. I ordered it by mail, and I guess there
has been some damned mixup. I'll tell you what it is – an ashtray with my
favorite Steinberg[2] drawing on it – the man drinking poison through a
straw. It will be a constant reminder of your dear friend, me, and my dour
disposition.

I[3] hope you are feeling quite decent by now. Do drop me a line on your
present condition & occupation. I have not been too hot – about a week ago
I got an infected antrum[4] and have been indoors since then except to go out
to F.H.[5] for Christmas lunch. Went up to Presbyterian at one point to see Dr.
A.[6] and a nose man. They gave me penicillin to take by mouth which made
me sick unto death & cost $7.50 – very unsatisfactory.

What a wonderful day it was I went up to the hospital. I don't think all
the time you were here we had such a day. It made me furious that I had to
be sick & not able to use it photographically. The atmosphere was so clear it
looked as if it had been removed – drained off – and there was nothing at all
between you and whatever you looked at. You could see across the river[7] as
clearly as you <would> ^can^ see the opposite bank of a brook. Smoke rose
straight up and was so precise in outline as the chimney. Everything was in
the full bloom of its own uniqueness.

Now we have had even more extraordinary weather as you may have read
– more snow than I have ever seen. One car is out on the street, and buried

---

1   Written in a second hand under date on p. 1: [1947].
2   Saul Steinberg (1914–1999), Romanian-American cartoonist. The image of a demented man
drinking poison through a straw appeared in the *New Yorker* (6 November 1943).
3   JSB inserts a paragraph mark before "I" to indicate there should be a line break.
4   Here apparently an infected chamber in the nose.
5   Far Hills, New Jersey.
6   Dr. Atchley. Presbyterian Hospital is likely Harkness Pavilion, New York.
7   Hudson River.

up above the fenders, almost to the level of the hood. Heaven knows when we can get it out.[1]

This is rather upsetting as we had hoped next week to drive to Pittsburgh.[2] Now we have to go by train which does ruinous things to our budget.

Miss Abbott[3] finally got here for dinner and she examined my recent photographs. She was most enthusiastic – (an attitude which is not at all natural with her) – She said among other things that I seemed well on the way to a style of real individuality and integrity. I really feel quite spurred on. As soon as I get back from Pittsburgh I get back to the job-hunting again. Wish me luck for '48 – perhaps I can push things a little and make life begin at 30![4]

I wish you a '48 you will look back on with satisfaction and thankfulness.

Much love,
Julia

---

1   Known as the "blizzard of 1947," on 26–27 December it snowed more than two feet.
2   The home of Thomas Bigham's parents.
3   Berenice Abbott, the famed photographer. See JSB's letter on 8 October 1944.
4   That is, a Happy New Year for 1948. JSB, who will be thirty in 1948, is twisting the popular sentiment that "life begins at 40." See Walter B. Pitkin (1878–1953), Columbia University professor, *Life Begins at Forty* (New York: Whittlesey House, 1932), a best-selling self-help book by the then guru of aging.

Life and Death

1948–1953

I don't know yet what the September schedule will be – if I am allowed any "vacation", perhaps we may still get together before we both move to our winter quarters.

[JSB to MKR, 20 August (1953)]

I'll drop you a note again in a few days. Meantime, all love

[MKR to JSB, 4 December 1953]

. . .

MKR to JSB, 4 January 1948. TLS, 2 pp. PM: SAINT AUGUSTINE
| JAN [day illegible] | 2^{30} PM | 1948 | FLA. AD: Mrs. Thomas J.
Bigham | 6 Chelsea Square | New York City 11. Air Mail Stamp.

Crescent Beach

Jan. 4, 1948

Dearest Julia:

It is a magnificent day, but the ocean is a wide blue barrier, too straight a demarcation between me and the horizon, and I find myself longing to be snow bound in the Yankee house,[1] looking out over icy but somehow friendly hills and valleys. I took out your picture of the view there and imagined the clean white field, and the lilac bush and apple trees in soft mounds. Then I thought, "You'd damn well better imagine that kitchen well-stocked with food, too!"

Martin[2] wrote me, before the Big Snow,[3] that the township was keeping the road ploughed, so that they had been going ahead with the plastering etc. I suppose it will be impossible for him to work there through the heaviest part of the winter.

I have thought of you so often. When I first reached home, I felt so well that I over-did, and found myself suddenly tiring unreasonably. One of Moe's sudden "woofs" would turn me inside out. Then my brother[4] flew from Seattle ten days before Christmas, and it was so exciting to see him again after more than ten years that we talked ourselves into utter exhaustion. He is really wonderful and having him here, warmed me through and through. He brought along two 16-millimeter films, running about 45 minutes each, that he has made in Alaska. You would have been fascinated. The newer one is all in color. His shots of the big Kodiak, or Alaskan brown bears, feeding are spectacular, as are other game shots and glacier shots. He is largely self-taught in photography, but being a perfectionist, has become expert. Among the few we invited to the "showing" was a professional photographer, who

---

1   MKR's home at Van Hornesville, New York.

2   Martin Egan, the contractor who did most of the restorations on MKR's Van Hornesville home.

3   The so-called Great Blizzard of 1947. In Upstate New York, where Van Hornesville is located, there were reports of four feet of snow or more, nearly twice what JSB experienced in New York City. See JSB's letter on 27 December 1947.

4   Arthur Houston Kinnan.

was most impressed. I showed Arthur the few of your pictures that I have, and he was all admiration and respect.

He gave me a message for you that is Greek to me, but you may understand. He noticed that the border around the print of the Van Hornesville view was uneven, and said to tell you that there is a new something-or-other to hold something-or-other during the printing, I think it is, so that you don't have to try to adjust it---avoiding slipping or whatever it is.

I wish I could remember for your information the types of cameras and lenses etc. that he uses, but I might as well try to recount the details of the atom bomb. You would also be interested in a description of his guns, but that too is beyond me. He has had one gun made especially to order for him, for use on the Kodiak bears---harder to kill, he says, than an elephant. He had to fly back the day after Christmas, but he promises to come next winter for a longer stay, and perhaps you can come down while he is here. His stories are delightful.

I am <u>thrilled</u> at Berenice Abbott's report[1] on your work. It should remove your timidity in job-hunting.

Arthur and Aunt Ida, Idella, Moe, Benny[2] and I drove to the Creek two days before Christmas. Norton joined us the afternoon of the 24th and we had our Christmas Celebration and dinner on Christmas Eve, as Norton had to be on the job the next day, and we all drove back together. I <u>had</u> to go back to Gainesville to finish shopping for the families at the Creek and I <u>had</u> to deliver the packages in person, so that after Arthur left, I felt quite feeble. I am feeling better now, but the nerves are still a bit jangly. I did not see Chet Crosby, but his kidney trouble is still serious.

I have to go to the Creek in a week or so, and will try then to get off to you a box of the tangerines that you liked.

You will never know how much it meant to me to have you come to the hospital so often. You were really the only one I wanted to see---and you came. Bless you.

With love,

<u>Marjorie</u>

---

1 Berenice Abbott's praise of JSB's photographs was a significant moment. See JSB's letter on 27 December 1947.

2 Arthur H. Kinnan, Aunt Ida Tarrant, Idella Parker, Moe the pointer, and Benny the cat.

MKR to JSB, 21 January 1948. TLS, 1 p. PM: SAINT AUGUSTINE |
JAN 21 | 5 PM | 1948 | FLA. AD: Mrs. Thomas J. Bigham, Jr. | 175 9th
Avenue | New York City 11. LH: Mrs. Norton Baskin | crescent
beach | st. augustine, florida.

Jan. 21, 1948

Dearest Julia:

The truly poisonous green of the Steinberg ash-tray[1] happens to be one
of the colors I am using in my studio (it is actually a good chartreuse) so it
is all right from the decorative angle. What the subject-matter will do to me
when I am working, futilely, is something else again---. I promise you that if
the example, and my own difficulties, prove too much for me, I too shall sip
my poison through a straw---.

Martha Gelhorn [*sic*] arrived about a week ago, and is putting in her
month of work against a dead-line in one of Verle Pope's tourist cottages---
while Edith, working against <u>her</u> dead-line, is in a similar dreary tourist
court at Silver Springs![2] Martha is the most sex-conscious creature I have
ever known in my life. Fortunately, she is so absorbed in her manuscript
that the local husbands are safe, although I did not like the way she said, in
refusing a social invitation, "AFTER I finish my work---." Since I am now
thoroughly recovered, I plan to have Norton completely worn-down by then,
and Edith will just have to shift for herself---.

After tomorrow with a stenographer on correspondence,[3] I shall be deep
in work in my lovely new studio. Poor Mopey[4] is at the Vet's with heart
worms. So many thanks for the delightful and ghastly gift.

Much love,

<u>Marjorie</u>

---

1   JSB sent MKR the ashtray for a Christmas present. See JSB's letter on 4 January 1948.

2   Martha Gellhorn, noted journalist and former wife of Ernest Hemingway, stayed in a rental
cottage owned by Verle Pope on St. Augustine Beach. While there, she worked on the manuscript
of *The Wine of Astonishment* (New York: Scribners, 1948), a World War II novel about the horrors
that took place at the Battle of the Bulge. Edith Pope stayed near the tourist mecca Silver Springs,
near Ocala, Florida. Her next novel was *River in the Wind* (New York: Scribners, 1954), a novel
about the Seminole wars.

3   Stenographer: Not identified.

4   Moe, MKR's pointer dog.

. . .

MKR to JSB, 21 February 1948. Envelope is missing. LH: Mrs.
Norton Baskin | crescent beach | st. augustine, florida.

Feb. 21, 1948

Dearest Julia:

The experience with your job is too horrid.[1] You are so honest that probably, in stressing the temporary angle of the job, the man thought you might
leave <u>him</u> at any time. Just keep plugging away.

I wish you were here, or I there, for you to do a photograph of my right
hand! I agreed to do one of those Parker pen things---I thought if Ernest
Hemingway could do one, it certainly was not beneath <u>my</u> dignity. Artzy-
bashoff (sp.?) makes a painting, or whatever it is, of the hand, from a photograph. The owner of the hand, holding the pen, does not endorse the product
except tacitly, and receives $500.[2]

I have been going through a grand mess at the Creek. You may remember my friend Thelma Shortridge,[3] erstwhile post-mistress at Citra. Her
husband[4] got tired of finding her boy-friend in bed with her, and Thelma
had moved next-door to the quarters she owned in conjunction with the
post office, which she rented to the government. About two months ago
she 'phoned me from a <local h> little hospital where she was getting over a
binge, and asked if I could join her at the Creek right away, and let her stay
there a few days while she got organized. That morning the living quarters,
all her belongings, her dog and the boy-friend, had been burned to ashes. I
was all sympathy, of course, and dashed over.

To make a ghastly story short, she, her literally insane mother, and an

---

1   The context here suggests that a letter from JSB is missing.

2   The "things" were advertisements for Parker ink pens, the most popular of which was the
"Parker '51,'" a "Demi-sized" fountain pen. The illustrations for the ads were done by Boris Artzy-
basheff (1899–1965), American illustrator, and they appeared widely in magazines such as *The
Saturday Evening Post*. See JSB's next letter on 15 April 1948.

3   Thelma Matilda Tompkins Shortridge (b. 1906), daughter of Fred D. Tompkins (1881–1943)
who was MKR's favorite hunting and fishing companion, was appointed postmistress at Citra on 2
February 1939 and was reappointed on 1 February 1946. Upon learning of Fred's death, MKR wrote
in a letter to NSB on 1 March 1943, "A letter from Thelma gives me the heart-breaking news about
Fred. I feel the most terrible sense of loss. He was one of the staunchest friends I ever had" (*Love
Letters* 75).

4   Thelma's husband, Robert Johnson "R. J." Shortridge (1906–1948) ran a truck-farm near Citra,
Florida, where MKR and JSB went often to get fresh produce.

uncle[1] who sat by the living-room fireplace and spat tobacco juice all over the white wood-work, simply took over at the Creek. I spent two days getting Thelma settled, left her my <j> fur jacket to wear, bought her other articles of clothing etc., and cleared out. She was not a heart-broken woman about the boy-friend by any means, but did seem to grieve for the dog! Well, I sent Idella over in a couple of weeks to get some things I needed. The floor of the bath-room was strewn with No. 2 (I refuse to use your favorite word). All the curtains and draperies were drawn tight and pinned together. Martha had been trying to keep up with things at my request, as I only expected them to stay a few days, and I told Martha I would make it right financially. The good old soul was almost crazy. Thelma vomited into the lavatory half a dozen times a day, and just left it there for Martha to clean out.

I had locked my liquor cupboard, but forgot about a dozen or so bottles of brandy, Cointreau,[2] etc. in the pantry that I used for flavoring in desserts. Those were all gone. She ran the Kohler[3] plant 24 hours a day, etc.

Fortunately, the shingles arrived for the new roof, and I had the work-men go right ahead on it, as the leaks were ruining the house. Also, I had long before told Mr. Young,[4] when he asked me if he and Louise could be put up at the Creek while he participated in the inaugural of an old friend of his as the new President of the University of Florida, that I should be delighted to do so. He never asks a favor, so I wrote Thelma that I would have to have the house.

She was furious, and only moved out when the work-men took off the roof!

Idella[5] and I went to the Creek last Monday, where a crew of four joined us for a thorough house-cleaning. We found Thelma's empty liquor bottles under and behind the bath-tub, behind doors, in the clothes closet, and in my dresser drawers---. She had used a casserole[6] under her bed for vomiting, and a metal waste-basket for urinating---. This, with her own bathroom a few steps away.

She and her mother had gone to a perfectly adequate house she owns, in

---

1 Thelma's mother, Annie Lee Smith Tompkins (1884–1964?), wife of Fred Tompkins whom he called the "Old Hen." She was a character in several of MKR's stories, most notably "Benny and the Bird Dogs," *Scribner's Magazine* 94.4 (October 1933): 193–200. See Tarr, *Bibliography*, C597, and *Short Stories*, pp. 198–215. The uncle is unidentified.

2 Cointreau, a French orange-flavored liqueur.

3 Kohler, brand name of MKR's gas-powered electric generator.

4 Owen D. Young. The new president of the University of Florida was J. Hillis Miller (1899–1953), who served from 1948 to 1953.

5 Idella Parker.

6 That is, a casserole dish.

Citra, and I went to see her there. She was utterly outraged at being forced out of my place! My neighbor Mrs. Glisson[1] had told me that Thelma had come to see her, and told her that from now on, my place at the Creek would be her (Thelma's) home!

I shouldn't spill out all this stuff to you, except that it is on my mind, and you probably will share my morbid interest in the depravity of human nature.

We are looking forward to seeing the Scribner's, pere et mere, here at the cottage, March 1.[2]

I'll send on the New Yorkers[3] again. I thought of sending you a subscription, but it seemed sensible to pass on my own copies instead.

Much love,

Marjorie

. . .

MKR to JSB, 28 February 1948. TLS, 2 pp. PM: SAINT AUGUSTINE | FEB 28 | 2 PM | 1948 | FLA. AD: Mrs. Thomas J. Bigham | 175 Ninth Avenue | New York City 11. LH: Mrs. Norton Baskin | crescent beach | st. augustine, florida.

Feb. 28, 1948

Dearest Julia:

The photographer flew here in his own 'plane day before yesterday, to take pictures for my co-operation (tacit endorsement) with the Parker pen people.[4] I told him about you and your work, and he said he would be very glad to have you go to see him at his New York studio, with samples of your work. He said that most studios, if not all, felt they had to have assistants with much experience, as when a job had to be done, it must be done right. I did not know your exact qualifications, so when or if you see him, don't be so fearfully modest. He indicated that he might have a job for you, and if not, might be able to steer you somewhere else.[5]

---

1 Pearlee Josey Glisson (1897–1980), wife of James "Tom" Glisson (1897–1950), and mother of James T. "Jake" Glisson Jr. (1927–2019), who served, in part at least, as an inspiration for Fodderwing in *The Yearling*.

2 French for father and mother, as in Charles Scribner III and Vera Scribner. For the visit, see JSB's letter on 15 April 1948.

3 The *New Yorker* magazine, in which many of MKR's short stories appeared.

4 See MKR's letter on 1 February 1948, and JSB's letter on 15 April 1948.

5 For JSB's visit to the photographer, William "Bill" Stone, see her letter on 15 April 1948.

He said, "I can do one thing for her, I can show her how the simplest technique gets the best results."

He was an awfully nice guy. Seems off-hand a bit of a sissy, in spite of having his lady-friend and her little girl with him, but was a glider pilot during the war, and finally told me he got Ernest Hemingway to cooperate on the Parker pen advertisements,[1] by matching war story for war story.

His visit was amusing. He called me here, at 1:20, and I made it clear that his little party would have to eat lunch before they took a taxi to the cottage. Norton and I were so charmed with the three of them, that it ended, after they had kept the taxi waiting for 3 hours, with our inviting them to have dinner and spend the night.

He was two and a half hours late in getting to the cottage for his pictures, had forgotten to bring flash-light bulbs (when he "did" Ernest in Cuba he forgot his light-meter, so on this trip he brought two), and when Norton drove them to the St. Augustine air-port to the 'plane, the guy vanished for 45 minutes. He had locked himself in the John---. Norton finally heard his feeble cries for help---. And as we check up, we have found that he left behind, two exposed plates, the contract he brought for me to sign about the advertisement, and my signature for reproduction.

I enclose his card with a notation.

Much love,

Marjorie

He left the card for your use.[2]

. . .

JSB to MKR, 15 April 1948. ALS, 5 pp. PM: NEW YORK, N.Y. | APR16 | 12³⁰PM | 1948 | AD: Mrs. Norton Baskin | Crescent Beach R.F.D. | St Augustine | Florida

April 15 – [1948][3]

Dearest Marjorie –

I hope you have not been thinking of me too badly in this long silence. If

---

1 The Parker Pen ad using Hemingway's hand appeared in *Life* 24.4 (26 January 1948), inside front cover.

2 In MKR's hand after the signature.

3 The year "[1948]" is inserted in another hand and is confirmed by MKR's previous letter on 28 February.

only I were a millionaire I would certainly invest in one of those talking letter machines and send you the "player" part. But then you would hear from me so often that it would no doubt prove more of a trial to our friendship than these unimpressive silences. The trouble is that when I don't write for a long time there is so much to tell I get discouraged at the thought.

Well, first off. Bill Stone.[1] I finally got to see him after overcoming several hurdles such as: though he says "I'm always here" he actually is never there. Incidentally – or rather, mainly, thank you for your <u>active</u> interest in my behalf.

It was a terribly queer interview – almost dreamlike – like K's interview with the painter in "The Trial[.]"[2] There were the interminable stairs – He has a whole bldg. on 3rd St. I climbed up about 11 flights of dark narrow rickety stairs and finally came out in a great farmlike attic room. The very apotheosis of pseudo-bohemianism. The lamps all made of pieces of driftwood with shades made of fishnet. On a center table some semi-consumed food and a couple of wickercovered chianti bottles[3] in which had been burned candles of all colors which had made an "artistic" drapery of multicolored wax around the bottles. In one corner was [a] bar the shelves of which were crowded with "interesting" empty bottles – there were three full bottles – scotch, rye & bourbon. I had some scotch & water (no ice – the most genuine bohemian touch) in an old fashioned glass. There were some very bad paintings and even worse photos around. We settled at the bar and he showed me his photos which were all of girls with little or nothing (two categories – not one) on. His work is mostly covers for magazines like "Real Life Stories" "Movie Stories" "Pageant"[4] etc. or sexy calendars. The pictures technically very good (all color) and I ohed & ahed and exclaimed over his technique till I was <u>quite</u> breathless. We must have looked at hundreds of girls – "This is Janey" "This is Suzy" "This is Jeanie"

I began to wonder when we were going to talk about <u>me</u>. Then somehow the subject got shifted to jazz. I said I really didn't know anything about it,

---

1   William "Bill" Stone, magazine photographer, published covers and photos in venues such as *Esquire* and *Screen Guide*. Stone took the photo of MKR's hand that was converted into a drawing for the Parker Pen ads discussed in MKR's previous letter on 21 February 1948.

2   Franz Kafka, *Der Process* [*The Trial*] (Berlin: Verlag Die Schmiede, 1925), in which the protagonist, "Josef K." is arrested and judged for an unspecified crime. At one point, "K." seeks legal advice from Titorelli, a mediocre painter who shows him one of his portraits of a judge. Titorelli admits the painting has been executed from the instructions of the client without actually seeing the subject matter.

3   JSB circles "chianti" and draws an arrow under and pointing to the right of "wickercovered" to indicate their transposition.

4   Cheap, lesser-known celebrity magazines, known for scintillating portraits of starlets.

but that only stimulated Bill and for <u>one</u> <u>hour</u> <u>and</u> <u>a</u> <u>half</u> I had to listen to one gem after another from his collection. Then we shifted to some Debussy preludes[1] he had just bought. I grew desperate and said I'd like to ask him some photographic questions. "Oh, yes," said he, "I haven't really been showing you the right pictures – not the most recent ones" and he started to hunt up more pictures. I grew more desperate and said that as he knew I was looking for a job – and then, thinking perhaps all the evasion was protective, assured him that I certainly didn't expect <u>him</u> to employ me, but thought perhaps he could give me some advice or leads. The upshot of this was that a. he couldn't afford to employ anyone b. he was about to employ someone from Calif. c. you couldn't get a job in commercial work unless you were very expert and had lots of "contacts" d. he offered me a job making color prints by a new process. This was all in such quick succession that I was in a state of confusion and hadn't had a chance to tell anything of what I had done, or show a single print. It was now after 8 PM and I decided the best thing I could do was get the hell home, so I gathered up my prints and did. The whole episode seems just as strange now as it did at the time. I feel as if I had wandered into a strange land of models and move starlets and stars where nothing is real – not even the sex.[2] I can see that commercial photography is not for me. You can't make a silk purse out of a sow's ear, particularly if one prefers the sow's ear.

Meanwhile, being unemployed, I have been doing a lot of portraits, some successful, more not. I have plenty of subject matter and am way behind both on printing and sittings. A great many people here <u>ask</u> me to take their pictures and of course many of them are most uninspiring, but then that in itself is good practice. I have been doing nothing <u>but</u> portraits – none of my favorite stuff: NYC.

The family came home absolutely raving, Muddy in particular, about the wonderful time they had with you and Norton. Everything was terrific – you, Norton, the house, the food, the ocean, the shells, Moe, etc. etc.[3]

I am fill of admiration for Scribners African and Indian books. "Cry the B. C."[4] left me a complete wreck. Anything noble or anything religious always makes me weep – this being both, I had to read it with a box of Kleenex beside me and wept so much I gave myself a mild sinus attack. I

---

1   Claude Debussy's *Préludes*, twenty-four short pieces for solo piano, composed between 1909 and 1913.

2   Compare Exodus 2:22: "I have been a stranger in a strange land."

3   See MKR's letter on 21 February 1948 and Silverthorne 285.

4   Alan Paton (1903–1988), South African writer and activist against the policies of racial discrimination known as apartheid, *Cry, the Beloved Country* (New York: Scribners, 1948).

think it is a really great book. Tom is quite as enthusiastic as I am and says he thinks it is the best novel dealing with religion or the religious point of view he has ever read. In an entirely different, <u>dry</u> way, I enjoyed every page of "The Prevalence of Witches".[1] Of course, anyone half Irish and half Indian <u>ought</u> to be capable of writing something extraordinary. I am anxious to read the A.L. Barker book now.[2] It has had such good reviews sounds like the sort of thing I enjoy. I haven't read a thing else except to keep up with the world weakly in Time.[3]

Our child is growing up fast and furiously.[4] Now that she can walk, she is capable of an impressive amount of destruction. She has such a forceful character I shudder at the thought of trying to impose the restrictions of civilization on her. I am about to try Tom's skill at opening the shutter and setting off flash, and if the resultant picture of Hildie and myself is good I'll send you one.

I really must go to bed now. I hope that your work is in a healthier condition than mine – And that you and Norton are well

Much love

Julia

. . .

JSB to MKR, 21 September 1948. ALS, 3 pp. PM: NEW YORK, N.Y. | SEP 21 | 4³⁰ PM | 1948. AD: Mrs. Norton Baskin | Van Hornesville / New York.

Tuesday [21 September 1948]

Dearest Marjorie –

Excuse the great delay in answering your invitation![5] Your letter arrived just as we were setting off for a week in Boston – then we arrived back here in the terrific swirl of preopening of seminary.

I would certainly love to come up and see you and see the house – also

---

1 Aubrey Menen (1912–1989), author and satirist of Irish and Indian descent, *The Prevalence of Witches* (New York: Scribners, 1947), the story of a British education official serving in India who confronts stupefying ignorance created by a fear of witchcraft.

2 A. L. [Audrey Lilian] Barker (1918–2002), prolific English novelist and short story writer, *Innocents: Variations on a Theme* (London: Hogarth Press, 1947; New York: Scribners, 1948), winner of the Somerset Maugham Prize, 1947.

3 *Time,* American news magazine published in New York since 1923.

4 The Bighams' daughter Hildreth.

5 From the context, there appears to be an MKR letter missing.

Moe and Idella[1] – I don't wish to commit myself on the new cat.[2] At the moment I don't see any opening in my life, but may I write you again in a week or ten days when I trust, existence will be more coherent? Would sometime in the first half of Oct be OK? It would only be for a couple of days.

We had a sort of mediocre summer. I have made a vow never to go out to the family's in Far Hills again. It's not that it's actively difficult – it's just <u>unsatisfactory</u>. Neither one of us got any work done, and on the other hand we didn't have anything that seemed like a <u>vacation</u>. The closest we came to the latter was 4 days in Boston (the first 3 days were spent at a conference). We spent our time looking at museums & "old Boston" and eating in good restaurants and saw a movie every night. We saw the Olivier <u>Hamlet</u>.[3] It is really a grand movie – play – performance. I don't know exactly what noun to use. Of course there are plenty of details to quibble about, but the total effect is thrilling – full of dramatic tension. And certain [illegible excision] things, the ghost, the soliloquies, can be much better realized in the movies than on the stage. Then there is <u>space</u> which is lacking on the stage.

---

1   Idella Parker, MKR's "perfect maid" from Florida who joined her in Van Hornesville. However, MKR continued to fear that Parker would once again leave her without notice. In a letter to NSB on 27 August 1948, MKR is enthusiastic, "Idella is crazy about it here. She said she couldn't understand how I could bear to leave it. And has she worked." There was a serious effort to integrate Parker into the Van Hornesville scene, as MKR observes in a letter 2 September: Mary Sickler, Louise Young's white maid, and Idella "became great buddies." On 6 September, MKR reported on Idella's interactions with Gertrude "Gertie" Sandvold, cook and wife of the Youngs' gardener, describing them as "together cozily." Yet in a letter to NSB on 13 September, MKR laments, "Idella is beginning to be a little anxious about getting home." On 14 October MKR is grateful that Parker seems happy again: "She has turned cheerful again, and has been very sweet to me." Parker did return briefly to Florida in early September to see her husband Bernard Young, but was back by 29 September to cook and to serve dinner for Louise Young, highlighted by "Japanese persimmon pudding." And Parker promised to stay for NSB's planned visit in October, as MKR writes on 4 October, Parker says "she will stay as long as [she] possibly could. It would make a great difference to our comfort to have her here when you are here, but I can't detain her when she is ready to go" (*Love Letters* 513–15, 517, 521). Parker's memories of her second summer in Van Hornesville are much different. To her, MKR had become irascible, particularly when she had been drinking. As Parker observes, "I was torn between being with my husband and trying to please Mrs. Baskin and stay with her because I knew she needed me. . . . Mrs. Baskin could not make me happy. Just the opposite. Her demands on me were enormous. I'm not talking about work, now, I'm talking about emotional demands. . . . She would go through depressions and bouts of sickness, dark moods and terrible drinking sprees, and here was Idella trying to cope with her day and night." However, "She was a good, kind woman who never meant anyone any harm. The person she hurt most was herself" (*Parker* 109–10). JSB, of course, witnessed these same outbursts, followed by professions of love.

2   Uki, MKR's Siamese cat.

3   Laurence Olivier (1907–1989), starred and directed in the 1948 British adaptation of *Hamlet* (written c. 1599–1601) by William Shakespeare (1564–1616). The film won the Best Picture and the Best Actor Academy Awards.

A movie we saw here in NY, and which you must make a great effort to see when you are here is a Danish film called Day of Wrath.[1] It is about witchcraft at the end of the 16th cent. In Denmark superficially and also about evil and guilt peculiar to no particular century. It is photographically I think the most beautiful film I've ever seen, and wonderfully played. It got perfectly terrible reviews when it opened, and folded in about a week. A couple of weekly mag reviewers (Sat Review of Lit. for one – I don't know who the others were) built up a demand for its return and it is now doing very well. Though in Cue,[2] for instance, it is still reviewed as "overlong, mediocre, tedious, poorly acted" – they reserve their enthusiasm for such movies as The Pirate with Judy Garland![3]

I am at the moment (doubtless not wisely, but too well)[4] immersed in existentialist literature. Have just finished Simone de Beauvoir's book,[5] now reading The Age of Reason,[6] and am headed for Sartre's next book, I forget the name, and Camus' The Plague.[7] Probably I'll have to have a slight course of shock therapy after this to restore my balance – or maybe I'll be mashed for life.

Saw Edith & Peggy Pope[8] a couple of days ago. She returned to Fla. yesterday. E looks very healthy and, for her, positively fat!

Will write very soon again, and hope to be more informative then.

Love,

Julia

---

1   *Day of Wrath*, filmed during the Nazi occupation of Denmark in 1943 and released in 1948, directed by the Danish filmmaker Carl T. Dreyer (1889–1968), plays witchcraft off against betrayal and abandonment.

2   *Cue*, the influential weekly magazine that covered the arts, film, and theater from 1948 until its demise in 1980.

3   *The Pirate* (1948), starring Judy Garland (1922–1969), directed by Vincente Minnelli (1903–1986), with music by Cole Porter (1891–1964).

4   Shakespeare, *Othello* (written c. 1603), where Othello confesses that he "loved not wisely, but too well" (5:2:344–45).

5   Simone de Beauvoir (1908–1986), *Le Sang des Autres* (1945), translated by Roger Senhouse (1899–1970) and Yvonne Moyse (1901–1986?) as *The Blood of Others* (New York: Knopf, 1948), an existential novel about the French Resistance.

6   Jean-Paul Sartre (1905–1980), *L'âge de raison* (1945), translated by Eric Sutton as *The Age of Reason* (New York: Knopf, 1947), an existential novel that pursues Sartre's belief that the ultimate aim of human kind is freedom.

7   Albert Camus (1913–1960), *La Peste* (1947), trans. Stuart Gilbert (1883–1969) as *The Plague* (London: Hamilton, 1948), a novel that highlights Camus' belief that freedom can only be found if the absurdist nature of the world were accepted.

8   Edith Pope and Margaret "Peggy" Pope Watson (b. 1938), daughter.

JSB to MKR, 6 October 1948. ALS, 2 pp. PM: NEW YORK, N.Y. |
OCT 7 | 5-PM | 1948. AD: Mrs. Norton Baskin | Van Hornesville |
New York.

Oct 6. [1948]

Dearest Marjorie –

Well, life just hasn't unsnarled itself much and I don't see at the moment
how I can get away. Right now I am suffering an infected antrum – or in
plain English sinus trouble – bad. In the good old days, you may remember,
I went down to Palm Beach[1] for this, but now I just stay indoors as much as
possible and take aspirin and leave the rest to the healing powers which, we
are told, do exist. The only medical treatment seems to be penicillin which I
tried last winter. Penicillin I then found out makes me sicker than anything
except that other formidable P, pregnancy. I trust I will be all well by next
Tues. as B. Abbott[2] wishes to begin photographing NY then.

I had longed to get out to Morristown to do some pictures of Granny's
house, garden, & chapel, as all of it must be sold as soon as possible.[3] Between
sinus & bad weather no luck so far. Perhaps I can go Fri, I am anxious to have
some pictures of the place which has so many happy memories for me, and
it looks lovely just now with masses of zinnias hardy chrysanthemums, (?),
marigolds, and other flowers which are beyond my knowledge.

This weekend I am taking care of Hildie which is a pretty full time affair,
taking in Sat, Sun & Mon which brings me up against Abbott. Maybe I'll
throw her over one day and go out.[4]

Life seems definately [sic] less bright without Granny. She was so full of
gaiety and her own dry outrageous humor. And of course I feel very keenly
the loss of my best friend for she really was that – The one person of whom I
felt sure that she was never at any time so involved in her own affairs as not
to be concerned with mine, and who gave me a great deal of both love and
material things with no demands for any sort of recompense or gratitude. I
shall always remember her wonderful example of unselfish love to me and
hope someday to equal it. Perhaps one has to be a grandmother first.

---

1   Palm Beach, Florida.

2   Berenice Abbott, the celebrated photographer, who is teaching JSB the tricks of the trade.

3   Louise Flagg Scribner lived at "The Gables" in Morristown, New Jersey. She died on 30 September 1948.

4   As in abandon her daughter Hildreth so she can go out to learn photographic techniques with Berenice Abbott.

I hope you are all over your grippe and that the week's work went – goes – well. I'll write again soon when I'm less mentally disheveled.

Much love,

Julia

. . .

MKR to JSB, 19 November 1948. TLS, 1 p. Envelope is missing. LH: Mrs. Norton Baskin | crescent beach | st. augustine, florida.

Nov. 19, 1948

Dearest Julia:

I was so disappointed that you didn't get to Van Hornesville and that I didn't make New York City. Just to see you. I was very ill for about six weeks with one of the old intestinal attacks,[1] but worked hard on a long story for POST and M.G.M. which Carl Brandt[2] thought was fine---only to have it heartily rejected by both.[3] It served me right, as I should never waste time on stuff that isn't reasonably creative. However, on the strength of Carl's approval, I had furnished my house recklessly, counting on the big sale---.

I continue to grieve with you and for you over your darling Granny's loss.[4] There are so few people in one's life who can give objective interest and sympathy, as she gave you. I like to think that I can offer you a fraction of the same sort of love and concern. Yet you could call on her at any moment, and I am so far away.

---

1   MKR suffered recurring bouts with diverticulosis from late September through November. In a letter to NSB on 24 September 1948, she complains, "I just had to wait for Idella [Parker] to leave, to have an old-fashion intestinal attack, the kind for which I used to go to the Riverside Hospital [Jacksonville, Florida]." Again, on 7 October, "Damn it, I had a day and a half free from pain and thought I was all right, then I was right back up to my ears in it again. I have watched everything carefully for some time, diet, liquor, even cigarettes. I must be tense as hell about something, and I can't figure it out." Once again, on 8 October, "Then last night and this morning the fiend hit again, and no amount of Phenobarbitol helped. . . . I have had worse attacks, but never a bad one that lasted so long---three weeks now." The attacks continued, as she reports on 14 October, "I had a marvelous day yesterday, entirely free from pain. Then I woke up at 5 A.M. today in agony again." (*Love Letters* 518, 521–23, 525).

2   MKR's New York literary agent.

3   The story, involving the canine corps in World War II, had a working title of "A Bad Name Dog" and was rejected by MGM, which wanted another story for another Lassie movie, and by the *Saturday Evening Post*. The whole experience MKR later described as a "fiasco" (*Love Letters* 591). See also Tarr, *Bibliography*, 267.

4   That is, the death of JSB's grandmother Louise Flagg Scribner. See JSB's letter on 6 October 1948.

It would be wonderful if you and Tom---even Hildy[1] and her nurse--- (Norton would say, <u>especially</u> Hildy) could have a vacation here with us this winter. I am sure I told you that Norton so enlarged the cottage that we have three bath-rooms and three bedrooms. If that does not work out, perhaps you could come down alone for a bit. I am full of Lecomte du Nouy's "Of Human Destiny" and of William Voght's "The Road to Survival".[2]

Much love, and my best to Tom,

Marjorie[3]

. . .

MKR to JSB, 5 January 1949. TLS, 1 p. Envelope is missing. LH:
MARJORIE KINNAN RAWLINGS | CROSS CREEK | HAWTHORN, FLORIDA.

Baskin
St. Augustine

Jan. 5, 1949

Dearest Julia:

Your box was terrific. I had read in the Tribune about the rare honey.[4] When I came to the six jelly jars, I thought, "It just can't be quince", but 'twas, and for supper one evening when I was alone, I ate a whole jar with bread and Cross Creek butter and tea. You were a darling to remember my tastes.

---

1   JSB's pet name for her daughter Hildreth.

2   Pierre Lecomte du Noüy (1883–1947), *Human Destiny* (London, Longmans, Green, 1947), argues that biological evolution naturally extends to the spiritual realm. MKR writes to NSB on 8 October 1948, "I am so happy and relieved that you have been suffering. Now is the time for you to read Lecomte de Noüy's 'Of Human Destiny.' You will realize why you are dissatisfied with yourself" (*Love Letters* 522). William Vogt (1902–1968), *The Road to Survival* (New York: Sloane, 1948), argues that the pressures of population are overwhelming the capacity to produce enough food. Vogt, a conservationist, believes that capitalism is responsible for the imbalance. MKR recommends Vogt's book to NSB, saying the conclusions have "stirred me deeply. It is both stimulating and terrifying. Not because of the atom bomb, but because of the world's destruction of its natural resources . . . so that if things continue as they are going, in a few decades, there will not be sufficient food or water supply for the whole earth. [Vogt] suggests practical remedies, and I must say they are drastic. They include . . . contraceptives!" (*Love Letters* 523). Vogt was the president of the Planned Parenthood Federation of America.

3   MKR types "Much love," then finishes the letter in pen.

4   Perhaps MKR is referring to "Rare Honeys Here Again from Several States." *New York Herald-Tribune* (18 February 1948).

Of course, last year's revolting gift of a man sipping poison through a straw, on a chartreuse background, also catered to my tastes.[1]

Suicide, with or without straw, often seems tempting just now, both because I cannot get to work on my book,[2] and because we have been involved in the most loathsome large parties, two of which we gave ourselves. One night we had champagne punch and buffet supper for 35 of the more respectable local element, and the next night we had hard liquor and buffet for 40 of the more disreputable, including the Popes.[3] The following night, we felt obliged to attend a New Year's Eve champagne party, where I became momentarily and drunkenly infatuated with a strange man, whom I found later to be a homo---.[4]

I am anxious to hear about your photography.

All my love,

Marjorie

· · ·

JSB to MKR, 10 January 1949. ALS, 5 pp. PM: NEW YORK, N.Y. | JAN 12 | 2^{30} PM | 1949. AD: Mrs. Norton Baskin | Crescent Beach | St Augustine | Florida. RA: J. Bigham | 6 Chelsea Sq. N.Y.C. 11. VIA AIR MAIL envelope.

Jan 10 [1949][5]

Dearest Marjorie –

How awful! Not only have I not yet answered your letter of what must be a month ago, but you get in the first Christmas present thank you letter.

I'm glad you are pleased with the honey etc. I can assure you that your oranges were received with the greatest joy. Hildie was rolling them all over the pantry as soon as we got the box open and has insisted on having an "onch" (sounds like conch without the first c) at least 3 times a day since then. They tasted <u>wonderful</u> to us – particularly as we had been having a long siege of tomato juice for breakfast for economy's sake. They really were very sweet & delicious – much better than anything we can buy here – Many thanks.

---

1 JSB gifted the ashtray to MKR on the previous Christmas. See her letter on 27 December 1947.
2 The manuscript of *The Sojourner.*
3 Verle Pope and Edith Pope.
4 Not identified.
5 Written in a second hand after date on p. 1: [49].

And thanks too for your sweet letter and the invitation to visit.[1] It is most tempting – but I don't see how it could be worked short of some mathematical miracles, that is, multiplying myself and time & our income. In this age of the revolution of concepts of matter[2] perhaps we shouldn't give up hope. I just can't leave Tom & Hildie and there isn't a prayer of T. getting away – and if we could, since Granny's death[3] and until her estate is settled, we are financially not in traveling condition! I am awfully disappointed because it would be heaven to get away for a little and particularly to Fla, but most of all because I so much miss seeing you. I do wish we didn't live so far apart. Well, anyway, it was a wonderful idea and you were sweet to ask us all.

Every year since we have been married it seems to me I have written you that "life is getting more hectic". I feel like an old phonograph record saying the same thing again, but, damn it, it's true – this year with a vengeance. Lately we have had weeks when we haven't had dinner together more than 3 nights in the week and then after it is with guests or in someone else's house! Poor Tom who has the constitution of an ox is finally beginning to show signs of wear[.]

He has just had a headache for a solid week and he never has headaches for more than an hour once in six months. The days are just a mad rush from one thing to another – often with not enough time to do each thing properly which is most tiring because it takes away the source of accomplishment. Of course, there is no time to do more than worry about his doctorate.

I have such a damn sympathetic nature that I get tired when he does even if I haven't done much. But I too seem to have got myself into a permanent rut behind life. I never catch up in things to be done both in and out of the house, and letters to be written and, worst of all, pictures to be taken, and prints to be made. Poor Hildie has had her bangs lopsided for 10 days – the front door has been painted on just one side for about 2 months. I won't go in to the photographic angle.

Actually in that field there is news. It looks as if in spite of myself I have at last started on my professional career. I did portraits of the children of two people I know in Far Hills at what will be my prices for a starter ($10 a print – 8×10 – or 6 for $50). They turned out very well, and have been raved over to a degree that quite surprises me. I have had rumors of two more assign-

---

1   See MKR's letter of invitation on 19 November 1948.

2   JSB might be referring to Graham Greene (1904–1991), *The Heart of the Matter* (London: Heinemann, 1948), a novel about personal responsibility and moral failure. On the other hand, she may be referring to current science on nuclear energy, the most famous of which was the so-called Atom Train in 1947–1948, where British scientists shared their knowledge of nuclear theory.

3   Louise Flagg Scribner died on 30 September 1948.

ments (coming from those) but they are not yet definite. In my more logical moments I can hardly see how even with such a "will to failure" as mine I can fail to get going – because the start was excellent and very strategic.

One of the parents of one photographee is a member of a very large family all of whom have to do whatever one has done – and they are also very much the leaders of Far Hills. Well, hope for the best.

I have been having a very bad time lately with my headaches, but I am not discouraged and even am hopeful that the bad period may be because I am getting closer and closer to the crux of the whole business.

I have had very little time for reading, but one thing which I must insist that you read too is "The Shaking of the Foundations" by Paul Tillich (This is a Scribner's book, maybe you can get Wallace to send it or Daddy.)[1] Tillich is considered by many knowing people (including my husband) to be the most profound Protestant theologian of the day – and one of the great ones of all times. He is also a most wonderful & lovable person. His theological writings are very tough reading, but this is a book of his sermons which put many of his ideas in a more human language. The ones you must read are "You are accepted" p. 153 and "The Yoke of religion" p. 93. I think these are both tremendous – they say so much that perhaps you can't get it all at once. I find myself thinking of them often, and getting more from them on each return. Do get this as soon as you can.

Much love to you,

Julia.

P.S. Of course love to Norton! And tell him Hildie says as soon as she gets a good picture of herself she'll send him one.

. . .

MKR to JSB, 24 February 1949. TLS, 2 pp. PM: SAINT AUGUSTNE | FEB 24 | 3³⁰ PM | 1949 | FLA. AD: Mrs. Thomas J. Bigham | 175 Ninth Avenue | New York City 11. LH: Mrs. Norton Baskin | CRESCENT BEACH | ST. AUGUSTINE, FLORIDA.

Feb. 24, 1949

Dearest Julia:

---

1   Paul Tillich (1886–1965), German American Christian existentialist and Lutheran theologian, *The Shaking of the Foundations* (New York: Scribners, 1948). Wallace Meyer and Charles Scribner III.

We have all been so disappointed that your mother and father[1] do not plan to stop here. Vera said over the 'phone that they might just possibly make a separate trip later, by car. I hope so. And if they do, why couldn't you come with them?

It is now full-fledged spring, and we have had no winter at all. I feel a bit cheated.

Edith plans April Fool's Day as the date for finishing the re-writing of her book.[2] I am so praying that it will be really good. I have made three <u>more</u> beginnings on mine, still all lousy.[3]

I am having a furnace put in the Van Hornesville house, and plan to go up very early, perhaps late April. I must be there, not only to work, but to catch the lilacs, iris and peonies.

I have a pitifully small flower garden here this year, stock, petunias, baby's breath and a dozen or so rose-bushes, including my beloved Pinnochios [*sic*], to which you introduced me. The truck-driver for the water-softener truck reported to Norton the other day that he had been looking forward all week to seeing my roses, but when he arrived, all expectancy, I had cut every one. He said, "I wish she'd of waited another day." So now I must adjust my flower-gathering to the water-softener man.

I followed one of awful [*sic*] impulses a few days ago. I went to call on my beloved James Cabell, and found him alone in the front room of their hotel suite, a bed-living-room, where his wife sleeps. We talked a while, and he called to his poor idiot son who was outside on the porch, that there was a letter for him. Ballard[4] collected his letter and said, "I'll leave you two alone. I know you want to talk." (He certainly is not <u>crazy</u>.) Mr. Cabell squirmed, and I realized that the most pornographic writer[5] in the country was having fits at being alone in a room with a woman. I happened to have in my coat pocket one Nylon stocking, that I had brought in for matching. So as I left the room, I rumpled up the stocking and surreptitiously dropped it on Mrs. Cabell's bed---. There will either be fireworks or it will fall completely flat. If the latter, I'll know what I've often suspected, that it's all in his mind---.[6]

I was appalled by your picture of utter poverty in the Bigham household, when you reported that you'd been using tomato juice for breakfast because

---

1 Charles Scribner III and Vera Scribner.

2 Edith Pope, most likely the manuscript of her novel *River in the Wind* (1954).

3 The manuscript of *The Sojourner* (1953).

4 James Branch Cabell (1879–1958); Priscilla Bradley Cabell (1875–1949); Ballard Hartwell Cabell (1915–1980), the son who became an accomplished painter.

5 MKR is referring to Cabell's novel, *Jurgen* (1919), which created a sensation for its graphic sexual content, and which was banned from display by the New York Society for the Prevention of Vice.

6 MKR is having fun with the adage that "sex is all in the mind."

you couldn't afford oranges. Something is hay-wire here, not only because I can't quite see you doling out bits of rice to a starving child, but because at that time Florida oranges were selling at so low a price that they weren't worth picking. Thanks to the California and Texas freezes, their loss will be our gain, and I hope to make some money on the grove this year.

Am still having a wonderful time with the quince jelly and marvelous honies,[1] but feel that you and yours must have lived on bread and water for a week, to pay for them. Ahem.

Much love,

Marjorie

. . .

JSB to MKR, 2 March 1949. ALS, 4 pp. PM: NEW YORK, N.Y. | MAR 2 | 6-PM | 1949. AD: Mrs. Norton Baskin | Crescent Beach RFD | St Augustine, Florida. RA: JULIA S. BIGHAM | 6 CHELSEA SQUARE | NEW YORK 11, N.Y. LH: CHELSEA 2-8467 [telephone] | JULIA S. BIGHAM | PHOTOGRAPHER | 6 CHELSEA SQUARE, NEW YORK 11, n.y. VIA AIR MAIL sticker.

March 2 [1949][2]

Dearest Marjorie –

Thought you'ld be interested to <say> ^see^ the latest step in the slow crawl from amateurism to professionalism. I'm rather depressed by it (the paper not the progress!). I seem to be in a rut of being gypped at the moment. The damn thing looks very shoestring instead of elegant as I had planned – all because the printer talked much faster than I protested and I just sat there being shoved around. I had to get some stuff printed because I've done a couple of jobs for dough and I don't get paid the dough!

Did anything come of the nylon stocking?[3] I have a passion for practical jokes, but I never indulge it because of my awful foresighted worry (the faculty that kept me from killing Buzz[4] as a kid). There was one occasion I passed up that frustrates me to this day: My No. 1 analyst (I am now with

---

1   Here the plural of honey, which JSB had sent as a Christmas present.

2   Written in a second hand at the top of p. 1: [3–2–59].

3   The one hose that MKR left on the bed of Priscilla Cabell as a joke. See MKR's letter on 24 February 1949.

4   Charles Scribner IV (aka Jr.), JSB's brother.

No. 2) (I guess I'm a tough nut to crack) (excuse it please) well, as I was saying – he acquired a nearly lifesize [*sic*] bust of Freud. One day as I was just
wading into my past, he said "I must show you something." I thought at least
he wanted my opinion on some photographs – but no. I had to see this bust
sitting in the place of honor in the living room – waiting room (he had home
& office combined). He was so impressed & delighted with the thing that immediately to the practical joke dept. of my mind there came the idea to get
one of those red religious vigil lights & set it burning in front of it. Damn it
I never did it because I was afraid it might upset a patient instead of him.

I am impressed to see that your novelist's intuition works even at a distance. How right you are to sense something wrong in our tomato-juice
drinking. It is something that has been wrong for some time & steadily gets
worse or in other words, the budget. As you know we live in great elegance
with a maid & a nurse – also we have a car. This leaves very little money over
to eat on, particularly now that I no longer get $50 a month from Granny.[1]
We eat in what you would no doubt consider a painfully economical way. We
have also given up such things as going to plays, music etc, buying books,
subscribing to magazines – My motto is any hardships so long as I have a
maid to help me bear them. Don't worry about Christmas. That comes under
"unsavable money"!

I have read a most fascinating book recently – <u>All Hallows Eve</u> by Chas.
Williams put out last fall I think by a new house: Pellegrini & Cudahy.[2] I
strongly recommend it to you. He is a favorite of the literary Anglicans T. S.
Eliot, D. Sayers, C. S. Lewis etc.[3] Now I am reading more about the devil –
<u>The Devil's Share</u> by deRougemont.[4] I cannot believe in the exterior devil of
Williams & deRougemont – I see evil as springing from man due to anxiety
as a result of sin – sin defined by Tillich[5] as separation. Have you read the
Tillich? I insist that you do. Immediately, deR's book is very interesting and
most perceptive & penetrating aside from his devil.

---

1 Louise Flagg Scribner, who died on 30 September 1948. The value of $50 in 1948 would be ap-
proximately $583 in 2022 dollars.

2 Charles Williams (1886–1945), English novelist, *All Hallows' Eve* [1945] (New York: Pellegrini &
Cudahy, 1948).

3 T. S. Eliot (1888–1965), English poet and essayist; Dorothy Sayers (1893–1957), English novelist
famous for her detective stories; C. S. Lewis (1898–1963), English essayist and fiction writer. Eliot
wrote introductions to the first three of Williams's novels.

4 Denis de Rougemont (1906–1985), *The Devil's Way* [*Le Part du Diable* 1942] (New York: Pantheon, 1944) addresses the paradox of believing in the existence of God but not in the existence of
Satan.

5 Paul Tillich, "sin as separation"—that is, separation from others, from one's self, and from God.

I'm sorry the book is being so stubborn.[1] Maybe the northern spring will thaw it. Van Hornesville must be just heaven in April & May – Maybe, if it accords with your pleasure, I could come & look at it?

My work is not progressing at all either. My "money" jobs were received with effusive acclaim, but no more orders! I am plotting self-promotion schemes at the moment.

Much love,

Julia

. . .

MKR to JSB, 2 May 1949. TLS, 1 p. Envelope is missing. LH: Marjorie Kinnan Rawlings | cross creek | hawthorn, florida.

St. Augustine

May 2, 1949

Dearest Julia:

Am picking up my new car[2] in Ocala tomorrow, ^Tuesday^ packing Wednesday, and leaving very early Thursday morning May 5, with Idella, dog and cat,[3] for Van Hornesville.

Want to speak of two things, hurriedly.

1. Hope you can come to see me soon after I get there, as I MUST spend the summer in Isolation, to get into the book that has tormented me for so long. Norton says he will not come near me until I am so deep in the book that he couldn't bother me---says he is tired of my alibis.

2. A long story that I'll have to tell you in person, but am obliged to head north before my new will is drawn up. Phil May my lawyer, and Norton, both know what I want, and I am naming you as my literary executor (executrix). Will explain the reasons when I see you, but one important angle is that you would never allow any of my trash, such as the serial "Mountain Prelude" to be published.[4]

---

1   MKR's manuscript of *The Sojourner*.

2   The Oldsmobile that replaced the one MKR wrecked. See MKR's letter on 25 April 1947.

3   Idella Parker, Moe, and Uki, MKR's Siamese cat.

4   "Mountain Prelude" appeared in serial in the *Saturday Evening Post* in 1947. MKR means that she never wants it published as a book.

Will phone you from Van Hornesville.

Much love,

Marjorie

. . .

MKR to JSB, 13 May 1949. TLS, 2 pp. Envelope is missing.

Van Hornesville

May 13, 1949

Dearest Julia:

I wrote you so hurriedly just before leaving Florida, and realize my note must have sounded as arbitrary as the Communist Manifesto.[1]

Of course, I hope you will come up to visit me <u>whenever</u> you can. If the still nebulous book[2] should ever reach a stage where it would be possible to interrupt it, I could only rejoice.

Moreover, you are not obliged to be my literary executor. My reason for pouncing on you is a longish story. I have been thinking about it, and feel that it would probably be an unwarranted imposition, and would be a great chore for you, while the other two applicants really want the job.[3] I do want to talk this over with you.

I should have 'phoned you, but was afraid I'd catch you at just the wrong moment. Wish you would call me collect any time this Sunday---Richfield Springs 377 F2. I'll be in all day, except for my afternoon walk if it isn't raining.

I do hope you can come soon, only because it is such a lovely time of year in the country. The 28 degree cold of two days ago presumably killed all the apple bloom around Van Hornesville, but up here on Mt. Tom[4] it is not harmed at all. My lilacs will be in full bloom in another week. Peonies and lilies of the valley are in bud. Iris is slow. I arrived too late for the blood-root, but have been gathering violets in three colors, trillium, jack-in-the-pulpit, rue anemone, foam-

---

1   Karl Marx (1818–1883), German socialist thinker, and Friedrich Engels (1820–1895), German Communist philosopher, *The Communist Manifesto* [*Manifest der Kommunistichen Partei*] (London: Burghard, 1848) espouses that capitalism, an offshoot of feudalism, must be replaced by socialism, and eventually by communism.

2   The manuscript of *The Sojourner*.

3   The one serious applicant was Clifford Lyons. The other was MKR's brother, Arthur Houston Kinnan.

4   Mount Tom, central New York, elevation 2,444 ft.

flower, and the tail end of the Dutchmen's breeches. And sprays of wild apple blossom. Still must make a serious search for yellow lady-slippers.

I had an oil-burning automatic furnace put in this spring, and while I'd prefer keeping the house cozy with the three fireplaces, it would take a constant procession of little colored boys toting in wood, rather impractical in these parts.

Idella[1] said yesterday after a repair-man left, "Don't these people up here sound funny!" I said, "Have you happened to think how we sound to them?" "No'm. How do we?" I said, "Funny".

Mary Sickler[2] has run away with a truck-driver. She has the little boy with her.

I haven't heard from you in so long, and have no idea how busy you are professionally, but I do want so much to see you.

Much love,

Marjorie

. . .

JSB to MKR, [10? June 1949]. ANS, 1 p. Envelope is missing. No date on letter.[3]

[10? June 1949]

Dearest Marjorie –

---

1   Idella Parker.

2   Mary Sickler, both cook and helper for the Owen D. Youngs, and on occasion for MKR.

3   Written in a second hand at the top of p. 1: July? 1949?, which is incorrect. The conjectured date of this letter, 10? June 1949, depends upon what MKR writes to NSB in the *Love Letters*, what JSB says in this letter, and what is said in the next letter. In a letter to NSB on 17 May 1949, MKR reports, "Julia phoned me Sunday [15 May], and will come up about the end of the month. On 1 June, MKR writes, "Haven't heard from Julia again. . . . Am not keen about having Julia just now, but having invited her, will let her come when she wants to." On 4 June, MKR is worried that the Norman Bergs will arrive when JSB is there and writes, "I 'phoned Julia this morning, and she is coming early this next week for a long week-end. She is taking Hildy [Hildreth] with the nurse to Far Hills on Monday [6 June], to be parked for the summer. . . . She is most anxious to come. It will be wonderful to have her." This would mean, according to JSB in this letter, that she was to arrive in Van Hornesville on Wednesday 8 June. Apparently, that did not happen, for MKR next mentions JSB to NSB is in her letter on 1 July: "Julia and I went down to the Young's [*sic*] last night after dinner," which means that they went to the Youngs on 30 June, a Thursday. Therefore, based on JSB's train dates in the above letter, she must have arrived in Van Hornesville on Wednesday 29 June and departed on Saturday 2 July for New York. These dates assume, of course, that she did not change her train dates, either coming, or going, or both. See *Love Letters* 529, 531–32. See also the notes to MKR's letter on 11 June 1949.

This will not be in any way an entertaining note – as I have just spent the most grueling gruesome morning afternoon and night in the darkroom – but I felt I had better get word to you at once of my plans. I called the station today & they say there is <not> no change to be made in the daily 3:48 EST train – So I will take that on Wed. and arrive in Fort Plain at 9:19 <She> daylight time.[1] I am sorry to keep you up later than the chickens this night – but then you shouldn't lose track of what the dark looks like. I figure on taking the morning train down on Sat – 8:40 standard – gets me to NYC 1:15 standard.

After contemplating trays of chemicals and other such dreary subjects it will be wonderful to get a look at a great big piece of country – And very good to see you after what seems like years!

Much love,

Julia

. . .

MKR to JSB, 11 June 1949. TLS, 2 pp. PM: FORT PLAIN | JUN 11 | 2 PM | 1949 | N.Y. AD: Mrs. Thomas J. Bigham, Jr. | 175 Ninth Avenue | New York City 11. LH: Van Hornesville, New York.

June 11, 1949

Dearest Julia:

Your note in the mail this morning,[2] and I am terribly disappointed that you plan to stay so short a time. This, for more than one reason.

Since you 'phoned me, I have talked with Norton on the 'phone, and he is coming up for a visit. I told him I was expecting you, and said I knew we would all have a good time if you over-lapped, but he said, no, that it had been so long since you and I had any real time together, that he wouldn't come until we had had our visit.[3] I didn't know then how long you could stay, but made this suggestion: that when you left here, since you didn't mind New York City traffic, you could drive me down in my car, to meet Norton. The best Florida train gets in to Penn Station about 2 P.M., E.S.T. Norton <u>has</u> made the connection with the Fort Plain train, at 3:48 out of the Grand

---

1   Fort Plain, New York. MKR would have had to drive from Van Hornesville to Fort Plain, approximately twelve miles, to pick JSB up.

2   That is, JSB's previous letter conjecturally dated [10? June 1949]. See 428, n. 3, for an accounting of JSB's actual arrival and departure.

3   NSB arrived on 17 June and departed on 28 June (see *Selected Letters* 334).

Central Station,[1] but when the Florida train is late getting into Penn, it is sometimes just too bad.

NOW, <if> if you positively must leave me Sat. A.M., I could not drive down to N.Y., as that evening I am having the big picnic supper and square dance for everybody (and their wives) who helped me on my house, about 24 people. They have already been invited for that date, June 18, so I must be here.[2]

I thought of three alternatives. The best would be for you to wait over until Sunday, or better yet, Monday,[3] when we would drive down to N.Y. to meet Norton. I have just written him, in case this works out, whether he would want to head straight out for here (I think he would) or spend the night in New York.

Another alternative, if you do have to leave here Saturday, would be for you to drive my car to New York, (it would save you half your railroad fare!) for Norton to come here in.[4]

I guess it is the third alternative, that in this latter case, Norton would either spend the night in N.Y.C. or again, would head directly here in my car. But I did write him that if you have to leave here on Saturday, it would probably be better for you to go home by train, and for him to come here by train.[5]

Let me know all about this, and please call me <u>collect</u>, Richfield Springs 377-F2. You didn't call me collect when I <u>asked</u> it.[6]

It will be so good to see you.

Much love,

<u>Marjorie</u>

1 The distance from Penn Station to Grand Central Station is just over a mile and takes approximately twelve minutes by taxi, assuming normal traffic.

2 At this juncture JSB has said, likely by telephone, that she has to leave on Saturday, June 18.

3 Sunday, 19 June, or Monday, 20 June. This plan was obviously scrapped because NSB arrived in Van Hornesville on 17 June (see 429, n. 3).

4 This plan was obviously also scrapped since NSB arrived in Van Hornesville on 17 June.

5 JSB did take the train, and did not arrive until 29 June, departing on 2 July (see MKR's letter dated [10? June], 428, n. 3). Thus, JSB and NSB did not see each other, which is what MKR hoped for in the first place, since she wanted JSB to herself, a fact that NSB recognized.

6 MKR wants JSB to call collect because she is aware of JSB's worry that she and Thomas Bigham have little money to spare. See JSB's lamentations about finances in letters on 10 January and 2 March 1949.

. . .

MKR to JSB, 7 and 12 July 1949. TLS, 2 pp. PM: VAN HORNESVILLE | JUL | 13 | A.M. | 1949 | N.Y. AD: Mrs. Thomas J. Bigham, Jr. | c/o Scribner | Far Hills | New Jersey. LH: Van Hornesville, New York.

July 7, 1949

Dearest Julia:

It was such fun, having you here even for so brief a time.[1]

With my usual disaffinity for everything mechanical, I've already blown an important fuse, wrecked the automatic coffee-maker, and found myself unable to cope with the electric oven, which turns itself off before I am done with it. And Gertrude,[2] who does a marvelous job of cleaning up, is driving me crazy because she takes from 3 to 3½ hours each morning instead of the 1½ to 2 hours I expected, and by the time I drive her home, it is still too early for the mail, so rather than make a second trip to Van Hornesville, I wait for it, and by the time I am back here, it is 11 o'clock, and my zest for writing is dissipated. Gertrude is not only very happy in her job, but I am paying her a very high price by the hour, and I am evidently buying a davenport or a refrigerator for her new home---.

I am returning the book you left with me, "God's Thumb Down".[3] It seemed to me a magnificent piece of work. With any luck at all, I think it will do extremely well. It is certainly infinitely beyond "The Girl on the Via Flaminia."[4]

Since you left, Moe has stopped making smells, the toilet has stopped sweating, and the field across from the house has been mowed, making good walking.[5]

Much love,

<u>Marjorie</u>

---

1 JSB was in Van Hornesville from 29 June to 2 July. See JSB's letter dated [10? June 1949] and MKR's letter on 11 June 1949.

2 Gertrude "Gertie" Sandvold (1909–1971) was a cook and a housemaid for the Owen D. Youngs and also on occasion for MKR.

3 Oscar de Liso (1916–1990), Italian-born writer, *God's Thumb Down* (New York: Scribners, 1949), a novel about the Communist threat in Italy, set against personal angst and despair and the glimmer of hope and redemption.

4 Alfred Hayes (1911–1985), British novelist, poet, and playwright, *The Girl on the Via Flaminia* (New York: Harper, 1949), a novel of romance set in Rome just after World War II.

5 Ellis J. and Lilian Frederick, who owned the farm next to MKR, also owned the field.

July 12

And Uki has returned to his own bed.[1]

Two other most welcome books arrived, and I have finished "The Stumbling Stone"[2] (most engaging, but not up to "Witches") and am nearly through the Diary of a Country Priest[3]---utterly touching.

I have pulled 9 bushel baskets of weeds, engaged a neighbor to cut all the grass with a power mower, but since the garden grass plot needed cutting again, he said I must get it raked this morning, when he would return to go over it. I did my haying from 6:30 to 8:15---. Also have made my currant jelly and picked wild raspberries for jam.

I had a charming note from Joan Sunderland[4]---what a smart bride to get it over with before the wedding--and she thanked me for "the very large old print". I should probably have sent her more goblets, and if you find Buzzie[5] doesn't share our enthusiasm for Audubons,[6] perhaps you can wangle the Havell[7] out of them for yourself. If not, I'll get you a nice one some other time.

I'll return the three books together as soon as I finish the Diary. And with great thanks.

I have enjoyed studying Hildy's portrait. Such a quizzical, earnest little face, questioning the world and everyone in it, but ready to be convinced---.

---

1   Uki, the Siamese cat, had been creating problems since MKR arrived in Van Hornesville. First it ran away and had to be rescued in the middle of the night from a tree. But more important to MKR, the cat refused at first to sleep in his appointed bed near the kitchen, with the hope that he would catch mice during the night. As MKR reports to NSB on 1 June 1949, "He caught nothing at all, and now will not speak to me after my cruelty." Instead, Uki demanded to sleep with either MKR or Idella Parker, or else "heart-broken" he "yowled and scratched" at various doors (Love Letters 530–31). Not that JSB would care, since she did not like cats, unless they remained at a distance and were not heard. MKR is reassuring JSB here that matters now seem to be under control. It should be noted here that MKR's trials and tribulations with Uki, whom NSB adored, provide some of the more comic moments in Love Letters.

2   Aubrey Menen (1912–1989), Anglo-India novelist The Stumbling Stone (New York: Scribners, 1949), a satire on faith; The Prevalence of Witches (New York: Scribners, 1948), a satire on education.

3   Georges Bernanos (1888–1948), French novelist, Journal d'un carécampagne [The Diary of a Country Priest] (1937). Trans. Pamela Morris (London: Boriswood, 1937), a novel about a disillusioned priest who begins to question his faith.

4   Joan Sunderland, Janette Kissel "Joan" Sunderland (1927–2012), wife of Charles Scribner IV (1921–1995).

5   Charles Scribner IV (aka Jr.), JSB's brother.

6   MKR sent an Audubon print to Scribner IV as a wedding present in 1949.

7   The print of John James Audubon's Birds of America. Robert Havell Sr. oversaw the printing and coloring, and Robert Havell Jr. did the engravings. See MKR's letter on 10 January 1945 for her evaluation of Audubon prints done by Havell and son.

JSB to MKR, [26?] July 1949. ALS, 4 pp. PM: NEW YORK, N.Y. | Jul 27 | 9-AM | 1949. AD: Mrs. Norton Baskin | Van Hornesville | New York.

Tuesday [26? July 1949][1]

Dearest Marjorie –

I hope your female intuition told you I was still alive – and I apologize for not giving you any evidence of the fact. Actually, I am alive only in the bare minimum sense. Pittsburgh was more exhausting even than I had thought possible. We were all tired before we left. The plane trip was terribly rough and we were all, including Hildie, within about one gulp of being sick. The Golden Wedding reception,[2] which entailed two days of desperate preparation, lasted from 2:30 to 11 PM!! And in all that time there wasn't 5 minutes when there weren't people coming and going. The only respite was ½ hour at supper time when we, (the family), went down to the cellar in shifts & ate sandwiches & drank milk and sat down. The older & younger generations survived marvelously, but the middle generation was almost dead. The next day there was a celebration of Holy Communion at the church where they were married & then a lunch and then we staggered onto the airplane – I had by that time a splitting headache – so bad for an hour before we left I was changing my mind every 2 minutes. I could make it – I couldn't make it. The only thing to be said about that airplane ride is that it was even worse than the preceding one. Hildie, however, enjoyed it thoroughly and ran up and down the aisle generally raising hell. At one point she stopped beside a man sleeping soundly with his mouth wide open – She evidently thought he was hungry, and as she is a very generous girl and as she had a piece of pretzel in her hand, she thrust it firmly into his mouth. Fortunately the man neither choked nor had apoplexy – but he stopped not far short of either. The worst of that incident was that I was too sick to enjoy it properly – but Tom and Marion[3] weren't.

I must say for Buzz's wedding[4] that it wasn't as bad as I thought it would be. (Incidentally, they do know it's an Audubon.)[5] Although it was very large

---

1   Written in a second hand at the top of p. 1: [7-27-49]
2   Golden wedding anniversary of Thomas and Ida Bigham, who were married on 11 July 1899.
3   Marion is not identified.
4   Charles Scribner IV married Janette Kissel "Joan" Sunderland (1927–2012) on 16 July 1949.
5   In MKR's letter to NSB on 12 July 1949, she bluntly questions whether Buzz and Joan appreciated the Audubon she gave them as a wedding present, "Had a note from young Charlie Scribner's

it was quite informal in spirit. I knew all the ushers, and some of them were quite warm admirers of me – so that was most relaxing and ego-boosting. Also Muddy didn't give me hell once – partly, I think, because the other bridesmaids were rather homely and so she felt quite pleased with me and that I did her credit!

My present period of relaxation is not so relaxed or pleasant as I had hoped. Martha[1] is on her vacation & doesn't return till Sunday. There is no doubt, Marjorie, that the weakest link in my chain is domesticity. I just do hate household chores and they do seem to take forever! I'm beginning to feel I'd rather give up eating than cook any more. (I hope this doesn't break up our friendship)

I keep wondering if you have gotten Gertrude[2] or yourself in any control yet. The situation sounded hopelessly stymied as far as creativity is concerned – Unless you take to writing in the middle of the night.

I have developed the pictures of your house & cat,[3] & they look OK. I'll send you pictures but not till this continual damn heatwave is over. This is certainly the worst summer ever. It's just murderous. I had thought that I could make T.[4] take off one or two days a week to go to Jones Beach[5] – but it just doesn't seem we'll ever get there. He is working day & night, poor thing, and I never even get to speak to him except at meals, poor me. And it still isn't thesis.

Well, time to think about cooking the damn dinner. I'm glad you liked the books. It is years since I read "The Diary"[6] but it made such an impression on me. I have perhaps wanted to read it again, so a couple of months ago I just decided to buy another copy and do it. (I had given it away).

Many thanks for the two days of country living you gave me – they still feel good.[7]

Much love,

Julia

---

bride-to-be, thanking me for 'the very large old print.' I should have sent the ash-trays---" (*Love Letters* 534).

1 Martha was the Bighams' cook.

2 Gertrude Sandvold, MKR's part time cook and housekeeper at Van Hornesville. In her letter on 7 and 12 July 1949, MKR complains that it takes her all morning to fetch and then to take home Sandvold, which as a result interrupts her "creative" period.

3 Uki.

4 Thomas Bigham, JSB's husband.

5 Jones Beach is located on the south shore of Long Island, New York.

6 Georges Bernanos, *The Diary of a Country Priest*.

7 JSB is referring to her visit with MKR in Van Hornesville from 28 June to 2 July 1949.

. . .

MKR to JSB, 28 July 1949. TLS, 3 pp. PM: VAN HORNESVILLE
| JUL | 29 | A.M. | 1949 | N.Y. AD: Mrs. Thomas J. Bigham, Jr. | 175
Ninth Avenue | New York City 11. LH: Van Hornesville, New York.

July 28, 1949[1]

Dearest Julia:

I almost had hysterics over Hildie's[2] cramming her pretzel down the sleeping man's maw.

Never think I should look askance at your disinclination for cooking. Since Idella[3] has been away, I have been living on scraps. And yesterday, when my first broccoli was ready, I cut it in famished expectation, put it to soak in cold salted water, and 16 (sixteen) fat green worms floated to the surface.

Things are working out wonderfully with Gertrude[4] since I mentioned casually to Mr. Young that they were <u>not</u> working out, and the next thing I knew he had arranged to have the assistant to their gardener (Gertrude's husband) deliver her here about 1 P.M., and while Gertrude cleans up, the man works in my garden, and then takes her home again. As a result, I am getting well along on my book, though suffering the torments of the damned. Norton wrote me, "No one seems to have invented twilight sleep[5] for book-bearing." Also, coming in the afternoon, Gertrude is anxious to get home again to prepare their own dinner, and the $25 I paid her the first week, has been cut down to about $17.[6] Of course, that still leaves me without anyone to cook for me.

Idella writes that she is ready to return at any time, but I want to wait until she is sure that she can stay with me in the fall, happily, until I go back to Florida. Last fall she went into a decline three weeks before I was ready to leave, and made me miserable, and I don't want it to happen again.[7]

---

1   Written in a second hand on the envelope: July 29, / 1949.

2   See JSB's letter dated [26?] July 1949.

3   Idella Parker had left temporarily to visit her husband, Bernard Young, in St. Augustine.

4   Gertrude Sandvold and her husband, Halvor Sandvold (1905–1983), the Owen D. Youngs' gardener.

5   A method for managing pain with amnesic drugs during childbirth, developed in Germany in the early twentieth century. First-wave feminists formed the National Twilight Sleep Association in 1914 in support of the procedure.

6   MKR complains to NSB in a letter on 5 July 1949, "Gertrude is doing a fine job of cleaning up, but she is having such a good time at it that she takes forever, and it is going to cost me as much as to have Idella do everything" (*Love Letters* 533). Owen D. Young likely heard the same complaint, but perhaps more subtly.

7   On 1 August, MKR shares the same sentiment with NSB, "A good letter from you, and one from Idella. She says she is ready to come any time, just to let her know. . . . She says she has lots to tell me some day. I suppose life with Bernard [Parker's husband] is almost unbearable. . . . I think it is

Gertrude has never lost her Norwegian accent. She "just woves my wittle wose-buds." She said people just didn't wealize how woses dwess up a womb. I passed this on to Norton, saying that it gave a picture of a naked Venus with woses draped across her navel.[1]

My garden is really lovely.

I have returned your three books.[2] And with great thanks.

I do hope that you and Tom can come here in the fall.

With love,

Marjorie

You know, I still have one of your choice books, "Thou and I",[3] at the cottage. I had not finished it. Reading it is an exalting but exhausting experience---you have to move almost into a new plane of thought.

I look forward to the picture of house and cat.[4]

. . .

JSB to MKR, [Mid-August? 1949]. ALS, 3 pp. Envelope is missing.

[Mid-August? 1949][5]

Dearest Marjorie –

Like most of the letters I write you this is staggering along weeks later than I wanted it to be. I was more delighted with your last letter than with any

---

her Reddick family that is the real pull" (*Love Letters* 537). Parker's memory is a bit different. She once had left MKR to be with her husband in New York, concluding, "A person gets weary carrying another person's misery and woe, and gradually I was beginning to feel that I could not carry Mrs. Baskin's much longer" (*Parker* 113).

1   Venus, or Aphrodite, the ancient Greek goddess of love, often depicted naked, but with her genitals covered, not her naval, as in *The Venus de Milo* (Louvre Museum, Paris), the Hellenistic-period statue where her lower half is covered by her robe, and in the Sandro Botticelli (c. 1445–1510), *The Birth of Venus* (c. 1484–1486), painting in which she covers herself with her own hair as she rises from the sea.

2   Georges Bernanos, *The Diary of a Country Priest*; Aubrey Menen, *The Stumbling Stone* and *The Prevalence of Witches*. See MKR's commentary on these works in her letter on 7 and 12 July 1949.

3   Martin Buber (1878–1965), German-Jewish philosopher, *I and Thou* [*Ich und Du*, 1923] (Edinburgh: Clark, 1937), a treatise about humankind's relationship with the multi-presences of God, but of equal importance humankind's existential relationship with the ever-shifting "I-You-It."

4   MKR's home at Van Hornesville and Uki, the cat. See MKR's letter on 7 and 12 July 1949, 432, n. 1, and Figure 9, 319.

5   Written in a second hand at the top of p. 1: [1949]. At the end of this letter, JSB, who is staying with her parents in Far Hills, relates that she cannot see beyond "Aug. 31" when the nurse returns to take care of Hildreth. The "difficult problems" she alludes to are her ever-present migraines that she believes are the result of stress. Since JSB had written to MKR on 26 July, it is likely that this letter was written around mid-August. See also 437, n. 7.

I've had from you in ages – sounds sadistic I know, but I was overjoyed to hear of your labor pains, I do hope that they are becoming harder and more frequent – I wish you the joy of much pain.[1]

I am out in Far Hills with Hildie. The nurse & the maid are vacationing and Tom is making a retreat at Holy Cross monastery. We are only here for a week so I dare say I shall survive, but, as I told you, at the moment parents are a great problem to me.

The books arrived safely and I am glad you liked them, I have the two Chas. Williams novels I told you about – if you haven't ordered them let me know & I can send them to you.[2] As to the Buber I and Thou,[3] it is available again, so keep my copy. I have been reading it again this summer and while it seemed to me wonderful when I first read it, I feel now that I only fractionally appreciated it. It is really something tremendous. I am also reading a sort of sequel to it, a volume of essays called Between Man and Man.[4] I can feel myself growing when I read them. I don't think this has been published here yet – if it has I will send it to you.

I am also reading Ignazio Silone's Bread and Wine[5] which is a very satisfying book. Have you read it? I must confess I haven't gotten very far in Hunters Horn.[6] I started to read it on the plane trip to Pittsburgh just as the going began to be rough, and the sight of it still makes me slightly nauseated.[7] Don't worry I won't forget it's yours – you're not in any hurry for it are you?

As you may have noticed there are some photos in this envelope. One ordinary "snapshot" of Uki and one which, while it may not look so much like him, turned out quite aesthetically. If you want more pictures of the house

---

1   MKR is trying to finish the manuscript of *The Sojourner*. JSB once compared the writing of a book to labor pains in childbirth, wishing that MKR's labor was "so severe that you can't stop anyway" (JSB's letter on 7 December 1949).

2   JSB sent MKR two of Charles Williams's novels. See MKR's response in her letter on 18 November 1949.

3   See MKR's letter on 28 July 1949, 436, n. 3.

4   Martin Buber, *Between Man and Man*. Trans. Ronald Gregor Smith (1913–1968), theologian (London: Kegan Paul, 1947), explores the subtle intricacies of man's relationship with man.

5   Ignazio Silone [Secondo Tranquilli] (1900–1978). Italian anti-Fascist, *Bread and Wine* (New York: Harper, 1937), contrasts the corporeal truth of Fascism and the transcendent truths of God.

6   Harriette Arnow, *Hunter's Horn*, which MKR sent JSB who just could not seem to finish reading the novel. See MKR's letter on 29 December 1949, 451, n. 5.

7   The Bighams attended the golden wedding anniversary of his parents in July 1949. See JSB's letter dated [26?] July 1949, in which she describes the rough airplane ride from New York to Pittsburgh. MKR refers to JSB's letter in her letter to NSB on 23 August, "Julia writes that she longs to come in the autumn, if I'm sure it won't interrupt me" (*Love Letters* 543), the date of which provides further evidence that this letter can be dated around mid-August.

to send to aunts or such, let me know and tell me how little or big you want them.[1]

This has been a difficult summer, full of trials, both inner & outer, and at the moment I haven't strength to look into the future any further than Aug. 31 when the nurse returns – so I really have no idea when or how I shall get up to see you again. But I have it in my mind as something I want to do – of course it is entirely contingent with how you feel about it and its not interfering in any way with your difficult delivery![2]

Must go and cope with Hildie now.

Much love,

Julia

. . .

JSB to MKR, [28?] October 1949. ALS, 4 pp. PM: NEW YORK, N.Y. | OCT 31 | 1[0]-AM | 1949. AD: Mrs. Norton Baskin | <Van Hornesville> | <New York> | Hawthorn | Fla. | Route 1[3]

Friday [28? October 1949][4]

Dearest Marjorie –

At last a quiet if somewhat superheated moment – under the hairdryer. I have still a few ergs of health left from my visit, but life has been awfully vigorous. The portraits I had to do of the 3 boys turned out to be even more exhausting than I had anticipated. The two older (14 & 7) were so furious at having to have their pictures done that they <u>both</u> were in tears on the way home from school. I fear the mother is not at all tactful – She even managed to make 14 miss his football practice. You can imagine the sort of icy & sullen expressions I was faced with. And I myself was in such a turmoil over the whole business that I was up most of the night before with a headache. The most that can be said for the pictures is that there are a few acceptable ones – and considering the circumstances I probably shouldn't view that as a largely negative result. (No pun intended) I have made the proofs for Idella & will send them off today. Here, too, it seems there are a few that are acceptable,

---

1   The photographs JSB alludes were taken by her when she visited MKR in Van Hornesville in the second week of October, as MKR tells NSB on 5 October (see *Love Letters* 551).

2   That is, the submission of the manuscript of *The Sojourner* to Scribners.

3   The letter is readdressed in another hand in pencil.

4   The inferred date is the closest Tuesday to 31 October. Written in a second hand at the top of p. 1: [10–31–49].

though they won't stand too much enlargement – as I had no tripod they're not really sharp. But a picture 5×7 on an 8×10 mount would be as large as she would want anyway, I guess[1]

I finished my bout with English "style" (Compton-Burnett[2]) and I can't feel it greatly influenced my life – quite a forgettable sort of book. But no doubt this is as much a comment on the "life" as the "style". You know I find Henry James[3] quite forgettable too, and I suppose it is only decent & patriotic to say that this shows a vitamin lacking in me and not in him.

I have started rereading "The Country Priest"[4] and this is no disappointment. It must be ten years since I read it, and I can understand it much better now. I remember being quite puzzled by some parts before. It really is a fine book.

I have a curious itch to read this peculiar sounding "Loving" by Henry Greene[5] – but I'm afraid it will be very Compton B'ish. Have you read it? Saturday – Far Hills – – – – – – – – – – – –[6]

Here is as far as I got Fri. Right after the hairdryer I had to go struggle with the Buick place about the underneath of my car. (I was in an accident on the Westside Highway[7] – damn car parked on it on a dark & rainy night – I saw it & put on the brakes, but the road was so greasy they took no hold at all and I slammed right into the back of it. Fortunately no one seriously hurt, but my friend, Ruth Wallach,[8] got a bad sprained ankle.) After finding the car had no hazardous injuries, I had to go home & work madly in the darkroom until time to leave for the country. Today I spent the morning running errands for Muddy, and all afternoon at the races. Rather dull & uneventful except for no reason that I know of I got two nosebleeds. Now I have about an hour before having to beautify myself for a large dinner here. Tomorrow I have to get up early & go to church, then go down to Orange[9] with Tom to his church, thence to lunch with some of his parishoners [sic] – then back here for dinner and

---

1 JSB took and developed pictures of and for Idella Parker. They have not been located.

2 Ivy Compton-Burnett (1884–1969), English novelist, *Two Worlds and Their Ways* (New York: Knopf, 1949), a novel about two sisters who are forced to face different cultures, brought upon them by their insistent parents.

3 Henry James (1843–1916), celebrated American expatriate, who is admired as much for his writing style as the content of his fiction.

4 Georges Bernanos, *The Diary of a Country Priest*. See MKR's evaluation in her letter on 7 and 12 July 1949.

5 Henry Green (1905–1973), *Loving* (London: Hogarth, 1945), a novel of conflicting social class in an Irish home during World War II.

6 October 29.

7 West Side Elevated Highway, part of New York State 9A, that ran along the Hudson River.

8 Ruth Wallach (1902–1992).

9 Orange, a city in Essex County, New Jersey.

then motor Buzz & his wife[1] to town. And then begin another week – When I think back to the time I used to have that wonderful stuff, leisure! Well maybe I'll manage to collect some again when I'm around 70.

I think I really must go downstairs & be sociable now – there are other houseguests here and no doubt I should bear my share of them. I would love to be sitting in your living room peacefully – even if I had to leave Uki[2] beside me! It seems awful that I can't look forward to seeing you & Norton when you are on your southern trek. If there is any change of place or anyway in which I could help you change the plan, let me know.

I am still, at this very late date, glowing gratefully (like a bloody, or should I say, ruddy, ember) over my Van Hornesville visit. Many thanks, Marge. Love to Norton, and very much to yourself.

Julia

P.S. Ruth Wallach & her brother, Hans,[3] who is a professor of psychology at Swathmore, are great admirers of yours. He particularly admires a short story you had in the NY'er (I seem to have missed it) about a halfwitted girl whose husband goes overseas in the war leaving her very lost – she finally wades out into the ocean to try to find him, (no doubt I have hacked up your plot in my version). He has lost his copy of this, or misplaced it in a pile of years of New Y'ers, or something, and asked me if I know when it appeared – which I didn't – but I said I'd ask you. I didn't give any guarantee that you'ld remember. Do you?

· · ·

MKR to JSB, 7 November 1949. TLS, 6 pp. Envelope, recto: PM: SAINT AUGUSTINE | NOV 7 | 4 PM / 1949 | FLA. AD: Mrs. Thomas J. Bigham | 175 Ninth Avenue | New York City 11. Envelope, verso, RA: Mrs. Norton Baskin | crescent beach | st. augustine, florida. LH: Mrs. Norton Baskin | crescent beach | st. augustine, florida

Nov. 7, 1949

Dearest Julia:

---

1 Charles Scribner IV and Janette Kissel "Joan" Scribner.
2 Uki, MKR's Siamese cat, which JSB did not like.
3 Hans Wallach (1904–1998), an experimental psychologist. The story is "The Shell." *New Yorker* 20 (19 December 1944), 29–31. See Tarr, *Bibliography*, C629, and *Short Stories*, pp. 338–43.

Norton and I left Van Hornesville last Tuesday morning early.[1] I battled all Sunday and Monday[2] to try to reach you by 'phone. Late Sunday evening, operator reported after several "busy" reports, that the Far Hills 'phone was listed as out of order, as someone had left a receiver off the hook. (No doubt Hildy). Monday[3] I kept missing you all around, and in the afternoon was told you had come and gone, but would be in about 7:30. We were having dinner with Mr. Young[4] that night, and I just gave up. I couldn't leave word for you to call me, as Norton and I were on the prowl. We had a simply marvelous time, mostly superb weather, even considerable color left, and I had to leave snapdragon and rose-buds behind in the garden.

Norton was fascinated by the Greek Orthodox church and we went twice. Louise Young had gone to Florida, and Mr. Young drank and dined with us at our house three times, all of them gala. Once was Oct. 27,[5] his actual birthday (celebrated formally two days later, so that all his children could be there) and our 8th anniversary. I replaced the grouse I gave you with a pheasant from a nearby game farm, and only the fact that we were already in the rosiest spirits and had what proved a superb vintage Champagne with supper, kept the meal from being a fiasco, for as Mr. Young told Norton afterward, Norton was the first man known ever to have tried to <u>carve</u> one pheasant. I had of course planned it just for two.

Mr. Young told us a hilarious story from his early days which I shall have to pass on in person, because of its length. He said we were the first people to whom he had ever been able to tell the story, from the necessity of using one of your favorite words repeatedly.[6] He said he had tried telling it once before, using a euphemism, and it had fallen flat, and he had been waiting 50 years for the Baskins. Who rolled in the aisles.

His birthday celebration again would have been a fiasco without the Baskins, if I may so modestly. Louise had drawn up a rough menu before she left, for the 72-year-old cook whose last job had been as a short-order cook in a joint. I looked over the menu to ask if I could help Gertie,[7] and we agreed that parsnips, at least, would have to go. I had taken Louise a fresh turkey from the turkey-farm a few weeks earlier when I got one for myself, thinking she'd enjoy using it at once and casually, but she had put it in her

---

1 Tuesday, 1 November 1949.
2 Sunday, 30 October 1949.
3 Monday, 31 October 1949.
4 Owen D. Young.
5 Thursday, 27 October 1949, the Baskins' eighth anniversary.
6 That is, "shit," which MKR, obviously with humorous intent, refused to say because the word was so much identified with JSB.
7 Gertrude Sandvold.

deep-freezer to save for the birthday party. It was a small turkey, and eventually served 16 people only because the carver was frightened by his responsibilities in the case. Louise had down for dessert, raspberry short-cake, and I assumed that Josephine Young Case[1] would bring a birthday cake or that Old Gertie understood that she was to provide one. Only Peggy Egan's[2] desire to contribute, if superfluously, saved the day, for her gay one with candles was the only one. I loaned Idella to help Gertie in the afternoon, to set the table and serve, for as you remember, Gertie left alone just dumps things on the table. Idella told me later of her utter defeat in trying to have things hot. She had won on the matter of having service plates on the table, Gertie protesting that there wasn't anything to put on them, but when she put the dinner plates in a warm place, Gertie snatched them away, saying she was supposed to take good care of Mrs. Young's[3] china. The delicious home-made rolls were served stone-cold, Idella with lifted eyebrows, as when she passed the home-grown frozen asparagus, which Gertie had cooked in little pieces, with milk over it.

Mr. Young's gifts were piled in front of his place, and if any one of them from his family, including Louise's $6.95 bed reading lamp, cost $10, I should never be allowed to add my own bank-account. The Philip Young's[4] gave him one nylon shirt with a note, pertinent and witty, I must say, since as a life-long Democrat he had come out for Dulles,[5] to the effect that he could now change shirts in mid-stream. And so it went down the family line.

Alfred Dunhill[6] came across magnificently. They wrote me that indeed they did know Mr. Young's choice in cigars, it was Upmann's Havana[7] mix-

---

1   Josephine Young Case (1907–1990), poet and director of RCA, daughter of Owen D. and Louise Young and wife of Everett N. Case, president of Colgate University.

2   Margaret "Peggy" Egan (1897–1974), the Irish-born nursemaid for the Youngs and later a maid for MKR. Martin Egan (1894–1979), Peggy's husband, the Irish-born contractor who did most of the restoration on MKR's home.

3   Louise Young, wife of Owen D. Young.

4   Philip Young (1910–1987), diplomat who served as the ambassador to the Netherlands, son of Owen D. and Louise Young.

5   John Foster Dulles (1888–1959), diplomat who served as secretary of state under President Dwight D. Eisenhower (1890–1969).

6   Alfred Dunhill of New York, a luxury store, known for its Humidor Room, where it stored, free of charge, over 400,000 cigars owned by the rich and famous. Unable to afford the rents to provide this luxury, Dunhill closed the Humidor Room in 1985.

7   Upmann's Havana, a prized hand-rolled cigar, cherished by smokers since the factory opened in Cuba in 1844. The German-born Upmanns lost control of the manufacture when they were convicted of espionage in World War II. However, the brand continues under various licenses and names and is so prized that President John F. Kennedy (1917–1963) bought over 1,400 of them before he issued the Cuban embargo in 1962. At one juncture Upmann enterprises made only two cigars, designated No. 1 and No. 2.

ture No. so and so, and since Norton had arrived by that time, we ordered two boxes, one for him to present, one for me, and while the price was not staggering, we felt satisfied that we were offering an adequate tribute.

Shortly before the celebration, I realized that as best I could remember, Norton and I had never been invited formally to join the family party. A phone call from Josephine, asking me to tell the cook the number of guests, took it for granted that we would be there, as I had done. We still had qualms, so when we arrived for drinks, Norton remarked that every family was supposed to have its bastards and we were appearing in that capacity.

I must tell you---. One day at the Van Hornesville house a few weeks ago, I had driven far away to a Home Bakery, and as I drove up to <the> my place, Mr. and Mrs. Young and a strange man emerged from the house, where they had been waiting for me. I was wind-blown and disheveled, unpowdered and un-painted. Moe leaped out of the car and jumped up all over the three visitors, I got out and approached them, tore open the top of the bag of doughnuts and said gustily, "Fresh doughnuts---have one!" Everyone refused with an odd coldness, so I said, "Well then, come on in for a drink." This invitation was also refused.

The next time I saw Mr. Young, he told me that the stranger was the leading banker of Herkimer,[1] of a very old family, who has been financing Louise on her restoration projects. The man had been delighted with my house, its furnishings, its immaculacy, the flowers, with Idella, who had appeared courteously in a pristine uniform and white organdy apron to make them welcome. My. Young puffed on his pipe. "And then," he said, "YOU drove up."

I could only say, "Of course, he was expecting Jane Austen".[2]

We had to put Idella on the Monday night train before we left Tuesday morning, as the 8:47 A.M. train now arrives so late, due to the coal strike,[3] that it does not make connections with the early afternoon train to St. Augustine. Norton and I had a good trip down, but terrible things happened our first night out, when we had reservations at a very nice tourist court at Gettysburg. We had not gotten off as early that morning as I had hoped, and on the road I remembered that I had not put the padlock on the wood-shed door, so that anyone could get into the house that way, and what with one thing and another, we were tired and jittery when we reached the Gettysburg alleged haven. We turned Moe loose to "run around", we had a couple of drinks, we freshened

---

1   Herkimer, New York, approximately 16 miles north of Van Hornesville.
2   Jane Austen (1774–1817), English novelist, known for her novels of manners.
3   Between 15 March 1949 and 15 March 1950, there were intermittent coal strikes throughout the United States, which affected coal supplies and in turn businesses, not the least of which were the railroads.

up, and I had on my hat and so on, ready for us to go back into Gettysburg (the tourist court is a couple of miles outside of the town) for dinner. I called Moe in. He appeared, covered with the most foul-smelling stuff I have ever encountered. Norton thought it could only be guano,[1] for it was a gray-white clay-like mixture, combining the odors of fecal matter and fish. I screamed imprecations against Moe. I stripped down to my brassiere and panties, in order to wash Moe under the shower. By Heaven's grace, I had put the shower-cap that you wore on your rainy walk with Moe, and that Norton had worn in picking my garden flowers for me in a heavy rain, when we were expecting everything to freeze, in my traveling kit, so I put that on to wash Moe.

At this moment, Norton, who has a stomach as touchy as yours, was obliged to go outside to be sick at his stomach. I did not notice his exit, since Moe, usually most obedient, refused to follow me to the shower. I grabbed Moe by his collar, especially thick with this ghastly stuff, and fought to drag him to his cleansing. And I had only those tourist cakes of soap with which to work.

Well, it seems that while Norton was being sick outside, he did recover, and attempted to enter the tourist cottage again, only to find that he was locked out. Meantime, a nice little man had driven up, to occupy the adjacent cottage. He saw Norton being sick at his stomach, he saw him beating on our cottage door, and asked Norton, "Are you in trouble?"

At that moment, I, struggling to drag Moe into the shower, screamed, "You WILL, you son of a bitch."

So the nice little man invited Norton to sit in his car to listen to his radio—

(Am without pencil, or pen)

So, love,
Marjorie[2]

. . .

MKR to JSB, 11 November 1949. PM: HAWTHORN | NOV 11 | 5 PM | 1949 | FLA. AD: Mrs. Thomas J. Bigham, Jr. | 175 Ninth Avenue | New York City 11. LH: Mrs. Norton Baskin | <Crescent Beach> | <St. Augustine, Florida.>

Cross Creek

---

1 Guano, by this time a generic term for fertilizer originally made primarily from the pungent feces of birds imported from South America by companies such as the Anglo-Continental Guano Works, founded in 1883.

2 Written on the verso of the envelope in MKR's hand: Forgot to say | could [underlined three times] I have, | 4 prints of the | Van Hornesville | House, and one | more each | of the cat | pictures???

Nov. 11, 1949

Dearest Julia:

Your letter to Van Hornesville was waiting here at the Creek, forwarded. I'm so sorry about your auto accident,[1] though you seem to have taken it in your stride. And I was deeply distressed to read in the paper that your nice cousin Fitzhugh Scribner,[2] was in the dreadful Washington crash. As I remember, he was supporting a rather strange female family. And to lose Helen Hokinson, too---.

It is good to be at the Creek again. Martha[3] had the house reasonably clean, and it seems as though I had never been away. The Turk's-cap and red hibiscus are brilliant, next to them the allananda is canary-yellow, and yellow butterflies continue the striking Spanish color scheme. A few roses in the garden, otherwise I'll have to start from scratch.

We'll go to the cottage for the week-end, but I sha'n't try to go over every week-end. Norton was the first to say that it wouldn't work. He will come here, which is a much nicer arrangement.

Early next week I'll brace myself and read the manuscript[4]---. Shall go on with it, no matter what.

Much love,

Marjorie

. . .

JSB to MKR, [11?] November 1949. ALS, 2 pp. PM: NEW YORK, N.Y. | NOV 15 | 11³⁰ AM | 1949. AD: Mrs. Norton Baskin | Cross Creek | Hawthorn | Florida.

Monday – [11? November 1949][5]

Dearest Marjorie –

I was quite entranced, not to say convulsed, by the saga of your night at

---

1 JSB wrecked her Buick. See JSB's letter dated [28?] October 1949.

2 An Eastern Airlines DC4 was hit by Bolivian Air Force plane on 2 November 1949 near Washington National Airport. All of the 55 people on board were killed, then the largest airplane disaster on record. Scribner Fitzhugh (1904–1949), JSB's cousin, was among the dead. Helen Hokinson (1893–1949), American cartoonist and staff cartoonist for the *New Yorker*, was also killed.

3 Martha Mickens.

4 The manuscript of *The Sojourner*.

5 Written in a second hand at the top of p. 1: [11-15-49]. The conjectured date is the first Monday before the PM.

Gettysburg. Of course I also felt deep sympathy for Norton – and you – and Moe, but I didn't allow it to interfere with my enjoyment of the account.[1] How do you so inevitably involve yourself in these affairs? No doubt you have read that one of the chief new interests of psychosomatic medicine is the study of people who are "accident prone." I think I must bring to the attention of some of my 'psychosomatic' friends a fascinating new category of persons, fully typified by you, people who are "incident prone." The truth is I can't think of anyone else who can compare with your 'proneness', which gives me an uncomfortable feeling that you may be unique – just sheer inexplicable genius![2] I do hope the rest of your trip was duller.

You didn't tell me several things I want to know. Did you read the Williams books,[3] and what do you think of them, if so? Did Idella like any of her pictures? It seemed to me one of the ones sitting inside was rather pleasant. And on the pictures – do you want the pictures of the Van H. house the size of the first one I sent you or somewhat smaller? It makes no difference in effort etc. so tell me what you want. – Also do you want the cats same size?

Still on the subject of pictures – Alan Paton (Cry the Beloved Country)[4] was down here Fri. Whitney D.[5] decided that, although the poor man had been endlessly photoed, he (W.D.) wanted _informal_ pictures of him. So in a mad tearing rush he was whipped down here between appointments, and I did a bunch of flash pictures. Unfortunately, Tom and he got off on a terribly profound conversation – first about the race question, and then about guilt – viewed psychologically, psychoanalytically & theologically. He got so wound up and excited that his face is all screwed around in _every_ picture. Not _one_ good one. The only faint consolation is that we all got on so well, I think he seemed quite eager to come down here again on his return from Calif. So maybe I can try again.

---

1   JSB is alluding to MKR's story of Moe, the dog, getting into guano, or fertilizer, the smell of which caused NSB to vomit, and which in desperation over the cleanup reduced MKR to a bra and panties. See MKR's letter on 7 November 1949.

2   A plethora of studies in 1949 demonstrated that "accident-prone" individuals do exist, approximately 1 in 29 have 50 percent more accidents than the other 28. The fact that JSB is reading such studies indicates the diversity of her interests and their application to her own experiences, even though she insists that it is MKR who is the more "accident-prone."

3   JSB actually recommended one by Charles Williams, _All Hallows' Eve_. See JSB's letter on 2 March 1949.

4   Alan Paton (1903–1988), South African novelist, _Cry, the Beloved Country_ (New York: Scribners, 1948), a novel about racial injustice and apartheid, ushered through the press by Maxwell Perkins before he died in 1947.

5   Whitney Darrow, then sales manager at Scribners.

Much love,

Julia

P.S. When you brace yourself and give yourself over to labor pains again – remember I am right there at your shoulder metaphysically – giving with the moral support.[1]

. . .

MKR to JSB, 18 November 1949. TLS, 3 pp. PM: HAWTHORN | NOV 19 | 5 PM | 1949 | FLA. AD: Mrs. Thomas J. Bigham | 175 Ninth Avenue | New York City 11. LH: Marjorie Kinnan Rawlings | cross creek | hawthorn, florida.

Nov. 18, 1949

Dearest Julia:

If you're sure you don't mind, would love the house and cat pictures the size they are in the copies you first sent me. I think both need to be that large for full effectiveness. "Cat in Clover" can remain same small size. The cats go to Marcia Davenport in Italy. The houses go to my brother, to Norton's Alabama family---he says he can't make them "see" it---and two sets to the aunties.[2]

Imagine Idella[3] has written you by now. Most of her shots were so solemn, but we all liked the half-smiling one very much, lots of character. She was hesitant about asking for more than two prints, but I assured her you would be happy to make her 6 or even 8. I have noticed that she and old Martha[4] are always crushed at first sight of a self-photo---I know they keep hoping they really don't look quite so <u>black</u>.

I should think that Paton's shots[5] with the screwed-up face would be im-

---

1   MKR in a letter on 11 November 1949 informs JSB that she is going to "brace myself and read the manuscript" of *The Sojourner* in an effort to rekindle her creative juices.

2   Marcia Davenport (1903–1996), American novelist, perhaps best known for *Valley of Decision* (New York: Scribners, 1942), about life in the steel mills of western Pennsylvania. Arthur H. Kinnan, MKR's brother. Florida Binney Sanford Baskin and Thomas Underwood Baskin, MKR's mother-in-law and father-in-law. Grace Kinnan, Marjorie Kinnan, and Wilmer Kinnan, MKR's aunts.

3   Idella Parker.

4   Martha Mickens.

5   JSB's photographs of Alan Paton. See JSB's letter on 11 November 1949.

mensely typical of him, showing his intensity. Or were you trying to make him look "Lost in the Stars"?[1]

About being "incident-prone", it seems to me you have pre-established and easily identifiable factors, at least in the Battle of Gettysburg situation, that would <u>guarantee</u> an "incident". Norton---as he calls himself, "Caspar Milquetoast"[2]---a violent hussy, and a dog that can be counted on to do the awkward thing. Mix that up on a 1,300-mile auto trip, and something has to happen---the reason I try to talk Norton out of "driving home to his little family".

I was utterly delighted with Charles Williams. I only had time to finish "All Hallows' Eve",[3] but shall order all of his books available in the U.S. He is quite literally "out of this world." Oddly, I have had a short story in mind that I thought would be unique in its subject matter---now I don't think I can write it, for everyone would say, "Oh, she's been reading Charles Williams." Perhaps I got it out of your mind after <u>you</u> had been reading Williams, just as the night when you announced with such terribly timeliness, "Marjorie, I smell smoke".

And do let me recommend to you Christopher Morley's "The Man Who Made Friends with Himself."[4] The reviews gave no conception of the delightful quality of the book---ribald and screamingly funny on the surface, but with a profound under-current.

What I think of as <u>your</u> tangerine tree, has a heavy crop this year, and as soon as the fruit, the Oneika Mandarin, is ripe, I'll send small boxes from time to time.

I finally screwed my courage to the sticking point and read over my manuscript.[5] It is no worse than I thought, but certainly no better. I see clearly what must be done in the eventual re-writing, but what disturbs me most is that more than anything I have done, it is so obviously written by a woman.

---

1   MKR is referring to a Broadway musical with lyrics by Maxwell Anderson (1888–1959) and music by Kurt Weill (1900–1950), which premiered in 1949, an adaptation of Alan Paton's *Cry, the Beloved Country*. See *Lost in the Stars* (New York: Sloane, 1950).

2   Caspar Milquetoast, a syndicated comic strip that ran from 1925–1953, created by H. T. Webster (1885–1952), who once described Caspar as the "man who speaks softly and gets hit with a big stick." The "violent hussy" is MKR and the dog is Moe.

3   Charles Williams (1886–1945), English poet, novelist, and essayist, *All Hallows' Eve* (London: Faber and Faber, 1945), a fantasy novel about two dead women who explore through art the nature of transcendence and harmony in an otherwise discordant world. JSB had sent MKR this and another novel, not identified. See JSB's letter dated [mid-August? 1949].

4   Christopher Morley (1890–1957), American essayist and novelist, *The Man Who Made Friends with Himself* (Garden City: Doubleday, 1949), a fantasy novel about the perverse and the unexpected effects of the atomic bomb.

5   The manuscript of *The Sojourner*.

To make the <u>faintest</u> pretense at being literature, a book must be sex-less as to style. (Needless to say, aside from a hundred other qualifications.) I shall have to do an immense amount of tightening.

Must pass on a comment of old Martha's, when I told her some "incident" or other. She said, "Sugar, it tasted like a story-book, the way you tell it."

Much love,

<u>Marjorie</u>

Norton's sister[1] brought her grand-nephew to the cottage to visit this summer. She prepared him for all the strange new relatives, describing "Uncle Norton" and his business, "Aunt so-and-so" and "Uncle this-and-that", and the cousins. Norton brought them by the Creek and she explained that it was where Aunt Marjorie lived, etc, etc. Old Martha did the honors of the house, and Norton and his sister both called her, with Southern courtesy, "Aunt Martha". As they drove away, little Dalby[2] said meditatively, "I did think Aunt Martha would be white."

. . .

JSB to MKR, 7 December 1949. ALS, 2 pp. PM: PITTSBURGH, PA | DEC 7. | 4-PM | 1949 | AIR MAIL FIELD. AD: Mrs. Norton Baskin | Cross Creek | Hawthorn | Florida. VIA AIR MAIL, TWA [Trans World Airlines] envelope. Air Mail stamp.

Wed <AM> PM [7 December 1949][3]

Dearest Marjorie –

You may be wondering why you haven't heard from me, & what has happened to your & Idella's pictures - Tues, the 29th my great aunt[4] died up in Nantucket, so I went up there with the family that night & didn't get home till Mon. evening. Just had yesterday home then got word this AM very early

---

1 Janise Adilon Baskin Ellis (1895?–1981).

2 Perhaps Joseph Dalby Ellis III (1939–1972?).

3 Written in a second hand at the top of p. 1: [12-7-49].

4 Rosalie Flagg Jaffray (1866–1949), married William Dexter Jaffray (1863–1949) in 1890 at the Episcopal Church of St. John the Baptist in New York City. In his 1890 passport, Jaffray listed his occupation as a "broker." In the 1900 census, he listed his residence as 8 Quince St., Nantucket, and in the 1920 census as 14 Quince St. They were childless, and according to family lore were "wildly eccentric." Upon Rosalie's death, 29 November 1949, JSB inherited her home on Nantucket. Unable to make meaningful use of the property, the Bighams "sold it immediately" (Hildreth Bigham McCarthy to Rodger Tarr, 13 January 2022). Rosalie was a sister of Louise Flagg Scribner, JSB's grandmother.

that Tom's father had died[1] – so we are now on the plane to Pittsburgh. Won't be home till Mon.

Haven't even made your pictures yet – you'll learn to practice the painful virtue – or complicated act of patience. Idella's are all done but not quite finished mounting & retouching – it is only a matter of an hour or so's work – please tell her I haven't forgotten or anything like that.

High altitude seems to dry up my mind. Will write you after I get settled back in NYC sea level. Hope the book is proving amenable – or if not, that your labor pains are so severe that you can't stop anyway.[2]

Much love,

Julia

· · ·

MKR to JSB, 29 December 1949. PM: ISLAND GROVE | DEC | 29 | P.M. | 1949 | FLA. AD: Mrs. Thomas J. Bigham | 175 Ninth Avenue | New York City 11. LH: MARJORIE KINNAN RAWLINGS | CROSS CREEK | HAWTHORN, FLORIDA.

Dec. 29, 1949

Dearest Julia:

I do not see how you managed to get off to me the grand books, to say nothing of Idella's "portraits,"[3] which reached her just the day before Christmas. She was so pleased, as they made up part of her Christmas gifts to her family. You must have stayed up late indeed to do this for her. I shall try to hit another grouse next season so that she can cook it for you.

I am delighted with the Hersholt translation of Andersen,[4] perhaps most of all with the illustrations, which seem exactly right. I have only dipped into the Betjeman, but what I have brought out so far has been fruity plums indeed. "Chintzy, chintzy cheeriness"---!!!!![5] You are a thoughtful dear and I do thank you.

---

1 JSB's father-in-law died on 7 December 1949.

2 Throughout the ordeal of writing, rewriting, and editing *The Sojourner*, MKR and JSB, with jocular nuance, equated it with the experience of labor pains and giving birth. The labor was long, more than seven years since inception. The birth officially took place on 5 January 1953. See Tarr, *Bibliography*, A8.

3 The photographs made of Idella Parker by JSB.

4 Hans Christian Andersen (1805–1875), Danish fairytale writer, *The Complete Andersen*. Trans Jean Hersholt (1886–1956). Illust. Fritz Syberg (1862–1939). New York: Heritage, 1949.

5 MKR is referring to "Death in Leamington" (1932) by John Betjemann (aka Betjeman, 1906–

Chet[1] has been over-worked and hasn't brought me small boxes for the special tangerines, so I'll go to the packing house for them myself. Anyway, the fruit is only now really sweet.

I spent Christmas at the beach with Norton, a dreary day for the most part, a terrific north-easter all day long with pouring rain, and Aunt Ida[2] for mid-day dinner at Marineland. (I took Idella home to Reddick for her Christmas.) After out-eating Norton and me together, and having ice cream on her pie, Aunt Ida (going on 90) said, "This old body needs nourishment. I get faint without food." Norton said later, "She shouldn't be weak for weeks."

Norton and I went to the usual Christmas night cocktail and buffet parties, but the real compensation for the week-end was a family game of bridge at the Owen Young's Monday.[3] I used quite casually my now-favorite, "Why, shit-fire, Honey", and realized with a jolt that I should always explain its origin before, instead of after, using it.[4] I do hope you can read "Hunter's Horn"[5] without getting plane-sick, so that you can send it on to Norton. He would love it, and you will, too, if you can manage.

I finally got around to ordering the Proust[6] for you. I think you will find, as I still do, that it must be taken in small doses.

I was sorry to hear of the death of Tom's father.[7] I wonder if a major break in a family is easier to bear at Tom's age, than at mine when I lost my father,[8] seventeen. Probably not.

Don't bother to write me until things calm down for you a bit, if ever. But I do love hearing from you.

Chet has taken Moe hunting, and reports him past reproach.[9] Uki the Siamese invalid is holding his own.

1984), a poem about the final insignificance of death. An old matron dies while crocheting and the poet is left to observe, "Oh! Chintzy, chintzy cheeriness" (l. 19), as the maid perfunctorily turns off the gas lamp, the light of life gone dark.

1   Chet Crosby.

2   Aunt Ida Tarrant.

3   Owen D. and Louise Young at their plantation, Washington Oaks, near Marineland, now a Florida State Park.

4   MKR enjoys pointing out that various forms of "shit" are among JSB's favorite words.

5   Harriette Simpson Arnow (1909–1986), Kentucky fiction writer, *Hunter's Horn* (New York: Macmillan, 1949), a novel about the trials and the tribulations of the Kentucky hill people. Arnow garnered further acclaim with her novel *The Dollmaker* (1954), about the departure and the aftermath of a destitute couple who leaves Kentucky for Detroit in search of sustenance.

6   Perhaps *In Search of Lost Time*. JSB was always recommending Proust to MKR; see, for example, her letter on 16 February 1945.

7   See JSB's letter on 7 December 1949.

8   Arthur Frank Kinnan died suddenly, from kidney disease, on 31 January 1913.

9   MKR reports similar news to NSB in a letter dated [5 December 1949], "Chet took Moe hunting

I realized too late that Hildy is now of an age to appreciate Christmas presents.[1] I'll not be remiss again.

Much love,

Marjorie

. . .

MKR to JSB, 30 January 1950. TLS, 3 pp. PM: ISLAND GROVE | JAN | 30 | P.M. | 1950 | FLA. AD: Mrs. Thomas J. Bigham | 175 Ninth Avenue | New York City 11.

Cross Creek

Jan. 30, 1950

Dearest Julia:

I am sure the Oneiko mandarins were ruined by the time you got them, if you ever did. If so, I'll put in a claim at least. Chet Crosby picked them and packaged them for me and took them to the express office in Island Grove. I typed down name and address. The next day I happened to notice on my express receipt which Chet had returned, that the stupid man in Island Grove who has given me so much trouble over the years, had put down 17 Ninth Ave, instead of 175. I was working, and sent Idella in with a request that Mr. Neil[2] wire New York making the correction. He said he would. Ten days later I had a notice from a N.Y. express office that they were unable to find you, and the address was still 17. Meantime, confusion at the Creek had become worse-confounded,[3] and Mr. Neil not being in his office when I stopped by, I left a note again insisting on a wire to N.Y., whoever paid for it. He probably thought it didn't matter, that 17 would certainly be next door to 175. If I ever kill a man, it will be Mr. Neil.

Will get off another box of tangerines soon.

Last Wednesday night Norman Berg,[4] who usually arrives inopportunely,

---

yesterday and said Moe was perfect. Retrieved, did everything right" (*Love Letters* 553).

1   JSB's daughter was almost three years old, having been born on 1 April 1947.

2   Mr. Neil, the husband of the postmistress in Island Grove, owed MKR $250 for a loan (*Love Letters* 463).

3   MKR is alluding to when Satan first saw Hell, "Confusion worst confounded" from John Milton (1608–1674), English poet and essayist, *Paradise Lost* (1667) 2.1.996.

4   Norman S. Berg, southeastern representative for Macmillan Publishing in Atlanta, became a confidant of MKR to whom she increasingly turned for literary and personal advice. His father was John George Berg (1879–1963).

fortunately arrived with his father for dinner and the night. At nearly bed-time, I heard screams of pain from Moe out in the dark. I grabbed a flashlight and we found him by the road holding up a terribly cut front leg. (Decided later he had plunged through barbed wire after one of the barn cats--found his hair on the wire.) Norman said it should be sewed up at once, and he drove me to the Vet's in Ocala, where we found one of the firm at the animal hospital giving a transfusion to a sick dog. The cut on Moe's leg had exposed and missed by a hair the largest vein in his body. Many stitches taken under local anaesthetic, Moe bandaged, doing well.

The next morning a 'phone message came from Island Grove for Idella, that her husband Bernard was in the St. Augustine hospital, seriously burned, and needed her.[1]

Up until then, I had been writing like mad, had allowed nothing to inter-fere with my schedule. Thought of just letting Idella take my car to go to St. A., but if she had to stay long, I'd be too marooned, also knew from having Norman here, the comfort of a friend at hand, so I dressed hurriedly and drove her over. What I was afraid of, had happened. Idella had reported a serious gas leak in the hot water heater in their apartment below the cot-tage, Norton had 'phoned the gas company twice. They claim they repaired the heater the morning before the accident. Anyway, Bernard, poor stupid fellow, when he found the water cold for his shower that night, decided the pilot light had blown out, and in spite of a strong smell of gas, touched a match---. He had on only shorts, so no upper clothing to catch fire. Second degree burns, and he will be all right, not even his childish beauty marred. But meantime, I felt obliged to leave Idella with him as long as necessary. Went to St. A. again over the week-end, it will be at least another week before Idella can leave, she wanted to send one of her sisters to take care of me, I said No, old Martha could do it.

Got here last night late, and this morning find that Martha's favorite grand-son who once worked for me, Adrenna's son Jack, "got shot" Satur-day night. Martha said, "Jack wasn't doin' a thing, another boy wanted to shoot another boy and Jack tried to stop him and caught the bullet." Have just sent Martha off to the hospital with all the cash I had, $74, as he will be thrown out if bill not paid. Martha utterly useless.[2]

---

1   Idella Parker and Bernard Young, then her husband.

2   MKR reports the shooting to NSB in a letter dated [30 January 1950], with the added caveat, "With people getting blown up [Bernard Young] and shot up [James "Jack" Mickens] all around me, I am lying low" (*Love Letters* 557). Mickens was first admitted to an Ocala white hospital, treated, and then transferred to Dr. J. L. Strange's black hospital in McIntosh. Adrenna Mickens is the daughter of Martha Mickens.

Am so sorry for all the injured <u>people</u>, Moe, Bernard and Jack, but can't help feeling sorry for me, too, as I just can't work.

Am also stuck with three sets of guests[1] in late February or early March---. Shit-fire, Honey.

<u>Love,</u>

<u>Marjorie</u>

. . .

MKR to JSB, 18 April 1950. TL, 3 pp. No closing. No signature. Envelope is missing.

Cross Creek

April 18, 1950

Dearest Julia:

If you ever do become "integrated" into "The Women of General", well, I have loved knowing you, and you can't imagine how I should miss you---. It must be like walking a tight-rope over Niagara, to maintain the fine balance necessary to be at least enough of "a good wife" not to harm Tom's career, and to avoid toppling into the whirlpool (from which no body has ever been recovered) of "women of (or in) general."[2]

Idella and I have finally solved my problem of keeping off the "fans" who stop by, while I am so hard at work. Having her tell them that I was "working" meant nothing at all, they still insisted. If the rumor reaches you that poor Mrs. Rawlings has become a chronic and bed-ridden invalid, it will be because these people, most of them so dreadful, believe her when she tells them that I [am] not well. Perhaps you are giving up your migraines at the wrong moment. You might hang on to them publicly---.

Chet Crosby doesn't expect a thank-you from you, but I told him I would

---

1 Wray Rawlings, MKR's ex-brother-in-law, who in the end could not come, and the Owen D. Youngs and the Everett Cases. MKR hoped for Robert Frost, the already celebrated poet, but the University of Florida, where he was giving a reading, was "hogging" him (*Love Letters* 564). In addition, there was an enmity on Frost's part toward Owen D. Young, who while at St. Lawrence University dated Elinor White, Frost's future wife. As MKR laments in a letter to NSB on 1 March 1950, "If it were not that Robert Frost so hates our dear Owen D. Young, we could have all of them at the Creek together" (*Love Letters* 564, n. 2).

2 The context of this paragraph suggests that MKR is responding to a letter, now missing, from JSB in complaint about the conflict between marital duties and the concurrent need for personal freedom.

let you know that the successful basket of fruit was from him, not from me, except that he used my plentiful tangerines. When I wanted to pay him for the basket, the express and the fancy fruit he used on top, he said it was a little thing he'd like to do for you himself.

We had been planning to leave for Van Hornesville the end of April or the first of May, until the sudden cold weather hit the whole East. Several mornings lately it has been 32 degrees, just missing hurting the orange bloom, so I have asked my neighbor Mrs. Fredericks[1] to keep me informed on the weather up there. I want to be on hand for the first wild apple-blossom, the first lilac bud, the first maple leaf, and for my new tulips and early iris, but I do not want or need to run into two or three weeks of utter bleakness.

I am so happy that you will be all summer at New Marlboro,[2] both because you love it so, and because we should be able to see more of each other. New M. is on a straight line across from Van H.,[3] and should be no more than a two or three hours' drive away. And cheers for your new car. Norton's new car is a De Soto[4] and he likes it very much. He said we should really swap cars, for his has that arrangement whereby the back seat folds out flat and makes the most enormous storage compartment, aside from the rear trunk. But I don't think Moe and Uki would like it as well---.

A Florida winter has so improved Uki's health that he is almost himself. He bats around the two half-wild farm cats, one of them a tough tom that could make mince-meat of him. Moe of course is well, and such an ass. He barks madly and ferociously whenever Norton and dear friends arrive, while the other night---a long story:

Tom Glisson,[5] my dearest neighbor and good friend, died most tragically

---

1   Lilian Frederick.

2   New Marlborough, Massachusetts.

3   Van Hornesville, New York. The distance between Van Hornesville and New Marlborough is approximately 125 miles.

4   DeSoto automobile production began in 1928 and ceased in 1961. NSB most likely purchased the DeSoto Custom Sportsman, with the innovation of not having a door pillar.

5   Tom Glisson (1889–1950) brought his family to Cross Creek in 1921. He was a proud man, and he and MKR on occasion had their differences. But they also trusted each other, and in the years prior to his death they became close friends. Carlton Glisson (1917–1994), the son mentioned above, went to the university, very unusual for a cracker boy at that time. Tom's daughter Marjorie Glisson (1921–2000), at one period served as a typist for MKR. Tom's wife, Pearlee Josey Glisson (1898–1980), whose sense of dignity was admired by MKR, was with Tom when he died a horrible death after "hours of unspeakable agony" from the effects of poison (*Selected Letters* 352). However, it was Tom's young son, James T. "Jake" Glisson (1927–2019), of whom MKR was particularly fond. At birth, J. T. suffered from an "affliction," most likely a club foot, and MKR watched him hobble up and down the road, but always with a bright smile and the word "Hey" when he saw her. A convinc-

early last Thursday morning. In his truck he had identical jugs, one containing drinking water, the other, tree-killer, whose lethal ingredient is a concentrated lead arsenate. Yes, he took a swig from the wrong jug, spit it out at once, rinsed out his mouth, and was certain he had not swallowed any of the stuff. He refused his son's urging to take eggs etc. as an emetic, did allow his wife to drive him to Gainesville to a doctor, and in spite of plasma, glucose solutions, etc., died horribly within twelve hours.

I went to the house to do what I could, and was able to be of some practical use, driving to a village some distance away to notify their daughter, sending telegrams, etc. I also told the family that I had plenty of room to take care of any over-flow of relatives who would drive in from Georgia. I said the beds would be made up, and I'd leave lights on in the house, so that latecomers could find their way. I went sound asleep about eleven o'clock and no one had come. Early in the morning I thought I heard a man cough. Later, I was SURE I heard a man cough. Nonsense, I thought, Moe ALWAYS barks, he's a WONDERFUL watchdog. Well, two Glisson male relatives had arrived late, been sent here, and had crawled in to the first available beds without the slightest arousing on Moe's part---.

My book[1] goes forward, but more slowly than I expected. For one thing, it will be longer than I thought. For another, the various interruptions have done the usual damage, so that I have been thrown off my stride for a week at a time. I gave up hope of finishing the first draft before I go north, and realized I was doing a worse job than was necessary, by trying to get a certain stint done each day and that it would be better to take more time. So, the revised manuscript will still be ready by fall (I decided I couldn't let anyone read the first draft) and if the thing is fit to be printed, publication would then be in early 1952.[2]

---

ing argument could be made that J. T. was the prototype for the "afflicted" boy Fodder-wing in *The Yearling*, the difference being that after a number of operations J. T.'s "affliction" was made well, while the fragile Fodder-wing tragically succumbed to his. After Tom's death MKR invited J. T. to spend the night with her. On the very porch where she had written *The Yearling*, they reminisced throughout the night, with MKR saying at one point about Tom, "He was one hell of a man" (Glisson, *The Creek* 254).

1   The manuscript of *The Sojourner*. The novel continued to cause MKR problems, with still more revisions to come. It was finally published on 5 January 1953.

2   The letter rather abruptly ends here, without a parting or a signature. MKR's next letter, 29 May 1950, provides the answer. This letter was put aside and never mailed. It was then included with the 29 May letter.

. . .

MKR to JSB, 29 May 1950. TLS, 3 pp. PM: VAN HORNESVILLE |
MAY | 29 | A.M. | 1950 | N.Y. AD: Mrs. Thomas J. Bigham | 175 Ninth
Avenue | New York City 11. RA: Baskin.

Van Hornesville, N.Y.

May 29, 1950

Dearest Julia:

Somewhere I have a several-page letter I began to you in Florida, about a
month ago.[1] I'll dig it out and send it along.

I suddenly discovered at the Creek that thirteen pages of single-spaced
factual notes for my book were missing. I went through all my files at the
cottage, then shortly before leaving the Creek, a new young friend I may
have mentioned, Gene Baroff[2] (he has been teaching at the University of
Fla. but is not going back, in order to write. He has already had very good
short stories and verses in "The American Scholar" and some of the "little"
magazines) helped me go through everything at the Creek---bureau drawers
full of manuscripts, etc. etc.---and there must have been a dozen letters I had
written and never sent. Gene said gravely, "Marjorie, when you die, I'd like
very much to edit your un-mailed letters."

The notes were not there, either---but I found them here, in among the
yellow second sheets. Such a relief--their loss would have meant needless
and stupid <u>weeks</u> of research. I won't need them until I do my re-writing,
when I'll check on accuracy among the other things.

I don't remember whether my house of cards[3] had fallen around my head
when I wrote earlier, but Idella has walked out once again, for the fourth
time, and always when I need her most. Norton was finally obliged to fire her
husband Bernard, or lose his valuable white bar tender, who said he simply
couldn't put up with Bernard another day. Bernard talked her into going to

---

1   Most likely MKR is referring to her letter dated 18 April, the one with no parting and no signature. If so, this would account for the lack of an envelope for the 18 April letter. Further, this would
also mean that JSB did not receive the 18 April letter until 30 May or 1 June 1930.

2   Gene Baro [Baroff] (1924–1982), an aspiring writer, was a frequent visitor at Cross Creek from
1949, while he was the curator of the Creative Writing Collection at the University of Florida. Baro
lived at MKR's home at Cross Creek for a period before becoming a professor of English at Ben-
nington College in 1958. He became a well-known critic and curator of the arts.

3   The expression "house of cards" dates to eighteenth-century England, if not before, but became
especially popular in America at the beginning of the twentieth century.

New York City with him to get a job as a couple, which she knows as well as I do, won't work. Bernard drives her crazy after more than a night together (she still seems to enjoy that) and is such a shirker that she knows she would find herself doing his work as well as her own. Also, which she may not be aware of, she isn't the sort of cook who could satisfy the type of household that has cook, butler, second maids etc. And I have spoiled her, and she would find herself unhappy with late dinner every night, to say nothing of all the extra time off I gave her, the use of my car and so on, although of course her wages would be higher.[1]

She swore she would slip away and join me at Van Hornesville and to let her know the date I was arriving here. Yet I found all her uniforms still in her cupboard at the Creek---. And I have had no word from her. (Oh yes, she left, leaving me all the packing and Creek cleaning to do.)

Dear Peggy Egan, Martin's wife,[2] found me a very nice, quiet white woman[3] in her early sixties who has taken on my job, and who came this morning to begin. Her daughter, with whom she lives in Van Hornesville, will bring her every morning early to bring my breakfast in bed, she will do the downstairs work while I write in my bedroom, cook a hot noon dinner (she is a noted cook and housekeeper) then wash up and do the upstairs, when I will take her home on my daily trip to the post-office.

(I have been running an ad in the Cooperstown and Richfield Springs papers, and the 'phone just rang, and a marvelous-sounding woman from near Cooperstown applied for the job. I shall go to see her, in case the local Mrs. Hulbert doesn't work out. Mrs. Hulbert will not come on Sundays, and I'll have to fix my own supper, and she rather held me up on the matter of wages, and if I like the other woman better, I know I could get rid of Mrs. Hulbert easily, by keeping her later and piling on the work!) My only suspi-

---

1   Idella Parker left MKR in late April 1950 to go with her husband, Bernard Young, to New York to seek employment as a couple. Even though MKR knew Parker was leaving, she still felt betrayed and obsessed about the reasons, as in her letter to NSB dated 24? April 1950, where she seeks NSB's counsel on what to do next. On 30 May, she informs NSB that she is removing Parker from her will, "I see no alternative but being through with Idella for good. If it didn't matter to her to abandon me at this point in my work, I could never depend on her to see me through my life---" (*Love Letters* 572). Parker's account is once again different, where she points out that MKR and NSB "took me to the bus in St. Augustine. . . . As the bus pulled out, she [MKR] waved and smiled, and that's the last time I ever saw Marjorie Rawlings" (Parker 113). MKR recounts in a letter to NSB on 1 May that she wrote a letter to Idella in New York, but felt that she had proof that Parker was "double-crossing" her (*Love Letters* 571). Still, MKR continued to write Parker as late as 6 December, with the underlying intention to convince Parker to leave New York and come back to Cross Creek. Parker did not.
2   Margaret Egan and Martin Egan, the former working as a part-time cook for MKR.
3   Edith Hulburt (1870–1956?), who left MKR at the end of July (see her letter to NSB on 15 July 1950, *Love Letters* 581).

cion about the woman[1] who just 'phoned, from her cultured accent, the fact that she drives a car, and her saying that she would be so happy to have me call, as it would be such a great pleasure at least to meet me, is that she, too, wants to write a book!!!!)

Hell, I'd rather do my own work than have an embryonic writer in the house.

Well, so Norton drove me north, with Moe and Uki, and we stopped off for two nights and a day with his family in Alabama,[2] adding some 500 miles to the trip---we did come up over the Sky Line Drive across the Blue Ridge, and if you and Tom ever have a chance to take it in the flowering time of Spring or the color time of Autumn, do so, it is superb. I promptly collapsed on arrival, from the winter's writing, the hard trip of nearly 2,000 miles, Idella's defalcation, worry about the book itself. Norton amazed me during my two days in bed, he cooked (brought my breakfast coffee with a pansy on the tray) cleaned up to a modest extent and was cheery throughout. Of course, he WAS feeling guilty, as he hadn't fired Bernard with any tact---. Unusual for him, yet I can't help feeling that the subtlest sort of male egoism was involved, both with the white bar tender, who couldn't control Bernard's elegant, if inefficient, loftiness, and with Norton, who has surely caught hell from living with me, but who feels obliged to get on his high horse now and again---.

Well, we had one warm afternoon during the ten days Norton was here, and he was washing the day's dishes, and he took off his Brooks Brothers silk bath-robe, then the top of his Brooks Bros. pajamas, and since he was still sweating, he opened the Dutch window over the kitchen sink. About that time a car-full of women drove by slowly, and (this is Norton's report) one of them called out, "This is her house" and then they saw Norton, apparently buck-naked. He said that since he has gotten so plump and really does need a brassiere, he is sure the "fans" were convinced they had seen the authoress, and that her personal habits were as odd as was to be expected---.

The season here is backward, and only now my new tulips are blooming, and the apple blossoms and lilacs.

Do write me.

Much love,

Marjorie

---

1   Perhaps Gertrude Sandvold, whose "Norwegian" accent MKR came to accept, if not to tolerate completely.
2   Union Springs, Alabama.

. . .

JSB to MKR, 25 June 1950. ALS, 4 pp. AD: Mrs Norton Baskin | Van Hornesville | New York. PM is torn away.

Sunday – June 25 – [1950]

Marjorie dear –

It seems better to write at least a note saying desperate forces of circumstance are preventing a letter, then just to leave a deadly silence.

How I sympathize with your domestic difficulties. I have been having them myself like mad. Hildy's nurse who had been with her since she was born left.[1] This created quite an emotional arise. I finally got a new one and we had just got over the difficulties of the change when she got sick & had to quit the job. Then I had to try to find another – much more difficult this time – plus Martha[2] was away on her vacation. To add to the general confusion I got another hemorrhage W^?^.[3] In the mean time a quite important estate business trip to Nantucket had to be cancelled and <out> our departure to the Berkshires postponed. I have now a terribly nice (I hope) young Danish girl.[4] But still confusion is almost in total control. Closing up this apt. plus deciding about work that has to be done here this summer (painting, papering etc) is driving me nuts. I still feel awfully weak, which is no doubt only normal as my hemoglobin ^???^[5] is in the 50's somewhere.[6]

I have looked on the map and Van H'ville seems to be less than 150 miles from New M[7] so we will surely see each other soon.

At present we expect to go up to New M next Wed, but also at present I mistrust all plans! The Sunday after we arrive T's whole family – mother, sister, brother & niece[8] are arriving for I trust not more than a week.[9] After

---

1   Nurse not identified.

2   JSB's cook.

3   JSB inserts a question mark above "hemorrhage," indicating a lack of confidence in her spelling.

4   Not identified.

5   JSB inserts the three question marks above "hemoglobin," indicating a lack of confidence in her spelling.

6   The normal hemoglobin level for an adult woman ranges between 12 and 16 grams per deciliter.

7   Van Hornesville, New York, to New Marlborough, Massachusetts, is approximately 125 miles.

8   Thomas Bigham's mother: Ida Newell Bigham; Ida's sister: Anna May Newell McCartney (1869–1946); Ida's brother: James Newell (1865–1927). Thomas Bigham did not have a brother. His only sibling was his sister, Mary Newell Bigham Porter (1902–1991), married to George DeVore Porter (1905–1976). Their daughter and JSB's niece, Marydee Porter, later married Steven J. Ojala.

9   The next Wednesday is 28 June and the following Sunday is 2 July. MKR writes in a letter to NSB on 15 July, "Julia 'phoned me yesterday afternoon and begged me to come to New Marlboro for the weekend. Her domestic problems have been straightened out . . . and the relatives wished

that I think I really must go to Nantucket. Well, to write more would only dismay and depress us both.

I hope you are settled with a gem of a domestic by now and able to work without distraction. I really will write a more civilized letter soon.

Much love,

Julia

. . .

JSB to MKR, [19? July 1950]. PM: NEW M[ARLBORO] / A[.M.] / 195[0] / MASS[.] AD: Mrs. Norton Baskin / Van Hornesville / New York.

[19? July 1950][1]

Dearest Marjorie –

I'm sorry about the orchids![2] Things got somewhat thick on Monday after you left, and I just never got to doing something about them. I will try to get them located sometime soon. Then I could bring you some in August. Perhaps it is better to transplant them after they are all finished blooming anyway. I know them very well, and don't need flowers for identification.

It was <u>such</u> fun having you here. You have no idea how happy we all are

---

off on her. Her mother and aunt are not coming for another two weeks. . . . I have decided to drive over. It appears about a 3 hour drive. . . . Julia had extra tickets for the Berkshire Music Festival . . . and in my depressed state of mind, think it will be smart to go" (*Love Letters* 581–82).

1   Part of the PM is torn away. The date here is a reconstruction. On 15 July 1950, MKR writes to NSB, "Julia 'phoned me yesterday afternoon and begged me to come to New Marlboro for the week-end [15–16 July]." MKR apparently arrived on Saturday and left after the Berkshire Music Concert on late Sunday [16 July] to stay with Bernice Gilkyson (1897–1986), a poet and editor at Scribners, and Walter Gilkyson (1880–1969), a lawyer and writer. On Tuesday 19 July, MKR was back at Van Hornesville and confesses to NSB, "I am evidently getting queerer and queerer, for I did not really enjoy my visits to Julia and the Gilkysons. I am uncomfortable with Tom Bigham. The Gilkysons were more than cordial, but . . . I have never come so close to starving to death, in both households" (*Love Letters* 581–82).

2   During the weekend in question, JSB apparently promised to locate some orchid plants for MKR to take back to Van Hornesville. But as JSB indicates in this letter, Monday 17 July got "somewhat thick" at home. On 21 July MKR writes in response to the above apology, "It is just as well you didn't find the orchids for me, as the distance out of my way would have been the finishing touch on my fatigue, for the driving time home from [the Gilkysons] proved to be more than four hours." Since MKR left the Bighams on Sunday 16 July and got home on 18 July, it seems likely that JSB's letter was written around 19 July.

that you came, (Hildy is included there – she is still carrying the bag every-time she goes out).[1]

Tania is coming up this weekend, and possibly Ruth, and definately [*sic*] not the poor Belgian cousin.[2] So we have another nice weekend coming up. I always say there's nothing nicer than <u>invited</u> guests!

Much love,

Julia

P.S. We have eaten our way very happily through the sausage meat & the mangoes - <u>trying</u> to take it easy on the strawberry jam – and saving the other mangos for an occasion. Thank you!!

. . .

MKR to JSB, 21 July 1950. TLS, 1 p. PM: COOPERSTOWN | JUL 22 | 8 AM | 1950 | N.Y. AD: Mrs. Thomas J. Bigham | c/o Willetts | New Marlboro | Mass. LH: VAN HORNESVILLE, NEW YORK.

July 21, 1950

Dearest Julia:

It is just as well you didn't find the orchids for me, as the distance out of my way would been the finishing touch on my fatigue---and a thrown-out sacro-iliac--for the drive home from the Gilkyson's [*sic*][3] proved to be more

---

1   MKR refers to this letter from JSB in a letter to NSB on 22 July, "Such an enthusiastic note from Julia about my visit, it made me feel better about it, and evidently my boredom---except for the music---went unnoticed. Did I write you that I have never seen a stronger personality in a child than 3-year Hildy? . . . She is gay and friendly when she accepts you, but seems to have no need or desire for demonstrative affection. . . . Will not stand for being kissed. Yet she is not a brat at all. Very likeable" (*Love Letters* 584). Strong words from MKR, who is on record as saying she much prefers male to female children.

2   Tania Crocker Whitman, close friend of JSB's at Foxcroft. Ruth, last name not identified, a prominent physio-therapist who worked with JSB after she broke her back falling from a horse at Foxcroft. Belgian cousin, likely a euphemism for Charles Leirens, the Belgian photographer whom JSB joked about. See JSB's letters on 14 June 1944 and 27 September 1944.

3   Bernice Lesbia Kenyon Gilkyson (1897–1982), American poet and editorial assistant at Scribners, shared the National Book Award with Robert Frost in 1950. Thomas Walter Gilkyson (1880–1969), American poet and playwright. In a letter to NSB on 15 July 1950, MKR relates that she is going to New Marlborough for the weekend of 15–16, and then hopes to stay with the Gilkysons on Monday, 17 July, at their home in New Hartford, Connecticut. On Tuesday 18 July MKR reports on her experiences to NSB, I could only introduce Tom as 'Father' Bigham, the title he uses. He is so High Church, and Julia has fallen in line with it, that he says a standing grace, and then he and Julia cross Hell out of themselves" (*Love Letters* 582). The distance from New Hartford, Connecticut, to Van Hornesville, New York, is approximately 150 miles.

than four hours. Am just back from the Cooperstown chiropractor and think he got things back in proper position.

It was so good to be with you and yours, and I hope to give you and Tom at least half as pleasant a time when you come here in August.

And I do hope you found the half-dozen lamb-kidneys I left behind! And ate them---.

The little old-fashioned grocery store in Van Hornesville had some pretty-well-aged cheese, and I ordered 5 lbs. of it sent to you, parcel post, which I presume you get without trouble at New Marlboro. (I sent it care of Willetts,[1] to make sure.)

Think I told you that alas, poor Mrs. Hulbert, whom I had just gotten used to, is leaving me at the end of the month, but the daughter[2] of my near-est neighbor,[3] down the hill a few yards, will take over.

Norton writes that Florida is unbelievably hot this summer.

Much love to all,

Marjorie

. . .

JSB to MKR, 17, 23 October 1950. ALS, 5 pp. PM: NEW YORK, N.Y. | OCT 23 | 5[30] PM | 1950 | GRAN[D CENTRAL | STATION]. AD: Mrs. Norton Baskin | Van Hornesville | New York.

Tuesday [17, 23 October 1950][4]

Dearest Marjorie –

Here I am going to this darn island again.[5] – On the boat at present – Louise Schieffelin is with me. This time I have to set the carpenter, plumber, electrician, etc in motion. I hope to have the house in order so that I can rent it next summer.[6] Though why anyone wants to go to a place so darn difficult to get to and so _full_ of other people who have braved the difficulties I will

---

1 JSB was staying with her Aunt Gladys Augusta Casey Willets, the sister of her mother Vera Gordon Scribner. Aunt Gladys had a country home in the Berkshires, near New Marlborough, Massachusetts.

2 Edith Hulburt.

3 Not identified. MKR's nearest neighbor would have been Ellis Frederick and Lilian Frederick.

4 Written in a second hand at the top of p. 1: [10-25-50], which is incorrect. Based upon the PM, Tuesday would be 17 October and the following Monday would be 23 October.

5 Nantucket, an island off Cape Cod, Massachusetts.

6 JSB's great aunt, Rosalie Flagg Jaffray, died on 29 November 1949. See JSB's letter on 7 December 1949, 449, n. 4.

never know. It seems that I can count on $1000 a season (June 15 – Sept) and possibly a bit more.

I heard from Daddy[1] you had finished the last line of the book – so you are now in a vacation period, no doubt. I hope the vacation is very nice – and that the domestic situation is smooth enough so you can really enjoy it. It must be perfectly beautiful up there now. The drive from N.Y. to New Bedford yesterday up the parkways was lovely – wonderful colors.

A couple of weeks ago I had another hemmorhage [*sic*] ^???^,[2] which has left me aenemic again (I can't cope with these words in the middle of the ocean). Quite enervating and, of course, upsets my plans for relieving Hildy's lonely status. I have loads of pills to take and hope to be normal again in about a month. Dr. Damon has been in Europe – to Rome of all places. Do you suppose his wife is a RC.?[3] Surely he <u>can't</u> be with all the birth control information & equipment he gives out.

One bright piece of news I received before I left yesterday is that Tom has <u>passed</u> his German Exam. This is a good step toward the Dr's degree. Nothing much to do now except write a book, and as you know that's fairly simple.

I have been having an awful time with Louise. She is a great wildlife lover and has been worrying about the seagulls following the boat. She wanted

---

1   Charles Scribner III. JSB is referring to MKR's manuscript of *The Sojourner*. As it turns out, MKR, or Scribner III, and/or both were being far too optimistic. In a letter to NSB on 20 September, MKR opines, "The beginning of the last chapter, which I reported so proudly, had to be torn up today. I began again, and it is more nearly right. I had not ripped the other out of my blood and guts. . . . Worked hard again this morning, and will work through Sunday, and the first draft will be finished then, perhaps even before. . . . On 19 October, MKR is still revising, "Find myself in pure Hell on the re-writing---. You see, I just read you the few chapters that do not offend me too much. The rest is ghastly. . . . The book is not *fluid* enough. . . , so much of the thing is dull and plodding, and now I must add even more stupid chapters. . . ." On 19 November, MKR confesses, "Have almost decided not to try to get my manuscript exactly as I want it . . . but to begin copying it right now. I have so many questions in my mind about it that it may be better to let Scribners see the moderately revised draft, then do more re-writing later" (*Love Letters* 597–99). Six months later MKR was still revising, as she reports to NSB in a letter on 11 June [1951], "The last few pages I did on my book were forced and valueless. . . . I am tired of beating my brains out." By 15 August 1951 she is still flustered, "Finished an important section of my new writing, and now am afraid it isn't right, either. It leaves a bad taste in my mouth" (*Love Letters* 608, 618). The saga of writing and re-writing continued throughout the rest of 1951. There were many setbacks, but none more wrenching than the news she received from JSB on 12 February 1952. Charles Scribner III, in her eyes second only as editor to Maxwell Perkins, had died on 11 February: "It is unspeakable. To lose Max and Charlie together in so few years. I don't see how I can bear it" (*Love Letters* 639).

2   JSB inserts the three question marks above her misspelling of hemorrhage.

3   Virgil Damon, MD, and Mary M. Damon (1901–1976), his wife. "RC," meaning Roman Catholic.

to go in and buy several sandwiches at 50 cents each to feed them. Thank heavens someone has just thrown over some garbage.

– – – – – – –

Monday the 23rd

That's the end of the boat letter. I just can't cope with writing on boats. I don't get exactly seasick – I just go into a decline. Couldn't even finish it on the way back. Now I am under the hairdryer, which is my one leisure spot.

Whether it is something which happens every five years to a household or whether I am in a compulsive fit I don't know, but my whole house seems to have to be reorganized down to the last inch. Of course, the living room & the bedroom were painted, and I got a lot of new furniture & bric a brac from Nantucket and from Granny's house & apt – these are physical facts which create a good deal of turmoil. Painting the living room meant removing all the books from the bookcases and that meant that reorganizing my library and heartlessly parting with lots of books – it took me about four days. Then I have a new desk after almost 20 years in the old one – that's not settled yet. I did go through all my clothes in a heroic manner – dispensing with things that I haven't been able to get into since before Hildy was born. They had been lying about partly through lethargy and partly through some idea about the possibility of a wasting illness which would leave me fitting them again. Dreadful things are yet to be faced like all my photography cabinets & drawers & closets and my tool closets & the medicine closet. However I expect to find on the other side of all this efficient labor a sensation of housekeeping righteousness that will make it all worthwhile!

Marjory [sic], I do hope you will stay in N.Y. <at> a bit, preferably with me, before you go back to Fla. in Nov. There are so many new things in my apt I would like to show you and I expect it will be looking very handsome by then. Muddy is giving me new curtains and recovering a sofa & loveseat, & a chair in the living room. With all the new stuff I have that becomes a new room. We could have a lovely time listening to the phonograph – which I hope will be magnificently installed by then.

Hildy is having a lovely time because a little girl named Bunny – just the same age – has moved into the apt upstairs. They are bosom friends. I didn't know this relationship existed at the age of 3½. It really is a great satisfaction to see them enjoying each other so much. H. pulled one the other day that floored me and that I think you & Norton would enjoy. Somehow the subject of babies came up between us. I was explaining (never mind how!) about grown up ladies & female animals having babies. H. said, "Do fathers have babies?". I carefully & soberly explained that they didn't – only mothers. "Do babies have babies?" said H. I started off carefully & soberly on the negative again – when I caught a wicked twinkle in her eye, "Ha, Mother" says she, "I was only teasing you." She's a great self appreciator too – went around for several minutes chuckling to herself and muttering "Do babies have babies, Ha Ha"[.]

Well, now my hair is dry. Must be off. Love to Norton if he is there and very much to you. And all kinds of very happy congratulations on the birth of the book. I hope the afterbirth will be as easy as the birth was hard –

Bless you,

Julia

. . .

MKR to JSB, 25 October 1950. TLS, 5 pp. Envelope is missing.

Van Hornesville, N.Y.

Oct. 25, 1950

Dearest Julia:

In my slow way, it took me some time to figure out what you were doing on a boat,[1] but it finally dawned. The rental proposition does sound good. When you begin spending that thousand for photographic and phonograph equipment, remember to save out for taxes and repairs!!!

I loved the story of Hildy's fast one, and have quoted it verbatim to Norton. If she can trap you at 3½, you'd better begin taking courses in counter-intelligence right now.

I did think until the very last page that I'd <u>never</u> finish my first draft[2]. The next to the end is all wrong, especially, and it seems <u>jerky</u>—too many jumps in between some of the chapters. I hate to think I'll have to add to it, for the sake of fluidness, as it already runs about 150,000 words, and is in deadly

---

1   A reference to JSB's explanation that she was on a boat to Nantucket in her letter on 17 October 1950. In her continuation of the letter on 23 October, JSB refers to her "boat letter" and then tells the story of Hildreth, at 3½, asking, "Do fathers have babies?", only to confess later that she was only teasing JSB. See JSB's letter on 17 and 23 October.

2   The first draft of the manuscript of *The Sojourner*.

peril of being dull in any case, except when things occasionally take an almost melodramatic turn. All this aside from the usual bad writing, which proves mostly a matter of over-writing, so that deleting like the devil solves much of <u>that</u> problem.

Norton dear soul came up the moment I gave the signal, but could stay only a week, and just passed in and out of N.Y.C. I so hope to finish the re-writing and slow painful copying,[1] with two carbons, by the end of November. I have two problems there, one that the weather will close in on me, my steep road become impassable, the house too cold, for even with the wonderful automatic oil furnace, the doors and windows have such cracks that a bitter wind (and it has been down to 28 degrees here already) pours in and I have to avoid one room or another for comfort. The other problem is of going direct to N.Y. by car with the animals, who would have to be parked at a city Vet's, poor things. Norton insists on returning to drive me back to Florida, and it may be, especially if I can't quite finish as planned and hoped, that we'd go straight to Florida, and then I'd go by train back to N.Y. with my manuscripts like a nest of vipers in my bosom. This arrangement would give me more leisure and peace of mind in the city, and in such a case, I'd love to stay with you. If Idella were here, I'd make a special train trip to N.Y. from here, leaving car and animals with her, but my country helper[2] can only come from 7:30 A.M. until about 2 or 3 P.M., or as much later as needed, but could not be on hand to take care of Moe and Uki 24 hours a day.

Don't know how much I've written you about my gal Grace, whom Norton and I are obliged to call privately, "Horsie." Comes of one of the good ancient farm families here, is five-ten or more, freckled, and sways from hoof to hoof when excited. (Did I ever write you that at the end of her first week the great big mare burst into tears and sobbed, "I'm not pleasing you."?) And only because I was so pleased to have her that I had sunk into the whirlpool of my work and almost forgotten her. Which I tried then to explain---. And did I write you about the little old maid[3] at Mrs. Young's weaving hall, the one who plays a home-made bamboo flute on the hills? She had mended a basket for me and would not let me pay her, so, since she is a noted local "flower arranger", I brought her home to take her pick of my best flowers, filling a huge basket for her, and then "entertained" her with a glass of sherry, which she sipped in mortal terror of losing her immortal soul, while I slugged down a stiff high-ball, being a bit exhausted by her. She gathered strength from the

---

1   That is, preparing a publisher's copy from the final draft, including two carbon copies.
2   Grace, last name not identified.
3   Not identified.

sherry and said, "You know, I've always thought I'd like to write a book. Just a little book, to sell for about a dollar." She sighed and finished the sherry and said, "But I don't know the words."

Oh yes, another problem has arisen that may change my plans. Late Sunday afternoon I set out on a moderately noble mission to deliver my magazines to two neighbors who read them and then pass them on to others. Stopped first at Redjives,[1] half-way down the road, looked both ways on the highway, no cars in sight, I was driving very slowly, was not drunk, and before I had completed my turn on the highway, going toward Van Hornesville, a car came roaring over the knoll that blocks complete vision at the ^left^ turn. What a hell of a crash---. Both cars totally wrecked. We had to wait an hour before the State Troopers arrived, and by then it was dark. So I called my great pal, the head of the Troopers in Cooperstown, and asked him to send his men again the next morning to make a better check. Result: turn, with blind spot, so dangerous that signs will probably be put up for warning. I took a slight blame for not having come to a dead stop, although troopers agreed that it undoubtedly wouldn't have made any difference, unless perhaps my delay at the dead stop might have allowed the other car to hit me amid-ship, instead of more or less a side-swiping. All agreed the other car was going too fast.

Much about the accident, which is recorded as "unavoidable", was most amusing. Moe was thrown out of my car, and with no concern for his mistress, who might have needed to be hauled out of a burning wreck by the alleged faithful Fido, simply high-tailed it up the road to home. The Redjives are Polish, and later the "Mama"[2] said to me, "We know something happen when Moe run by so fast, and you just been here. Moe not even stop play with Fanny." (Their dog.)

The other amusing angle was that the driver and owner of the car that hit me was a Syracuse University student. He and his friend with him were not remotely hurt, and he came and sat with me in the car through the one door that could be opened, and we exchanged information, as we were both fully insured. He looked up from copying my name from my driver's license and said, "Could you possibly be the Marjorie Rawlings who's the author of 'The Yearling'? It's compulsory reading at college." I said, Yes, and with satisfaction he said, "This is a very great pleasure."

I could only interpret this to mean that it was well worth his wreck of his own car, to have knocked out an author responsible for compulsory reading---.

---

1 Ruth and Johnnie Redjives, a prosperous farm family.
2 Ruth Redjives.

Anyway, my car was towed off by a wrecker, to the nearest large Oldsmobile agency, where I had already asked about a trade for a new car. So now I shall definitely try to get a new one, and an "8" this time, as the total lack of power in the "6" is too annoying. My Grace has her own car, and she and other neighbors will transport me when necessary.

I thought at first I had only a minor cut and bruise below my left knee, but it turned out to be quite a mess and extremely painful, along with bruises and soreness back of left hip and over kidney, etc., so Grace took me to the Cooperstown hospital yesterday for examination and many X-rays. Apparently nothing broken or chipped, but the doctor wants me again for more leg X-rays when the swelling has gone down, blood in bruise absorbed etc., to make certain. I was in such pain that he gave me tablets of codine [*sic*] to bring home, but after all, I didn't dare take one, as I'd hate to be knocked out while all alone in the house. Am quite comfortable today, except when I have to stand up to go to the bathroom. Uki, of course, is hell-bent on sleeping on the sore leg at night.[1]

Norton was marooned by the hurricane at Marineland[2] and the next day had to drive 63 miles to get to the cottage, where he found the east side of the roof ripped off to a depth of five feet. Nothing important, such as books or pictures, damaged, only sopping wet rugs and furniture.

I can't spell hemorrhage or aenemia, either, but I know what you mean, and do hope you finish soon with both.[3] I am delighted that Hildy has found a pal of her own age, but I am afraid it may give Bunny an inferiority complex---.

Congratulations on Tom taking the German hurdle,[4] and tell him not to let a trifle like writing a book slow him up on his doctorate. There's nothing to it---one only needs to know the words---.

I'll let you know later more definitely about when I'll be in N.Y.

Much love,

Marjorie

---

1   MKR complains to NSB in a letter on 3 November about the unexpected aftermath of the accident, "Thought I had no jitters from the wreck, but yesterday a car darted out from a side road and Stad just missed it, and I had a minor convulsion. . . . Will be damn glad to have you do the driving back to Florida" (*Love Letters* 599). Albert "Stad" Stadler (1923–2000), American painter, was a leading figure in the movement of color abstraction. Stadler and his friend, Gene Baro, were constant visitors at Cross Creek while they were at the University of Florida.

2   Hurricane King, a Category 4 with sustained winds of 130 MPH, hit Miami on 18 October and then proceeded inland doing major damage well into Georgia. The distance from Marineland to Crescent Beach is approximately seven miles.

3   See JSB's letter on 25 June 1950.

4   JSB reports that Bigham passed his German exam in her letter on 17–23 October 1950.

JSB to MKR, 12 February 1951. ALS, 4 pp. PM: NEW YORK, N.Y. | FEB 14 | 9³⁰ AM | 1951. AD: Mrs. Norton Baskin | Crescent Beach R.F.D. | St Augustine | Florida. RA: Mrs. T. Bigham | 6 Chelsea Sq. | N.Y.C. 11. LH (embossed): 6 Chelsea Square | New York 11, N.Y. VIA AIR MAIL envelope.

Monday [12 February 1951][1]

Dearest Marjorie –

I have been meaning to write you daily for almost 2 weeks! The psyche was willing but the soma[2] raised pure hell – I had a mountainous migraine followed by endless hills of headaches – now I'm down to the molehill stage at last. Of course the damn continual seasickness is with me, and makes any effort of brain or brawn seem totally unreasonable – oddly the brain effort seems the worst.

The reason I waited to write you is that Daddy called me up when he was about 2/3rds through your book and he was so full of enthusiasm.[3] He said he really thought it was some of the finest writing you had ever done – that your writing about the country and life in it was truly wonderful, and he was feeling a better man just from having read it. I suppose he must have written all this to you before he left, but I wanted to tell you how happy I was to hear that after all the awful pains you had – bearing and birthing – that the baby is so pretty. I can't wait to see it.

I hope everything is well with you. I don't suppose Idella has wandered back into the fold?[4] Anyway, I hope you have someone to take care of things comfortably after your rather desperate summer.

---

1   The first Monday before the PM is 12 February 1951. Written in a second hand at the top of p. 1: [2-14-51], which is the PM date, not the composition date. The last known letter from MKR is dated 25 October 1950, which suggests that there are letters missing before this one.

2   Soma, from the ancient Greek *sôma*, meaning "body."

3   At this point, incredibly good news for MKR, who for more than five years had suffered authorial labor pains, as JSB referred to them. However, the enthusiasm of Charles Scribner III was short-lived. In April MKR was called to New York to meet with Scribner and John Hall Wheelock, poet and editor, who in 1947 succeeded Maxwell Perkins as senior editor at Scribners. In a letter to NSB on 21 April 1951, she reports somewhat cavalierly that she is in New York and will soon meet with "Charlie . . . and the boys" (*Love Letters* 606). The meeting, which JSB attended, did not go well. The verdict was devastating. The manuscript of *The Sojourner* needed extensive revision, a crushing blow to her already fragile psyche. MKR had been in Harkness Pavilion just days before for tests, under the supervision of Dr. Atchley.

4   Idella Parker had not returned.

I don't know whether you are at the beach or at the Creek fussing away on that poor child of yours – I'd better send this to the beach. By the way, have you ever received the Times Literary Supplement – Tom gave it to <u>me</u> for Xmas and it didn't start coming till last week. Let me know if you didn't and I'll write a complaining letter – or make Tom do it. I hope you don't <u>have</u> the damn thing already, but I couldn't remember ever seeing it in any of your houses.[1]

My house is driving me nuts and gulping down money as though it were a government project.

Also being an heiress drives me nuts, (of course, I'm not quite in the Barbara Hutton[2] class). Granny's estate[3] has been partly settled and I have to fuss around with books and investment advisory services and custodian accounts etc. etc. I have decided I am quite unambitious. I was perfectly happy when I didn't own anything just got some money handed to me occasionally. I'm just a frustrated 'lost woman' or an unkept 'kept woman' or some such thing.

Anyway, heartfelt congratulations from one mother to another – and thank heaven mine will be easier to bear!

Much love,

Julia

. . .

JSB to MKR, 13 February 1951. PM: NEW YORK, N.Y. | FEB 14 | 5-PM | 1951. AD: Mrs. Norton Baskin | Crescent Beach R.F.D. | St. Augustine | Florida. RA: Mrs. T. Bigham | 6 Chelsea Sq. | N.Y.C. 11. VIA AIR MAIL envelope.

Tuesday [13 February 1951][4]

Dearest Marjorie –

I was in Scribners today on an errand and saw Wallace Meyer[5] – We always exchange news of you, and he said he had just had a telegram from

---

1   JSB had apparently given MKR a subscription to *The Times Literary Supplement* (London) as a Christmas present.
2   Barbara Hutton (1912–1979), socialite and heiress to the Woolworth fortune, lived a lavish life-style, including seven marriages.
3   Louise Flagg Scribner died in 1948.
4   Written in a second hand at the top of p. 1: [2-14-51], which is the PM date, not the composition date of 13 February.
5   Wallace Meyer, an editor at Scribners.

you – and from this he told me of your disturbing letter from Carl Brandt etc.[1] I was quite enraged, and disturbed for you, as I certainly hadn't gotten any such opinion or impression from Daddy. Afterwards, I thought to myself that my last night's[2] letter being so coincidental might look horribly unspontaneous. Marjorie, forgive me if my paranoia imagination far outstrips yours – Anyway. Mine insists that I assure you that any coincidence is purely para-psychological or extra-sensory or what have you. In a way I feel like a fool even writing you this – but I have such a very strong feeling against there ever being even a smell of business entering into our friendship.

If this does seem idiotically paranoid to you – as I said, forgive it. And remember the love –

Julia

. . .

MKR to JSB, 7, 19, and 21 February 1951. PM: SAINT AUGUSTINE | FEB 22 | 3 PM | 1951 | FLA. AD: Mrs. Thomas J. Bigham | 6 Chelsea Square | New York City 21 [11].

Crescent Beach
St. Augustine, Florida

Fab. [*sic*] 7, 1951[3]

Dearest Julia:

I am sorry not to have both congratulated and commiserated with you earlier, but my own birth pangs were coming too thick and fast. And your morning nausea cannot be quite as severe as my constant seasickness.[4]

---

1   Carl Brandt, MKR's New York literary agent, who had a frequent habit of trying to interject himself, no doubt with good intentions, into MKR's compositional trials, much to the consternation of Maxwell Perkins. Brandt did not refrain when it came to her stumbling blocks with the manuscript of *The Sojourner*, and when he offered to come to Van Hornesville, MKR's frustration became evident: "You are sweet, as always, to want to help me, but with Max gone, it seems to me now only God can help me, and I doubt whether He's interested" (Silverthorne 309).

2   In her previous letter to MKR, JSB told her how much Charles Scribner III was enjoying reading the manuscript of *The Sojourner*. See JSB's letter on 12 February 1951.

3   This letter was written partly on 7 February 1951, then only dated without text on 19 February, completed on 21 February, and mailed on 22 February.

4   From the context of this paragraph, JSB seems to have alerted MKR that she is pregnant, which then permits MKR to say that she is also giving birth, to *The Sojourner*. JSB's letter about her second pregnancy is missing.

Seriously, I'm terribly depressed that the very best medical help in the country, if not the world, can't stop your pregnant nausea. I thought this was supposed now to be under control. I have always known of your, usually, admirable uniqueness, but you're carrying it a bit too far. Again, <u>most</u> seriously, I'm so sorry that you aren't carrying the baby comfortably. You were very brave to create a new soul, after the punishment you took with Hildy.

I had a notice from England that you have ordered the Literary Supplement of the London Times for me.[1] So many thanks. It has not begun coming yet. I'll wait a decent interval, at least until the mail embargo is ended, and then write the Times. (It has begun coming—a great treat.)[2]

I gave out of phenobarbitol [sic] and got a new bottle. This came close to being a mistake. I made a great effort to get my manuscript off to your father, for him to read <it> before he left on the long cruise, as I did want him to have something tangible now. I had told him nothing of the nature of themes of the book. I had a wire from him, within a hundred pages of finishing the reading, to which I have clung like mad. I had warned him that it wasn't his sort of book, but he said, "It is a joy to read such a book about the good earth".[3] A lengthy letter, he said, would follow before the end of the week.

So, what happens? His letter is evidently still resting quietly in one of the mail sacks at Penn. Station, while a bitch of a letter got through, from Carl Brandt,[4] to whom I had your father send the first carbon of the manuscript, when Jack Wheelock[5] was through with it. It may be the greatest compliment possible, that Carl was left stone-cold by the as yet not edited or necessarily re-written draft. If Carl couldn't see it for the Ladies' Home Journal or for the movies, it would automatically to him be a poor book. (At least, that's the way I'm rationalizing.)

I forget when I last wrote you, and whether, if so, I told of the[6]

---

1   See JSB's letter on 12 February 1951.

2   The parenthetical comment is inserted in MKR's hand. In 1951 there was, for a brief period, a mail embargo between Great Britain and the United States, which permitted only First Class, Air Mail, and other restricted mails to pass freely, which did not include printed matter like *The Times Literary Supplement*, even though it began to arrive shortly after MKR's caution. The comment in parenthesis is inserted in holograph.

3   Charles Scribner III might have in the back of his mind Pearl S. Buck (1892–1973), *The Good Earth* (New York: Day, 1931), awarded the Pulitzer Prize in 1932, a novel about the emerging conflicts in early twentieth-century China between old wealth and peasant poverty.

4   Carl Brandt, MKR's literary agent.

5   John Hall Wheelock.

6   This portion of the letter ends in mid-sentence. MKR continues on 19 February and then again

Feb. 19!!!!

And Feb. 21------

Needless to say, I have no idea what I started to tell you---

Meantime, your two good letters came in the same mail[1]. I happened to open the second one first, puzzling myself no end in the process. I still don't understand why you felt concerned that there might have been <u>anything</u> in the least out of the way. No idea of "business" would ever occur to me. For me, you are quite accidentally the daughter of my publisher.[2] The accident is a pleasant one, since I love him, too.

Actually, your first letter is the most cheering thing I have had about my manuscript. Your father had wired and written me, but I had the uneasy feeling that knowing how depressed I was, he was only trying to give me a temporary lift, and that the full bad news would follow later. His having spoken even more generously to you than to me about the book, reassured me that I do have something not too dreadful to go on working with.

I seem not to have written the book I wanted to write, as "the good earth" has apparently taken over, where I intended it only to be a natural background for the story of this particular man's mind.

I still have not heard from Jack and Wallace[3] in lengthy comment. Jack must have had a serious siege with the virus pneumonia.

Dr. Atchley is coming for a day in mid-March,[4] which is wonderful, except for the too-short time.

I had to fire the unspeakable colored woman Norton had for me.[5] I have never been through such a nerve-wracking experience. I finished editing and copying my first draft without any help except for a twice weekly cleaning woman. Then an odd thing happened. A colored friend[6] 'phoned me from the North and said that a young colored woman, a friend of hers, was in serious trouble. The young woman has been successful in her profession, but the brutal husband she had left, traced her to our mutual friend's studio

---

on 21 February.

1   JSB's letters on 12 and 13 February 1951.

2   Charles Scribner III.

3   John Hall Wheelock and Wallace Meyer, editors at Scribners.

4   Dr. Atchley, by this time a good friend, was making a personal visit, no doubt with the underlying intent of speaking to her about her continuing bouts with diverticulosis. She was admitted to Harkness Pavilion in New York in late April for a battery of tests.

5   The woman is not identified.

6   Perhaps Pearl Eileen Primus (1919–1994). Trinidad-born American dancer and choreographer, and anthropologist, who helped establish the importance of African dance and music in American culture. Lucille, last name not identified, may be the "colored woman" who came to live with MKR at Crescent Beach. Christine was Lucille's daughter.

and held a knife to her throat, etc. Help came, and he left, threatening to kill her another time. So, would I take her on here for a year, under an assumed name, with or without pay, by way of refuge. My friend vouched for her personality, for her character, immaculacy and good cooking. Having never done domestic work of any sort, she was willing and anxious to do anything I needed done, from scrubbing to typing.

She took a train the next day, arriving with trunk and all belongings. She is <u>charming</u>. She assumed at once the attitude of the self-respecting servant. She appeared from her apartment in one of Idella's half-buttonless old uniforms, worn as gracefully and casually as a tea frock. I showed her over the cottage and when we reached the studio, where the typewriter was open on the desk, she said, "I assume this is the room where you won't want to be disturbed at certain hours."

She is so superior to Idella that it's funny. She is too young and inexperienced in that line to plan and carry out a full dinner without suggestions and advice, but once is enough for her to learn anything. And she makes some superb West Indian dishes, including a broiled curried chicken with a sauce, that is simply delicious. She sings in French (not her native tongue, either) as she washes dishes. She takes the southern Jim Crow[1] in her stride. Since the arrangement is only temporary, I sha'n't try to teach her too much while I am so hard at work. Our domestic life is most pleasant once again.

However, you might know, the fly in the ointment---. To make a very long story short, a week or so ago she asked desperately if I could possibly consider letting her bring her child here, a little girl almost four. An aunt in St. Thomas, Virgin Islands, had been keeping the child, but was obliged to go now where she could not have her any longer. With plenty of room in the garage apartment, and considering Lucille's inevitable loneliness and anxiety (of which she shows publicly no sign) it would have taken a harder heart than mine to refuse. So again the next day she flew from Jacksonville to Miami, to San Juan, to St. Thomas, returning two days later with offspring.

Offspring is smart as a whip, with enormous eyes and a pointed chin, looking exactly like a wombat. Norton is enchanted with her. Norton gets only an hour a day with her---. Being too little to be left alone in the apartment, she must necessarily accompany the mother everywhere, which means <u>here</u>. Lucille keeps her sternly away from me, but she makes little sorties when unwatched, and I can't go out of the door without her rushing to grab my hand, to go with me apparently 'til death do us part. A certain amount of

---

1   Jim Crow, local and state laws and edicts passed, primarily in the South, to enforce segregation at all levels of the social fabric.

this is engaging, but <u>anything</u> ubiquitous becomes tiring, and the day-long patter of tiny feet and chatter of tiny tongue, to say nothing of anything but tiny tantrums, is not too much to my taste. She is as confirmed a No girl as Hildy ever dreamed of being.

But considering the enormous risk I took in committing myself to a full year of a total stranger, I am extremely well off.

I am reasonably certain that I shall be able to do my re-writing here in the studio. I can't leave Norton for months again---so soon! I go seldom to the Creek, to spare myself the pain and longing. I took Lucille there for two days, and when we left, she said, "There's something there I can't put my finger on, but whatever it is, it's good."

Norton has been putting out feed for the birds outside the <ge>terrace, and we are getting indigo buntings, towhees, redbirds, song sparrows, an occasional finch, and a mocking-bird who at this moment is auditioning for spring.

What did you think of the James Jones book?[1] It seems to me a magnificent thing. Norman Berg is so enthused that on a recent trip calling on the Macmillan trade, he found himself talking the Jones, and getting around only incidentally to commenting on the Macmillan list!

Moe and Uki are thriving.

All my love, my dear Julia, and many thanks indeed for your helpful letter.

<u>Marjorie</u>

.   .   .

MKR to JSB, 19 June 1951. TLS, 2 pp. Envelope is missing.

Van Hornesville, N.Y.

June 19, 1951

Dearest Julia:

We must have been worrying about each other at the same time. Last Thursday afternoon I 'phoned your apartment, and when there was no answer, I decided you were in Far Hills. I called there on Saturday, and was told you were in Nantucket.[2] Your card came yesterday.

---

1   James Jones (1921–1977), American novelist, *From Here to Eternity* (New York: Scribners, 1951). When he died in 1947, Maxwell Perkins had at his bedside the manuscript of the novel. See MKR's letter to NSB on 19 June 1951, n. 4 (*Love Letters* 609).

2   JSB was in Nantucket dealing with the estate of her great aunt, Rosalie Flagg Jaffray. See JSB's

You must be in fair condition to be battling the house. And to have progressed from detective stories to "War and Peace"[1] surely shows mental improvement---.

I have been all but sweating blood / ^on my re-writing^ for the month since Norton left.[2] Then yesterday I had one of those flashes of light that showed me not only that I had been on the wrong road from the beginning, but pointed unmistakeably [sic] to the right one.

It is so clear now, that I look at myself and say, "You stupid fool, you just can't be <u>trusted</u> to write."

Gertrude[3] has been coming for two weeks now and that side of life is calm and comfortable. Martin Egan's wife[4] drives here at 7 in the morning, I have my breakfast tray and then work in the bed all morning, Gertrude does everything downstairs in utter quiet, cleaning, laundry, mending, has a hot noon meal for me of her own planning, and I take her home in the early afternoon when I go for my mail. She fixes things for supper, ahead, if I want them, and as I was having five of Mr. Young's family[5] for supper Sunday, when Gertrude doesn't come, she prepared everything, jellied chicken, salad, strawberries, baked a cake, and all I had to do was put it on the table.

Mr. Young and Louise have not arrived yet, and things are quite complicated. They had expected to arrive here last week. Then Louise's mother, Mrs. Powis,[6] had a sudden operation for breast cancer--at the age of 87. She went home from the hospital one day, and at 3 the next morning Louise was taken to the hospital with an acute gall bladder attack. However, Norton reports that operation did not seem to be called for, and she would be in the hospital only a few days.

I happened to see Idella's best friend in Cooperstown, and Hattie[7] said that Idella had written her two weeks before, "What a fool I was ever to leave Mrs. Baskin. Do you suppose she'd take me back? I'm too ashamed to ask her, after the way I treated her." Hattie asked, "<u>Would</u> you take her back?" and I heard myself say, "Of course." I hastened to add that I was committed for the summer, and very satisfactorily. Hattie said, "But when you go back to Florida in the fall?" and I said "Yes."

---

letter on 7 December 1949, 449, n. 4. The card MKR refers to is missing.

1 Leo Tolstoy (1828–1910), Russian writer, *War and Peace* (1869), the celebrated novel that uses as the backdrop the invasion of Russia by Napoleon Bonaparte (1769–1821) in 1812.

2 NSB was in Van Hornesville for a "few days" in May 1951 (*Selected Letters* 366).

3 Gertrude Sandvold.

4 Margaret Egan.

5 Owen D. and Louise Young.

6 Julia Dunham Powis (1864–1954).

7 Not identified.

Idella has definitely left Bernard.[1] She took a course in catering this spring, after she left him and of course she may only be working it to come back to me long enough to dare to ask for the loan of money on some pretext, to head out again and set up as a cateress. Norton said, "Never mind, we might get in two or three years of comfort."

I went to Utica for my first eye check-up and the report was of vision and tension normal.[2] However, I got so upset about my work that my eyes have been paining me the past week or so. The doctor told me not to worry about the glaucoma, "Worry is bad for glaucoma," and I said, "Can I worry about other things?" and he looked confused and said he supposed everybody had to worry about something.

Much love,

Marjorie

. . .

MKR to JSB, 5 September 1951. TLS, 2 pp. Envelope is missing.

Van Hornesville, N.Y.

Sept. 5, 1951

Dearest Julia:

Such a relief to have your long portage safely over. I gather that you didn't have to have any surgery this time.

I do think it's awfully nice to have a little sister for Hildy.[3] There doesn't seem to be much community when a girl is four years older than a brother, as I was. I was 21 before Arthur[4] and I liked each other!

It will be fascinating to watch Hildy's reactions. If Mary Kirkpatrick develops as strong a nature, there'll be fireworks!

I have never been such a hermit as this summer. I've liked it, too. The book[5]

---

1 Bernard Young, Parker's husband.

2 MKR had been checked for glaucoma when she entered Harkness Pavilion in April 1951 (*Love Letters* 605).

3 Mary Kirkpatrick Bigham was born at Harkness Pavilion on Wednesday, 29 August 1951. In a letter to NSB on 31 August, MKR laments, partly in jest, "Another girl, damn it" (*Love Letters* 620). Mary Kirkpatrick later attended Chapin School, Garrison Forest School, and the University of Pennsylvania. She married Alan Penrose Langdale Blinks and was employed as a guide for Abercrombie and Kent safaris in Nairobi and Kenya.

4 Arthur H. Kinnan, MKR's brother.

5 The revisions of the manuscript of *The Sojourner*.

does go so slowly, but I hope this time I've made sense. I simply can't tell how much longer it will take me, but my aim is for early November. I think I'll run down to New York in mid-or late October for the Scribner folks to see what I've done, even if I'm not quite through.[1]

Gertrude[2] has made me very comfortable. She leaves in a week to return to her regular job at the school cafeteria, but I have such a sweet young Irish woman coming who will be satisfactory I know, if I can get used to her strange high voice. Katherine[3] will live here, she drives a car, loves house-keeping, and I am most hopeful about her.

I had the entire Young family for buffet supper Sunday, 31 of them, but have ducked all company otherwise.[4] One of my oldest and best friends from college days will spend at least two weeks, late September or early October, but I plan to go on with my work just the same. Her husband, also an old friend, died suddenly of a heart attack late in the spring, and Lois[5] is naturally still at sea. She wants to spend some time with me, and it's one of the times when you just couldn't let a friend down. I told her that she can amuse herself mornings while I work in bed, then we'll ramble around afternoons.

---

1   In a letter to NSB on 11 October, MKR informs, "I have practically decided to run down to New York for a few days at the end of the coming week or the first of the next one. I want Charlie and Jack Wheelock to see what I've done. If they approve so far, it will encourage me. If not, I'll know that I am stuck for the winter" (*Love Letters* 626). The meeting with Charles Scribner III and John Wheelock was a success, with MKR being asked to do some revisions before she went to final draft.

2   Gertrude Sandvold.

3   Catherine (Katherine) Mulligan. In a letter to NSB on 20 August 1951, MKR comments enthu-siastically, "I think I have found the answer to the sweet, capable, lifelong-loyal help that I once thought I had in Idella. Her name is Katherine Mulligan." The honeymoon did not last long. By 6 December, MKR is at wit's end: "Katherine finally drove me to it. Violence. Her motives are the kindest in the world, but I am exhausted from never getting my way," causing the weight-conscious MKR in righteous despair to throw "two blasted boxes of Fanny Farmer" cookies at her. Yet two days later, MKR was praising Mulligan as an "expert" in "planning the house closing. . . . It is defi-nite that she is to be with me next summer." Next summer came with this comment to NSB a letter on 7–14? June 1952, "I *cannot* put up with Katherine much longer" (*Love Letters* 619, 629–30, 640).

4   MKR relates to NSB in a letter on 8 September 1951, "My party went off splendidly, I am sure, as far as the guests quests were concerned, but it was a fatality for me. I couldn't get anyone to help me. . . . I reached for the Old Forrester [bourbon] as automatically as a rabbit breeds---." MKR goes on to explain that "I thought no one noticed, (!!!!), but the next day Louise [Young] said with arched eyebrows, 'Are you on the wagon again?'" She then confesses to NSB, "I probably shouldn't have told you about my fall from grace, but wanted to get it off my chest" (*Love Letters* 621–22).

5   Lois Clark Hardy, MKR's sorority sister at the University of Wisconsin. James Edward Hardy, Lois's husband, president of the Brimley-Hardy farm implement company in Louisville, Kentucky, died in 1951. MKR visited them often, especially to attend the Kentucky Derby.

I got my annual grouse with the car again. Wished you had been here to share it.[1]

Don't try to write me. I'll write again, or telephone.

Much love,

<u>Marjorie</u>

. . .

MKR to JSB, 1 October 1951. TLS, 1 p. Envelope is missing.

Van Hornesville

Oct. 1, 1951

Dearest Julia:

I wanted to 'phone you, but a letter from your father[2] said that you were to stay put in bed for a week, and I don't remember a 'phone by your bed.

How ghastly to have such a serious hemorrhaging so long after the birth.[3] I suppose it must have come with your first period. I do hope you have your strength back now.

I have been wonderfully well all summer, but have been having my first cold or minor flu in years, and I think it's because I over-did my serious reducing. I have lost 35 pounds, with about 7 more to go, and these are so obstinate that I repeated within ten days a strenuous 2-day diet that is probably only safe to do about once a month.

Gertrude[4] had to return to her winter job at the school cafeteria, and I have, living here, the strangest young Irish woman.[5] She is 31, very pretty, immaculate, a born servant in the old-fashioned way, and has a mind, or

---

1 MKR is likely not joking. Eating fresh road kill is a habit she picked up from the crackers of Florida, where such a practice was not uncommon, especially in the making of purloo (pronounced pur-low), the ingredients of which were always left to the preparer's imagination, a soup/stew that very well might include, possum, racoon, squirrel, even rattlesnake, seasoned with swamp cabbage, wild garlic, and bacon drippings, and complemented with rice, potato, or both. The key is the kill must be fresh. The best purloo is that which is boiled outdoors in an iron kettle over a jack-oak fire.

2 Charles Scribner III.

3 Mary Kirkpatrick Bigham was born on 29 August 1951.

4 Gertrude Sandvold.

5 Catherine (Katherine) Mulligan. In a letter dated [28 September 1951], MKR alerts NSB that she is thinking about bringing Mulligan to Florida, "It was necessary to speak to Katherine about Florida after all. . . . For sweetness, willingness, workingness, even the very servant-ness, I couldn't do better, and in time I may be able to make an efficient cook and housekeeper of her, which she certainly is not now" (*Love Letters* 624).

lack of one, that is always one jump ahead of itself. She never answers a direct question, but makes a remark that would apply, as I finally figured out, to a second question that might have followed the first if she had answered it. There are horrifying gaps in her cooking knowledge, but she is anxious to learn and to please me, and seems teachable. She loves the animals and drives the car and I am quite well off.

The work[1] is taking longer than I hoped, but I still think I'll make a jaunt to N.Y.C. late in October.

I had wanted Norton to come up this week, but he is holding out for the trip when I am about ready to return to Florida.

I think of you often, always with love.

Marjorie

· · ·

MKR to JSB, 26 January 1952. TLS, 1 p. Envelope is missing.
LH: Marjorie Kinnan Rawlings / cross creek / hawthorn, florida.[2]

January 26, 1952[3]

Dearest Julia:

I do hope you received the Mandarin oranges, tangerines. I took them in to that dreadful express man[4] at Island <Gorve> Grove and having typed out specifically the address twice, the man typed <off> on the express label "Ninth Street^"^ instead of ^"^Ninth Avenue".[5] I screamed and he corrected it.

Do tell me what happened about the <green> ^dream^ house.

Love,

Marjorie

---

1 On the revision of the manuscript of *The Sojourner*.

2 The next letter, 31 January, contains the language of this letter, plus additional information. It is possible that this letter was a start-up letter and was never sent.

3 The gap in dates between this letter and the last letter suggests that there are letters missing, most notably the usual Christmas letters exchanged between MKR and JSB. It is also possible that the fruit was sent much earlier as a Christmas gift and that JSB has yet to acknowledge it.

4 Mr. Neil at the Island Grove post office, who once before sent citrus to the wrong address in New York. See MKR's letter on 30 January 1950.

5 The excision of "off" and the insertions of the quotation marks are in MKR's hand.

MKR to JSB, 31 January 1952. TLS, 1 p. PM: ISLAND GROVE | JAN | 31 | 19[52] | FLA. AD: Mrs. Thomas J. Bigham | 175 Ninth Avenue | New York City 11. LH: Marjorie Kinnan Rawlings | Cross Creek | Hawthorn, Florida.[1]

[31 January 1952]

Dearest Julia:

I had a basket picked of the Oneiko Mandarins (tangerines) for you, and Chet Crosby's wife[2] packed them, and I took them to that awful express and telegram man at Island Grove, and I myself typed the two labels to go on the basket, and I JUST HAPPENED to notice that when Mr. Neil[3] was making out the express ticket, here, where I had 175 Ninth AVENUE typed plain as day, he wrote Ninth STREET, and I tried to tell him about N.Y.C. streets and avenues, and he said, "It's all New York City, isn't it?"

So I hope you received the tangerines.

And I hope also that you do not let anything deter you from the dream house.[4] Do not buy a substitute. Heaven and Hell can be coped with, but the Purgatory of a compromise, never---.

My love,

Marjorie

. . .

MKR to JSB, 19 February 1952. TLS, 3 pp. [Envelope is missing]. LH: Mrs. Norton Baskin | crescent beach | st. augustine, florida.[5]

Sunday, Feb 19.[6]

Dearest Julia:

---

1 MKR's letter on 26 January is likely the start-up for this letter on 31 January.

2 Helen Crosby.

3 Mr. Neil, the expressman in Island Grove whom MKR disliked and distrusted. Neil had sent tangerines to the incorrect address before. See MKR 30 January 1950.

4 The context of this comment suggests that there is a letter or letters missing from JSB about this contemplated real estate purchase.

5 MKR types in "Mrs." to convert NSB's stationery to her own.

6 MKR writes in the month and day: "Feb. 17."

Just felt I wanted to write you at once.

How good to hear your voice, and to realize that you will be tough enough to see Vera through.[1] I have an idea that you will be able to help Buzzie, too. For him, aside from the anguish, there will be the shock of so great a responsibility coming upon him, years before any of us were prepared for it. I say "us", for the Scribner "family", whether or no, includes the devoted writers and people like Whitney and Jack and Wallace.[2] It may be of some comfort to have us share the pain.

The more I think of it, the more I think (and Norton was sure of it at once) that you would do well, if you come South en famille, to tuck in at the cottage, first of all, and if the March weather is warm enough, just stay here as long as you are happy. If March is inclement, you and Vera could mosey on farther south and find just what you want, and then move, with bassinet, diapers, pap and Pablum.[3]

I do not believe you could be more comfortable than here, if it is warm enough for the beach. On a separate sheet, I'll enclose a diagram of the enlarged cottage. The only draw-back I can see as to domestic arrangements, is that the studio, where the nurse[4] and Hildy and Mary would undoubtedly park, has, in the bathroom, only a shower, with no tub. Norton, who, I think, (know!) is terribly hoping you will come, rather snapped at me. He said he assumed the nurse was young and could use a shower, and surely, after you and Vera were through with your respective bathrooms, the nurse could bathe Hildy in one of them, and a bit sardonically, that he imagined Mary would have a canvas bath instead of being dunked in a large porcelain one.

Norton has a cleaning woman[5] twice a week, who would continue to come, on his own-payroll, as he could not afford to lose her by dropping her for a while, and we can find you a cook. The maid's apartment, at the foot of

1   MKR is referring to the death of JSB's father Charles Scribner III on 11 February. Vera was his wife, and Buzzie his son, Charles Scribner IV (aka Jr.), brother of JSB. It is clear from the context that MKR and JSB spoke over the telephone, although JSB also sent telegrams. In MKR's letter dated [12 February], she laments to NSB, "Mail did come, and in it telegrams from Julia and Whitney Darrow that Charles Scribner had died suddenly. Three days before his death, Scribner wrote to MKR complementing her on *The Sojourner*: "And in the mail today, so shocking, what must have been one of Charlie's last letters. . . . [He] had done his usual delightful scribbling all around in pencil. . . . And he had had too much to do and was so tired" (*Love Letters* 639).

2   Whitney Darrow, Scribner's sales manager; John Hall Wheelock, a Scribner's editor; Wallace Meyer, a Scribner's editor.

3   Pap, soft food for infants, and Pablum, a trademarked cereal for infants.

4   Not identified.

5   Not identified.

our dune, is comfortable, as Norton enlarged that, too, and the cook would stay there.

And if Vera changes her mind, and wants just to go here or there, trying to escape the inescapable, you might well do the same thing, stop at the cottage, or, of course, at Cross Creek, except that the Creek is no place for your mother. I was surprised when you said that the ocean, or ocean air, did not agree with her, as she seemed to be so happy hunting shells on the beach.

By God, another idea occurs to me. Sanibel Island,[1] on the West Coast of Florida. The choicest shells in the world are found there, and I have a friend there (if she isn't dead or gone,[2] I haven't been in contact with her for many years) and it is a grand place, and I'll check on that. The Gulf Coast is almost always warm.

I was so tempted to fly North, for the funeral, and Edith Pope was, too, but I felt that your father would want me to finish my belated book[3] by April, for fall publication.

Keep in touch with Norton and me, and I can give you a <u>telegraph</u> address for Cross Creek, <where I must finish my book:> which will really reach me:

Marjorie Rawlings
c/o Williams, Cross Creek Groves
Island Grove, Florida

The Williams'[4] will bring me any wires.

All my love,
<u>Marjorie</u>

. . .

MKR to JSB, 29 February 1952. ALS, 5 pp. PM: SAINT AUGUSTINE | MAR 1 | 7 [am/pm blurred] | 1952 | FLA. AD: Mrs. Thomas J. Bigham | c/o Scribner | Far Hills | New Jersey.

---

1 Sanibel Island is a barrier island on the west coast of Florida, approximately 295 miles south of Cross Creek.

2 Not identified.

3 *The Sojourner.*

4 George H. "Hugh" Williams (1893–1966) and Grace Flora Brice Williams (1892–1992), ran a store in Island Grove, FL, called Cross Creek Groves (Stephens 5, n. 22). The Williamses "lived down the road" from MKR (*Selected Letters 292).*

Feb. 29, 1952

Flagler Hospital
St. Augustine, Fla.

Dearest Julia:—

What a darling you are. With all your own trouble, to worry about me. (Must admit, I was worried, too!) Your good letter came today.[1] And a few days ago, the most gorgeous red roses from you and Vera—18 of them. They are full-bloom now, but still fresh and lovely. Either you and your mother were frightfully extravagant, or roses aren't as high in Florida as New York, but I'm afraid it was the former. And very much appreciated. I'll write Vera with my next burst of strength.[2]

I am doing wonderfully well, and begin to feel rested and relaxed. I had planned a perfectly lovely collapse when I finished my book, rather gauging it for Harkness[3] in mid-April, just in time to luxuriate there and then go on to Van Hornesville in early May. I seem to have tripped over my own feet. I certainly never planned anything like this. That night at the Creek alone with that ghastly pain, unable to call anyone, is something I shall be most careful not to repeat, if possible.

No residual damage was done, and there will not be any from similar spasms (which I may be able to avoid entirely.) The doctor explained the type of attack—it sounded related to angina pectoris[4]—and said a spasm must never be allowed to last too long, else an occlusion occurs. I am not to consider myself an invalid in any way—it is just that I must never allow myself to pass a certain limit, in strength, or in mental tension. And no one but I can recognize that limit. I shall do so. Cigarettes are forbidden

---

1   JSB's letter is missing.

2   MKR experienced a "coronary spasm." On Saturday, 16 February, she drove from Cross Creek to Crescent Beach, where she began to suffer from what she thought was "indigestion." On Sunday, 17 February, she insisted, in spite of NSB's protestations, to drive back to Cross Creek, where she was in the final throes of revising her manuscript of *The Sojourner*. That night the pain became "unbearable," and in her state she was unable to rouse Adrenna Mickens from the tenant house and thus suffered through the night. On Monday, 18 February, a doctor was summoned from Gainesville, and she was taken by ambulance to Flagler Hospital in St. Augustine, where the doctors told her she barely escaped a "coronary occlusion." She remained in the hospital for nearly three weeks, at which time she was put on a strict diet, and as she confirms to JSB, told smoking was "forever forbidden," and liquor in "moderation" only after a full recovery (*Selected Letters* 370–71). As MKR concludes in this letter to Norman Berg on 2 March, "I am fortunate in many things---this was a warning, in time" (*Selected Letters* 373).

3   Harkness Pavilion, the hospital in New York.

4   Angina pectoris, severe pain in the chest, often radiating to the shoulder and to the arm and often a signal that a heart attack is in progress.

forever. Liquor is allowed "in moderation", but it is easier for me to abstain entirely than to be moderate, so liquor is out entirely, at least for a long time to come. I said to Gene Baroff[1] "It's simply ridiculous to be sensible." But I must be.

I was within two days of finishing my book, ready for copying. However, since I had planned to do the copying myself, and now must use a stenographer, I may not be too far behind after all. I had a dear note, and a wire, from Jack Wheelock,[2] telling me not to worry about anything.

My sweet little Irish Catherine Mulligan lost her mother a week before I got myself into trouble, and wanted to come to me, so it seemed "intended" and Norton 'phoned her and told her to come ahead. A sister and brother-in-law were driving South, and she came with them, and they are due in today. She drives a car, well, and will be a great help and comfort.

I will have to go from the hospital (probably early this coming week) to the cottage, instead of the Creek, because of the telephone. And being so much closer to doctors etc. I'll go at my work very gradually and cautiously, and if it seems safe, a little later, will go to the Creek.

Something depends on which place I can get a good stenographer.

I am so relieved that you will not try to travel with two babies and a nurse! A good jaunt by car with your mother will help her as much as anything can, and you will be so much better off. If I am at the cottage, Norton and I would want you to be our guests at Marineland. The Court there is attractive and comfortable.[3]

I do think Edith's[4] idea of Sarasota on the West Coast is promising. At least take Vera there to see the Ringling Museum and to look in on the art classes.[5] And the famous Sanibel Island is not far from there,[6] where some of the world's finest and rarest shells are found. If I'm not mistaken, there is a good hotel there. Plan to stop off at our beach, and Norton will have some information on Sanibel.

From your father's last letter,[7] I gathered that you had actually bought a place. Was it the dream-house?

Do keep up, my dear.

---

1 Gene Baroff [Baro], then curator of the University of Florida Creative Writing Collection.
2 John Hall Wheelock.
3 The Marine Village Court motel, managed by NSB's brother Tom Baskin, was located on A1A next to the Dolphin Restaurant, managed by NSB. Both were located just to the south of Marine Studios.
4 Edith Pope.
5 The Circus Museum at The Ringling and Ca' d'Zan Museum of Art, both in Sarasota.
6 Sarasota to Sanibel Island is approximately 108 miles.
7 Charles Scribner III's last letter to MKR was dictated on 8 February 1952.

(over)

When the ambulance called for me at the Creek, ill as I was, I thought to tell Adrenna to leave a rear door of my car open all the time, so Moe could jump in and out. (As long as my car is around, he does not run away.) She wrote me the other day, "Moe take a ride in the car every day he thinks he be goin I wush you could see him."

Norton will take Catherine to the Creek Sunday to get my clothes, my papers, and the animals, and she will drive my car back here.

Much love and I look forward so much to seeing you.

And all thanks again for the wonderful roses.

Marjorie

I don't need a thing.

. . .

MKR to JSB, 1 April 1952. ALS, 4 pp. PM: SAINT AUGUSTINE | APR 7 | 5 PM | 1952 | FLA. AD: Mrs. Thomas J. Bigham | 175 Ninth Avenue | New York City 11.[1]

Crescent Beach
St. Augustine, Fla.

April 1, 1952

Dearest Julia:—

It was so good to hear your voice. And the good news that Buzzie is being released[2]—and will live at Far Hills.[3] This seems perhaps the one thing that would take Vera out of herself, since you were not free to give your own whole life to her.

For a while, she will feel so old, Julia, but I hope she will soon pass out of that stage and take her former interest in things.

I think I told you of the time Edith[4] was visiting me at the Creek, and she called out from the yard, "What kind of snake is this?" and here I found her, sans spectacles, with her puss practically pushed into that of a deadly coral snake. Well, she did the same thing early yesterday morning. She was out in

---

1   Envelope and text are in pencil. On the envelope below the address are 11 Xs.
2   That is, Charles Scribner IV (aka Jr. or Buzzie) was released from his military duty upon the death of his father, Charles Scribner III.
3   Far Hills, New Jersey, the home of the Scribner family estate.
4   Edith Pope and Verle Pope, her husband.

a negligee, admiring the scenery, and calling one of the cats, and stooped to pull a weed from beside the steps. This time it was a rattlesnake. She said, "A small one". Of course, there is no such things as a small rattler, for their venom is just as deadly as that of a 5-footer. Verle came and killed it and was terribly amazed with her when she threw up a little later and hated to admit it was from the shock. She went to her doctor just to be sure it was psychosomatic, and he said "If it had been I, I should have had a coronary thrombosis and would now be dead."

I am not behaving as well as I should,[1] but must be past the danger point, as nothing more has happened. A wonderful secretary has begun work copying my book. (I thought I was going to have Mr. Young's secretary, with the loan of his electric typewriter, but she backed out.) This woman[2] is a professional typer of manuscripts and said it is such a joy to be typing good English, as most of her would-be-writer-customers are illiterate.

I am doing very little editing. I have gone stale on the thing and feel sure it is best, as your father urged, to get it into print. I can then relax for a bit, before the proofs begin coming.

My Irish Catherine[3] is driving me mad.

(over)

You sounded thriving, in spite of all your burdens.

I am furious that you aren't coming South, but we'll get together soon. Dana[4] wants me to stop off in N.Y. to see him and I may do so. Can't wait to see the Mass. place.[5]

Much love,

Marjorie

---

1   That is, MKR had gone back to drinking and smoking, against the advice of her doctors at Flagler Hospital, where she was treated for her "coronary spasm" in February–March 1952.

2   Nike Grafstrom (b. 1908?) was a copyeditor from Chicago, Illinois, who had moved to St. Augustine, Florida. In 1953, she helped type MKR's notes for her projected biography of Ellen Glasgow (Silverthorne 321; Selected Letters 392–93).

3   Catherine (Katherine) Mulligan.

4   Dr. Atchley.

5   The Bighams' new home in Sheffield, Massachusetts.

MKR to JSB, 3 May 1952. TLS, 3 pp. PM: SAINT AUGUSTINE | MAY 3 | 4³⁰ PM | 1952 | FLA. AD: Mrs. Thomas J. Bigham | 6 Chelsea Square | New York City 11. LH: MRS. NORTON BASKIN | CRESCENT BEACH | ST. AUGUSTINE, FLORIDA. <u>Via Air Mail.</u>[1]

May 3, 1952

Dearest Julia:

This is how things are lined up, if nothing happens:

Norton and the animals[2] and I leave here early Monday morning May 14 [12]. (I have a new car.) He will deliver me at Harkness Pavilion some time Wednesday May 14. (We will use the new N.J. turnpike which takes us right to the George Washington bridge.) He will drive on to my place at Van Hornesville that day, no matter how late at night he may get in. (On account of the animals. My Catherine and Peggy Egan[3] begin this Monday to get the house ready, and Catherine will be there when Norton gets in.)

I will use the hospital as a hotel. I hope and really expect that the mornings of Thursday and Friday May 15 and 16 will be enough for the X-rays and checks that Dr. Atchley wants, and I have written him asking if he can so arrange it. I have written Jack Wheelock[4] asking if we can have our session on my book the afternoon of Thursday May 15. I disapproved thoroughly of the photography of me he was planning to use for publicity,[5] said I had hoped you would get a chance to work on me, to get something not so formal, and he said Fine, but also what about their regular photographer taking pictures, so I have suggested that Jack make that appointment for Friday afternoon, May 16, mid- or late by preference.

I want to take the 9 A.M. train Saturday ^May 17^[6] morning for Ft. Plain, where Norton will meet me.

Now of course when I am through with the proofs on my book this sum-

---

1 "Via Air Mail" is inserted in MKR's hand.

2 Moe and Uki, the Siamese cat.

3 Catherine Mulligan, MKR's fulltime housekeeper, and Margaret Egan, part-time housekeeper and cook at Van Hornesville, New York.

4 John Hall Wheelock.

5 The publicity photograph by Erich Hartmann (1922–1999), German-born American portrait photographer, was finally used, and is the one that appears on the back cover of the dust jacket of *The Sojourner*. Whether or not JSB did any photographs of MKR has not been established.

6 The date is inserted in MKR's hand.

mer, I'll be as free as a runaway bal^l^oon,[1] and will expect to dash here and there, seeing your new place in Mass., making a visit to Robert Frost,[2] etc. etc., but also hope we can get together this time, even though I am sort of skipping through.

If Dr. Atchley and Jack Wheelock accept my schedule, I'll be free Thursday and/or Friday evenings. I say and/or, in case Dr. Atchley wants me to go to Englewood[3] for dinner one of those nights. Wait a minute, it would <u>not</u> be Thursday, he has a regular club dinner meeting. So can you and I have dinner and the evening Thursday May <16?> 15? If so, I'd love to have you come to Harkness and have dinner with me in my room. All of this is going to tire me (I am completely well, but I do tire easily, and I am supposed to <u>quit</u> whenever I feel so) and if you don't mind the trip up, I could even climb into bed if I am too exhausted.

I'll 'phone you from the hospital Wednesday ^May 14^[4] after I get in, to check.

Much love,

<u>Marjorie</u>

.   .   .

MKR to JSB, 21 May 1952. TLS, 1 p. Envelope is missing.

May 21, 1952

Dearest Julia:

Yesterday's TRIBUNE backs up my sea horse story.[5]

I meant to call you before I left, but things stayed complicated. However, all is well with me, as I was sure, and I wish I had my money back.[6]

---

1   The "l" is inserted in MKR's hand.

2   Robert Frost lived near Ripton, Vermont, in 1952.

3   Atchley lived in Englewood, New Jersey, approximately eleven miles north of New York City.

4   The date is inserted in MKR's hand.

5   *New York Herald-Tribune* (20 May 1952): story and reference to it in the *Tribune* not located.

6   MKR had just left Harkness Pavilion, where she had undergone tests under the supervision of Dr. Atchley. MKR apparently did not see JSB during and after her stay in Harkness. In a letter to NSB on 4 June, she reports, "Dana had sent me the prescription for Dexedrine. Said it was likely to make one very jittery. . . . I didn't dare try it, as I have never been so jittery in my life. . . . Simply could not stand it so Saturday began drinking again, and after knocking myself out last night, feel relaxed this morning for the first time. Will go back on the wagon again today" (*Love Letters* 640).

Norton left yesterday. Seems he had planned to spend part of his vacation with his family on his way home.[1] <home.>

Cold and rainy here, tulips and apple blossoms just opening.

Catherine[2] does better here, but I am still fighting the battle of the poached egg. She must try to take them out of the water with a fork---.

The first of my proofs came into Jack Wheelock's office while I was there,[3] giving me the creeps. When I have them out of the way, can't you come here to get your breath?

Julia, Buzz[4] is <u>wonderful</u>. He is going to make a <u>superb</u> President. I only hope he will be able to delegate some authority and not work himself to death.

Much love,

Marjorie

Dr. Atchley said he tried so hard to get Buzz out of the Navy before your father died, and I said, "That might have saved Charlie's life", and Dr. Atchley said, "Nothing would have saved him."

. . .

MKR to JSB, 20 August 1952. TLS, 2 pp. Envelope is missing. LH: VAN HORNESVILLE, N.Y.

August 20, 1952

Dearest Julia:

You should be a writer of serialized mystery stories. You have the damndest trick of leaving your correspondents dangling in suspense. I have squirmed at hearing nothing more from you since you were two-thirds through my book, certain that the last part disappointed you. Now Buzz writes me that you are enthusiastic, and I can relax.[5]

I think I have not written you since you and Tom were here, and how I

---

1 The Baskin family lived in Union Springs, Alabama.

2 Catherine (Katherine) Mulligan.

3 MKR would have seen John Hall Wheelock at Scribners on Monday, 19 May, or perhaps the Friday before, 16 May.

4 Charles Scribner IV (aka Jr.) succeeded his father, Charles Scribner III, as president of Scribners.

5 The content of this paragraph suggests that MKR has not been hearing from JSB on a regular basis. And, of course, there is always the possibility that letters from JSB are missing. Buzz is Charles Scribner IV (aka Jr.), who had already undertaken his duties as president of Scribners. JSB would be reading the proof of *The Sojourner*.

did enjoy seeing you. And I thank you deeply, either or both, for the book of Common Prayer and for the St. Augustine's Prayers. I read night and morning in the Common Prayer, and say either the Lord's prayer or a despairing one of my own, hoping for some sign of grace. It has not yet come, but surely it will. I don't understand what I might call my spiritual sterility. It is not a matter of crying, "I believe. Help Thou my unbelief",[1] for I do believe. But I have a dullness which I should be unwilling to offer.[2]

The visit of my brother and his baby[3] did not help me, and I was unable to give there any help. My brother is a man obsessed, and his terrible possessive love for the most attractive and bright little boy is doing only harm to the child. None of the legal or friendly advice, to return west and fight the court battle for custody, even registers on Arthur. Having a ticket, and bedroom, for Chicago, at which point he said he would decide whether to continue by 'plane or train, he left the train precipitously at a New York state town, and writes now of starting a business there.

Relatives, as such, leave me very cold, but no one is closer than a brother, and my heart is torn for him, and for the boy.

After they left, I was desolate, and 'phoned Robert Frost in Vermont,[4] and he wanted me to come, and I spent two days with him, and as you would

---

1 Mark 9:24.

2 JSB and Thomas Bigham had visited MKR at Van Hornesville after MKR's appeal in her letter on 21 May 1952. MKR writes to NSB on 14 July 1952, "I had asked Julia and Tom to come for a few days, and she accepted with real delight" (*Love Letters* 643). The gifts likely did not have the impact MKR is claiming, given her negative opinion of Bigham's High Church Episcopal orthodoxies, and even though it seems clear that JSB came increasingly to endorse them.

3 Arthur Houston Kinnan had been plaguing MKR for years. He seemed unable to support himself and routinely asked for monies to keep him alive or to underwrite his various projects and schemes. He had just been divorced by his wife Grace V. Campbell Kinnan (1917–1996) in September 1952. In violation of court orders Kinnan took his infant son, Arthur Jeffrey "Jeff" Kinnan (b. 1951), and fled to Florida. While MKR was in Van Hornesville, New York, finishing the reading of the proof of *The Sojourner*, Arthur, with Jeff, stayed briefly with NSB at Crescent Beach. NSB loved the child and tentatively agreed with MKR that they should adopt him. Various reasons, most prominently MKR's failing health, led them to reconsider, although they did tell Arthur that they would take Jeff in an emergency. Arthur and Jeff, as this letter indicates, visited MKR in Van Hornesville. MKR is not complimentary about her brother in a letter to NSB on 10–11 August 1952, "I expect Arthur to phone me any day, reproaching me for not writing or calling. But I don't see how I can write, for I have nothing to offer but hell, and ass-child that he is, it still isn't fair to kick him when he is down" (*Love Letters* 649). Apparently, Arthur and Jeff lived in Syracuse, New York, for a while, finally ending up on Vashon Island, King County, Washington. Employing a detective agency, Grace Kinnan, who was living in Seattle, finally found Jeff (*Seattle Daily Chronicle*, 2 December 1953: 2). The newspaper used this leader: "Mother's Hunt for Baby Ends." During the whole ordeal, MKR, who wittingly and unwittingly aided Arthur in his deceptions, remained unsympathetic to the plight of Grace Kinnan, the boy's mother.

4 Frost lived near Ripton, Vermont. MKR describes her visit with Frost in a letter to NSB dated

know, he gives, restores, a sense of balance. I told him of going to Florida and Ohio for Aunt Ida's death[1] and burial, and as against her 92 years, we figured that he had <14y> 14 years more to go, and I, 36, and we both agreed we'd never make it. How I love him. He read me a new long poem that made my hair stand on end. He thinks he may possibly not publish again except posthumously.[2]

I am waiting to hear when Norton can come, and whether he still wants to go to England and Ireland.[3]

Mail time approaches, so, as Adrenna[4] ended her last letter to me from Cross Creek, "Good by an stay sweet."

Much love,

Marjorie

. . .

MKR to JSB, 29 October 1952. ALS, 4 pp. Envelope is missing. LH: SHELBOURNE HOTEL. | DUBLIN. | TEL. 66471-7. 14 LINES. | TELEGRAMS: | "SHELOTEL, DUBLIN."

Oct. 29, 1952

Dearest Julia:—

We have had marvelous luck for the most part, as to weather and inns.[5] Our few personal contacts have been delightful. The Canterbury Tales translator, Nevill Coghill,[6] did Oxford University up brown[7] for us. We were

---

[10 August 1952]. The poem Frost read to MKR was "Gold for Christmas" (see MKR's letter to Gene Baro, 16–17 August 1952, Baro Papers, Special Collections, University of Florida).

1 Aunt Ida McFarland Tarrant died on 23 June 1952, and was buried in Cincinnati, Ohio.

2 Frost published four more collections of poems before his death in 1963.

3 JSB was helping MKR and NSB with their planned trip to Ireland.

4 Adrenna Mickens.

5 The Baskins left New York on the luxury ocean liner *United States* on 3 October 1952 (*U.S. Departing Passenger Lists*). They embarked in first class, but owing to MKR's parsimony returned on the less expensive *Mauretania* on 20 November 1952 (*New York Passenger Lists*). The expenses caused a pre-sailing tiff between the two, settled by MKR, as she reports to Norman Berg in a letter on 19 September 1952: "I said, all right, we'd go on the damn boat [*United States*], but since we are sharing expenses, he could pay for the trip over, and I'd get us back on a cheaper and _nicer_ small boat" (*Selected Letters* 379).

6 Nevill Coghill (1899–1980), British literary scholar, known especially for his modernization of Geoffrey Chaucer (1340?–1400), *The Canterbury Tales* (1387–1400).

7 "Up brown," British idiom for "just right."

thrilled by the Epstein "Lazarus"[1] in the chapel of New College. It is completely right in its, what is it, 12[th.] Century milieu.

Yorkshire was literally grand. My friend-by-correspondence drove us for miles over the moors, and took us to tea at his sister's place, Mortham Tower,[2] an early Norman smallish castle she restored. And with dozens of bathrooms! She invited me to visit her next summer, to have the North tower suite, and was serious about it. I invited her to visit me, and as we drove away, Major Morritt[3] said to me, "You're probably in trouble. Violet[4] accepts invitations."

I had found Violet fascinating, 60-ish, lost her husband in the first war (the first Air Corps V.C.) and her only child, a son, as a flier in the Battle of Britain.[5] She used to fly her own 'plane, hunted big game, as her brother put it, "sat in trees all night for leopards and all that sort of thing". It turns out that Violet is "rather eccentric" as well, being a theosophist[6] "and all that sort of thing".

We missed the worst Irish Channel gale in years. The night boat before ours had three ambulances waiting at Dublin for the stricken passengers! Our crossing last night was most pleasant. The sun was bright this morning, we have a huge, high room overlooking St. Stephens green,[7] with private bathroom, and we had no sooner put on coats to go out tramping than the rain began to pour down. We shall probably just go riding after lunch.

---

1   Jacob Epstein (1880–1959), American-born sculptor and artist, whose "Lazarus" is in the New College, Oxford University. Epstein's cultural milieu was that of the Classical Age of India.

2   Mortham Tower, Rokeby, County Durham, England, a fourteenth-century tower turned into a fortified manor.

3   Major H. E. [Henry Edward] Morritt (1880–1960), most famous for *Fishing Ways and Wiles* (London: Methuen, 1929).

4   Linda Beatrice Morritt Rhodes-Moorhouse (1886–1973).

5   The first airman to receive the Victoria Cross, the highest honor awarded in the British military, was William Barnard Rhodes-Moorhouse (1887–1915). He married Linda Beatrice Morritt on 25 June 1912 and was mortally wounded by ground fire while dropping bombs on a railway station in Courtrai, France, on 26 April 1915. He was awarded the V.C. posthumously on 22 May. Their son, William Henry "Willie" Rhodes-Moorhouse (1914–1940), was shot down while in a dogfight with a German fighter plane over Tunbridge Wells, approximately 30 miles southeast of London, on 6 September 1940. He had been awarded the Distinguished Flying Cross in late July for shooting down two German bombers and a fighter plane in southern England. This and his fatal encounter occurred during the Battle of Britain, July–October 1940, a series of decisive air engagements that prevented the Germans from invading England and determined Allied air supremacy over Europe for the remainder of the war.

6   Theosophist, one who addresses Divinity through mystical insight.

7   Shelbourne Hotel, a luxury hotel, overlooks St. Stephen's Green, a square in central Dublin, Ireland.

We came by boat so that we could bring our rented car with all our 9 pieces of assorted luggage.

In a couple of days we'll begin working South.

I am so glad that we came. We are really enjoying all of it. We haven't minded the food, as soon as we learned NOT to order "sausages" for breakfast. They are made of used hay.[1]

We loved the Cotswolds, too.[2] We took one dash over into Wales, & found a sudden poverty.

A piece of bad luck like yours—the bride-to-be who was to honeymoon at my house at Van H., has been operated on, 2 days before the wedding, & is seriously ill![3]

Love,

Marjorie

. . .

JSB to MKR, 4 March 1953. ALS, 4 pp. PM: NEW YORK, N.Y. | MAR 6 | 10³⁰ AM | 1953. AD: Mrs. Norton Baskin | 5 Paxton Road | Richmond | Virginia. LH (embossed): 6 CHELSEA SQUARE | NEW YORK 11, N.Y.

I hope this makes sense – I fear I am a bit overdosed with headache cures[4]

March 4, [1953][5]

Dearest Marjorie –

---

1 MKR's insult of the staple of the British and the Irish breakfast, "The Banger," cannot be forgiven.

2 Cotswolds, rolling hills and verdant vales, most notably in Gloucestershire and Oxfordshire in England, made famous by the pastoral elegy "The Scholar Gypsy" (1853) by Matthew Arnold (1822–1888).

3 Lois Jean Hardy (1926–2010), daughter of Edward and Lois Hardy of Louisville, Kentucky, married Heath Licklider (1917–1982) on 20 December 1952, not 25 October as MKR reports. MKR writes to NSB on 28 August that she offered her Van Hornesville home for their honeymoon (*Love Letters* 657) and that they accepted. The *Louisville Courier-Journal* (21 December 1952): Section 4, p. 58, announces that the couple will honeymoon in Florida. Licklider was a professor of architecture at Princeton University.

4 JSB inserts this postscript at the top of p. 1.

5 Written in a second hand at the top of p 1: [3-6-53], which is the mailing date, not the composition date.

Here is the letter that was to be awaiting your arrival in Richmond[1] – another paving block in the road to you know where.[2]

First off, thank you <u>very</u> much for the tangerines. I think they were the best ever.[3] This must have been a very good tangerine year, as even the ones in the stores were very sweet. I am going to send you a jar of tangerine dust[4] – I'm sure you will like it. Just <springle> sprinkle it on hot buttered toast as if it were cinnamon & sugar. Don't you have to entertain some elegant old dames at tea? That would be a good time to show it off.

I have just put in a brute of a month – 3 straight weeks with not one single night home alone. Ended up with T's[5] sister and b.-in-law and niece here for a 5 day visit.[6] My head has been aching for 10 days straight. After a week one begins to doubt that it will ever unache again. A dire future is looming up too. At the moment Hildy is quite sick with chickenpox. Neither Tom, Martha, Ester or Mary has ever had same.[7] I can just see Hildy & me dashing around two weeks from today. They say adults are quite ill with it!

I am enclosing two pictures of the old homestead.[8] (I) shows the N side which faces out on the view. (II) shows the W and S sides. I am very anxious to get up and try and stimulate the workmen a bit. It is <u>far</u> from finished inside. Of course, the well may have entirely caved in my now.

Also here's a recent picture of H & M.[9] I'm full of snapshots at the moment. Don't you think they look amusingly alike? Their temperaments are rather reversed in this picture – H is usually the serious one, and Mary bursting with pleasure in herself. Mary may grow up (woe on us) to calculate her effects or lose <them> her charms altogether, but right now to

---

1   MKR went to Richmond, Virginia, to interview the relatives and the friends of Ellen Glasgow (1873–1945) for the biography she was intending to write about the celebrated Virginia novelist. See the seminal study of Ashley Lear, *The Remarkable Kinship of Marjorie Kinnan Rawlings and Ellen Glasgow* (University Press of Florida, 1988).

2   JSB is alluding to the English proverb: "The road to you know where [Hell] is paved with good intentions."

3   For years MKR had been sending JSB tangerines from her grove for Christmas or shortly thereafter, depending on when they came to full ripeness.

4   Recipe for tangerine dust: Dry a sliced tangerine in the oven. Puree the slices in a blender after adding ½ teaspoon of sugar and a pinch of Kosher salt.

5   Thomas Bigham.

6   Mary, George, and Marydee Porter. See JSB's letter on 25 June 1950, 460, n. 8.

7   Martha was a cook for the Bighams and Ester served as a nanny for their daughters Hildreth Julia and Mary Kirkpatrick. Martha and Ester's last names are not identified.

8   The home the Bighams bought in Massachusetts. Two photos of the home are enclosed with this letter.

9   JSB's daughters Hildreth Julia and Mary Kirkpatrick.

my unobjective eye she is the ne plus ultra of human personality. Almost everyone succumbs, which is sometimes hard for Hildy, but Mary makes up as best she can by considering H. the finest person she knows. It really works too.

At the moment Muddy is on a motor tour of the south with a couple of friends – New Orleans is the goal, but there was some talk of Mexico. I hope it will be a good change for her.[1]

Is there any chance of your coming up here before you go back? Well, we'll see each other in the summer surely.

Much love,
Julia

. . .

JSB to MKR, [17 April 1953]. ALS 3 pp. PM: NEW YORK 1, N.Y. | Apr 17 | 4 - PM | 1953. AD: Mrs. Norton Baskin | Crescent Beach RFD | St Augustine | Florida. LH [embossing is backward and upside down] 6 CHELSEA SQUARE | NEW YORK 11, N.Y. VIA AIR MAIL sticker.

[17 April 1953][2]

Dearest Marjorie –

I was going to 'do' another piece of paper, but decided to leave this one as quite symbolic of things here.[3]

I do apologize for not writing you at once about the tangerine dust.[4] – Such a great honor to be asked![5] I have the distinct feeling of teaching my grandmother to suck eggs – sending you cooking instructions. It's a free country, and you can dry the skins any way you want to. I do it on a cookie sheet atop my largest radiator – that's not much of a help in Fla. is it? The main thing is that it should be done quickly & thoroughly. I tried the compartment next to the oven in the gas stove – you know, the pan

---

1   Vera Scribner's husband, and JSB's father, Charles Scribner III, had died the previous year, on 11 January 1952.

2   Written in a second hand at the top of p. 1: [17 Apr. 1953], date inferred from the PM.

3   JSB is referring to the incorrect positioning of the embossing on the LH of p. 1. She began the letter on the verso, making the embossing upside down and backward, a metaphor she uses for her current condition.

4   See JSB's letter on 4 March 1953, where she informs MKR that she is sending her some tangerine dust. This reference confirms that the date for this letter is 1953.

5   MKR must have asked for the recipe. That letter appears to be missing.

storage place. It didn't work a bit well. The skins got brown spots & smelled horrible. The pulverization is done with a meat grinder, and then put the dust through a sieve to remove large pieces. Then half and half with sugar – that's it.[1]

We have been very unhealthy. Hildy with the joyous cruelty of children gave chicken pox to her small sister & her father[,] the latter was quite ill & miserable – 2 weeks in bed. I have been having a desperate time with my darn headaches.

Much struggling & planning to try to get the house in Sheffield[2] ready for the end of May. I think we will make it.

Best love to you & Norton,
Julia

. . .

MKR to JSB, 18 March 1953. TLS, 3 pp. Envelope is missing. LH:
MARJORIE KINNAN RAWLINGS

I leave here March 27th.[3]

5 Paxton Road
Richmond, Va.[4]

March 18, 1953

Dearest Julia:

You are a good girl! You said you would send me some of the powdered tangerine peel and you did it! It is the most delectable stuff I ever tasted. I used it properly, sugar and butter on the toast. If you had discovered it in time for my Cookery,[5] it would have made an enormous hit. If you didn't already have so many irons in the fire, you could produce it commercially at a good profit. But it must be a lot of work to roll it out so powder-soft. I don't dare ask you to repeat just how long the drying takes, and whether you hurry the drying pan by putting the peel in a pan on the radiator;

---

1 JSB's recipe contains an enormous amount of sugar, but perfectly typical of the time period.

2 Sheffield, Berkshire County, Massachusetts, the location of the recently purchased Bigham home, is approximately 122 miles north of New York City.

3 MKR writes this postscript at the top of p. 1, to indicate that she is leaving Richmond, Virginia, on 27 March to return to Cross Creek, Florida.

4 This is MKR's temporary address while in Richmond.

5 *Cross Creek Cookery* (1942).

and whether you do roll it out with a rolling pin or put it through the finest chopper of a meat-grinder. It is surely too fine to have been ground. I thought it would be nice to do some for the summer, when I return to Florida. The tangerines still on the trees will by now be pithy and inedible, but the rind would be as good as ever. If you'll tell me again, I'll make some for your summer, too. I hadn't really taken you seriously!

The picture of Hildy and Mary[1] is simply enchanting. They exude personality. You are in for a merry life and probably a short one.[2] They will be a handful.

No, I shall not be in N.Y. again, except perhaps to go once in the summer from Van H. to do some Glasgow research at the N.Y. Public Library. But we must get together at Van H. or at your Mass. place.

I shall have to talk with you to give you not only the Glasgow story but what Norton calls the Richmond story. I gave Carl Van Vechten[3] a resumé, as he opened the way for me to get much valuable material, and he wrote, "You will have enough material for another book-NOT about Ellen Glasgow." The cream of Richmond is curdled with malice and indiscretion. They tell me all they know and do not know about Ellen Glasgow, and try like mad to pump me. Even with those who knew Ellen well, it is impossible to keep them on track. They end up inevitably with totally irrelevant genealogy. One grande dame got started on the subject of Mrs. Lavender[4] (sic). She ended, "We were all mowed down when Mrs. Lavender went to the poorhouse." I suppose it never occurred to them that if they got together they could have saved Mrs. Lavender from the poorhouse.

I have written this story to Norton and to our Irish friend and hostess,[5] but I shall repeat it to you, at the risk, if MY letters are ever published, of the reader's noting with lifted eyebrows, as I did in reading Katherine Mansfield's letters,[6] how often a writer in correspondence tells again and again

---

1 See JSB's letter on 4 March 1953, 496, n. 9.

2 Little could MKR know that JSB would die from cancer eight years later at the age of forty-three.

3 Carl Van Vechten (1880–1964), American writer, photographer, and critic, perhaps best known for his novel *Nigger Heaven* (New York: Knopf, 1926) that helped give definition to the Harlem Renaissance.

4 Mrs. Lavender: Not identified.

5 Major H. E. Morritt and his sister Linda "Violet" Rhodes-Moorhouse, who hosted the Baskins during their trip to Great Britain. Morritt's father, Robert Ambrose Morritt (1816–1890) was born in Ireland, but moved to Rokeby, England, before the birth of H. E. and Violet. See MKR's letter on 29 October 1952.

6 Katherine Mansfield (1888–1923), New Zealand short story writer, known for her experiments in technique, particularly steam-of-consciousness. MKR had written an introduction to the *Katherine Mansfield Stories*, ed. J. Middleton Murry ([1899–1957] New York: World, 1946). See Tarr, *Bibliography*, B9, and *Uncollected Writings*, 315–18.

the same incident. If you remember my nasty and favorite short story "The Pelican's Shadow",[1] I spoke of the habit of writers, when uttering a bon mot,[2] to "recognize it as a precious nut to be stored away and brought out later in the long hard winter of literary composition."[3] But this should be so much up your alley:

I don't remember whether I wrote you that strange woman here read in an interview with me in one of the local papers that I was "between Siamese cats", and gave me a six months' old unrelated pair. The precocious little female came in heat early, and the big stupid male simply could not figure it out. He tried until he collapsed from exhaustion, and then ran and hid from her under the flounces of the poster bed where I sleep and work. I wrote Norton that the female was not giving enough cooperation, as at the first, when she knew precisely what was called for, she would sit down with her tail over the adit.[4] Norton and I work the N.Y. Sunday papers' crossword puzzles, and when you find a 4-letter word for "entrance", the answer is always "adit".

Also, Norton picked up from his British friends in India and Burma the expression, Cockney, I suppose, "I've 'ad it," or "'e's 'ad it," meaning that something is over and done with.

So, I was able at last to report to him, "The adit's adit."[5]

The work has gone well here for the most part. Three of the most important human sources are still being a bit reticent, but things come out, things come out---. And I was finally kissed by an 82-year-old gentleman who had been engaged to Ellen, (that romance being broken up by his love affair with Queen Marie of Roumania.)[6] We have visited back and forth, and he gave me much interesting material--but refused outright to discuss his relations with Ellen.

I must go now for another visit with a mere child of 70---.[7]

---

1   "The Pelican's Shadow" *New Yorker* 15 (6 January 1940): 17–19, a story about a perfectionist husband and a less than perfect bride, in part at least about the marriage of Charles Rawlings and MKR. See Tarr, *Bibliography*, C611, and *Short Stories*, 290–87.

2   That is, a witty remark.

3   "The Pelican's Shadow," 294.

4   An "adit" is a horizontal entrance to a mine serving as a means to access or for drainage.

5   In other words, the female cat has finally "had it" from the male.

6   Henry Anderson, Glasgow's suitor, met Queen Marie of Rumania (Marie Alexandra Victoria [1875–1938]), the daughter of Queen Victoria (1819–1901) of Britain, in September 1917. Richmond gossip assumed that they had become lovers, and Glasgow was devastated. MKR writes to NSB on 16 February about her meeting with Anderson, "Well, Col Anderson won't talk. I got blunt and he got blunt. I had tried to lead him on---fatuous fancy---by wondering why Ellen never married. He said she gave everything to her work" (*Love Letters* 666–67).

7   Not identified.

Much love and thanks,

Marjorie.

. . .

JSB to MKR, 20 August [1953]. ALS, 2 pp. Envelope is missing.

August 20. [1953][1]

Dearest Marjorie –

I am writing you from Bucks Co. Pa. where I am in the midst of another 'psychological week'.[2] This has been a most desperate summer, but I am so much improved that it is well worth the struggle. I don't know yet what the September schedule will be – if I am allowed any "vacation", perhaps we may still get together before we both move to our winter quarters.

So far, I have been here every other week all summer. In the month of July Tom was on vacation so he held the fort while I was away. This month it seemed at first we wouldn't see each other at all as he would have to go back to N.Y. as soon as I returned from here and vice versa. However I got his sister & b-in law[3] to come and spend their vacation of 3 weeks in Sheffield[4] so T & I were able to be away at the same time and home at the same time. You can imagine how heartwrenching it is to only see him & the children[5] only half the summer when that is our time to be together. And it is just dreadful to leave Ford Hill[6] just as I get going on the mountains of work to be done. It is terribly 'in the rough' there still. I am horrified at the thought of having to close the place up when I haven't really got it opened.

You will be interested – and shocked – to hear that I read my first Jane Austen novel this summer of confusion – <u>Northanger Abbey</u>.[7] I loved it and am looking forward to the rest. Right now I am reading my first Trollope,

1   The year is inferred by the context of the letter.
2   JSB is undergoing biweekly psychological counseling in Bucks County, Pennsylvania. "Why?" would be unfounded speculation, although it is clear from the content of her letters that she feels overwhelmed by her duties as wife and as parent, and to a certain extent finds these duties in conflict with her passion to become a professional photographer.
3   Mary and George Porter. See JSB's letter on 4 March 1953, 496, n. 6.
4   Sheffield, Massachusetts, the location of the Bighams' new home.
5   Hildreth Julia and Mary Kirkpatrick, JSB's daughters.
6   Ford Hill Road, Sheffield, Massachusetts, the location of the Bighams' new home.
7   Jane Austen (1775–1817), English novelist, *Northanger Abbey* (London: Murray, 1817), a satire on Gothic novels, completed in 1803 but published posthumously, concerns a woman who does not seek social frills but instead a moral life.

The Warden – wonderful.[1] I have had very little time for reading, and most of it has been occupied ^? ?^ by "work". I have complained some to the editors at CSS[2] that while I am sure Scribner's publishes excellent books I never get a chance to read them because I am kept busy reading all the awful books we <u>don't</u> publish.[3]

I am colossally (can't spell today) fed up with motoring. This is a very long trip to make every single week. I generally stop off in Far Hills[4] coming and going for a meal. Muddy is very busy with plans [for the][5] new house. She is completely moved ou[t] [o]f the old one into a rented one, and the new one will be begun any week now. The cottage and barns are already up – nearly complete.

I do hope this has been a good summer for you and that you are very healthy. It must have been a bit hectic with all your kittens.[6] When I find out what will go on in Sept I will give you a call. Till then Love to my friend Moe[7] and lots of same to you –

Julia

---

1 Anthony Trollope (1815–1882), English novelist, *The Warden* (London: Longman, Brown, and Green, 1855), a social novel set in Barsetshire about the need for compassion and understanding, made more famous by Trollope's caricature of Thomas Carlyle as "Dr. Pessimist Anticant" and of Charles Dickens (1812–1870) as "Mr. Popular Sentiment."

2 Charles Scribner's Sons.

3 This comment suggests that JSB undertook, at least to some extent, editorial evaluation of submitted manuscripts to Scribners, a role of significant importance to the well-being of the press.

4 The distance from Far Hills, New Jersey, the family home of the Scribners, to Sheffield, Massachusetts, is approximately 152 miles.

5 There is a hole in the MS and part of the text is missing.

6 Uki, MKR's beloved Siamese cat, went missing during the holidays in Florida. A Virginia woman read about the ordeal in a Richmond newspaper and brought MKR two Siamese kittens, Ditty and Chi, the former a gregarious female and the latter a love-starved but incompetent male. MKR was so enamored of the kittens that she penned a poem about the sex lives of the kittens, "A Defensive Ditty for a Defenseless Ditty" (see *Love Letters* 674).

7 Moe, MKR's pointer dog, who had to be left in Florida while MKR was in Richmond interviewing people for her biography of Ellen Glasgow and while the Baskins traveled abroad in Great Britain. JSB's expression "my friend Moe" alludes to MKR's *Cross Creek*, ch. 12, "My Friend Moe," 108–21. So JSB's friend Moe is a pointer dog, and MKR's friend Moe Sykes was a local carpenter whom she befriended in her early days at Cross Creek. He once borrowed $40 from MKR just to see if she would lend him the money (*Cross Creek* 117–18).

MKR to JSB, 19 November 1953. TLS, 3 pp + enclosure. PM: SAINT AUGUSTINE | NOV 19 | 5 PM | 1953 | FLA. AD: Mrs. Thomas J. Bigham | 6 Chelsea Square | New York City 11 | N.Y. RA: Crescent Beach | St. Augustine, Fla. LH: Marjorie Kinnan Rawlings.

Crescent Beach
St. Augustine, Fla.

Nov. 19, 1953

Dearest Julia:

This, of course, is Perry Patterson again, in one of his better efforts. It is also obvious that he went off with Quentin Reynolds' typewriter, too---. Carried it away with him.[1]

The wife and two small children are a bit out of character, but after all, he has had time since we last heard from him to have acquired two or three wives without appropriate bastards, and no doubt has.[2]

---

1 The saga of Perry Patterson became part of the conversation as early as 1942. He first duped MKR by mail, claiming that he was a struggling writer in need of help. She fell for his blather almost immediately. Patterson claimed to be a wounded war veteran in a hospital in Canada. MKR was so taken in that she arranged for him to come to New York, with JSB as his sponsor, to meet the Scribners. He was even invited to Far Hills to meet with Charles Scribner III, who was so duped by Patterson's stories of woe that he offered him a preliminary contract, apparently with the barest of writing samples. In repayment, Patterson absconded with JSB's typewriter, and then had the temerity to continue to carry on his correspondence with JSB and with MKR. See, for example, the commentary on Patterson in letters on 22 August 1942, 29 August 1942, [13?] October 1942, [26 October 1942], [7? November 1942], and 11 November 1942. When MKR and JSB finally realized, a painful realization, that they had been deceived, it was too late. Patterson subsequently became a metaphor for deception in their letters. Quentin Reynolds (1902–1965) was an American sports writer who became a noted war correspondent. MKR seems to be referring to Reynolds's typewriter being stolen from the newspaper account entitled "The Great Literary Hoax" accompanying this letter. MKR writes at the top of the clipping: "Perry Patterson!!" Reynolds published the elaborate wartime account of a Canadian George Dupre (1903–1982) under the title *The Man Who Wouldn't Talk* (New York: Random House, 1953), only to learn later that the whole story was a hoax, exposed by the *Calgary Herald*. Bennett Cerf (1898–1971), the editor at Random House, ordered the book be moved from nonfiction to fiction and the sales increased markedly. *Reader's Digest* published a condensation of the story, but later retracted it, issuing a three-page apology for falling prey to the hoax. The clipping is a summary of the DuPre story.

2 MKR seems to be referring to another newspaper account of Dupre, "wife and two small children." If so, the account has not been found. MKR could also be responding to something JSB has written. If so, that letter is missing. MKR's contention about the linking of Perry Patterson and George Dupre has not been authenticated, although the stories the two weave are remarkably

It is dreadful that the summer passed without our seeing each other. We must not let it happen again. I miss you too much. But I do expect to get to New York this late winter or very early spring for two or three weeks, staying preferably at a quiet apartment hotel near or at Gramercy Park.[1] I may ask you later to look at two or three for me, if not too much trouble.

I had steady company at Van Hornesville from Aug. 1st on.[2] Norton drove up in his own car, so that he could drive the animals directly here, while I stopped off in Virginia for nearly a month, to finish the personal Glasgow research. I had kept all four kittens for him to see, hoping he would back me up in my desire to renege on giving away three of them. On the contrary, tired as he was from his drive, he insisted that we set out the day after his arrival to deliver them. Did you see the cartoon in last week's New Yorker, of a woman with fourteen countable cats, saying to a female visitor who was looking at a portrait over the mantel of a sad-eyed man and dog, "They just went out for a walk one morning, and that's the last I ever saw of them"?

Norton had almost suspicious hysterics over it.

He had a fiendish time on his drive south. Moe rode standing up all the way, with his head in a corner. The three cats escaped three times. The first time, he turned up a side road and walked up it to sit down for his picnic lunch. He heard cats speaking, and looked back to see Everardus, Chi-Chi and Marco Polo stalking toward him in single file, tails tall and stiff. Then they escaped at two filling stations. However, they were amiable and ready to be caught. Moe would not eat his canned dinner the second night, and showed that he had committed a crime. In repacking the car, Norton discovered why. Moe had had enough of pampered cats, and had made a fine meal from the fried chicken in the picnic basket. And Norton's first night out, he was turned away by three motor courts. He 'phoned ahead to a fourth and asked if there was any objection to pets. The owner said Not at all, he had one of his own. When he saw the car after Norton had paid and registered, he said, My God, I thought you had one pet, not a menagerie. Norton showed him Moe's special blanket, the cats' basket and their sanitary pan of a gravelly

---

similar. See "'Cloak and Dagger' Hoax Embarrasses Author," *The West Australian* (16 November 1953): 1, and "John Darton, "Literary Hoaxes of the Past," *New York Times* (13 February 1972): 56.

1   A fenced-in private park in New York City, the surrounding area of which is also known as Gramercy Park.

2   Most notable among them was Carrie Duke (1883–1955?), who came to give MKR more material for her biography of Ellen Glasgow, but in the end as MKR wrote to NSB on 17 August 1953, Carrie "is really a dear, and the best of company," but she "had very little material to give me" (*Love Letters* 687–88).

"Kitty Litter" and was admitted. The man walked in with ice, in time to hear Moe lapping noisily from the toilet; one cat biting a lamp-shade; the other two sharpening their claws on the upholstered chairs; and in bringing in the pan of Kitty Litter, Norton had strewn the gravel clear across the room. Norton says he will now feel free to go anywhere in the world, as he could never again feel so unwelcome.

My time in Virginia was most profitable. I finished my job of ingratiating myself with the last three "hold-outs", and was rewarded with rich and sometimes shocking material.[1]

I had a comfortable and expensive suite at the Jefferson Hotel in Richmond, where I could entertain the old ladies. All of this, fortunately, can be deducted from income tax. The Captain of waiters was a dear white-haired old-time Negro who took care of me and my parties beautifully.

From this comfort, I returned to the beach[2] to a daily woman only, who arrives at 9:30 and leaves at 2, being transported in one of Norton's Marineland station wagons that ferries his help. I shall probably find excuses to stay in New York as long as possible—.

Edith Pope has had the most stunning pictures taken for the jacket of her book.[3] I have never seen her more beautiful. Until shortly before I arrived here, she was still seeking a title for the book, which I cannot understand, as to me, the title is an integral part of the story one must tell. She wanted a Biblical title, and on a visit to Norton, borrowed his Bible with the Concordance, and at the same time, Polly Adler's "A House is Not a Home".[4] Leaving, she thanked Norton for the Good Book and the good book.

I did not get one lick of work done this summer.

I do hope the so-distant psychiatrist[5] has you straightened out.

Much love,
Marjorie

---

1   As MKR is about to leave Richmond, she expresses a mixture of disappointment and of hope about her research on Ellen Glasgow, writing to NSB on 4 November 1953, "It is a pity not to have gotten more from these few still-living friends and relatives, but I imagine that when I go over my card file, I will find that I have a great deal . . ." (*Love Letters* 692).

2   Crescent Beach.

3   Edith Pope, *The River in the Wind* (New York, Scribners, 1954).

4   Pearl "Polly" Adler (1900–1962), *A House Is Not a Home* (New York: Rinehart, 1953), about Adler's life as a madam of multiple houses of prostitution.

5   JSB was under the care of a psychiatrist in Bucks County, Pennsylvania, during the summer of 1953. See her letter dated [20] August 1953.

MKR to JSB, 4 December 1953. TLS, 2 pp. PM: SAINT AUGUSTINE | DEC 4 | 4 PM | 1953 | FLA. AD: Mrs. Thomas J. Bigham | Harkness Pavilion | Presbyterian Hospital | 180 Fort Washington Avenue | New York, N.Y. LH: Marjorie Kinnan Rawlings. [Written on the envelope in MKR's hand]: <u>Air Mail</u> | <u>Special Delivery</u>. Stamped on the envelope: Special Delivery - Air Mail.

Crescent Beach
St. Augustine, Fla.

December 4, 1953

Dearest Julia:

Buzz just phoned me to tell me that you are in Harkness,[1] after an operation, not serious or dangerous, he said.

I do feel rather a grievance against life that with all your other complications you should have to have even a minor operation. But thank heavens you are at Harkness![2]

When you are fully recovered, but not before, give me a blow-by-blow account. I called Edith Pope to tell her about it, so that she can write you too.

I have just played another dirty trick on Moe. I took him to the Creek without any of my cats day before yesterday. He was so happy to be there, the lord of all he surveyed once again. Then Norman Berg came by with the most adorable Siamese kitten that he was taking to his sister in New Jersey. The cute little thing had never been out of its commercial pen and was starved for affection. I put Moe to sleep on his blanket in Norman's room, while I kept the kitten with me. I must say that Moe took it in his stride, although when we headed for the Creek alone I'm sure he thought he was through with cats at last! But all is well amongst them, and each of the three cats presents itself to Moe to be nibbled in turn. It keeps him awfully busy.

My dear, I do hope you recover soon from this set-back. Again, I shall not send flowers to the hospital, as I know you will be deluged with them, but shall wait to send you some when you are back at home.[3]

---

1 Buzz, Charles Scribner IV (aka Jr.), JSB's brother and now president of Scribners.

2 Harkness Pavilion.

3 Sheffield, Massachusetts.

I'll drop you a note again in a few days. Meantime, all love,

<u>Marjorie</u>

And Chet Crosby will send you my tangerines when you return home.[1]

. . .

JSB to NSB, 15 December 1953. Telegram.

WESTERN UNION
AA01
A.NG084 PD=NEW YORK NY 15 439 PWE= 1953 DEC 15 PM 4 56.

NORTON BASKIN=
CRESCENT BEACH PHONE CRESCENT BEACH FLO=

DEAR NORTON I CAN HARDLY TAKE IN THE SHOCKING NEWS
ALL MY THOUGHTS AND SYMPATHY ARE WITH YOU LOVE=

JULIA=

Marjorie Kinnan Rawlings died suddenly of an aneurysm on 14 December
1953 at the age of 57.

Julia Scribner Bigham died after a long battle with breast cancer on 24
October 1961 at the age of 43.

---

1   The postscript is in MKR's hand. This is MKR's last communication with JSB.

Bibliography

Action, Patricia Nassif, Lady. *Invasion of Privacy: The* Cross Creek *Trial of Marjorie Kinnan Rawlings.* Gainesville: University Presses of Florida, 1988.

Kinser, Brent E. "'I'd Much Rather Write You Instead': The Letters of Marjorie Kinnan Rawlings to Bertram C. Cooper." *The Marjorie Kinnan Rawlings Journal of Florida Literature* 13 (2004): 1–33.

———. "'The least touch of butter': Marge and Emily on Manners." *The Marjorie Kinnan Rawlings Journal of Florida Literature* 10 (2001): 1–9.

Lear, Ashley Andrews. *The Remarkable Kinship of Marjorie Kinnan Rawlings and Ellen Glasgow.* Gainesville: University Press of Florida, 2018.

Lillios, Anna. *Crossing the Creek: The Literary Friendship of Zora Neale Hurston and Marjorie Kinnan Rawlings.* Gainesville: University Press of Florida, 2010.

McCutchan, Ann. *The Life She Wished to Live: A Biography of Marjorie Kinnan Rawlings, Author of* The Yearling. New York: Norton, 2021.

Nolan, David. *The Houses of St. Augustine.* Sarasota: Pineapple Press, 1995.

Rawlings, Marjorie Kinnan. *Blood of My Blood,* edited by Anne Blythe Meriwether. Gainesville: University Press of Florida, 2002.

———. *Cross Creek.* New York: Scribners, 1942.

———. *Cross Creek Cookery.* New York: Scribners, 1942.

———. *Cross Creek Sampler: A Book of Quotations,* selected and edited by Rodger L. Tarr and Brent E. Kinser. Gainesville: University Press of Florida, 2011.

———. *Golden Apples.* New York: Scribners, 1935.

———. *The Marjorie Rawlings Reader,* edited by Julia Scribner Bigham, New York: Scribners, 1956.

———. *Max and Marjorie: The Correspondence between Maxwell E. Perkins and Marjorie Kinnan Rawlings,* edited by Rodger L. Tarr. Gainesville: University Press of Florida, 1999.

———. *Poems. Songs of a Housewife,* edited by Rodger L. Tarr. Gainesville: University Press of Florida, 1997.

———. *The Private Marjorie: The Love Letters of Marjorie Kinnan Rawlings to Norton S. Baskin,* edited by Rodger L. Tarr. Gainesville: University Press of Florida, 2004.

———. *The Secret River,* edited by Julia Scribner Bigham. New York: Scribners, 1955.

———. *Selected Letters,* edited by Gordon E. Bigelow and Laura V. Monti. Gainesville: University Presses of Florida, 1983.

————. *Short Stories,* edited by Rodger L. Tarr. Gainesville: University Press of Florida, 1994.

————. *The Sojourner.* New York: Scribners, 1953.

————. *South Moon Under.* New York: Scribners, 1933.

————. *The Uncollected Writings of Marjorie Kinnan Rawlings,* edited by Rodger L. Tarr and Brent E. Kinser. Gainesville: University Press of Florida, 2007.

————. *When the Whippoorwill—.* New York: Scribners, 1940.

————. *The Yearling.* New York: Scribners, 1938.

Silverthorne, Elizabeth. *Marjorie Kinnan Rawlings: Sojourner at Cross Creek.* Woodstock: Overlook Press, 1988.

Stephens, James M. *Cross Creek Reader's Guide: An Illustrated Quick-Reference Guide to Cross Creek.* Privately printed, 2003.

Tarr, Rodger L. *Marjorie Kinnan Rawlings: A Descriptive Bibliography.* Pittsburgh: University of Pittsburgh Press, 1988.

————. "Marjorie Kinnan Rawlings and the Rochester (N.Y.) Magazine *Five O'Clock.*" *American Periodicals* 1, no. 1 (Fall 1991): 83–85.

————. "Marjorie Kinnan Rawlings and the *Washington Post.*" *Analytical and Enumerative Bibliography,* n.s., 4, no. 4 (1990): 163–68.

Turcotte, Florence M. "'For This is an Enchanted Land': Marjorie Kinnan Rawlings and the Florida Environment," *Florida Historical Quarterly* 90, no. 4 (Spring 2012): 488–504.

————. "Racial Politics and the Publication of *The Secret River* by Marjorie Kinnan Rawlings," *Marjorie Kinnan Rawlings Journal of Florida Literature* 27 (2020): 5–24.

Index

Page numbers in *italics* indicate illustrations.

The Closed Garden (Green), 237–38
Coghill, Nevill, 493, 493n6
Cohen-Portheim, Paul, 128n1
Colcorton (Pope), 253, 253n2, 258, 258n1
Coleridge, Samuel Taylor, 172n2
Collier's Magazine, 342n1
The Communist Manifesto (Marx and Engels), 427, 427n1
The Complete Andersen (Hersholt), 450, 450n4
Compton-Burnett, Ivy, 439, 439n2
Cone, Frederick P., 62n1, 97n1
Confessions of St. Augustine (Sheed), 262, 262n7
Conrad, Joseph, 175, 175n1
The Conspiracy of the Carpenters, 209, 210n1
The Constant Nymph (Kennedy), 46, 46n6
Cook, James M., 287n1
Cooper, Bertram Cleveland: aboard USS Bountiful, 326, 327n1, 356; birth of child, 376n2; career change and, 350–51, 362; correspondence with JSB, 290, 302, 306; correspondence with MKR, 290n1, 294n1, 326–27; dislike of Thomas Bigham, 353, 355–56; friendship with JSB, 295, 356; friendship with MKR, 274–75, 302n1, 356; interest in JSB, 295n2, 306n2; marriage to Constance Lang, 361, 361n5, 362, 365; MKR's matchmaking with Julia, 274n5, 294, 296n1, 306n2, 324n3; as Navy chaplain, 274n5, 351; visit with MKR, 365
Cooper, Bertram Cleveland, III, 376n2
Cooper, Gary, 201n2
Cooper, James Fenimore, 389, 389n3
Coughlin, Charles E., 239, 239n1
Counter Attack in Spain (Sender), 258, 267
Cowley, Malcolm, 262, 262n4
Crawlings-by-the-Sea, 102, 102n1
Crescent Beach, Florida: additions to, 346, 385; Arthur Houston Kinnan visit to, 32; Berg's request for honeymoon at, 63–64; hurricane damage at, 397, 399, 469; JSB visit to, 9, 31, 64n1; maid apartment at, 52, 52n3, 77, 386n1; Norton and MKR visit to, 21; Willkie visits to, 74n5
Le crève-coeur (Aragon), 232
Cronin, A. J., 319, 319n5
Crosby, Helen, 482
Crosby, James "Chet," 244, 246n4, 254–55, 259–60, 260n3, 273, 311, 330, 338, 351, 372, 380, 451, 454, 507
Cross Creek (Rawlings): Camp illustrations

for, 53n2, 102n4, 121, 121n1; correspondence with Maxwell Perkins on, 94n1, 96n1, 102, 102n2; difficulties with, 94, 99, 102n2; Ferdinand the bull in, 61n4; Julia on progress with, 18, 96; lawsuit by Zelma Cason, 162, 207, 207n2, 209n6, 305n1, 310, 310n4, 356, 356n4, 359–61, 363; Maxwell Perkins and, 70, 70n5, 74n1, 108, 108n2, 114n3; MKR trouble with narrative chronology, 76, 76n2; MKR work on, 48n4, 65; proofs for, 114n3, 119, 121
Cross Creek, Florida: Black culture at, 17–18; Cracker culture at, 15–18; flowers at, 124, 210, 326, 380; frontier life at, 16; interactions of Cracker and Black workers at, 17–18, 71; MKR home at, 15–16; orange groves in, 124, 326, 358; snake adventures at, 344, 344n5; Thelma Shortridge's destruction of cottage, 408–9; workers at, 71, 346, 349–50, 350n2, 358
Cross Creek Groves, 484n4
Crowe, Della, 53n2
Cry, the Beloved Country (Paton), 413, 413n4, 446, 446n5
Culture and Anarchy (Arnold), 98n3
Culver, Henry Brundage, 120, 120n2
Culver, Irma Asch, 120, 120n2
Cunha, Euclides da, 263, 263n2, 267, 267n3, 287n1

Dahon, Renée, 93n5
Daisy Miller (James), 353, 353n3
Damon, Mary M., 464n4
Damon, Virgil, 162n3, 366, 383, 464, 464n4
The Dark Journey (Green), 215, 237
Darrow, Charles Whitney: Alan Paton and, 446; cribner sales manager, 237n2; Cross Creek Cookery and, 125, 129, 137, 323; death of Charles Scribner III and, 483, 483n1; marriage of MKR and Norton, 112–13; Norton's verse and, 237; as Scribner sales manager/ vice president, 112n3, 125n1, 323n3, 342n4; Wine Advisory Board advertisement and, 342
Davenport, Marcia, 182, 182n5, 200, 200n5, 201, 398, 401, 447, 447n2
Davenport, Russell, 182, 182n5
Davis, Clint, 188, 188n4, 188n6
Davis, George, 166n2, 166n8
Davis, Jeff, 57n2
Day of Wrath, 416, 416n1

Rachmaninoff, Sergei, 92, 92n3

Racine, Jean-Baptiste, 141, 141n4

Rainbow Springs, Florida, 66, 66n4

Randall, David A., 171, 171n5

"The Raven" (Poe), 60n4

Rawlings, Charles "Chuck," 19, 44n5, 47n2, 65, 65n7, 117n2, 161n2

Rawlings, Marjorie Kinnan: alcohol abuse and, 18–19, 251n1, 415n1; anger issues, 2, 109n2; archive of, 5–13; attempt to fly Norton home from India, 307n2; bond with JSB, 14–16, 20–21, 24, 30; conflicted prejudice and, 17–18, 250n1, 311, 333; correspondence style, 1–2; Cracker lore and, 52n3; Cross Creek home of, 15–16; death of, 9, 32; death of Aunt Ida Tarrant and, 32; death of Charles Scribner III and, 31; death of Maxwell Perkins and, 31; dependence on Idella Parker, 325n3, 338n5, 415n1; dislike of Vera Scribner, 171n2; drinking and driving, 249–52, 270n1, 381, 381n1; experience of patriarchy, 27; friendship with Hamilton Holt, 93n4; Gone With the Wind premiere, 48n2; guest of Eleanor Roosevelt, 99n3; at Harkness Pavilion, 107n1, 107n2, 109n2, 111n1, 162, 162n3, 165n5, 170, 170n8, 200n1, 470n3, 474n4, 489–90; health issues, 31–32, 418n1; ineligibility to be a godmother, 29–30, 375, 377, 377n1; infatuation with Perry Patterson, 25–26; intended biography of Ellen Glasgow, 32, 488n2, 496n1, 502n7, 504n2, 505; killing a mule with car, 250–51, 251n1; lecture at University of Wisconsin, 65, 65n2; literary success and, 19–20; maid problems, 205, 205n2, 206; Margaret Mitchell and, 20, 48; marriage of JSB and Thomas, 28–29; marriage to Charles Rawlings, 19, 286n1, 500n1; marriage to Norton Baskin, 21, 28, 111, 111n3, 111n6, 112–13, 286n2; meeting with Julia, 44–45n5; meeting with Vera Scribner, 44n5; Otto Lange and, 180n2; problems with diverticulosis, 51n4, 75n4, 111n1, 162n3, 200n1, 401n3, 418n1, 474n4; Pulitzer Prize for The Yearling, 15, 20; racist outbursts and, 16–17, 310, 310n3, 311; relationship with mother, 7, 20, 161, 161n2; relationship with Scribners, 112n2; shooting of Samson and, 211n4; with Siamese cats, 317; social justice and, 16–17, 22; support for American troops, 22; travel with JSB, 24–25; trip to Ireland and England, 32, 493, 493n3; unpublished

works, 5; U.S. Forest Service trip, 131n4, 135n3, 139, 140n2, 141, 142n7, 146n4, 188n3; visit to cotton field, 316; Wine Advisory Board advertisement and, 342, 342n4, 343; work with Charles Scribner III, 31, 44n5; work with Maxwell Perkins, 70n5, 72n4

—correspondence with Bertram Cooper, 296n1, 327n1

—correspondence with Carl Brandt, 472n1

—correspondence with Ida Tarrant: on Julia's visit at ocean cottage, 71n4; on operation in NY, 164n2; on stay at Marion Hotel, 320n3; on visit to Scribners at Dew Hollow, 44n5

—correspondence with JSB: on accident-prone people, 448; on Adrenna Mickens, 61–62, 67; on alligator cooking, 145; on Animated Magazine, 93; on Aragon, 212; on art, 69–70; on artistic torment, 174–76, 178; on barbecue cloth, 247; on beau "Dave," 75, 75n2; on being forbidden to smoke and drink, 485–86, 488, 488n1; on Benny (cat), 395, 395n3, 398–99; on Bergs, 64, 78, 106, 278, 452–53, 506; on Bert Cooper, 294, 306n2, 326–27, 355–56, 361–62, 365, 376; on Bill Stone, 410–11; on bird feeder, 181, 312; on birth of Hildreth, 375, 378–79, 384; on birth of Mary Kirkpatrick, 478; on blackouts, 120, 120n1; on brother's visit, 405–6, 492; on buying Sheffield dishes, 59, 65, 65n5; on Buzz, 487, 491; on car accidents, 381, 468–69; on Castle Warden, 114, 118–20, 125, 129–30, 338–39, 347–48; on Catherine Gilpin, 153–54; on Chet Crosby, 338, 351, 380, 452, 454, 507; on Christmas dinner, 369–70, 451; on citizen defense, 97, 97n1; on citrus groves, 76, 169, 179, 370, 376, 448, 451, 455; confession of love for married man, 28; conservative views, 98n2; on cookery, 163, 379, 435; on coronary spasm, 485, 485n2, 486–87; on correspondence from troops, 341, 341n2; correspondence style, 1–4; on Under Cover, 233; on cows, 52, 52n4, 53; on Crescent Beach cottage, 77, 102, 136, 333; on Cross Creek, 65, 65n1, 76, 76n2, 94, 99, 102, 119, 121; on Cross Creek Cookery, 129, 137, 139; on Cross Creek lawsuit, 207, 310, 356, 359–61; on Dave, 100, 100n1; on day dreaming, 235; on death of Charles Scribner III, 483, 483n1, 484; on death of Louise Flagg Scribner, 418; on death of Maxwell Perkins, 394n1; on death

Rawlings family, 3

The Razor's Edge (Maugham), 304, 304n2

Rebellion in the Backlands (Cunha), 263, 263n2, 267, 267n3, 287, 287n1

Redjives, Johnnie, 468

Redjives, Ruth, 468

Reflections in a Golden Eye (McCullers), 166, 166n3

Revere, Anne, 60n2

The Revolt of the Masses (Ortega y Gasset), 44, 44n4

Reynolds, James Russel "Jimmy," 271

Reynolds, Quentin, 503, 503n1

Reynolds, Robert Rice, 233, 233n1

Rhodes-Moorhouse, Linda Beatrice Morritt, 494n5, 494n, 499, 499n5

Rhodes-Moorhouse, William Barnard, 494, 494n5

Rhodes-Moorhouse, William Henry "Willie," 494n5

Ribault, Jean, 160, 160n3

Richardson, Samuel, 258, 258n7

Richard Wagner (Pourtalès), 287, 287n1

Richeson, Elizabeth "Betty" Norvelle, 268n3

Riggs, Ethel Traphagen, 200n2, 202n4, 203

Riggs, Isabel A., 202n4

Riggs, Marion Gertrude, 202n4

The Road to Survival (Vogt), 419, 419n2

Robbery Under Arms (Browne), 259, 259n8, 261, 321, 321n3, 372

Robbins, Jerome, 266n1

Robeson, Paul, 236n4, 237

Rochester Times-Union, 19

Rollins College, 86, 86n1, 88, 88n1, 89, 91, 91n2, 93, 93n4, 326, 326n1

Rollins Sandspur, 86n1, 93n4

Romains, Jules, 258, 258n5

Roosevelt, Eleanor, 79n4, 80, 99n3, 214n2, 307n2

Roosevelt, Franklin D., 74, 74n5, 79, 79n4, 82n4, 98n1, 98n2, 102n3, 114n4, 118n3, 121n5, 239n1, 307, 307n6, 307n7

Rose, Billy, 80, 80n3

Rossie, Allia Nora, 186, 219

Rougemont, Denis de, 425, 425n4

The Rover Boys (Winfield), 121, 121n4

Ryerson, Florence, 306n1

Sabin, Cecil, 303, 303n2

Sabin, Dossie, 303, 303n2

Sabin, Tommy, 303, 303n2

Saki, 204, 204n4, 211, 211n1

Sampson, B. J., 57n2

Sandvold, Gertrude, 415n1, 431, 431n2, 434, 434n2, 435, 435n4, 436, 441–42, 459, 477, 479–80

Sandvold, Halvor, 397, 397n4, 435n4

Sanibel Island, 484, 484n1, 486

Santayana, George, 331, 331n4, 361

Sartre, Jean-Paul, 416, 416n6

Saturday Evening Post, 342n1, 367n4, 408, 426n4

Sayers, Dorothy, 425, 425n3

Schieffelin, George McKay, 297, 297n1

Schieffelin, Louise Scribner, 94, 94n5, 157, 157n3, 177n3, 276n1, 297, 297n1, 298, 300, 463–64

Schieffelin, Louise Winterbotham, 297, 297n1

Schiefflin, George M., Jr., 56, 56n5

Schnabel, Artur, 255, 255n2

Scott, Robert L., Jr., 326, 326n3

The Screwtape Letters (Lewis), 290n2

Scribner, Charles I (1821–1871), 3, 236n2

Scribner, Charles II (1854–1930), 3, 99n2, 184

Scribner, Charles III (1890–1952), 3; on Burma business, 264n3; on *Cross Creek Cookery,* 131; *Cross Creek* lawsuit and, 162; death of, 31, 464n1, 483, 483n1; on death of Maxwell Perkins, 386n5, 387; fall and broken rib, 247, 247n3; Julia's wedding and, 328n4; Perry Patterson and, 25–26, 138, 147, 151n5; publication of *The Yearling,* 15; relationship with MKR, 112n2; on *The Sojourner,* 470, 470n3, 472n2, 474, 479n1, 483n1; stay with MKR at Cross Creek, 45n1; visits with Moores in South Beach, 81n4; work with MKR, 31, 44n5

Scribner, Charles IV (Buzz) (1921–1995), 3; on Julia as invalid, 34; literature suggestions from MKR, 178; love affairs and, 84, 84n5, 85, 138; marriage to Joan Sunderland, 432n6, 433, 433n4, 434; MKR archive and, 7, 10; Navy service and, 131n4, 135n3, 182, 197; as president of Scribners, 32, 491, 491n5; reading Niebuhr, 186; release from military duty, 487, 487n2, 491

Scribner, Charles V (III) (1951–), 3, 5, 7–10, 12–13

Scribner, Julia (1918–1961). *See* Bigham, Julia Scribner

Scribner, Louise Flagg: birthday presents and, 177; on Christmas gifts, 157; closeness with

RODGER L. TARR is University Distinguished Professor of English, Emeritus, Illinois State University. He has published extensively on Victorian literature and on Rawlings, including *Max and Marjorie: The Correspondence between Maxwell E. Perkins and Marjorie Kinnan Rawlings* and *The Private Marjorie: The Love Letters of Marjorie Kinnan Rawlings to Norton S. Baskin.* Other work includes editions of Rawlings's short stories and poems and the definitive bibliography of her works.

BRENT E. KINSER is professor of literature and head of the Department of English Studies at Western Carolina University. He has published extensively on Rawlings, including *The Uncollected Writings of Marjorie Kinnan Rawlings* and *Cross Creek Sampler*, both coedited with Rodger L. Tarr, and on Victorian literature, in particular as an editor of the Carlyle Letters Project, Duke University Press, which is comprised of the Duke-Edinburgh Edition of *The Collected Letters of Thomas and Jane Welsh Carlyle,* and the *Carlyle Letters Online* (carlyleletters.dukeupress.edu).

FLORENCE M. TURCOTTE is the literary manuscripts archivist at the George A. Smathers Libraries, University of Florida, Gainesville. She has served as curator of the Marjorie Kinnan Rawlings Papers since 2005.